THE

LINCOLN

READER

THE

LINCOLN

READER

———◦•◦———

Edited, with an Introduction, by

PAUL M. ANGLE

A DA CAPO PAPERBACK

Library of Congress Cataloging in Publication Data

The Lincoln reader / edited, with an introduction by Paul M. Angle.
    p.   c. — (A Da Capo paperback)
    Reprint. Originally published: Westport, Conn.: Greenwood Press, 1947.
    ISBN 0-306-80398-4
    1. Lincoln, Abraham, 1809-1865. 2. Presidents — United States-Biography.
I. Angle, Paul M. (Paul McClelland), 1900-1975.
E457.L745   1990   89-71447
973.7'092 — dc20   CIP

Published by Da Capo Press, Inc.
A Subsidiary of Plenum Publishing Corporation
233 Spring Street, New York, New York 10013

Manufactured in the United States of America

CONTENTS

Acknowledgments   ix

Preface   xi

1   Kentucky Childhood   3
ABRAHAM LINCOLN. CARL SANDBURG. IDA M. TARBELL.
ALBERT J. BEVERIDGE. WILLIAM E. BARTON.

2   Youth in Indiana   16
JOHN G. NICOLAY AND JOHN HAY. CARL SANDBURG.
WARD HILL LAMON. WILLIAM E. BARTON. ALBERT J.
BEVERIDGE.

3   New Salem   36
ABRAHAM LINCOLN. WILLIAM H. HERNDON. BENJAMIN
P. THOMAS. JOHN G. NICOLAY AND JOHN HAY. THOMAS
P. REEP. WILLIAM E. BARTON.

4   The DeWitt Clinton of Illinois   65
JOHN G. NICOLAY AND JOHN HAY. HARRY E. PRATT.
WILLIAM H. HERNDON. WARD HILL LAMON. ALBERT J.
BEVERIDGE. THOMAS FORD.

5   Attorney and Counsellor-at-Law   89
ALBERT A. WOLDMAN. PAUL M. ANGLE. JOHN G. NICOLAY
AND JOHN HAY. ALBERT J. BEVERIDGE.

6   Romance and Marriage   113
CARL SANDBURG. ABRAHAM LINCOLN TO MARY OWENS
AND TO MRS. O. H. BROWNING. CARL SANDBURG AND
PAUL M. ANGLE.

7   Mr. Lincoln of Illinois   132
    BENJAMIN P. THOMAS. SAMUEL C. BUSEY. WILLIAM H.
    TOWNSEND. JOHN G. NICOLAY AND JOHN HAY. WILLIAM
    H. HERNDON.

8   Leader of the Illinois Bar   162
    BENJAMIN P. THOMAS. HENRY C. WHITNEY. JESSE W.
    WEIK. ALBERT A. WOLDMAN. HARRY E. PRATT. JOHN H.
    LITTLEFIELD. THOMAS DRUMMOND.

9   The House on Eighth Street   188
    WARD HILL LAMON. WILLIAM H. HERNDON. JESSE W.
    WEIK. CARL SANDBURG. WILLIAM E. BARTON.

10 Rebirth in Politics: 1854–1858   201
    JAMES MINER. JAMES S. EWING. JOSEPH FORT NEWTON.
    ABRAHAM LINCOLN TO E. B. WASHBURNE AND TO JOSHUA
    F. SPEED. WILLIAM H. HERNDON. HENRY C. WHITNEY.
    NOAH BROOKS. CARL SANDBURG.

11 The Great Debates   226
    WILLIAM H. HERNDON. ISAAC N. ARNOLD. HORACE
    WHITE. THE CHICAGO TIMES. THE CHICAGO TRIBUNE.
    JOSEPH MEDILL. CARL SCHURZ. GUSTAVE KOERNER.
    PAUL M. ANGLE. JAMES G. RANDALL.

12 "The Taste Is In My Mouth a Little": Nomina-
    tion, 1860   255
    CARL SANDBURG. RICHARD J. OGLESBY. MURAT HAL-
    STEAD. WARD HILL LAMON. CHARLES CARLETON COFFIN.
    LORD CHARNWOOD.

13 Candidate and President-Elect   282
    ABRAHAM LINCOLN TO A. G. HENRY. HELEN NICOLAY.
    CARL SCHURZ. WILLIAM E. BARINGER. HENRY VILLARD.
    DONN PIATT. JAMES A. CONNOLLY. WILLIAM H. HERN-
    DON. PHILIP VAN DOREN STERN.

14 The New President   310
WARD HILL LAMON. ELIHU B. WASHBURNE. ALBERT G.
RIDDLE. MARGARET LEECH. L. E. CHITTENDEN. A PUBLIC
MAN. CARL SANDBURG. ABRAHAM LINCOLN.

15 The Momentous Issue   337
MARGARET LEECH. JOHN G. NICOLAY AND JOHN HAY. A
PUBLIC MAN. EDWARD BATES. JAMES G. RANDALL. STE-
PHEN D. LEE. ABRAHAM LINCOLN.

16 The War Begins   355
GEORGE ASHMUN. JOHN HAY. JOHN G. NICOLAY AND
JOHN HAY. HELEN NICOLAY. WILLIAM H. RUSSELL.

17 Search for a General   377
JOHN HAY. MONTGOMERY C. MEIGS. L. E. CHITTENDEN.
LORD CHARNWOOD. GIDEON WELLES. NOAH BROOKS. A. K.
MCCLURE.

18 Emancipation   403
THOMAS T. ECKERT. GIDEON WELLES. FRANCIS B. CAR-
PENTER. ABRAHAM LINCOLN. SALMON P. CHASE. JOHN
G. NICOLAY AND JOHN HAY.

19 Life in the White House   415
WARD HILL LAMON. ELIZABETH TODD GRIMSLEY. JULIA
TAFT. ELIZABETH KECKLEY. NOAH BROOKS. JOHN HAY.

20 Gettysburg   439
CARL SANDBURG. CLARK E. CARR. JOHN HAY. ABRAHAM
LINCOLN.

21 Years of Victory   450
LORD CHARNWOOD. GIDEON WELLES. JOHN G. NICOLAY
AND JOHN HAY. JOHN G. NICOLAY. CARL SANDBURG.

22 The Second Election   476
NOAH BROOKS. JOHN G. NICOLAY. JOHN HAY. ABRAHAM
LINCOLN. LORD CHARNWOOD.

23 Peace   496

CARL SANDBURG. WILLIAM TECUMSEH SHERMAN. D. D. PORTER. LLOYD LEWIS. MARGARET LEECH.

24 Death—and a People's Grief   520

WARD HILL LAMON. FREDERICK W. SEWARD. JOHN G. NICOLAY. GIDEON WELLES. CARL SANDBURG. PAUL M. ANGLE.

Epilogue   538

LORD CHARNWOOD.

References   540

Bibliography   544

Index   549

ACKNOWLEDGMENTS

The Publishers acknowledge with appreciation to the following permission to reprint material in this volume:

To The Abraham Lincoln Association, Springfield, Illinois, for permission to reprint from *Lincoln's New Salem* by Benjamin P. Thomas, copyright 1934; from *Here I Have Lived* by Paul M. Angle, copyright 1935; from *Lincoln: 1847–1853* by Benjamin P. Thomas, copyright 1936; from *Lincoln: 1809–1839* by Harry E. Pratt, copyright 1941; from *The Personal Finances of Abraham Lincoln* by Harry E. Pratt, copyright 1943; and from *A House Dividing* by William E. Baringer, copyright 1945.

To D. Appleton-Century Company, New York, for permission to reprint from *Washington in Lincoln's Time* by Noah Brooks, copyright 1894 by the Century Company; from *Abraham Lincoln,* two volumes, by William H. Herndon and Jesse W. Weik, copyright 1896 by D. Appleton and Company; from an article by J. McCan Davis in the *Century Magazine,* copyright 1900 by the Century Company; from *Short Life of Abraham Lincoln* by John G. Nicolay, copyright 1902 by the Century Company; from *Lincoln in the Telegraph Office* by David Homer Bates, copyright 1907 by the Century Company; and from *Personal Traits of Abraham Lincoln* by Helen Nicolay, copyright 1912 by the Century Company.

To The Bobbs-Merrill Company, Indianapolis, for special permission to reprint from *Life of Abraham Lincoln,* Volume I, by William E. Barton, copyright 1925; and from *Lincoln and His Wife's Home Town* by William H. Townsend, copyright 1929.

To Brown, Hay and Stephens, Springfield, Illinois, for permission to reprint from *One Hundred Years of Law* by Paul M. Angle, copyright 1928.

To Dodd, Mead & Company, New York, for permission to reprint from *Lincoln and the Civil War in the Letters and Diaries of John Hay* by Tyler Dennett, copyright 1939; and from *Lincoln the President,* Volume I, by James G. Randall, copyright 1945.

To Harcourt, Brace and Company, Inc., New York, for permission to reprint from *Abraham Lincoln, The Prairie Years*, Volumes I and II, by Carl Sandburg, copyright 1926; from *Myths After Lincoln* by Lloyd Lewis, copyright 1929; from *Abraham Lincoln, The War Years*, Volumes I, II, III, and IV, by Carl Sandburg, copyright 1939; and from *Mary Lincoln, Wife and Widow* by Carl Sandburg and Paul M. Angle, copyright 1932.

To Harper & Brothers, New York, for permission to reprint from *Recollections of President Lincoln* by L. E. Chittenden, copyright 1891; from *In the Footsteps of the Lincolns* by Ida M. Tarbell, copyright 1924; and from *Reveille in Washington* by Margaret Leech, copyright 1941.

To D. C. Heath and Company, Boston, for permission to reprint from *The Civil War and Reconstruction* by James G. Randall, copyright 1937.

To Houghton Mifflin Company, Boston, for permission to reprint from *Memoirs of Henry Villard*, Volume I, by Henry Villard, copyright 1904; from *The Diary of Gideon Welles*, Volumes I and II, copyright 1911; from *The Real Lincoln* by Jesse W. Weik, copyright 1922; from *Abraham Lincoln, 1809–1858*, Volume I, by Albert J. Beveridge, copyright 1928; and from *Lawyer Lincoln* by Albert A. Woldman, copyright 1936.

To Little, Brown & Company, Boston, for permission to reprint from *Tad Lincoln's Father* by Julia Taft Bayne, copyright 1931.

To David Lloyd, New York, and the estate of Lord Charnwood for permission to reprint from *Abraham Lincoln* by Lord Charnwood, copyright 1917 by Henry Holt and Company.

To G. P. Putnam's Sons, New York, for permission to reprint from *Recollections of War Times* by Albert G. Riddle, copyright 1895; and from *Reminiscences of a War-Time Statesman and Diplomat* by Frederick W. Seward, copyright 1916.

To Random House, Inc., New York, for permission to reprint from *The Life and Writings of Abraham Lincoln* by Philip Van Doren Stern, copyright 1940.

To Thomas P. Reep, Petersburg, Illinois, for permission to reprint from *Lincoln at New Salem* by Thomas P. Reep, copyright 1927 by Old Salem Lincoln League.

To The Torch Press, Cedar Rapids, Iowa, for permission to reprint from *Memoirs of Gustave Koerner*, copyright 1909; and from *Lincoln and Herndon* by Joseph Fort Newton, copyright 1910.

Foreword

The Lincoln Reader is a biography written by sixty-five authors. From their writings one hundred seventy-nine selections have been chosen and arranged to form an integrated narrative. Great names in Lincoln biography—Carl Sandburg, Ida M. Tarbell, Lord Charnwood, Albert J. Beveridge, William H. Herndon, John G. Nicolay, and John Hay—stand out prominently; others, like James G. Randall and Benjamin P. Thomas, are better known to scholars than to the general public. Quite a few whose writings appear here have been forgotten by almost everyone, and at least two who wrote contemporary news stories which I have included have never emerged from anonymity. And I suppose there are not many readers who would include Lincoln himself in a list of Lincoln biographers, yet some of his writings have notable biographical significance.

I wish I could formulate the standard of selection by which I have been guided. It would be gratifying, though presumptuous, to be able to assert that here is the "best" of Carl Sandburg, or Lord Charnwood, or Nicolay and Hay, but I make no such claim. I have simply taken from each author what seemed to fit best at a given point in the book—a fine piece of narrative here, a vivid reminiscence there, a penetrating character study or a contemporary diary entry at other places. Beyond that, all I can say is that I have taken pains to see that no author is unworthily represented.

In making any book one acquires many obligations; in this my debts are unusually numerous. I am well aware of the fact that in *The Lincoln Reader* I have been no more than a kind of literary midwife to those who have really labored, and to them, and, in many instances, their publishers also, I am forever indebted. From my own publishers, the Rutgers University Press, I have received far more aid than even an unreasonable author could possibly expect. Jay Monaghan and Margaret A. Flint of the Illinois State Historical Library have given me assistance cheerfully and efficiently whenever I requested it, while Margaret Scriven, June Rosen, and Teresa Krutz of the Chicago Historical Society have helped me to weather one crisis after another. Finally, a long-suffering family has once more accepted all the consequences of authorship—and they are many—without complaint.

A word as to references. The sources from which all the selections in this book have been taken are listed under the heading, *References*, at the end of the text. The listing, which follows the same order in which the selections appear, is by short title only. Full titles, with other bibliographical information, will be found in the *Bibliography*.

PAUL M. ANGLE

Chicago Historical Society
October 1, 1946

THE
LINCOLN
READER

CHAPTER ONE

Kentucky Childhood

ON THE TWELFTH of February, 1809, Abraham Lincoln was born in central Kentucky. His
family lived in primitive surroundings. He enjoyed none
of the advantages that even then were not uncommon—
good schooling, wealth, family influence. Yet he rose above
his environment to leadership in the law, to political prominence, to the Presidency. There, in little more than four
years, his supreme fitness was proved. And when he died,
at the end of the severest crisis in the nation's history, all
mankind called him great.

Biographers, baffled by the gap between his humble
origin and enduring fame, have sought to find an explanation for his genius in heredity. On the paternal side, his
ancestry has been traced to Samuel Lincoln, a weaver's ap-
prentice who emigrated from England to the New World
and settled at Hingham, Massachusetts, in 1637. For
nearly a century and a half the family line was carried on
by sturdy, respectable citizens in Massachusetts, New
Jersey, Pennsylvania, and Virginia. Then one named
Abraham yielded to the lure of the West and crossed the
mountains to Kentucky, where his son Thomas grew to
manhood and married Nancy Hanks. Of this union the
sixteenth President of the United States was born.

As far as the records show, no other Lincoln gave any
sign of greatness. On the other hand, none possessed qualities that require apology.

The maternal ancestry of Abraham Lincoln remains
obscure. Nancy Hanks, his mother, may have been the il-

*legitimate daughter of Lucy Hanks; she may also have
been born in wedlock before her mother became a widow.
The evidence is inconclusive. Neither hypothesis, however,
accounts for the greatness of her son. The Hankses, an
undistinguished family, never attained even the modest
status of the Lincolns; and those who subscribe to the
theory of Nancy's illegitimacy can give no good reason for
believing that Abraham Lincoln's unknown grandfather
was possessed of extraordinary capacity.*

*When not even the bare record of a man's ancestry can
be established, and when what little is known reveals no
continuity of personality between himself and his for-
bears, the story of his life is best begun with his own birth.*

1

IN SENTENCES as bare of ornament as the cabin in which he
was born, Abraham Lincoln described his birth and early childhood,
and related all the family history that he knew. The autobiography,
written in the third person, was prepared for John Locke Scripps
of Chicago, who was gathering material for a campaign biography
of the Republican nominee.

A BRAHAM LINCOLN was born February 12, 1809, then in
Hardin, now in the more recently formed county of La Rue, Kentucky. His father, Thomas, and grandfather, Abraham, were
born in Rockingham County, Virginia, whither their ancestors
had come from Berks County, Pennsylvania. His lineage has been
traced no farther back than this. The family were originally
Quakers, though in later times they have fallen away from the
peculiar habits of that people. The grandfather, Abraham, had
four brothers—Isaac, Jacob, John, and Thomas. So far as known,
the descendants of Jacob and John are still in Virginia. Isaac
went to a place near where Virginia, North Carolina, and Tennessee join; and his descendants are in that region. Thomas came to
Kentucky, and after many years died there, whence his descendants went to Missouri. Abraham, grandfather of the subject of
this sketch, came to Kentucky, and was killed by Indians about
the year 1784. He left a widow, three sons, and two daughters.
The eldest son, Mordecai, remained in Kentucky till late in life,

when he removed to Hancock County, Illinois, where soon after he died, and where several of his descendants still remain. The second son, Josiah, removed at an early day to a place on Blue River, now within Hancock County, Indiana, but no recent information of him or his family has been obtained. The eldest sister, Mary, married Ralph Crume, and some of her descendants are now known to be in Breckenridge County, Kentucky. The second sister, Nancy, married William Brumfield, and her family are not known to have left Kentucky, but there is no recent information from them. Thomas, the youngest son and father of the present subject, by the early death of his father, and very narrow circumstances of his mother, even in childhood was a wandering laboring-boy, and grew up literally without education. He never did more in the way of writing than to bunglingly write his own name. Before he was grown he passed one year as a hired hand with his uncle Isaac on Watauga, a branch of the Holston River. Getting back into Kentucky, and having reached his twenty-eighth year, he married Nancy Hanks—mother of the present subject—in the year 1806. She also was born in Virginia; and relatives of hers of the name of Hanks, and of other names, now reside in Coles, in Macon, and in Adams counties, Illinois, and also in Iowa. The present subject has no brother or sister of the whole or half blood. He had a sister, older than himself, who was grown and married, but died many years ago, leaving no child; also a brother, younger than himself, who died in infancy.

2

OF LINCOLN'S BIRTH and childhood little more is known than what he himself wrote. A great artist, however, needs few materials. From neighborhood traditions, old men's memories, and a poet's understanding of men and women, Carl Sandburg amplifies the sparse facts of Lincoln's own record.

I N MAY AND THE BLOSSOMTIME of the year 1808, Tom and Nancy with little Sarah moved out from Elizabethtown to the farm of George Brownfield, where Tom did carpenter work and helped farm.

The Lincolns had a cabin of their own to live in. It stood among wild crab apple trees.

And the smell of wild crab apple blossoms, and the low crying of all wild things, came keen that summer to the nostrils of Nancy Hanks.

The summer stars that year shook out pain and warning, strange laughters, for Nancy Hanks.

The same year saw the Lincolns moved to a place on the Big South Fork of Nolin's Creek, about two and a half miles from Hodgenville. They were trying to farm a little piece of ground and make a home. The house they lived in was a cabin of logs cut from the timber near by.

The floor was packed-down dirt. One door, swung on leather hinges, let them in and out. One small window gave a lookout on the weather, the rain or snow, sun and trees, and the play of the rolling prairie and low hills. A stick-clay chimney carried the fire smoke up and away.

One morning in February of this year, 1809, Tom Lincoln came out of his cabin to the road, stopped a neighbor and asked him to tell "the granny woman," Aunt Peggy Walters, that Nancy would need help soon.

On the morning of February 12, a Sunday, the granny woman was there at the cabin. And she and Tom Lincoln and the moaning Nancy Hanks welcomed into a world of battle and blood, of whispering dreams and wistful dust, a new child, a boy.

A little later that morning Tom Lincoln threw some extra wood on the fire, and an extra bearskin over the mother, went out of the cabin, and walked two miles up the road to where the Sparrows, Tom and Betsy, lived. Dennis Hanks, the nine-year-old boy adopted by the Sparrows, met Tom at the door.

In his slow way of talking—he was a slow and a quiet man— Tom Lincoln told them, "Nancy's got a boy baby." A half sheepish look was in his eyes, as though maybe more babies were not wanted in Kentucky just then.

The boy, Dennis Hanks, took to his feet, down the road to the Lincoln cabin. There he saw Nancy Hanks on a bed of poles cleated to a corner of the cabin, under warm bearskins.

She turned her dark head from looking at the baby to look at Dennis and threw him a tired, white smile from her mouth and gray eyes. He stood by the bed, his eyes wide open, watching the even, quiet breaths, of this fresh, soft red baby.

"What you goin' to name him, Nancy?" the boy asked.

"Abraham," was the answer, "after his grandfather."

Soon came Betsy Sparrow. She washed the baby, put a yellow petticoat and a linsey shirt on him, cooked dried berries with wild honey for Nancy, put the one-room cabin in better order, kissed Nancy and comforted her, and went home.

Little Dennis rolled up in a bearskin and slept by the fireplace that night. He listened for the crying of the newborn child once in the night and the feet of the father moving on the dirt floor to help the mother and the little one. In the morning he took a long look at the baby and said to himself, "Its skin looks just like red cherry pulp squeezed dry, in wrinkles."

He asked if he could hold the baby. Nancy, as she passed the little one into Dennis's arms, said, "Be keerful, Dennis, fur you air the fust boy he's ever seen."

And Dennis swung the baby back and forth, keeping up a chatter about how tickled he was to have a new cousin to play with. The baby screwed up the muscles of its face and began crying with no let-up.

Dennis turned to Betsy Sparrow, handed her the baby, and said to her, "Aunt, take him! He'll never come to much."

3

WITH A WOMAN'S INTUITION, Ida M. Tarbell pictures the life of Nancy Hanks Lincoln on the Sinking Spring farm, where the Lincoln family lived during the first two years of Abraham's life.

THE LIFE THAT NANCY HANKS with her children led in this cabin was in all its details the same life that she was to lead up to her death. Here on her hillside farm there were none even of the simple excitements that she may have enjoyed in E-town. She was more alone here, though she had neighbors at no great distance. But her life was like that of them all, and in many of its details like the life of the Lincolns who first came to this country, Samuel and his wife Martha in Hingham, Massachusetts, in the middle of the seventeenth century.

Here, as there, the fireplace of the cabin was the very heart of the place. Nancy's fireplace, as we see it today, was deep and wide, with a long stone mantel and big hearthstone. The chimney was outside—a cat-and-clay chimney, as it was called, made by mixing cut straw or grass with stiff clay and laying it in alternate layers with split lathes of hard wood. Within, hooks were fitted and the long crane from which to suspend pots.

The feeding of the fireplace was one of the essential tasks of a pioneer home. And it was one of the tasks that later was to fall to the baby that now lay in Nancy's arms. He was to learn that a woodpile was only one degree less important to the life of the home than the cupboard. He was to learn to gather for the fireplace for months before winter set in, as Nancy did for her larder. There must be logs as long as the opening, of a half dozen different sizes; they must be green and dry, hard and soft, and there must be chips to kindle a low fire, brush to make a blaze. He was to learn that a fire must never go out after cold sets in. And he was to master all the ceremonials of the fireplace—putting on the back log, packing the coals at night, stirring them in the morning, and choosing just the right wood for quick heat. The baby Abraham was to learn all this, and to learn—who ever better?—the joys of the fireside, and how it might light one on the way to knowledge.

Nancy was not troubled at her fireplace with a multiplicity of cooking utensils like a housewife of today. Her chief reliance was the Dutch oven, a big iron pot with a cover, standing on long legs and kept continuously on the coals. After the Dutch oven, the most important article was her long-handled frying pan. On this she roasted the game with which the larder of her home was always filled, both in Kentucky and later in Indiana. Here, too, she fried the salt pork and bacon which the pioneer always preferred to venison, rabbit or wild turkey, and, of course, it was on this frying pan that she made the hot bread and cakes which went with the meats. . . .

Her bread baking she did in a clay oven—not so good an oven as that which Thomas's mother had used back in Virginia, for that was brick, but it was an oven of the same kind. Nancy had an outside fireplace, too, where in summer she kept her Dutch oven going, and in the fall tried out lard, and made soap and prepared the tallow for the candles. All through the summer, like every pioneer housewife, she gathered wild berries and dried them. All though the fall she cut and strung apples and pumpkins to dry. . . . In the fall, too, she wrapped up in dry leaves or bits of paper apples and pears to keep for her children's Christmas. . . .

She was skilled in spinning and weaving, and there were few days that did not find her at her loom or wheel, or cutting up and making into garments for Thomas, little Sarah, the baby Abraham, the linsey-woolsey she had spun. From her loom, too, came woolen blankets in the fine and simple designs of her time. When she collected by long patience enough pieces of cotton for a quilt she patched it in some famous pattern, and as she worked she rocked her baby in the simple cradle we can well believe Tom Lincoln had made for her.

4

IN 1811, Thomas Lincoln moved to a farm ten miles north and east of the one on which Abraham was born. Albert J. Beveridge, with fine feeling for the rugged country in which it was located, describes the new farm and its surroundings, and relates something of the boy's life there.

Some seven or eight miles north and east from the Sinking Spring farm, a tremendous stone escarpment called Muldraugh's Hill divides the Barrens from the lower and heavily timbered land to the northward. This vast cliff is pierced by a valley four miles in length and from one fourth of a mile to two miles broad. High hills, abrupt, and mountainous in appearance, rise on either side. Lengthwise through the valley a deep and rapid stream, Knob Creek, hurries to the Rolling Fork, a large stream at the valley end; and the Rolling Fork, in turn, flows into Salt River which empties into the Ohio.

From the gorges of the lofty elevations on either side of the valley smaller streams feed Knob Creek which has its rise in the cliffs that separate the valley from the higher land of the Barrens. For five hundred feet this eminence sharply falls to land and streams below; and the abutting hills, stretching out from the parent cliff like gnarled and knotted arms of a giant, are almost as imposing.

Formed as it is of the silt carried from the surface of the hills, the product of decomposing vegetation throughout ages of time, the soil of this valley is extremely rich and productive. Some of the little triangles of land that project from Knob Creek into the hills on either side are not surpassed in fertility—the mere dropping of seed with the slightest cultivation suffices to yield a crop. In 1813,[1] when Thomas Lincoln moved to Knob Creek from his sterile farm on the edge of the Barrens, the main stream and tributaries teemed with fish and the surrounding hills were full of game. A more ideal spot for the winning of a livelihood with the least possible exertion could not be found.

At the end of such a hollow projecting from Knob Creek into the cliff-like hills, two and one half miles from the Rolling Fork, Thomas Lincoln set up his new home. . . . Seven miles southwest of his Knob Creek cabin, was Hodgen's mill, where Thomas Lincoln took his corn to be ground, although other grist mills were nearer to his cabin. There were thirty acres in the hill-enclosed triangle that Lincoln occupied. Not all of the small farm could be cultivated, however, since part of the thirty acres ran up into the encompassing hills. Dennis Hanks thus describes Lincoln's Knob Creek holding: "The 30-acre farm in Kentucky was Knotty— Knobby—as a piece of land could be, with deep hollows and ravines, cedar trees covering the . . . Knobs as thick as trees could grow." At least half of the farm was on the bottom, for Thomas tilled fourteen acres "running up and down the branch about 40 feet on either side." His cabin was much like the one by the Sinking Spring.

This valley was comparatively well settled, and neighbors were more numerous and not so distant as had been the case in the region of the Sinking Spring. Sometime during the sojourn of the Lincoln family on Knob Creek a school was opened in the vicinity by one Zachariah Riney, a Catholic; and Sarah accompanied by her little brother went to this school for a few weeks. Later another school, taught by one Caleb Hazel, was attended by the Lincoln children for an even briefer period.

"It was from that place [Knob Creek cabin]," writes Haycraft to Herndon, "that young Abraham commenced trudging his way to school to Caleb Hazel with whom I was well acquainted and

---

[1] Correct date: 1811.

could perhaps teach spelling, reading and indifferent writing and perhaps could cypher to the Rule of three—but he had no other qualification of a teacher except large size and bodily strength to thrash any boy or youth that came to his School."

Humble indeed was the appearance of these children of the poverty-burdened pioneers, Abraham being clad in "a one piece long linsey shirt" without other garments, since school was held only in warm weather. Three months, at best, was the extent of the instruction the girl and boy thus received. These schools, like all others at that time, were subscription affairs, a very small charge being made for each child taught. But, admits Dennis Hanks, "Abe had no books in Ky."

Abraham's experiences on Knob Creek were, however, of far greater value than any premature schooling could have been. Lovely and noble were his surroundings, perfect and healthful conditions. The steep and rocky heights that rose from the yard of the Lincoln cabin and all about the valley, were clad with majestic trees, mostly of cedar, two and more feet in diameter, their crests from seventy to a hundred feet above the earth. Clear as light was the water of the streams—so clear that through them pebbles in deep pools could be seen as plainly as on the surface of the ground.

There was no bustle of hurrying people, no noise, no tumult, no distraction. It was a place of peace, calm, silent, and serene. A still and tranquil grandeur was the most intimate companion with which destiny supplied Abraham Lincoln at the time of his first impressions of life and the world.

5

IN THE HILL REGIONS of Kentucky and Tennessee the people change slowly. Attending college there many years after the removal of the Lincoln family, and later preaching to the mountain folk, William E. Barton was unwittingly preparing himself to understand Lincoln's early boyhood.

LIFE IN THE KNOB CREEK CABIN proceeded along a line so well defined by the conditions of frontier life, and so familiar to those who have known life of that character that we have no uncertainty concerning its essential details. Thomas Lincoln annually scratched the surface of his three little fields, the largest of which contained seven acres, using a wooden plow shod with iron. His main crop was corn; but he had some beans, and he dropped a pumpkin seed into every third hill of corn. Abraham when a small boy was taught the art of corn-dropping, and instructed to remember the pumpkin seed in the third hill. The corn was cultivated with a "bull-tongue" plow, Abraham in his last year in Kentucky riding the horse to plow between the corn rows. Thomas also planted some potatoes and a few onions, and Nancy may have had a small garden and a few flowers.

Thomas Lincoln was a good judge of horses. The Estray Books contain for the most part stereotyped notices to the effect that John Smith took up as an estray at his farm on Bull Skin Creek, a bay mare, or a brindle cow. When Thomas Lincoln reported an estray, he measured the height in hands, and looked at the teeth for age, and noted all the marks and brands. He was never without horses after his coming of age, and on Knob Creek he owned a stallion and several brood mares.

He attended the auction sale of the personal property of Jonathan Joseph in 1814. Three heifers were sold at auction, and Thomas Lincoln bought the best one, as judged by the price. He habitually attended auctions, and with sufficient money in his pocket to be a successful bidder, and his purchases were sensible.

With one possible exception:

On July 19, 1814, he attended the auction sale of the estate of Thomas Hall and made several purchases. A sword which he bought is easily accounted for; he wanted to make it over into a drawing-knife. But he bought a "truck-waggon" for eight and one half cents. What kind of wagon could he have bought for that price? No kind of wagon, so far as I know, but a toy. Abraham was then five years and five months of age. I imagine Abraham was the happiest lad on Knob Creek that night. . . .

While actual details are lacking, we have no difficulty in supplying the essential facts of the life of the Lincoln family on Knob Creek from our knowledge of the nature of the farm and of frontier life of the period. . . .

It is not probable that Nancy Lincoln had a button to her back. Her dresses were of linsey-woolsey and they were put on and re-

moved without any needless enlarging or closing of the aperture
at the neck. One or two pins may have been used at the throat, but
pins were a luxury. Nor did she possess a hairpin. She probably
wore a horn comb, and it may have been ornamental. In that
region, the hair of a woman is always slipping from its one moor-
ing, and coming loose. The owner must frequently remove her
back comb, run it through her hair a few times, coil up the hair
again, and refasten it with her comb. A woman in the hills of
Kentucky never starts any new occupation without first winding
herself up in this fashion.

Cows were cheap. A good cow and calf could usually be bought
for ten dollars. Feed for cattle cost nothing from early spring
until late in the fall; for the cattle ranged freely in the woods, but
usually came home at night to their calves. When they did not
come home, some one had to hunt for them; and that was likely to
be a wearisome quest. Nancy milked the cows until Sarah was old
enough to relieve her of this duty; does not the word "daughter"
mean "milker?" This is the way Sarah milked. First of all, she
drove the cow into a fence corner, and then led the calf out of the
pen, and permitted the calf to begin its meal. This induced the
cow to let down her milk. The prospect of a speedy meeting with
the calf was a strong inducement to the cow to come home at
night; one cow with a young calf could usually be depended upon
to lead the entire herd to the fence at milking time. When the
milk was ready to flow freely, Sarah led the protesting calf back
into the pen or shed, and proceeded to secure the family's share
of the milk. She did not use a milking stool, but stood and with
her right hand milked into a gourd which she held in her left hand.
Now and then she stopped to empty the gourd into a bucket
placed in an adjacent fence corner, safe from the danger of being
kicked over. After she had obtained as much milk as she deemed
equitable, she brought back the calf; and the calf had the
rich strippings, while the mother contentedly licked her offspring. . . .

Of duties inside the house, we also know the daily routine.

Thomas worked his little farm, not industriously, but with
sufficient labor to produce each season a little crop of corn; now
and then he cheerfully went by invitation to do an odd job of
carpenter work; but Nancy worked at home every day. If Thomas

had sheep, she carded, spun and wove. In the absence of wool, she knew the uses of buffalo wool. The chafing dish was unknown to her, but she was on terms of intimate friendship with its predecessor, the skillet. She laid hold of the spindle and her hands knew the distaff. She ate not the bread of idleness. But . . . Nancy was able to finish all her necessary work early in the afternoon; and having no rocking chair, she held her baby in her arms as she sat in a low splint-bottomed chair whose front legs thumped the puncheon floor, if indeed, the Knob Creek cabin had such a floor. There was a certain unhurried spirit about the labor of the pioneer household. . . . The pioneer did not fret because he could not cut down the whole forest in a single year. He accepted his situation, and when his day's work was done, he rested and visited and took life as comfortably as he was able. Nancy knew what to do in her hours of ease. . . .

Nor was life in those conditions devoid of a certain simple luxury. Now and then Thomas cut down a bee tree, and then the family had honey, some of which was kept in a crock against the time of need. Occasionally he did a day's work in Bardstown and took his pay in unbolted wheat flour. Who that has never lived long on hoecake and corn pone with sorghum molasses (a plural noun) for "long-sweetening" can know the sheer delight of hot biscuit and honey? And there was wild turkey, and in time there were chickens to fry. The creek furnished fish. The Knob Creek farm provided a reasonably sure living with a minimum of physical exertion.

Nor were occasions of special festivity lacking. There were cornhuskings and frolics and raisings and weddings and camp meetings and funerals. And there was the monthly preaching service.

Besides all this, the Knob Creek farm was on the main road from Louisville to Nashville. Travelers went by every day, and sometimes stopped and talked. There was a mill on Knob Creek as early as 1797, and that was an important social center. Moreover, Caleb Hazel, father of Lincoln's schoolteacher of the same name, kept a tavern, where he provided things to eat and also to drink. Sometimes he paid his license, and sometimes he paid his fine.

Life on Knob Creek was not so dull as has been imagined. Compared with Nolin Creek, the Knob Creek farm was located on Main Street of the Kentucky wilderness.

The Knob Creek farm was more fertile and more easily tilled than that on Nolin Creek; and here Abraham had his first experience in riding a horse to plow corn. The farm was subject to sudden rise of water, which sometimes flooded the valley almost without warning when a heavy storm broke over the hill, and the plain would be submerged when there had been little or no rain at the cabin. One such storm came just after corn planting and seemed to wash all the seed and soil away, and to leave instead only sand and clay. . . .

Of Abraham Lincoln's life in this environment few authentic traditions remain. The years were uneventful. The labored efforts of later decades to fill in this gap bear on their face the marks of invention. But these were not lost years in Lincoln's life. . . .

Much more romantic than Nolin, Knob Creek was a place to stir the boyish imagination. In some fashion, the strength of the hills became his in those years in the Knob Creek cabin. . . . Child that he was, and with a narrowed horizon walled in by almost insuperable heights that shut him from contact with the outer world, save as that world plodded along the rough road down Muldraugh's Hill and along the creek, he was not wholly out of touch with the beginnings of imagination and aspiration and nascent achievement.

CHAPTER TWO

Youth In Indiana

T HROUGHOUT *his residence in Kentucky Thomas Lincoln was a decent, respected, though far from prominent citizen. He had credit with merchants and paid his bills; he served on juries and in other public capacities; he owned livestock, and supported his little family as well as other men of his station in life. But he had constant trouble with the titles to the farms on which he lived. In 1816, with a suit to deprive him of title to the Knob Creek farm pending in court, he decided to move to Indiana. There, on land acquired directly from the United States government, a man could be sure that no technical flaw would cause him to lose a farm into which he had put years of hard work.*

So the Lincoln family moved in 1816 to an undeveloped region in the southwestern corner of Indiana, there to remain through fourteen years that took a tenacious hold on Lincoln's memory. Long afterward, when he summarized these years in his third person autobiography, .he wrote with clear recollection of the "unbroken forest" in which the family settled, and of the clearing away of timber that was "the great task ahead." Of himself he said that though very young he "was large of his age, and had an ax put into his hands at once; and from that till within his twenty-third year he was almost constantly handling that most useful instrument—less, of course, in plowing and harvesting seasons."

One small incident burned itself into his mind. "A few days before the completion of his eighth year," he wrote,

"in the absence of his father, a flock of wild turkeys ap-
proached the new log cabin, and Abraham with a rifle-gun,
standing inside, shot through a crack and killed one of
them. He has never since pulled a trigger on any larger
game."

1

THE REMOVAL from Kentucky to Indiana, and the hard times
that the family endured at the beginning of their residence, are
described by John G. Nicolay and John Hay, two men who in later
years were to know Lincoln intimately and to become his "official"
biographers. In their youth both Nicolay and Hay had been close
enough to frontier conditions to write of them with realism.

By the time the boy Abraham had attained his seventh
year, the social condition of Kentucky had changed considerably
from the early poineer days. Life had assumed a more settled and
orderly course. The old barbarous equality of the earlier time was
gone; a difference of classes began to be seen. Those who held
slaves assumed a distinct social superiority over those who did not.
Thomas Lincoln, concluding that Kentucky was no country for
a poor man, determined to seek his fortune in Indiana. He had
heard of rich and unoccupied lands in Perry County in that State,
and there he determined to go. He built a rude raft, loaded it with
his kit of tools and four hundred gallons of whisky, and trusted
his fortunes to the winding watercourses. He met with only one
accident on his way: his raft capsized in the Ohio River, but he
fished up his kit of tools and most of the ardent spirits and arrived
safely at the place of a settler named Posey, with whom he left
his odd invoice of household goods for the wilderness, while he
started on foot to look for a home in the dense forest. He selected
a spot which pleased him in his first day's journey. He then
walked back to Knob Creek and brought his family on to their new
home. No humbler cavalcade ever invaded the Indiana timber.
Besides his wife and two children, his earthly possessions were of
the slightest, for the backs of two borrowed horses sufficed for the
load. Insufficient bedding and clothing, a few pans and kettles,
were their sole movable wealth. They relied on Lincoln's kit of

tools for their furniture, and on his rifle for their food. At Posey's they hired a wagon and literally hewed a path through the wilderness to their new habitation near Little Pigeon Creek, a mile and a half east of Gentryville, in a rich and fertile forest country.

Thomas Lincoln, with the assistance of his wife and children, built a temporary shelter of the sort called in the frontier language "a half-faced camp"; merely a shed of poles, which defended the inmates on three sides from foul weather, but left them open to its inclemency in front. For a whole year his family lived in this wretched fold, while he was clearing a little patch of ground for planting corn, and building a rough cabin for a permanent residence. They moved into the latter before it was half completed; for by this time the Sparrows had followed the Lincolns from Kentucky, and the half-faced camp was given up to them. But the rude cabin seemed so spacious and comfortable after the squalor of "the camp," that Thomas Lincoln did no further work on it for a long time. He left it for a year or two without doors, or windows, or floor. The battle for existence allowed him no time for such superfluities. He raised enough corn to support life; the dense forest around him abounded in every form of feathered game; a little way from his cabin an open glade was full of deer licks, and an hour or two of idle waiting was generally rewarded by a shot at a fine deer, which would furnish meat for a week, and material for breeches and shoes. His cabin was like that of other pioneers. A few three-legged stools; a bedstead made of poles stuck between the logs in the angle of the cabin, the outside corner supported by a crotched stick driven into the ground; the table, a huge hewed log standing on four legs; a pot, kettle, and skillet, and a few tin and pewter dishes were all the furniture. The boy Abraham climbed at night to his bed of leaves in the loft, by a ladder of wooden pins driven into the logs.

2

TWO YEARS PASSED, and prospects brightened for the Lincolns. Then came the milksickness, intermittent scourge of the pioneers, and with it, death and sorrow. Carl Sandburg reconstructs these grim weeks.

Hardly a year had passed [since their arrival], however, when both Tom and Betsy Sparrow were taken down with the "milk sick," beginning with a whitish coat on the tongue. Both died and were buried in October on a little hill in a clearing in the timbers near by.

Soon after, there came to Nancy Hanks Lincoln that white coating of the tongue; her vitals burned; the tongue turned brownish; her feet and hands grew cold and colder, her pulse slow and slower. She knew she was dying, called for her children, and spoke to them her last choking words. Sarah and Abe leaned over the bed. A bony hand of the struggling mother went out, putting its fingers into the boy's sandy black hair; her fluttering guttural words seemed to say he must grow up and be good to his sister and father.

So, on a bed of poles cleated to the corner of the cabin, the body of Nancy Hanks Lincoln lay, looking tired . . . tired . . . with a peace settling in the pinched corners of the sweet, weary mouth, silence slowly etching away the lines of pain and hunger drawn around the gray eyes where now the eyelids closed down in the fine pathos of unbroken rest, a sleep without interruption settling about the form of the stooped and wasted shoulder bones, looking to the children who tiptoed in, stood still, cried their tears of want and longing, whispered "Mammy, Mammy," and heard only their own whispers answering, looking to these little ones of her brood as though new secrets had come to her in place of the old secrets given up with the breath of life.

And Tom Lincoln took a log left over from the building of the cabin, and he and Dennis Hanks whipsawed the log into planks, planed the planks smooth, and made them of a measure for a box to bury the dead wife and mother in. Little Abe, with a jackknife, whittled pine wood pegs. And then, while Dennis and Abe held the planks, Tom bored holes and stuck the whittled pegs through the bored holes. This was the coffin, and they carried it the next day to the same little timber clearing near by, where a few weeks before they had buried Tom and Betsy Sparrow. It was in the way of the deer run leading to the saltish water; light feet and shy hoofs ran over those early winter graves.

So the woman, Nancy Hanks, died, thirty-six years old, a pioneer sacrifice, with memories of monotonous, endless everyday chores, of mystic Bible verses read over and over for their promises, and with memories of blue wistful hills and a summer when the crab apple blossoms flamed white and she carried a boy-child into the world.

3

THOMAS LINCOLN soon discovered that life in a backwoods cabin, with the hardships it brought to two small children deprived of a mother's care, was next to impossible. In little more than a year after the death of Nancy Hanks Lincoln he went back to Kentucky on a quest that is traced by Ward Hill Lamon.

THIRTEEN MONTHS after the burial of Nancy Hanks . . . Thomas Lincoln appeared at Elizabethtown, Kentucky, in search of another wife. Sally Bush had married Johnston, the jailer, in the spring of the same year in which Lincoln had married Nancy Hanks. She had then rejected him for a better match, but was now a widow. In 1814, many persons in and about Elizabethtown had died of a disease which the people called the "cold plague," and among them the jailer. Both parties being free again, Lincoln came back very unexpectedly to Mrs. Johnston, and opened his suit in an exceedingly abrupt manner. "Well, *Miss* Johnston," said he, "I have no wife, and you have no husband. I came a purpose to marry you: I knowed you from a gal, and you knowed me from a boy. I have no time to lose; and, if you are willin', let it be done straight off." To this she replied, "Tommy, I know you well, and have no objection to marrying you; but I cannot do it straight off, as I owe some debts that must first be paid." "The next morning," says Hon. Samuel Haycraft, the clerk of the courts and the gentleman who reports this quaint courtship, "I issued his license, and they were married *straight* off on that day, and left, and I never saw her or Tom Lincoln since." From the death of her husband to that day, she had been living, "an honest, poor widow," "in a round log-cabin," which stood in an "alley" just below Mr. Haycraft's house. Dennis Hanks says that it was

only "on the earnest solicitation of her friends" that Mrs. Johnston consented to marry Lincoln. They all liked Lincoln, and it
was with a member of her family that he had made several voyages
to New Orleans. Mr. Helm, who at that time was doing business in
his uncle's store at Elizabethtown, remarks that "life among the
Hankses, the Lincolns, and the Enlows was a long ways below life
among the Bushes." Sally was the best and the proudest of the
Bushes; but, nevertheless, she appears to have maintained some
intercourse with the Lincolns as long as they remained in Kentucky. . . .

Mrs. Johnston has been denominated a "poor widow"; but
she possessed goods, which, in the eyes of Tom Lincoln, were of
almost unparalleled magnificence. Among other things, she had a
bureau that cost forty dollars; and he informed her, on their arrival in Indiana, that, in his deliberate opinion, it was little less
than sinful to be the owner of such a thing. He demanded that
she should turn it into cash, which she positively refused to do.
She had quite a lot of other articles, however, which he thought
well enough in their way, and some of which were sadly needed in
his miserable cabin in the wilds of Indiana. Dennis Hanks speaks
with great rapture of the "large supply of household goods"
which she brought out with her. There was "one fine bureau, one
table, one set of chairs, one large clothes-chest, cooking utensils,
knives, forks, bedding, and other articles." It was a glorious day
for little Abe and Sarah and Dennis when this wondrous collection
of rich furniture arrived in the Pigeon Creek settlement. But all
this wealth required extraordinary means of transportation; and
Lincoln had recourse to his brother-in-law, Ralph Krume, who
lived just over the line, in Breckinridge County. Krume came
with a four-horse team, and moved Mrs. Johnston, now Mrs. Lincoln, with her family and effects, to the home of her new husband
in Indiana. When she got there, Mrs. Lincoln was much "surprised" at the contrast between the glowing representations which
her husband had made to her before leaving Kentucky and the real
poverty and meanness of the place. She had evidently been given
to understand that the bridegroom had reformed his old Kentucky
ways, and was now an industrious and prosperous farmer. She was
scarcely able to restrain the expression of her astonishment and

discontent; but, though sadly overreached in a bad bargain, her lofty pride and her high sense of Christian duty saved her from hopeless and useless repinings. On the contrary, she set about mending what was amiss with all her strength and energy. Her own goods furnished the cabin with tolerable decency. She made Lincoln put down a floor, and hang windows and doors. It was in the depth of winter; and the children, as they nestled in the warm beds she provided them, enjoying the strange luxury of security from the cold winds of December, must have thanked her from the bottoms of their newly comforted hearts. She had brought a son and two daughters of her own—John, Sarah, and Matilda; but Abe and his sister . . . , the ragged and hapless little strangers to her blood, were given an equal place in her affections. They were half naked, and she clad them from the stores of clothing she had laid up for her own. They were dirty, and she washed them; they had been ill-used, and she treated them with motherly tenderness. In her own modest language, she "made them look a little more human." "In fact," says Dennis Hanks, "in a few weeks all had changed; and where every thing was wanting, now all was snug and comfortable. She was a woman of great energy, of remarkable good sense, very industrious and saving, and also very neat and tidy in her person and manners, and knew exactly how to manage children. She took an especial liking to young Abe. Her love for him was warmly returned, and continued to the day of his death. But few children loved their parents as he loved his stepmother. She soon dressed him up in entire new clothes, *and from that time on he appeared to lead a new life.* He was encouraged by her to study, and any wish on his part was gratified when it could be done. The two sets of children got along finely together, as if they had all been the children of the same parents. Mrs. Lincoln soon discovered that young Abe was a boy of uncommon natural talents, and that, if rightly trained, a bright future was before him, and she did all in her power to develop those talents." When, in after years, Mr. Lincoln spoke of his "saintly mother," and of his "angel of a mother," he referred to this noble woman, who first made him feel "like a human being"— whose goodness first touched his childish heart, and taught him that blows and taunts and degradation were not to be his only portion in the world.

4

ABRAHAM LINCOLN had gone to school in Kentucky, but the major part of his scanty store of formal education was acquired in an Indiana "blab" school. William E. Barton, familiar in his youth with vestigial schools, draws from his own experience to portray the young Lincoln.

ABRAHAM LINCOLN attended school in Indiana. His first teacher was Andrew Crawford, his second a man named Sweeney, and his third was Azel W. Dorsey. The school which Lincoln attended was one and one fourth miles from the home. Like the Kentucky schools, it was a "blab" school. The system of silent study was beginning to be recognized, but how was the teacher to know that a boy was studying unless the boy kept repeating his lesson aloud as he studied?, And how was he to be persuaded to continue his industrious application to his spelling book unless the teacher passed about the room, whip in hand, and gently or otherwise whipped those who were silent?

Abraham's schoolmates in after years remembered that he had been an apt pupil, eager to learn, and that he quickly surpassed his companions. His sister Sarah, who accompanied him, was also a bright pupil, of good mind, and was more industrious than her brother. For while Abraham loved books, he did not love hard work; and when study became work, he became for a time less eager for learning, and gave himself to fun.

Of Lincoln's school days in Indiana, the most definite memories appear to be those of the school kept by Andrew Crawford. This teacher endeavored to impart not only the education contained in books, but the principles which underlie the usages of polite society. One pupil was required to go out-of-doors, and to be met at the door by another pupil who inquired his name, and then escorted him about the room, presenting him to the pupils one by one.

In his first schools Abraham used only the spelling book. It was the custom in that day for a pupil to spell the book through several times before he began to read. He knew how to spell "incomprehensibility," a "word of eight syllables, accented on the sixth" long before he could read that interesting statement that

"Ann can spin flax." At first he used Dillworth's Speller, then
Webster's *Old Blueback*. After long and faithful use of the speller,
he learned to use the reader, and in time became familiar with
Murray's *English Reader*, which he believed to have been the best
textbook ever supplied to an American boy. . . .

The whole of his schooling, as he has informed us, was less
than a year. What he has told and what is otherwise known of
his teachers has caused some authors to question whether his
teaching was of any considerable value to him. . . . But I know
the kind of schools Lincoln attended, and in spite of their grave
limitations I have a high sense of their value. Even the discipline
of those schools, severe as it was, and combining "lickin' and
l'arnin' " with a liberal allowance for the licking, was not without
its worth. If the teachers were ignorant, so were the pupils and
their parents; if the teacher could cipher to the rule of three, that
was quite as far as most of the pupils had any occasion to go. The
schoolhouses were bare, log buildings, with the cracks unchinked.
They were built upon slopes high enough at one end for hogs to
rest under the floor and fill the place with fleas—a situation only
partly remedied by the pennyroyal which the pupils brought in
by the armful and tramped upon in the aisle. The benches were
of puncheon and had no backs, and it was thought a needless concession to the love of luxury to saw off the legs where they projected upward through the surface of the seat. But the children
departed from those schools a little less ignorant than they were
when they entered.

The books that Lincoln read and reread in his boyhood had a
marked influence upon his life. There was the Bible, first of all,
the basis of his pure literary style, and the foundation of his
system of righteousness expressed in law. There were *Pilgrim's
Progress* and *Æsop's Fables*. There was Weems' *Life of Washington*, at which people smile, but which did good to Abraham
Lincoln and many another lad. There was *Robinson Crusoe*, and
a History of the United States. If we could substitute a better
life of Washington and a modern History of the United States,
it would be for the profit of any American boy if he were shut up
with these half-dozen books and no others until he thoroughly
mastered them. They were an almost ideal selection. To this short

list he later added Franklin's *Autobiography* and Weems' *Life of Marion.*

It has become common to refer mirthfully to Weems' *Life of Washington*, and in truth it has no great merit as critical biography; but . . . . Lincoln read this pompous and highly colored book with none of the disdain of the modern critic. In 1861, in addressing the Senate of the State of New Jersey, he said:

"May I be pardoned if, upon this occasion, I mention that away back in my childhood, the earliest days of my being able to read, I got hold of a small book, such a one as few of the younger members have ever seen—Weems' *Life of Washington*. I remember all the accounts there given of the battle-fields and struggles for the liberties of the country, and none fixed themselves upon my imagination so deeply as the struggle here at Trenton, New Jersey. The crossing of the river, the contest with the Hessians, the great hardships endured at that time, all fixed themselves on my memory more than any single Revolutionary event; and you all know, for you have all been boys, how these early impressions last longer than any others. I recollect thinking then, boy even though I was, that there must have been something more than common that these men struggled for."

Abraham Lincoln became the owner of Weems' *Life of Washington* through an accident. He borrowed the book from Josiah Crawford, a neighbor reputed to have been close-fisted. The book was placed upon a little shelf below an unchinked crack between the logs of the Lincoln home and was damaged by rain. Lincoln offered to pay for it, and had to pull fodder three days at twenty-five cents a day to purchase the book. . . .

At school Abraham was a leader. He stood well in his studies. He was a good reader, an excellent speller, a good penman, and was able to compose well. Very early he had a desire to write out his opinions on many topics; and his essays attracted attention at once. He won the respect of his teachers and also of his fellow students. His habitual and well-known fairness caused him to be chosen to decide mooted questions, and his decisions were accepted without appeal. Altogether it is an attractive young giant who emerges from our study of the conditions of Lincoln's boyhood. He was rude and uncultured; but he had a good mind, a warm heart, a love of justice and fair play, and a high sense of honor that won for him the lasting respect of those who knew him.

5

LINCOLN once reduced his life in Indiana to four short words. "There," he wrote, "I grew up." What growing up meant is described by Ward Hill Lamon, whose account was based on reminiscences by old residents of Spencer County which William H. Herndon gathered soon after Lincoln's death.

ABE HAD A VERY RETENTIVE MEMORY. He frequently amused his young companions by repeating to them long passages from the books he had been reading. On Monday mornings he would mount a stump, and deliver, with a wonderful approach to exactness, the sermon he had heard the day before. His taste for public speaking appeared to be natural and irresistible. His stepsister, Matilda Johnston, says he was an indefatigable "preacher." "When father and mother would go to church, Abe would take down the Bible, read a verse, give out a hymn, and we would sing. Abe was about fifteen years of age. He preached, and we would do the crying. Sometimes he would join in the chorus of tears. One day my brother, John Johnston, caught a land terrapin, brought it to the place where Abe was preaching, threw it against the tree, and crushed the shell. It suffered much—quivered all over. Abe then preached against cruelty to animals, contending that an ant's life was as sweet to it as ours to us."

But this practice of "preaching" and political speaking, into which Abe had fallen, at length became a great nuisance to old Tom. It distracted everybody, and sadly interfered with the work. If Abe had confined his discourses to Sunday preaching, while the old folks were away, it would not have been so objectionable. But he knew his power, liked to please everybody, and would be sure to set up as an orator wherever he found the greatest number of people together. When it was announced that Abe had taken the "stump" in the harvest field, there was an end of work. The hands flocked around him, and listened to his curious speeches with infinite delight. "The sight of such a thing amused all," says Mrs. Lincoln; though she admits that her husband was compelled to break it up with the strong hand; and poor Abe was many times dragged from the platform, and hustled off to his work in no gentle manner.

Abe worked occasionally with Tom Lincoln in the shop; but he did it reluctantly, and never intended to learn even so much of the trade as Lincoln was able to teach him. The rough work turned out at that shop was far beneath his ambition, and he had made up his mind to lead a life as wholly unlike his father's as he could possibly make it. He therefore refused to be a carpenter. But he could not afford to be idle; and, as soon as he was able to earn wages, he was hired out among the neighbors. He worked for many of them a few months at a time, and seemed perfectly willing to transfer his services wherever they were wanted, so that his father had no excuse for persecuting him with entreaties about learning to make tables and cupboards.

Abe was now becoming a man, and was, in fact, already taller than any man in the neighborhood. He was a universal favorite, and his wit and humor made him heartily welcome at every cabin between the two Pigeon Creeks. Any family was glad when "Abe Linkern" was hired to work with them; for he did his work well, and made them all merry while he was about it. The women were especially pleased, for Abe was not above doing any kind of "chores" for them. He was always ready to make a fire, carry water, or nurse a baby. But what manner of people were these among whom he passed the most critical part of his life? We must know them if we desire to know him.

There lived in the neighborhood of Gentryville a Mrs. Elizabeth Crawford, wife to the now celebrated Josiah with the sour temper and the blue nose. Abe was very fond of her, and inclined to "let himself out" in her company. . . . We have from her a great mass of valuable, and sometimes extremely amusing, information . . . :

"You wish me to tell you how the people used to go to meeting —how far they went. At that time we thought it nothing to go eight or ten miles. The old ladies did not stop for the want of a shawl, or cloak, or riding dress, or two horses, in the wintertime; but they would put on their husbands' old overcoats, and wrap up their little ones, and take one or two of them up on their beasts, and their husbands would walk, and they would go to church, and stay in the neighborhood until the next day, and then go home. The old men would start out of their fields from their work, or out of the woods from hunting, with their guns on their shoulders, and go to church. Some of them dressed in deerskin pants and moccasins, hunting shirts with a rope or leather strap around them. They would come in laughing, shake hands all around, sit down and talk about their game they had killed, or some other work they had done, and smoke their pipes together with the old ladies. If in warm weather, they would kindle up a little fire out in the meeting-house yard, to light their pipes. If in wintertime, they would hold church in some of the neighbors' houses. At such times they were always treated with the utmost of kindness: a bottle of whisky, a pitcher of water, sugar and glass, were set out, or a basket of apples, or turnips, or some pies and cakes. Apples were scarce them times. Sometimes potatoes were used as a treat. (I must tell you that the first treat I ever received in old Mr. Linkern's house, that was our President's father's house, was a plate of potatoes, washed and pared very nicely, and handed round. It was something new to me, for I never had seen a raw potato eaten before. I looked to see how they made use of them. They took off a potato, and ate them like apples.) Thus they spent the time till time for preaching to commence, then they would all take their seats: the preacher would take his stand, draw his coat, open his shirt collar, commence service by singing and prayer; take his text and preach till the sweat would roll off in great drops. Shaking hands and singing then ended the service. The people seemed to enjoy religion more in them days than they do now. They were glad to see each other, and enjoyed themselves better than they do now."

Society about Gentryville was little different from that of any other backwoods settlement of the same day. The houses were scattered far apart; but the inhabitants would travel long distances to a log-rolling, a house-raising, a wedding, or any thing else that might be turned into a fast and furious frolic. On such occasions the young women carried their shoes in their hands, and only put them on when about to join the company. The ladies drank whisky toddy, while the men took it straight; and both sexes danced the livelong night, barefooted, on puncheon floors.

The fair sex wore "cornfield bonnets, scoop-shaped, flaring in front, and long though narrow behind." Shoes were the mode when entering the ballroom; but it was not at all fashionable to scuff them out by walking or dancing in them. "Four yards of linsey-woolsey, a yard in width, made a dress for any woman." The waist was short, and terminated just under the arms, while the skirt was long and narrow. "Crimps and puckering frills" it had none. The coats of the men were homemade; the materials, jeans or linsey-woolsey. The waists were short, like the frocks of the women, and the long "claw-hammer" tail was split up to the waist. This, however, was company dress, and the hunting shirt did duty for every day. The breeches were of buckskin or jeans; the cap was of coonskin; and the shoes of leather tanned at home. If no member of the family could make shoes, the leather was taken to someone who could, and the customer paid the maker a fair price in some other sort of labor.

The state of agriculture was what it always is where there is no market, either to sell or buy; where the implements are few and primitive, and where there are no regular mechanics. The Pigeon Creek farmer "tickled" two acres of ground in a day with his old shovel plough, and got but half a crop. He cut one acre with his sickle, while the modern machine lays down in neat rows ten. With his flail and horse tramping, he threshed out fifteen bushels of wheat; while the machine of today, with a few more hands, would turn out three hundred and fifty. He "fanned" and "cleaned with a sheet." When he wanted flour, he took his team and went to a "horse-mill," where he spent a whole day in converting fifteen bushels of grain.

The minds of these people were filled with superstitions, which most persons imagine to be, at least, as antiquated as witch-burning. They firmly believed in witches and all kind of witch-doings. They sent for wizards to cure sick cattle. They shot the image of the witch with a silver ball, to break the spell she was supposed to have laid on a human being. If a dog ran directly across a man's path while he was hunting, it was terrible "luck," unless he instantly hooked his two little fingers together, and pulled with all his might, until the dog was out of sight. There were wizards who took charmed twigs in their hands, and made them point to springs of water and all kinds of treasure beneath the earth's surface. There were "faith doctors," who cured diseases by performing mysterious ceremonies and muttering cabalistic words. If a bird alighted in a window, one of the family would speedily die. If a horse breathed on a child, the child would have the whooping cough. Every thing must be done at certain "times and seasons," else it would be attended with "bad luck." They must cut trees for rails in the early part of the day, and in "the light of the moon." They must make fence in "the light of the moon"; otherwise, the fence would sink. Potatoes and other roots were to be planted in the "dark of the moon," but trees, and plants which bore their fruits above ground, must be "put out in the light of the moon." The moon exerted a fearful influence, either kindly or malignant, as the good old rules were observed or not. It was even required to make soap "in the light of the moon," and, moreover, it must be stirred only one way, and by one person. Nothing of importance was to be begun on Friday. All enterprises inaugurated on that day went fatally amiss. A horse-colt could be begotten only "in the dark of the moon," and animals treated otherwise than "according to the signs in the almanac" were nearly sure to die.

Such were the people among whom Abe grew to manhood. With their sons and daughters he went to school. Upon their farms he earned his daily bread by daily toil. From their conversation he formed his earliest opinions of men and things, the world over. Many of their peculiarities became his; and many of their thoughts and feelings concerning a multitude of subjects were assimilated with his own, and helped to create that unique character, which, in the eyes of a great host of the American people, was only less curious and amusing than it was noble and august.

6

IN THE LAST YEARS of his youth, Lincoln began to see something of the world beyond the limits of the frontier farm in Spencer County. For a time he helped to operate a ferry on the Ohio River; often he worked as a hired man for farmers in the neighborhood. Then, in 1828, a great chance came. Albert J. Beveridge tells the story.

THE RICHEST MAN in Carter Township was James Gentry, a native of North Carolina who in April, 1818, had come from Kentucky with his young wife to the Pigeon Creek settlement. He

entered a thousand acres of land and afterward bought several
hundred acres more. He had a large family, two of whom married
into the family of another wealthy man, Gideon W. Romaine.
Gentry soon began to keep a small stock of goods for sale at his
farm house; thus began the town of Gentryville. Soon William
David, a blacksmith, came and in time a few cabins were built
near by. Gentryville became the social as well as the trading centre
of the countryside.

Gentryville was less than a mile and a half from the Lincoln
cabin; and to the backwoods hamlet young Lincoln would speed
like a homing pigeon when work was done for the day. For there
gathered other youth and men who craved companionship and the
storytelling, talk, and discussion which took place in country
stores. About this time, one, William Jones, came from Vincennes
and opened a little store. Soon he and Lincoln became fast friends
and Jones hired the boy to help him. But it was the village blacksmith who was "Abe's pertickler friend." Gentry and Jones
formed a partnership, with Abraham sometimes assisting as man
of all work.

As long as Gentry or Jones would keep the candles lighted and
the log fire burning, Abraham would remain, talking, forever talking, relating his jokes, telling his rude and often unsavory tales;
flashing his kindly repartee, propounding his theories about
everything. "He was so odd, original and humorous and witty
that all the People in town would gather around him," Dennis
Hanks told Herndon. "He would Keep them there till midnight
or longer telling Stories and cracking jokes. . . . I would get
tired, want to go home, cuss Abe most heartily." And "Sumtimes
we Spent a Little time at grog piching waits," says Dennis.

Lincoln had great physical strength, so great that tales of his
performances are well-nigh unbelievable. Long afterward one
elderly person recalled that the young Hercules of Pigeon Creek
bore away easily heavy posts which "some of the men" were preparing to carry by means of bars. "Abe could sink an axe deeper
in wood . . . He could strike with a mall a heavier blow than any
man I ever saw," testifies William Wood. Stature, physical power,
good humor, intellect, integrity, are the outstanding features of
the picture of Abraham Lincoln during these years.

In April, 1828, James Gentry hired this strong, capable, and trustworthy youth to go with his son, Allen, on a flatboat loaded with produce to New Orleans, then the best market for such things as the upper Mississippi country had to sell. The boat started from Gentry's landing on the Ohio, about three quarters of a mile from Rockport. Lincoln acted as a bow hand, "working the foremost oar and was paid eight dollars per month from the time of starting to his returning home." It was no ignorant lout but a fairly well-informed young person of grasping and absorbing mind, who, with quip and quiddity, droll story and quaint common sense, enlivened the hours, as Gentry's flatboat floated down the Ohio and Mississippi to the great Southern mart.

Nothing happened, it seems, to disturb that placid voyage until one night, when tied to the shore at the plantation of a Madame Duchesne, not far from New Orleans, a company of Negroes armed with hickory clubs and bent on plunder, came upon the flatboat when the occupants were asleep. Aroused by the noise, Lincoln seized a club and furiously attacked the marauders. He knocked several into the river and the others fled, Lincoln and Gentry in hot pursuit. They, too, were wounded, it appears, for they were bleeding when they got on board again. Also they feared that the Negroes would return; so they "hastily swung into the stream and floated down the river till daylight."

So came Abraham Lincoln to New Orleans, the first city and the first place bigger than the Boonville or Rockport, Indiana, of 1828, he had ever seen. It was then a remarkable city of narrow streets, foreign-built houses, with colored stuccoes and iron railings, broad avenues lined by handsome houses, a cathedral, and immense warehouses for receiving, pressing, and storing cotton. From the levee, a much used causeway, could be seen nearly two miles of various descriptions of vessels, arks and flatboats from the north, steamboats still giving a sense of novelty, three-masters for foreign trade, with their broadsides to the shore—expressing the growing commerce of the river and people and offering "one of the most singularly beautiful" sights that could be conceived.

At the market, the common place of meeting, could be found nuts and fruits of the tropics; fish from lake and gulf; sugar, grain, and meats. Lincoln saw and heard the bustle and heaving labor on the river front, sea-going vessels made ready, crews of strange speech. He could note the medley of people and dress—

French, Spanish, Mexicans, Creoles, even Indians, and slaves, from the full Negro through many degrees of mixed blood. It all gave a new experience to the two youths from the backwoods of Indiana, but there is no evidence of the impression made upon Lincoln by this, his second contact with slavery.

The cargo sold, the young men returned to their Indiana homes in June, making the journey up stream on one of the big and sumptuous steamboats of the time, the elder Gentry paying the fare. On Pigeon Creek Lincoln took up again the old routine, unchanged in speech or manner by his trip to the metropolis of the South. He was still the avid reader of books, the incessant talker, the bubbling fountain of good cheer.

7

BUT NEITHER LINCOLN nor his father were to remain on Pigeon Creek much longer. Another move was imminent. Carl Sandburg follows the family as its members seek a new home.

In the fall of 1829, Abraham Lincoln was putting his ax to big trees and whipsawing logs into planks for lumber to build a house on his father's farm. But his father made new plans; the lumber was sold to Josiah Crawford; and the obedient young axman was put to work cutting and sawing trees big enough around to make wagon wheels, and hickories tough enough for axles and poles on an ox wagon.

The new plans were that the Lincoln family and the families of Dennis Hanks and Levi Hall, married to Abe's stepsisters, thirteen people in all, were going to move to Macon County over in Illinois, into a country with a river the Indians named Sangamo, meaning "the land of plenty to eat." The Lincoln farm wasn't paying well; after buying eighty acres for $2.00 an acre and improving it for fourteen years, Tom Lincoln sold it to Charles Grigsby for $125.00 cash before signing the papers.

The "milk-sick" was taking farm animals; since Dennis Hanks lost four milk-cows and eleven calves in one week, besides having a spell of the sickness himself, Dennis was saying, "I'm goin' t' git out o' here and hunt a country where the 'milk-sick' is not; it's like to ruined me."

In September Tom Lincoln and his wife had made a trip down

to Elizabethtown, Kentucky, where they sold for $123.00 the lot which Mrs. Lincoln had fallen heir to when her first husband died; the clerk, Samuel Haycraft, filled out the deed of sale, declaring that she "was examined by me privately and apart from her said husband" and did "freely and willingly. subscribe to the sale." And Tom, with the cash from this sale and the money from the sale of his own farm, was buying oxen, or young steers, and trading and selling off household goods.

Moving was natural to his blood; he came from a long line of movers; he could tell about the family that had moved so often that their chickens knew the signs of another moving; and the chickens would walk up to the mover, stretch flat on the ground, and put up their feet to be tied for the next wagon trip.

The menfolk that winter, using their broadaxes and drawknives on solid blocks of wood, shaping wagon wheels, had a church scandal to talk about. Tom Lincoln and his wife had been granted by the Pigeon church a "letter of Dismission," to show they had kept up their obligations and were regular members. Sister Nancy Grigsby had then come in with a "protest" that she was "not satisfied with Brother and Sister Lincoln." The trustees took back the letter, investigated, gave the letter again to Brother and Sister Lincoln, and to show how they felt about it, they appointed Brother Lincoln on a committee to straighten out a squabble between Sister Nancy Grigsby and Sister Betsy Crawford. And it was jotted down in the Pigeon church records and approved by the trustees.

The ox wagon they made that winter was wood all through, pegs, cleats, hickory withes, and knots of bark, holding it together, except the wheel rims, which were iron. Bundles of bedclothes, skillets, ovens, and a few pieces of furniture were loaded, stuck, filled and tied onto the wagon; early one morning the last of the packing was done. It was February 15, 1830; Abraham Lincoln had been four days a full-grown man, a citizen who "had reached his majority"; he could vote at elections from now on; he was lawfully free from his father's commands; he could come and go now; he was footloose.

At Jones' store he had laid in a little stock of pins, needles, buttons, tinware, suspenders, and knickknacks, to peddle on the way to Illinois.

And he had gone for a final look at the winter dry grass, the ruins of last year's wild vine and dogwood over the grave of Nancy Hanks. He and his father were leaving their Indiana home that day; almost naked they had come, stayed fourteen years, toiled, buried their dead, built a church, toiled on; and now they were leaving, almost naked. Now, with the women and children lifted on top of the wagonload, the men walked alongside, curling and cracking their whiplashes over the horns or into the hides of the half-broken young steers.

And so the seven-yoke team of young steers, each with his head in a massive collar of hardwood, lashed and bawled at with "Gee," "Haw," "G' lang" and "Hi thar, you! Git up!" hauled the lumbering pioneer load from the yellow and red clay of Spencer County, in Southern Indiana, to the black loam of the prairie lands in Macon County, Illinois.

CHAPTER THREE

New Salem

WITH THE MIGRATION *of his family from Indiana to Illinois, Lincoln's boyhood and youth came to an end. Now twenty-one, he was free to strike out for himself. First, however, he did what he could to help his father get established. John Hanks, who had picked out the site on which the Lincolns located, had logs for a cabin already on the ground, but rails for fences had to be split and the prairie broken so that a crop of corn—a necessity for the coming winter—could be planted.*

With the family settled—although, as it turned out, they were to move within a year—Lincoln worked at such odd jobs as the deep drifts of the most celebrated winter in the history of Illinois permitted. Eventually the snow melted and the streams flowed again. Then it was that Abraham Lincoln, a hired boathand, moved for the first time on the currents of his own life.

1

LINCOLN'S AUTOBIOGRAPHY includes a concise account of his first year in Illinois.

MARCH 1, 1830, Abraham having just completed his twenty-first year, his father and family, with the families of the two daughters and sons-in-law of his stepmother, left the old homestead in Indiana and came to Illinois. Their mode of conveyance was wagons drawn by ox teams, and Abraham drove one of the teams. They reached the county of Macon, and stopped there some time within the same month of March. His father and family settled a new place on the north side of the Sangamon River, at the junction of the timberland and prairie, about ten miles westerly from Decatur. Here they built a log cabin, into which they removed, and made sufficient of rails to fence ten acres of ground, fenced and broke the ground, and raised a crop of sown corn upon it the same year. . . .

The sons-in-law were temporarily settled in other places in the county. In the autumn all hands were greatly afflicted with ague and fever, to which they had not been used, and by which they were greatly discouraged, so much so that they determined on leaving the county. They remained, however, through the succeeding winter, which was the winter of the very celebrated "deep snow" of Illinois. During that winter Abraham, together with his stepmother's son, John D. Johnston, and John Hanks, yet residing in Macon County, hired themselves to Denton Offutt to take a flatboat from Beardstown, Illinois, to New Orleans; and for that purpose were to join him—Offutt—at Springfield, Illinois, so soon as the snow should go off. When it did go off, which was about the first of March, 1831, the county was so flooded as to make traveling by land impracticable; to obviate which difficulty they purchased a large canoe, and came down the Sangamon River in it. This is the time and the manner of Abraham's first entrance into Sangamon County. They found Offutt at Springfield, but learned from him that he had failed in getting a boat at Beardstown. This led to their hiring themselves to him for twelve dollars per month each, and getting the timber out of the trees and building a boat at Old Sangamon town on the Sangamon River, seven miles northwest of Springfield, which boat they took to New Orleans, substantially upon the old contract.

During this boat-enterprise acquaintance with Offutt, who was previously an entire stranger, he conceived a liking for Abraham, and believing he could turn him to account, he contracted with him to act as clerk for him, on his return from New Orleans, in charge of a store and mill at New Salem, then in Sangamon, now in Menard County. . . . Abraham's father, with his own family and others mentioned, had, in pursuance of their intention, removed from Macon to Coles County. John D. Johnston, the stepmother's son, went to them, and Abraham stopped indefinitely and for the first time, as it were, by himself at New Salem, before mentioned. This was in July, 1831.

2

WILLIAM H. HERNDON, who knew New Salem when it was a thriving village, depicts the arrival of Lincoln and the first weeks he spent there. Fortunately, Herndon's nostalgic description of the village site (written in 1889) no longer fits: it is now an Illinois state park, with all the original cabins restored and furnished.

I N   A U G U S T [1] the waters of the Sangamon River washed Lincoln into New Salem. This once sprightly and thriving village is no longer in existence. Not a building, scarcely a stone, is left to mark the place where it once stood. To reach it now the traveler must ascend a bluff a hundred feet above the general level of the surrounding country. The brow of the ridge, two hundred and fifty feet broad where it overlooks the river, widens gradually as it extends westwardly to the forest and ultimately to broad pastures. Skirting the base of the bluff is the Sangamon River, which, coming around a sudden bend from the southeast, strikes the rocky hill and is turned abruptly north. . . .

The country in almost every direction is diversified by alternate stretches of hills and level lands, with streams between each struggling to reach the river. The hills are bearded with timber—oak, hickory, walnut, ash, and elm. Below them are stretches of rich alluvial bottom land, and the eye ranges over a vast expanse of foliage, the monotony of which is relieved by the alternating swells and depressions of the landscape. Between peak and peak, through its bed of limestone, sand, and clay, sometimes kissing the feet of one bluff and then hugging the other, rolls the Sangamon River. The village of New Salem, which once stood on the ridge, was laid out in 1828; it became a trading place, and in 1836 contained twenty houses and a hundred inhabitants. In the days of land offices and stagecoaches it was a sprightly village with a busy market. Its people were progressive and industrious. Propitious winds filled the sails of its commerce, prosperity smiled graciously

---

[1] July, 1831, by Lincoln's statement.

on its every enterprise, and the outside world encouraged its
social pretensions. It had its day of glory, but, singularly enough,
contemporaneous with the departure of Lincoln from its midst it
went into a rapid decline. A few crumbling stones here and there
are all that attest its former existence. "How it vanished," observes one writer, "like a mist in the morning, to what distant
places its inhabitants dispersed, and what became of the abodes
they left behind, shall be questions for the local historian."

Lincoln's return [2] to New Salem in August, 1831, was, within
a few days, contemporaneous with the reappearance of Offutt, who
made the gratifying announcement that he had purchased a stock
of goods which were to follow him from Beardstown. He had again
retained the services of Lincoln to assist him when his merchandise
should come to hand. The tall stranger—destined to be a stranger
in New Salem no longer—pending the arrival of his employer's
goods, lounged about the village with nothing to do. Leisure never
sat heavily on him. To him there was nothing uncongenial in it,
and he might very properly have been dubbed at the time a
"loafer." He assured those with whom he came in contact that he
was a piece of floating driftwood; that after the winter of deep
snow, he had come down the river with the freshet; borne along by
the swelling waters, and aimlessly floating about, he had accidentally lodged at New Salem. . . .

His introduction to the citizens of New Salem, as Mentor
Graham the schoolteacher tells us, was in the capacity of clerk of
an election board. Graham furnishes ample testimony of the facility, fairness, and honesty which characterized the new clerk's
work, and both teacher and clerk were soon bound together by the
warmest of ties. During the day, when votes were coming in slowly,
Lincoln began to entertain the crowd at the polls with a few attempts at storytelling. . . .

"In the afternoon," my cousin relates, "as things were dragging
a little, Lincoln the new man, began to spin out a stock of Indiana
yarns. One that amused me more than any other he called the
lizard story. 'The meeting-house,' he said, 'was in the woods and
quite a distance from any other house. It was only used once a
month. The preacher—an old line Baptist—was dressed in coarse

---

[2] He had first seen New Salem that spring when Offutt's flatboat, with Lincoln
aboard, was held up temporarily by the New Salem mill dam.

linen pantaloons, and shirt of the same material. The pants, manufactured after the old fashion, with baggy legs and a flap in front,
were made to attach to his frame without the aid of suspenders.
A single button held his shirt in position, and that was at the
collar. He rose up in the pulpit and with a loud voice announced
his text thus: "I am the Christ, whom I shall represent today."
About this time a little blue lizard ran up underneath his baggy
pantaloons. The old preacher, not wishing to interrupt the steady
flow of his sermon, slapped away on his legs, expecting to arrest
the intruder; but his efforts were unavailing, and the little fellow
kept on ascending higher and higher. Continuing the sermon, the
preacher slyly loosened the central button which graced the waistband of his pantaloons and with a kick off came that easy-fitting
garment. But meanwhile Mr. Lizard had passed the equatorial
line of waistband and was calmly exploring that part of the
preacher's anatomy which lay underneath the back of his shirt.
Things were now growing interesting, but the sermon was still
grinding on. The next movement on the preacher's part was for
the collar button, and with one sweep of his arm off came the tow
linen shirt. The congregation sat for an instant as if dazed; at
length one old lady in the rear of the room rose up and glancing
at the excited object in the pulpit, shouted at the top of her
voice: "If you represent Christ then I'm done with the Bible." ' "

A few days after the election Lincoln found employment with
one Dr. Nelson, who after the style of dignitaries of later days
started with his family and effects in his "private" conveyance—
which in this instance was a flatboat—for Texas. Lincoln was
hired to pilot the vessel through to the Illinois River. Arriving at
Beardstown the pilot was discharged, and returned on foot across
the sand and hills to New Salem. In the meantime Offutt's long expected goods had arrived, and Lincoln was placed in charge. Offutt
relied in no slight degree on the business capacity of his clerk. In
his effusive way he praised him beyond reason. He boasted of his
skill as a business man and his wonderful intellectual acquire-
ments. As for physical strength and fearlessness of danger, he
challenged New Salem and the entire world to produce his equal.
In keeping with his widely known spirit of enterprise, Offutt rented
the Rutledge and Cameron mill, which stood at the foot of the hill,
and thus added another iron to keep company with the half

dozen already in the fire. As a further test of his business ability Lincoln was placed in charge of this also. William G. Greene was hired to assist him, and between the two a life-long friendship sprang up. They slept in the store, and so strong was the intimacy between them that "when one turned over the other had to do likewise." At the head of these varied enterprises was Offutt, the most progressive man by all odds in the village. He was certainly an odd character, if we accept the judgment of his contemporaries. By some he is given the character of a clear-headed, brisk man of affairs. By others he is variously described as "wild, noisy, and reckless," or "windy, rattle-brained, unsteady, and improvident." Despite the unenviable traits ascribed to him he was good at heart and a generous friend of Lincoln. His boast that the latter could outrun, whip, or throw down any man in Sangamon County was soon tested, as we shall presently see, for, as another has truthfully expressed it, "honors such as Offutt accorded to Abe were to be won before they were worn at New Salem." In the neighborhood of the village, or rather a few miles to the southwest, lay a strip of timber called Clary's Grove. The boys who lived there were a terror to the entire region—seemingly a necessary product of frontier civilization. They were friendly and good-natured; they could trench a pond, dig a bog, build a house; they could pray and fight, make a village or create a state. They would do almost anything for sport or fun, love or necessity. Though rude and rough, though life's forces ran over the edge of the bowl, foaming and sparkling in pure deviltry for deviltry's sake, yet place before them a poor man who needed their aid, a lame or sick man, a defenseless woman, a widow, or an orphaned child, they melted into sympathy and charity at once. They gave all they had, and willingly toiled or played cards for more. Though there never was under the sun a more generous parcel of rowdies, a stranger's introduction was likely to be the most unpleasant part of his acquaintance with them. They conceded leadership to one Jack Armstrong, a hardy, strong, and well-developed specimen of physical manhood, and under him they were in the habit of "cleaning out" New Salem whenever his order went forth to do so. Offutt and Bill Clary—the latter skeptical of Lincoln's strength and agility—ended a heated discussion in the store one day over the new clerk's ability to meet the tactics of Clary's Grove, by a bet

of ten dollars that Jack Armstrong was, in the language of the
day, "a better man than Lincoln." The new clerk strongly opposed
this sort of an introduction, but after much entreaty from Offutt,
at last consented to make his bow to the social lions of the town in
this unusual way. He was now six feet four inches high, and
weighed, as his friend and confidant, William Greene, tells us
with impressive precision, "two hundred and fourteen pounds."
The contest was to be a friendly one and fairly conducted. All
New Salem adjourned to the scene of the wrestle. Money, whisky,
knives, and all manner of property were staked on the result. It
is unnecessary to go into the details of the encounter. Everyone
knows how it ended; how at last the tall and angular rail-splitter,
enraged at the suspicion of foul tactics, and profiting by his
height and the length of his arms, fairly lifted the great bully by
the throat and shook him like a rag; how by this act he established himself solidly in the esteem of all New Salem, and secured
the respectful admiration and friendship of the very man whom he
had so thoroughly vanquished. From this time forward Jack
Armstrong, his wife Hannah, and all the other Armstrongs became
his warm and trusted friends. None stood readier than they to
rally to his support, none more willing to lend a helping hand.
Lincoln appreciated their friendship and support, and in after
years proved his gratitude by saving one member of the family
from the gallows.

3

BEFORE LINCOLN had lived in New Salem a year the Black Hawk
War broke out. Although he had recently announced that he was a
candidate for election to the State Legislature, he promptly volunteered for service. His experiences as a militiaman—often bordering
on the comic—are related by Benjamin P. Thomas.

F OR SOME TIME [before 1832] trouble had been brewing
in northwestern Illinois between white settlers and Indians. In
1804, the Sauk and Fox tribe had ceded their lands in the Rock
River valley to the United States with the provision that they
might remain on them as long as they were the property of the
government. As squatters moved into the region there were argu-

ments and minor outbreaks. In 1831, hostilities almost broke out, but the Indians were finally persuaded to move west of the Mississippi and to agree never to return without permission from the President of the United States or the Governor of Illinois. Nevertheless, in April, 1832, Chief Black Hawk recrossed the river with five hundred braves. They came ostensibly to plant corn; but they were well mounted and well armed, and their coming spread terror along the Illinois frontier. A detachment of United States troops at Fort Armstrong on Rock Island watched their movements suspiciously, and an overt act by nervous militiamen precipitated hostilities.

Governor Reynolds immediately called for volunteers from the state militia to help repel the Indians. At that time all male white inhabitants between the ages of eighteen and forty-five were required to enroll in the militia and to provide themselves with "proper accoutrements." Refusal to enroll made one liable to punishment as a deserter. Those physically unfit or "conscientiously scrupulous of bearing arms" were exempt in peace time on payment of seventy-five cents a year. The men chose their own officers. . . .

Lincoln promptly volunteered for thirty days. He was enrolled at Richland, near New Salem, on April 21, 1832. His company was composed chiefly of his friends and neighbors. The Clary's Grove boys constituted a large part of it. Lincoln was elected captain by an overwhelming majority. In each of the two brief autobiographies which he later wrote he asserted that this honor gave him more satisfaction than any subsequent success in his life.

Jack Armstrong was first sergeant of the company. William F. Berry, soon to be Lincoln's partner in business, and Alexander Trent were corporals. In the ranks were Hugh Armstrong, David Pantier, George Warburton, John M. Rutledge, Bill Clary, Bill Greene, Royal Clary, Pleasant Armstrong, David Rutledge and Isaac Golliher. A soldier of another command described Lincoln's company as "the hardest set of men he ever saw." William Cullen Bryant, who was traveling in Illinois in 1832, said that the volunteers "were a hard-looking set of men, unkempt and unshaved, wearing shirts of dark calico, and sometimes calico capotes." Some of the settlers whose farms they passed complained that they "made war on the pigs and chickens." For elected officers to exact obedience from such a group was no small task, and it is said that Lincoln's first command drew forth a request to "go to the devil."

The volunteers assembled at Beardstown, where Lincoln's company was attached to the Fourth Regiment of Mounted Volunteers of the Brigade of Samuel Whiteside. They were mustered into state service on April 28. From Beardstown the brigade marched to Rock Island, where Lincoln's company was sworn into Federal service on May 9.

From Rock Island they marched along the Rock River to Dixon's Ferry, then south to Ottawa, where they were disbanded on May 27, their thirty days having expired. The march was uneventful. Lincoln saw no fighting. Once he was arrested and deprived of his sword for a day for disobeying an order prohibiting the discharge of firearms within fifty yards of camp. And when some of his men, without his knowledge, broke into the officers' quarters, stole their liquor and got too drunk to march next day, Lincoln was again put under arrest and made to carry a wooden sword for two days. One day he saved the life of an old Indian who wandered into camp. The Indian had a letter from General Cass certifying that he was friendly to the whites; but this meant nothing to the frontier soldiers to whom "the only good Indian was a dead one." They had enlisted to kill Indians, and saw no reason why they should not start with this one. But Lincoln intervened. When some of the men denounced him as a coward, he, "swarthy with resolution and rage," offered to disillusion them. The Clary's Grove boys supported him, as they always did in a pinch, and the others sullenly gave in.

All of Lincoln's resourcefulness and adaptability were needed to supplement his scanty knowledge of military tactics. On one occasion, when he was leading his company across a field, twenty abreast, they came to a fence with a narrow gate. Unable to think of the proper command to "turn the company endwise," Lincoln shouted, "Halt! This company will break ranks for two minutes and form again on the other side of that gate!" Herndon said that the movement was successfully executed.

In their leisure moments the volunteers sang, wrestled, raced, gambled and played pranks upon each other. About the campfires Lincoln enhanced his reputation as a story teller. He wrestled with champions from other companies, and at Beardstown met his match in Lorenzo D. Thompson.

When his term of enlistment expired, he re-enlisted in Captain Alexander White's Company, on May 26. He served in this company only one day; and on the twenty-seventh enlisted again, this time as a private in the mounted company of Captain Elijah Iles. He was mustered into Iles' company by Second Lieutenant Robert Anderson, of the Third U. S. Artillery, famous later as the commander of Fort Sumter. Iles' command was made up of "generals, colonels, captains and distinguished men" from disbanded detachments. It was attached to a "spy battalion" or scouting detachment. While it was encamped near Ottawa, word came that the Indians had cut off the town of Galena, and it and other companies were immediately despatched to the rescue. Proceeding by forced marches, they reached the town without encountering the Indians, and found the inhabitants frightened but unharmed.

When Lincoln's enlistment expired on June 16, he re-enlisted for another thirty days, this time in Jacob M. Earley's company. Still he saw no fighting, but at Kellogg's Grove he helped bury five men who had been killed and scalped the day before. Their appearance made a lasting impression on him. Years later he recalled that "the red light of the morning sun was streaming upon them as they lay heads towards us on the ground. And every man had a round, red spot on top of his head, about as big as a dollar where the redskins had taken his scalp. It was frightful, but it was grotesque, and the red sunlight seemed to paint everything all over. I remember that one man had on buckskin breeches."

Lincoln was mustered out of the service at Black River, Wisconsin, on July 16. His horse and that of his messmate, George Harrison, having been stolen the previous night, the two men made their way to Peoria, most of the way on foot. Harrison said: "I laughed at our fate, and he joked at it, and we all started off merrily. The generous men of our Company walked and rode by turns with us, and we fared about equal with the rest." John T. Stuart, Lincoln's future law partner, was one of those who accompanied him. At Peoria Lincoln and Harrison bought a canoe and paddled down the Illinois River to Havana. From there Lincoln trudged across country to New Salem.

In later years he treated his military career lightly. In 1848 in a speech in Congress in which he ridiculed the attempts of the Democrats to magnify the military record of Lewis Cass, their candidate for president, he said: "By the way, Mr. Speaker, did you know I am a military hero? Yes, sir; in the days of the Black Hawk War I fought, bled, and came away. Speaking of General Cass's career reminds me of my own. I was not at Stillman's defeat, but I was about as near it as Cass was to Hull's surrender; and, like him, I saw the place very soon afterward. It is quite certain I did not break my sword, for I had none to break; but I bent a musket pretty badly on one occasion. If Cass broke his sword, the idea is he broke it in desperation; I bent the musket by accident. If General Cass went in advance of me in picking huckleberries, I guess I surpassed him in charges upon the wild onions. If he saw any live, fighting Indians, it was more than I did; but I had a good many bloody struggles with the mosquitoes, and although I never fainted from loss of blood, I can truly say I was often hungry. Mr. Speaker, if I should ever conclude to doff whatever our Democratic friends may suppose there is of black-cockade federalism about me, and therefore they shall take me up as their candidate for the presidency, I protest they shall not make fun of me, as they have of General Cass, by attempting to write me into a military hero."

Yet in spite of Lincoln's bantering attitude toward his military service, Herndon believed that "he was rather proud of it after all."

4

THE STORY of Lincoln's first political campaign—seriously interrupted by his Black Hawk War service—is told by Nicolay and Hay, who rightly considered it one of the important events of his life.

THE DISCHARGED VOLUNTEER arrived in New Salem only ten days before the August election, in which he had a deep personal interest. Before starting for the wars he had announced himself, according to the custom of the time, by a handbill circular, as a candidate for the Legislature from Sangamon County. He had done this in accordance with his own natural bent for public life and desire for usefulness and distinction, and not without strong encouragement from friends whose opinion he valued. He had even then considerable experience in speaking and think- ing on his feet. He had begun his practice in that direction before leaving Indiana, and continued it everywhere he had gone. Mr. William Butler tells us that on one occasion, when Lincoln was a farm hand at Island Grove, the famous circuit-rider, Peter Cart- wright, came by, electioneering for the Legislature, and Lincoln at once engaged in a discussion with him in the cornfield, in which the great Methodist was equally astonished at the close reasoning and the uncouth figure of Mr. Brown's extraordinary hired man. At another time, after one Posey, a politician in search of office, had made a speech in Macon, John Hanks, whose admiration of his cousin's oratory was unbounded, said that "Abe could beat it." He turned a keg on end, and the tall boy mounted it and made his speech. "The subject was the navigation of the Sangamon, and Abe beat him to death," says the loyal Hanks. So it was not with the tremor of a complete novice that the young man took the stump during the few days left him between his return and the election.

He ran as a Whig. . . . Without discussing the merits of the party or its purposes, we may insist that his adopting them thus openly at the outset of his career was an extremely characteristic act, and marks thus early the scrupulous conscientiousness which shaped every action of his life. The State of Illinois was by a large majority Democratic, hopelessly attached to the person and policy of Jackson. Nowhere had that despotic leader more violent and unscrupulous partisans than there. They were proud of their very servility, and preferred the name of "whole-hog Jackson men" to that of Democrats. The Whigs embraced in their scanty ranks the leading men of the State, those who have since been most distinguished in its history, such as S. T. Logan, Stuart, Browning, Dubois, Hardin, Breese, and many others. But they were utterly unable to do anything except by dividing the Jackson men, whose very numbers made their party unwieldy, and by throwing their votes with the more decent and conservative por- tion of them. In this way, in the late election, they had secured the success of Governor Reynolds—"the Old Ranger"—against Governor Kinney, who represented the vehement and proscriptive spirit which Jackson had just breathed into the party. He had

visited the General in Washington, and had come back giving
out threatenings and slaughter against the Whigs in the true
Tennessee style, declaring that "all Whigs should be whipped
out of office like dogs out of a meat-house"; the force of southwestern simile could no further go. But the great popularity of
Reynolds and the adroit management of the Whigs carried him
through successfully. A single fact will show on which side the
people who could read were enlisted. The "whole-hog" party
had one newspaper, the opposition five. Of course it would have
been impossible for Reynolds to poll a respectable vote if his
loyalty to Jackson had been seriously doubted. As it was, he
lost many votes through a report that he had been guilty of
saying that "he was as strong for Jackson as any reasonable man
should be." The Governor himself, in his naïve account of the
canvass, acknowledges the damaging nature of this accusation,
and comforts himself with quoting an indiscretion of Kinney's,
who opposed a projected canal on the ground that "it would
flood the country with Yankees."

It showed some moral courage, and certainly an absence of
the shuffling politician's fair weather policy, that Lincoln, in his
obscure and penniless youth, at the very beginning of his career,
when he was not embarrassed by antecedents or family connec-
tions, and when, in fact, what little social influence he knew would
have led him the other way, chose to oppose a furiously intolerant
majority, and to take his stand with the party which was doomed
to long continued defeat in Illinois.

In the circular in which he announced his candidacy he made
no reference to national politics, but confined himself mainly to
a discussion of the practicability of improving the navigation of
the Sangamon, the favorite hobby of the place and time. He had
no monopoly of this "issue." It formed the burden of nearly every
candidate's appeal to the people in that year. The excitement
occasioned by the trip of the *Talisman*[3] had not yet died away,
although the little steamer was now dust and ashes, and her bold
commander had left the State to avoid an awkward meeting with
the sheriff. The hope of seeing Springfield an emporium of commerce was still lively among the citizens of Sangamon County,

---

[3] A small steamer which made its way up the Sangamon as far as Springfield
in the spring of 1832. Later, while docked at St. Louis, it burned.

and in no one of the handbills of the political aspirants of the season was that hope more judiciously encouraged than in the one signed by Abraham Lincoln. It was a well-written circular, remarkable for its soberness and reserve when we consider the age and the limited advantages of the writer. It concluded in these words: "Upon the subjects of which I have treated, I have spoken as I have thought. I may be wrong in regard to any or all of them; but holding it a sound maxim that it is better only sometimes to be right than at all times wrong, so soon as I discover my opinions to be erroneous I shall be ready to renounce them. . . . Every man is said to have his peculiar ambition. Whether it be true or not, I can say for one, that I have no other so great as that of being truly esteemed of my fellow-men, by rendering myself worthy of their esteem. How far I shall succeed in gratifying this ambition is yet to be developed. I am young, and unknown to many of you. I was born and have ever remained in the most humble walks of life. I have no wealthy or powerful relations or friends to recommend me. My case is thrown exclusively upon the independent voters of the county; and, if elected, they will have conferred a favor upon me, for which I shall be unremitting in my labors to compensate. But if the good people in their wisdom shall see fit to keep me in the background, I have been too familiar with disappointments to be very much chagrined. . . ."

Of course, in the ten days left him after his return from the field, a canvass of the county, which was then—before its division—several thousand square miles in extent, was out of the question. He made a few speeches in the neighborhood of New Salem, and at least one in Springfield. He was wholly unknown there except by his few comrades-in-arms. We find him mentioned in the county paper only once during the summer, in an editorial note adding the name of Captain Lincoln to those candidates for the Legislature who were periling their lives on the frontier and had left their reputations in charge of their generous fellow citizens at home. On the occasion of his speaking at Springfield, most of the candidates had come together to address a meeting there to give their electors some idea of their quality. These were severe ordeals for the rash aspirants for popular favor. Besides those citizens who came to listen and judge, there were many whose only object was the free whisky provided for the occasion,

and who, after potations pottle-deep, became not only highly un-
parliamentary but even dangerous to life and limb. This wild
chivalry of Lick Creek was, however, less redoubtable to Lincoln
than it might be to an urban statesman unacquainted with the
frolic brutality of Clary's Grove. Their gambols never caused
him to lose his self-possession. It is related that once, while he
was speaking, he saw a ruffian attack a friend of his in the crowd,
and the *rencontre* not resulting according to the orator's sympathies, he descended from the stand, seized the objectionable fighting man by the neck, "threw him some ten feet," then calmly
mounted to his place and· finished his speech, the course of his
logic undisturbed by this athletic parenthesis. Judge Logan
saw Lincoln for the first time on the day when he came up to
Springfield on his canvass this summer. He thus speaks of his
future partner: "He was a very tall, gawky, and rough-looking
fellow then; his pantaloons didn't meet his shoes by six inches.
But after he began speaking I became very much interested in
him. He made a very sensible speech. His manner was very much
the same as in after life; that is, the same peculiar characteristics
were apparent then, though of course in after years he evinced
more knowledge and experience. But he had then the same novelty
and the same peculiarity in presenting his ideas. He had the same
individuality that he kept through all his life."

There were two or three men at the meeting whose good opinion
was worth more than all the votes of Lick Creek to one beginning life: Stephen T. Logan, a young lawyer who had recently
come from Kentucky with the best equipment for a *nisi prius*
practitioner ever brought into the State; Major Stuart, whom we
have met in the Black Hawk war, once commanding a battalion
and then marching as a private; and William Butler, afterwards
prominent in State politics, at that time a young man of the
purest Western breed in body and character, clear-headed and
courageous, and ready for any emergency where a friend was to
be defended or an enemy punished. We do not know whether
Lincoln gained any votes that day, but he gained what was far
more valuable, the active friendship of these able and honorable
men, all Whigs and all Kentuckians like himself.

The acquaintances he made in his canvass, the practice he
gained in speaking, and the added confidence which this ex-

perience of measuring his abilities with those of others gave, were all the advantages which Lincoln derived from this attempt. He was defeated, for the only time in his life, in a contest before the people. The fortunate candidates were E. D. Taylor, J. T. Stuart, Achilles Morris, and Peter Cartwright, the first of whom received 1,127 votes and the last 815. Lincoln's position among the eight defeated candidates was a very respectable one. He had 657 votes, and there were five who fared worse, among them his old adversary Kirkpatrick. What must have been especially gratifying to him was the fact that he received the almost unanimous vote of his own neighborhood, the precinct of New Salem, 277 votes against 3,[4] a result which showed more strongly than any words could do the extent of the attachment and the confidence which his genial and upright character had inspired among those who knew him best.

5

THE CAMPAIGN over, Lincoln was forced to think about making a living. With fatal ease, he became a partner in one of New Salem's stores. A homespun version of the disastrous venture is provided by Thomas P. Reep, lifelong resident of Petersburg, the nearby town which prospered as New Salem withered.

THE EXPERIENCES of this campaign . . . encouraged him to remain in the county and to try his political fortune again. In the meantime, it was necessary that he should have some employment—a means of livelihood—preferably at a place and under conditons where he could meet and mingle with the people, and he sought employment as a clerk in a New Salem store. Nothing of this kind offered and it appearing that one of the Herndon brothers, James, had sold his half interest in a store owned by them at New Salem to William F. Berry, and Rowan Herndon, the other brother, being dissatisfied with Berry, and desiring to leave the place—he having accidentally shot and killed his wife a short time before—sold his interest in the store to Lincoln, taking his promissory note in payment of the purchase price. Thus Lincoln, for the first time in his life, became a mer-

---

[4] By Lincoln's statement, 277 to 7.

chant in his own right and one of the business fraternity of the village.

A short time before this the Chrisman brothers had failed and a portion of their stock of groceries had been taken over by James Rutledge upon a debt. This stock was purchased from Rutledge by Berry and Lincoln, they giving their notes in payment. A few months later, probably in January, 1833, Reuben Radford incurred the enmity of the Clary's Grove boys, which resulted in Berry and Lincoln securing his stock of goods and moving into the store. The circumstance was as follows: Radford was a large man of great physical strength and announced his ability to look after his own rights and to protect them. He was told that such an attitude would cause the Clary's Grove boys to try him out and they would surely "lick" him; if one couldn't then two or three together could and would. On the day in question, Radford, having occasion to go to the country, left his younger brother in charge of the store, admonishing him to be careful and directing him to sell the Clary's Grove boys, in case any of them came in, but two drinks of liquor. Sure enough, the Clary's Grove boys came and in peace got their two drinks of liquor. Being denied more, they shoved the protesting youth out of their way, stepped behind the counter and helped themselves, with the result that they all got "rip-roaring" drunk, and turned things in the store topsy-turvy, broke the crockery and knocked out the windows, leaving chaos and ruin in their wake. Then they leaped on their horses and yelling like wild Indians, left the town for their homes. A bunch of them passed a short distance from where Radford was stopping in the country and, hearing their yells, he immediately feared the worst and, leaping on his horse, ran him all the way to New Salem, where he dismounted from his panting and lathered steed and rushed into his store. Broken glass and crockery-ware covered the floor and the contents seemed to be a total wreck. Stepping outside, Radford declared that he would sell out to the first man who made him an offer. Just at that moment William G. Greene, the erstwhile Offutt clerk, came along, having been sent on horseback, with some grist to the mill. Hearing Radford's words, he replied, "Sell out to me." Radford replied, "I will. How much will you give?" Greene rode up to the side of the store and, sticking his head through a broken window, surveyed the contents and offered Radford $400.00 for the stock, which Radford accepted. The news of the purchase traveled fast in New Salem and soon Lincoln came over to see his old friend and new competitor. Looking over the contents, he announced that they must take an inventory and Greene, not understanding the term and guessing that it might mean some sort of a celebration along the line followed by the Clary's Grove boys just before, replied, "Abe, I don't believe this store will stand another one just at this time." Lincoln explained that by inventory he meant the listing of the goods and the setting opposite each item, the value thereof. So they at once proceeded to make the inventory. Greene paid $23.00 cash and for the balance gave two notes each for $188.50, which was secured by a mortgage drawn and witnessed by Lincoln on the real estate, viz.: the west half of Lot 5 north of Main Street. Before the inventory was completed, it was evident that the stock would run to nearly $900.00, and Berry and Lincoln bought it from Greene, paying him $265.00 cash, principally in silver, assuming the payment of his notes for $377.00 to Radford and, by turning over a horse, saddle and bridle owned by Berry. Berry and Lincoln then moved their stock into the new store building and bid fair to make considerable money, as competition had now been reduced to but one other store—that owned and operated by Hill.

In later life William G. Greene took delight in telling his experience at home on the night of his purchase of the Radford store and stock. He had sent a boy home with the meal his father had sent *him* after and this boy had carried the news of "Billy's" purchase. The taking of the inventory and fixing of the papers covering the purchase from Radford and the sale to Berry and Lincoln kept young Greene till quite late that night and when he arrived home the family had retired. His father, however, was awake, waiting for him. When he stepped into the fireplace room where his parents slept, Greene, Sr., said: "So, Billy, you are a merchant are ye? You git along to bed now and in the morning I will thrash the merchant out you mighty quick." Young Bill held his peace until he had stirred up the coals and lighted the room with fresh kindling. Then, reaching into his pockets, he began stacking up his silver on the floor with considerable "jingle." His father's curiosity being aroused and desiring an excuse for raising up to look, he said: "I'll just take a chaw of tobacco," and lifted up his head from the pillow and reached under it for his twist. Bill thought the psychological moment to speak had arrived and he said: "Pap, I was a merchant but I've sold out and cleared this." Whereupon Greene, Sr., reached over and awaking his wife, said: "Liz, (Billy's mother) git up and git Billy a *fust rate* supper. He's had a hard day of it."

But Lincoln and Berry's venture in the mercantile business did not bring in the returns anticipated. A considerable part of the stock purchased by them from their predecessors consisted of liquors, and because of Lincoln's prejudice against its sale and use had hindered the disposal thereof to an appreciable extent, their failing circumstances gave Berry the opportunity he craved and being the senior partner, he applied for and secured in the name of Berry and Lincoln a license to keep a tavern, which meant solely in this case, the right to sell liquor by the drink. This permit was granted on the sixth day of March, 1833, by the County Commissioners' Court of Sangamon County and the bond in the case, while purporting to be signed by Lincoln, the name is not in his handwriting and appears to have been written there by Berry. The bond is signed by Bowling Green as surety. Shortly afterward Lincoln sold his interest in the store to Berry, taking Berry's notes, one of which he turned over to James Rutledge in payment of his part of the indebtedness of the firm to Rutledge. Afterwards, when Berry had sold out to the Trent Brothers and they had left, leaving their notes unpaid and Berry had died insolvent, Lincoln offered his personal note to Rutledge for the amount due him. This Rutledge refused, stating that he had agreed to take Berry's note for the debt of Lincoln to him and proposed to keep his agreement; if he failed to get his money from Berry's estate, he would lose it. . . .

Within a year after becoming sole owner, Berry sold out the store to the Trent Brothers, taking their notes, and about the time these came due, they paid them by slipping away while others were sleeping. One morning in the late fall of 1834 the village awoke. Smoke spirals arose from the chimneys, but none from the Trent Brothers' store. Its absence and the closed door attracted the attention of the inhabitants. An examination was made and no one was seen about the building. Further investigation showed the families to have disappeared with their household goods during the night, leaving Berry and their other creditors to hold the bag. This method of paying debts was of common occurrence in those days and did not excite the inhabitants, provided the remnant of goods on hand were left. Berry took over the store and operated it until he failed and was closed out. . . . On January 10, 1835, he died, leaving Lincoln to shoulder the burden of all their debts.

6

ONCE MORE LINCOLN cast about for something to do. Good fortune was with him, as Benjamin P. Thomas reveals.

AT THIS TIME LINCOLN'S FORTUNES were at low ebb. In debt and out of a job, he said in his autobiography that he was reduced to the elemental problem of securing bread to keep body and soul together. Many men in similar circumstances would have blamed the town for their failure, and moved away, leaving their debts unpaid. But Lincoln remained. He believed that if he could succeed anywhere he could do so at New Salem. He had no intention of evading his obligations, and he wished to remain with his friends.

Except for the problem of debt he was not badly off, for with his strength and skill and reputation for honesty he had no trouble getting work. Travelers in Sangamon County in the early thirties remarked time and again about the scarcity of laborers and the good wages paid to them. Patrick Shirreff, a Scotsman, stated that "labor is scarce and highly remunerated. A good farming help obtains $120, an indifferent one $100 a year, with bed and board." He calculated that this was equivalent to eighty acres of land a year, and in proportion to the cost of living and of land, about eight hundred times as much as English farm laborers got. Clarke [5] pleaded with his family to send one of the boys to Illinois. "If he will learn house carpenters trade and come into this country," he wrote, "I will warrant him a rich man in a few years, finally tradesmen of all kinds are in great demand here and will be for many years, they get from two to five dollars

---

[5] C. J. F. Clarke, a settler who lived near New Salem.

pr. day." Under such circumstances Lincoln could have had no difficulty in earning a living, and certainly there was little chance of his being in want.

But he was looking for a chance to become something more than a laborer; and on May 7, 1833, his ambition was gratified to some extent when he was appointed postmaster at New Salem, succeeding Samuel Hill. His explanation of his securing the position under President Jackson when he was "an avowed Clay man," was that the office was "too insignificant to make his politics an objection." He retained the position until the removal of the office to Petersburg on May 30, 1836.

According to one story, Lincoln's appointment was the result of a petition circulated by the New Salem women. Irked at the treatment accorded them by Hill, who neglected the distribution of mail while he sold liquor to the men, they petitioned the Post Office Department for his removal. Herndon did not know whether Lincoln solicited the appointment or whether it came to him without effort on his part. Upon appointment, Lincoln, like other postmasters, was required to furnish bond of $500. Nelson Alley and Alexander Trent were his bondsmen.

New Salem was on a mail route which ran from Springfield through Sangamontown, Athens, New Salem, Havana, Lewistown, Jackson Grove, Canton and Knox Courthouse (Knoxville) to Warren Courthouse (Monmouth), a distance of about one hundred and twenty-five miles. The mail was scheduled to leave Springfield on Saturday at four A.M. and to arrive at Warren Courthouse at six A.M. on Tuesday and arrived in Springfield at ten P.M. on Thursday, if on time. It was carried on horseback by Harvey L. Ross, whose father, Ossian Ross, of Havana, held the contract for the route. After the stage line was established, the mail was carried by it.

Postal rates varied with the distance traversed and the number of pages in a letter. A single sheet cost six cents for the first thirty miles, ten cents for thirty to eighty miles, twelve and a half cents for eighty to one hundred and fifty miles, eighteen and three-quarters cents for one hundred and fifty to four hundred miles, and twenty-five cents for more than four hundred miles. Two sheets cost twice as much, three sheets three times as much, and so on. Neither stamps nor envelopes were used. Letters were simply folded and sealed, and the postage charge was written in the upper right hand corner on the outside. Postage was paid by the addressee.

The high rates on letters elicited numerous complaints. To conserve space people frequently covered a sheet, then turned it sidewise and wrote across what they had already written, sometimes following this by writing obliquely across the page. Postmasters had difficulty in determining the number of sheets in a folded and sealed letter; and if the receiver questioned the rate charged he could open the letter in the postmaster's presence and have the error, if any, corrected.

As postmaster, Lincoln was exempt from militia and jury duties, was permitted to send and receive personal letters free, and to receive one newspaper daily without charge. The law provided, however, that "if any person shall frank any letter or letters, other than those written by himself, or by his order, on the business of the office, he shall, on conviction thereof, pay a fine of ten dollars." A letter of September 17, 1835, from Mathew S. Marsh to George M. Marsh, his brother, throws light on Lincoln's conduct of his office. "The Post Master (Mr. Lincoln)," wrote Marsh, "is very careless about leaving his office open and unlocked during the day—half the time I go in and get my papers, etc., without anyone being there as was the case yesterday. The letter was only marked twenty-five and even if he had been there and known it was double, he would not have charged me any more—luckily he is a very clever fellow and a particular friend of mine. If he is there when I carry this to the office—I will get him to 'Frank' it. . . ." Lincoln was there, and did frank it, thereby making himself liable to a ten dollar fine; for on the outside of the letter, in Lincoln's hand, is written: "Free, A. Lincoln, P. M. New Salem, Ill., Sept. 22."

A note from Lincoln to George Spears also reveals his indifference to postal regulations. "At your request," wrote Lincoln, "I send you a receipt for the postage on your paper—I am somewhat surprised at your request—I will however comply with it—The law requires Newspaper postage to be paid in advance and now that I have waited a full year you choose to wound my feelings by insinuating that unless you get a receipt I will probably make you pay it again—"

The postal law required every postmaster to maintain an office "in which one or more persons shall attend on every day on which a mail shall arrive." By the time that Lincoln became postmaster he had terminated his connection with the Lincoln and Berry store, and there is doubt as to whether his office was ever located there. Possibly it was for awhile. Later it was in Hill's store. According to Harvey Ross, Lincoln kept his receipts in a wooden chest under the counter in an old blue sock.

Lincoln gave general satisfaction in his administration of the office. He was always anxious to please and accommodate. When he thought that someone was especially anxious to receive a letter, he would walk several miles, if necessary, to deliver it. Herndon recalled that "Mr. Lincoln used to tell me that when he had a call to go to the country to survey a piece of land, he placed inside his hat all the letters belonging to people in the neighborhood and distributed them along the way." The practice of carrying papers and letters in his hat became a habit with him.

As postmaster, Lincoln could read all the newspapers that came to New Salem. At this time he formed the habit of newspaper reading which he continued through life, and through which, in part, he learned to interpret public opinion. His position also enabled him to become acquainted with almost every settler in that part of the country and made more formidable his subsequent candidacies for the Legislature.

Financially the job was not much help to him. His remuneration depended upon the receipts of his office, which were small. More than a year after the New Salem office was discontinued, and after he had moved to Springfield, he turned over the balance of his receipts to William Carpenter, the Springfield postmaster. Carpenter's account book contains the following entry under date of June 14, 1837: "For Cash recd of A. Lincoln late P. M. New Salem $248.63." We do not know how long this sum had been accumulating; but if it was the receipts of the office for a year, Lincoln's commissions for that year would have totaled about seventy-five or eighty dollars. If it represented the total receipts of the office for the three years of Lincoln's tenure, his commissions were about twenty-five or thirty dollars a year.

The *Sangamo Journal* of April 9, 1834, published the receipts of some of the Illinois post offices for 1833. The Jacksonville office took in $956. That at Springfield received $681. The Chicago office received $369; that at Beardstown $187; Peoria, $136; Pekin, $178; Vandalia, $426. On the New Salem route the Havana office took in $54; Knoxville, $36; Lewistown, $130. No figures are given for the New Salem office, but in comparison with these figures the estimate of twenty-five or thirty dollars a year as Lincoln's remuneration seems more likely to be correct.

The position of postmaster was not confining, and Lincoln supplemented his commissions by doing all sorts of odd jobs, such as splitting rails, helping at the mill, harvesting and tending store for Hill. In December, 1834, he succeeded Doctor Allen as local agent for the *Sangamo Journal.* On election days he often made a dollar by serving as clerk, and sometimes returned the poll book to the Court House in Springfield, for which service he was paid $2.50.

In the latter part of 1833, he secured employment as a deputy to John Calhoun, the county surveyor. Calhoun was one of the most prominent Jacksonian politicians in the county and Herndon says that Lincoln probably got the job through the recommendation of some Democrat. Knowing Calhoun's political affiliation, Lincoln hesitated to accept the job at first, but upon being assured that it would entail no political commitment, he did so.

Surveying in those days, when the country was rapidly filling with settlers and the division lines of farms were being run for the first time, when speculators were buying large tracts and laying off towns, and when miles of wagon road were being opened, was an important and responsible job. Lincoln knew nothing about it; but borrowing books from Calhoun and enlisting the help of Mentor Graham, he went to work. Using Robert Gibson's *Theory and Practice of Surveying* and Flint's *Treatise on Geometry, Trigonometry and Rectangular Surveying* as texts, he studied day and night. Often he and Graham were up until midnight, interrupting their calculations only when Mrs. Graham ordered them out for a fresh supply of wood for the fire. But he mastered the books, obtained a fifty-dollar horse on credit, procured a compass and chain, and by the end of the year was ready to start work.

7

HANDLING THE MAILS and making occasional surveys kept
Lincoln occupied. But neither these activities nor any others prevented him from drawing the essentials of a further education from
the New Salem environment. William E. Barton identifies the influences that contributed to his development.

LINCOLN WENT TO SCHOOL, as he said, "by littles." His
two short terms of schooling in Kentucky and his three in Indiana
totaled less than a year of formal instruction. When he went to
Congress in 1848, and filled out a concise blank whose catch words
were intended to suggest the outlines of a brief biography, he entered opposite the title "Education," the single word "Defective."
But when we consider him as he was toward the end of his experience in New Salem, we are impressed not so much by the meager-
ness of his equipment as by the extent of his preparation for a
successful life. . . .

New Salem greatly encouraged his love of learning. We can not
pursue the history of Lincoln's six years at New Salem intelli-
gently and confine our study to the financial adventures of the
firm of Lincoln and Berry, or the vicissitudes of Denton Offutt
and his rough-and-tumble encounters with the Clary Grove boys.
Lincoln was in an environment that gave him adequate mental
stimulus and encouragement.

Among Lincoln's friends was Jack Kelso, a peculiar, unpracti-
cal genius, who bore the reputation of having a fine education.
Kelso introduced him to Shakespeare, Burns and Byron. Kelso
was married but childless. He was not fond of labor, but was a
good fisherman. Fishing was about the only job at which he
worked industriously, and he rather resented it when any one intruded upon his vocation with an offer of remunerative employment. Lincoln had no musical ability, but had an ear for rhythm.
He fished now and then with Kelso, and oftener sat with Jack and
visited in the evening. Lincoln's taste in poetry up to this time had
been principally for jingles, and rhymed nonsense. He began to
appreciate some of the real beauties to be found in the writings of
great poets.

Lincoln early formed the acquaintance and close friendship of Bowling Green. Green was a half-brother of Jack Armstrong. His father had lived in Tennessee, and his mother, whose maiden name was Nancy Potter, bore him prior to her marriage to Robert Armstrong by whom she had eight children. Bowling Green was a very large man, weighing over two hundred pounds, and had a singularly pink and white skin, his complexion being like that of a woman. He was easy-going and hospitable, and Lincoln was much in his home. Green and Lincoln both were inclined to be Whigs in a community where most men were Democrats. Green was a justice of the peace, and had a few law books which he willingly loaned to Lincoln. . . .

Among the agencies which affected Lincoln during his residence in New Salem was a debating society, organized under the direction of James Rutledge, and including in its membership the literary lights of the community. Lincoln attained considerable skill as a debater and he set himself to the work of preparation of essays on a wide variety of themes, philosophical, scientific and religious.

Although one of the founders of New Salem was a preacher of the Cumberland Presbyterian faith, and the coming of the Bale family brought two Baptist preachers, Abraham and Jacob Bale, as residents of the town, and although Peter Cartwright and other Methodist preachers came frequently and preached in the schoolhouse or in the Rutledge tavern, there was in New Salem a rather strong tendency toward what was called infidelity. Paine's *Age of Reason* and Volney's *Ruins* were in active circulation. Lincoln read them, and they were not without their influence upon his thinking. . . .

One of Lincoln's best friends in New Salem, and one of the strongest forces for righteousness, was Doctor John Allen, who came to New Salem from Vermont before August 28, 1831. He was a strict Sabbatarian, whose principles in this regard were strengthened by an incident that occurred on his westward journey. Coming down the Ohio River, he stopped on Saturday night and waited for the next boat. The boat on which he had been traveling sank next day with loss of life. Doctor Allen practised his profession on Sunday, but gave his fees for that day to religion and charity. He organized the first Sunday School in New

Salem, and was its superintendent. He organized a Temperance Society, which was looked upon with disfavor. Mentor Graham became a member; and for his membership in it was expelled from the New Salem Baptist Church: the same church meeting, by way of even-handed justice, expelled three other members for drunkenness. . . .

The social life of New Salem in those days was a revelation to Lincoln. It was far beyond anything he had known in Spencer County, Indiana. Gentryville never supposed that it was going to become a great city. It never cherished a hope that brought to it any such group of people as made up the population of New Salem. This mushroom village on the Sangamon, which disappeared from the map almost as soon as it found a place there, combined in itself during its short lifetime, those elements which made it for Lincoln the portal to new experiences. It had almost as many different types of people as it had log cabins. There were preachers and infidels, earnest advocates of temperance like Doctor Allen, and swaggering bullies of the backwoods like the Clary Grove boys. There were men who drifted along the river, "half horse, half alligator," not all of them gamblers and thugs, but men who regarded the life of the river as providing a law of its own. There were people who made a cross instead of signing their names, and there were others who read the classics and were at home among the poets. In all of this remarkable heterogeneity there was a strange kind of social unity. . . . It was a place where, to quote the not over-nice but accurately expressive language of the period, "kin and kin-in-law did not count a cuss." It was no disgrace to be poor, and there was little to encourage a man in making any hypocritical pretense of more piety than he actually possessed.

8

BY THE SPRING OF 1837, Lincoln had definitely outgrown the moribund village on the Sangamon. As he takes leave of it, we draw once more on Benjamin P. Thomas, this time for a summary of what he owed to its hospitable inhabitants.

I N   H I S   S I X   Y E A R S at New Salem Lincoln had gone far. He could justly take pride in his progress. Coming to the village like "a piece of floating driftwood," as he said, he had worked his way up to a position of leadership not only in New Salem but in the State as well. He was recognized as a skilful politician. He had made valuable friendships in the county and the State at large. He had learned to think straight and express himself with force and clarity. He had equipped himself to make a living with his brain instead of his hands.

To New Salem he owed much. His associations there were more varied than any he had known in Kentucky, Indiana or his earlier home in Illinois. His advent there was a definite step forward— one that freed him from the retarding influence of his family and revealed to him the possibility of betterment.

The New Salem years left a lasting impress. To the end of his life the rural background of his early years colored his writings and speech. Many of the similes and metaphors which enrich his literary style smack of the countryside. The "twang of the cross-roads" was in his anecdotes. Often in later life he illustrated his remarks with rural analogies drawn from his New Salem experiences.

In New Salem as well as in his former homes in Kentucky and Indiana, Lincoln lived in a Southern pioneer atmosphere. His contact with its people helped him understand the Southern temperament and point of view. He entered with zest into the theological discussions of the community, and profited by the niceties of thought, the subtle distinctions and fine-spun argument that they necessitated. Yet, while he enjoyed them as a mental exercise, and while he eventually attained to a deep faith, emotionally the bitterness of sectarian prejudice must have been repellent to him, and was probably a cause of his lasting reluctance to affiliate with any sect.

The New Salem environment, typical of that of the West in general, offered opportunities which Lincoln would not have had in an older community. Humble origin and lack of schooling were no handicaps, for they were common deficiencies. A newcomer had no difficulty in establishing himself, for no one had been there

long, no propertied class had emerged, and social castes were unknown. Equality of opportunity was in large degree a fact, and
democracy and nationalism were the political ideals.

Lincoln accepted these ideals, and benefited by the opportunities that the frontier afforded. But at the same time he avoided
the frontier's weaknesses or, learning from experience, outgrew
them. He became self-reliant without becoming boastful and without overestimating himself; analytical and conservative rather
than opportunistic and impulsive. He realized the value of law,
and was respectful of form and tradition, in a region where men
sometimes made their own law, where informality prevailed, and
where people were concerned with the present and future rather
than the past.

His support of Clay rather than Jackson, his defense of the
old Indian in the Black Hawk War, his stand on slavery show that
he was thinking for himself, and that here—as later in his opposition to the Mexican War and in the tolerant and forgiving spirit
that he maintained toward the South in the prevailing bitterness
of Civil War—he dared stand against the crowd. His standards
and ambitions transcended those of the community. At New
Salem, as in later life, his individuality stands out. Yet while becoming a leader of his fellows Lincoln never lost touch with them.
He grew beyond his associates, but not away from them.

CHAPTER FOUR

"The DeWitt Clinton of Illinois"

WHILE LINCOLN WAS earning a living at New Salem, growing in knowledge, and finding new interests, he was also discovering in politics an interest that was to absorb him for most of his life. By winning the practically unanimous vote of his precinct when he ran for the legislature in 1832 he had established his right to run again at the next opportunity. He had also given the political wiseacres of the county good reason to believe that his second try would be successful.

1

NICOLAY AND HAY analyze the sources of Lincoln's political popularity, as revealed in his day-by-day living and in his first successful campaign.

THOUGH IT IS evident that the post office and the surveyor's compass were not making a rich man of him, they were sufficient to enable him to live decently, and during the year he greatly increased his acquaintance and his influence in the county. The one followed the other naturally; every acquaintance he made became his friend, and even before the end of his unsuccessful canvass in 1832 it had become evident to the observant politicians of the district that he was a man whom it would not do to leave out of their calculations. There seemed to be no limit to his popularity nor to his aptitudes, in the opinion of his admirers. He was continually called on to serve in the most incongruous capacities. Old residents say he was the best judge at a horse race the county afforded; he was occasionally second in a duel of fisticuffs, though he usually contrived to reconcile the adversaries on the turf before any damage was done; he was the arbiter on all controverted points of literature, science, or woodcraft among the disputatious denizens of Clary's Grove, and his decisions were never appealed from. His native tact and humor were invaluable in his work as a peacemaker, and his enormous physical strength, which he always used with a magnanimity rare among giants, placed his offhand decrees beyond the reach of contemptuous question. He composed differences among friends and equals with good-natured raillery, but he was as rough as need be when his wrath was roused by meanness and cruelty. We hardly know whether to credit some of the stories, apparently well-attested by living witnesses, of his prodigious muscular powers. He is said to have lifted, at Rutledge's mill, a box of stones weighing over half a ton! It is also related that he could raise a barrel of whisky from the ground and drink from the bung—but the narrator adds that he never swallowed the whisky. Whether these traditions are strictly true or not, they are evidently founded on the current reputation he enjoyed among his fellows for extraordinary strength, and this was an important element in his influence. He was known to be capable of handling almost any man he met, yet he never sought a quarrel. He was everybody's friend and yet used no liquor or tobacco. He was poor and had scarcely ever been at school, yet he was the best-informed young man in the village. He had grown up on the frontier, the utmost fringe of civilization, yet he was gentle and clean of speech, innocent of blasphemy or scandal. His good qualities might have excited resentment if displayed by a well-dressed stranger from an Eastern state, but the most uncouth ruffians of New Salem took a sort of proprietary interest and pride in the decency and the cleverness and the learning of their friend and comrade, Abe Lincoln.

It was regarded, therefore, almost as a matter of course that Lincoln should be a candidate for the Legislature at the next election, which took place in August, 1834. He was sure of the united support of the Whigs, and so many of the Democrats also wanted to vote for him that some of the leading members of that party came to him and proposed they should give him an organized support. He was too loyal a partisan to accept their overtures without taking counsel from the Whig candidates. He laid the matter before Major Stuart, who at once advised him to make the canvass. It was a generous and chivalrous action, for by thus encouraging the candidacy of Lincoln he was endangering his own election. But his success two years before, in the face of a vindictive opposition led by the strongest Jackson men in the district, had made him somewhat confident, and he perhaps thought he was risking little by giving a helping hand to his comrade in the Spy Battalion. Before the election Lincoln's popularity developed itself in rather a portentous manner, and it required some exertion to save the seat of his generous friend. At the close of the poll, the four successful candidates held the following relative positions: Lincoln, 1,376; Dawson, 1,370; Carpenter, 1,170; and Stuart, at that time probably the most prominent young man in the district, and the one marked out by the public voice for an early election to Congress, 1,164.

2

UNDER THE FIRST constitution of Illinois, in force until 1848, elections for members of the Legislature were held on the first Monday of August in the even-numbered years. Ordinarily the Legislature convened in early December and remained in session until the latter part of the following February. Its meeting place was Vandalia, capital of Illinois from 1820 to 1839, which Harry E. Pratt pictures as Lincoln saw it in the early winter of 1834.

LATE IN NOVEMBER LINCOLN was seated in the stage-coach bound for Vandalia, attired in a new sixty-dollar suit made for him by a Springfield tailor, with the remainder of Coleman Smoot's $200 loan [1] in his pocket to tide him over until the legislators voted themselves a partial salary payment at Christmas time.

Ahead lay new adventures and opportunities undreamed of four years earlier when he entered the State of Illinois. Seated

---

[1] Coleman Smoot, a farmer living near New Salem, lent Lincoln this sum so that he could pay his debts, buy clothing, and live decently during his first weeks in Vandalia.

with him in the stage were Sangamon County's other three representatives, John Todd Stuart, John Dawson and William Carpenter. The first two had each served a term in the House and
knew what was ahead. Stuart, like Lincoln, was Kentucky-born,
and only two years older, while Dawson was born in Virginia in
1791 and Carpenter in Pennsylvania in 1787. The older men were
both farmers and Democrats. . . .

   Lincoln's career at New Salem had qualified him to handle the
local problems of roads and the improvement of the Sangamon
River, but his experience had not taken him deeply into the major
problems that were to confront him in the Legislature: the problems of slavery and abolitionism, state banks, temperance, public
education, tariff, public lands, the creation of courts, building of
railroads and canals, and the cause and cure of a panic that would
leave the state treasury bankrupt. To listen, and to participate in
the discussion and solution of these questions on the floor of the
House and in the "Lobby," was to give him a training for his
subsequent career as a politician and statesman which no college
could have supplied. He was now about to enter his freshman
course in politics, government, and statesmanship. He was to
make new acquaintances and friendships and to learn and practice
the subtleties of the politician under the example and tutelage of
old and experienced practitioners.

   Completing its twenty-hour run from Springfield to Vandalia,
the stage driver, on entering town, whipped up his horses and
blew a blast on his horn as he drew up to the new Vandalia Inn at
the corner of the public square.

   Vandalia, a quiet, sleepy village of eight hundred during nine
months of the year, sprang into life with the opening of the Legislature and the convening of the Federal and Illinois Supreme
Courts. Lincoln found himself among many office seekers who
flocked to the capital. Their activities were described in a letter
dated at Vandalia on December 1, 1834, which reads: "yesterday,
last night, all night nearly this town has been a scene of busy,
buzzing bargaining etc. It is said 150 persons, some from the distant parts of the State [are seeking] . . . the appointment of
Sergeant at Arms of the Senate and Doorkeeper of the House of
Representatives."

Situated on a bluff sixty feet above the west bank of the Kaskaskia River, recently spanned with a new bridge, Vandalia was well laid out with a public square and streets eighty feet wide. The streets were muddy or dusty, dependent on the weather, despite three days' labor during the year by each adult male. Several good grist mills were near at hand and building activity may be gauged by the presence of thirty-four carpenters and seven masons and plasterers. The Presbyterians had the only resident minister, and a frame church building worthy of the name. With the exception of the State House, the only brick structure in town was a two-story brick building, formerly used by the state bank, but now occupied by several state offices. The State House, a two-story building, was unprepossessing and gave the impression of great age, despite its erection in 1824.

3

DURING HIS FIRST TERM, as William H. Herndon points out, Lincoln was content to listen, observe—and learn.

At this session of the Legislature he was anything but conspicuous. In reality he was very modest, but shrewd enough to impress the force of his character on those persons whose influence might some day be of advantage to him. He made but little stir, if we are to believe the record, during the whole of this first session. Made a member of the Committee on Public Accounts and Expenditures, his name appears so seldom in the reports of the proceedings that we are prone to conclude that he must have contented himself with listening to the flashes of border oratory and absorbing his due proportion of parliamentary law. He was reserved in manner, but very observant; said little, but learned much; made the acquaintance of all the members and many influential persons on the outside. The lobby at that day contained the representative men of the State—men of acknowledged prominence and respectability, many of them able lawyers, drawn thither in advocacy of some pet bill. Schemes of vast internal improvements attracted a retinue of logrollers, who in later days seem to have been an indispensable necessity in the movement of complicated legislative machinery. Men of capital and brains were there. He early realized the importance of knowing all these, trusting to the inspiration of some future hour to impress them with his skill as an organizer or his power as an orator. Among the members of the outside or "third body" was Stephen A. Douglas, whom Lincoln then saw for the first time. Douglas had come from Vermont only the year before, but was already undertaking to supplant John J. Hardin in the office of States Attorney for the district in which both lived. What impression he made on Lincoln, what opinions each formed of the other, or what the extent of their acquaintance then was, we do not know. It is said that Lincoln afterwards in mentioning their first meeting observed of the newly arrived Vermonter that he was the "least man he had ever seen." The Legislature proper contained the youth and blood and fire of the frontier. Some of the men who participated in these early parliamentary battles were destined to carry the banners of great political parties, some to lead in war and some in the great council chamber of the nation. Some were to fill the Governor's office, others to wear the judicial ermine, and one was destined to be Chief Magistrate and die a martyr to the cause of human liberty.

The society of Vandalia and the people attracted thither by the Legislature made it, for that early day, a gay place indeed. Compared to Lincoln's former environments, it had no lack of refinement and polish. That he absorbed a good deal of this by contact with the men and women who surrounded him there can be no doubt. The "drift of sentiment and the sweep of civilization" at this time can best be measured by the character of the legislation. There were acts to incorporate banks, turnpikes, bridges, insurance companies, towns, railroads, and female academies. The vigor and enterprise of New England fusing with the illusory prestige of Kentucky and Virginia was fast forming a new civilization to spread over the prairies. At this session Lincoln remained quietly in the background, and contented himself with the introduction of a resolution in favor of securing to the State a part of the proceeds of sales of public lands within its limits.

With this brief and modest record he returned to his constituents at New Salem.

4

IN THE COURSE of its regular session the Legislature passed a resolution providing that it be called together for a second session in December, 1835, for the purpose of apportioning the State into legislative districts under the census of 1835. Four days before the second session was to convene one of the State's two senators died, so the duty of electing a successor also fell upon the legislators. Nicolay and Hay, unable to disguise their own strong prejudices in their characterization of Stephen A. Douglas, reveal Lincoln's part in this session.

LINCOLN RETURNED to New Salem, after this winter's experience of men and things at the little capital, much firmer on his feet than ever before. He had had the opportunity of measuring himself with the leading men of the community, and had found no difficulty whatever in keeping pace with them. He continued his studies of the law and surveying together, and became quite indispensable in the latter capacity—so much so that General Neale, announcing in September, 1835, the names of the deputy surveyors of Sangamon County, placed the name of Lincoln before that of his old master in the science, John Calhoun. He returned to the Legislature in the winter of 1835–36, and one of the first important incidents of the session was the election of a senator to fill the vacancy occasioned by the death of Elias Kent Kane. There was no lack of candidates. A journal of the time says: "This intelligence reached Vandalia on the evening of the 26th of December, and in the morning nine candidates appeared in that place, and it was anticipated that a number more would soon be in, among them 'the lion of the North,' who, it is thought, will claim the office by pre-emption." It is not known who was the roaring celebrity here referred to, but the successful candidate was General William L. D. Ewing, who was elected by a majority of one vote. Lincoln and the other Whigs voted for him, not because he was a "White" man, as they frankly stated, but because "he had been proscribed by the Van Buren party." Mr. Semple, the candidate for the regular Democratic caucus, was beaten simply on account of his political orthodoxy.

A minority is always strongly in favor of independent action and bitterly opposed to caucuses, and therefore we need not be surprised at finding Mr. Lincoln, a few days later in the session, joining in hearty denunciation of the convention system, which had already become popular in the East, and which General Jackson was then urging upon his faithful followers. The missionaries of this new system in Illinois were Stephen A. Douglas, recently from Vermont, the shifty young lawyer from Morgan County, who had just succeeded in having himself made circuit attorney in place of Colonel Hardin, and a man who was then regarded in Vandalia as a far more important and dangerous person than Douglas, Ebenezer Peck, of Chicago. Peck was looked upon with distrust and suspicion for several reasons, all of which seemed valid to the rural legislators assembled there. He came from Canada, where he had been a member of the provincial parliament; it was therefore imagined that he was permeated with secret hostility to republican institutions; his garb, his furs, were of the fashion of Quebec; and he passed his time indoctrinating the Jackson men with the theory and practice of party organization, teachings which they eagerly absorbed, and which seemed sinister and ominous to the Whigs. He was showing them, in fact, the way in which elections were to be won; and though the Whigs denounced his system as subversive of individual freedom and private judgment, it was not long before they were also forced to adopt it, or be left alone with their virtue. The organization of political parties in Illinois really takes its rise from this time, and in great measure from the work of Mr. Peck with the Vandalia Legislature. There was no man more dreaded and disliked than he was by the stalwart young Whigs against whom he was organizing that solid and disciplined opposition. But a quarter of a century brings wonderful changes. Twenty-five years later Mr. Peck stood shoulder to shoulder with these very men who then reviled him as a Canadian emissary of tyranny and corruption, —with S. T. Logan, O. H. Browning, and J. K. Dubois—organizing a new party for victory under the name of Abraham Lincoln.

The Legislature adjourned on the eighteenth of January, having made a beginning, it is true, in the work of improving the State by statute, though its modest work, incorporating canal and bridge companies and providing for public roads, bore no relation to the ambitious essays of its successor. Among the bills passed at this session was an Apportionment Act, by which Sangamon County became entitled to seven representatives and two senators, and early in the spring eight "White" statesmen of the county were ready for the field—the ninth, Mr. Herndon, holding over as State Senator.

5

THE YEAR 1836 was the year of a Presidential election, so it was inevitable that local and national politics should be inextricably mixed. Ward Hill Lamon discloses the tactics which returned Lincoln to the Legislature and gave Sangamon County to the Whigs, although Illinois and the nation at large voted Martin Van Buren, the Democratic candidate, into the White House.

I N 1836 Mr. Lincoln was again a candidate for the Legislature; his colleagues on the Whig ticket in Sangamon being, for Representatives, John Dawson, William F. Elkin, N. W. Edwards, Andrew McCormick, Dan Stone, and R. L. Wilson; and for Senators, A. G. Herndon and Job Fletcher. They were all elected. . . .

Mr. Lincoln opened the campaign by the following manifesto:

New Salem, June 13, 1836.
To the Editor of "The Journal."

In your paper of last Saturday, I see a communication over the signature of "Many Voters," in which the candidates who are announced in the "Journal" are called upon to "show their hands." Agreed. Here's mine.

I go for all sharing the privileges of the government who assist in bearing its burdens. Consequently, I go for admitting all *whites* to the right of suffrage who pay taxes or bear arms (*by no means excluding females*).

If elected, I shall consider the whole people of Sangamon my constituents, as well those that oppose as those that support me.

While acting as their Representative, I shall be governed by their will on all subjects upon which I have the means of knowing what their will is; and upon all others I shall do what my own judgment teaches me will best advance their interests. Whether elected or not, I go for distributing the proceeds of the sales of the public lands to the several States, to enable our State, in common with others, to dig canals and construct railroads without borrowing money and paying the interest on it.

If alive on the first Monday in November, I shall vote for Hugh L. White for President.

Very respectfully,

A. LINCOLN.

The elections were held on the first Monday in August, and the campaign began about six weeks or two months before. Popular meetings were advertised in the *Sangamo Journal* and the *State Register*—organs of the respective parties. Not infrequently the meetings were joint—composed of both parties—when, as Lincoln would say, the candidates "put in their best licks," while the audience "rose to the height of the great argument" with cheers, taunts, catcalls, fights, and other exercises appropriate to the free and untrammelled enjoyment of the freeman's boon.

The candidates traveled from one grove to another on horseback; and, when the "Long Nine" (all over six feet in height) took the road, it must have been a goodly sight to see.

"I heard Lincoln make a speech," says James Gourly, "in Mechanicsburg, Sangamon County, in 1836. John Neal had a fight at the time: the roughs got on him, and Lincoln jumped in and saw fair play. We stayed for dinner at Green's, close to Mechanicsburg,—drank whisky sweetened with honey. There the questions discussed were internal improvements, Whig principles." (Gourly was a great friend of Lincoln's, for Gourly had had a foot race "with H. B. Truett, now of California," and Lincoln had been his "judge"; and it was a remarkable circumstance that nearly everybody for whom Lincoln "judged" came out ahead.)

"I heard Mr. Lincoln during the same canvass," continues Gourly. "It was at the Court House, where the State House now stands. The Whigs and Democrats had a general quarrel then and there. N. W. Edwards drew a pistol on Achilles Morris." But Gourly's account of this last scene is unsatisfactory, although the witness is willing; and we turn to Lincoln's colleague, Mr. Wilson, for a better one. "The Saturday evening preceding the election the candidates were addressing the people in the Court House at Springfield. Dr. Early, one of the candidates on the Democratic side, made some charge that N. W. Edwards, one of the candidates on the Whig side, deemed untrue. Edwards climbed on a table, so as to be seen by Early, and by every one in the house, and at the top of his voice told Early that the charge was false. The excitement that followed was intense—so much so, that fighting men thought that a duel must settle the difficulty. Mr. Lincoln, by the program, followed Early. He took up the subject in dispute, and handled it fairly, and with such ability that every one was astonished and pleased. So that difficulty ended there. Then, for the first time, developed by the excitement of the occasion, he spoke in that tenor intonation of voice that ultimately settled down into that clear, shrill monotone style of speaking that enabled his audience, however large, to hear distinctly the lowest sound of his voice."

It was during this campaign, possibly at the same meeting, that Mr. Speed heard him reply to George Forquer. Forquer had been a leading Whig, one of their foremost men in the Legislature of 1834, but had then recently changed sides, and thereupon was appointed Register of the Land Office at Springfield. Mr. Forquer was an astonishing man: he not only astonished the people by "changing his coat in politics," but by building the best frame house in Springfield, and erecting over it the only lightning rod the entire region could boast of. At this meeting he listened attentively to Mr. Lincoln's first speech, and was much annoyed by the transcendent power with which the awkward young man defended the principles he had himself so lately abandoned. "The speech" produced a profound impression, "especially upon a large number of Lincoln's friends and admirers, who had come in from the country" expressly to hear and applaud him.

"At the conclusion of Lincoln's speech" (we quote from Mr. Speed), "the crowd was dispersing, when Forquer rose and asked to be heard. He commenced by saying that the young man would have to be taken down, and was sorry that the task devolved upon him. He then proceeded to answer Lincoln's speech in a style,

which, while it was able and fair, yet, in his whole manner, asserted and claimed superiority. Lincoln stood near him, and
watched him during the whole of his speech. When Forquer concluded, he took the stand again. I have often heard him since, in
court and before the people, but never saw him appear so well
as upon that occasion. He replied to Mr. Forquer with great dignity and force; but I shall never forget the conclusion of that
speech. Turning to Mr. Forquer, he said, that he had commenced
his speech by announcing that 'this young man would have to be
taken down.' Turning then to the crowd, he said, 'It is for you,
not for me, to say whether I am up or down. The gentleman has
alluded to my being a young man: I am older in years than I am
in the tricks and trades of politicians. I desire to live, and I desire
place and distinction as a politician; but I would rather die now,
than, like the gentleman, live to see the day that I would have to
erect a lightning rod to protect a guilty conscience from an offended God.' "

He afterwards told Speed that the sight of that same rod "had
led him to the study of the properties of electricity and the utility
of the rod as a conductor."

Among the Democratic orators stumping the county at this
time was Dick Taylor, a pompous gentleman, who went abroad
in superb attire, ruffled shirts, rich vest, and immense watch
chains, with shining and splendid pendants. But Dick was a severe
Democrat in theory, made much of "the hard-handed yeomanry,"
and flung many biting sarcasms upon the aristocratic pretensions
of the Whigs—the "rag barons" and the manufacturing "lords."
He was one day in the midst of a particularly aggravating decla-
mation of this sort, "when Abe began to feel devilish, and thought
he would take the wind out of Dick's sails by a little sport." He
therefore "edged" slyly up to the speaker, and suddenly catching
his vest by the lower corner, and giving it a sharp pull upward, it
opened wide, and out fell upon the platform, in full view of the
astonished audience, a mass of ruffled shirt, gold watch, chains,
seals, and glittering jewels. Jim Matheny was there, and nearly
broke his heart with mirth. "The crowd couldn't stand it, but
shouted uproariously." It must have been then that Abe delivered
the following speech, although Ninian W. Edwards places it in
1840:

"While he [Colonel Taylor] was making these charges against the Whigs over the country, riding in fine carriages, wearing ruffled shirts, kid gloves, massive gold watch chains, with large gold seals, and flourishing a heavy gold-headed cane, he [Lincoln] was a poor boy, hired on a flatboat at eight dollars a month, and had only one pair of breeches to his back, and they were buckskin —'and,' said Lincoln, 'if you know the nature of buckskin, when wet and dried by the sun, they will shrink—and mine kept shrinking, until they left several inches of my legs bare between the tops of my socks and the lower part of my breeches; and, whilst I was growing taller, they were becoming shorter, and so much tighter, that they left a blue streak around my legs that can be seen to this day. If you call this aristocracy, I plead guilty to the charge.' "

Hitherto Sangamon County had been uniformly Democratic; but at this election the Whigs carried it by an average majority of about four hundred, Mr. Lincoln receiving a larger vote than any other candidate. The result was in part due to a transitory and abortive attempt of the anti-Jackson and anti-Van Buren men to build up a third party, with Judge White, of Tennessee, as its leader. This party was not supposed to be wedded to the "specie circular," was thought to be open to conviction on the bank question, clamored loudly about the business interests and general distress of the country, and was actually in favor of the distribution of the proceeds of the sales of the public lands. In the nomenclature of Illinois, its members might have been called "nominal Jackson men"; that is to say, men who continued to act with the Democratic party, while disavowing its cardinal principles—traders, trimmers, cautious schismatics who argued the cause of Democracy from a brief furnished by the enemy. The diversion in favor of White was just to the hand of the Whigs, and they aided it in every practicable way. Always for an expedient when an expedient would answer, a compromise when a compromise would do, the "hand" Mr. Lincoln "showed" at the opening of the campaign contained the "White" card among the highest of its trumps. "If alive on the first Monday in November, I shall vote for Hugh L. White for President." A number of local Democratic politicians assisting him to play it, it won the game in 1836, and Sangamon County went over to the Whigs.

6

THE LEGISLATURE of 1836–37 was the most important of the four in which Lincoln served. Largely through his efforts—for he had now become a leading member—it relocated the capital of the State and passed a system of internal improvements that was soon to become the most voracious of white elephants. Before it adjourned, it took a strong stand on the slavery question. It is fitting, therefore, that its leading members should be characterized with care, as they are by Albert J. Beveridge.

THIS LEGISLATURE was remarkable not only in what was done but in the quality of its members. There was a strange mingling of vision and blindness, of fine ability bloated with unreasoning optimism; and through all ran the poisonous filaments of the politician's deals and trades. Of the more than one hundred members of House and Senate, not one had been born in Illinois; and this was true, too, of the three members of the Supreme Court, the many lawyers in attendance upon it, and the throng of lobbyists who came to Vandalia whenever the General Assembly met, and who, since great enterprises were at hand, were especially numerous during this session.

Most conspicuous were the members of the Supreme Court— William Wilson, Chief Justice, able and learned; Samuel D. Lockwood, highly educated and a fine lawyer; Thomas C. Brown, "the Falstaff of the bench," who never refused nor offered a drink, and made up for his total ignorance of the law by a quick, audacious wit and friendly good nature. All three Justices were ardent Whigs.

Among the attorneys at Vandalia, the most prominent was Justin Butterfield, of Chicago, who was attending the Supreme Court, a good lawyer and a cultivated man of sparkling humor, and Josiah Lamborn who was afterwards elected Attorney General. Gurdon S. Hubbard was an example of the lobbyists. Born in New England, he had become an Indian trader in Illinois, spoke several Indian dialects perfectly, and during the session, with others scarcely less qualified, performed an Indian war dance for the amusement of the legislators. Former Governor John Reynolds, the "Old Ranger," was there, too, cordial and grave, with the mingled reserve and heartiness of the frontier.

Of all those in Vandalia during that memorable winter, John T. Stuart was the best known. He was over six feet tall, the "handsomest man in Illinois," an able, and resourceful lawyer, deferential in manner, benignant of countenance and, for years to come, an influential man in the State. But he was known as a plotter and manipulator—"Jerry Sly," his political enemies called this closest associate of Lincoln. The reverse of Stuart in appearance and method was Reverend John Hogan, of Alton, of Irish birth, once a Methodist preacher, florid of face, boisterous of manner, bold and outspoken, an incessant talker, frequently in debate, aggressively optimistic, looking at all things through rose-colored spectacles.

Ninian W. Edwards, of Springfield, who was "naturally and constitutionally an aristocrat, and . . . hated democracy . . . as the devil is said to hate holy water," was an example of the class-conscious higher orders of society. With a manner lofty and aloof, vain, proud of his name and family, he was unpopular. His attire was of the best material, made in the latest mode of fashion. In the State Senate was Cyrus Edwards, of Madison County, uncle of Ninian W. Edwards, and his equal in apparel and conduct. "The great Edwards family" was well represented in the General Assembly of 1836–37. Into this family Lincoln was to marry within five years.

Of the same type was another Whig, Edwin B. Webb, of White County, born in Kentucky of an old Virginia family, refined, undersized, alert. He was devoted to Lincoln, who returned his affection. Another friend of Lincoln in the House whose adherence grew ever closer through the years, was "a slim, handsome young man, with auburn hair, sky-blue eyes, with the elegant manners of a Frenchman," Jesse K. Dubois, of Lawrence County. John A. McClernand, then of Shawneetown and a fighting Democrat who, twenty-five years later, was to bear so gallant and distinguished a part in the Civil War, was also a member of the House. He was only twenty-four years old, was uncommonly able, a fluent speaker, and quickly developed into one of the Democratic leaders.

The Speaker, James Semple, originally a tanner but now a

lawyer, was a Democrat of outstanding note and influence, strong-willed, domineering, but highly capable, though neither eloquent nor learned. Orlando B. Ficklin, of Wabash County, was also a member of the House, well-informed, resourceful and, like Lincoln, a notable mimic, wag, and story teller. One of the most popular members was a slender young man only twenty-six but already a veteran, having been dangerously wounded while serving as a soldier in Florida, James Shields, with whom, in a few years, Lincoln was to have a serious personal difficulty. Shields spoke and wrote French, was a hard student, generous, frank, engaging, and utterly without physical fear. He was a thorough-going Democrat, and was thrice to become a Senator of the United States from three different states and to hold more offices, civil and military, than almost any other man in American history.

More of Lincoln's mold was Archibald Williams, of Adams County, over six feet tall, angular and uncouth. He and Lincoln sat near to each other in the southeast corner of the House and were friends and confidants. So striking was their ungainly appearance that a stranger asked, "Who in the hell are those two ugly men?" Years afterward Lincoln declared that Williams was "the strongest-minded and clearest-headed man he ever saw." One of the most picturesque figures in the House and a member of power and influence was Usher F. Linder, who, many years later, wrote descriptions of his fellow members in this historic session. He, too, was more than six feet in stature, slender, raw-boned, and as awkward as Lincoln. He was born in Kentucky a few weeks after the birth of Lincoln and in the same county. He was well-educated, a good lawyer, almost irresistible before a jury, a vigorous partisan, formidable in debate, and a "terror on the stump."

At this session appeared a young representative from Morgan County who, soon thereafter, pressed Lincoln hard for the Whig leadership of the House and within five years passed him in political career. He was a college graduate and a lawyer, able, combative, and courageous, but without Lincoln's adroitness and political cleverness. Tall, well-dressed, with dark eyes, thick black hair and bold, determined, intellectual face, John J. Hardin was an attractive, manly figure. His father was Martin D. Hardin, Secretary of State of Kentucky, where the son was born. In exactly a decade after Hardin entered the Legislature of Illinois, it was to be his fortune to be killed in battle while leading his regiment at Buena Vista.

With Cyrus Edwards in the State Senate, was Orville H. Browning, of Quincy, a stalwart Whig. He was a finely educated man, a careful and successful lawyer, a good politician, stately and courteous, always dressed with scrupulous care. He was to become one of the founders of the Republican party and, during the War, Lincoln's mouthpiece in the United States Senate. His wife was with him and Linder makes particular mention of her as "an elegant and accomplished lady. . . ." In the Senate also was William H. Davidson, of White County, a brother-in-law of Chief Justice Wilson, a handsome man, well-educated, wealthy, of the old Virginia school, and, of course, an unyielding Whig.

Of all members of the General Assembly, however, the most curious in appearance was a newly elected Democratic member from Morgan County, Stephen A. Douglas, who, from the first, attracted more attention than any other person in Vandalia. Only slightly more than five feet tall, he seemed a dwarf among the stalwart men about him—"looked like a boy," his colleagues said. A mighty head covered with a great mass of thickly growing dark brown hair, powerful neck and shoulders and deep chest, made more conspicuous his short stature. His voice was a deep baritone —some said a vibrant bass. Strong, aggressive jaws and chin added to the impression of singular force, even bellicosity, given by his whole physical make-up; but the friendly, generous mouth softened the severity of his appearance.

If, aside from his small height, one feature was more striking than others, it was his eyes of deepest blue, which were uncommonly large, intelligent, bold, alert, and so brilliant that a newspaper correspondent describes them as "shooting out electric fires." He was, if possible, more ambitious than Lincoln, an incessant talker, fecund in plan, adroit in management. With the vision of the statesman he was already an adept in the tricks of the politician. As ingratiating as he was combative, he made friends quickly and on every hand, and these friends stuck to him through thick and thin.

Born in Vermont, April 23, 1813, he was twenty-three years of age. His father was a physician, and tradition says his grandfather had been one of Washington's soldiers at Valley Forge.

Educated in the common schools of his native state and at
Brandon Academy, he had also learned the trade of cabinet-mak-
ing. He studied law in New York and thence went to Illinois to
practice his profession. He arrived, practically destitute, at Winchester, Morgan County, where at first he taught school for a
living. He soon removed to Jacksonville, opened a law office, and
quickly growing in popularity, took active and vigorous part in
politics. A local quarrel resulted in his election as State's Attorney, which office he resigned when elected to the Legislature. Because of an effective speech at a Democratic meeting at Jacksonville in 1834 when all others in his party were disheartened and
despondent, he had been given the title of "The Little Giant"—
a title which his work in the Legislature was to confirm and establish permanently. Stephen A. Douglas was now to make his first
appearance as a law maker, and, on a larger stage than his
county, as a politician and a statesman.

Such in general was the Legislature, the lobby and the surroundings in the midst of which Lincoln found himself in his
third session of the General Assembly.

7

WILLIAM H. HERNDON examines the legislative session of
1836–37 and Lincoln's part in it. It is worth noting that as late as
the summer of 1860 Lincoln was to say in his autobiography, that
the statement on slavery, with which Herndon's account ends, still
defined his position on that vexing question.

THE LEGISLATURE of which Mr. Lincoln thus became a
member was one that will never be forgotten in Illinois. Its legislation in aid of the so-called internal improvement system was
significantly reckless and unwise. The gigantic and stupendous
operations of the scheme dazzled the eyes of nearly everybody, but
in the end it rolled up a debt so enormous as to impede the otherwise marvelous progress of Illinois. The burdens imposed by this
Legislature under the guise of improvements became so monu-
mental in size it is little wonder that at intervals for years afterward the monster of repudiation often showed its hideous face

above the waves of popular indignation. These attempts at a settlement of the debt brought about a condition of things which it is said led the Little Giant, in one of his efforts on the stump, to suggest that "Illinois ought to be honest if she never paid a cent." However much we may regret that Lincoln took part and aided in this reckless legislation, we must not forget that his party and all his constituents gave him their united endorsement. . . .

One of his biographers, describing his legislative career at this time, says of him: "He was big with prospects: his real public service was just now about to begin. In the previous Legislature he had been silent, observant, studious. He had improved the opportunity so well that of all men in this new body, of equal age in the service, he was the smartest parliamentarian and cunningest 'logroller.' He was fully determined to identify himself conspicuously with the liberal legislation in contemplation, and dreamed of a fame very different from that which he actually obtained as an anti-slavery leader. It was about this time he told his friend Speed that he aimed at the great distinction of being called the 'DeWitt Clinton of Illinois.' "

The representatives in the Legislature from Sangamon County had been instructed by a mass convention of their constituents to vote "for a general system of internal improvements." Another convention of delegates from all the counties in the State met at Vandalia and made a similar recommendation to the members of the Legislature, specifying that it should be "commensurate with the wants of the people." Provision was made for a gridiron of railroads. The extreme points of the State, east and west, north and south, were to be brought together by thirteen hundred miles of iron rails. Every river and stream of the least importance was to be widened, deepened, and made navigable. A canal to connect the Illinois River and Lake Michigan was to be dug, and thus the great system was to be made "commensurate with the wants of the people." To effect all these great ends, a loan of twelve million dollars was authorized before the session closed. Work on all these gigantic enterprises was to begin at the earliest practicable moment; cities were to spring up everywhere; capital from abroad was to come pouring in; attracted by the glowing reports of marvelous progress and great internal wealth, people were to come swarming in by colonies, until in the end Illinois was to outstrip all the others, and herself become the Empire State of the Union.

Lincoln served on the Committee on Finance, and zealously labored for the success of the great measures proposed, believing they would ultimately enrich the State and redound to the glory of all who aided in their passage. In advocating these extensive and far-reaching plans he was not alone. Stephen A. Douglas, John A. McClernand, James Shields, and others prominent in the subsequent history of the State, were equally as earnest in espousing the cause of improvement, and sharing with him the glory that attended it. Next in importance came the bill to remove the seat of government from Vandalia. Springfield, of course, wanted it. So also did Alton, Decatur, Peoria, Jacksonville, and Illiopolis. But the "Long Nine," by their adroitness and influence, were too much for their contestants. They made a bold fight for Springfield, entrusting the management of the bill to Lincoln. The friends of other cities fought Springfield bitterly, but under Lincoln's leadership the "Long Nine" contested with them every inch of the way. The struggle was warm and protracted. "Its enemies," relates one of Lincoln's colleagues (R. L. Wilson), "laid it on the table twice. In those darkest hours when our bill to all appearances was beyond resuscitation, and all our opponents were jubilant over our defeat, and when friends could see no hope, Mr. Lincoln never for one moment despaired; but collecting his colleagues to his room for consultation, his practical common sense, his thorough knowledge of human nature, then made him an overmatch for his compeers and for any man that I have ever known." The friends of the bill at last surmounted all obstacles, and only a day or two before the close of the session secured its passage by a joint vote of both houses.

Meanwhile the great agitation against human slavery, which like a rare plant had flourished amid the hills of New England in luxuriant growth, began to make its appearance in the West. Missionaries in the great cause of human liberty were settling everywhere. Taunts, jeers, ridicule, persecution, assassination even, were destined to prove ineffectual in the effort to suppress or exterminate these pioneers of Abolitionism. These brave but derided apostles carried with them the seed of a great reform. Perhaps, as was then said of them, they were somewhat in advance of their season, and perhaps too, some of the seed might be sown in sterile ground and never come to life, but they comforted themselves with the assurance that it would not all die. A little here and there was destined to grow to life and beauty.

It is not surprising, I think, that Lincoln should have viewed this New England importation with mingled suspicion and alarm. Abstractly, and from the standpoint of conscience, he abhorred slavery. But born in Kentucky, and surrounded as he was by slave-holding influences, absorbing their prejudices and following in their line of thought, it is not strange, I repeat, that he should fail to estimate properly the righteous indignation and unrestrained zeal of a Yankee Abolitionist. On the last day but one of the session, he solicited his colleagues to sign with him a mild and carefully worded protest against the following resolutions on the subject of domestic slavery, which had been passed by both houses of the Legislature in answer to the Southern protests:

"Resolved by the General Assembly of the State of Illinois:

"That we highly disapprove of the formation of Abolition societies and of the doctrines promulgated by them,

"That the right of property in slaves is sacred to the slave-holding States by the Federal Constitution, and that they cannot be deprived of that right without their consent,

"That the General Government cannot abolish slavery in the District of Columbia without the consent of the citizens of said District, without a manifest breach of good faith,

"That the Governor be requested to transmit to the States of Virginia, Alabama, Mississippi, New York, and Connecticut, a copy of the foregoing report and resolutions."

All the members declined, however, save one, Dan Stone, who with his associate will probably be known long after mention of all other members of the "Long Nine" has dropped from history. The language and sentiment are clearly Lincolnian, and over twenty years afterward, when it was charged that Lincoln was an Abolitionist, and this protest was cited as proof, it was only necessary to call for a careful reading of the paper for an unqualified and overwhelming refutation of the charge. The records of the Legislature for March 3, 1837, contain this entry:

"Resolutions upon the subject of domestic slavery having passed both branches of the General Assembly at its present session, the undersigned hereby protest against the passage of the same.

"They believe that the institution of slavery is founded on both injustice and bad policy, but that the promulgation of abolition doctrines tends rather to increase than abate its evils.

"They believe that the Congress of the United States has no power under the Constitution to interfere with the institution of slavery in the different States.

"They believe that the Congress of the United States has the power under the Constitution to abolish slavery in the District of Columbia, but that the power ought not to be exercised unless at the request of the people of the District.

"The difference between these opinions and those contained in the above resolutions is their reason for entering this protest.

                              "Dan Stone,
                              "A. Lincoln,
"Representatives from the County of Sangamon."

This document so adroitly drawn and worded, this protest pruned of any offensive allusions, and cautiously framed so as to suit the temper of the times, stripped of its verbal foliage reveals in naked grandeur the solemn truth that "the institution of slavery is founded on both injustice and bad policy." A quarter of a century later finds one of these protesters righting the injustice and correcting the bad policy of the inhuman and diabolical institution.

The return of the "Long Nine" to Springfield was the occasion of much enthusiasm and joy. The manifestations of public delight had never been equalled before, save when the steamer *Talisman* made its famous trip down the Sangamon in 1832. The returning legislators were welcomed with public dinners and the effervescent buncombe of local orators. Amid the congratulations of warm friends and the approval of their enthusiastic constituents, in which Lincoln received the lion's share of praise, they separated, each departing to his own home.

8

TEN YEARS AFTER the legislative session of 1836–37 Thomas Ford, who had just finished a term as governor of Illinois, wrote a history of the State in which he expressed his opinions with a degree of freedom and incisiveness rare among chroniclers. What he had to say of the Legislature in which Lincoln bore so conspicuous a part still has relevance.

THE MEANS USED in the Legislature to pass the system, deserve some notice for the instruction of posterity. First, a large portion of the people were interested in the success of the canal, which was threatened, if other sections of the State were denied the improvements demanded by them; and thus the friends of the canal were forced to logroll for that work by supporting others which were to be ruinous to the country. Roads and improvements were proposed everywhere to enlist every section of the State. Three or four efforts were made to pass a smaller system, and when defeated, the bill would be amended by the addition of other roads, until a majority was obtained for it. Those counties which could not be thus accommodated were to share in the fund of two hundred thousand dollars. Three roads were appointed to terminate at Alton, before the Alton interest would agree to the system. The seat of government was to be removed to Springfield. Sangamon county, in which Springfield is situated, was then represented by two senators and seven representatives, called "the Long Nine," all Whigs but one. Among them were some dexterous jugglers and managers in politics, whose whole object was to obtain the seat of government for Springfield. This delegation, from the beginning of the session, threw itself as a unit in support of, or opposition to, every local measure of interest, but never without a bargain for votes in return on the seat of government question. Most of the other counties were small, having but one representative, and many of them with but one for a whole district; and this gave Sangamon county a decided preponderance in the logrolling system of those days. It is worthy of examination whether any just and equal legislation can ever be sustained where some of the counties are great and powerful and others feeble. But by such means "the Long Nine" rolled along like a snowball, gathering accessions of strength at every turn, until they swelled up a considerable party for Springfield, which party they managed to take almost as an unit in favor of the internal improvement system, in return for which the active supporters of that system were to vote for Springfield to be the seat of government. Thus it was made to cost the State about six millions of dollars to remove the seat of government from Vandalia to Springfield, half which sum would have purchased all the real estate in that town at three prices; and thus by logrolling on the canal measure, by multiplying railroads, by terminating three railroads at Alton, that Alton might become a great city in opposition to St. Louis, by distributing money to some of the counties, to be wasted by the county commissioners, and by giving the seat of government to Springfield, was the whole State bought up and bribed, to approve the most senseless and disastrous policy which ever crippled the energies of a growing country.

CHAPTER FIVE

Attorney and Counsellor at Law

A BRAHAM LINCOLN *left New Salem in the spring of 1837 partly because the town was dying, but mainly because he was now ready to begin the practice of the law. For that, New Salem was barren territory. Springfield, on the other hand, promised every advantage. In addition to a partnership with one of the best known lawyers of the State there were the alluring opportunities that would come as soon as the town took on its new status as a capital—opportunities to practice in the Supreme Court of the State and in the federal courts, the certainty of frequent companionship with leading men from all parts of Illinois who would often visit the seat of government. And who should make more of those opportunities than the legislator who had done so much to create them?*

But the story of Lincoln the lawyer must begin long before the day when he rode into Springfield on a borrowed horse to hang out his shingle. We need not hold with those who go back to his Indiana boyhood to find the germ of his decision to study law, but we must revert at least to the year 1834, when John T. Stuart convinced him that his lack of formal education would not be a material handicap.

1

ALBERT A. WOLDMAN, a Cleveland attorney whose study of Lincoln the lawyer has supplanted all earlier investigations dealing exclusively with Lincoln's professional career, recounts his struggle with the law and his eventual admission to the bar.

Sᴛʀᴇᴛᴄʜᴇᴅ ᴜɴᴅᴇʀ an ancient shade tree which stood just outside the door of his store, his long bare feet resting high on the bark of the tree, Abe Lincoln read aloud from his law book. "Municipal law," he recited, "is a rule of civil conduct prescribed by the supreme power in a state, commanding what is right and prohibiting what is wrong."

The primary and principal objects of the law, he read in the *Commentaries*, are rights and wrongs. Rights are divided into rights of persons and rights of things. Rights of persons include the rights of personal security or the legal enjoyment of life, limbs, body, health, and reputation; personal liberty; and the right to acquire property. Wrongs are simply violations of rights, and are divided into private wrongs and public wrongs.

To the few straggling customers who came to his store, Abe Lincoln could explain by referring to the pages of his Blackstone how absolute rights of individuals can be preserved through the writ of habeas corpus. He could discuss the merits of different forms of government—democracy, aristocracy, and monarchy. He could answer: Can slavery subsist anywhere consistently with reason and the principles of natural law?

He became familiar with crimes and punishments and with domestic relations of husband and wife, parent and child, guardian and ward, and master and servant. He read of the history and purposes of the common law and the struggle for Anglo-Saxon liberty, the formulation of the Magna Charta, trial by jury, the Petition of Rights, the Bill of Rights, and the development of that system of jurisprudence which has ever been a bulwark of defense against oppression and injustice.

In the Indiana *Revised Statutes* he had read laws and documents which were confined exclusively to American institutions. Now he was drinking from the very well head of these institutions.

There was a popular saying that three books—the Bible, Shakespeare, and Blackstone, embodying the best in religion, philosophy, literature, and law—constituted a sufficient library. Now the unschooled pioneer youth was adding a comprehensive study of the commentaries of the famous English jurist to his knowledge of the Bible and the writings of the immortal Bard of Avon. With tireless industry and ever-widening horizon he explored the abun-

dant stores of legal learning which chance had brought to his
door. . . .

Law now became the greatest absorbing interest of Lincoln's
life, never again to go out of his mind. As he expressed it, he now
"went at it in good earnest." He served no office apprenticeship.
His legal education was to be even less formal than his academic
training. He became an articled clerk to himself, so to speak. He
walked or rode on horseback to Springfield to borrow Major
Stuart's books for study.

He borrowed the few law books owned by Squire Bowling
Green, at whose home he boarded for a while, and mastered them.
Although compelled to continue surveying to pay board and
clothing bills, he took advantage of every leisure moment to pursue his studies at home, in the fields, and on the road between New
Salem and Springfield. Persons who in later years recalled Lincoln's studious habits in New Salem often observed him reading
his law books while walking between New Salem and Springfield,
and "so intense was his application and so absorbed was he in his
study that he would often pass his best friends without observing
them." Some, noticing his sunken cheeks and bleary, red eyes, said
Lincoln was going crazy with hard study. Sometimes he read
forty pages or more on a trip between two towns. Often persons
saw him wandering at random across fields repeating aloud salient
points of what he read.

In season and out he added to his legal knowledge. From a form
book he learned to draw up deeds, mortgages, leases, contracts,
and bills of sale. Soon he felt that he could make some practical
application of this training and offered his services in drafting
such legal instruments for his friends and neighbors.

"In 1834," says Daniel Green Burner, "my father Isaac Green
Burner sold out to Henry Onstott and he wanted a deed written.
I knew how handy Lincoln was that way and suggested that we
get him. We found him sitting on a stump. 'All right,' said he,
when informed what we wanted. 'If you will bring me a pen and
ink and a piece of paper I will write it here.' I brought him these
articles and picking up a shingle and putting it on his knee for a
desk, he wrote out the deed."

He drafted a will for Joshua Short, of Sangamon County. The
instrument, which bears Lincoln's signature as an attesting wit-

ness, is an early characteristic specimen of his simple yet classic style of expression.

He continued the habit formed at Boonville, and frequently attended the trials at the justice of peace court of his friend Bowling Green. As there was no practicing attorney residing in New Salem, the friendly squire permitted him to act as sort of "next friend" to parties and plead the cases of his neighbors. His knowledge of the *Revised Laws of Illinois* sufficed to enable him to handle these cases capably and impressively. The Justice of the Peace seemed deeply impressed by the legal knowledge and reasoning of the embryonic practitioner. Weighing three hundred pounds and "given to mirth," Squire Green especially enjoyed Lincoln's droll stories and ludicrous tales. This unofficial practice proved a valuable experience to Lincoln, despite the fact that the Justice of the Peace often overrode both law and evidence to arrive at his common-sense decisions. Squire Green is reported to have decided a hog case known as Ferguson *vs.* Kelso by declaring that the plaintiff's witnesses were "damned liars," the court being well acquainted with the shoat in question and knowing it to belong to Jack Kelso.

One day Lincoln left his surveying to go to the justice of the peace court of Squire Berry at Concord and plead a bastardy case for a young unmarried mother. The man's character, Lincoln argued, was like a piece of white cloth, which though soiled could again be made clean by washing and hanging in the sun to dry. But the character of the girl, who was probably less to blame than the man, was like a broken and shattered bottle or glass vase, which could never be restored and made whole again.

Of course, Lincoln, without a license to practice law, received no fees for "pettyfogging," as he called it, before Squires Green and Berry, nor for his services in drafting legal instruments for his neighbors.

However, this practical experience in the justice of the peace courts proved very valuable training. It was the only apprenticeship to the law that Lincoln could afford. He continued to borrow books and continued to study. No one examined him. He simply read on until he completed the prescribed texts. The number of books he read, while not large, constituted the necessary volumes for preparation for the bar. He never regarded this method as ideal, and was often to refer to himself as a "mast-fed lawyer."

We get some idea of how Lincoln pursued his law studies from letters he wrote in later years to students who asked his advice regarding the best method of preparing for the bar. To one young man he wrote:

"If you are resolutely determined to make a lawyer of yourself, the thing is more than half done already. It is but a small matter whether you read with anybody or not. I did not read with anyone. Get the books and read and study them till you understand them in their principal features; and that is the main thing. It is of no consequence to be in a large town while you are reading. I read at New Salem, which never had three hundred people living in it. The books, and your capacity for understanding them, are just the same in all places. Always bear in mind that your own resolution to succeed is more important than any other one thing."

To another student's inquiry as to the "best method of obtaining a thorough knowledge of the law," Lincoln advised: "The mode is very simple, though laborious and tedious. It is only to get the books and read and study them carefully. Begin with Blackstone's *Commentaries* and after reading it through, say twice, take up Chitty's *Pleadings*, Greenleaf's *Evidence* and Story's *Equity*, etc., in succession. Work, work, work, is the main thing."

When Lincoln completed the standard texts which law students of the period usually read in order to qualify for the practice of law, he was not required to pass any examination. Not until March, 1841—about four years after Lincoln's admission to the bar—did the Supreme Court adopt the rule requiring all applicants for admission to the bar to appear for examination in open court.

In the absence of any record of formal examination, much confusion and controversy exists over the exact date of his admission to the bar. In the records of the Circuit Court of Sangamon County, dated March 24, 1836, is found this entry: "It is ordered by the court that it be certified that Abraham Lincoln is a person of good moral character." This was but a preliminary formality, complying with a statute enacted in 1833, under which the only requirement for the granting of a license to practice was a certificate procured from the court of some county certifying to the applicant's good moral character. On September 9, 1836, a license to practice law was issued to Lincoln by two of the justices of the Supreme Court, and a number of biographers designate this as the date of his formal admission to the bar. Manifestly this is incorrect, for the statute made necessary not only the securing of the license, but also the additional step of appearing before the clerk of the Supreme Court for enrolment. It was weeks later before Lincoln presented himself to the clerk and took the oath to support the Constitution of the United States and of Illinois. After this formality, the license, with the oath endorsed thereon, was duly presented to the clerk, and on March 1, 1837, the name of Abraham Lincoln was formally enrolled as an attorney or counsellor, licensed to practice law in all the courts of the State of Illinois.

Thus did the backwoodsman, farm laborer, clerk, flatboat hand, storekeeper, captain, postmaster, and deputy surveyor become "the Hon. A. Lincoln, Esquire, Attorney and Counsellor at Law."

2

WHEN THE *Sangamo Journal*, Springfield's Whig newspaper, came off the press on April 15, 1837, it carried a new notice in its column of professional cards: "J. T. Stuart and A. Lincoln, Attorneys and Counsellors at Law, will practice conjointly in the courts of this Judicial Circuit. Office No. 4 Hoffman's Row upstairs. Springfield, April 12, 1837." Angle describes Lincoln's first law partnership and also the beginnings of that distinctive feature of his practice—his circuit riding.

S TUART'S PREDOMINATING interest was politics. In 1836 he had been a candidate for election to the National House of Representatives, but had been defeated. Early in 1838 his candidacy was again announced. His opponent was Stephen A. Douglas. Between these two ensued a contest the like of which has rarely been seen. Though the Springfield District comprised thirty-four counties and covered nearly half the State, the contestants spoke in every corner, frequently traveling together and speaking from the same platform. Commencing amicably enough, the campaign became exceedingly bitter before its end. When the returns were finally in it was found that Stuart had defeated his opponent by the microscopic margin of thirty-six votes.

While Stuart was thus engaged, Lincoln was handling the business of the firm. The account book, in his handwriting, shows the sort of work in which he was engaged and the fees charged. Typical entries follow:

E. C. Ross
   To Stuart & Lincoln   Dr.
   1837—April—To attendance at trial of right of
             J. F. Davis' property before Moffett $5.00

Mather, Lamb & Co.
   To Stuart & Lincoln   Dr.
   1837—April—To attendance at trial of right of
             J. F. Davis' property before Moffett $5.00

Lucinda Mason
   To Stuart & Lincoln   Dr.
   1837—Oct—To obtaining assignment of Dower $5.00

Wiley & Wood
   To Stuart & Lincoln   Dr.
   1837–8 To defence of Chancery case of Ely $50.00
   Credit by coat to Stuart—   15.00
                                 $35.00

Peyton L. Harrison
   To Stuart & Lincoln   Dr.
   1838 March—To case with Dickinson— $10.00

Allen & Stone
   To Stuart & Lincoln   Dr.
   1838 Oct. To case with Centre $2.50

In 1839 Stuart left for Washington. Lincoln signalized his departure by writing across the top of a fresh page in the account book, "Commencement of Lincoln's administration, 1839. Nov. 2." The entries continued for a while, but the junior partner soon found such an orthodox method of bookkeeping too arduous. Milton Hay, at that time a student in the office, later described the system to which he resorted. Hay was present when Stuart returned to Springfield at the end of his first term in Congress. The two partners held a long conversation—Stuart describing events in Washington, Lincoln giving an account of local happenings. When the conversation ended Stuart got up to leave, but Lincoln asked him to sit down again. "Lincoln then went to a little cherry-colored desk and pulled out sundry packages. They contained money and represented Stuart's half of the firm's earnings during his absence in Washington. Each was labeled with the amount of money contained therein and the name of the client from whom it was obtained. This was duly turned over to Major Stuart."

It is easy to imagine, from this incident, the manner in which Lincoln conducted the firm's business. The following letter, written to Stuart soon after his departure for Washington, makes the picture increasingly vivid. "I write this," Lincoln opened, "about some little matters of business. You recollect you told me you had drawn the Chicago Musick money & sent it to the claimants. A damned hawk-billed Yankee is here, besetting me at every turn I take, saying that Robert Kinzie never received the $80 to which he was entitled. Can you tell any thing about the matter?—Again old Mr. Wright, who lives up South Fork somewhere, is teasing me continually about some *deeds* which he says he left with you, but which I can find nothing of. Can you tell me where they are?"

It was during the time of his partnership with Stuart that Lincoln commenced the circuit travels later to become so famous. Since Stuart had made his first round of the circuit courts, many changes had taken place. Illinois was growing, new counties were being organized, more courts and longer terms were becoming necessary. As a result new circuits were being added and the existing ones frequently reorganized. There were now nine circuits instead of the five in existence when Stuart began practice. Sangamon County was no longer a part of the First, having been transferred to the Eighth Circuit upon its formation in 1839.

From the time of its formation the Eighth Circuit was the scene of most of the circuit work of the Springfield bar. For many years it covered a vast territory. Originally comprising eight counties, it was made larger year by year until 1845, when the original eight counties had increased to seventeen, which, if shaded on a map, would have darkened more than a fifth of the area of the State.

Rarely did an Eighth Circuit court convene without a Springfield lawyer present. Traveling was a real hardship—so real that the words of old lawyers, describing early days, become fresh and vivid when the circuit is the subject. "Between Fancy Creek and Postville, near Lincoln," wrote James C. Conkling, "there were only two or three houses. Beyond Postville, for thirteen miles was a stretch of unbroken prairie, flat and wet, covered with gopher hills, and apparently incapable of being cultivated for generations. For fifteen or eighteen miles this side of Carlinville, the country was of a similar character, without a house or an improvement along the road. For about eighteen miles between South Fork and Shelbyville, there was only one clearing. I have travelled between Decatur and Shelbyville from nine o'clock in the morning until after dark over a country covered with water, from recent rains, without finding a house for shelter or refreshment. It may well be supposed that with such a sparse population the courts were not overburdened with business. At the first term in Christian County there were only two or three cases on the docket. The court met and adjourned on the same day." Incidentally, Conkling was the only lawyer in attendance—which probably accounts for the rare honor the clerk accorded him by writing his name in the record book along with those of the court officers.

Then, and throughout the period of circuit traveling, the courts were primitive institutions. According to our standards population was sparse, and a courthouse no larger than an ordinary dwelling was quite sufficient for the needs of almost any county. In the small court room the judge usually sat upon a raised platform at one end. To the side was a small table for the clerk, and occasionally, for the lawyers, a larger one—adorned with feet as frequently as papers. Of course there were no libraries. Litigation, however, was simple, and usually susceptible of determination on principle rather than through the citation of parallel cases.

Yet in spite of its hardships, there were many fascinations in circuit practice. With the people court days were gala days. Everyone who could attended court, whether or not business called him there, for other types of amusement were infrequent. The attorneys took on heroic roles in the eyes of the spectators, each prominent advocate having a group of enthusiastic supporters who gloried in his prowess. And among themselves the lawyers found much entertainment. No circuit traveler who has recorded his experiences has failed to mention the irresponsible gaiety, the hearty amusements and the firm friendships of those who rode from court to court together,

But Lincoln, during his first partnership, was undergoing an initiation in other courts than those of the circuit. The State offices were transferred from Vandalia to Springfield in 1839, and during that year the Supreme Court held its first session in the new capital. Since the State House was not yet completed the court sat for the time being in St. Paul's Episcopal Church. During the same year the United States Circuit and District Courts also removed from Vandalia to Springfield, likewise occupying a church until permanent quarters were found in one of the town's new business houses.

Lincoln, for the firm, at once commenced practice in these courts. On December 3, 1839, he was admitted to practice before the courts of the United States, while in the Supreme Court he tried seven cases before the termination of his partnership with Stuart.

Four years served to orient Lincoln in the law. During these years politics had occupied the major part of Stuart's time, permitting him to give no more than incidental attention to the problems of his office. It is possible that his first experiences in the Supreme and Federal Courts taught Lincoln how deficient was his own legal education, and how badly he needed the guidance that Stuart, whose mind was on his political career, was unable to give him. At any rate, there was forewarning of a change early in 1841, when Lincoln wrote his partner in Washington that other things being equal, he would "rather remain at home with Judge Logan." The change came upon Stuart's return to Springfield in April, when formal notice of the dissolution of the partnership appeared in the *Sangamo Journal*.

3

THROUGHOUT HIS PARTNERSHIP with Stuart, Lincoln divided his time between the law and the Legislature, where the in-

ternal improvement system was already a sore subject. Nicolay
and Hay set forth factors that were rapidly deflating the DeWitt
Clinton of Illinois.

L INCOLN WAS NOT yet done with Vandalia, its dinners of
game, and its political intrigue. The archives of the State were
not removed to Springfield until 1839, and Lincoln remained a
member of the Legislature by successive re-elections from 1834
to 1842. His campaigns were carried on almost entirely without
expense. Joshua Speed told the writers that on one occasion some
of the Whigs contributed a purse of two hundred dollars which
Speed handed to Lincoln to pay his personal expenses in the
canvass. After the election was over, the successful candidate
handed Speed $199.25, with the request that he return it to the
subscribers. "I did not need the money," he said. "I made the canvass on my own horse; my entertainment, being at the houses of
friends, cost me nothing; and my only outlay was seventy-five
cents for a barrel of cider, which some farm hands insisted I
should treat them to." He was called down to Vandalia in the
summer of 1837, by a special session of the Legislature. The
magnificent schemes of the foregoing winter required some repair-
ing. The banks throughout the United States had suspended
specie payments in the spring and, as the State banks in Illinois
were the fiscal agents of the railroads and canals, the Governor
called upon the lawmakers to revise their own work, to legalize the
suspension, and bring their improvement system within possible
bounds. They acted as might have been expected: complied with
the former suggestion, but flatly refused to touch their masterpiece. They had been glorifying their work too energetically to
destroy it in its infancy. It was said you could recognize a legislator that year in any crowd by his automatic repetition of the
phrase, "Thirteen hundred—fellow citizens!—and fifty miles of
railroad!" There was nothing to be done but to go on with the
stupendous folly. Loans were effected with surprising and fatal
facility, and, "before the end of the year, work had begun at many
points on the railroads. The whole State was excited to the highest
pitch of frenzy and expectation. Money was as plenty as dirt.
Industry, instead of being stimulated, actually languished. We
exported nothing," says Governor Ford, "and everything from

abroad was paid for by the borrowed money expended among us." Not only upon the railroads, but on the canal as well, the work was begun on a magnificent scale. Nine millions of dollars were thought to be a mere trifle in view of the colossal sum expected to be realized from the sale of canal lands, three hundred thousand acres of which had been given by the general Government. There were rumors of coming trouble, and of an unhealthy condition of the banks; but it was considered disloyal to look too curiously into such matters. One frank patriot, who had been sent as one of a committee to examine the bank at Shawneetown, when asked what he found there, replied with winning candor, "Plenty of good whisky and sugar to sweeten it."

But a year of baleful experience destroyed a great many illusions, and in the election of 1838 the subject of internal improvements was treated with much more reserve by candidates. The debt of the State, issued at a continually increasing discount, had already attained enormous proportions; the delirium of the last few years was ending, and sensible people began to be greatly disquieted. Nevertheless, Mr. Cyrus Edwards boldly made his canvass for Governor as a supporter of the system of internal improvements, and his opponent, Thomas Carlin, was careful not to commit himself strongly on the other side. Carlin was elected, and finding that a majority of the Legislature was still opposed to any steps backward, he made no demonstration against the system at the first session. Lincoln was a member of this body, and, being by that time the unquestioned leader of the Whig minority, was nominated for Speaker, and came within one vote of an election. The Legislature was still stiff-necked and perverse in regard to the system. It refused to modify it in the least, and voted, as if in bravado, another eight hundred thousand dollars to extend it.

But this was the last paroxysm of a fever that was burnt out. The market was glutted with Illinois bonds; one banker and one broker after another, to whose hands they had been recklessly confided in New York and London, failed, or made away with the proceeds of sales. The system had utterly failed; there was nothing to do but repeal it, stop work upon the visionary roads, and endeavor to invent some means of paying the enormous debt. This work taxed the energies of the Legislature in 1839, and for some years after. It was a dismal and disheartening task. Blue Monday had come after these years of intoxication, and a crushing debt rested upon a people who had been deceiving themselves with the fallacy that it would somehow pay itself by acts of the Legislature.

Many were the schemes devised for meeting these oppressive obligations without unduly taxing the voters; one of them, not especially wiser than the rest, was contributed by Mr. Lincoln. It provided for the issue of bonds for the payment of the interest due by the State, and for the appropriation of a special portion of State taxes to meet the obligations thus incurred. He supported his bill in a perfectly characteristic speech, making no effort to evade his share of the responsibility for the crisis, and submitting his views with diffidence to the approval of the Assembly. His plan was not adopted; it was too simple and straightforward, even if it had any other merits to meet the approval of an assembly intent only upon getting out of immediate embarrassment by means which might save them future trouble on the stump. There was even an undercurrent of sentiment in favor of repudiation. But the payment of the interest for that year was provided for by an ingenious expedient which shifted upon the Fund Commissioners the responsibility of deciding what portion of the debt was legal, and how much interest was therefore to be paid. Bonds were sold for this purpose at a heavy loss.

This session of the Legislature was enlivened by a singular contest between the Whigs and Democrats in relation to the State banks. Their suspension of specie payments had been legalized up to "the adjournment of the next session of the Legislature." They were not now able to resume, and it was held by the Democrats that if the special session adjourned *sine die* the charter of the banks would be forfeited, a purpose the party was eager to accomplish. The Whigs, who were defending the banks, wished to prevent the adjournment of the special session until the regular session would begin, during the course of which they expected to renew the lease of life now held under sufferance by the banks— in which, it may be here said, they were finally successful. But on one occasion, being in the minority, and having exhausted every other parliamentary means of opposition and delay, and seeing the vote they dreamed imminent, they tried to defeat it by leaving the house in a body, and, the doors being locked, a number of them, among whom Mr. Lincoln's tall figure was prominent, jumped from the windows of the church where the Legislature was then holding its sessions. "I think," says Mr. Joseph Gillespie, who was one of those who performed this feat of acrobatic politics, "Mr. Lincoln always regretted it, as he deprecated everything that savored of the revolutionary."

Two years later the persecuted banks, harried by the demagogues and swindled by the State, fell with a great ruin, and the financial misery of the State was complete. Nothing was left of the brilliant schemes of the historic Legislature of 1836 but a load of debt which crippled for many years the energies of the people, a few miles of embankments which the grass hastened to cover, and a few abutments which stood for years by the sides of leafy rivers, waiting for their long delaying bridges and trains.

4

POLITICS ALSO took its toll from the law. On December 2, 1839—nearly a year in advance of the Presidential election—the Whigs nominated William Henry Harrison as their candidate. The campaign, including Lincoln's participation in it, is reconstructed by Albert J. Beveridge.

THE SESSION over, Lincoln plunged into the Presidential compaign of 1840, the most picturesque, perhaps, in American history. Senator White had been dropped by the Whigs as their candidate, and, solely as a matter of the politician's cherished "availability," the one outstanding Whig leader and statesman, Henry Clay, had been rejected for a somewhat colorless, inoffensive person who, however, had the high political assets of poverty and a military record. Harrison and Tyler became the Whig candidates for President and Vice-President, against Van Buren and Johnson.

Although delighted by the defeat of Clay because he was a slave holder, the Abolitionists, as a whole, would not support the Whig ticket and a section of them organized the Liberty party pledged to immediate emancipation, and placed its standard in the hands of James G. Birney of New York and Thomas Earle of Pennsylvania.

The Whigs adopted no platform and Harrison said no word.

They agreed in nothing except hostility to Van Buren and all things Democratic. But fate and circumstances supplied better campaign materials than principles or policies could afford. A sneer at Harrison in a Democratic paper at Baltimore gave the Whigs their campaign battle cry. Harrison, said the contemptuous editor, would be content if somebody would give him enough money to live on in a log cabin with plenty of hard cider.

So the campaign became a volcanic eruption of volatile and unintelligent sentimentalism. Harrison was the poor man's friend, the farmer's champion, the log cabin and hard cider candidate; Van Buren, an aristocrat who ate his meals from gold plates and drank his champagne from crystal goblets. Meetings of incredible size were held, barbecues given, monster processions formed. No other political contest produced so many popular songs, most of them without sense.

June 4, 1840, a "monster" Whig demonstration took place in Springfield. Processions paraded the streets. Hardin marched holding high a banner with the device of a dead rooster lying on its back. On its way to Springfield, the Chicago delegation had captured a Democratic emblem and hilariously displayed it on a pole in the form of a petticoat. "While we write," chronicles the Springfield Democratic paper, "we are surrounded by log cabins on wheels, hard cider barrels, canoes, brigs, and every description of painted device, which, if a sober Turk were to drop among us would induce him to believe we were a community of lunatics or men run mad. . . . We never before saw such an exhibition of humbug."

Whig orators covered the State, attacking Van Buren's financial plans, but mostly appealing to passion and prejudice. The people cared for no arguments.

> "Without a why or a wherefore
> We'll go for Harrison therefore,"

rang the refrain of a Whig campaign song. Democratic newspapers and speakers were in despair. "We speak of the divorce of bank and state; the Whigs reply with a dissertation on the merits of hard cider. We defend the policy of the administration; the Whigs answer 'log cabin.' " We urge the "honesty, sagacity, statemanship" of Van Buren, and the unfitness of Harrison; "the Whigs answer that Harrison is a poor man."

In this popular emotionalism one Whig speaker, at least, kept his head and appealed to his audiences with fact and reason. The Illinois Whig convention, under the perfect control of Stuart and the "Whig Junto," nominated Lincoln as one of the Illinois Harrison and Tyler electors, and he spoke all over the State. Thus his acquaintance and friendships broadened. No reports of his campaign speeches exist, but it is practically certain that they were substantially the same as his argument in the debate already described, modified, of course, to suit the humor of his audiences. Often he and Douglas travelled and spoke together.

Behind the storm of popular fervor, there were genuine forces —the forces of hard times, desire for a change, anger over patronage. The Whigs denounced Democratic extravagance, Democratic "maladministration," Democratic "accumulation of executive power," the outcome of which would surely be "an Elective Monarchy." What the country needed, what the people demanded, was "Reform." Down with Van Buren with his "English carriage, English horses, and English driver."

Lincoln did other and far more effective work for the Whigs than to make stump speeches. Long before the campaign got under way and even while the Legislature was still in session, he wrote instructions to picked men throughout the State; and these orders, in the form of a confidential party circular signed by the Whig committee at Springfield, were sent to every county. "We have appointed you the Central Whig Committee of your county," began Lincoln. Watch and work; your reward will the be "glory" of having helped to beat the Democrats, those "corrupt powers that now control our beloved country." The Whig candidates deserve the support of "every true patriot who would have our country redeemed." The whole State must be so well organized, "that every Whig can be brought to the polls." This cannot be done without your help.

So divide your county into "small districts" and appoint in each a subcommittee; make a "perfect list of all the voters," and "ascertain with certainty for whom they will vote." Designate doubtful voters "in separate lines," indicating their probable choice. Each subcommittee must "keep a constant watch on the doubtful voters" and "have them talked to by those in whom they have the most confidence"—also Whig documents must be given them.

These subcommittees must report to the County Committee "at least once a month . . . and on election days see that every Whig is brought to the polls." Let the subcommittees be appointed "immediately" and let them make their first report not later than the last day of April. "On the first of each month hereafter we shall expect to hear from you;" and when "we" have heard from all the counties "we" will advise you of the outlook.

The Whig State Committee will get out a party paper for the campaign, says Lincoln, and encloses a prospectus. "It will be superintended by ourselves, and every Whig in the State must take it. . . . You must raise a fund and forward us for extra copies—every county ought to send fifty or one hundred dollars —and the copies will be forwarded to you for distribution among our political opponents. The paper will be devoted exclusively to the great cause in which we are engaged. . . ."

"You must inform us of results" of any election in your county "immediately." The next Legislature will elect a United States Senator, so "let no local interests divide you; but select candidates that can succeed. Our plan of operations will of course be concealed from every one except our good friends."

In such practical fashion Lincoln went about the work of organizing the Whig party throughout Illinois. To Stuart he hurried off a letter asking for a "Life of Harrison" and other campaign data—"everything you think will be a good 'war club.' " He adds that he believes the Whigs will carry Illinois; "the nomination of Harrison takes first-rate." Large numbers of "the grocery sort of Van Buren men [frequenters of saloons] . . . are out for Harrison." Lincoln tells Stuart of the joint debate: "I made a big speech which is in progress of printing in pamphlet form."

Lincoln frequently wrote his partner on the political situation. "I have never seen the prospects of our party so bright in these parts as they are now," says Lincoln, though his own political outlook is not "very flattering, for I think it probable I shall not be permitted to be a candidate. . . . Subscriptions to the *Old Soldier* pour in without abatement." Lincoln gives Stuart a list of Democrats who will vote for Harrison, so that Stuart can send them Whig campaign literature.

Again he reports to the Illinois Whig chieftain in Washington: After all, the Whig Convention did nominate him for the House again and Baker for the Senate, but only because the delegates thought Lincoln and Baker "necessary to make stump speeches." He tells other local political news and adds a postscript that a prominent Springfield Democrat "has come out for Harrison. Ain't that a caution?"

As election day approached the Democrats carefully guarded the voting. "Democrats, watch the polls," admonished the *State Register*. "The Federalists [Whigs] . . . are not to be trusted. By fraud alone they expect to succeed. Challenge every voter who is not known to be an inhabitant of the State for the last six months. See that no one votes twice or oftener. . . . 'eternal vigilance is the price of liberty.' "

In spite of seemingly insurmountable disadvantages, and in spite of the crushing Whig victory in the nation, the Democrats carried Illinois. This extraordinary State triumph was due to Douglas more than to any other man. With that political dexterity and resourcefulness in which he was unequalled, Douglas advanced two issues peculiar to Illinois and fresh in the minds of the people. These issues were the partisan decision of the Whig majority of the Supreme Court by which, in practical effect, the Whig Secretary of State was given a life tenure of office, and the Whig effort to disfranchise the so-called "alien vote" in the State—both questions, which, as we shall see, were to cause an unprecedented upheaval in the next Legislature. Illinois went for Van Buren by a heavy majority and the Legislature was overwhelmingly Democratic. But the Whigs won in Sangamon County and Lincoln was once more a member of the House.

5

LINCOLN'S LAST TERM as a member of the Illinois Legislature was anticlimactic. By this time he had lost his zest for lawmaking, and troubles of the heart further diverted his attention from the affairs of the State of Illinois. By the spring of 1841, however, he had recovered his normal equilibrium sufficiently to form a new partnership, this time with Stephen T. Logan. Albert A. Woldman gives that association its important place in Lincoln's life.

INDEPENDENT AND SELF-RELIANT to an extraordinary degree, Lincoln nevertheless felt keenly the deficiencies of his own legal education when pitted against the leaders of the Illinois bar. It was then that he needed the advice and guidance of an older and more experienced man. Judge Logan stood out as a truly great advocate—the greatest natural lawyer of his day, according to David Davis, later Justice of the Supreme Court of the United States. He stood at the very head of the Illinois bar. In his office many leading lawyers were developed, including four future United States Senators and three governors of States. Powerful was his influence as a preceptor, and great his faculty for recognizing latent ability. From the viewpoint of Lincoln's advancement in the law, the association with Judge Logan was indeed fortunate.

Judge Logan had found ample opportunity to recognize the qualifications of Lincoln. As judge of the circuit court, he had made the order admitting Lincoln to the bar; he had signed the journal entry which terminated Lincoln's first case, Hawthorne *vs.* Wooldridge; he had met the novice in a number of legal battles in the justice of the peace and circuit courts, and the Supreme Court, and had found the novice worthy of his steel. In fact, in all three cases in which Lincoln opposed Judge Logan in the Supreme Court, the younger man emerged the victor.

Stephen T. Logan was about ten years older than Lincoln. He had come to the Springfield bar from Kentucky in 1833, with no mean reputation as a lawyer. For ten years previously he had practiced his profession in his native State. And though he came to compete with such giants as Douglas, Stuart, Baker, Bledsoe, McDougall, Strong, Edwards, Lamborn, and many others then rising into eminence, all soon recognized his masterly ability and willingly accorded him the leadership.

From 1835 to 1837 he served as circuit judge, and resigned the office, then paying seven hundred and fifty dollars a year, to build up what became for some years to come probably the largest private law practice at the Illinois bar. He could be found on one side or another of nearly every leading case that went to the State Supreme Court.

He was a small, thin man, with a little, wrinkled, wizened face, set off by an immense head of hair which might be called frowsy, and Elihu B. Washburne also recalls that "he was dressed in linsey-woolsey and wore heavy shoes. His shirt was of unbleached cotton and unstarched and he never incumbered himself with a cravat. His voice was shrill, sharp, and unpleasant, and he had not a single grace of oratory; but when he spoke he always had interested and attentive listeners. Underneath this curious and grotesque exterior there was a gigantic intellect."

Stephen T. Logan was perhaps the most constructive influence in Lincoln's life. Stuart had been indifferent to Lincoln's carelessness, lack of method, and slipshodness. Placing politics above law, Stuart had been inclined to rely on his own native wit and ability, rather than on study and preparation, to win cases. He trusted to the spur of the moment; and the junior partner had adopted the same haphazard methods.

But Judge Logan was different. Unlike many lawyers of the day, he did not regard the law as merely a steppingstone to political preferment. In fact he lacked the elements of a successful politician and needed an orator like Lincoln to assist him. But to an eminent degree he possessed the true qualities of a great advocate. Well grounded in the law as a science, he was devoted equally to its philosophy and art, rereading Blackstone every year. He pursued the practice for its own sake, and deservedly had the reputation of being the best *nisi prius* lawyer in the State.

Methodical, industrious, particular, painstaking, and precise, Logan could not tolerate Lincoln's disorderly ways. He immediately exercised influences that were of great worth in inculcating a habit of closer application and deeper study of the principles underlying a lawsuit. He compelled the junior partner to study the authorities and prepare each case carefully in advance. Attention to details, thoroughness, and exactitude became more prominent in his practice. The younger man appreciated the soundness of judgment, accuracy of learning, and brilliancy of legal conceptions of his senior associate. He observed the intuitive vision with which Logan could see the strong point in his own case or the weak one of his opponent; how logically and tersely he stated his points to the court; and how with the same terse logic, the same hugging of the point of his case "but adding a mesmeric force often overwhelming," he argued his cause to the jury.

Association with so able a lawyer inevitably produced a speedy and beneficial effect upon Lincoln. It stimulated him to unusual endeavors, and soon he began to adopt the methods of Judge Logan. He studied his cases with greater care and diligence. He examined the law both of his side and that of his opponent. We have his own statement for the fact that he was never thereafter surprised by the strength of an opponent's case. By analyzing it he often found it weaker than he first feared. This ability to foresee and comprehend an adversary's contention was to stand him in good stead in the momentous days to come, memorably so in his now historic debates with Douglas, where he so mastered the arguments of his adversary that frequently he was able to turn the contentions of his great rival to his own advantage. He began to comprehend a case in all its fullness of circumstances. He became a formidable adversary not only in pleading to the jury but in the presentation of legal arguments as well. Judge Logan had expected little from his new partner other than that he would be a great help in pleading before juries, but he was pleasantly surprised to find Lincoln develop into an able all-round lawyer.

6

THE FIRM of Logan and Lincoln lasted from the spring of 1841 until the fall of 1844. Then, because Logan desired to take his son into partnership and because Lincoln felt himself strong enough to head his own firm, it was dissolved. The succeeding partnership—Lincoln's last—is portrayed by Woldman.

IMMEDIATELY AFTER the firm of Logan and Lincoln was dissolved, a shingle bearing the legend "Lincoln & Herndon" appeared in the dingy stairway of a building opposite the courthouse square in Springfield. It was to remain hanging for twenty-two years. . . .

Lincoln had known William Henry Herndon long and intimately. They had first met in 1832 when William's cousin, Rowan

Herndon, pilot of the *Talisman*, had chosen Abe Lincoln as his assistant to navigate the steamer through the Sangamon River from near Springfield to the Illinois River.

After this chance meeting on the banks of the Sangamon, Herndon often saw Lincoln in New Salem and in Springfield, where Herndon attended school and worked at odd times in Joshua Speed's store. Later he attended Illinois College at Jacksonville. When the Abolitionist editor, Elijah Lovejoy, was shot by a mob at Alton while defending his press, the students at the college were aroused to a fever heat.

Edward Beecher, brother of Harriet Beecher Stowe, author of *Uncle Tom's Cabin*, and of the Reverend Henry Ward Beecher, eminent clergyman, was president of the institution. He had been one of Lovejoy's stanchest supporters, and now the college, ablaze with righteous anger, became the center of Abolition sentiment. Indignant students and faculty joined in denouncing the outrage. William, in a fiery speech to his fellow students, accused the institution of slavery with the direct responsibility for the brutal crime, and bitterly denounced the attempts to gag the press by mob rule.

Archer G. Herndon, William's father, was strongly pro-slavery and when he heard of his son's speech he declared that he would have no share in the education of a "damned Abolitionist pup" and ordered him to leave college at once and return to Springfield. If he thought he was thus saving his son from further infection with the poison of Abolitionism, he was mistaken, "as it was too late," Herndon wrote. "My soul had absorbed too much of what my father believed was rank poison." From then on, the destruction of slavery became to him his most absorbing political objective.

He was nineteen years of age when he returned to Springfield. He induced Speed to re-employ him as a clerk in his store. He slept in a large room above the establishment, also used as sleeping quarters by Speed, Lincoln, and Charles R. Hurst. The future partners saw much of each other, and a degree of intimacy neighboring on brotherly affection developed between them. "There was something in his tall and angular frame, his ill-fitting garments, honest face and lively humor that imprinted his individuality on my affection and regard," Herndon said of his friend and idol. Both joined the debating and literary society which met in Speed's room or in a lawyer's office. They were also members of the Young Men's Lyceum, where Lincoln delivered his famous address on "The Perpetuation of Our Free Institutions."

After Lincoln became associated with Judge Logan, he invited Herndon to study law in their office; and even before the latter received a license to practice law, Lincoln one day, greatly agitated, informed him of his determination to leave Logan, and invited the young man to become his partner. This occurred in the autumn of 1844. Not until December 9 of that year was Herndon admitted to the bar.

What a strange thing for Lincoln to do—to leave the association of one of the ablest lawyers in the whole mid-West and then ally himself with an inexperienced novice! There were undoubtedly a dozen well-trained and successful attorneys in Springfield who would gladly have accepted the opportunity to form a partnership with him. But it was apparent that he desired just such an associate as Herndon—a young man whom he could train according to his own methods. He longed for independence from the restraint of a peer or superior. He wished to be his own master.

There are many indications that throughout his partnership with Logan the judge kept the reins of authority in his hands, and that Lincoln chafed under the restraint. With a junior, the condition would be reversed. Lincoln was politically ambitious. Logan, himself desirous of a seat in Congress, preferred that Lincoln devote more of his time to law. With young Herndon it would be different. What he lacked in experience as a lawyer would be more than compensated by his political sagacity.

He was then in his twenty-fifth year, nine years Lincoln's junior; a fine-appearing young man, five feet six inches tall, handsome, energetic, and an all-around good fellow. He had a knack of winning friends, and had already become uncommonly strong and influential in molding the political opinions of the young men of Springfield. He was a leader in the ranks of the young Whigs, and Lincoln felt his aggressiveness would be a great help to him in the political arena as well as in the law office and in the courts of justice.

"I confess I was surprised when he invited me to become his partner," Herndon later wrote. "I was young in the practice and was painfully aware of my want of ability and experience; but when he remarked in his earnest honest way, 'Billy, I can trust you, if you can trust me,' I felt relieved and accepted his generous proposal. It has always been a matter of pride with me during our long partnership, continuing on until it was dissolved by the bullet of the assassin Booth, we never had any personal controversy or disagreement."

Unlike in temperaments, habits, and natures, it is a mystery how two such conflicting personalities managed to get along for so many years in harmonious friendship. It was a curious alliance. Lincoln always called his junior "Billy," while the latter addressed him as "Mr. Lincoln." The senior associate was a conservative, while Herndon was a radical and militant enthusiast. Lincoln was a total abstainer, while Herndon all through his career was a victim of the drink habit. Lincoln hated slavery but believed that by confining it to the States where it already had a foothold it would gradually disappear in the natural course of events; Herndon, an agitator and abolitionist, was intent upon the immediate destruction of the institution. "Choke down slavery" was his constant cry.

And yet they possessed much in common. They respected each other as comrades, and Billy almost worshiped his friend as a hero. They helped each other by their fellowship and contact. Herndon's self-effacement in his senior's behalf was nobly self-sacrificing. He was his man Friday. If such a thing be possible, he was more ambitious politically for Lincoln than Lincoln himself. So despite the dissimilarities in their thoughts, habits, and temperaments, they were mutually helpful and formed a well-nigh perfect combination both from a business and a political standpoint.

CHAPTER SIX

Romance and Marriage

*I*N LINCOLN'S LIFE *there were three women—
Ann Rutledge, Mary Owens, and Mary Todd. The
blond, blue-eyed girl of New Salem died in her early twen-
ties, and thus made of her romance with Lincoln an immortal legend. Mary Owens—older, of sturdier character
and more independent mind—took warning from Lincoln's awkward and introspective love-making, and rejected him. Mary Todd—proud, imperious, ambitious—
walked to the altar with him, but whether she found truth
in the words inscribed on the ring he gave her, "Love is
Eternal," is an open question.*

*Of few people, even living people, can others know the
full story of inner intimacies. Almost thirty years were to
pass after the death of Ann Rutledge before it was revealed that she and Abraham Lincoln had loved each
other. By that time it was too late to disentangle fact from
fiction. Some who had lived at New Salem remembered
that Lincoln and Ann had been deeply in love and that her
death had driven him to the edge of derangement; others
could recall nothing of the kind. And no one since then has
been able to say with certainty what feeling existed between these two, and how deeply affected, how permanently scarred, the one was by the other's death.*

*With Lincoln and Mary Owens there is no uncertainty,
for Lincoln himself revealed the full extent of his affections. But with Mary Todd even what happened in the
course of an uneasy courtship, to say nothing of the emotions of those concerned, remains clouded. Did Lincoln fail*

to appear for his own wedding, as the traditional story has it, or did he merely break the engagement on the day to which he himself referred as "the fatal 1st of January, 1841"? What caused his indecision? Distrust of his own feelings? A premonition that there were qualities in Mary Todd that would make her hard to live with? The lingering image of Ann Rutledge? These questions, too, remain unanswered.

1

THE STORY of Ann Rutledge, eighteen-year-old daughter of one of New Salem's two founders, begins when Lincoln met her there in 1831. Soon afterward she became engaged to John McNeil, the village's richest resident. By 1834, when Lincoln went to Vandalia for the first time, McNeil had been absent in the East for many months. There Carl Sandburg takes up the narrative.

H E W A S N O W A W A Y from New Salem and Ann Rutledge. And the girl Ann Rutledge had been engaged to marry John McNeil, the storekeeper and farmer who had come to New Salem and in five years acquired property worth $12,000.00. In money and looks McNeil was considered a "good catch"; and he and Ann Rutledge were known as betrothed, when McNeil started on a trip East. In a short time, as soon as he could visit his father and relatives in New York, he would come back and claim his bride. This was the promise and understanding.

And it was known to Lincoln, who had helped McNeil on deeds to land holdings, that McNeil's real name was McNamar. This was the name put in the deeds. He said he had come West taking another name in order that he might make his fortune without interference from his family back East. He had, for convenience, kept his name off election poll books, and never voted.

McNamar had been away for months and sent few letters, writing from Ohio that he was delayed by an attack of fever, writing again from New York that his father had died and he could not come West till the estate was settled. Thus letters came, with excuses, from far off. Whisperers talked about it in New Salem. Had his love died down? Or was a truthful love to be expected from a man who would live under a false name?

Days were going hard for the little heart under the face framed in auburn hair over in New Salem, as Lincoln had his thoughts at his desk in the capitol at Vandalia. She had sung to him, clear-voiced, a hymn he liked with a line, "Vain man, thy fond pursuits forbear."

He introduced a bill limiting the jurisdiction of justices of the peace; he introduced a bill to authorize Samuel Musick to build a toll bridge across Salt Creek; he moved to change the rules so that it should not be in order to offer amendments to any bill after the third reading; he offered a resolution relating to a state revenue to be derived from the sale of public lands; he moved to take from the table a report submitted by his committee on public accounts. And he had his thoughts. The line had been sung for him clear-voiced, "Vain man, thy fond pursuits forbear."

Back to New Salem he came in the spring of 1835. And there was refuge for Ann Rutledge, with her hand in a long-fingered hand whose bones told of understanding and a quiet security. She had written McNamar that she expected release from her pledge to him. And no answer had come; letters had stopped coming. Her way was clear. In the fall she was to go to a young ladies' academy in Jacksonville; and Abraham Lincoln, poor in goods and deep in debts, was to get from under his poverty; and they were to marry. They would believe in the days to come; for the present time they had understanding and security.

The cry and the answer of one yellowhammer to another, the wing flash of one bluejay on a home flight to another, the drowsy dreaming of grass and grain coming up with its early green over the moist rolling prairie, these were to be felt that spring together, with the whisper, "Always together."

He was twenty-six, she was twenty-two; the earth was their footstool; the sky was a sheaf of blue dreams; the rise of the blood-gold rim of a full moon in the evening was almost too much to live, see, and remember. . . .

August of that summer came. Corn and grass, fed by rich rains in May and June, stood up stunted of growth, for want of more rain. The red berries on the honeysuckles refused to be glad. The swallows and martins came fewer.

To the homes of the settlers came chills and fever of malaria. Lincoln had been down, and up, and down again with aching bones, taking large spoons of Peruvian bark, boneset tea, jalap, and calomel. One and another of his friends had died; for some, he had helped nail together the burial boxes.

Ann Rutledge lay fever-burned. Days passed; help arrived and was helpless. Moans came from her for the one man of her thoughts. They sent for him. He rode out from New Salem to the Sand Ridge farm. They let him in; they left the two together and alone a last hour in the log house, with slants of light on her face from an open clapboard door. It was two days later that death came.

There was what they called a funeral, a decent burial of the body in the Concord burying ground seven miles away. And Lincoln sat for hours with no words for those who asked him to speak to them. They went away from him knowing he would be alone whether they stayed or went away.

A week after the burial of Ann Rutledge, Bill Green found him rambling in the woods along the Sangamon River, mumbling sentences Bill couldn't make out. They watched him and tried to keep him safe among friends at New Salem. And he rambled darkly and idly past their circle to the burying ground seven miles away, where he lay with an arm across the one grave.

"Vain man, thy fond pursuits forbear." As the autumn weeks passed, and the scarlet runners sent out signals across the honey locust and the sycamore tree where they had sat together on the Salem hilltop, and the sunsets flamed earlier in the shortening afternoons, the watchers saw a man struggling on a brink; he needed help. Dr. Allen said rest would help. They took him to the home of Bowling and Nancy Green, at the foot of a bluff climbed by oak-timber growths. A few days he helped in the field at corn-husking; most of the time Nancy had him cutting wood, picking apples, digging potatoes, doing light chores around the house, once holding the yarn for her as she spun.

In the evenings, it was useless to try to talk with him. They asked their questions and then had to go away. He sat by the fire one night as the flames licked up the cordwood and swept up the chimney to pass out into a driving stormwind. The blowing weather worked some sort of lights in him and he went to the door and looked out into a night of fierce tumbling wind and black horizons. And he came back saying, "I can't bear to think of her

In the backwoods schools of Indiana pupils had no money for textbooks. Like the others, Lincoln made his own arithmetic. This is one of the pages of that unique volume.

HERBERT GEORG STUDIO, SPRINGFIELD, ILL.

In a building identical with the one in the right foreground Lincoln and Berry kept their general store at New Salem. The picture shows a part of the reconstructed village, now an Illinois State Park.

By this document Abraham Lincoln, Captain of Illinois volunteers, granted an honorable discharge to a soldier of his company.

ORIGINAL IN ILLINOIS STATE HISTORICAL LIBRARY

I CERTIFY, That *Lewis W Farmer* Volunteered and served
as a Private in the Company of Mounted Volunteers under my
command, in the Regiment commanded by Col. SAMUEL M. THOMPSON, in the Brigade under the command of Generals S. WHITESIDE and H. ATKINSON, called into the service of the United States by the Commander-in-Chief of the Militia of the State, for the protection of the North Western Frontier against an Invasion of the British Band of Sac and other tribes of Indians,—that he was enrolled on the *21st* day of *April* 1832, and was HONORABLY DISCHARGED on the *7th* day of *June* thereafter, having served *48 days.*

Given under my hand, this *21st* day of *September* 1832
A Lincoln Capt

On November 4, 1842, Abraham Lincoln and Mary Todd were married at the home of Ninian W. Edwards in Springfield. Here is the license issued by Noah W. Matheny, Clerk of Sangamon County, and the certification of the officiating minister, the Rev. Charles Dresser of the Episcopal Church. One week later Lincoln was to write to one of his good friends: "Nothing new here except my marrying, which to me, is matter of profound wonder."

Washington and the Capitol as they looked in 1848, when Lincoln was a Member of Congress.

In Mrs. Spriggs's boarding house in this row of buildings, located where the Library of Congress now stands, Lincoln lived during his term in Congress.

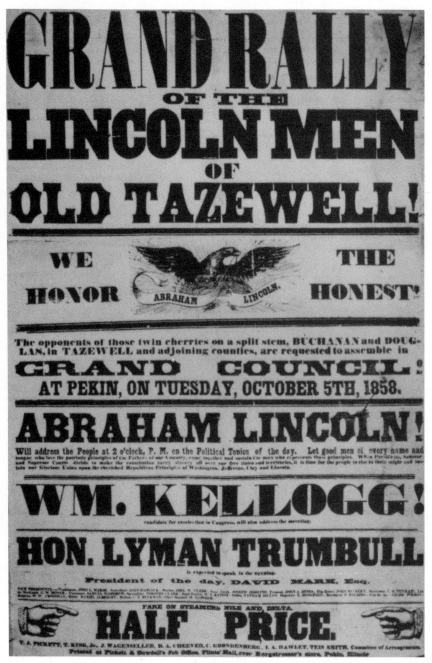

A handbill featuring Abraham Lincoln as a speaker at a political meeting held during the course of the Lincoln-Douglas Debates. As far as is known, this is the only handbill of that campaign which has been preserved.

Stephen A. Douglas, the "Little Giant" who defeated Lincoln for election to the United States Senate in 1858.

The Illinois State House, where Lincoln received visitors after his nomination for the Presidency in 1860. In the left background are the Sangamon County Courthouse, in which Lincoln had tried many law suits, and the Springfield Marine and Fire Insurance Company, where he had his modest bank account.

The Wigwam, built by the people of Chicago for the Republican National Convention of 1860. In this building Lincoln was nominated for the Presidency.

The Lincoln home, at Eighth and Jackson streets, Springfield, as a photographer recorded it in 1860. Lincoln and one of his sons stand inside the fence.

The Lincoln home as a lithographer depicted it in a print widely circulated during the campaign of 1860.

The Republican candidate as he was pictured for the people of the United States during the campaign of 1860. This lithograph, by the famous printmakers Currier & Ives, was widely circulated.

The "Rail Splitter" on canvas. The painting, by an unknown artist, was made for use during the 1860 campaign. A few months later a company of Indiana volunteers carried it as a banner in the battle of Belmont, their first engagement of the Civil War. There a Confederate rifleman put a bullet hole, still plainly visible, through Lincoln's forehead, whereupon the portrait was sent back home.

The biggest rally of the 1860 campaign was held at Springfield on August 8, 1860. This picture shows the procession passing in front of the Lincoln home. Lincoln, wearing a white suit and black bow tie, stands at the right side of the doorway.

Lincoln's cabinet after Stanton replaced Cameron, as pictured in a contemporary lithograph. Left to right: the President, Gideon Welles, Salmon P. Chase, Montgomery Blair, William H. Seward, Caleb B. Smith, Edward Bates, and Edwin M. Stanton.

Pennsylvania Avenue, Washington, as it appeared in 1861, when Lincoln rode along it from the White House to the Capitol for his first inauguration.

The White House as it appeared during Lincoln's occupancy.

The Soldiers' Home on the outskirts of Washington. Here Lincoln and his family spent the summer months during his administration.

Mrs. Abraham Lincoln as she was photographed shortly after her husband's inauguration.

Mrs. Lincoln with Willie and Tad.

HERBERT GEORG STUDIO, SPRING-
FIELD, ILL.

Robert Lincoln, the oldest son. During the campaign of 1860 press correspondents often referred to him as the "Prince of Rails."

HERBERT GEORG STUDIO, SPRING-
FIELD, ILL.

RECRUITS WANTED!

"Time is Everything."

Having been authorized by

GOV.YATES

To raise a Company of men, for three years or during the war, I have opened an Office in the building lately occupied by Mr. R. Bills,

On Hamilton St., adjoining 'Peoria House,'

for the purpose of recruiting said company.

Forty Dollars Cash

paid on being mustered into the U. S. Service.

Dont wait until DRAFTING commences

but come up like MEN, and show your PATRIOTISM by enlisting and helping with all your power to restore again to its once proud position, that

GLORIOUS OLD FLAG!

The STARS AND STRIPES.

PEORIA, July 19th, 1862.　　　　　**M. V. HOTCHKISS.**

B. Foster, Printer and Bookbinder, Peoria.

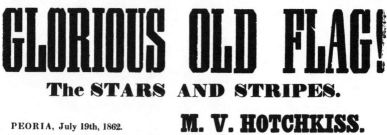

A Civil War recruiting poster calling for volunteers from Lincoln's own State.

out there alone." And he clenched his hands, mumbling, "The rain
and the storm shan't beat on her grave."

Slowly, as the weeks passed, an old-time order of control came
back to him—only it was said that the shadows of a burning he
had been through were fixed in the depths of his eyes, and he was
a changed man keeping to himself the gray mystery of the change.

2

IN THE SUMMER of 1836, a year after the death of Ann Rutledge, Lincoln was drawn to another woman, Mary Owens, of Greene
County, Kentucky. While Mary Owens was visiting her sister, Mrs.
Bennett Able, in New Salem, Lincoln showed an interest which soon
reached the stage of courtship. Before many months, however, he
was beset by the doubts that he revealed in the two letters which
follow.

Springfield, May 7, 1837.
Friend Mary: I have commenced two letters to send you before
this, both of which displeased me before I got half done, and so
I tore them up. The first I thought was not serious enough, and
the second was on the other extreme. I shall send this, turn out as
it may.

This thing of living in Springfield is rather a dull business,
after all; at least it is so to me. I am quite as lonesome here as I
ever was anywhere in my life. I have been spoken to by but one
woman since I have been here, and should not have been by her
if she could have avoided it. I've never been to church yet, and
probably shall not be soon. I stay away because I am conscious
I should not know how to behave myself.

I am often thinking about what we said about your coming to
live at Springfield. I am afraid you would not be satisfied. There
is a great deal of flourishing about in carriages here, which it
would be your doom to see without sharing it. You would have to
be poor, without the means of hiding your poverty. Do you believe you could bear that patiently? Whatever woman may cast
her lot with mine, should any ever do so, it is my intention to do
all in my power to make her happy and contented; and there is
nothing I can imagine that would make me more unhappy than

to fail in the effort. I know I should be much happier with you than the way I am, provided I saw no signs of discontent in you. What you have said to me may have been in the way of jest, or I may have misunderstood it. If so, then let it be forgotten; if otherwise, I much wish you would think seriously before you decide. What I have said I will most positively abide by, provided you wish it. My opinion is that you had better not do it. You have not been accustomed to hardship, and it may be more severe than you now imagine. I know you are capable of thinking correctly on any subject, and if you deliberate maturely upon this before you decide, then I am willing to abide your decision.

You must write me a good long letter after you get this. You have nothing else to do, and though it might not seem interesting to you after you had written it, it would be a good deal of company to me in this "busy wilderness." Tell your sister I don't want to hear any more about selling out and moving. That gives me the "hypo" whenever I think of it. Yours, etc.,

LINCOLN.

Springfield, August 16, 1837.

Friend Mary: You will no doubt think it rather strange that I should write you a letter on the same day on which we parted, and I can only account for it by supposing that seeing you lately makes me think of you more than usual; while at our late meeting we had but few expressions of thoughts. You must know that I cannot see you or think of you with entire indifference; and yet it may be that you are mistaken in regard to what my real feelings toward you are. If I knew you were not, I should not trouble you with this letter. Perhaps any other man would know enough without further information; but I consider it my peculiar right to plead ignorance, and your bounden duty to allow the plea. I want in all cases to do right, and most particularly so in all cases with women. I want at this particular time, more than anything else, to do right with you; and if I knew it would be doing right, as I rather suspect it would, to let you alone, I would do it. And for the purpose of making the matter as plain as possible, I now say that you can now drop the subject, dismiss your thoughts (if you ever had any) from me forever, and leave this letter unanswered, without calling forth one accusing murmur from me. And I will even go further, and say that if it will add anything to your comfort or peace of mind to do so, it is my sincere wish that you should. Do not understand by this that I wish to cut your acquaintance. I mean no such thing. What I do wish is that our further acquaintance shall depend upon yourself. If such further acquaintance would contribute nothing to your happiness, I am sure it would not to mine. If you feel yourself in any degree bound to me, I am now willing to release you, provided you wish it; while, on the other hand, I am willing and even anxious to bind you faster, if I can be convinced that it will, in any considerable degree, add to your happiness. This, indeed, is the whole question with me. Nothing would make me more miserable than to believe you miserable—nothing more happy than to know you were so.

In what I have now said, I think I cannot be misunderstood, and to make myself understood is the only object of this letter.

If it suits you best to not answer this, farewell. A long life and a merry one attend you. But if you conclude to write back, speak as plainly as I do. There can be neither harm nor danger in saying to me anything you think, just in the manner you think it.

My respects to your sister. Your friend,

LINCOLN.

3

THE SEQUEL? That was revealed a year later, when Lincoln whiled away an idle evening by writing the whole story of the romance to the wife of one of his friends—indiscreetly, but to the great benefit of history.

Springfield, April 1, 1838.

Dear Madam: Without apologizing for being egotistical, I shall make the history of so much of my life as has elapsed since I saw you the subject of this letter. And, by the way, I now discover that in order to give a full and intelligible account of the things I have done and suffered since I saw you, I shall necessarily have to relate some that happened before.

It was, then, in the autumn of 1836 that a married lady of my acquaintance, and who was a great friend of mine, being about to pay a visit to her father and other relatives residing in Kentucky, proposed to me that on her return she would bring a sister of hers with her on condition that I would engage to become her brother-in-law with all convenient despatch. I, of course, accepted the proposal, for you know I could not have done otherwise had I really been averse to it; but privately, between you and me, I was most confoundedly well pleased with the project. I had seen the said sister some three years before, thought her intelligent and agreeable, and saw no good objection to plodding life through hand in hand with her. Time passed on, the lady took her journey and in due time returned, sister in company, sure enough. This astonished me a little, for it appeared to me that her coming so readily showed that she was a trifle too willing, but on reflection it occurred to me that she might have been prevailed on by her married sister to come, without anything concerning me ever having been mentioned to her, and so I concluded that if no other objection presented itself, I would consent to waive this. All this occurred to me on hearing of her arrival in the neighborhood — for, be it remembered, I had not yet seen her, except about three years previous, as above mentioned. In a few days we had an interview, and, although I had seen her before, she did not look as my imagination had pictured her. I knew she was over-size, but she now appeared a fair match for Falstaff. I knew she was called an "old maid," and I felt no doubt of the truth of at least half of the appellation, but now, when I beheld her, I could not for my life avoid thinking of my mother; and this, not from withered features — for her skin was too full of fat to permit of its contracting into wrinkles — but from her want of teeth, weatherbeaten appearance in general, and from a kind of notion that ran in my head that nothing could have commenced at the size of infancy and reached her present bulk in less than thirty-five or forty years; and, in short, I was not at all pleased with her. But what could I do? I had told her sister that I would take her for better or for worse, and I made a point of honor and conscience in all things to stick to my word, especially if others had been induced to act on it, which in this case I had no doubt they had, for I was now fairly convinced that no other man on earth would have her, and hence the conclusion that they were bent on holding me to my bargain. "Well," thought I, "I have said it, and, be the consequences what they may, it shall not be my fault if I fail to do it." At once I determined to consider her my wife, and this done, all my powers of discovery were put to work in search of perfections in her which might be fairly set off against her defects. I tried to imagine her handsome, which, but for her unfortunate corpulency, was actually true. Exclusive of this, no woman that I have ever seen has a finer face. I also tried to convince myself that the mind was much more to be valued than the person, and in this she was not inferior, as I could discover, to any with whom I had been acquainted.

Shortly after this, without attempting to come to any positive understanding with her, I set out for Vandalia, when and where you first saw me. During my stay there I had letters from her which did not change my opinion of either her intellect or intention, but, on the contrary, confirmed it in both.

All this while, although I was fixed "firm as the surge-repelling rock" in my resolution, I found I was continually repenting the rashness which had led me to make it. Through life I have been in no bondage, either real or imaginary, from the thraldom of which I so much desired to be free. After my return home I saw nothing to change my opinion of her in any particular. She was the same, and so was I. I now spent my time in planning how I might get along in life after my contemplated change of circumstances should have taken place, and how I might procrastinate the evil day for a time, which I really dreaded as much, perhaps more, than an Irishman does the halter.

After all my sufferings upon this deeply interesting subject, here I am, wholly, unexpectedly, completely out of the "scrape," and I now want to know if you can guess how I got out of it — out, clear, in every sense of the term — no violation of word, honor, or conscience. I don't believe you can guess, and so I might as well tell you at once. As the lawyer says, it was done in the manner following, to wit: After I had delayed the matter as long as I thought I could in honor do (which, by the way, had brought me round into the last fall), I concluded I might as well bring it to a consummation without further delay, and so I mustered my resolution and made the proposal to her direct; but, shocking to relate, she answered, No. At first I supposed she did it through an affectation of modesty, which I thought but ill became her under the peculiar circumstances of her case, but on my renewal of the charge I found she repelled it with greater firmness than before. I tried it again and again, but with the same success, or rather with the same want of success.

I finally was forced to give it up, at which I very unexpectedly found myself mortified almost beyond endurance. I was mortified, it seemed to me, in a hundred different ways. My vanity was deeply wounded by the reflection that I had so long been too stupid to discover her intentions, and at the same time never doubting that I understood them perfectly; and also that she, whom I had taught myself to believe nobody else would have, had actually rejected me with all my fancied greatness. And, to cap the whole, I then for the first time began to suspect that I was really a little in love with her. But let it all go! I'll try and outlive it. Others have been made fools of by the girls, but this can never with truth be said of me. I most emphatically, in this instance, made a fool of myself. I have now come to the conclusion never again to think of marrying, and for this reason—I can never be satisfied with any one who would be blockhead enough to have me.

When you receive this, write me a long yarn about something to amuse me. Give my respects to Mr. Browning.

Your sincere friend,

A. LINCOLN.

Mrs. O. H. Browning.

4

SOME YEARS AGO a bundle of old letters bearing on the courtship of Lincoln and Mary Todd came to light. In the hands of Sandburg and Angle, the letters led to a new interpretation of the tangled story of Lincoln's marriage. The following narrative is Sandburg's.

WHEN MARY TODD, twenty-one years old, came in 1839 to live with her sister, Mrs. Ninian W. Edwards [Elizabeth Todd], she was counted an addition to the social flourish of the town. They spoke in those days of "belles." And Mary was one. Her sister told how she looked. "Mary had clear blue eyes, long lashes, light brown hair with a glint of bronze, and a lovely complexion. Her figure was beautiful and no Old Master ever modeled a more perfect arm and hand." Whatever of excess there may be in this sisterly sketch it seems certain that Mary Todd had gifts, attractions, and was among those always invited to the dances and parties of the dominant social circle. Her sister's husband once remarked as to her style, audacity or wit, "Mary could make a bishop forget his prayers."

A niece of Mary Todd wrote her impression of how her aunt looked at twenty-two in the year 1840, when her eyes first lighted on Abraham Lincoln. As an impression it has its value, serving as the viewpoint and testimony of some of those who found adorable phases in Mary Todd. In this presentation she is a rare and cherished personage with "faint wild rose in her cheeks," tintings that came and went in the flow of her emotions. "Mary although not strictly beautiful, was more than pretty. She had a broad white forehead, eyebrows sharply but delicately marked, a straight nose, short upper lip and expressive mouth curling into an adorable slow coming smile that brought dimples into her cheeks and glinted in her long-lashed, blue eyes. Those eyes, shaded by their long, silky fringe, gave an impression of dewy violet shyness contradicted fascinatingly by the spirited carriage of her head. She was vital, brilliant, witty and well trained in all the social graces from earliest childhood. She could now without rebuke, wear the coveted hoop skirts of her childish desire, and with skirts frosted with lace and ruffles she ballooned and curtsied in the lovely French embroidered swisses and muslins brought up to her from New Orleans by her father. In stockings and slippers to match the color of her gown, all pink and white, she danced and swayed as lightly and gayly as a branch of fragrant apple blossoms in a gentle spring breeze. From her pink dimpled cheeks to her sophisticated pink satin slippers, she was a fascinating alluring creature." Such, in one viewpoint, was the woman Lincoln gathered in his arms some time in 1840 when they spoke pledges to marry and take each other for weal or woe through life.

For two years Mary Todd haunted Lincoln, racked him, drove him to despair and philosophy, sent him searching deep into himself as to what manner of man he was. In those two years he first became acquainted with a malady of melancholy designated as hypochondriasis, or "hypo," an affliction which so depressed him that he consulted physicians. What happened in those two years?

Some time in 1840, probably toward the end of the year, Lincoln promised to marry Miss Todd and she was pledged to take him. It was a betrothal. They were engaged to stand up and take vows at a wedding. She was to be a bride; he was to be a groom. It was explicit.

Whether a wedding date was fixed, either definitely or approximately, does not appear in Mary Todd's letter to Mercy Levering in December of 1840. Whether in that month they were engaged at all or not also fails to appear. In this letter, however, we learn of Mary Todd, her moods and ways, at that time. She writes from Springfield, giving the news to her friend, mentioning Harriet Campbell who "appears to be enjoying all the sweets.of married life." She refers to another acquaintance as ready to perpetrate "the crime of matrimony." This is light humor, banter, for the surmise is offered, "I think she will be much happier."

Certain newly married couples, she observes, have lost their "silver tones."

She raises the question, "Why is it that married folks always become so serious?"

She is puzzled, perplexed, about marriage; it is one of life's gambles; there seem to be winners and losers. Her moods shift. Her head is full of many events and people that may affect her fate. She sees time plowing on working changes. She reports what the marching months have done to a prairie stream. "The icy hand of winter has set its seal upon the waters, the winds of Heaven visit the spot but roughly, the same stars shine down, yet not with the same liquid, mellow light as in the olden time, some forms and memories that enhanced the place have passed by."

Reading along in this December letter of Mary Todd one may gather an impressionistic portrait of her, a little mezzotint. She can speak with grace. "Pass my imperfections lightly as usual," she writes Mercy. "I throw myself on your amiable nature, knowing that my shortcomings will be forgiven." She is aware of her tendency to be chubby. "I still am the same ruddy *pineknot*, only not quite so great an exuberance of flesh, as it once was my lot to contend with, although quite a sufficiency."

Mary Todd made a little forecast in this letter. "We expect a very gay winter," she wrote. "Evening before last my sister gave a most agreeable party; upwards of one hundred graced the festive scene." Matilda Edwards, a cousin of Ninian Edwards, had come on from Alton. The party was for her. "A lovelier girl I never saw," writes Mary Todd.

It wasn't so gay a winter, however, either for one or the other of the engaged couple. Lincoln was uneasy, worried. Months of campaigning, traveling in bad weather, eating poorly cooked food and sleeping in rough taverns had made his nerves jumpy. He saw reasons why marriage would not be good for him or for Mary Todd. He wrote a letter to her, begging off. Then he showed the letter to Speed, whose reputation was lively for falling in love and falling out again. Speed threw the letter into the fire, saying in effect that such feelings of the heart shouldn't be put onto paper and made a record that could be brought up later. It was New Year's Day, 1841. Lincoln went to the Edwards house and came back to Speed. He explained that he had told Mary all that was in the letter. And Mary broke into tears, Lincoln took her into his arms, kissed her, and the engagement was on again.

But Lincoln was wretched. He had yielded to tears, had sacrificed a reasoned resolve because he couldn't resist the appeal of a woman's grief. Mary Todd saw his condition, saw that he was not himself, saw further that anything between them was impossible until he should recover. And so, regretfully but without bitterness, she released him from the engagement.

Over Springfield in the circles of these two principal persons the word spread that Mary Todd had jilted Lincoln. After leading him on, encouraging him, she suddenly had decided it was not for the best. So there would be no wedding. And both were content to let the bald fact stand without explanation.

Then Lincoln broke down completely. Two weeks after the night he had tried to tell Mary Todd how he felt and had failed, he took to his bed, miserably sick. Only Speed and Doctor Henry saw him. Six days later he was up and around, due, it was said, to the strong brandy which the doctor had prescribed in large quantities. But he was not the old-time Lincoln. How he looked to others was told by James C. Conkling in a letter to his fiancée, Mercy Levering, Mary Todd's close friend. "Poor Lincoln! How are the mighty fallen!" wrote Conkling. "He was confined about a week but though he now appears again he is reduced and emaciated in appearance and seems scarcely to possess strength enough to speak above a whisper. His case is at present truly deplorable but what prospect there may be for ultimate relief I cannot pretend to say." No keen or quick sympathy for Lincoln stands forth from Conkling's letter. He writes as though he and others of a limited circle were watching a man recovering from punishment received in the tangles of an ancient trap, suffering of a sort all men and women must know in the pilgrimage of life. As one of Bobby Burns' poems declares none has the right to expect sympathy for toothache, thus also there is a sort of unwritten law that those smitten with love, and rejected by the ones loved, must expect kindly laughter rather than tears from their friends. Howsoever that may be we have Conkling's letter saying of Lincoln, "I doubt not but he can declare 'That loving is a painful thrill. And not to love more painful still,' but would not like to intimate that he has experienced 'That surely 'tis the worst of pain To love and not be loved again.' "

Lincoln wrote two letters to his law partner, Congressman John T. Stuart at Washington, D. C. In one letter he notes, "I have within the last few days, been making a most discreditable exhibition of myself in the way of hypochondriasm." In the second letter: "I am now the most miserable man living. If what I feel were equally distributed to the whole human family, there would not be one cheerful face on the earth. Whether I shall ever be better I cannot tell; I awfully forbode I shall not. To remain as I am is impossible; I must die or be better, it appears to me."

His doctor, A. G. Henry, advised a change of scene, a complete break from his present surroundings. He would go to Bogota, Colombia, if Stuart could get him the consulate at that South American port. He wrote, referring to the effort Stuart was making to have him appointed consul, "The matter you spoke of on my account you may attend to as you say, unless you shall hear of my condition forbidding it. I say this because I fear I shall be unable to attend to any business here, and a change of scene might help me. If I could be myself, I would rather remain at home with Judge Logan. I can write no more."

Stuart failed to land the consulate. And Lincoln never saw the shores of South America.

In weeks and months that followed, the limited circle of insiders who believed they knew "what was going on," whispered, spoke and wrote to each other about Lincoln's being jilted by Mary Todd. "Poor A—," wrote Mercy Levering in February. "I fear his is a blighted heart! perhaps if he was as persevering as Mr. W—he might be finally successful." And Conkling replied, "And L. poor hapless swain who loved most true but was not loved again—I suppose he will now endeavor to drown his cares among the intricacies and perplexities of the law."

The memory of Lincoln, the story teller, the gay one, remained fresh, and Conkling recalled it. "No more will the merry peal of laughter ascend *high in the air*, to greet his listening and delighted ears. He used to remind me sometimes of the pictures I formerly saw of old Father Jupiter, bending down from the clouds, to see what was going on below. And as an agreeable smile of satisfaction graced the countenance of the old heathen god, as he perceived the incense rising up—so the face of L. was occasionally distorted into a grin as he succeeded in eliciting applause from some of the fair votaries by whom he was surrounded. But alas! I fear his shrine will now be deserted and that he will withdraw himself from the society of us inferior mortals."

Mary Todd meantime moved gayly and serenely through the little social whirl of Springfield. "Miss Todd and her cousin, Miss Edwards," Conkling wrote to Mercy Levering, "seemed to form the grand centre of attraction. Swarms of strangers who had little else to engage their attention hovered around them, to catch a passing smile." And with what he meant to be humor of some sort Conkling added, "By the way, I do not think they were received, with even ordinary attention, if they did not obtain a broad grin or an obstreperous laugh."

A letter of Mary's written to Mercy Levering in June of the summer of 1841 shows that her heart was not so gay after all. And furthermore, she didn't believe that everything was over and the past all sealed so far as she and Lincoln were concerned.

"The last three months have been of *interminable* length," she confesses. "After my gay companions of last winter departed, I was left much to the solitude of my own thoughts, and some *lingering regrets* over the past, which time can alone overshadow with its healing balm. Thus has my *spring time* passed. Summer in all its beauty has come again. The prairie land looks as beautiful as it did in the olden time, when we strolled together and derived so much of happiness from each other's society—this is past and more than this."

Meantime also rumors traveled that Mary Todd was seriously interested in Edwin B. Webb, a widower. Mary assures her friend Mercy these rumors are mistaken. She writes in this June letter that many visitors are in Springfield for the court sessions. "But in their midst the *winning widower* is not. Rumor says he with some others will attend a supreme court next month."

Mercy Levering in her last letter to Mary Todd had intimated that Mary and the widower were "dearer to each other than friends." Now Mary proceeds to put herself on record as to this. "The idea was neither new nor strange, dear Merce. The knowing world, have coupled our names for months past, merely through the folly and belief of another, who strangely imagined we were attached to each other. In your friendly and confiding ear allow me to whisper that my *heart can never be his.* I have deeply regretted that his constant visits, attention etc. should have given room for remarks, which were to me unpleasant. There being a slight difference of some eighteen or twenty summers in our years, would preclude all possibility of congeneality of feeling, without which I would never feel justifiable in resigning my happiness into the safe keeping of another, even should that other be, far too worthy for me, with his two *sweet little objections.*"

Was she at this time keeping Lincoln in mind and heart for marriage? We can only guess and surmise. . . .

And now though Mary Todd had sent him a letter releasing him from their engagement, Mary in her June letter of 1841 to Mercy Levering is referring to Joshua Speed, Lincoln's friend and roommate. She has had a letter from Speed who is visiting his old home in Kentucky. Speed brings to mind Lincoln and she writes of him "*His* worthy friend [Lincoln], deems me unworthy of notice, as I have not met *him* in the gay world for months. With the usual comfort of misery, [I] imagine that others were as seldom gladdened by his presence as my humble self, yet I would that the case were different, that he would once more resume his station in Society, that 'Richard should be himself again.' Much, much happiness would it afford me."

The implication was there in her letter that time would bring her and Lincoln together again. Though she had been in the social whirl, danced with other men, had her name linked with suitors for marriage, Lincoln was talked of as solitary. Her hope was, so she wrote Mercy Levering, that "Richard should be himself again," that Lincoln would recover from the bad health, the nervous exhaustion, which marked him in the winter of 1840. . . .

Early in 1841 Speed sold his store in Springfield and went to Kentucky. In August Lincoln went to visit him, to rest for weeks in the big Speed home near Louisville. There he met Fanny Henning, the young woman Speed was planning to marry. The wedding date was set, Lincoln went back to Springfield but for months he and Speed were haunted by the approaching wedding. Speed was as shaken and worried about it as Lincoln had been about his affair with Mary Todd. Speed returned to Springfield for a long visit but on leaving for Kentucky again Lincoln handed him a letter to read on the stage to St. Louis and the steamboat for Louisville. The letter was an argument fortifying Speed and giving him reasons and courage for going through with his wedding as planned. "I know what the painful point is with you at all times when you are unhappy: it is an apprehension that you do not love her as you should. What nonsense!"

Speed reached home, found his intended bride sick, the doctors worried. He wrote Lincoln he was in the depths of misery. Lincoln replied, "Why, Speed, if you did not love her, although you might not wish her death, you would most certainly be resigned to it." He asked pardon if he was getting too familiar. "You know the hell I have suffered on that point, and how tender I am upon it."

Speed married Fanny Henning in February of 1842, and Lincoln's letter of congratulation declared, "I tell you, Speed, our forebodings (for which you and I are peculiar) are all the worst sort of nonsense." Speed had written that something indescribably horrible and alarming still haunted him. He implied marriage was no good to him. Lincoln predicted, "You will not say *that* three months from now, I will venture. When your nerves get steady now, the whole trouble will be over forever. Nor should you become impatient at their being very slow in becoming steady." Thus the recovering victim of "nerves" assured one struggling.

Also in this advice to Speed Lincoln includes a little argument that both he and Speed had been dreaming fool dreams about marriage bringing an impossible paradise. They had overrated the benefits and romance of matrimony. "You say, you much fear that the Elysium of which you and I dreamed so much is never to be realized. Well, if it shall not, I dare swear it will not be the fault of her who is now your wife. I now have no doubt, that it is the peculiar misfortune of both you and me to dream dreams of Elysium far exceeding all that anything earthly can realize."

When, a month later, Speed wrote that he was happy and Lincoln's predictions had come true, Lincoln replied, "Your last letter gave me more pleasure than the sum total of all I have enjoyed since that fatal first of January, 1841." Again he refers to Mary Todd. She still haunts him. "Since then it seems to me that I should have been entirely happy, but for the never absent idea that there is *one* still unhappy whom I have contributed to make so. That still kills my soul. I cannot but reproach myself for even wishing to be happy while she is otherwise. She accompanied a large party on the railroad cars to Jacksonville last Monday, and on her return spoke, so that I heard of it, of having enjoyed the trip exceedingly. God be praised for that!"

Speed now sent a warning that Lincoln must either soon make up his mind to marry Miss Todd or put her out of his thoughts completely, forget her. This was correct advice, Lincoln wrote back. "But, before I resolve to do one thing or the other, I must gain my confidence in my own ability to keep my resolves when they are made. In that ability, you know I once prided myself, as the only or chief gem of my character; that gem I lost, how and where you know too well. I have not yet regained it; and, until I do, I cannot trust myself in any matter of much importance."

Perhaps Lincoln used some of these very words to Mary Todd when later in 1842 they were brought together at the home of Mrs. Simeon Francis, wife of Lincoln's friend, the editor of the *Sangamo Journal*. Neither Lincoln nor Mary Todd knew beforehand they were to be brought face to face by Mrs. Francis, so it was said. It was a pleasant surprise. The first meeting was followed by many others. Among the very few who knew of these meetings was Julia Jayne, a close friend of Mary Todd. With these two young women Lincoln joined in the fall of 1842 in writing pieces for the *Sangamo Journal* satirizing James Shields, state auditor, who challenged Lincoln to a duel which at the finish dissolved into apologies that meant nothing in particular. Yet it was an adventure with fresh excitements daily; it drew the couple closer.

Early in October Lincoln wrote Speed he knew well that Speed was happier than when first married. He could see in Speed's letters "the returning elasticity of spirits" resulting from marriage. "But," he wrote, "I want to ask you a close question. 'Are you now in *feeling*, as well as *judgment*, glad you are married as you are?' From anybody but me this would be an impudent question, not to be tolerated; but I know you will pardon it in me. Please answer it quickly, as I am impatient to know."

Speed's answer to Lincoln, it seemed, was yes, he was glad both in feeling and judgment that he had married as he did.

A few weeks later, on November 4, 1842, Lincoln and Mary Todd were married at the Ninian W. Edwards home. The Reverend Charles Dresser in canonical robes performed the ring ceremony for the groom, thirty-three years old, and the bride, twenty-three years old.

Mary Todd was now to have fresh light on why newly married couples lose their "silver tones," if they do. She was to know more clearly the reply to her query of two years previous, "Why is it that married folks always become so serious?"

In one of his letters advising Speed to marry, Lincoln had written that his old father used to say, "If you make a bad bargain, hug it all the tighter."

In a letter five days after his wedding to a Shawneetown lawyer regarding two law cases, Lincoln closed with writing, "Nothing new here, except my marrying, which, to me, is a matter of profound wonder."

Twenty-four years later Joshua Speed wrote Herndon, "If I had not been married and happy—far more happy than I ever expected to be—Lincoln would not have married."

CHAPTER SEVEN

Mr. Lincoln of Illinois

WITH FOUR TERMS *in the State Legislature to his credit, and many stanch supporters among the Whigs of central Illinois, Lincoln set his heart upon election to Congress. His ambition, however, was not to be realized immediately. In 1843 he was thwarted by the Whigs of his own county, who instructed their delegates to the district convention to vote for his good friend, Edward D. Baker. Then they made matters worse by electing Lincoln a delegate, leaving him, as he said, "a good deal like a fellow who is made a groomsman to a man that has cut him out and is marrying his own dear 'gal.'" But Baker's good fortune turned out to be of short duration, for the district convention rejected him in favor of John J. Hardin who was duly elected.*

After Hardin's turn came Baker's, so it was not until 1846 that Lincoln had his chance. Even then there were obstacles. Hardin, out of office two years, was feeling the lure of Washington, and Lincoln was barely able to induce him to withdraw from the contest for the nomination. Moreover, Peter Cartwright, the famous Methodist circuit-rider whom the Democrats nominated, turned out to be a troublesome opponent. Nevertheless, when the votes were counted, Lincoln was found to have received 6,340 to 4,829 for Cartwright—the largest majority by which the district had ever been carried.

Three months after the election Lincoln wrote to his old friend, Joshua F. Speed: "Being elected to Congress has not pleased me as much as I expected." No wonder, for the

*Thirtieth Congress was not to convene until December of
the next year. But time passed, and at last, in late October, 1847, there came a day when Abraham Lincoln, his
wife, and two small children boarded the stage for the first
lap of their journey to Washington. Their destination was
Mrs. Lincoln's home in Lexington, Kentucky, where they
stayed for several weeks. Then another tiresome trip, by
stage and rail, and the little family of the new Congressman from Illinois found itself installed in lodgings in
Brown's Hotel, Washington.*

<h2 style="text-align:center">1</h2>

FOR TWO YEARS Lincoln's life was to center in a national capital
in which evidences of raw youth were mingled with omens of future
magnificence. The scene is set by Benjamin P. Thomas.

As LINCOLN FIRST SAW IT, Washington was a dirty,
sprawling town of 40,000, often cold in winter and humid and
malarial in summer. Three-fourths of the population were whites,
while 8,000 free negroes and 2,000 slaves made up the balance.
Georgetown, close by, had an additional 8,500 inhabitants.

So far as improvements and conveniences were concerned, the
town was little better than Springfield. Privies, pigsties, and
cowsheds cluttered the back yards; while streets and alleys were
littered with garbage. Chickens, geese and pigs roamed at will,
feasting on the refuse. Water was supplied by wells; while produce was brought in from Maryland and Virginia farms in carts
driven by slaves, and sold at the market, which was just off
Pennsylvania Avenue midway between the Capitol and the White
House.

Few streets were paved, and sidewalks consisted of gravel or
ashes. The north side of Pennsylvania Avenue, where bricks had
been laid from the Capitol to the White House, was the city's
promenade. The only street lights were along a part of Pennsylvania Avenue, where oil lamps shed a smoky glow; but even
these were dispensed with when Congress was not in session. The
four hotels provided omnibus service to and from the depot, and
other buses connected the depot and the Capitol with the wharves
of Georgetown; but the only other street conveyances were

antiquated hackney carriages. Almost everyone got about on "Shank's mare"; while a colored maid or nurse could not get a ride at any price unless she had a white child with her.

Fifteen policemen were on duty at night; and when fires broke out not only the volunteer companies, but "men, women, children, dogs, and every living and creeping beast . . . ran pell-mell to the scene of the conflagration."

The White House was essentially as it is today; but neither wing of the Capitol had been built and an old wooden dome still surmounted its central portion. Only the front part of the Treasury Building had been completed, and the foundation of the Smithsonian Institution had just been laid. The State Department occupied a two-story house on the site of the north front of the Treasury, while the War and Navy departments were housed in two-story dwellings on the site of the present State, War and Navy Building.

A disgrace to the capital in the eyes of many Northerners was the domestic slave trade of which it was the center. Lincoln was deeply impressed by seeing gangs of slaves shuffling through the street in chains and in his Peoria address, six years later, recalled the "sort of Negro livery-stable," plainly visible from the Capitol, "where droves of Negroes were collected, temporarily kept, and finally taken to Southern markets, precisely like droves of horses."

Two quasi-official newspapers with national circulation—the *Union,* Democratic organ, and the *National Intelligencer,* the mouthpiece of the Whigs—were published in the capital; and the *National Era,* the abolition sheet, was also printed there.

The influence of the thirty-seven churches, of eight denominations, was offset by the numerous saloons and gambling houses which lined Pennsylvania Avenue. There were some shops along this thoroughfare; but most ladies and gentlemen shopped in Baltimore.

Balls, receptions and dinners provided most of the social life. Cabinet members, the Speaker of the House, and local business and social leaders entertained; but the fact that only five Senators and four Representatives had houses and the austerity of the Presidential levees during Polk's occupancy of the White House were deterrents to social life. Social position depended on manners, family and official position rather than wealth. Mrs. John Sherwood summed up Washington life at this time as "a strange jumble of magnificence and squalor. Dinners were handsome and very social, the talk delightful, but the balls were sparsely furnished with light and chairs. The illumination was of wax and stearine candles, which used to send down showers of spermaceti on our shoulders. Brilliant conversation was the order of the day, and what Washington lacked of the upholsterer it made up in the manners and wit of its great men . . . [but] some of the Southwestern members got fearfully drunk at dinners."

2

ALTHOUGH THE MEXICAN WAR was practically over by the time Lincoln took his seat, it was still the burning question in Congress. To the Whigs, it was an unholy piece of Democratic perfidy and a national shame ; the Democrats took the position that no nation mindful of its honor could have tolerated Mexico's aggressions. To Lincoln, in Springfield, the controversy had not been a disturbing one. He had had doubts from the first about the justness of the war, but he had joined with other speakers in at least one mass meeting to encourage enlistments. Now, in Washington, he discovered that he had to take sides. Thomas plots the course he took and what his constituents thought about it.

U PON TAKING HIS SEAT in Congress Lincoln found that he could not remain passively acquiescent even if he so desired. On the second day of the session the President in his message reasserted that Mexico had struck the first blow and had shed the blood of American citizens on American soil. Two weeks later, Richardson of Illinois, one of the Administration's most aggressive supporters, introduced a resolution declaring the war to be just and necessary, and that the amount of indemnity must depend on Mexico's obstinacy in protracting it. On this resolution Lincoln and practically all the other Whigs unhesitatingly voted no. Lincoln was a practical politician ; and as such would probably have gone along with the Whig majority in any event. But by this time he had come to the conclusion that the President was in the wrong. A few days after Richardson's resolution was defeated Lincoln entered the Whig lists by introducing a series of resolutions calculated to embarrass the President by forcing him to admit that Mexico and not the United States had jurisdiction over the "spot" where the first blood of the war was shed. About three weeks later he clarified his position in his first important speech.

Accepting Polk's contention that the Rio Grande had been the western boundary of the Louisiana Purchase, he contended that this was immaterial, because by our treaty of 1819 we had sold all the territory between the Rio Grande and the Sabine to Spain. He admitted that Texas, after obtaining independence from Mexico, claimed the Rio Grande as her boundary; but pointed out that Mexico had never recognized this claim. True, Santa Anna, after his capture by the Texans, had recognized it; but he had done so under duress, in a document having "none of the distinguishing features of a treaty"; and his action had been repudiated by the Mexican government. Furthermore, the document had stipulated that the Texan army should not go within five leagues of the Rio Grande, a singular feature if it intended to make that river the boundary. He admitted that Texas had exercised jurisdiction beyond the Nueces, but denied that her jurisdiction had extended as far as the Rio Grande. And this, the exercise of jurisdiction, was the real test. "The extent of our territory in that region depended not on any treaty-fixed boundary (for no treaty had attempted it), but on revolution. Any people anywhere being inclined and having the power have the right to rise up and shake off the existing government, and form a new one that suits them better. This is a most valuable, a most sacred right—a right which we hope and believe is to liberate the world . . . All Mexico, including Texas, revolutionized against Spain; still later Texas revolutionized against Mexico. In my view, just so far as she carried her revolution by obtaining the actual, willing or unwilling, submission of the people, so far the country was hers, and no farther. Now, sir, for the purpose of obtaining the very best evidence as to whether Texas had actually carried her revolution to the place where the hostilities of the present war commenced, let the President answer the interrogatories I proposed." The reasoning here advanced shows the influence of Lincoln's study of Jeffersonian philosophy; and it is worthy of note that some recent writers on the subject are of the opinion that the United States' claim to the territory in question was at least of doubtful validity. Polk, however, completely ignored the interrogatories.

Throughout the session, until the treaty of peace was ratified, Lincoln voted with the Whigs on all resolutions designed to put the Administration in the wrong on the origin of the war, and to capitalize on its mistakes in waging it. On January 3, 1848, he voted for Ashmun's amendment which added the phrase "in a war unconstitutionally and unnecessarily begun by the President" to a resolution of thanks to General Taylor for his victory at Buena Vista. On the fourth he voted Aye on a resolution requesting information regarding instructions sent to our naval officers to permit Santa Anna to return to Mexico—a most embarrassing subject, since Santa Anna, once within the country, had immediately put himself at the head of the Mexican army instead of suing for peace as the Administration had supposed he would do. On the thirty-first Lincoln supported a resolution requesting information as to why Scott had been removed from his command, and again voted for a similar resolution on April 17. This also was a delicate subject for the Administration, because Scott's victories had made him extremely popular, and many persons suspected that he was the victim of political jealousy. Lincoln voted to print copies of a memorial from Quakers of New England praying for a speedy termination of the war, and also for the printing of ten thousand copies of an abstract of war contracts—always inflammable political material—which had been let by the Administration. But whenever supply bills were presented, he, like most other Whigs, voted for them rather than risk popular disfavor. Furthermore, he took a practical view regarding annexation of territory, and refused to vote for a resolution sponsored by the extreme anti-expansionist group which demanded that our army be withdrawn to a defensive line on the east bank of the Rio Grande, and that peace be made without indemnity.

Lincoln's "spot" resolutions, his anti-Administration speech, and his attitude on the war in general created surprise and resentment in his district. At first criticism was relatively mild.

The *Register* warned that the obstructionists in Congress "will find that the masses—the honest and patriotic citizens of Illinois—will mark their course and condemn them to an infamy as deep as that which rests upon the opposers of the last war. . . . Thank Heaven, Illinois has eight Representatives who will stand by the honor of the nation. Would that we could find Mr. Lincoln in their ranks doing battle on the side of his country as valiantly as did the Illinois volunteers on the battle fields of Buena Vista and Cerro Gordo. He will have a fearful account to settle with them, should he lend his aid in an effort to neutralize their achievements and blast their fame."

The Whig press attempted to defend Lincoln, but its support merely goaded the opposition. Warnings and regrets were followed by denunciation. The *Ottawa Free Trader* expressed its shame that an Illinois Representative had broken the State's united and patriotic front. A mass meeting in Pinckneyville passed resolutions declaring that those who tried to render their own government odious "deserved to be regarded as little better than traitors to their country." Another meeting in Clark County denounced Lincoln for the stain he had placed on the "patriotism and glory" of his State. Never before had such "black odium and infamy" been heaped upon the "living brave and illustrious dead." A Morgan County meeting resolved that "this Benedict Arnold of our district be known here only as the Ranchero Spotty of one term." Other Democratic meetings passed similar resolutions.

The Sangamon County Democratic Convention, in congratulating Illinois on the patriotism of its citizens and Representatives, felt "compelled to recognize one unfortunate exception, in the person of the Hon. Abraham Lincoln, present Whig Representative from this congressional district; who, contrary to the expectations and wishes of his constituents, and in contempt of the two gallant regiments which they furnished for the war, has lent himself to the schemes of such men as Corwin, Giddings, Hale and others, apologists and defenders of Mexico, and revilers of their own country."

"Out Damned Spot!" screamed the *Register*, which duly reprinted every denunciation and also added comments of its own. To an article on a peculiar disease called "spotted fever," which was prevalent in Michigan, it appended the observation: "This fever does not prevail to any very alarming extent in Illinois. The only case we have heard of that is likely to prove fatal, is that of 'spotty Lincoln,' of this state. This 'spotty' gentleman had a severe attack of 'spotted fever' in Washington city not long since, and fears were entertained that the disease would 'strike in,' and carry him off. We have not heard of any other person in Washington being on the 'spotted' list—and it is probable that the disease died with the patient.—What an epitaph: 'Died of Spotted Fever.' Poor Lincoln!"

The defense of the *Journal* and other Whig papers was weak and unavailing in the face of the overwhelming opinion in favor of the war. The appellation "Spotty Lincoln" stuck, with devastating effect on Lincoln's future political aspirations. Even in the presidential campaign of 1860, it was occasionally applied to him.

Herndon, frightened by the indignation which Lincoln's course had aroused, and disagreeing with his attitude, warned him of the consequences. In reply Lincoln wrote a confidential letter explaining and defending his position. "I will stake my life that if you had been in my place you would have voted just as I did," he declared. "Would you have voted what you felt and knew to be a lie? I know you would not. Would you have gone out of the House—skulked the vote? I expect not. If you had skulked one vote, you would have had to skulk many more before the end of the session. Richardson's resolutions, introduced before I made any move or gave any vote upon the subject, make the direct question of the justice of the war; so that no man can be silent if he would. You are compelled to speak; and your only alternative is to tell the truth or a lie. I cannot doubt which you would do. . . . The Locos are untiring in their efforts to make the impression that all who vote supplies or take part in the war do of necessity approve the President's conduct in the beginning of it; but the Whigs have from the beginning made and kept the distinction between the two."

Still fearful and unconvinced, Herndon attempted to defend Polk's action as a defensive measure to repel a threatened invasion. Lincoln replied that the President himself had never gone this far; and even so, "Allow the President to invade a neighboring nation whenever he shall deem it necessary to repel an invasion . . . and you allow him to make war at pleasure . . . Your view . . . places our President where kings have always stood."

Lincoln further attempted to justify himself in letters to Usher F. Linder and J. M. Peck; but for the most part his defense consisted in sending copies of Whig speeches on the war to the Whig newspapers of his district. Most of these never saw the light; because the editors, realizing the strength of local sentiment, foresaw the disastrous political consequences which would result from further publicizing the attitude of the Whig Representatives in Congress.

During the early weeks of his term Lincoln, informed by Herndon that some of his constituents favored his renomination, had expressed a willingness to run again if no one else desired the nomination. But his hopes for a second term were speedily withered by the Democratic blasts.

3

THE OTHER ISSUE which disturbed the first session of the Thirtieth Congress was slavery—an issue made acute by the prospect of large acquisitions of territory as the result of the Mexican defeat. When Lincoln, in 1855, wrote to Joshua Speed; "When I was in Washington, I voted for the Wilmot proviso as good as forty times," he was indulging in hyperbole, but the following account, from Thomas's summary of Lincoln's Congressional experience, shows that he was consistent and forthright in his opposition to the spread of slavery.

O N February 28, 1848, he expressed his attitude on the Wilmot Proviso when he voted against a motion to table a resolution, practically identical with the Proviso, which would have prohibited slavery in any territory which might be acquired from Mexico. On July 28, he voted against a Senate bill to establish territorial governments in Oregon, California and New Mexico. This bill would have continued in effect the anti-slavery laws of Oregon; but would have enjoined the legislatures of the other territories from passing any law relating to slavery, thus leaving the question to be settled by appeal to the Supreme Court. It was tabled, 105–93, on a vote which split both parties. Having rejected this bill, the House then formulated one of its own, giving territorial government to Oregon alone, and providing that the Ordinance of 1787 should be extended over it. Lincoln voted against an amendment striking out this provision, and for the passage of the bill with the provision included. It passed in this form; but the Senate struck out the provision and substituted a section extending the Missouri Compromise line to the Pacific. The House likewise rejected this, again on a sectional vote. The House bill was finally accepted by the Senate and signed by President Polk, although he preferred the Missouri Compromise provision.

Early in the second session, on December 13, 1848, Lincoln voted for a resolution which instructed the Committee on Territories to report a bill establishing territorial governments in California and New Mexico, and excluding slavery. Toward the close of the session such a bill was introduced, and passed; but the Senate rejected it, and in its place attached a rider, the so-called Walker amendment, to the general appropriations bill. This provided temporary governments for the two territories and extended over them the Constitution and laws of the United States. As the Constitution recognized the right of property in slaves, this would have been a tacit victory for the South. The anti-slavery majority in the House, including Lincoln, voted the amendment down; and on the last day of the session debated an amendment continuing in effect the laws of Mexico, one of which excluded slavery. Throughout the night Polk waited with a veto message, resolved to kill the whole appropriation bill if this amendment was included. But in the early morning the House receded, and the appropriations bill was passed with both the Walker and the House amendments deleted. With this dramatic finale the stage was set for the great struggle in the next Congress which ended in the Compromise of 1850.

Despite his stand on slavery in the territories, Lincoln was obviously opposed to unnecessary agitation of the slavery question. He took no part in the debates on the subject and maintained a conciliatory attitude whenever possible. . . . In April, 1848, when a mob threat to dismantle the press of the *National Era* led to a bitter debate on slavery, Lincoln with other moderates, both North and South, voted to end the discussion to prevent the matter's going "to the country to a greater extent than it had already gone out."

Lincoln's vote for a petition for a law appropriating the proceeds of the sale of public lands for the extinction of slavery indicates that already he believed compensated and gradual emancipation to be the best solution of the problem. And this is confirmed by his position on slavery and the slave trade in the District of Columbia. . . .

Early in the second session . . . Palfrey of Massachusetts asked permission to introduce a resolution directing the Committee on the District of Columbia to report a bill abolishing the slave trade in the District. Lincoln voted against giving leave to introduce, although most Northern members favored it. Five days later, Lincoln voted to table a resolution, offered by Giddings, of Ohio, which would have authorized a referendum by the people of the District on the further toleration of slavery. This vote can be explained by the fact that he already had in mind a similar plan of his own, with more moderate features.

Again, on December 21, Lincoln voted against a resolution directing the Committee on the District to report a bill abolishing slavery. The resolution passed, but on January 10, 1849, before the committee had had time to draw a bill, Lincoln gave notice of an amendment which he proposed to add to the resolution of instruction. His plan would direct the committee to bring in a bill confining slavery in the District to such slaves as were already there and such as might be brought in temporarily by government officials. Children born of slave mothers after January 1, 1850, should be free, but should serve as apprentices to their masters until they reached a certain age. If any master wished to free a slave already in the District he should be paid the fair value of the slave, such value to be determined by a slave-valuation board consisting of the President, Secretary of State and the Secretary of the Treasury. His plan also contemplated that the municipal authorities would provide efficient means for apprehending and delivering to their owners all fugitive slaves escaping into the District—a provision which aroused the ire of the Abolitionists and later caused Wendell Phillips to denounce him as "that slave hound from Illinois." The final and most significant stipulation was that all white male citizens, twenty-one years old or over, who had lived in the District for one year, should vote for or against the project, which, if accepted, should be put into effect at once.

Lincoln stated that his plan had the approval of fifteen leading citizens of the District; but when called upon to give their names he made no answer. Three days after his presentation of the plan, he gave notice that he would introduce it as a bill; but he never did so.

On January 31, 1849, the committee reported its bill—a disappointment to the radicals since it merely prohibited the slave trade. A motion to table was defeated, 72–117, Lincoln voting with the majority. Bitter debate followed and the Southern members became so alarmed that they held a conference at which they determined to appeal to their constituents to resist the "aggressions" of the North. Throughout the remainder of the session the debate flared up at intervals; but nothing further had been done when the Congress adjourned on March 4.

4

AT THE SAME TIME that Lincoln was making the record of a stanch party member in the House he was winning for himself the name of an amiable companion. Samuel C. Busey, a young physician who lived in the same boardinghouse, characterizes him as he appeared to his messmates.

F INALLY . . . I took the office on A Street, S. E., now included in the eastern park of the Capitol, vacated by Dr. Francis M. Gunnell, who had a week before passed the Medical Examining Board for the Navy, at the head of the list, and took my meals at a boardinghouse kept by Mrs. Sprigg, occupying a seat at the table nearly opposite Abraham Lincoln, whom I soon learned to know and admire for his simple and unostentatious manners, kindheartedness, and amusing jokes, anecdotes, and witticisms. When about to tell an anecdote during a meal he would lay down his knife and fork, place his elbows upon the table, rest his face between his hands, and begin with the words "that reminds me," and proceed. Everybody prepared for the explosions sure to follow. I recall with vivid pleasure the scene of merriment at the dinner after his first speech in the House of Representatives, occasioned by the descriptions, by himself and others of the Congressional mess, of the uproar in the House during its delivery. . . .

There was a large number of boarders at the Sprigg house, among whom may be named, besides Mr. Lincoln, Messrs. McIlvaine, Dick, Blanchard, and Pollack, members of the House of Representatives from Pennsylvania, and Thompkins, M. C., from Mississippi, the Green family, Nathan Sargent—better known as "Oliver Oldschool"—Edmund French, a private citizen, and myself. All the members of the House of Representatives were Whigs. The Wilmot Proviso was the topic of frequent conversation and the occasion of very many angry controversies. Dick, who represented the Lancaster district in Pennsylvania, afterward represented by Thaddeus Stevens, was a very offensive man in manner and conversation, and seemed to take special pleasure in ventilating his opinions and provoking unpleasant discussions with the Democrats and some of the Whigs, especially Thompkins, who held adverse opinions on the Wilmot Proviso. Nathan Sargent was also a radical, but was so interested in the success of the Whigs and the election of Zachary Taylor that he restrained himself and followed Mr. Lincoln, who may have been as radical as either of these gentlemen, but was so discreet in giving expression to his convictions on the slavery question as to avoid giving offence to anybody, and was so conciliatory as to create the impression, even among the pro-slavery advocates, that he did not wish to introduce or discuss subjects that would provoke a controversy. When such conversation would threaten angry or even unpleasant contention he would interrupt it by interposing some anecdote, thus diverting it into a hearty and general laugh, and so completely disarrange the tenor of the discussion that the parties engaged would either separate in good humor or continue conversation free from discord. This amicable disposition made him very popular with the household.

Congressman Lincoln was very fond of bowling, and would frequently join others of the mess, or meet other members in a match game, at the alley of James Casparis, which was near the boardinghouse. He was a very awkward bowler, but played the game with great zest and spirit, solely for exercise and amusement, and greatly to the enjoyment and entertainment of the other players and bystanders by his criticisms and funny illustrations. He accepted success and defeat with like good nature and humor, and left the alley at the conclusion of the game without a sorrow or disappointment. When it was known that he was in the alley there would assemble numbers of people to witness the fun which was anticipated by those who knew of his fund of anecdotes and jokes. When in the alley, surrounded by a crowd of eager listeners, he indulged with great freedom in the sport of narrative, some of which was very broad. His witticisms seemed for the most part to be impromptu, but he always told the anecdotes and jokes as if he wished to convey the impression that he had heard them from some one; but they appeared very many times as if they had been made for the immediate occasion.

Congressman Lincoln was always neatly but very plainly dressed, very simple and approachable in manner, and unpretentious. He attended to his business, going promptly to the House and remaining till the session adjourned, and appeared to be familiar with the progress of legislation.

5

AT THE END of the winter Mrs. Lincoln took the two children, Robert and Edward Baker, and returned to her home in Lexington. From letters which passed between her and Lincoln, now alone, we learn much about his life in Washington, and not a little about two different temperaments. William H. Townsend amplifies the letters with brief explanatory comments.

A T THEIR GRANDFATHER TODD's comfortable residence on West Main and out at "Buena Vista" on the Leestown Pike, Robert and little Eddie, with small pickaninnies to do their bidding, found much in contrast to the cramped quarters at Widow Spriggs' boardinghouse. The Todd summer home was a tall, rambling, frame house, surrounded by large locust trees, situated on a beautiful knoll, a quarter of a mile from the highway. It had a double portico in front and a long porch on the side that connected two stone slave cabins with the main portion of the dwelling. A tiny brook meandered from a stone "spring house" through the rolling woodland at the foot of the knoll, and from the porticoes the view was magnificent.

The "long Whig" and his wife were regular correspondents, and one of the letters that he wrote her ran as follows:

"Washington, April 16, 1848.

"Dear Mary:

"In this troublesome world, we are never quite satisfied. When you were here, I thought you hindered me some in attending to business but now, having nothing but business—no vanity—it has grown exceedingly tasteless to me. I hate to sit down and direct accounts, and I hate to stay in the old room by myself. You know I told you in last Sunday's letter I was going to make a little speech during the week and the week has passed away without my getting a chance to do so and now my interest in the subject has passed away too. Your second and third letters have been received since I wrote before. Dear Eddy thinks father is gone tapets. Has any further discovery been made as to the breaking into your grandmother's house? If I were she I would not remain there alone. You mention that your Uncle John Parker is likely to be at Lexington. Don't forget to present him my very kindest regards.

"I went yesterday to hunt the little plaid stockings as you wished, but found that McKnight has quit business and Allen had not a single pair of the description you gave and only one plaid pair of any sort that I thought would fit 'Eddy's dear little feet.' I have a notion to make another trial tomorrow morning. If I could get them, I have an excellent chance of sending them. Mr. Warrick Tunstall, of St. Louis is here. He is to leave early this week and to go by Lexington. He says he knows you, and will call to see you, and he voluntarily asked if I had not some package to send to you.

"I wish you would enjoy yourself in every possible way, but is there no danger of wounding the feelings of your good father, by being openly intimate with the Wickliffe family? Mrs. Broome has not removed yet, but she thinks of doing so tomorrow.

"All the house or rather all with whom you were on decided good terms send their love to you. The others say nothing. Very soon after you went away, I got what I think a very pretty set of shirt bosom studs—modest little ones jet set in gold only costing 50 cents a piece or 1.50 for the whole.

"Suppose you do not prefix the 'Hon.' to the address on your letters to me any more. I like the letters very much but I would rather they should not have that upon them. It is not necessary as I suppose you have thought to have them come free.

"And you are entirely free from headache? That is good—considering it is the first spring you have been free from it since we were acquainted—I am afraid you will get so well and fat and young as to be wanting to marry again. Tell Louisa I want her to watch you a little for me. Get weighed and write me how much you weigh. I did not get rid of the impression of that foolish dream about dear Bobby, till I got your letter written the same day.

"What did he and Eddie think of the little letters father sent them? Don't let the blessed fellows forget father. A day or two ago Mr. Strong, here in Congress said to me that Matilda would visit here within two or three weeks. Suppose you write her a letter, and enclose it in one of mine, and if she comes I will deliver it to her, and if she does not, I will send it to her.

"Most affectionately

"A. LINCOLN."

And on a warm May evening, by her window that opened into the garden, filled with lilacs and honeysuckle, Mary scribbled a long, newsy letter to her husband:

"Lexington, May—, 48.

"My Dear Husband:

"You will think indeed that old age has set its seal upon my humble self, that in few or no letters I can remember the day of the month. I must confess it is one of my peculiarities.

"I feel wearied and tired enough to know that this is Saturday night, our babies are asleep, and as Aunt Maria B. is coming for me tomorrow morning, I think the chances will be rather dull that I should answer your last letter tomorrow.

"I have just received a letter from Frances W., it related in especial manner to the box I had desired her to send, she thinks with you (as good persons generally agree) that it would cost more than it would come to, and it might be lost on the road. I rather expect she has examined the special articles and thinks, as Levi says, they are rather hard bargains. But it takes so many changes to do children, particularly in summer, that I thought it might save me a few stitches. I think I will write her a few lines this evening, directing her to send them. She says Willie is just recovering from another spell of sickness, Mary or none of them are well. Springfield, she reports, as dull as usual—Uncle S. was to leave there on yesterday for Ky.

"Our little Eddie has recovered from his spell of sickness— Dear boy, I must tell you a little story about him. Bobby in his wanderings today, came across in a yard a little kitten, your hobby; he says he asked a man for it. He brought it triumphantly to the house. So soon as Eddie spied it, his tenderness broke forth, he made them bring it water, fed it with bread himself with his own dear hands, he was a delighted little creature over it. In the midst of his happiness Ma came in. She, you must know, dislikes the whole cat race. I thought in a very unfeeling manner, she ordered the servant near to throw it out which of course was done —Ed screaming and protesting loudly against the proceeding. She never appeared to mind his screams, which were long and loud, I assure you. 'Tis unusual for her nowadays to do anything quite so striking, she is very obliging and accommodating, but if she thought any of us were on her hands again, I believe she would be worse than ever. In the next moment she appeared in a good humor, I know she did not intend to offend me. By the way, she has just sent me up a glass of ice-cream, for which this warm evening I am duly grateful.

"The country is so delightful I am going to spend two or three weeks out there, it will doubtless benefit the children. Grandma has just received a letter from Uncle James Parker of Miss. saying he & his family would be up by the twenty-fifth of June, would remain here some little time and go on to Philadelphia to take their oldest daughter there to school. I believe it would be a good chance to pack up and accompany them. You know I am so fond of sight-seeing & I did not get to New York or Boston, or travel the lake route. But, perhaps, dear husband, like the irresistible Col. Mc. cannot do without his wife next winter and must needs take her with him again. I expect you would cry aloud against it.

"How much I wish, instead of writing, we were together this evening, I feel very sad away from you.

"Ma & myself rode out to Mr. Bell's splendid place this afternoon to return a call. The house and grounds are magnificent. Frances W. would have died over their rare exotics.

"It is growing late, these summer eves are short, I expect my long scrawls, for truly such they are, weary you greatly. If you come on in July or August, I will take you to the Springs. Patty Webb's school in S. closes the first of July. I expect Mr. Webb will come for her. I must go down about that time & carry on quite a flirtation (you know we always had a penchant that way).

"I must bid you goodnight. Do not fear the children have forgotten you. I was only jesting. Even E's eyes brighten at the mention of your name.

> "My love to all.
> "Truly yours
> "M. L."

Lincoln did not forget to provide his family with funds even though, under the circumstances, they were at practically no expense.

> "Washington, May 24, 1848.

"My dear Wife:

"Enclosed is the draft as I promised you in my letter of Sunday. It is drawn in favor of your father, and I doubt not he will give you the money for it at once. I write this letter in the post office, surrounded by men and noise, which, together with the fact that there is nothing new, makes me write so short a letter.

> "Affectionately
> "A. LINCOLN."

Mary's letters from Lexington were full of local happenings, doubtlessly interesting to the lonely man at the Widow Spriggs'. Thieves had broken into "Grandma" Parker's residence and had stolen a gold watch and a quantity of monogrammed silverware. Mrs. Parker had offered a reward of a hundred dollars for their detection. "Has any further discovery been made as to the breaking into your grandmother's house?" wrote Lincoln. "If I were

she I would not remain there alone." Cassius M. Clay, on his return from Mexico, had renewed warfare on his old enemies by
suing the leaders of the committee of sixty, for damages to his
printing press and, upon a change of venue to Jessamine County,
was awarded judgment for twenty-five hundred dollars. Henry
Clay, having been defeated in the Philadelphia convention by
General Taylor, was being urged to stand for election to the
Senate, and John J. Crittenden had resigned his seat in that body
to become the Whig candidate for governor of Kentucky.

Another letter from Lincoln to his wife, during these months,
has been preserved:

"Washington, July 2, 1848.

"My dear wife:

"Your letter of last sunday came last night—On that day
(sunday) I wrote the principal part of a letter to you, but did
not finish it, or send it till tuesday, when I had provided a draft
for $100 which I sent in it—It is now probable that on that day
(tuesday) you started to Shelbyville; so that when the money
reaches Lexington you will not be there—Before leaving, did you
make any provision about letters that might come to Lexington
for you? Write me whether you got the draft, if you shall not
have already done so, when this reaches you—Give my kindest regards to your uncle John, and all the family. Thinking of them
reminds me that I saw your acquaintance, Newton, of Arkansas,
at the Philadelphia Convention—We had but a single interview,
and that was so brief, and in so great a multitude of strange faces,
that I am quite sure I should not recognize him, if I were to meet
him again—He was a sort of Trinity, three in one, having the
right, in his own person, to cast the three votes of Arkansas—Two
or three days ago I sent your uncle John, and a few of our other
friends each a copy of the speech I mentioned in my last letter;
but I did not send any to you, thinking you would be on the road
here, before it would reach you—I send you one now—Last wednesday P. H. Hood & Co. dunned me for a little bill of $8.50 for
goods which they say you bought—I hesitated to pay them, because my recollection is that you told me when you went away,
there was nothing left unpaid—Mention in your next letter
whether they are right."

At some length the letter runs along in chatty fashion. The Richardsons have a new baby. Interest in the Saturday night concerts on the Capitol grounds is dwindling. Two girls that he and Mrs. Lincoln had seen at the exhibition of the Ethiopian Serenaders were still in Washington, . . . And then closes:

"I have had no letter from home, since I wrote you before except short business letters, which have no interest for you.

"By the way, you do not intend to do without a girl, because the one you had last left you? Get another as soon as you can to take charge of the dear codgers—Father expected to see you all sooner; but let it pass; stay as long as you please, and come when you please—Kiss and love the dear rascals.

                              "Affectionately
                                   "A. LINCOLN"

6

LIKE MOST OF HIS FELLOW MEMBERS of Congress, Lincoln was as much interested in the approaching Presidential election as in legislative matters. Benjamin P. Thomas presents him as a party stalwart.

DURING THE ENTIRE TERM of the Congress the main concern of the Whigs was the Presidential election of 1848. No sooner had General Taylor's victories begun to bring him popularity than the Whig leaders began to consider his availability. He had never taken an active part in politics, had never announced any views, was an exponent of the military spirit which they denounced, a slaveowner, and an advocate of annexation of Mexican territory. In fact, his prominence rested altogether on his success in the "illegal, unrighteous and damnable war." But his vote-getting potentialities were great.

Early in 1846 the Taylor boom got under way, and gathered momentum as election year approached. The Whigs were mindful that the only Presidential election they had won was that of 1840, when they passed over Henry Clay, their recognized leader, and rode to victory on the military reputation of William Henry Harrison. Now, with their opponents divided, and victory once more within their reach, they again relegated Clay to the background to take advantage of the popularity of a "military chieftain."

Since Lincoln's entry into politics, Henry Clay had been his idol. Keenly sensitive to the feelings of the people, however, and practical, as ever, in his views, he recognized Taylor's pulling powers and was not slow to clamber on the Taylor bandwagon. On February 9, 1848, he declined an invitation to attend a Taylor meeting at Philadelphia; but announced himself as "decidedly in favor of General Taylor as the Whig candidate for the next Presidency." He also stated that during the previous summer the Whig representatives at the Illinois State Constitutional Convention had gone on record overwhelmingly for Taylor and that this, "together with other facts falling within my observation, leave no doubt in my mind that the preference of the Whigs of the State is the same."

On February 17, he explained his position in a letter to T. S. Florney. "In answer to your inquiries," he wrote, "I have to say I am in favor of General Taylor as the Whig candidate for the Presidency because I am satisfied we can elect him, that he will give us a Whig administration, and that we canot elect any other Whig. In Illinois his being our candidate, would *certainly* give us one additional member of Congress, if not more; and *probably* would give us the electoral vote of the state. That with him, we can, in that state, make great inroads among the rank and file of the Democrats, to my mind is certain; but the majority against us there, is so great, that I can do no more than express my *belief* that we can carry the state."

Through the early months of 1848, Lincoln kept in close touch with the trend of opinion, particularly in Illinois, and did what he could to swing the Clay men over to Taylor; "not," as he explained to Jesse Lynch of Magnolia, "because I think he would make a better president than Clay, but because I think he would make a better one than Polk, or Cass, or Buchanan, or any such creatures, one of whom is sure to be elected, if he is not." To E. B. Washburne, Archibald Williams and other influential Whigs in Illinois he sent letters urging them to send Taylor delegates to the Whig National Convention. In his letter to Williams, dated April 30, he analyzed the situation. "Mr. Clay's chance for an election is just no chance at all," he urged. "He might get New York, and that would have elected him in 1844, but it will not now, because he must now, at the least, lose Tennessee, which he had then, and in addition the fifteen new votes of Florida, Texas, Iowa, and Wisconsin. I know our good friend Browning is a great admirer of Mr. Clay, and I therefore fear he is favoring his nomination. If he is, ask him to discard feeling, and try if he can possibly, as a matter of judgment, count the votes necessary to elect him."

Early in June Lincoln left Washington to attend the Whig National Convention at Philadelphia. Here he had the pleasure of witnessing Taylor's nomination, and of seeing Illinois contribute to it. On the first ballot the Illinois votes were cast three for Clay, one for Scott, and four for Taylor (one district was not represented); on the second and third ballots there was no change; but on the fourth and final ballot the whole delegation voted for the General.

From June until Election Day Lincoln labored hard. In another letter to Williams on June 12, he portrayed the situation as he saw it. "By many, and often," he wrote, "it had been said they would not abide the nomination of Taylor; but since the deed has been done, they are fast falling in, and in my opinion we shall have a most overwhelming, glorious triumph. One unmistakable sign is that all the odds and ends are with us—Barnburners, Native Americans, Tyler men, disappointed Locofocos, and the Lord knows what. This is important, if in nothing else, in showing which way the wind blows. Some of the sanguine men have set down all the States as certain for Taylor but Illinois, and it is doubtful. Cannot something be done even in Illinois?"

Illinois gave him his greatest anxiety; and much of his time was devoted to it. Of friends in various counties he requested the names of both Whigs and Democrats who might be persuaded to switch their votes. Their replies enabled him further to analyze the situation and to send campaign literature to those whose minds were not made up. Upon Herndon, who was pessimistic about the outcome in Sangamon County, he urged the necessity of getting the young men together in a "Rough and Ready Club." "Take in everybody you can get . . . as you go along gather up all the shrewd, wild boys about town, whether just of age or a little under age . . . Let everyone play the part he can play best—some speak, some sing, and all 'holler.' " He was impatient with Herndon for asking for Whig speeches when he had been regularly sending him the *Congressional Globe*. This he had also sent to the Whig papers; "yet, with the exception of my own little speech, which was published in two only of the then five, now four, Whig papers, I do not remember having seen a single speech, or even abstract from one, in any single one of those papers. With equal and full means on both sides, I will venture that the 'State Register' has thrown before its readers more of Locofoco speeches in a month than all the Whig papers of the district have done of Whig speeches during the session."

But Herndon "was not easily warmed up." He knew of the defections from the party which Lincoln's course had caused, of the discouragement which prevailed among the Whigs in Springfield, and of the dissatisfaction of the young men "at the stubbornness and bad judgment of the old fossils in the party, who were constantly holding the young men back." These sentiments, together with newspaper clippings, he forwarded to Lincoln. Under date of July 10, Lincoln wrote a fatherly reply, disclaiming any intention on the part of the "old men" to act ungenerously, and advising that the "way for a young man to rise is to improve himself every way he can, never suspecting that anybody wishes to hinder him. Allow me to assure you that suspicion and jealousy never did help any man in any situation."

Herndon was mollified; and he and others set to work, but with discouraging results. The Congressional election on August 6, seemed to indicate the outcome. Stephen T. Logan, Whig candidate to succeed Lincoln, was defeated by Thomas L. Harris, of Petersburg, 7,095 to 7,201.

Lincoln tried to explain the result on the ground that Logan was unpopular with many Whigs, while Harris was looked on as a hero by reason of his war record. "That there is any political change against us in the district I cannot believe," he said.

Yet the *Register* probably had a more accurate explanation. "The whigs about Springfield are attributing their defeat to Judge Logan solely," it observed, "alleging that the Judge's unpopularity brought about the result. This will not do, gentlemen, you must put the saddle on the right horse. It was the crushing load Logan had to carry in the shape of whig principles, and the course of the whig party for the past two years. Besides his own dead weight, Logan had to carry the votes of the whig party, including Lincoln, that the war was unconstitutional and unnecessary. If this whig reasoning will apply to Logan, why not to Stuart and Edwards? The former received but 22 and the latter but 16 more votes than the Judge in Sangamon. 'Acknowledge the corn,' whiggery is getting in bad odor."

Meanwhile Lincoln labored on. He sent copies of the *Battery*, a Whig campaign paper, to constituents, and flooded his district with government documents. On July 27, he made a speech in Congress ridiculing the efforts of the Democrats to extol the military qualities of Lewis Cass, their Presidential candidate, by comparing Cass's military record to his own experiences in the Black Hawk War. In the more serious part of his speech he defended Taylor's attitude on the exercise of the veto power, and his failure to announce his position on the questions of the day.

At the end of the first session of Congress Lincoln remained in Washington, franking documents and writing letters to such men as William Schouler and Thaddeus Stevens, in order to keep in touch with the political trend. In this he was probably acting in close co-operation with the National Committee, although not a member of it.

In the latter part of August and the first week of September he made a few speeches in and around Washington and on September 9, began a speaking tour in New England. Here his efforts were directed to proving that the Whigs and Free-Soilers occupied the same ground with respect to the extension of slavery, that a Democratic victory would facilitate extension, and that the Free-Soilers, by voting for Van Buren, would split the anti-extension vote and conduce to the election of Cass. Lincoln closed his tour at a huge meeting at Tremont Temple, where he and William H. Seward spoke from the same platform. He was deeply impressed with Seward's remarks, and upon taking leave of him next day expressed the opinion that politicians of all parties must give more attention to the slavery problem in the future. In fact, his contact with New England leaders and sentiment and his experiences in Congress were major factors in awakening him to the immediacy of the slavery problem and to the necessity of uniting the various anti-slavery factions upon a definite and practicable program.

His New England tour ended, Lincoln headed for home. Traveling leisurely to Chicago, he spoke there at a Whig rally. On August 23, he had been selected as an assistant Taylor elector with the understanding that he would assist in the campaign in Illinois. On October 21, he opened his campaign at Jacksonville and proceeded from there through the northern part of the Congressional district. Here, as in New England, he tried to unite the Whigs and Free Soilers, but whenever an opposition speaker appeared on the same platform he diverted Lincoln and put him on the defensive by bringing up his record on the war. A correspondent of the *Register* claimed that "Lincoln has made nothing by coming to this part of the country to make speeches. He had better have stayed away." Nevertheless, on Election Day, Taylor carried the district by 1,500 votes, a result for which Lincoln, in his autobiography, assumed a large measure of credit.

7

LINCOLN'S COURSE in the second session of the Thirtieth Congress, which convened on December 4, 1848, and adjourned on the 4th of March following, is of far less interest than what happened after his term ended. Nicolay and Hay tell the story.

For a few weeks in the spring of 1849 Mr. Lincoln appears in a character which is entirely out of keeping with all his former and subsequent career. He became, for the first and only time in his life, an applicant for an appointment at the hands of the President. His bearing in this attitude was marked by his usual individuality. In the opinion of many Illinoisans it was important that the place of Commissioner of the General Land Office should be given to a citizen of their State, one thoroughly acquainted with the land law in the West and the special needs of that region. A letter to Lincoln was drawn up and signed by some half-dozen of the leading Whigs of the State asking him to become an applicant for that position.

He promptly answered, saying that if the position could be secured for a citizen of Illinois only by his accepting it, he would consent; but he went on to say that he had promised his best efforts to Cyrus Edwards for that place, and had afterwards stipulated with Colonel Baker that if J. L. D. Morrison, another Mexican hero, and Edwards could come to an understanding with each other as to which should withdraw, he would join in recommending the other; that he could not take the place, therefore, unless it became clearly impossible for either of the others to get it. Some weeks later, the impossibility referred to having become apparent, Mr. Lincoln applied for the place; but a suitor for office so laggard and so scrupulous as he, stood very little chance of success in contests like those which periodically raged at Washington during the first weeks of every new administration. The place came, indeed, to Illinois, but to neither of the three we have mentioned. The fortunate applicant was Justin Butterfield, of Chicago, a man well and favorably known among the early members of the Illinois bar, who, however, devoted less assiduous attention to the law than to the business of office-seeking, which he practiced with fair success all his days.

It was in this way that Abraham Lincoln met and escaped one of the greatest dangers of his life. In after days he recognized the error he had committed, and congratulated himself upon the happy deliverance he had obtained through no merit of his own. The loss of at least four years of the active pursuit of his profession would have been irreparable, leaving out of view the strong probability that the singular charm of Washington life to men who have a passion for politics might have kept him there forever. . . . Yet if Justin Butterfield had not been a more supple, more adroit, and less scrupulous suitor for office than himself, Abraham Lincoln would have sat for four inestimable years at a bureau desk in the Interior Department, and when the hour of action sounded in Illinois, who would have filled the place which he took as if he had been born for it? Who could have done the duty which he bore as lightly as if he had been fashioned for it from the beginning of time?

His temptation did not end even with Butterfield's success. The Administration of General Taylor, apparently feeling that some compensation was due to one so earnestly recommended by the leading Whigs of the State, offered Mr. Lincoln the governorship of Oregon. This was a place more suited to him than the other, and his acceptance of it was urged by some of his most judicious friends on the ground that the new Territory would soon be a

State, and that he could come back as a Senator. This view of the matter commended itself favorably to Lincoln himself, who, however, gave it up on account of the natural unwillingness of his wife to remove to a country so wild and so remote.

This was all as it should be. The best place for him was Illinois, and he went about his work there until his time should come.

8

LINCOLN'S UNSUCCESSFUL ATTEMPT to secure a federal office had at least one good result: it gave rise to two stories so characteristic of their subject, so revealing as far as personality is concerned, that they deserve to be perpetuated. One is related by William H. Herndon in a letter to his collaborator, Jesse W. Weik.

I N 1850 Mr. Lincoln was an applicant, under Taylor's Administration, for Commissioner of the General Land Office; he made arrangements to start for Washington and started from Ramsdell's tavern in this city; he had a companion in the stage, for it was in old stage times, who was a gentleman from Kentucky, educated, cultured, and a man of accomplishments, but, like all warm and goodhearted men, he loved the good and cheerful. The two men, Lincoln and his friend, started for Washington early in the morning, eating their breakfast before day. After they had got in the stage and had ridden some miles, the Kentucky gentleman pulled out of his pocket a small plug of the very best tobacco from the "sacred soil of Virginia," and handed it to Mr. Lincoln, with a fine tortoise-shell penknife, and said to Lincoln: "Stranger, will you take a chew?" and to which Mr. Lincoln said: "Thank you, I never chew." The two rode on for some miles. When they got near Taylorville, some twenty-five miles from this place and east of it, the Kentucky gentleman pulled out a fine cigar case filled with the very best and choicest of Havana cigars, opened it, got out his lighter, and said to Lincoln: "Please have a fine Havana cigar," and to which Mr. Lincoln replied in his kindest manner: "Thanks, stranger, I never smoke." The gentleman lit his cigar and very leisurely rode along thumping and bumping over the rough road, smoking and puffing away, conversing all the while. Lincoln and his Kentucky companion became very much attached to each other. Lincoln had told some of his best jokes and the man had spun out his best ideas. They were really much pleased with each other, seemed to fit one another. The Kentucky gentleman was graceful and Lincoln graceless, but somehow or other they fitted each other like brother chums. They rode on merrily and pleasantly for a long, long while to them, for it was a tiresome journey. The stand where the two were to eat their dinners was being approached, was seen in the distance. The Kentucky man threw out of the stage the stub of his cigar, opened his satchel or other thing, and took out a silver case filled with the very best French brandy, took out the cork, got a silver cup, and handing them to Lincoln, saying: "Stranger, take a glass of the best of French brandies, won't you?" and to which Mr. Lincoln said: "No, I thank you, mister, I never drink." This peculiarity seemed to amuse the Kentucky gentleman very much; he threw himself back against the front of the stage and good-naturedly and laughing said: "See here, stranger, rather, my jolly companion, I have gone through the world a good deal and have had much experience with men and women of all classes, and in all climes, and I have noticed one thing—" Mr. Lincoln, here breaking in anxiously, asked his companion: "What is it, what is it?" "It is this," said the Kentucky man. "My observation, my experience, is, among men, that those who have no vices have damned few virtues." Lincoln was fond of a joke as you know, looked at his friend sharply to see if it was a joke or was intended for an insult, intending to pitch him out of the stage if it was an insult, and to laugh over it if a joke. Lincoln was quickly convinced that the man was good-natured, kind, gentlemanly, etc.; and then he burst out into a loud laugh saying: "It's good, it's too good to be lost, and I shall tell it to my friends." Lincoln really laughed himself tired, kicked out, in fact, the bottom of the stage, tore out the crown of his hat by running his hand through it, etc., etc. The two friends became bosom ones and landed in Washington together.

9

THE OTHER ANECDOTE of Lincoln's quest for office is also told in Herndon's words.

DURING THIS SAME JOURNEY occurred an incident for which Thomas H. Nelson, of Terre Haute, Indiana, who was appointed Minister to Chile by Lincoln when he was President, is authority. "In the spring of 1849," relates Nelson, "Judge Abram Hammond, who was afterwards Governor of Indiana, and I arranged to go from Terre Haute to Indianapolis in the stage coach. An entire day was usually consumed in the journey. By daybreak the stage had arrived from the West, and as we stepped in we discovered that the entire back seat was occupied by a long, lank individual, whose head seemed to protrude from one end of the coach and his feet from the other. He was the sole occupant, and was sleeping soundly. Hammond slapped him familiarly on the shoulder, and asked him if he had chartered the stage for the day. The stranger, now wide awake, responded, 'Certainly not,' and at once took the front seat, politely surrendering to us the place of honor and comfort. We took in our travelling companion at a glance. A queer, odd-looking fellow he was, dressed in a well-worn and ill-fitting suit of bombazine, without vest or cravat, and a twenty-five cent palm hat on the back of his head. His very prominent features in repose seemed dull and expressionless. Regarding him as a good subject for merriment we perpetrated several jokes. He took them all with the utmost innocence and good-nature, and joined in the laugh, although at his own expense. At noon we stopped at a wayside hostelry for dinner. We invited him to eat with us, and he approached the table as if he considered it a great honor. He sat with about half his person on a small chair, and held his hat under his arm during the meal. Resuming our journey after dinner, conversation drifted into a discussion of the comet, a subject that was then agitating the scientific world, in which the stranger took the deepest interest. He made many startling suggestions and asked many questions. We amazed him with words of learned length and thundering sound. After an astounding display of wordy pyrotechnics the dazed and bewildered stranger asked: 'What is going to be the upshot of this comet business?' I replied that I was not certain, in fact I differed from most scientists and philosophers, and was inclined to the opinion that the world would follow the darned thing off! Late in the evening we reached Indianapolis, and hurried to Browning's hotel, losing sight of the stranger altogether. We retired to our room to brush and wash away the dust of the journey. In a few minutes I descended to the portico, and there descried our long, gloomy fellow traveler in the center of an admiring group of lawyers, among whom were Judges McLean and Huntington, Edward Hannigan, Albert S. White, and Richard W. Thompson, who seemed to be amused and interested in a story he was telling. I inquired of Browning, the landlord, who he was. "Abraham Lincoln, of Illinois, a member of Congress," was the response. I was thunderstruck at the announcement. I hastened upstairs and told Hammond the startling news, and together we emerged from the hotel by a back door and went down an alley to another house, thus avoiding further contact with our now distinguished fellow traveler. Curiously enough, years after this, Hammond had vacated the office of Governor of Indiana a few days before Lincoln arrived in Indianapolis, on his way to Washington to be inaugurated President. I had many opportunities after the stage ride to cultivate Mr. Lincoln's acquaintance, and was a zealous advocate of his nomination and election to the Presidency. Before leaving his home for Washington, Mr. Lincoln caused John P. Usher and myself to be invited to accompany him. We agreed to join him in Indianapolis. On reaching that city the Presidential party had already arrived, and upon inquiry we were informed that the President-elect was in the dining room of the hotel, at supper. Passing through, we saw that every seat at the numerous tables was occupied, but failed to find Mr. Lincoln. As we were nearing the door to the office of the hotel, a long arm reached to my shoulder and a shrill voice exclaimed, "Hello, Nelson! do you think, after all, the world is going to follow the darned thing off?" It was Mr. Lincoln.

CHAPTER EIGHT

Leader of the Illinois Bar

*L**INCOLN HAD ENTERED** Congress with high hopes; he finished his term a disillusioned man. As a member of the House of Representatives he had succeeded only in alienating his constituents; as an office seeker he had been snubbed. He resolved to have no more to do with politics, and to practice law with greater earnestness than ever before.*

During his partner's absence in Washington, Herndon had succeeded in holding most of the firm's clients. When Lincoln returned, he remonstrated that he had no right to share in the profits for this period. Herndon replied that the older man had given him a chance when he was young and unknown, and that he wanted to continue the partnership as if there had been no hiatus in it. Lincoln was willing, so the old relationship was resumed.

Two years in the nation's capital had left Lincoln unchanged in appearance and manner. "When he returned from Washington in 1849," wrote Isaac N. Arnold, who knew him well, "he would have been instantly recognized in any court room in the United States, as being a very tall specimen of that type of long, large-boned men produced in the northern part of the Mississippi valley, and exhibiting its most peculiar characteristics in the mountains of Virginia, Tennessee, Kentucky, and in Illinois. He would have been instantly recognized as a Western man, and his stature, figure, dress, manner, voice, and accent indicated that he was from the Northwest. In manner he was cordial, frank, and friendly, and, although not without dignity, he put every one perfectly at ease. The first impression a stranger meeting him or hearing him speak would receive, was that of a kind, sincere and genuinely good man, of perfect truthfulness and integrity. He was one of those men whom everybody liked at first sight. If he spoke, before many words were uttered, the hearer would be impressed with his clear, direct good sense, his simple, homely, short Anglo-Saxon words, by his wonderful wit and humor."

1

AFTER LINCOLN'S RETURN from Washington he resumed his circuit practice, spending nearly six months out of every twelve accompanying the judge from court to court in the Eighth Judicial Circuit. Benjamin P. Thomas follows the circuit, and recreates the conditions under which Lincoln conducted his nomadic practice.

W HEN LINCOLN RESUMED the practice of law, the Eighth Judicial Circuit comprised fourteen counties in central and eastern Illinois. As he made his first trip around the circuit in the fall of 1849, he found it not much different from what it had been before. Population was increasing rapidly; log cabins were giving place to frame dwellings; some farmers were wearing boots and clothes of manufactured cloth, instead of brogans and homespun. But farm implements were still crude and insufficient, although the more progressive farmers were replacing scythes, cradles and wooden plows with reapers, mowers and steel-shod plows, and were using horses in place of oxen. While buggies, carryalls and stage coach lines were gradually supplanting or supplementing saddle horses as a means of conveyance, travel was still hazardous and slow, for little or no improvement had been made in the roads, which were muddy and often impassable in winter, dusty in summer and fall, and rutted all year round.

The rate of speed depended on the roads. Under favorable conditions an average of four to five and a half miles an hour was good time; when roads were bad a mile an hour was about all a struggling team could make. Thirty-five miles was a good day's drive. Frequently Judge Davis and the lawyers had to rise before dawn and drive all day and into the night to reach the next court on time. Often in early spring and late autumn the weather was uncomfortably cold, with occasional flurries of snow. Sometimes lawyers arrived in town drenched to the skin by a shower which had overtaken them on the open prairie. Again, it was necessary to drive all day in the rain. Wooden bridges were often carried away by freshets, in which case swollen streams must be forded or swum. Runaways and breakdowns were frequent. Houses were sometimes miles apart; inns were small, cold and cheerless, villages unkempt, crude and at certain seasons almost isolated.

Little change had taken place in social life. Men still gathered at the stores or groceries to discuss crops, weather, roads, politics, letters from friends who had gone to California in the Gold Rush, and the latest news and local gossip. Around the stove in winter and on the porch in summer one could always find a group whittling, smoking, bespattering the surrounding terrain with tobacco juice, as they talked, joked and ruminated. Here was the forum of the people, where Lincoln, as he traveled from town to town, could learn the workings of their minds, how their ideas changed from one court term to the next, how they reacted to certain conditions and circumstances.

Old recreations and social festivities like hunting, house-raisings, cornhuskings and quilting bees were being supplemented by sewing societies, charivaries, spirit-rappings and lyceums and debating societies. But books and newspapers were few, and intellectual indeed was the home which boasted more than a five-foot bookshelf.

Under such conditions court week was a gala time for villagers and farmers. The latter flocked to town by scores to purchase supplies, renew friendships and enjoy the court proceedings. Judge and lawyers were looked on as celebrities, and a popular lawyer with political ambitions could build up a large potential following from acquaintances and admirers.

When the circuit lawyers arrived in town they were met by the local lawyers who wished to obtain their assistance. These associations were usually not permanent, but merely for the trial of a particular case. Lincoln's only permanent connection on the circuit was made with Ward Hill Lamon, of Danville, in 1853.

The Supreme Court Library at Springfield was the only collection of legal books on the circuit, and after leaving Springfield, lawyers were dependent on their memories or such books as they carried with them. For the most part, however, cases were simple and were decided on principle rather than by legal precedent. With little time for preparation, common sense and sound reasoning were the principal requisites of success.

The need for volume, accentuated by the prevailing low fees, prevented lawyers from specializing to any extent. Most of them took whatever cases they could get. Lincoln, for example, handled partition suits, foreclosures, appeals from justices' courts, actions in debt, trespass, replevin, suits over dower rights. Most of his cases were of the dull, humdrum sort, typical of farming communities, with an occasional slander suit or divorce case providing some sensation.

Although civil suits made up the bulk of Lincoln's practice, he did some criminal work. He defended a man who was accused of keeping a disorderly house, an adulterer, three persons charged with gambling and one charged with keeping a gambling house. He defended two larceny suits, two perjury suits, four indictments for illegal sales of liquor, three assault cases and two murder cases. As attorney for the plaintiff he secured a verdict of guilty in a bastardy case. His reputation as a prosecutor is attested by his being appointed special prosecuting attorney at Pekin in May, 1853, in order to insure a conviction in a vicious rape case.

One might assume that the local lawyers wrote the pleadings and did the preparatory work, leaving the court work to the circuit lawyers who assisted them; but this was not the case, at least so far as Lincoln was concerned. Hundreds of pleadings in Lincoln's handwriting have been found in the various courthouses of the circuit, and hundreds more have disappeared from the files. Always neatly and carefully drawn, and usually signed by Lincoln with his own last name and that of his associate, they prove that besides conducting the trials, Lincoln also did his full share of the laborious formal work.

So far as the firm of Lincoln and Herndon was concerned, Lincoln did most of the circuit work. The firm had a large practice in Menard County, and after that county was transferred from the circuit Herndon handled practically all the firm's business there. When the circuit was reorganized in 1853 he also finished the pending cases in some of the counties which were transferred to other circuits and which Lincoln could no longer visit because of conflict in court dates. Most of the time, however, he remained in Springfield. . . .

By 1853, the growth of population had brought such an increase in the volume of litigation that it was necessary to decrease the circuit's size from fourteen counties to eight; and Shelby, Macon, Christian, Moultrie, Edgar and Piatt were transferred to other circuits. . . .

By the end of the decade of the fifties the increase in population, with the resulting volume of business, and the building of a railroad net, which made travel quick and easy, were destined to bring an end to circuit life; but the influence of these factors, especially the latter, was little felt as yet. While a few of the more successful lawyers were giving up circuit practice, and some were confining themselves to counties contiguous to their homes, most of them, like Lincoln, still found it necessary to travel the whole circuit.

2

THE EIGHTH CIRCUIT was more than a means of livelihood to Lincoln: it was a way of life. It is portrayed as such by Henry C. Whitney, who first met Lincoln at Urbana in the fall of 1854, and practiced with him in eastern Illinois counties for the next several years. In Whitney's picture, Lincoln divides honors with Judge David Davis, who presided over the circuit after 1849.

T HE J U D G E W A S A S P O N D E R O U S in his excellent judgment and commonsense, as in his physique: (300 plus): and he endeavored to rid cases of their technicalities, and to get down to the actual merits, as expeditiously as possible. He was full of vim and energy on the bench, when there was a necessity for it: but when the evening was come, he would gather his courtiers about him, and make a night of it, similar to the knights of the Round Table, or the Pickwick Club.

As for Lincoln, he had three different moods: first, a *business* mood, when he gave strict and close attention to business, and banished all idea of hilarity, i.e., in counselling or in trying cases, there was no trace of the joker; second, his *melancholy* moods, when his whole nature was immersed in Cimmerian darkness; third, his *don't-care-whether-school-keeps-or-not* mood; when no irresponsible "small boy" could be so apparently careless, or reckless of consequences.

To illustrate the "style" of business in court by something very common: the first term of Davis' court I attended, the Judge was calling through the docket for the first time, in order to dispose of such cases as could be done summarily, and likewise to sort the chaff from the wheat, when he came across a long bill in chancery, drawn by an excellent, but somewhat indolent lawyer, on glancing at which, he exclaimed, "Why, brother Snap, how *did* you rake up energy enough to get up such a long bill?" "Dunno, Jedge," replied the party addressed, squirming in his seat and uneasily scratching his head. The Judge unfolded and held up the bill: "Astonishing, ain't it? Brother Snap did it. Wonderful, eh! Lincoln?" This amounted to an order on Lincoln to heave a joke in at this point, and he was ready of course; he had to be, he never failed. "It's like the lazy preacher," drawled he, "that used to write long sermons, and the explanation was, he got to writin', and was too lazy to stop." This was doubtless improvised and forgotten at once, as I never heard of his repeating it. It was rather feeble, but it was better than the stock word "Humph!" so often printed as a reply, but never really uttered, and it is literally true that

". . . he could not ope
His mouth, but out there flew a trope."

He *always* had a reply, and it was *always* pertinent, and frequently irresistibly funny, but the pity is that his funniest stories don't circulate in polite society or get embalmed in type.

In the evening, all assembled in the Judge's room, where the blazing faggots were piled high, and the yule log was in place, and there were no estrays there, although the door was not locked. Davis' methods were known, and his companions well defined, and, if a novice came, he soon found out both. For instance, an unsophisticated person might be attracted to the Judge's room by our noise, supposing it to be "free for all." If Davis wanted him, he was warmly welcomed, the fatted calf was killed, and the ring put on his finger; but if he really was not desired, he was frozen out by the Judge thus: "Ah! Stop a minute, Lincoln! Have you some business, Mr. Dusenberry?" If Dusenberry should venture: "Well, no! I came designin'—" Davis would interrupt him, "Swett, take Mr. Dusenberry out into the hall, and see what he wants, and come right back yourself, Swett. Shut the door. Now, go ahead, Lincoln! You got as far as—Ha! Ha!! Ha!!! 'She slid down the hill, and—' but wait for Swett. Swett!! Swett!!!" called he. "Hill," (to Lamon) "call Swett in. Now, Lincoln, go ahead," etc. "She slid down the hill, you know. Ho! Ho! Ho!!!" Any one who knew Davis would recognize this.

Would we do nothing but listen to Lincoln's stories? Oh! yes, we frequently talked philosophy, politics, political economy, metaphysics and men; in short, our subjects of conversation ranged through the universe of thought and experience.

One night, we discussed Washington at length, and some speculation was ventured as to whether he was perfect, whether he, too, was not fallible, being human, but Lincoln protested—"Let us believe, as in the days of our youth, that Washington was spotless; it makes human nature better to believe that one human being was perfect: that human perfection is possible."

The Judge had an *orgmathorial* [1] court (as he called it) to try us for any breach of decorum. I wish I could properly narrate some of the proceedings of these courts, some of Swett's speeches, and Lincoln's interjections; they were better than the sketches of the Pickwick Club. Of course, all this was desultory and evanescent, and so designed by the actors; the seal of secrecy was necessarily implied. While, of course, nothing wrong was said or done, yet it would have been atrocious to disclose the secrets of the Judge's coterie in their entertainments, nor do I recollect of ever having heard anything we discussed there mentioned, or alluded to, outside. The Judge did not hesitate to advert to court matters in his hands for action, thus: Some section hands on the Illinois Central Railroad had caught a setter on the prairie, and tied it to a stake, and set fire to the dry grass around it, so that the dog burned to death. As I was attorney for the railway, the rascals, when the case got into court, looked to me for counsel, and I advised them to plead guilty, leaving it for the court to act. This matter coming up in the room, the Judge remarked drily: "This court considers the wanton burning of a bird-dog as a very serious

---

[1] A made-up word.

matter," and I knew by that, that my men would catch it good, unless I could, in some way, hedge against it, which I did next day. At another time, the doctrine of metempsychosis was discussed by the whole crowd, i.e., the doctrine that when one man dies, a child is born which inherits the vital principle—the soul— of the departing one, when suddenly, the conversation was diverted to the character of a mean lawyer on our circuit whom I will call Quirk, but not of our coterie, and after we had picked his character to pieces, so that there was nothing left to it, we resumed on metempsychosis, and as we had about exhausted our ideas about it, it was noticed that Lincoln had ventured nothing on the subject, either of metempsychosis or Quirk, and so (of course, that wouldn't do) Davis gave Lincoln his usual nudge: "Queer doctrine! Queer doctrine!! Eh! Lincoln?" The latter had been rather reticent and abstracted through the evening, but we knew he didn't like Quirk better than the rest of us did, but he was ready as usual; as I have said, he never let Davis' check on his resources go to protest: "I rayther reckon, that's good doctrine, and it's nothin' agin' it, that when Quirk was born, no one died."

In point of fact, the country hotels, wherein were the scenes of our revelries, are all demolished, and ugly brick blocks are substituted in their places, and Samuel of Posen spreads his wares and net for country merchants, where Lincoln, and Davis, and Swett, and Lamon, and the rest were wont to congregate. At Danville, the county seat of Vermilion County, the Judge, and Lincoln, and I used to occupy the ladies' parlor of the old McCormick House, changed to a bedroom during court, the former occupying a three-quarter bed, and Lincoln and I occupying the other one, jointly. This parlor was an "annex" to the main building, and one door opened out directly on the sidewalk, and as the fall term was held in cold weather, we had a hearth wood fire to heat our room. One morning, I was awakened early—before daylight—by my companion sitting up in bed, his figure dimly visible by the ghostly firelight, and talking the wildest and most incoherent nonsense all to himself. A stranger to Lincoln would have supposed he had suddenly gone insane. Of course I knew Lincoln and his idiosyncracies, and felt no alarm, so I listened and laughed. After he had gone on in this way for, say, five minutes, while I was awake, and I know not how long *before* I was awake, he sprang out of bed, hurriedly washed, and jumped into his clothes, put some wood on the fire, and then sat in front of it, moodily, dejectedly, in a most sombre and gloomy spell, till the breakfast bell rang, when he started, as if from sleep, and went with us to breakfast. Neither Davis nor I spoke to him; we knew his trait; it was not remarkable for Lincoln.

At another time, in this same place: one evening, Lincoln was missing immediately after supper: he had no place to go, that we could think of, no friend to visit, no business to do, no client to attend to, and certainly no entertainment to go to; hence "Where is Lincoln?" was the question. I visited all the law offices and stores, but got no trace whatever; and at nine o'clock—an early hour for us—Davis and I went, grumbling and hungry for mental food, to bed, leaving the problem unsolved. Now Lincoln had a furtive way of stealing in on one, unheard, unperceived and unawares; and on this occasion, after we had lain for a short time, our door latch was noiselessly raised, the door opened and the tall form of Abraham Lincoln glided in noiselessly. "Why Lincoln, where *have* you been?" exclaimed the Judge. "I was in hopes you fellers would be asleep," replied he. "Well, I have been to a little show up at the Academy," and he sat before the fire, and narrated all the sights of that most primitive of country shows, given chiefly to school children. Next night, he was missing again; the *show* was still in town, and he stole in as before, and entertained us with a description of new sights—a magic lantern, electrical machine, etc. I told him I had seen all these sights at school. "Yes," he said, sadly, "I now have an advantage over you in, for the first time in my life, seeing these things which are of course common to those, who had, what I did not, a chance at an education, when they were young."

3

IN LINCOLN'S TIME specialization, at least as far as Western lawyers were concerned, was still years in the future. Therefore his practice included almost every kind of case that Illinois and Federal law provided for. Jesse W. Weik offers a sampling, mainly from the 'fifties.

By the time mr. lincoln was nearing the end of his career as a practicing lawyer, the modern damage suit against common carriers and other corporations, especially where based on personal injury, was coming into vogue. Lincoln's experience in that line, as indicated by several cases to which Herndon called my attention, was necessarily limited. One of the earliest was an action brought by him during the partnership with Stuart in which George Stockton demands of James Tolby a hundred dollars for damages to "a cooking stove" in transit between Beardstown and Springfield. Tolby drove "a conveyance for hire" between the points named and was therefore liable as a common carrier. Another case, and probably the first personal injury suit he ever brought against a common carrier, was that of Grubb *vs.* Frink and Walker tried in 1852. The defendants were operating a stagecoach between Rushville and Frederick which overturned one day resulting in a serious injury to one of the passengers. In his account of the accident Mr. Lincoln is sufficiently careful and minute in his averments. After describing the plaintiff's long list of "cuts, bruises, wounds, and divers broken bones," he recites the payment by him of large sums of money paid for the services of physicians and surgeons in the endeavor to be cured of the fractures, bruises, and injuries, and concludes with a demand for damages of one thousand dollars. Another action, that of Jasper Harris *vs.* Great Western Railway Company, was tried in Sangamon County in 1854. The plaintiff was a brakeman whose "right foot, ankle, leg, and thigh while in the service of said company, were so greatly torn, crushed and broken that amputation of his said right limb above the knee was necessary." It was Lincoln's first suit against a railroad company for personal injury and included a demand for ten thousand dollars in damages. The declaration, though signed Lincoln and Herndon, was written by Lincoln, and when contrasted with the phraseology of a bill of complaint as lawyers now word such things is about as crude and primitive as the machinery and appliances of that early period appear when compared to the ponderous and elaborate equipment now in use by the railroads of this day.

Perhaps no case in which Lincoln figured awakened his interest more readily and completely than an action, entitled Hildreth *vs.*

Turner, appealed to the Supreme Court of Illinois from Logan County in the spring of 1854. It related to the validity of a patent, but involved no great legal principle and was otherwise of no especial significance save as Lincoln's connection therewith gave it prominence. In February, 1853, one Alexander Edmonds, a mechanical genius in the town of Mount Pulaski, invented what he called "The Horological Cradle," a contrivance to be "rocked by machinery with a weight running on one or more pulleys; the cradle constituting the pendulum and which, being wound up, would rock itself, thus saving the continual labor to mother and nurses of rocking the cradle." The brief description by the inventor suffices to indicate the objects and character of the proposed apparatus, but notwithstanding its doubtful value from a practical standpoint there was something about it that attracted the interest and attention of Mr. Lincoln. Eventually a disagreement between the inventor of the machine and a man who was induced to advance capital for its manufacture led to a lawsuit in which Lincoln and Herndon represented one side of the controversy when it reached the Supreme Court. "Although Lincoln and I were duly retained," related Herndon, "Mr. Lincoln, owing to his natural bent for the study of mechanical appliances, soon became so enamoured of the case that he assumed entire charge of our end of it. The model of the machine was for a time exhibited in a store window in town and eventually reached our office where Mr. Lincoln became deeply absorbed in it. He would dilate at great length on its merits for the benefit of our callers or any one else who happened into the office and manifested the least interest in it. Although the papers in the case indicated that Lincoln and Herndon were of counsel, I recall that I had but little beyond a nominal part in it. All the papers were drawn by Mr. Lincoln himself, a division of our labors to which I readily consented because, in view of my apparent lack of faith in the enterprise, I apprehend he suspected I was willing that he should assume the entire responsibility of winning or losing the suit."

The record of the case recites that the inventor professed to have obtained a "patent for said invention and had been exhibiting a model of the same; that the patent right would be valuable and could be sold for a large amount of money, etc."; but before the case was decided it was discovered that Edmonds had no letters of patent for the cradle, its machinery or mode of operation, but only for an ornamental design for a "horological cradle" as set out in the specifications. The court ruled against the patentability of the contrivance, holding that every one should be presumed to know that a baby cradle would not be patentable by the description so far as the application of its use is concerned.

While the case was under consideration by the Supreme Court, the model was brought into the room and set to going—a proceeding in which Lincoln was plainly interested as shown by his willingness to enlighten the judges, some of whom ventured to make inquiries regarding the *modus operandi.* Although the inventor claimed to have disposed of his rights in the States of Mississippi, Georgia, Alabama, Florida, and South Carolina for ten thousand dollars, he made no mention of his interest in Illinois, Indiana, Missouri, and other near-by states, probably because the people in those localities, like Herndon, had seen the device at a range close enough to make them more or less cautious in the investment of their surplus capital. . . .

The shrinkage in a lawyer's practice in Lincoln's day attributable to the lack of bodily injury suits was more than counterbalanced by the then popular slander suit. It was a most abundant source of litigation and hardly a term of court was allowed to pass without one or more actions of that kind. The money demanded for damages was invariably large, and even though the injured party sometimes recovered judgment for the full amount demanded, he frequently waived payment of all but a nominal sum. Of these primitive and sprightly contests Lincoln had his proportionate share. In Coles County, Illinois, in the fall of 1843, in conjunction with Usher F. Linder, he appeared for the plaintiff in the slander suit of Bagley *vs.* Vanmeter. Evidently Lincoln's prospects, so far as a generous fee is concerned, were not very encouraging, for a document written by him and signed by his client, the plaintiff, has been found in which the latter, referring to the judgment in his behalf which he expects, makes the following pertinent reservation regarding the pay due his attorneys: "I assign twenty dollars to Usher F. Linder and thirty dollars to Logan & Lincoln if said judgment shall amount to so much." Unfortunately for all concerned, when the records were all made and the money paid in, the judgment yielded a total of eighty dollars.

In the case of Thomas McKibben, who brought suit against Jonathan Hart demanding two thousand dollars damages because the
latter had called him a horsethief, Mr. Lincoln represented the
plaintiff. Trial took place during the May term, 1845, of the Circuit Court of Coles County, Illinois. Mr. Lincoln's father, Thomas
Lincoln, lived a few miles south of Charleston, the county seat,
which will doubtless account for the fact that the latter's son figured so frequently in the litigation of that locality. In the case
mentioned, Lincoln secured for his client a judgment for about
two hundred dollars, of which thirty-five dollars was assigned to
him for his fee and which he deposited with the clerk of the court
with instructions to pay the same to his father. In due time
Thomas Lincoln trudged over to Charleston, where the money
which, doubtless, was a welcome addition to the old gentleman's
meager income, was turned over to him. The receipt, drawn up by
the clerk, was duly signed, but the name, Thomas Lincoln, was
written by his stepson, John D. Johnston. . . .

One [other suit] was the case of Dungey *vs.* Spencer tried at
the town of Clinton, in Dewitt County, in the spring of 1855.
Lincoln represented Dungey, the plaintiff, and Lawrence Weldon,
afterwards a member of the United States Court of Claims, the
defendant. The basis of the action, as set out in the declaration in
Lincoln's hand, and for which several thousand dollars in damages
was asked, was the charge that the defendant "in the presence of
divers good citizens falsely and maliciously spoke and uttered of
and concerning the plaintiff, these false scandalous, malicious,
and defamatory words: 'Black Bill (meaning the plaintiff) is a
Negro and it will be easily proved if called for.' " It was a family
quarrel, Dungey, who was a Portuguese and somewhat dark com-
plexioned, having married Spencer's sister. The law of Illinois
made it a crime for a Negro to marry a white woman, and hence
the words were slanderous. It is unnecessary to dwell on the details
of the trial. It suffices to state that Lincoln won, recovering for his
client, the plaintiff, a judgment for six hundred dollars, of which
amount the latter on the advice of his counsel remitted four hundred dollars; the defendant meanwhile assuming payment of Lincoln's fee and the costs of the suit.

"At this juncture," related Mr. Weldon, "Mr. Lincoln proposed to leave the question of the amount of his fee to my asso-

ciates, Mr. C. H. Moore and myself. We protested against this and insisted that he should fix the amount of his own fee. After a few moments' thought he said: 'Well, gentlemen, don't you think I have honestly earned twenty-five dollars?' We were astonished, and had he said one hundred dollars it would have been nearer what we expected. The judgment was a large one for those days; he had attended the case at two terms of court, had been engaged for two days in a hotly contested suit, and his client's adversary was going to pay the bill. The simplicity of his character in money matters is well illustrated by the fact that for all this service he only charged twenty-five dollars."

4

AS FAR AS LINCOLN'S practice is known to laymen, his most famous feat was his successful defense of William, or "Duff" Armstrong. Duff, a son of his old friend Jack Armstrong of New Salem days, was charged with murder as the result of a killing which had occurred at a camp meeting in the summer of 1857. The case was tried in the spring of the following year at Beardstown, Cass County. There, as Woldman makes clear, Lincoln rose to heights of eloquence rare even for him.

LINCOLN WAS ANXIOUS that the jury be composed of young men, believing that youthful hot blood would be more sympathetic to the plight of his young client. He was successful in selecting a venire whose members averaged less than thirty years of age. The jury impaneled, the trial began with Judge James Harriot presiding. There were about twenty-five witnesses. . . .

The State's star witness was Charles Allen. He had already testified at the trial of James H. Norris, also accused of participating in the murder. Norris was found guilty of manslaughter largely through Allen's testimony that under the bright moonlight he had seen Norris hit Metzker on the back of the head with a club-like object and Armstrong strike him in the right eye with a slingshot. Now Allen repeated the same story, and the prosecution's case was seemingly clinched.

"Lincoln sat with his head thrown back, his steady gaze apparently fixed upon one spot of the blank ceiling, entirely oblivious to what was happening about him, and without a single variation of feature or noticeable movement of any muscle of his face," is the recollection of Judge Abram Bergen, then a young lawyer present in the court room.

Lincoln took over the witness for cross-examination. With apparent unconcern he questioned Allen regarding unimportant details. Then as to the fatal blows themselves; tell about them again.

Did you actually see the fight? Yes. Well, where were you standing at the time? About one hundred fifty feet away from the combatants. Describe this weapon again. The slingshot was pictured in detail. And what time did you say all this occurred? Eleven o'clock at night. How could you see from a distance of one hundred and fifty feet at eleven o'clock at night? The moon was shining real bright. A full moon? Yes, a full moon, and as high in the heavens as the sun would be at ten o'clock in the morning. He was positive about that.

Then with dramatic suddenness Lincoln requested the sheriff to bring him an almanac for the year 1857. Turning to the date of August 29, the night of the murder, he pointed a long forefinger to the page and bade Allen to read. Did not the almanac specifically say that the moon on that night was barely past the first quarter instead of being full? And wasn't it a fact that the almanac also revealed that instead of the moon being high in the heavens in the position of the morning sun, it had actually disappeared by eleven o'clock? And wasn't it a further fact that it was actually so dark at the time that it was impossible to see distinctly from a distance of fifty feet, let alone one hundred and fifty feet?

These revelations caused a tremendous sensation. Of course, the court took judicial notice of the almanac, but Lincoln desired to have it introduced in evidence. He submitted it to the inspection of the prosecutors and the judge and then it was handed to the jury. The jury smiled and nodded approvingly. Allen as a witness was destroyed. But the case was not yet over. The prosecution strove valiantly to make up for lost ground, but there were no other eye witnesses.

The defense then called a number of witnessses—persons to testify as to Duff's good reputation; witnesses who had seen Metzker fall from his horse; a Dr. Charles E. Parker, who declared that just such a fall or blow struck by Norris could very likely have caused the fatal injury. But extremely damaging to the State's case was the testimony of one Watkins, who swore that the slingshot in evidence belonged not to Duff but to him; that it was continuously in his own possession on the night of the fight, but that he had thrown it away the following day, at the very spot where it had been found.

Then followed the arguments of counsel to the jury. The prosecutors reviewed all the sordid details of the "atrocious crime"; denounced the young ruffians who had been terrorizing the countryside; urged that the jury make an example of Duff, and demanded that they inflict upon him the penalty of death.

After Walker's argument, Lincoln arose. The silence of the room was broken only by the heartbreaking sobs of Duff's grief-stricken mother. Tall, gaunt, and homely, Lincoln had risen to great heights both at the bar and in the political arena in Illinois. And now he was about to begin the greatest jury speech of his career. The crowd in the courtroom had been attracted not so much by the case itself as by the prominence of Lincoln. It was a sultry hot day and the audience was sweltering. Unconcernedly Lincoln took off his coat and vest and removed the stock that clung uncomfortably to his large Adam's apple.

"Slowly and carefully," relates Walker, "he reviewed the whole testimony and picked it all to pieces." Allen's story should be given no credence, Lawyer Lincoln urged the members of the jury. Having been mistaken about the light of the moon, he was undoubtedly mistaken as to other points of his testimony, he declared. Soon one of his suspenders fell from a shoulder, but paying no attention to it, he allowed it to hang during the rest of the speech. When he spoke "his eyes brightened perceptibly, and every facial movement seemed to emphasize his feeling and add expression to his thoughts," is the testimony of Judge Abram Bergen. "Then vanished all consciousness of his uncouth appearance, his awkward manner, or even his high-keyed unpleasant voice, and it required an extraordinary effort of the will to divert attention to the man, so concentrated was every mind upon what he was saying."

Lincoln had mastered some technical questions in anatomy and explained his theory that it was more likely that Metzker had died, not from any wound inflicted by Duff, but rather from the blow of Norris's club or from repeated falls from his horse. And he especially emphasized Watkins' testimony that he, and not the defendant, was the owner of the slingshot. Lincoln cut open the weapon and demonstrated to the jury that it was made exactly as Watkins had sworn he had made it.

After completely analyzing the evidence for nearly an hour, Lincoln devoted another ten minutes to an appeal that melted the hearts of the jury and brought joy to the sorrowing mother and freedom to her erring son. He was not arguing this case for a fee, he declared. In fact, he was indebted to Duff Armstrong's mother and deceased father in a manner he could never repay. When he was a stranger in New Salem, penniless, homeless, and alone, Jack and Hannah Armstrong, struggling pioneers though they were, had opened wide the doors of their humble cabin and had given him shelter and food. He had rocked this very defendant, as an infant, to sleep in his rough-hewn cradle. Their home had been his home. He had virtually been one of the family. Deep in his heart he felt that the son of such kindly, lovable parents could be no base murderer. And now that big-hearted Jack Armstrong was in his grave, the grief-stricken widow, alone in her plight, should be saved further sorrow. He drew a touching picture of the hopelessness, suffering, and desolation in store for the poor old mother, if the jury saw fit to deprive her of her boy. As a pleader for her son's life, God willed he should repay his debt to his old benefactors. He prayed that he would not be unworthy of the task.

Real tears trickled down his homely face. "But they were genuine," insists Mr. Shaw, the special prosecutor. "His terrible sincerity could not help but rouse the same passion in the jury. I have said it a hundred times that it was Lincoln's speech that saved that criminal from the gallows." For when Lincoln sat down some of the jurors were seen to wipe misty eyes with their rough toil-worn hands. The prosecutor concluded the State's case, and Lincoln handed Judge Harriott two carefully written requests for special instructions to the jury. Neither one referred to the moon incident, but dealt with the question of reasonable doubt and the endeavor of the defense to shift the guilt to Norris, already found guilty of the murder.

With the instructions completed, Duff's fate was soon in the hands of the jury.

"They'll clear him before dark, Hannah," Lincoln was heard to encourage the heartbroken mother as with his arm around her shoulder, he tenderly escorted her from the courtroom. He was right. By their first ballot the jurors acquitted the defendant.

5

ALMOST AS WELL KNOWN as the Armstrong case is Lincoln's suit against the Illinois Central Railroad for $5,000, the largest fee he ever received. That suit and the case out of which it grew are summarized by Harry E. Pratt.

T HE CHARTER of the Illinois Central . . . provided that the company should pay to the State each year 5 per cent of its gross receipts. In return, all its property was exempted from taxation for six years. At the end of this period the charter provided that "an annual tax for State purposes shall be assessed by the auditor upon all the property and assets of every kind and description belonging to said corporation."

Construction of the railroad began as soon as it was chartered, and in May, 1853, the line from the Illinois River to Bloomington was completed and in operation. In August, 1853, McLean County started proceedings to force the Illinois Central to pay taxes on the property it owned within the county. A county tax in addition to the payment of 5 per cent of its gross earnings to the State would have been practically impossible, and would have endangered the life of the road. The company refused to pay and brought suit in the McLean County Circuit Court to enjoin collection. Lincoln saw the importance of the issue and was anxious to have a part in the litigation.

Champaign County also considered taxing the railroad's property and Lincoln talked the question over with T. R. Webber, the circuit clerk. When the railroad sought to obtain his services he felt under obligation to Webber and wrote to him on September 12, 1853, suggesting that the two counties make common cause. "I am somewhat trammeled by what has passed between you and me," he wrote, "feeling that you have the first right to my services, if you choose to secure me a fee something near such as I can get from the other side.

"The question in its magnitude to the Co. on the one hand and the counties in which the Co. has land on the other is the largest law question that can now be got up in the State, and therefore in justice to myself, I can not afford, if I can help it, to miss a fee altogether."

Three weeks later he wrote to Mason Brayman, one of the Illinois Central attorneys: "Neither the county of McLean nor any one on its behalf has yet made any engagement with me in relation to its suit with the Illinois Central Railroad on the subject of taxation. I am now free to make an engagement for the road, and if you think of it you may 'count me in.' "

In due course Lincoln was retained by the railroad, and argued the charter case in the McLean County Circuit Court in the fall of 1854. The case was decided against him, and an appeal was taken to the Supreme Court. It was stipulated "that the only question to be made in the Supreme Court" was whether the road could be taxed by the county.

In the Supreme Court, on February 28, 1854, the case was argued orally by Lincoln and James F. Joy for the railroad, and by Stephen T. Logan and John T. Stuart for McLean County. It was continued, and reargument was ordered. Two years later, on January 16–17, 1856, the case was heard again, with Lincoln making the opening argument and Joy concluding for the railroad. The court unanimously held that, under the constitution, the Legislature could make exceptions from the rule of uniformity in taxation, and that the provision in the road's charter requiring payment to the State of a percentage of its gross earnings was such an exception; and therefore counties could not tax the road. Accordingly the decision of the McLean court was reversed. Thus Lincoln and Joy were sustained.

Up to this point in the discussion of the case writers agree, but in the subsequent details which relate to Lincoln's efforts to collect his fee they differ widely. Herndon said Lincoln went to Chicago and presented a bill for $2,000 in addition to the retainer fee. Joy, Lincoln's associate, who had been paid a salary of $10,000 a year by the railroad in 1854, but had resigned soon after, received $1,200 for his services in the case. Joy said Lincoln wrote to him asking that his fee be "a particularly beautiful section of land belonging to the company." This assertion, made by Joy many years after the trial, is hard to reconcile with Lincoln's lack of interest in the acquisition of land.

At any rate, Lincoln eventually submitted a bill for $5,000 for his fee, to which the officials of the company objected as being excessive. From the standpoint of the amount saved to the company it was not excessive, but the payment of a $5,000 fee was unheard of in the West, and it is probable that few Eastern lawyers had received so large a fee up to that time. After waiting nearly a year for his money, Lincoln determined to bring suit against the company. In January, 1857, he filed an affidavit with the circuit clerk of McLean County, stating that he desired to take the depositions of seven lawyers to be read in evidence. Lincoln prepared his case for the March, 1857, term of the McLean court, but the entire time of the court was taken up with a murder trial, so a special term was set for June 15th.

Before this date an official of the Illinois Central called on Lincoln and discussed the settlement of his fee. If a compromise was suggested, it was refused by Lincoln. Moreover the railroad official was made to understand the strength of the latter's position. For more than twenty years Lincoln had been a close friend of Jesse K. Dubois, the State Auditor, who could reject the railroad's estimate of the value of its property for tax purposes; he was the acknowledged adviser of Governor Bissell, and on very friendly terms with Ozias M. Hatch, the Secretary of State. In plain words, Lincoln was in a position where he could do the Illinois Central a great deal of good, if he chose, or a great deal of harm. This was recognized by the railroad and definite steps, the character of which are not clear, were taken to keep Lincoln's influence on the side of the railroad. This is brought out in a letter written by Ebenezer Lane, resident director in Chicago, to W. H. Osborn, the president of the Illinois Central, on May 14, 1857.

"We can now look back and in some degree estimate the narrow escape we have made (I hope and believe entirely) from burdens of the most serious character. While Lincoln was prosecuting his lawsuit for fees, it was natural for him to expect a dismissal from the Company's service and being a politician aspiring to the Senate, to entertain plans of making an attack upon the company not only in a revengeful spirit, but as subservient to his future advancement. He had seen the obscurity of those sections of our charter relating to taxation, which, unexplained by the History of the Charter, seem to bear (even more naturally) such a construction as would impose on us an amount not exceeding 3/4/100 in addition to the 5 per cent. He kept this to himself, but before our settlement with him, the Auditor, a vain, self-sufficient but weak man, approached him with a view to retain him for the State for consultation. Lincoln answered he was not free from his engagement to us, but expected a discharge. He therefore gave him no detailed opinion, but expressed his sense of the great magnitude which the Auditor was bound to protect. This had no other effect probably than to raise still higher the Auditor's opinion of himself.

"Meanwhile we settled with Lincoln and fortunately took him out of the field, or rather engaged him in our interests. This is the more fortunate, as he proves to be not only the most prominent of his political party, but the acknowledged special adviser of the Bissell administration."

If Lincoln was specially retained by the railroad in May, 1857, it is natural to ask why he continued his suit against the railroad for the collection of his fee. The explanation is that the officials of the railroad in the West had to convince the board of directors in New York that the fee had to be paid, and paid at a time when the company was very short of funds.

At the special term of the McLean court, presided over by Judge Jesse O. Norton by exchange of circuits with Judge David Davis, the case of Abraham Lincoln *vs.* Illinois Central Railroad was called on June 18, 1857. No one appeared for the railroad and judgment was rendered by default. But John M. Douglass, general counsel for the company, appeared that afternoon and asked that the judgment be set aside. When called again, Lincoln told the history of the services which he had rendered the railroad, and by permission of Douglass, read the statement of six attorneys that the $5,000 fee was reasonable. The trial, according to the recollections of several who were present, was a mere formality. Douglass reminded Lincoln of the retainer fee, which both men seem to have remembered was $200 instead of $250. Judgment was entered in Lincoln's favor for $4,800.

Lincoln waited a month, but still the fee was not paid. It was, perhaps, with some hope of collecting it that he went to New York

City in late July. Disgusted with his reception by the Illinois Central officials, he returned home, and on August 1, an execution was issued to the sheriff of McLean County to seize enough property of the railroad to satisfy the judgment. The fee was then paid. The panic of 1857 struck a month later, and had he not collected when he did it is doubtful if he would have received his money for a considerable time.

6

THE COLORFUL ASPECTS of Lincoln's circuit practice have tended to obscure the fact that for at least half of each year he practiced law in Springfield. His office—both workshop and place of refuge—is sketched by John H. Littlefield, a student there in the last years of Lincoln's practice.

M Y BROTHER MET MR. LINCOLN in Ottawa, Illinois, one day, and said to him: "I have a brother who I would very much like to have enter your office as a student." "All right!" was his reply; "send him down and we will take a look at him." I was then studying law at Grand Rapids, Michigan, and on hearing from my brother I immediately packed up and started for Springfield. I arrived there on Saturday night. On Sunday Mr. Lincoln was pointed out to me. I well remember this first sight of him. He was striding along, holding little Tad, then about six years old, by the hand, who could with the greatest difficulty keep up with his father. In the morning I applied at the office of Lincoln and Herndon for admission as a student. The office was on the second floor of a brick building on the public square, opposite the courthouse. You went up one flight of stairs and then passed along a hallway to the rear office, which was a medium-sized room. There was one long table in the center of the room, and a shorter one running in the opposite direction, forming a "T" and both were covered with green baize. There were two windows which looked into the back yard. In one corner was an old-fashioned secretary with pigeonholes and a drawer, and here Mr. Lincoln and his partner kept their law papers. There was also a bookcase containing about two hundred volumes of law as well as miscellaneous books. The morning I entered the office Mr. Lincoln and his partner, Mr.

Herndon, were both present. Mr. Lincoln addressed his partner thus: "Billy, this is the young man of whom I spoke to you. What- ever arrangement you make with him will be satisfactory to me." Then, turning to me, he said, "I hope you will not become so enthusiastic in your studies of Blackstone and Kent as did two young men whom we had here. Do you see that spot over there?" pointing to a large ink stain on the wall. "Well, one of these young men got so enthusiastic in his pursuit of legal lore that he fired an inkstand at the other one's head, and that is the mark he made." I immediately began to clean up about the office a little. Mr. Lincoln had been in Congress and had the usual amount of seeds to distribute to the farmers. These were sent out with Free- Soil and Republican documents. In my efforts to clean up, I found that some of the seeds had sprouted in the dirt that had collected in the office. Judge Logan and Milton Hay occupied the front offices on the same floor with Lincoln and Herndon, and one day Mr. Hay came in and said with apparent astonishment: "What's happened here?" "Oh, nothing," replied Lincoln, pointing to me, "only this young man has been cleaning up a little." One of Lin- coln's striking characteristics was his simplicity, and nowhere was this trait more strikingly exhibited than in his willingness to re- ceive instruction from anybody and everybody. One day he came into the office and addressing his partner, said: "Billy, what's the meaning of antithesis?" Mr. Herndon gave him the definition of the word, and I said: "Mr. Lincoln if you will allow me, I will give you an example." "All right, John, go ahead," said Mr. Lincoln in his hearty manner. "Phillips says, in his essay on Napoleon, 'A pretended patriot, he impoverished the country; a professed Catholic, he imprisoned the Pope,' " etc. Mr. Lincoln thanked me and seemed very much pleased. Returning from off the circuit once he said to Mr. Herndon: "Billy, I heard a good story while I was up in the country. Judge——was complimenting the land- lord on the excellence of his beef. 'I am surprised,' he said, 'That you have such good beef. You must have to kill a whole critter when you want any.' 'Yes,' said the landlord, 'we never kill less than a whole critter.' "

Lincoln's favorite position when unraveling some knotty law point was to stretch both of his legs at full length upon a chair in front of him. In this position, with books on the table nearby and in his lap, he worked up his case. No matter how deeply interested in his work, if any one came in he had something humorous and pleasant to say, and usually wound up by telling a joke or an ancedote. I have heard him relate the same story three times within as many hours to persons who came in at different periods, and every time he laughed as heartily and enjoyed it as if it were a new story. His humor was infectious. I had to laugh because I thought it funny that Mr. Lincoln enjoyed a story so repeatedly told.

There was no order in the office at all. The firm of Lincoln and Herndon kept no books. They divided their fees without taking any receipts or making any entries on books. One day Mr. Lincoln received $5,000 as a fee in a railroad case. He came in and said: "Well, Billy," addressing his partner, Mr. Herndon, "here is our fee; sit down and let me divide." He counted out $2,500 to his partner, and gave it to him with as much nonchalance as he would have given a few cents for a paper. Cupidity had no abiding place in his nature.

I took a good deal of pains in getting up a speech which I wanted to deliver during a political campaign. I told Mr. Lincoln that I would like to read it to him. He sat down in one chair, put his feet into another one, and said: "John, you can fire away with that speech; I guess I can stand it." I unrolled the manuscript, and proceeded with some trepidation. "That's a good point, John," he would say, at certain places, and at others: "That's good—very good indeed," until I felt very much elated over my effort. I delivered the speech over fifty times during the campaign. Elmer E. Ellsworth, afterwards Colonel of the famous Zouaves, who was killed in Alexandria, early in the war, was nominally a student in Lincoln's office. His head was so full of military matters, however, that he thought little of law. Of Ellsworth, Lincoln said: "That young man has a real genius for war!"

7

AN ESTIMATE of Lincoln's standing as a lawyer is given by Thomas Drummond, judge of the United States District Court for the last ten years of Lincoln's practice.

I T IS NOT NECESSARY to claim for Mr. Lincoln attributes
or qualities which he did not possess. He had enough to entitle
him to the love and respect and esteem of all who knew him. He
was not skilled in the learning of the schools, and his knowledge
of the law was acquired almost entirely by his own unaided study
and by the practice of his profession. Nature gave him great
clearness and acuteness of intellect and a vast fund of common-
sense; and as a consequence of these he had much sagacity in
judging of the motives and springs of human conduct. With a
voice by no means pleasing, and, indeed, when excited, in its shrill
tones sometimes almost disagreeable; without any of the personal
graces of the orator; without much in the outward man indicating
superiority of intellect; without great quickness of perception—
still, his mind was so vigorous, his comprehension so exact and
clear, and his judgments so sure, that he easily mastered the intricacies of his profession, and became one of the ablest reasoners and
most impressive speakers at our bar. With a probity of character
known to all, with an intuitive insight into the human heart, with
a clearness of statement which was itself an argument, with an
uncommon power and facility of illustration, often, it is true, of
a plain and homely kind, and with that sincerity and earnestness
of manner to carry conviction, he was perhaps one of the most
successful jury lawyers we have ever had in the State. He always
tried a case fairly and honestly. He never intentionally misrep-
resented the testimony of a witness or the arguments of an opponent. He met both squarely, and, if he could not explain the one
or answer the other, substantially admitted it. He never misstated
the law according to his own intelligent view of it. Such was the
transparent candor and integrity of his nature that he could not
well or strongly argue a side or a cause that he thought wrong. Of
course, he felt it his duty to say what could be said, and to leave
the decision to others; but there could be seen in such cases the
inward struggle in his own mind. In trying a cause he might occasionally dwell too long or give too much importance to an incon-
siderable point; but this was the exception, and generally he went
straight to the citadel of a cause or a question, and struck home
there, knowing if that were won the outwork would necessarily
fall. He could hardly be called very learned in his profession, and

yet he rarely tried a cause without fully understanding the law applicable to it. I have no hesitation in saying he was one of the ablest lawyers I have ever known. If he was forcible before the jury he was equally so with the court. He detected with unerring sagacity the marked points of his opponents' arguments, and pressed his own views with overwhelming force. His efforts were quite unequal, and it may have been that he would not on some occasions strike one as at all remarkable; but let him be thoroughly aroused, let him feel that he was right and that some great principle was involved in his case, and he would come out with an earnestness of conviction, a power of argument, and a wealth of illustration, that I have never seen surpassed. . . . Simple in his habits, without pretensions of any kind, and distrustful of himself, he was willing to yield precedence and place to others, when he ought to have claimed them for himself. He rarely, if ever, sought office except at the urgent solicitations of his friends. In substantiation of this, I may be permitted to relate an incident which now occurs to me. Prior to his nomination for the Presidency, and, indeed, when his name was first mentioned in connection with that high office, I broached the subject upon the occasion of meeting him here. His response was, "I hope they will select some abler man than myself."

CHAPTER NINE

The House on Eighth Street

A LITTLE MORE than a year after he was married, Lincoln bought a home. It was a frame cottage, a story and a half in height, on Eighth Street at the corner of Jackson Street. The owner and occupant at the time of the purchase was the Reverend Charles Dresser, the Episcopal clergyman who had performed his marriage.

In this residence, later enlarged to two full stories, Lincoln, Mrs. Lincoln, and their sons lived until their departure for Washington. (In strict accuracy, one should except a year during Lincoln's term in Congress, when the house was leased.) What went on within the walls of this modest home has long since ceased to be a purely personal matter. When a man attains Lincoln's stature in history every facet of his private life, including his relations with his wife, becomes a matter of legitimate inquiry. One could also say that Mrs. Lincoln, by her conduct both before and after Lincoln's death, forfeited whatever claim to privacy she might otherwise have had.

But to ascertain just what did go on within the walls of the house on Eighth Street is by no means easy. Human likes and dislikes colored the observations of those who had first-hand knowledge; one-sided evidence and their own prepossessions have sometimes made the writings of biographers not wholly credible—although discerning readers of the following pages will find unwritten reactions to the strong personality of Mrs. Lincoln, even in the biased words some biographers have set down.

1

THAT LINCOLN HAD LITTLE TIME for discharging domestic
duties is evident in the following picture of a dreary Lincoln home.
However, there were always moments—even days—which he gave over
in their entirety to occupying himself with his children. An engaging sketch of the paternal Lincoln is offered by Ward Hill
Lamon.

H IS H O U S E W A S an ordinary two-story frame building, with
a stable and a yard: it was a bare, cheerless sort of a place. He
planted no fruit or shade trees, no shrubbery or flowers. He did
on one occasion set out a few rose bushes in front of his house; but
they speedily perished, or became unsightly for want of attention.
Mrs. Wallace, Mrs. Lincoln's sister, undertook "to hide the naked-
ness" of the place by planting some flowers; but they soon withered and died. He cultivated a small garden for a single year,
working in it himself; but it did not seem to prosper, and that
enterprise also was abandoned. He had a horse and a cow; the one
was fed and curried, and the other fed and milked, by his own
hand. When at home, he chopped and sawed all the wood that was
used in his house. Late one night he returned home, after an absence of a week or so. His neighbor, Webber, was in bed; but,
hearing an ax in use at that unusual hour, he rose to see what it
meant. The moon was high; and by its light he looked down into
Lincoln's yard, and there saw him in his shirt sleeves "cutting
wood to cook his supper with." Webber turned to his watch, and
saw that it was one o'clock. Besides this house and lot, and a small
sum of money, Mr. Lincoln had no property, except some wild
land in Iowa, entered for him under warrants, received for his
service in the Black Hawk War.

Mrs. Wallace thinks "Mr. Lincoln was a domestic man by
nature." He was not fond of other people's children, but was extremely fond of his own; he was patient, indulgent, and generous
with them to a fault. On Sundays he often took those that were
large enough, and walked with them into the country, and, giving
himself up entirely to them, rambled through the green fields or
the cool woods, amusing and instructing them for a whole day at
a time.

2

IN A LETTER to Jesse W. Weik, William H. Herndon, who at best had no love for Mrs. Lincoln, handles the Lincoln household without restraint. Even though thirty years have passed—the letter was written in 1886—his irritation at juvenile vandalism is still alive.

I T W A S T H E H A B I T, custom, of Mrs. Lincoln, when any big man or woman visited her house, to dress up and trot out Bob, Willie, or Tad and get them to monkey around, talk, dance, speak, quote poetry, etc., etc. Then she would become enthusiastic and eloquent over the children, much to the annoyance of the visitor and to the mortification of Lincoln. However, Lincoln was totally blind to his children's faults. After Mrs. Lincoln had exhausted the English language and broken herself down in her rhapsodies on her children, Lincoln would smooth things over by saying: "These children may be something sometimes, if they are not merely rare-ripes, rotten-ripes, household plants. I have always noticed that a rare-ripe child quickly matures, but rots as quickly." He, Lincoln, used to come down to our office on a Sunday when Mrs. Lincoln had gone to church, *to show her new bonnet,* leaving Lincoln to care for and attend to the children. Lincoln would turn Willie and Tad loose in our office, and they soon gutted the room, gutted the shelves of books, rifled the drawers, and riddled boxes, battered the points of my gold pens against the stairs, turned over the inkstands on the papers, scattered letters over the office, and danced over them and the like. I have felt many a time that I wanted to wring the necks of these brats and pitch them out of the windows, but out of respect for Lincoln and knowing that he was abstracted, I shut my mouth, bit my lips, and left for parts unknown.

3

A SERVANT'S VIEW of a household is proverbially jaundiced, but it deserves to be considered. Here is the testimony of Harriet Hanks, entrusted to her letters to Herndon and placed in evidence by Weik.

I cannot pass from the subject of Lincoln's family in the early days without mention of one member whom I personally knew and from whose lips I learned much that has escaped biographers and historians save what she imparted to Herndon. I refer to Harriet Chapman, a daughter of Dennis Hanks, who became the wife of Augustus H. Chapman and who died not long since in Charleston, Illinois, being past eighty years of age. The lady in her youth was for a time a member of Abraham Lincoln's household in Springfield. It was not long after Mr. Lincoln's marriage to Mary Todd when the children were still small. Mr. Lincoln had invited her to come to Springfield and make her home with him, with which generous invitation she finally complied. . . . Her purpose was to attend school while in Springfield, and she lived with the Lincolns as a member of the household for about a year and a half; but in time her relations with Mrs. Lincoln became so strained, if not intolerable, she found it a relief at last to withdraw and return to her home in Charleston. The letters she wrote to Mr. Herndon between 1865 and 1868, and which are still in my possession, afford such characteristic and relevant glimpses into Lincoln's home life after his marriage to Mary Todd that I venture to quote a few lines.

In a letter written at Charleston, Illinois, November 21, 1866, she says: "You ask me how Mr. Lincoln acted at home. I can say, and that truly, he was all that a husband, father, and neighbor should be. Always kind and affectionate to his wife and child (Bob being the only one when I was with them) and very pleasant to all about him. Never did I hear him utter an unkind word to any one. For instance, one day he undertook to correct his child and his wife was determined that he should not, and attempted to take it from him; but in this she failed. She tried tongue-lashing, but met with the same fate, for Mr. Lincoln corrected his child, as a father ought to, in the face of his wife's anger, and that too without changing his countenance once or making any reply to her. His favorite way of reading when at home was lying on the floor. I fancy I see him now lying full length in the hall of his old home. He would turn a chair down on the floor with a pillow on it. He was very fond of reading poetry and would often, when he appeared to be in a brown study, commence reading aloud 'The

Burial of Sir John Moore,' and so on. He often told laughable
jokes and stories when he thought we were looking sad and
gloomy." The letter contains this additional paragraph: "Anything I can tell you regarding Mr. Lincoln will be cheerfully
given, but I would rather omit further mention of his wife, as I
could say but little in her favor."

In a letter dated December 10, 1866, she writes: "Mr. Lincoln
was remarkably fond of children. One of his greatest pleasures
when at home was that of nursing and playing with his little boy.
He was what I would call a hearty eater and enjoyed a good meal
of victuals as much as any one I ever knew. I have often heard
him say that he could eat corn cakes as fast as two women could
make them, although his table at home was set very sparingly.
Mrs. Lincoln was very economical; so much so that by some she
might have been pronounced stingy. Mr. Lincoln seldom ever wore
his coat when in the house at home and often went to the table in
his shirt-sleeves, which practice greatly annoyed his wife who, by
the way, loved to put on style."

4

ALTHOUGH THE FOLLOWING PASSAGE is from Ward Hill
Lamon's biography, the author's indebtedness to Herndon, for both
substance and point of view, is apparent.

On a winter's morning, this man [Lincoln] could be
seen wending his way to the market, with a basket on his arm, and
a little boy at his side, whose small feet rattled and pattered over
the ice-bound pavement, attempting to make up by the number of
his short steps for the long strides of his father. The little fellow
jerked at the bony hand which held his, and prattled and questioned, begged and grew petulant, in a vain effort to make his
father talk to him. But the latter was probably unconscious of the
other's existence, and stalked on, absorbed in his own reflections.
He wore on such occasions an old gray shawl, rolled into a coil,
and wrapped like a rope around his neck. The rest of his clothes
were in keeping. "He did not walk cunningly—Indian-like—but
cautiously and firmly." His tread was even and strong. He was a
little pigeon-toed; and this, with another peculiarity, made his

walk very singular. He set his whole foot flat on the ground, and in turn lifted it all at once—not resting momentarily upon the toe as the foot rose, nor upon the heel as it fell. He never wore his shoes out at the heel and the toe more, as most men do, than at the middle of the sole; yet his gait was not altogether awkward, and there was manifest physical power in his step. As he moved along thus silent, abstracted, his thoughts dimly reflected in his sharp face, men turned to look after him as an object of sympathy as well as curiosity; "his melancholy," in the words of Mr. Herndon, "dripped from him as he walked." If, however, he met a friend in the street, and was roused by a loud, hearty "Good morning, Lincoln!" he would grasp the friend's hand with one or both of his own, and, with his usual expression of "Howdy, howdy," would detain him to hear a story: something reminded him of it; it happened in Indiana, and it must be told, for it was wonderfully pertinent.

After his breakfast hour, he would appear at his office, and go about the labors of the day with all his might, displaying prodigious industry and capacity for continuous application, although he never was a fast worker. Sometimes it happened that he came without his breakfast; and then he would have in his hands a piece of cheese, or Bologna sausage, and a few crackers, bought by the way. At such times he did not speak to his partner or his friends, if any happened to be present: the tears were, perhaps, struggling into his eyes, while his pride was struggling to keep them back. Mr. Herndon knew the whole story at a glance: there was no speech between them; but neither wished the visitors to the office to witness the scene; and, therefore, Mr. Lincoln retired to the back office, while Mr. Herndon locked the front one, and walked away with the key in his pocket. In an hour or more the latter would return, and perhaps find Mr. Lincoln calm and collected; otherwise he went out again, and waited until he was so. Then the office was opened, and every thing went on as usual.

5

BY BALANCING TESTIMONY and drawing upon his own rich understanding of the ways of men and women, Carl Sandburg comes to conclusions that are realistic without being harsh.

F OUR BABIES WERE BORNE by Mary Todd Lincoln in ten years, all boys, Robert Todd (1843), Edward Baker (1846), William Wallace (1850), Thomas (1853). They made a houseful. Their mother had maids for housework but until the family went to the White House to live, she usually sewed her own dresses, did much of the sewing for the children, and took on herself many of the thousand and one little cares and daily chores that accompany the feeding and clothing of babies, and upbringing of lusty and mischievous boys. She had hours, days, years of washing and nursing these little ones, tending their garments, overseeing their school studies, watching their behavior, instructing them as to the manners of gentlemen, keeping an eye on their health, working and worrying over them when they were sick. Even those who could not see her as pleasant company, even the ones who believed her a vixen and a shrew, gave testimony that she was an exceptional mother, brooding over her offspring with a touch of the tigress.

Her little Eddie died in 1850, not quite four years old; that was a grief. Thomas, nicknamed Tad, had a misshapen palate and lisped; he had brightness, whimsical bold humor; he was a precious burden to his mother and father.

Mrs. Lincoln knew that her husband understood her faults. She believed she knew his failings and instructed him. Across their twenty-two years of married life there were times when she was a help. Often too she knew she presumed on his patience and good nature, knowing that when calm settled down on the household he would regard it as "a little explosion" that had done her good. In the matter of faults she may have heard him tell of meeting a farmer who wanted Lincoln to bring suit against a next door neighbor. And Lincoln suggested that the farmer should forget it; neighbors are like horses; they all have faults and there is a way of accommodating yourself to the faults you know and expect; trading a horse whose faults you are used to for one who has a new and a different set of faults may be a mistake. Undoubtedly Lincoln had a theory that a turbulent woman and an unruly horse must be met with a patience much the same for either the woman or the horse.

She terrorized housemaids, icemen, storekeepers, delivery boys, with her tongue lashings. He knew these tempers of hers connected directly with the violent headaches of which she complained for many years. He knew they traced back to a deep-seated physical disorder, sudden disturbances that arose and shook her controls till she raved and was as helpless as a child that has spent itself in a tantrum. Sentences of letters she wrote show that she felt guilty and ashamed over her outbreaks of hysteria; she wished they had never happened, felt deeply that she had made a fool of herself. If Lincoln ever suspected that these habitual brainstorms were the result of a cerebral disease eating deeper into the tissues from year to year, it is not revealed in any letter or spoken comment in the known record.

In the courting days and in the earlier years of marriage his nickname for her was "Molly." After the children came he called her "Mother." When complaints were raised against her he tried to smooth out the trouble, telling one man who had been tongue-lashed that he ought to be able to stand for fifteen minutes what he [Lincoln] had stood for fifteen years. Much can be inferred from a letter he wrote to the editor of a new Republican newspaper which Mrs. Lincoln had thrown out of the house in a huff. "When the paper was brought to my house," he explained, "my wife said to me, 'Now are you going to take another worthless little paper?' I said to her *evasively*, 'I have not directed the paper to be left.' From this, in my absence, she sent the message to the carrier."

Did she on one occasion chase him out of the house with a broomstick? One woman told of it years afterward. It may have been so, though no other witness has come forward to tell about it, and the next door neighbors, the Gourleys, recalled no affair of the broomstick. "I think the Lincolns agreed moderately well," said James Gourley. "As a rule Mr. Lincoln yielded to his wife— in fact, almost any other man, had he known the woman as I did, would have done the same thing. She was gifted with an unusually high temper and that usually got the better of her. She was very excitable and when wrought up had hallucinations." Once she was afraid of rough characters doing violence to her and the maid. Her wailing brought Gourley over and he spent the night guarding the house. "The whole thing was imaginary," said Gourley. Though others living farther away emphasized her bad peculiarities, Gourley declared, "I never thought Mrs. Lincoln was as bad as some people here in Springfield represented her." When one of her spells of temper came on Lincoln at first seemed to pay no attention. "Frequently he would laugh at her, which is a risky thing to do in the face of an infuriated wife; but generally, if her impatience continued, he would pick up one of the children and deliberately leave home as if to take a walk. After he had gone, the storm usually subsided, but sometimes it would break out again when he returned."

Did she throw a bucket of water on his head from a second-story window as he stood at the front door asking to be let in? Such a tale has been told and was once published in a foreign language newspaper—printed as fun for the readers who for years laughed at one stage jester asking another, "Who was that lady I seen you with last night?" "That wasn't no lady; that was my wife." There are legends which grow by what they feed on. Possibly once during the eighteen or nineteen years of the married life of the Lincolns in Springfield she threw a bucket of water on him at the front door—possibly once—though Herndon and others never heard of it.

Though the talk and the testimony blame the woman chiefly there seems to have been one time that the man too lost his control. Lincoln was at the office one morning before Herndon arrived. His hat over his eyes he gave a short answer to Herndon's "Good morning," sat slumped till noon, and then made a meal of crackers and cheese. On the day before, on a Sunday morning, Mrs. Lincoln was in a bad mood, one thing led to another and after repeated naggings Lincoln took hold of her and pushed her toward an open door facing Jackson Street, calling in his peculiar high-pitched voice, "You make the house intolerable, damn you, get out of it!" Churchgoers coming up Jackson Street might have seen and heard all. How would they know it was the first and only time in his life he had laid rough hands on his wife and cursed her? Even letting it pass that people had seen and heard what happened how could he blame himself enough for letting himself go in such cheap behavior? So Sunday had been a day of shameful thoughts. The night had brought no sleep. And at daybreak he had come to the law office, without breakfast, without hope.

The marriage contract is complex. "Live and let live," is one of its terms. It travels on a series of readjustments to the changes of life recurring in the party of the first part and the party of the second part. Geared to incessant ecstasy of passion, the arrangement goes smash. Mutual ambitions, a round of simple and necessary duties, occasional or frequent separations as the case may be, relieved by interludes of warm affection—these are the conditions on which many a longtime marriage has been negotiated. The mood and color of this normal married life permeate the letters that passed between Lincoln and his wife when he was in Congress. Their household talk across the twenty-two years must have run along many a day and hour in the mood of these letters; exchanges of news, little anxieties about the children and the home, the journeyings of each reported to the other. When he hurried home from the law office during a thunderstorm, knowing that she was a terror-struck and sick woman during a thunderstorm, it was an act of accommodation by one partner for another. Likewise when a man appeared at the office saying the wife wanted a tree in their home yard cut down, it was accommodation again in his saying, "Then for God's sake let it be cut down!"

All romance is interrupted by the practical. The most passionate of lovers must either go to a hotel or set up housekeeping. And either is a humdrum piece of business in a sheer romance. Many a woman has said, "I love you, but the roast is burning and we must leave our kisses till after dinner." Managing a family and household is the work and care of a husband and wife as distinguished from two lovers. The husband must attend to the "husbandry," the bread-and-butter supply, while his wife loves, cherishes and obeys him; that is the theory; an ancient Saxon verb has it that she "wifes" him. We know from the 1848 letters of Lincoln and his wife that he was husbanding their resources and that she "wifed" him.

We can be sure, too, that for much of the time Lincoln and his wife went about their concerns peacefully and with quiet affection for each other. Domestic flareups, nerve-snappings, come to all couples; perhaps to these two they simply came more frequently and more violently. Authentic records—letters written without any thought of future readers—contain many glimpses of placid relations. One can read nothing but calm contentment into Lincoln's sentence about a novel he had received from a friend: "My wife got hold of the volume I took home, read it half through last night, and is greatly interested in it." Only the comradeship that comes to those who understand each other can be inferred from Mrs. Lincoln's comment on a trip east: "When I saw the large steamers at the New York landings I felt in my heart inclined to sigh that poverty was my portion. How I long to go to Europe. I often laugh and tell Mr. Lincoln that I am determined my next husband shall be rich."

6

NO FAMILY—at least no urban family—lives in a vacuum. William E. Barton sees the Lincolns in the context of Springfield's social life.

L I N C O L N   S P E N T most of his day at his office, and his evening with companions at the store or State House. But his habits about the house are well defined. He was not quite at home in his own house. . . . The habit he had learned in the "blab school" never left him; and it was not easy for him to read or write silently. He read aloud; and when he wrote, he spoke the words as he slowly wrote them, weighing each one as he uttered and recorded it. Lying on the floor, coatless, and with hair awry, he sometimes answered a knock at the door, much to the displeasure of Mrs. Lincoln. She had a maid, and wanted her callers to know that the maid was properly aware of her duties. But Lincoln, if he was lying on the floor of the living room, would rise, welcome the callers, and excuse himself while he went back to "trot out" Mrs. Lincoln. . . .

Lincoln and his wife were both of a generous nature, but their home was one of somewhat restricted hospitality. Mrs. Lincoln had the problem of limited resources, and in addition the long and frequent absences of her husband, and his lack of social graces. Lincoln was not wholly wrong when he wrote to Mary Owens that if she married him she would see other people enjoying wealth, and be unable to share it.

I have heard it said in Springfield, "Lincoln never felt free to invite a guest to his home; his poverty and Mrs. Lincoln's inability to keep help prevented any hospitality." But this is not true. I find in Senator Browning's *Diary* many such entries as these:

Springfield, Monday, [1852 January]

At night delivered a lecture in 3rd Presbyterian church for the benefit of the poor. After the lecture went to Mr. Lincoln's to supper.

Thursday July 22 [1852]

After tea Mrs B & self called at Mr. Ridgleys, Mr. Edwards, & spent the evening at Lincolns.

Thursday Feby 5 [1857]

. . . At night attended large & pleasant party at Lincolns.

Wednesday Feby 2, 1859.

. . . At large party at Lincoln's at night.

Thursday June 9, [1859]

. . . Went to a party at Lincolns at night.

The Lincolns did less entertaining than some of their more prosperous neighbors, but they did their share.

When there was company at the Lincoln home, Mrs. Lincoln had her trials. She was never sure that her husband would use the butter knife, and not reach for butter with his own knife. He tried to please her, but if he got interested in telling stories, he sometimes forgot and reverted to his early habits. There was no separate knife for the butter in the home of Nancy Hanks, and probably none in the Rutledge tavern, nor was there always one in the "City Hotel" at the county seat where Lincoln attended court.

Still, Lincoln acquired some measure of what may truly be called culture. One who knew him well said that whatever Mr. Lincoln lacked of social grace was made up by his kindness of heart; he was so inherently kind that he could not help being a gentleman. . . .

Springfield had its social laws and requirements. Mary Todd was a born aristocrat, and her marriage to a man socially her inferior did not demote her socially. Her husband was not of prominent family as she was, but he was an increasingly popular politician, and from the beginning he stood well in the capital city of Illinois. The social set in which they both moved prior to their marriage was the best in Springfield, and that is saying much; and during their married life they maintained their position.

Springfield was a town with a fashionable life of its own; and Lincoln and his wife were not outside the fashionable group. Lincoln's little eccentricities did not make him unwelcome in even the best homes in Springfield; indeed, he had a kind of adaptation which made him feel at home even when he did not know all the details of what might be required of him socially.

The Lincolns had visiting cards. Those of Mrs. Lincoln were neat and of the proper size and style; Lincoln's were written, and neatly written; and that, also, was good form. He did not make many social calls with her, but she left his card with her own, and it was a proper card.

While Mr. Lincoln in his personal appearance and attire was not all that a vain and society-loving woman might have desired, he and Mrs. Lincoln had their full share in the best social life of Springfield, and she had far more frequent occasion to be pleased with him than to be ashamed of him. Indeed, she was inordinately proud of him; nor did she ever see any other man whose social graces made sufficient compensation for Lincoln's more important qualifications to cause her to regret having married him. And Lincoln was proud of his plump little wife, and was happy when his increasing prosperity enabled her to dress as became her station. Not that she ever had dressed shabbily; Mary Todd always made a good appearance in society; but there came a time when Lincoln could afford to provide her money to buy for herself some things which he could not have afforded when they were first married.

They had as much social life as she cared for, and perhaps rather more than Lincoln cared for, and it was of the best.

CHAPTER TEN

Rebirth in Politics: 1854—1858

*I F , I N 1854, two men now remembered only by close
students of American history had not been bitter rivals
for a seat in the United States Senate, Abraham Lincoln
might now be known only as an able Illinois lawyer.*

*In January of that year Stephen A. Douglas, chairman
of the Senate's committee on territories, introduced a bill
to organize the territories of Kansas and Nebraska. At the
instigation of Senator David R. Atchison, of Missouri,
who was being strenuously opposed for re-election by
Thomas H. Benton, Douglas included a provision which
repealed the Missouri Compromise. (Atchison, strongly
pro-slavery, thought the repeal would strengthen his candidacy.) By Douglas's bill, in its final form, slavery was no
longer to be prohibited north of the line of 36° 30', but was
to be adopted or rejected by the people of the new territories.*

*The introduction of the Kansas-Nebraska Bill raised a
storm rarely if ever equalled in American political history.
Throughout the North the popular protest was vociferous
and lasting; in Congress opponents of the measure battled
it at every step. The Pierce Administration, however,
threw all its influence in support of the bill. After almost
five months of debate it was passed and signed by the
President.*

*One of the many thousands who considered the Kansas-
Nebraska Bill a menacing reversal of national policy was
Abraham Lincoln. "In 1854," he wrote of himself, "his
profession had almost superseded the thought of politics*

*in his mind, when the repeal of the Missouri Compromise
aroused him as he had never been before." He took to the
stump, thinking only of re-electing Richard Yates, a vigorous Anti-Nebraska Representative, to Congress, and
unaware that he himself was starting on a course that
would lead to a far higher goal.*

1

LINCOLN MADE his first Anti-Nebraska speech on August 26,
1854, at the little town of Winchester in Scott County, Illinois.
Years later James Miner, who heard the speech, wrote down his
recollections of the occasions, and what he remembered of Lincoln's
argument.

ONE DAY IN THE SUMMER of 1854 my father and I were
walking along the north side of the "Square" when we met Col.
N. M. Knapp. He stopped us and said to my father: "Miner, Abe
Lincoln is over at the Akin house and wants to see you. He is
going to speak in the courthouse this afternoon. He has got up a
speech on the Kansas-Nebraska bill which he has never made before and he has come down here to 'try it on the dog' before he
delivers it to larger audiences." My father laughed and passed on,
going to the Akin hotel. . . .

Lincoln and Richard Yates, Sr., had driven to Winchester
from Jacksonville that morning. In the afternoon about one hundred and fifty or two hundred persons gathered in the upper room
of the old courthouse. . . . On the west side of the old courtroom
there was a dais or raised platform for the judge's seat and desk.
Lincoln stood in front of this platform on the floor and made his
speech, which was a reply to various arguments advanced by
Senator Douglas in favor of his Kansas-Nebraska bill. . . .
[That bill] was a shock to the feelings of the people in the North
and especially in the State of Illinois, where it caused a revolt
among a large portion of Douglas' Democratic following and compelled him to hurry home from Washington to "mend his fences";
in consequence he had been making speeches at various places in
the northern part of the State, Chicago, Galesburg and other
points.

I can only recall the outlines of Mr. Lincoln's speech. He began by telling how in the minds of the people the Missouri Compromise was held as something sacred, more particularly by the citizens of Illinois, as the bill had been introduced in the senate in 1820 by a senator from Illinois, Jesse B. Thomas. He spoke of the aggressiveness of the slave-holding party, their eagerness to acquire more slave territory; alluded to several arguments Douglas had made in his speeches in favor of the Kansas-Nebraska bill and replied to them. He used several illustrations in making his points, one in particular I remember, because it was the only time he laughed during his whole speech; otherwise he was as earnest and solemn as though he had been delivering a funeral oration. I remember he impressed me with the feeling that the country was on the brink of a great disaster. Douglas, in his speeches, had introduced the Squatter Sovereignty idea, that the people of a territory should be allowed to settle the question of slavery, or any other question, among themselves, and that the people of the South had as much right to go into these territories as the people of the North. Mr. Lincoln said: "Let us see about equal rights of the North and South. How is it in Congressional representation? The South has representation for three-fifths of its slave population." He then took up the comparison of one of the Congressional districts in the black belt of Georgia where there were five black persons to one white one, and compared the ratio of white representation in Congress of its representatives to the ratio of white representation by our representatives in the sixteenth Congressional district in Illinois. One white man's vote in Georgia was equal to three white men's votes in Illinois. "Talk about equal rights," said he, "I would like some man to take a pointer dog, and nose around, and snuff about, and see if he can find my rights in such a condition."

After the meeting was over my father asked Yates what he thought of Lincoln's speech. He said: "Miner, I have heard this winter, all the big men in Congress talk on this question, but Lincoln's is the strongest speech I ever heard on the subject."

2

LINCOLN'S SPEECHES in Yates's behalf, marked with new seriousness and high purpose, soon attracted attention beyond the Con-

gressional district, and he was urged to speak in other parts of the
State. In late September he was at Bloomington, where Douglas
was scheduled to make an address in defense of his Nebraska policy.
In a reminiscence of the occasion by James S. Ewing there are
glimpses of two men moving toward rivalry, as well as a fore-
shadowing of the great debate that bears both their names.

I n 1854, Judge Stephen A. Douglas came to Bloomington to
make a speech defending the principles of the Kansas-Nebraska
Bill. Judge Lawrence Weldon, who was then a young lawyer at
Clinton, and who had come up to hear the speech, went with Mr.
Stevenson and myself to pay our respects to the "Little Giant."
We were presented to Judge Douglas by Mr. Amzi McWilliams,
then a prominent Democratic lawyer of this city. After we had
been in Mr. Douglas's room a few minutes, Mr. Lincoln came in,
and the Senator and he greeted each other most cordially as old
friends, and then Mr. Douglas introduced Mr. Lincoln to Judge
Weldon. He said: "Mr. Lincoln, I want to introduce you to Mr.
Weldon, a young lawyer who has come to Illinois from Ohio, and
has located at Clinton." Mr. Lincoln said: "Well, I am glad of
that; I go to Clinton sometimes myself, and we will get acquainted. . . ."

At this same meeting I heard Mr. Lincoln define his position
on the liquor question. . . . The committee had placed on the
sideboard of Judge Douglas's room (probably without his knowledge) a pitcher of water, some glasses and a decanter of red
liquor. As visitors called they were invited to partake; most of
the Democrats declined. When Mr. Lincoln rose to go, Mr. Douglas said: "Mr. Lincoln, won't you take something?" Mr. Lincoln
said: "No, I think not." Mr. Douglas said: "What! are you a
member of the Temperance Society?" "No," said Mr. Lincoln, "I
am not a member of any temperance society; but I am temperate,
in this, that I don't drink anything."

At the same meeting, another incident occurred. One of the
visitors who came to call on Senator Douglas was the Hon. Jesse
W. Fell. He was an old friend, and had known Douglas when he
first came to the State. I remember very well their cordial meeting
and recall clearly a part of their conversation. After talking a
while of old times and mutual friends, Mr. Fell said: "Judge

Douglas, many of Mr. Lincoln's friends would be greatly pleased to hear a joint discussion between you and him on these new and important questions now interesting the people, and I will be glad if such a discussion can be arranged." Mr. Douglas seemed annoyed, and, after hesitating a moment, said: "No, I won't do it! I come to Chicago, and there I am met by an old-line Abolitionist; I come down to the center of the State, and I am met by an old-line Whig; I go to the south end of the State, and I am met by an anti-Administration Democrat. I can't hold the Abolitionist responsible for what the Whig says; I can't hold the Whig responsible for what the Abolitionist says, and I can't hold either responsible for what the Democrat says. It looks like dogging a man over the State. This is my meeting; the people have come to hear me, and I want to talk to them." Mr. Fell said: "Well, Judge, you may be right; perhaps some other time it can be arranged."

3

THE CLIMAX OF THE CAMPAIGN, as far as Lincoln was concerned, came during the first week of October, when the state fair was in progress at Springfield. There, on the afternoon of the third, Douglas made a spirited defense of the Kansas-Nebraska Bill, to which Lincoln replied on the following day. The episode—a debate in fact if not in form—is developed by Joseph Fort Newton.

DOUGLAS WAS AT THIS TIME the most striking figure in the public eye—the most popular leader since Henry Clay—and in view of the estrangement of a large part of his constituency, he put forth all his powers of persuasion. He defended the Kansas-Nebraska Bill by appealing to his panacea of "popular sovereignty," which, he said, only sought to establish in the territories a policy already existing in the states. Why, he asked, should not the people of the territories have the right to form and regulate their domestic institutions in their own way? Moving from their old homes to new ones did not incapacitate them for self-government. If the citizens of a territory decided by vote to admit slaves as property, no state had a right to interfere. After this manner he argued, using all the arts at his command, and in ordinary times his eloquence would have been conclusive; but he had reckoned by the wrong star. His political compass, never very steady, had been deflected, perhaps unawares, by the subtle attraction of personal and partisan interest. His fallacy lay in the assumption that property in slaves did not differ from other kinds of property; and that the nation could deal with an historic evil by evasion. None the less his speech, delivered with great vitality and charm, swayed men by its blend of plausibility and power.

It was therefore upon no ordinary occasion that Lincoln found himself pitted against his old adversary—his rival on many occasions and for many things. Much interest attached to his reply, not only from the fact that he was crossing swords with a famous debater, but because he was a candidate against James Shields— his old dueling antagonist—for the Senate; and for the further reason that such a discussion involved, necessarily, a survey of slavery in all its phases. While he was known to be a Whig of anti-slavery leanings, up to this time there had been no demand that he declare himself on that question as a national political issue. He had now to define his position, and he did not hesitate to tell the plain truth, so far at least as the public mind was ready for the whole truth; and the telling of it made his speech one of the imperishable utterances of that critical period, if not of our whole history. When he had finished men of all parties realized that a new leader had appeared, the equal of Douglas in debate, calm, strong, and fearless, with a sure grasp of the problem—a man of genius ablaze with passion.

For four hours the circuit-riding lawyer unfolded and described the great issue with a mastery of facts, a logical strategy, and a penetration of insight that astonished even his friends. Evidence of careful study was apparent in the compactness of his thought and the lucidity of his style, and there was a total absence of the story-telling, of the grotesque humor, which had marred his earlier efforts. There were occasional playful passages, keen logical thrusts and bright metaphorical sallies, but as a whole the speech was charged with deep feeling, the speaker becoming at times intense and solemnly prophetic as the far-reaching nature of the issue was unveiled. Unlike the Abolitionist orators, he did not recite the cruelties of slavery, but held himself to the legal aspects of the question, arraigning Douglas and his party for

violating the pledge of the Compromise, and for opening the way
for the extension of slavery into new territory. While he did not
plead for the abolition of slavery, he had none of the spirit of
concession to property interests that had ruined Webster, and he
spoke as one to whom the moral issue was vividly alive. Restrict
slavery, he argued, and time would work its abolition by natural
process. For the pet dogma of Douglas he had a profound scorn,
and his epigrams pierced it like flashes of lightning. He turned it
over and over, inside and out, tearing off its mask and exhibiting
it in such a light that no one could fail to see the deception em-
bodied in it. No political dogma ever received a more merciless
exposure, while the Senator himself sat on a front bench, not
twelve feet away, intently listening. There were warm, but for
the most part good-humored passages between them as the afternoon ran along. Lincoln kept his temper, even under the most
provoking taunts, and his readiness and ease of retort delighted
the immense audience. It was a great triumph, and thunders of
applause greeted him; but what impressed men was the granitic
solidity of his argument, made luminous by a passionate earnestness all the more effective for its restraint. One who was present
[Horace White] has left this picture of the orator:

"It was a warmish day in early October, and Mr. Lincoln was in
his shirt sleeves when he stepped on the platform. I observed that,
although awkward, he was not in the least embarrassed. He began
in a slow and hesitating manner, but without any mistakes of
language, dates, or facts. It was evident that he had mastered
his subject, that he knew what he was going to say, and that he
knew he was right. He had a thin, high-pitched, falsetto voice of
much carrying power, and could be heard a long distance in spite
of the bustle and tumult of the crowd. He had the accent and
pronunciation peculiar to his native State, Kentucky. Gradually
he warmed up with his subject, his angularity disappeared, and
he passed into that attitude of unconscious majesty that is so
conspicuous in Saint-Gaudens's statue at the entrance of Lincoln
Park in Chicago. . . . Progressing with his theme, his words
began to come faster and his face to light up with the rays of
genius and his body to move in unison with his thoughts. His
gestures were made with his body and head rather than with his
arms. They were the natural expression of the man, and so per-

fectly adapted to what he was saying that anything different
would have been quite inconceivable. Sometimes his manner was
very impassioned, and he seemed transfigured with his subject.
Perspiration would stream down his face, and each particular
hair would stand on end. . . . In such transfigured moments as
these he was the type of the Hebrew prophet.

"I heard the whole speech. It was superior to Webster's reply
to Hayne, because its theme is loftier and its scope wider. . . .
I think also that Lincoln's speech is the superior of the two as an
example of English style. It lacks something of the smooth, com-
pulsive flow which takes the intellect captive in the Websterian
diction, but it excels in the simplicity, directness, and lucidity
which appeal both to the intellect and to the heart. The speech
made so profound an impression on me that I feel under its spell to
this day."

When Lincoln closed, Owen Lovejoy, the leader of the Abolitionists—then holding a convention in the city—announced a
meeting in the same place that evening of all the "friends of
liberty," with a view to organizing the Republican party in
Illinois, as it had already been organized in Wisconsin and
Ohio. The scheme was to induce Lincoln to address them, and
thus publicly to commit him as of their faith. But the astute
Herndon, though in their counsels and as radical as any of them,
was more of a politician, and knew the danger to Lincoln of
consorting just then with Abolitionists. So he hunted up his
partner and said: "Go home at once! Take Bob with you and
drive somewhere in the country, and stay till this thing is over."
Lincoln, always alert and politic, did take Bob in his buggy and
drove to Tazewell County, where Judge Davis was holding court.
Thus he escaped the dilemma, since either joining, or refusing
to join, the Abolitionists would have been perilous in view of the
approaching contest for the senatorship.

4

TO THEIR SURPRISE, the Anti-Nebraska forces won a majority
of the Illinois Legislature in the fall elections of 1854, and thus found
a senatorship within their reach. Lincoln soon came to the front as
the leading candidate against James Shields, whose term was ex-

piring. How he was thwarted, and how he swung the prize to Lyman Trumbull, an Anti-Nebraska Democrat, comes out best in his own words.

Springfield, February 9, 1855.

Hon. E. B. Washburne.

My dear Sir: The agony is over at last, and the result you doubtless know. I write this only to give you some particulars to explain what might appear difficult of understanding. I began with 44 votes, Shields 41, and Trumbull 5—yet Trumbull was elected. In fact, 47 different members voted for me—getting three new ones on the second ballot, and losing four old ones. How came my 47 to yield to Trumbull's 5? It was Governor Matteson's work. He has been secretly a candidate ever since (before, even) the fall election. All the members round about the canal were Anti-Nebraska, but were nevertheless nearly all Democrats and old personal friends of his. His plan was to privately impress them with the belief that he was as good Anti-Nebraska as any one else—at least could be secured to be so by instructions, which could be easily passed. In this way he got from four to six of that sort of men to really prefer his election to that of any other man—all *sub rosa*, of course. One notable instance of this sort was with Mr. Strunk of Kankakee. At the beginning of the session he came a volunteer to tell me he was for me and would walk a hundred miles to elect me; but lo! it was not long before he leaked it out that he was going for me the first few ballots and then for Governor Matteson.

The Nebraska men, of course, were not for Matteson; but when they found they could elect no avowed Nebraska man, they tardily determined to let him get whomever of our men he could, by whatever means he could, and ask him no questions. In the mean time Osgood, Don Morrison, and Trapp of St. Clair had openly gone over from us. With the united Nebraska force and their recruits, open and covert, it gave Matteson more than enough to elect him. We saw into it plainly ten days ago, but with every possible effort could not head it off. All that remained of the Anti-Nebraska force, excepting Judd, Cook, Palmer, Baker and Allen of Madison, and two or three of the secret Matteson men, would go into caucus, and I could get the nomination of that caucus.

But the three senators and one of the two representatives above named "could never vote for a Whig," and this incensed some twenty Whigs to "think" they would never vote for the man of the five. So we stood, and so we went into the fight yesterday — the Nebraska men very confident of the election of Matteson, though denying that he was a candidate, and we very much believing also that they would elect him. But they wanted first to make a show of good faith to Shields by voting for him a few times, and our secret Matteson men also wanted to make a show of good faith by voting with us a few times. So we led off. On the seventh ballot, I think, the signal was given to the Nebraska men to turn to Matteson, which they acted on to a man, with one exception, my old friend Strunk going with them, giving him 44 votes. Next ballot the remaining Nebraska man and one pretended Anti went over to him, giving him 46. The next still another, giving him 47, wanting only three of an election. In the mean time our friends, with a view of detaining our expected bolters, had been turning from me to Trumbull till he had risen to 35 and I had been reduced to 15. These would never desert me except by my direction; but I became satisfied that if we could prevent Matteson's election one or two ballots more, we could not possibly do so a single ballot after my friends should begin to return to me from Trumbull. So I determined to strike at once, and accordingly advised my remaining friends to go for him, which they did and elected him on the tenth ballot.

Such is the way the thing was done. I think you would have done the same under the circumstances; though Judge Davis, who came down this morning, declares he never would have consented to the forty-seven men being controlled by the five. I regret my defeat moderately, but I am not nervous about it. I could have headed off every combination and been elected, had it not been for Matteson's double game—and his defeat now gives me more pleasure than my own gives me pain. On the whole, it is perhaps as well for our general cause that Trumbull is elected. The Nebraska men confess that they hate it worse than anything that could have happened. It is a great consolation to see them worse whipped than I am. I tell them it is their own fault—that they had abundant opportunity to choose between him and me, which they declined, and instead forced it on me to decide between him and Matteson.

With my grateful acknowledgments for the kind, active, and continued interest you have taken for me in this matter, allow me to subscribe myself

Yours forever,
A. LINCOLN.

5

AS LINCOLN'S VERSION of his Senatorial defeat shows, parties were in flux in 1854 and 1855, and many a man did not know where he stood or in what company he would eventually find himself. In a letter to Joshua F. Speed, Lincoln reveals his own uncertainties, at the same time setting forth the cardinal points of his political creed.

Springfield, August 24, 1855.

Dear Speed: You know what a poor correspondent I am. Ever since I received your very agreeable letter of the 22d of May I have been intending to write you an answer to it. You suggest that in political action, now, you and I would differ. I suppose we would; not quite as much, however, as you may think. You know I dislike slavery, and you fully admit the abstract wrong of it. So far there is no cause of difference. But you say that sooner than yield your legal right to the slave, especially at the bidding of those who are not themselves interested, you would see the Union dissolved. I am not aware that any one is bidding you yield that right; very certainly I am not. I leave that matter entirely to yourself. I also acknowledge your rights and my obligations under the Constitution in regard to your slaves. I confess I hate to see the poor creatures hunted down and caught and carried back to their stripes and unrequited toil; but I bite my lips and keep quiet. In 1841 you and I had together a tedious low-water trip on a steamboat from Louisville to St. Louis. You may remember, as I well do, that from Louisville to the mouth of the Ohio there were on board ten or a dozen slaves shackled together with irons. That sight was a continued torment to me, and

I see something like it every time I touch the Ohio or any other slave border. It is not fair for you to assume that I have no interest in a thing which has, and continually exercises, the power of making me miserable. You ought rather to appreciate how much the great body of the Northern people do crucify their feelings, in order to maintain their loyalty to the Constitution and the Union. I do oppose the extension of slavery because my judgment and feeling so prompt me, and I am under no obligations to the contrary. If for this you and I must differ, differ we must. You say, if you were President, you would send an army and hang the leaders of the Missouri outrages upon the Kansas elections; still, if Kansas fairly votes herself a slave State she must be admitted, or the Union must be dissolved. But how if she votes herself a slave State unfairly, that is, by the very means for which you say you would hang men? Must she still be admitted, or the Union dissolved? That will be the phase of the question when it first becomes a practical one. In your assumption that there may be a fair decision of the slavery question in Kansas, I plainly see you and I would differ about the Nebraska law. I look upon that enactment not as a law, but as a violence from the beginning. It was conceived in violence, is maintained in violence, and is being executed in violence. I say it was conceived in violence, because the destruction of the Missouri Compromise, under the circumstances, was nothing less than violence. It was passed in violence, because it could not have passed at all but for the votes of many members in violence of the known will of their constituents. It is maintained in violence, because the elections since clearly demand its repeal; and the demand is openly disregarded.

You say men ought to be hung for the way they are executing the law; I say the way it is being executed is quite as good as any of its antecedents. It is being executed in the precise way which was intended from the first, else why does no Nebraska man express astonishment or condemnation? Poor Reeder is the only public man who has been silly enough to believe that anything like fairness was ever intended, and he has been bravely undeceived.

That Kansas will form a slave constitution, and with it will ask to be admitted into the Union, I take to be already a settled question, and so settled by the very means you so pointedly condemn. By every principle of law ever held by any court North or South, every negro taken to Kansas is free; yet, in utter disregard of this—in the spirit of violence merely—that beautiful legislature gravely passes a law to hang any man who shall venture to inform a negro of his legal rights. This is the subject and real object of the law. If, like Haman, they should hang upon the gallows of their own building, I shall not be among the mourners for their fate. In my humble sphere, I shall advocate the restoration of the Missouri Compromise so long as Kansas remains a Territory, and when, by all these foul means, it seeks to come into the Union as a slave State, I shall oppose it. I am very loath in any case to withhold my assent to the enjoyment of property acquired or located in good faith; but I do not admit that good faith in taking a negro to Kansas to be held in slavery is a probability with any man. Any man who has sense enough to be the controller of his own property has too much sense to misunderstand the outrageous character of the whole Nebraska business. But I digress. In my opposition to the admission of Kansas I shall have some company, but we may be beaten. If we are, I shall not on that account attempt to dissolve the Union. I think it probable, however, we shall be beaten. Standing as a unit among yourselves, you can, directly and indirectly, bribe enough of our men to carry the day, as you could on the open proposition to establish a monarchy. Get hold of some man in the North whose position and ability is such that he can make the support of your measure, whatever it may be, a Democratic party necessity, and the thing is done. Apropos of this, let me tell you an anecdote. Douglas introduced the Nebraska bill in January. In February afterward there was a called session of the Illinois legislature. Of the one hundred members composing the two branches of that body, about seventy were Democrats. These latter held a caucus, in which the Nebraska bill was talked of, if not formally discussed. It was thereby discovered that just three, and no more, were in favor of the measure. In a day or two Douglas's orders came on to have resolutions passed approving the bill; and they were passed by large majorities!!! The truth of this is vouched for by a bolting Democratic member. The masses, too, Democratic as well as Whig, were even nearer unanimous against it; but, as soon as the party necessity of supporting it became apparent, the way the Democrats began to see the wisdom and justice of it was perfectly astonishing.

You say that if Kansas fairly votes herself a free State, as a Christian you will rejoice at it. All decent slaveholders talk that way, and I do not doubt their candor. But they never vote that way. Although in a private letter or conversation you will express your preference that Kansas shall be free, you would vote for no man for Congress who would say the same thing publicly. No such man could be elected from any district in a slave State. You think Stringfellow and company ought to be hung; and yet at the next presidential election you will vote for the exact type and representative of Stringfellow. The slave-breeders and slave-traders are a small, odious, and detested class among you; and yet in politics they dictate the course of all of you, and are as completely your masters as you are the master of your own negroes. You inquire where I now stand. That is a disputed point. I think I am a Whig; but others say there are no Whigs, and that I am an Abolitionist. When I was at Washington, I voted for the Wilmot proviso as good as forty times; and I never heard of any one attempting to unwhig me for that. I now do no more than oppose the extension of slavery. I am not a Know-nothing; that is certain. How could I be? How can any one who abhors the oppression of negroes be in favor of degrading classes of white people? Our progress in degeneracy appears to me to be pretty rapid. As a nation we began by declaring that "all men are created equal." We now practically read it "all men are created equal, except negroes." When the Know-nothings get control, it will read "all men are created equal, except negroes and foreigners and Catholics." When it comes to this, I shall prefer emigrating to some country where they make no pretense of loving liberty — to Russia, for instance, where despotism can be taken pure, and without the base alloy of hypocrisy.

Mary will probably pass a day or two in Louisville in October. My kindest regards to Mrs. Speed. On the leading subject of this letter, I have more of her sympathy than I have of yours; and yet let me say I am

Your friend forever,
A. LINCOLN.

6

BY 1856 new political alignments were fast replacing those which
the passage of the Kansas-Nebraska Bill had disrupted. The Republican party, born in 1854, was losing its pristine radicalism and
gaining many converts from the old Whig and Democratic organizations. One of these was Lincoln. How he joined the ranks, and
signalized his adherence by the most dramatic speech of his career,
is explained by William H. Herndon.

F INDING HIMSELF DRIFTING about with the disorgan-
ized elements that floated together after the angry political
waters had subsided, it became apparent to Lincoln that if he
expected to figure as a leader he must take a stand himself. Mere
hatred of slavery and opposition to the injustice of the Kansas-
Nebraska legislation were not all that were required of him.
He must be a Democrat, Know-Nothing, Abolitionist, or Republican, or forever float about in the great political sea without compass, rudder, or sail. At length he declared himself. Believing the
times were ripe for more advanced movements, in the spring of
1856 I drew up a paper for the friends of freedom to sign, calling
a county convention in Springfield to select delegates for the
forthcoming Republican State Convention in Bloomington. The
paper was freely circulated and generously signed. Lincoln was
absent at the time and, believing I knew what his "feeling and
judgment" on the vital questions of the hour were, I took the
liberty to sign his name to the call. The whole was then published
in the Springfield *Journal*. No sooner had it appeared than John
T. Stuart, who, with others, was endeavoring to retard Lincoln
in his advanced movements, rushed into the office and excitedly
asked if "Lincoln had signed the Abolition call in the *Journal?*"
I answered in the negative, adding that I had signed his name
myself. To the question, "Did Lincoln authorize you to sign it?"
I returned an emphatic "No." "Then," exclaimed the startled and
indignant Stuart, "you have ruined him." But I was by no means
alarmed at what others deemed inconsiderate and hasty action.
I thought I understood Lincoln thoroughly, but in order to
vindicate myself if assailed I immediately sat down, after Stuart

had rushed out of the office, and wrote Lincoln, who was then in Tazewell County attending court, a brief account of what I had done and how much stir it was creating in the ranks of his conservative friends. If he approved or disapproved my course I asked him to write or telegraph me at once. In a brief time came his answer: "All right; go ahead. Will meet you—radicals and all." Stuart subsided, and the conservative spirits who hovered around Springfield no longer held control of the political fortunes of Abraham Lincoln.

The Republican party came into existence in Illinois as a party at Bloomington, May 29, 1856. The State convention of all opponents of Anti-Nebraska legislation had been set for that day. Judd, Yates, Trumbull, Swett, and Davis were there; so also was Lovejoy, who, like Otis of colonial fame, was a flame of fire. The firm of Lincoln and Herndon was represented by both members in person. The gallant William H. Bissell, who had ridden at the head of the Second Illinois Regiment at the battle of Buena Vista in the Mexican War, was nominated as Governor. The convention adopted a platform ringing with strong Anti-Nebraska sentiments, and then and there gave the Republican party its official christening. The business of the convention being over, Mr. Lincoln, in response to repeated calls, came forward and delivered a speech of such earnestness and power that no one who heard it will ever forget the effect it produced. In referring to this speech some years ago I used the following rather graphic language: "I have heard or read all of Mr. Lincoln's great speeches, and I give it as my opinion that the Bloomington speech was the grand effort of this life. Heretofore he had simply argued the slavery question on grounds of policy—the statesman's grounds—never reaching the question of the radical and the eternal right. Now he was newly baptized and freshly born; he had the fervor of a new convert; the smothered flame broke out; enthusiasm unusual to him blazed up; his eyes were aglow with an inspiration; he felt justice; his heart was alive to the right; his sympathies, remarkably deep for him, burst forth, and he stood before the throne of the eternal Right. His speech was full of fire and energy and force; it was logic; it was pathos; it was enthusiasm; it was justice, equity, truth, and right set ablaze by the divine fires of a soul maddened by the wrong; it was hard, heavy, knotty, gnarly, backed with wrath. I attempted for about fifteen minutes as was usual with me then to takes notes, but at the end of that time I threw pen and paper away and lived only in the inspiration of the hour. If Mr. Lincoln was six feet, four inches high usually, at Bloomington that day he was seven feet, and inspired at that. From that day to the day of his death he stood firm in the right. He felt his great cross, had his great idea, nursed it, kept it, taught it to others, in his fidelity bore witness of it to his death, and finally sealed it with his precious blood." The foregoing paragraph, used by me in a lecture in 1866, may to the average reader seem somewhat vivid in description, besides inclining to extravagance in imagery, yet although more than twenty years have passed since it was written I have never seen the need of altering a single sentence. I still adhere to the substantial truthfulness of the scene as described.

7

OF THE ESSENCE OF DRAMA is the contrast between the wild cheering that greeted the "Lost Speech" and the manner in which word came to Lincoln that he was enough of a national figure to be seriously considered for the Republican Vice-Presidential nomination. The scene is Henry C. Whitney's.

O NLY SEVENTEEN DAYS from the incident narrated just now, the National Convention met at Philadelphia to nominate a national ticket, whose nominees should be inimical to the further spread of human slavery.

At the same time an extra session of the circuit court of Champaign County convened at Urbana, Illinois, to dispose of a large mass of unfinished business. Judge Davis held the court, and Lincoln, having a few cases to try, attended.

At the Judge's request I secured a room for Lincoln, him and myself at the American House, kept by one John Dunaway. This primitive hostelry had three front entrances from the street, but not a single hall downstairs; one of these entrances led directly into the ladies' parlor and from it an entrance was obtained to the dining room, and also from another corner a flight of stairs conducted us to our room. Close by the front and dining-room doors was kept a gong which our vulgar boniface was wont to beat vigorously, as a prelude to meals, he standing in the door-way immediately under our windows and thereby causing us great annoyance.

This term of court was extremely prosaic, having for trial cases meagre both in amount and incident, tried usually by the court without the aid of a jury.

The weather was dry and hot; our surroundings were not con-ducive to comfort, and I don't recollect having ever attended a more uninteresting term of court.

The way we appropriated the news was thus: The *Chicago Press* used to reach town by the noon mail. Lincoln and Davis would go to the room direct from court, while I would go to the post office and get Judge Cunningham's paper. I would then read the news to them in our room.

While coming in one day with the paper I met Dunaway, our host, coming down from our room, where he had been and still was searching anxiously for his gong, which some ruthless hand had, alas, abstracted. When I had reached the room I was in the presence of the culprit. Lincoln sat awkwardly in a chair tilted up after his fashion, looking amused, silly and guilty, as if he had done something ridiculous, funny and reprehensible.

The Judge was equally amused; but said to him: "Now, Lin-coln, that is a shame. Poor Dunaway is the most distressed being. You must put that back," etc., etc.

It seems that Lincoln, in passing through the dining room, had seen the offending and noisy instrument; and in a mischievous freak had secreted it between the top and false bottom of a center table, where no one would have thought of looking for it. But he and I immediately repaired to the dining room and while I held the two contiguous doors fast Lincoln restored the gong to its accustomed place, after which he bounded up the stairs, two steps at a time, I following.

I think it was on that very day—at any rate it was on Thurs-day, June 19th—I read from the Chicago paper the following: "John C. Fremont was nominated for President on the first ballot. All the New England states went bodily for Fremont, except eleven votes for McLean. New York gave 93 for Fremont." Next day at noon I was on hand with the paper again, from which I read the following, viz.: "The convention then proceeded to an informal ballot for Vice-President, which resulted as follows: Dayton, 259; Lincoln, 110; Ford, 7; King, 9; Banks, 29; Sumner, 30; Collamer, 15; Johnson, 2; Pennington, 7; Carey, 3. Mr. Eliot, of Massachusetts, withdrew the names of Sumner, Wilson and Banks at their request. Wilmot's name was then withdrawn. The motion was then carried to proceed to a final ballot. Dayton was then unanimously nominated for Vice-President with the following exceptions: New York, Pennsylvania and Connecticut 20 for Lincoln," etc. Davis and I were greatly excited, but Lincoln was phlegmatic, listless and indifferent; his only remark was: "I reckon that ain't me; there's another great man in Massachusetts named Lincoln, and I reckon it's him."

Next day I got the paper, as usual, and not only saw that it was our Lincoln, but learned what remarks were made in the convention. The Judge and I were especially incensed at Palmer's reply to a question proposed, it being that we could carry Illinois either with or without Lincoln. The inquiry was made about Lincoln: "Will he fight?" Lincoln betrayed no other feeling except that of amusement at the sole qualification demanded.

I may observe, that we had not expected Lincoln to be a candidate at this time; all talk about his candidacy was abstract, and not concrete as yet; our favorite was Judge McLean.

The succeeding day I got the paper early and started to court with it before its adjournment. I met Lincoln at the west gate of the courthouse square, quite alone, coming from court, which had not even then adjourned. He was grave, gloomy, thoughtful and abstracted. I handed him the paper, which contained a woodcut of Fremont, and remarked: "It's a shame for a man with such a head as that to beat Judge McLean." Lincoln took the paper quite mechanically, and looked at it for a moment with no show of interest, and then handed it back, with the remark: "I don't see anything wrong about that head." I felt rebuked, for my remark was really unjust; but, looking again, I said, handing him back the paper, "I think that a man who parts his hair in the middle, like a woman, ain't fit to be President." He took the paper again, quite mechanically, looked at the picture for a moment, and then, with no remark at all, handed it back, and resumed his walk, gloomy and abstracted.

A day or two later he was ready to return home. He had collected $25 or $30 for that term's business thus far and one of our clients owed him $10, which he felt disappointed at not being able to collect; so I gave him a check for that amount, and went with him to the bank to collect it. The cashier, T. S. Hubbard, who paid it, is still living in Urbana and will probably remember it. I do not remember to have seen him happier than when he had got his little earnings together, being less than $40, as I now recollect it, and had his carpetbag packed, ready to start home.

8

LINCOLN THREW HIMSELF into the campaign of 1856 without reserve, although he was too much of a realist in politics to expect victory. How he impressed a young newspaperman at one of the many meetings he addressed is reported by Noah Brooks.

DURING THE PRESIDENTIAL CAMPAIGN of 1856 I lived in Northern Illinois. As one who dabbled a little in politics and a good deal in journalism, it was necessary for me to follow up some of the more important mass meetings of the Republicans. At one of these great assemblies in Ogle County, to which the country people came on horseback, in farm wagons, or afoot, from far and near, there were several speakers of local celebrity. Dr. Egan of Chicago, famous for his racy stories, was one, and "Joe" Knox of Bureau County, a stump speaker of renown, was another attraction. Several other orators were "on the bills" for this long-advertised "Fremont and Dayton rally," among them being a Springfield lawyer who had won some reputation as a shrewd, close reasoner and a capital speaker on the stump. This was Abraham Lincoln, popularly known as "Honest Abe Lincoln." In those days he was not so famous in our part of the state as the two speakers whom I have named. Possibly he was not so popular among the masses of the people; but his ready wit, his unfailing good humor, and the candor which gave him his character for honesty, won for him the admiration and respect of all who heard him. I remember once meeting a choleric old Democrat striding away from an open-air meeting where Lincoln was speaking, striking the earth with his cane as he stumped along and exclaiming, "He's a dangerous man, sir! a damned dangerous man! He makes you believe what he says, in spite of yourself!" It was Lincoln's manner. He admitted away his whole case, apparently, and yet, as his political opponents complained, he usually carried conviction with him. As he reasoned with his audience, he bent his long form over the railing of the platform, stooping lower and lower as he pursued his argument, until, having reached his point, he clinched it (usually with a question), and then suddenly sprang upright, reminding one of the springing open of a jack-knife blade.

At the Ogle County meeting to which I refer, Lincoln led off, the raciest speakers being reserved for the later part of the political entertainment. I am bound to say that Lincoln did not awaken the boisterous applause which some of those who followed him did, but his speech made a more lasting impression. It was talked about for weeks afterward in the neighborhood, and it probably changed votes; for that was the time when Free-Soil votes were being made in Northern Illinois. I had made Lincoln's acquaintance early in that particular day; after he had spoken, and while some of the others were on the platform, he and I fell into a chat about political prospects. We crawled under the pendulous branches of a tree, and Lincoln, lying flat on the ground, with his chin in his hands, talked on, rather gloomily as to the present, but absolutely confident as to the future. I was dismayed to find that he did not believe it possible that Fremont could be elected. As if half pitying my youthful ignorance, but admiring my enthusiasm, he said, "Don't be discouraged if we don't carry the day this year. We can't do it, that's certain. We can't carry Pennsylvania; those old Whigs down there are too strong for us. But we shall, sooner or later, elect our president. I feel confident of that."

"Do you think we shall elect a Free-Soil president in 1860?" I asked.

"Well, I don't know. Everything depends on the course of the Democracy. There's a big antislavery element in the Democratic party, and if we could get hold of that, we might possibly elect our man in 1860. But it's doubtful—*very* doubtful. Perhaps we shall be able to fetch it by 1864; perhaps not. As I said before, the Free-Soil party is bound to win in the long run. It may not be in my day; but it will in yours, I do really believe."

9

IN A STRICT SENSE, the pessimism which Lincoln expressed to Brooks was justified: Buchanan defeated both Fremont and Fillmore, the candidate of the American party. Yet Fremont received 1,300,000 votes to 1,800,000 for Buchanan and 900,000 for Fillmore, and carried all except four Northern states. The Republican party had demonstrated that it was no weakling. In 1857, it found another opportunity to prove itself. The Supreme Court presented the opponents of slavery extension with a new issue by its decision in the case of Dred Scott. Carl Sandburg calculates the effect of that decision on Lincoln's career.

FIVE MONTHS after the people had by their ballots spoken more decisively than ever before against slavery extension into new territory, with a majority of 400,000 votes against slavery extension, there came from the Supreme Court at Washington a decision that Congress did not have power to prohibit slavery in the territories; a slave was property and if a slave owner took that property into a territory, where the United States Constitution was the high law, the law of that territory could not take away from him his property.

A defense of this decision was made by Senator Douglas in a speech in Springfield in June; he said: "The courts are tribunals prescribed by the Constitution and created by the authority of the people to determine, expound, and enforce the law. Hence, whoever resists the final decision of the highest judicial tribunal aims a deadly blow at our whole republican system of government."

Lincoln replied, first quoting from a message of President Jackson disregarding a Supreme Court bank decision. "Again and again," said Lincoln, "have I heard Judge Douglas denounce that bank decision and applaud General Jackson for disregarding it."

And, having eaten many meals with judges and having slept in the same hotel bedrooms with judges, and having himself on a few occasions sat on the bench by appointment during the absence of a judge for a day or two, Lincoln ventured to say, "Judicial decisions are of greater or less authority as precedents according to circumstances. That this should be so accords both with common sense and the customary understanding of the legal profession."

He pointed to the fact that the Supreme Court had often overruled its own decisions, and said, "We shall do what we can to have it overrule this."

Then he went into the history of court decisions and state laws regulating slaves. It had not been so far back that state legislatures had the unquestioned power to abolish slavery. "Now it is becoming quite fashionable to withhold that power."

There had been days when the Declaration of Independence was held sacred. "But now, to aid in making the bondage of the negro universal and eternal, it is assailed and sneered at and construed, and hawked at and torn, till, if its framers could rise from their graves, they could not at all recognize it."

As to the slave, and the operation of law, civilization, the schools, colleges, churches, fine arts and men of learning and women of culture, and their ways of thought and action toward the slave, Lincoln delivered himself of a swift and terrible verbal cartoon, a sardonically sketched poem.

Of the chattel slave, he said: "All the powers of earth seem rapidly combining against him. Mammon is after him, ambition follows, philosophy follows, and the theology of the day is fast joining the cry. They have him in his prison house; they have searched his person, and left no prying instrument with him. One after another they have closed the heavy iron doors upon him; and now they have him, as it were, bolted in with a lock of a hundred keys, which can never be unlocked without the concurrence of every key—the keys in the hands of a hundred different men, and they scattered to a hundred different and distant places; and they stand musing as to what invention, in all the dominions of mind and matter, can be produced to make the impossibility of his escape more complete than it is."

From this he advanced to challenge Judge Douglas's argument that Republicans who insisted that the Declaration of Independence included all, black as well as white men, were so insisting "only because they want to vote, and eat, and sleep, and marry with negroes!"

And he mixed logic and human passion in declaring: "I protest against the counterfeit logic which concludes that, because I do not want a black woman for a slave, I must necessarily want her for a wife. I need not have her for either. I can just leave her alone. In some respects she certainly is not my equal; but in her natural right to eat the bread she earns with her own hands without asking leave of any one else, she is my equal, and the equal of all others."

Did the men who wrote the Declaration of Independence mean to say that all men are equal in all respects, equal in color, size, intellect, moral development, social capacity? No, hardly that. Then what did they mean? "They meant to set up a standard maxim for free society, which should be familiar to all and revered by all. The assertion that 'all men are created equal' was of no practical use in effecting our separation from Great Britain; and it was placed in the Declaration, not for that, but for future use. Its authors meant it to be—as, thank God, it is now proving itself—a stumbling block to those who in after times might seek to turn a free people back into the hateful paths of despotism. They knew the proneness of prosperity to breed tyrants, and they meant when such should reappear in this fair land and commence their vocation, they should find left for them at least one hard nut to crack."

He took up Judge Douglas's argument that the Declaration of Independence referred to the white race alone, in which Douglas said: "When they declared all men to have been created equal, they were speaking of British subjects on this continent being equal to British subjects born and residing in Great Britain; the Declaration was adopted for the purpose of justifying the colonists in the eyes of the civilized world in withdrawing their allegiance from the British crown."

To which Lincoln replied, "Why, according to this, not only negroes but white people outside of Great Britain and America were not spoken of in that instrument. The English, Irish, and Scotch, along with white Americans, were included, to be sure, but the French, Germans, and other white people of the world are all gone to pot along with the judge's inferior races! I had thought the Declaration promised something better than the condition of British subjects; but no, it only meant that we should be equal to them in their own oppressed and unequal condition. According to that, it gave no promise that, having kicked off the king and lords of Great Britain, we should not at once be saddled with a king and lords of our own."

And he came to the matter of Judge Douglas being horrified at the mixing of blood by the white and black races. He too would be horrified. "Agreed for once—a thousand times agreed. There are white men enough to marry all the white women, and black men enough to marry all the black women; and so let them be married."

But—he wished to note there were 405,751 mulattoes in the United States in 1850. "Nearly all have sprung from black slaves and white masters."

He quoted statistics, and argued that the Supreme Court by its decision in degrading black people was promoting race amalgamation. "Could we have had our way, the chances of these black girls ever mixing their blood with that of white people would have been diminished at least to the extent that it could not have been without their consent. But Judge Douglas is delighted to have them decided to be slaves, and not human enough to have a hearing, even if they were free, and thus left subject to the forced concubinage of their masters, and liable to become the mothers of mulattoes in spite of themselves; the very state of case that produces nine-tenths of all the mulattoes—all the mixing of blood in the nation."

The speech had leaps of ironic humor; it laid the blame for slavery on the love of money, and closed: "The plainest print cannot be read through a gold eagle; and it will be ever hard to find many men who will send a slave to Liberia, and pay his passage, while they can send him to a new country—Kansas, for instance—and sell him for fifteen hundred dollars, and the rise."

And because Illinois and the Northwest and Lincoln were becoming more important nationally, the *New York Times* printed the speech in full.

CHAPTER ELEVEN

The Great Debates

D*OUGLAS'S TERM in the Senate was to expire in 1858. Since he personified the policy against which the Republicans had risen in revolt, his defeat would be a stinging check to it. Lincoln, by common consent, was to be the Republican candidate.*

Yet it was clear that it would not be an easy contest. For a time it seemed that Douglas himself might win Republican support for re-election. In the fall of 1857 a pro-slavery convention meeting at Lecompton, Kansas, framed a carefully devised constitution which included a clause permitting slavery in the new State. Only that clause was to be submitted to popular vote, but even if it were rejected, other provisions in the constitution would protect slave-holders already there. To Douglas, this was a clear violation of his cherished principle of popular sovereignty. When Buchanan made the admission of Kansas under the Lecompton Constitution a party measure, Douglas broke with the Administration. By his course he won the respect of many Republicans, especially in the East, and there was considerable feeling that he should not be opposed for re-election.

In Lincoln's opinion, such sentiment was a threat to Republican integrity and a menace to his own candidacy. Douglas was right in opposing the Lecompton Constitution, but he was still an advocate of popular sovereignty, still a morally insensitive politician who did not care whether slavery was voted up or down. Gradually it became apparent that the Republicans of Illinois were of

Lincoln's mind. By the middle of May, 1858, he was able to write to Elihu B. Washburne: "I think our prospects gradually and steadily grow better, though we are not yet clear out of the woods by a great deal."

Douglas's position was even more difficult than Lincoln's. Buchanan, thoroughly aroused, resolved to crush the rebel, and threw the whole weight of federal patronage in Illinois behind a hastily formed organization of administration Democrats, or Danites, as they were called. Even though the great majority of his followers remained loyal, Douglas thus had to fight an unscrupulous Democratic opposition as well as an able Republican contestant backed by a young and virile party.

The contest, of course, was for the election of members of the Legislature—all members of the House of Representatives, and half of the State Senators—who were pledged to vote for Lincoln, Douglas, or a Buchanan Democrat.

1

WILLIAM H. HERNDON DEPICTS the nomination of Lincoln, and particularly the dramatic and controversial speech in which he accepted the honor.

W E REACH APRIL, 1858, at which time the Democratic State Convention met and, besides nominating candidates for State offices, endorsed Mr. Douglas's services in the Senate, thereby virtually renominating him for that exalted office. In the very nature of things Lincoln was the man already chosen in the hearts of the Republicans of Illinois for the same office, and therefore with singular appropriateness they passed, with great unanimity, at their convention in Springfield on the 16th of June, the characteristic resolution: "That Hon. Abraham Lincoln is our first and only choice for United States Senator to fill the vacancy about to be created by the expiration of Mr. Douglas' term of office." There was of course no surprise in this for Mr. Lincoln. He had been all along led to expect it, and with that in view had been earnestly and quietly at work preparing a speech in acknowledgment of the honor about to be conferred on him. This speech he wrote on stray envelopes and scraps of paper, as ideas suggested themselves, putting them into that miscellaneous and convenient receptacle, his hat. As the convention drew near he copied the whole on connected sheets, carefully revising every line and sentence, and fastened them together, for reference during the delivery of the speech and for publication. The former precaution, however, was unnecessary, for he had studied and read over what he had written so long and carefully that he was able to deliver it without the least hesitation or difficulty. A few days before the convention, when he was at work on the speech, I remember that Jesse K. Dubois, who was Auditor of State, came into the office and, seeing Lincoln busily writing, inquired what he was doing or what he was writing. Lincoln answered gruffly, "It's something you may see or hear sometime, but I'll not let you see it now." I myself knew what he was writing, but having asked neither my opinion nor that of anyone else, I did not venture to offer any suggestions. After he had finished the final draft of the speech, he locked the office door, drew the curtain across the glass panel in the door, and read it to me. At the end of each paragraph he would halt and wait for my comments. I remember what I said after hearing the first paragraph, wherein occurs the celebrated figure of the house divided against itself: "It is true, but is it wise or politic to say so?" He responded: "That expression is a truth of all human experience, 'a house divided against itself cannot stand,' and 'he that runs may read.' The proposition also is true, and has been for six thousand years. I want to use some universally known figure expressed in simple language as universally well-known, that may strike home to the minds of men in order to raise them up to the peril of the times. I do not believe I would be right in changing or omitting it. I would rather be defeated with this expression in the speech, and uphold and discuss it before the people, than be victorious without it. . . ."

Before delivering his speech he invited a dozen or so of his friends over to the library of the State House, where he read and submitted it to them. After the reading he asked each man for his opinion. Some condemned and not one endorsed it. One man, more forcible than elegant, characterized it as a "damned fool utterance"; another said the doctrine was "ahead of its time"; and still another contended that it would drive away a good many voters fresh from the Democrats ranks. Each man attacked it in his criticism. I was the last to respond. Although the doctrine announced was rather rank, yet it suited my views, and I said, "Lincoln, deliver that speech as read and it will make you President." At the time I hardly realized the force of my prophecy. Having patiently listened to these various criticisms from his friends—all of which with a single exception were adverse—he rose from his chair, and after alluding to the careful study and intense thought he had given the question, he answered all their objections substantially as follows: "Friends, this thing has been retarded long enough. The time has come when these sentiments should be uttered; and if it is decreed that I should go down because of this speech, then let me go down linked to the truth—let me die in the advocacy of what is just and right." The next day, the seventeenth, the speech was delivered just as we had heard it read. Up to this time Seward had held sway over the North by his "higher-law" sentiments, but the "house-divided-against-itself" speech by Lincoln in my opinion drove the nail into Seward's political coffin. . . .

Lincoln had now created in reality a more profound impression than he or his friends anticipated. Many Republicans deprecated the advanced ground he had taken, the more so as the Democrats rejoiced that it afforded them an issue clear and well-defined. Numbers of his friends distant from Springfield, on reading his speech, wrote him censorious letters; and one well-informed co-worker (Leonard Swett) predicted his defeat, charging it to the first ten lines of the speech. These complaints, coming apparently from every quarter, Lincoln bore with great patience. To one complainant who followed him into his office he said proudly, "If I had to draw a pen across my record, and erase my whole life from sight, and I had one poor gift or choice left as to what I should save from the wreck, I should choose that speech and leave it to the world unerased."

2

THREE WEEKS after Lincoln's "House Divided" speech Douglas opened his own campaign with an address from the balcony of Chicago's Tremont House. Lincoln was present by invitation, and on the next night spoke in reply at the same place. Two weeks later

Lincoln, again in Chicago, challenged Douglas to a series of joint discussions. Douglas accepted, and agreed to appear on the same platform with Lincoln in six of the state's eight Congressional districts. (Both men had already spoken in the other two.) Ottawa, Freeport, Jonesboro, Charleston, Galesburg, Quincy, and Alton were designated as suitable locations. Douglas was to open the first debate—at Ottawa on August 21—with a speech of an hour's duration, Lincoln was to have an hour and a half for his reply, and Douglas was to close in thirty minutes. Thereafter, the speakers were to take turns in opening the discussions. With the arrangements agreed upon and rules stipulated, the rival candidates are introduced by Isaac N. Arnold, who had known both of them for almost a quarter of a century.

A T   T H E   T I M E of these discussions, both Lincoln and Douglas were in the full maturity of their powers. Douglas was forty-five, and Lincoln forty-nine years of age. Physically and mentally, they were as unlike as possible. Douglas was short, not much more than five feet high, with a large head, massive brain, broad shoulders, a wide, deep chest, and features strongly marked. He impressed every one at first sight, as a strong, sturdy, resolute, fearless man. Lincoln's herculean stature has been already described. A stranger who listened to him for five minutes would say: "This is a kind, genial, sincere, genuine man; a man you can trust, plain, straightforward, honest, and true." If this stranger were to hear him make a speech, he would be impressed with his clear good sense, by his wit and humor, by his general intelligence, and by the simple, homely, but pure and accurate language he used.

Douglas was, in his manners, cordial, frank, and hearty. The poorest and humblest found him friendly. In his younger days he had a certain familiarity of manner quite unusual. When he was at the bar, and even after he went on the bench, it was not unusual for him to come down from the bench, or leave his chair at the bar, and take his seat on the knee of a friend, and, with an arm thrown familiarly around the neck of his companion, have a social chat, or a legal or political consultation.

Such familiarity had disappeared before 1858. In his long residence at Washington, Douglas had acquired the bearing and manners of a perfect gentleman and man of the world. But he was always a fascinating and attractive man, and always and everywhere personally popular. He had been, for years, carefully and thoroughly trained; on the stump, in Congress, and in the Senate, to meet in debate the ablest speakers in the state and nation. For years he had been accustomed to meet on the floor of the Capitol, the leaders of the old Whig and Free-Soil parties. Among them were Webster and Seward, Fessenden and Crittenden, Chase, Trumbull, Hale, and others of nearly equal eminence, and his enthusiastic friends insisted that never, either in single conflict, or when receiving the assault of the Senatorial leaders of a whole party, had he been discomfited. His style was bold, vigorous, and aggressive, and at times even defiant. He was ready, fluent, fertile in resources, familiar with national and party history, severe in denunciation, and he handled with skill nearly all the weapons of debate. His iron will and restless energy, together with great personal magnetism, made him the idol of his friends and party. His long, brilliant, and almost universally successful career, gave him perfect confidence in himself, and at times he was arrogant and overbearing.

Lincoln was also a thoroughly trained speaker. He had met successfully, year after year, at the bar, and on the stump, the ablest men of Illinois and the Northwest, including Lamborn, Stephen T. Logan, John Calhoun, and many others. He had contended in generous emulation with Hardin, Baker, Logan, and Browning, and had very often met Douglas, a conflict with whom he always courted rather than shunned. He had at Peoria, and elsewhere, extorted from Douglas the statement, that in all his discussions at Washington, he had never met an opponent who had given him so much trouble as Lincoln. His speeches, as we read them today, show a more familiar knowledge of the slavery question, than those of any other statesman of our country. This is especially true of the Peoria speech, and the Cooper Institute speech. Lincoln was powerful in argument, always seizing the strong points, and demonstrating his propositions with a clearness and logic approaching the certainty of mathematics. He had, in wit and humor, a great advantage over Douglas. Douglas's friends loved to call him "the little giant"; Lincoln was physically and intellectually the big giant.

3

TO BOTH CANDIDATES, the formal debates were to be high points in a continuous Senatorial campaign. Lincoln's engagements began at Beardstown on August 12. That meeting, with others that culminated in the first debate at Ottawa, is described by Horace White, who covered the whole campaign for the pro-Lincoln *Chicago Tribune*.

D OUGLAS HAD BEEN THERE the previous day, and I had heard him. His speech had consisted mainly of tedious repetitions of "popular sovereignty," but he had taken occasion to notice Lincoln's conspiracy charge, and had called it "an infamous lie." He had also alluded to Senator Trumbull's charge that he (Douglas) had, two years earlier, been engaged in a plot to force a bogus constitution on the people of Kansas without giving them an opportunity to vote upon it. "The miserable, craven-hearted wretch," said Douglas, "he would rather have both ears cut off than to use that language in my presence, where I could call him to account. . . ."

Mr. Douglas's meeting at Beardstown was large and enthusiastic, but was composed of a lower social stratum than the Republican meeting of the following day. Mr. Lincoln came up the Illinois River from the town of Naples in the steamer *Sam Gaty*. Cass county and the surrounding region was by no means hopeful Republican ground. Yet Mr. Lincoln's friends mustered forty horsemen and two bands of music, beside a long procession on foot to meet him at the landing. Schuyler county sent a delegation of three hundred, and Morgan county was well represented. These were mostly old-line Whigs who had followed Lincoln in earlier days. Mr. Lincoln's speech at Beardstown was one of the best he ever made in my hearing, and was not a repetition of any other. . . .

The next morning, August 13, we boarded the steamer *Editor* and went to Havana, Mason County. Mr. Lincoln was in excellent spirits. Several of his old Whig friends were on board, and the journey was filled up with politics and storytelling. In the latter branch of human affairs, Mr. Lincoln was most highly gifted. From the beginning to the end of our travels the fund of anecdotes never failed, and, wherever we happened to be, all the people within earshot would begin to work their way up to this inimitable storyteller. His stories were always *apropos* of something going on, and oftenest related to things that had happened in his own neighborhood. He was constantly being reminded of one, and, when he told it, his facial expression was so irresistibly comic that the bystanders generally exploded in laughter before he reached what he called the "nub" of it. Although the intervals between the meetings were filled up brimfully with mirth in this way, Mr. Lincoln indulged very sparingly in humor in his speeches. I asked him one day why he did not oftener turn the laugh on Douglas. He replied that he was too much in earnest, and that it was doubtful whether turning the laugh on anybody really gained any votes.

We arrived at Havana while Douglas was still speaking. The deputation that met Mr. Lincoln at the landing suggested that he should go up to the grove where the Democratic meeting was going on and hear what Douglas was saying. But he declined to do so, saying: "The Judge was so put out by my listening to him at Bloomington and Clinton that I promised to leave him alone at his own meetings for the rest of the campaign. I understand that he is calling Trumbull and myself liars, and if he should see me in the crowd he might be so ashamed of himself as to omit the most telling part of his argument." I strolled up to the Douglas meeting just before its conclusion, and there met a friend who had heard the whole. He was in a state of high indignation. He said that Douglas must certainly have been drinking before he came on the platform, because he had called Lincoln "a liar, a coward, a wretch and a sneak."

When Mr. Lincoln replied on the following day, he took notice of Douglas's hard words in this way:

"I am informed that my distinguished friend yesterday became a little excited, nervous (?) perhaps, and that he said something about fighting, as though looking to a personal encounter between himself and me. Did anybody in this audience hear him use such language? (Yes, Yes.) I am informed, further, that somebody in his audience, rather more excited or nervous than himself, took off his coat and offered to take the job off Judge Douglas's hands and fight Lincoln himself. Did anybody here witness that warlike proceeding? (Laughter and cries of 'yes.') Well, I merely desire to say that I shall fight neither Judge Douglas nor his second. I shall not do this for two reasons, which I will explain. In the first place a fight would prove nothing which is in issue in this election. It might establish that Judge Douglas is a more muscular man than myself, or it might show that I am a more muscular man than Judge Douglas. But this subject is not referred to in the Cincinnati platform, nor in either of the Springfield platforms. Neither result would prove him right or me wrong. And so of the gentleman who offered to do his fighting for him. If my fighting Judge Douglas would not prove anything, it would certainly prove nothing for me to fight his bottle-holder. My second reason for not having a personal encounter with Judge Douglas is that I don't believe he wants it himself. He and I are about the best friends in the world, and when we get together he would no more think of fighting me than of fighting his wife. Therefore, when the Judge talked about fighting he was not giving vent to any ill-feeling of his own, but was merely trying to excite—well, let us say enthusiasm against me on the part of his audience. And, as I find he was tolerably successful in this, we will call it quits."

At Havana I saw Mrs. Douglas (*née* Cutts) standing with a group of ladies a short distance from the platform on which her husband was speaking, and I thought I had never seen a more queenly face and figure. I saw her frequently afterward in this campaign, but never personally met her till many years later, when she had become the wife of General Williams of the Regular Army, and the mother of children who promised to be as beautiful as herself. There is no doubt in my mind that this attractive presence was very helpful to Judge Douglas in the campaign. It is certain that the Republicans considered her a dangerous element.

From Havana we went to Lewistown and thence to Peoria, still following on the heels of "the little giant," but nothing of special interest happened at either place. As we came northward Mr. Lincoln's meetings grew in size, but at Lewistown the Douglas gathering was much the larger of the two and was the most considerable in point of numbers I had yet seen.

The next stage brought us to Ottawa, the first joint debate, on August 21. Here the crowd was enormous. The weather had been very dry and the town was shrouded in dust raised by the moving

populace. Crowds were pouring into town from sunrise till noon
in all sorts of conveyances, teams, railroad trains, canal boats,
cavalcades, and processions on foot, with banners and inscrip-
tions, stirring up such clouds of dust that it was hard to make out
what was underneath them. The town was covered with bunting,
and bands of music were tooting around every corner, drowned
now and then by the roar of cannon. Mr. Lincoln came by railroad
and Mr. Douglas by carriage from La Salle. A train of seventeen
passenger cars from Chicago attested the interest felt in that city
in the first meeting of the champions. Two great processions escorted them to the platform in the public square. But the eagerness to hear the speaking was so great that the crowd had taken
possession of the square and the platform, and had climbed on
the wooden awning overhead, to such an extent that the speakers
and the committees and reporters could not get to their places.
Half an hour was consumed in a rough-and-tumble skirmish to
make way for them, and, when finally this was accomplished, a
section of the awning gave way with its load of men and boys, and
came down on the heads of the Douglas committee of reception.
But, fortunately, nobody was hurt. . . .

At the conclusion of the Ottawa debate, a circumstance occurred which, Mr. Lincoln said to me afterwards, was extremely
mortifying to him. Half a dozen Republicans, roused to a high
pitch of enthusiasm for their leader, seized him as he came down
from the platform, hoisted him upon their shoulders and marched
off with him, singing *The Star-Spangled Banner*, or *Hail Columbia*, until they reached the place where he was to spend the night.
What use Douglas made of this incident, is known to the readers
of the joint debates. He said a few days later, at Joliet, that Lincoln was so used up in the discussion that his knees trembled, and
he had to be carried from the platform, and he caused this to be
printed in the newspapers of his own party. Mr. Lincoln called
him to account for this fable at Jonesboro.

The Ottawa debate gave great satisfaction to our side. Mr. Lincoln, we thought, had the better of the argument, and we all came
away encouraged. But the Douglas men were encouraged also. In
his concluding half hour, Douglas spoke with great rapidity and
animation, and yet with perfect distinctness, and his supporters
cheered him wildly.

4

ON AUGUST 27, six days after the Ottawa debate, Lincoln and Douglas met again at Freeport. The *Chicago Times*, Douglas's organ, gilds the scene with the typically partisan journalism of the period.

THE CAMPAIGN.—THE DISCUSSION AT FREEPORT

Douglas and Lincoln.—15,000 Present!—Lincoln on Pledges.— Lincoln "Aint Pledged" to Anything! Lincoln Asks Questions! Lincoln Gets Answered!—A Leak Takes Place.—The "Lion" Frightened the "Dog"!—Lincoln Gets Weak! Lincoln a Fountain!!—Speeches of the Candidates

Friday was the day appointed for the joint discussion at Freeport between Douglas and Lincoln.

On Thursday night Judge Douglas reached Freeport from Galena, and was met at the depot by a vast multitude of persons. As he stepped upon the platform, he was greeted with tremendous shouts and cheers. A grand salute was fired at the same time, which, as it resounded through the city, gave notice to the people that the champion of popular rights had arrived, and thousands of persons flocked from the hotels and from all parts of the city, swelling the assemblage to not less than five thousand persons. A procession was formed, and, with not less than a thousand torches, music, the cheers of people, and the thunders of the cannon, Judge Douglas was escorted to the Brewster House. When the head of the procession reached the hotel, the ranks opened, and the carriage containing the people's guest drove up to the door. At this moment the scene was the grandest ever beheld in Freeport. The whole area of the streets in the vicinity of the hotel was densely packed; a few squares off, the cannon was belching forth its notes of welcome; a thousand torches blazed with brilliancy; the crowd cheered lustily, and from windows, balconies, house-tops, etc., there were to be seen the smiling faces and waving handkerchiefs of ladies. . . .

FRIDAY'S PROCEEDINGS

On Friday the day was heavy, and weather chilly and damp, yet, at two o'clock, there had assembled at the grove on the outskirts of the town, a multitude numbering not less than 15,000 persons, many of them ladies. Hon. Thomas J. Turner was moderator on the part of the Republicans, and Col. Mitchell on the part of the Democrats. At two o'clock the discussion commenced. . . .

During the delivery of Douglas' speech Lincoln was very uneasy; he could not sit still, nor would his limbs sustain him while standing. He was shivering, quaking, trembling, and his agony during the last fifteen minutes of Judge Douglas' speech was positively painful to the crowd who witnessed his behavior. The weather was lowering, and occasionally showering, and this, together with the fearful blows of Douglas, had a terrible effect upon Lincoln. He lost all his natural powers, and it was discovered that wherever he moved about the stand there was a leak from the roof or elsewhere. The leak seemed to be confined to the "spot" where Lincoln stood; his boots glistened with the dampness, which seemed to have the attribute of mercy for

> It droppeth like the gentle *rain*
> Upon the *place beneath.*

5

WHOLLY DIFFERENT IN TONE, but probably no closer to accuracy, was the *Tribune's* account of the Freeport debate.

GREAT DEBATE BETWEEN LINCOLN AND DOUGLAS AT FREEPORT

Fifteen Thousand Persons Present.—The Dred Scott Champion "Trotted out" and "Brought to His Milk."—It Proves to Be Stump-Tailed.—Great Caving-in on the Ottawa Forgery.— He Was "Conscientious" about It.—Why Chase's Amendment Was Voted Down.—Lincoln Tumbles Him All over Stephenson County.—Verbatim Report of Lincoln's Speech.—Douglas' Reply and Lincoln's Rejoinder.

The second great debate between Lincoln and Douglas came off at Freeport, on Friday afternoon. The day broke chilly, cloudy and lowering. Alternations of wind, and sunshine filled up the forenoon. At twelve o'clock the weather settled dismally, cold and damp, and the afternoon carried out the promise of the morning with the single exception of the rain.

The crowd, however, was enormous. At nine o'clock the Carroll County delegation came in with a long procession headed by a band of music and a banner on which was inscribed:

CARROLL COUNTY
For
ABRAHAM LINCOLN

At ten o'clock a special train from Amboy, Dixon and Polo, arrived with twelve cars crowded full. Mr. Lincoln was on this train, and some two thousand citizens of Freeport and vicinity had assembled to escort him to the Brewster House. Six deafening cheers were given as our next Senator stepped from the cars; after which the whole company formed in procession and escorted him around the principal streets to the elegant hotel. Here the reception speech was delivered by Hon. Thomas J. Turner—to which Mr. Lincoln responded in a few appropriate remarks. Half an hour later a train of eight cars arrived from Galena. Another procession was formed, preceded by a banner on which was inscribed:

THE GALENA LINCOLN CLUB

The delegation marched to the Brewster House and gave three rousing cheers for Abraham Lincoln. Mr. L. appeared on the balcony and returned his thanks amid a storm of applause. But the special train on the Galena road from Rockford, Marengo and Belvidere, eclipsed the whole—*consisting of sixteen cars and over a thousand persons*. They also marched to the Brewster House with a national flag bearing the words:

WINNEBAGO COUNTY
For
"OLD ABE"

Mr. Lincoln was again called out and received with loud cheers.

Douglas arrived in the town on Thursday evening and was escorted from the depot by what purported to be a torchlight procession. It was held to be a torchlight procession by a number of Dred Scottites who were in the secret, but with the mass of the

community it passed for a small pattern, candle-box mob of Irish-
men and street urchins. "Plenty of torches, *gentlemen!*" cried the
chief lictor—"plenty of torches; won't cost you a cent." "Don't
be afraid of 'em." He succeeded in "passing" about seventy-five
of them. The rest will be good for the next time.

At two o'clock the people rushed to the grove, a couple of
squares in the rear of the Brewster House. The crowd was about
one-third larger than that at Ottawa. It formed a vast circle
around a pyramid of lumber in the center, which had been erected
for the speakers and reporters. . . .

In the essence of billingsgate DOUGLAS transcended his Ottawa performance. He threw mud in great handfuls. So disgust-
ing was his language that the people on the ground peremptorily
hushed him up, three times. After a copious volley of phrases from
the cock-pit, he bellowed out "You Black Republicans" to his audience, who stopped him right in his tracks, and ordered him to
say "white," or to leave off the adjective entirely. Twice did he
essay to go on, and twice did the people bring him to, and make
him take a fresh start. Good for old Stephenson!

6

THE FREEPORT DEBATE has gone down in history because of
the second of four questions which Lincoln propounded to Douglas
on that occasion—a question given sharp point by the Dred Scott
decision of the preceding year: "Can the people of a United States
Territory, in any lawful way, against the wish of any citizen of the
United States, exclude slavery from its limits prior to the formation
of a State constitution?" Something of the background of that question is furnished by Joseph Medill, then and for many years later one
of the publishers of the *Chicago Tribune*.

I TRAVELED AROUND with Mr. Lincoln after the Ottawa
discussion to Freeport. He addressed three or four meetings during that time, one of them at Galesburg, where he had an immense
audience; another at Macomb in McDonough county, where the
crowd was comparatively small. As I recollect it we proceeded directly from Macomb to Freeport on the morning of August 27.
On the way north on the cars Mr. Lincoln beckoned to me to take

a seat beside him—I was sitting a few seats behind him at the time
—which I did. He took a half sheet of writing paper out of his
pocket and, handing it to me, said: "I am going to answer Mr.
Douglas's questions today in our discussion which he put to me
at Ottawa and I intend to ask him a few questions in return, and
I jotted them down this morning at the hotel before I left there.
I wish you to read them over and tell me what you think of my
questions." I did so, reading one of them several times. After a
considerable pause he said: "Well, how do those interrogatories
strike you?" I replied: "Mr. Lincoln, I do not like the second
question." "What's the objection to it?" Mr. Lincoln asked. I
replied: "It opens the door through which Senator Douglas will
be enabled to escape from the tight place in which he finds himself
on the slavery question in this State since he succeeded in getting
the Missouri Compromise repealed (which excluded slavery from
the territories north of 36°30′, and that included, of course,
Kansas and Nebraska)."

We argued at some further length, but I could make no impression whatever on Mr. Lincoln's mind. He said that he wouldn't
change the form of the question, and that he intended "to spear it
at Douglas that afternoon." In due time we arrived at Freeport
and there was a great crowd of Lincoln's friends at the depot with
a carriage to take him up to his hotel. The town was swarming
with people, great numbers coming from all the adjoining counties. I found at the hotel the Republican member of Congress from
that district, E. B. Washburne, with whom I was intimately acquainted, and Norman B. Judd, of Chicago, who was chairman of
the Republican State Central Committee.

I took each of them aside and related what passed between Lincoln and myself on the cars, and repeated the language of the second question which he intended to propound to Douglas, and both
of them said that they feared the ill effects from it, and they would
try and persuade Lincoln to leave it out or modify its language.
They followed Mr. Lincoln upstairs into his apartments, where
he was making his toilet for dinner, as the road had been dusty on
the way up, and they spent a considerable time with him. When
they came downstairs I saw both of them again, and they informed
me that they had argued the impolicy of putting question two to

Douglas as strongly as they could, but were not able to change his purpose. Other leaders saw Mr. Lincoln before the debate began and urged him not to give Douglas such an opportunity to get out of the tight place it was believed he was in before the people of Illinois on the slavery question.

Mr. Lincoln opened the discussion in the afternoon, and first replied to Douglas' seven questions put to him at Ottawa, and then said:

"I now proceed to propound to the Judge interrogatories so far as I have framed them. I will bring forward today an installment, only to number four, and reserve the other questions to our next debate."

And thereupon he read his four questions, including the question two, to which I have referred. He went on and finished his speech, and Mr. Douglas arose in reply and proceeded to answer the four questions. When he came to question two he realized in his reply my worst fears. He said in substance:

"It matters not what way the Supreme Court may hereafter decide as to the abstract questions whether slavery may or may not go into a territory under the Constitution; a majority of the people thereof have the lawful means to introduce or exclude it as they please, for the reason that slavery cannot exist a day or an hour anywhere unless it is supported by local police regulations. These police regulations can only be established by the local legislature and if the majority of the people of the territory are opposed to slavery they will elect representatives to that body who will by unfriendly legislation, effectually prevent the introduction of it into their midst. If, on the contrary, they are for slavery, their legislature will favor its admission and extension. Hence, no matter what the decision of the Supreme Court may be on that abstract question, still the right of the people to make a slave territory or free territory is perfect and complete under the Nebraska bill. I hope Mr. Lincoln deems my answer satisfactory on that point."

That was Senator Douglas's reply to Mr. Lincoln's sharp question, and it so pleased the thousands of Democrats present that they cheered and shouted and kept it up so long it was with difficulty the chairman of the meeting, aided by Mr. Douglas himself, could induce them to stop applauding in order that he might proceed with his speech, while Republicans maintained an absolute silence.

The Democratic papers all over Northern Illinois quoted and applauded Douglas's triumphant reply to Mr. Lincoln's interrogatory.

7

TWO MONTHS PASSED, and both candidates still campaigned with undiminished fervor. After Freeport, they had met in debate at Jonesboro, Charleston, and Galesburg, and had spoken almost daily, and on some days several times, in the intervals between formal meetings. On October 13 they met for the sixth time at Quincy. There Carl Schurz, a German university graduate and liberal who in six years in the United States had already made a political reputation, had his first meeting with Abraham Lincoln.

T H E Republican State Committee of Illinois asked me to make some speeches in their campaign, and, obeying that call, I found myself for the first time on a conspicuous field of political action. . . . One of the appointments called me to Quincy on the day when one of the great debates between Lincoln and Douglas was to take place there, and on that occasion I was to meet Abraham Lincoln myself. On the evening before the day of the debate, I was on a railroad train bound for Quincy. The car in which I traveled was full of men who discussed the absorbing question with great animation. A member of the Republican State Committee accompanied me and sat by my side.

All at once, after the train had left a way station, I observed a great commotion among my fellow passengers, many of whom jumped from their seats and pressed eagerly around a tall man who had just entered the car. They addressed him in the most familiar style: "Hello, Abe! How are you?" and so on. And he responded in the same manner: "Good evening, Ben! How are you, Joe? Glad to see you, Dick!" and there was much laughter at some things he said, which, in the confusion of voices, I could not understand. "Why," exclaimed my companion, the committeeman, "there's Lincoln himself!" He pressed through the crowd and introduced me to Abraham Lincoln, whom I then saw for the first time.

I must confess that I was somewhat startled by his appearance. There he stood, overtopping by several inches all those surrounding him. Although measuring something over six feet myself, I had, standing quite near to him, to throw my head backward in order to look into his eyes. That swarthy face with its strong features, its deep furrows, and its benignant, melancholy eyes, is now familiar to every American. . . . At that time it was clean-shaven, and looked even more haggard and careworn than later when it was framed in whiskers.

On his head he wore a somewhat battered stovepipe hat. His neck emerged, long and sinewy, from a white collar turned down over a thin black necktie. His lank, ungainly body was clad in a rusty black dress coat with sleeves that should have been longer; but his arms appeared so long that the sleeves of a store coat could hardly be expected to cover them all the way down to the wrists. His black trousers, too, permitted a very full view of his large feet. On his left arm he carried a gray woolen shawl, which evidently served him for an overcoat in chilly weather. His left hand held a cotton umbrella of the bulging kind, and also a black satchel that bore the marks of long and hard usage. His right he had kept free for handshaking, of which there was no end until everybody in the car seemed to be satisfied. I had seen, in Washington and in the West, several public men of rough appearance; but none whose looks seemed quite so uncouth, not to say grotesque, as Lincoln's.

He received me with an offhand cordiality, like an old acquaintance, having been informed of what I was doing in the campaign, and we sat down together. In a somewhat high-pitched but pleasant voice he began to talk to me, telling me much about the points he and Douglas had made in the debates at different places, and about those he intended to make at Quincy on the morrow.

When, in a tone of perfect ingenuousness, he asked me—a young beginner in politics—what I thought about this and that, I should have felt myself very much honored by his confidence, had he permitted me to regard him as a great man. But he talked in so simple and familiar a strain, and his manner and homely phrase were so absolutely free from any semblance of self-con-

sciousness or pretension to superiority, that I soon felt as if I had
known him all my life and we had long been close friends. He in-
terspersed our conversation with all sorts of quaint stories, each
of which had a witty point applicable to the subject in hand, and
not seldom concluding an argument in such a manner that nothing more was to be said. He seemed to enjoy his own jests in a
childlike way, for his unusually sad-looking eyes would kindle
with a merry twinkle, and he himself led in the laughter; and his
laugh was so genuine, hearty, and contagious that nobody could
fail to join in it.

When we arrived at Quincy, we found a large number of friends
waiting for him, and there was much handshaking and many familiar salutations again. Then they got him into a carriage, much
against his wish, for he said that he would prefer to "foot it to
Browning's," an old friend's house, where he was to have supper
and a quiet night. But the night was by no means quiet outside.
The blare of brass bands and the shouts of enthusiastic, and not
in all cases quite sober, Democrats and Republicans, cheering and
hurrahing for their respective champions, did not cease until the
small hours.

The next morning the country people began to stream into
town for the great meeting, some singly, on foot or on horseback,
or small parties of men and women, and even children, in buggies
or farm wagons; while others were marshaled in solemn procession
from outlying towns or districts with banners and drums, many
of them headed by maidens in white with tricolored scarfs, who
represented the Goddess of Liberty and the different States of
the Union, and whose beauty was duly admired by everyone, including themselves. On the whole, the Democratic displays were
much more elaborate and gorgeous than those of the Republicans,
and it was said that Douglas had plenty of money to spend for
such things. He himself also traveled in what was called in those
days "great style," with a secretary and servants and a numerous
escort of somewhat loud companions, moving from place to place
by special train with cars specially decorated for the occasion, all
of which contrasted strongly with Lincoln's extremely modest
simplicity. There was no end of cheering and shouting and jostling on the streets of Quincy that day. But in spite of the excite-

ment created by the political contest, the crowds remained very good-natured, and the occasional jibes flung from one side to the other were uniformly received with a laugh.

The great debate took place in the afternoon on the open square, where a large, pine-board platform had been built for the committee of arrangements, the speakers, and the persons they wished to have with them. I thus was favored with a seat on that platform. In front of it many thousands of people were assembled, Republicans and Democrats standing peaceably together, only chaffing one another now and then in a good-tempered way.

As the champions arrived they were demonstratively cheered by their adherents. The presiding officer agreed upon by the two parties called the meeting to order and announced the program of proceedings. Mr. Lincoln was to open with an allowance of one hour. . . . His voice was not musical, rather high-keyed, and apt to turn into a shrill treble in moments of excitement; but it was not positively disagreeable. It had an exceedingly penetrating, far-reaching quality. The looks of the audience convinced me that every word he spoke was understood at the remotest edges of the vast assemblage. His gesture was awkward. He swung his long arms sometimes in a very ungraceful manner. Now and then he would, to give particular emphasis to a point, bend his knees and body with a sudden downward jerk, and then shoot up again with a vehemence that raised him to his tiptoes and made him look much taller than he really was—a manner of enlivening a speech which at that time was, and perhaps still is, not un-usual in the West, but which he succeeded in avoiding at a later period.

There was, however, in all he said, a tone of earnest truthful-ness, of elevated, noble sentiment, and of kindly sympathy, which added greatly to the strength of his argument, and became, as in the course of his speech he touched upon the moral side of the question in debate, powerfully impressive. Even when attacking his opponent with keen satire or invective, which, coming from any other speaker, would have sounded bitter and cruel, there was still a certain something in his utterance making his hearers feel that those thrusts came from a reluctant heart, and that he would much rather have treated his foe as a friend.

8

TWO DAYS later, at the last debate of the series, another German-American intellectual and liberal, Gustave Koerner, had an opportunity to form his impressions.

I ATTENDED ONLY the last joint meeting, shortly before the election, at Alton. I arrived there in the morning, and found Lincoln in the hotel sitting room. He at once said: "Let us go up and see Mary." I had not seen Mrs. Lincoln, that I recollected, since meeting her at the Lexington parties, when she was Miss Todd. "Now, tell Mary what you think of our chances! She is rather dispirited." I was certain, I said, of our carrying the State and tolerably certain of our carrying the Legislature. St. Clair was perfectly safe. The outlook in Madison was good. We had just then been reading the St. Louis morning papers, where it was announced that more than a thousand Douglas men had chartered a boat to attend the Alton meeting, and that they represented the Free-Soil party in Missouri and were enthusiastic for Douglas's election. We discussed fully the singular position that party had taken under the lead of Frank Blair, who had been the great champion of the cause of our party in Missouri, ever since the repeal of the Missouri Compromise. I found Lincoln a little despondent. He had come quietly down from Springfield with his wife that morning, unobserved, and it was not until an hour or so that his friends were made aware of his arrival. He was soon surrounded by a crowd of Republicans; but there was no parade or fuss, while Douglas, about noon, made his pompous entry, and soon afterwards the boat from St. Louis landed at the wharf, heralded by the firing of guns and the strains of martial music.

The speaking commenced at two o'clock. The stand was on the public square. It was occupied by the speakers and by the Lincoln and Douglas Reception Committees of Alton. Mr. Lincoln took me with him on the platform. Here I met, for the first time since 1856, Judge Douglas, who in his genial manner shook hands with me, apparently quite cordially. But I was really shocked at the condition he was in. His face was bronzed, which was natural enough, but it was also bloated, and his looks were haggard, and his voice almost extinct. In conversation he merely whispered. In addressing his audience he made himself understood only by an immense strain, and then only to a very small circle immediately near him. He had the opening and conclusion. His speech, however, was as good as any he had delivered. Lincoln, although sunburned, was as fresh as if he had just entered the campaign, and as cool and collected as ever. Without any apparent effort he stated his propositions clearly and tersely, and his whole speech was weighted with noble and deep thoughts. There were no appeals to passion and prejudice.

The Alton speech contained, by general admission, some of the finest passages of all the speeches he ever made. When Douglas's opening speech had been made, he was vociferously cheered. When, after Lincoln's speech, which made a powerful impression, Douglas made his reply, there was hardly any applause when he closed.

9

IN A FEW PARAGRAPHS, Angle carries the rivalry through the last days of the campaign, Lincoln's concluding speech at Springfield, and the outcome.

A T   L A S T   T H E   C A M P A I G N   neared its close. The Douglas meeting of October 20 was the last big effort of the Democrats, and the final Republican rally took place on the thirtieth. Its pattern was familiar—delegations from nearby cities, fluttering flags and banners, parades and fireworks. During the afternoon Lincoln spoke from a stand on the east side of the square, concluding with an eloquent and touching reference to his own part in the contest. "In some respects the contest has been painful to me," he said. "Myself, and those with whom I act have been constantly accused of a purpose to destroy the Union; and bespattered with every imaginable odius epithet; and some who were friends as it were but yesterday have made themselves most active in this. I have cultivated patience, and made no attempt at a retort.

"Ambition has been ascribed to me. God knows how sincerely I prayed from the first that this field of ambition might not be opened. I claim no insensibility to political honors; but today could the Missouri restriction be restored, and the whole slavery question be replaced on the old ground of 'toleration' by *necessity* where it exists, with unyielding hostility to the spread of it, on principle, I would, in consideration, gladly agree, that Judge Douglas should never be *out*, and I never *in*, an office, so long as we both or either, live."

After Lincoln came Richard Yates, who spoke until six o'clock, and that evening a succession of speakers held forth in the rotunda of the State House. Late that night, when finally the town was quiet, the campaign came to an end.

On November 2, rain fell throughout the day and the streets were in a terrible condition, but the largest vote ever polled in the city was turned out in spite of the weather. The next day it was apparent that Douglas had won his re-election. Over the State as a whole the Republican candidates had received a majority of the popular vote, but the apportionment favored their opponents, and Douglas's re-election was a certainty. In Springfield and Sangamon County the vote was close, but the Douglas candidates had clear majorities over their Republican and Danite opponents.

Two months later the General Assembly of Illinois met in joint session. Before crowded galleries James W. Barrett, of Sangamon, nominated Stephen A. Douglas for the United States Senate; Norman B. Judd, of Cook, nominated Abraham Lincoln. A few minutes later the vote was announced: Douglas, 54; Lincoln, 46. "Glory to God and the Sucker Democracy," Lanphier wired to his chief in Washington. A short time afterward he sent a second telegram: "Announcement followed by shouts of immense crowd present. Town wild with excitement. Democrats firing salute. Guns, music, and whiskey rampant." Back from Washington came the message: "Let the voice of the people rule."

10

WHAT WAS IT ALL ABOUT—the parades and rallies, the oratory, the long columns of newsprint? James G. Randall dispassionately weighs the arguments of the rival candidates.

I T IS SURPRISING how little attention has been given to the actual content of the debates. The canvass had been conducted in dead earnest, yet it has always been easier to relate its picturesque features than to analyze its substance. It was symptomatic of the times that the debaters were not concerned with a representative coverage of national questions, but almost entirely with slavery, and with only a limited and comparatively unimportant aspect of that subject. Public attention is seldom devoted to a balanced and fully rounded estimate of public problems. It takes some selected issue and concentrates on that. So do political parties, with the added factor that parties make it appear that they are more opposite than they really are, that their points of difference on an incomplete statement of issues are the only things the people need to contemplate, and that party voting is the infallible method of accomplishing large results. One may distinguish between a discussion that strives always for a solution of governmental problems and a "canvass" in which the participants engage in sparring for popular effect and party advantage. In the main the joint debates between Lincoln and Douglas belong in the latter category.

Swinging up and down and back and forth across Illinois, making the welkin ring and setting the prairies on fire, Lincoln and Douglas debated—what? That is the surprising thing. With all the problems that might have been put before the people as proper matter for their consideration in choosing a Senator— choice of government servants, immigration, the tariff, international policy, promotion of education, westward extension of railroads, the opening of new lands for homesteads, protection against greedy exploitation of those lands (a problem to which Congress gave insufficient attention), encouragement to settlers, and the bettering of agriculture, not to mention such social problems as guarding against economic depression, improving the condition of factory workers, and alleviating those agrarian grievances that were to plague the coming decades—with such issues facing the country, these two candidates for the Senate talked as if there were only one issue. Thus instead of a representative coverage of the problems of mid-century America, the debaters gave virtually all their attention to slavery in the territories. More specifically, they were concentrating on the question whether Federal prohibition of slavery in western territories, having been dropped after full discussion in 1850, should be revived as if it were the only means of dealing with the highly improbable chance that human bondage would ever take root in such a place as Kansas, Nebraska, or New Mexico. It is indeed a surprising thing to suppose that the negligible amount of human bondage in Kansas, or the alleged inability of the people of that nascent state to decide the matter for themselves, constituted the only American question of sufficient importance to occupy nearly all the attention of senatorial candidates in one of the most famous forensic episodes of the century. Remembering that slavery in the large was not the subject of the debates, it may be said that if the highly unlikely inflow of slavery into Kansas was the main topic of national concern, the American people were more fortunate than they knew.

It was not that any frontal attack upon slavery in the states was involved. Lincoln was far from being an abolitionist, and nothing was more obvious in the controlling counsels of Lincoln's party in that period than the avoidance of any "ultra"—i.e., strongly abolitionist—tone. The "peculiar institution" was not being assailed by the Republican party in the commonwealths where it existed. Nor was it a case of one side demanding full civil and social equality for the Negro while the other side opposed such equality. Big and fundamental things about slavery and the Negro were not on the agenda of national parties. Each speaker could swell or mute the discussion on those fundamentals as he saw fit, and they were usually muted so far as commitments or constructive proposals were concerned. Despite all this, the intensity of the discussion baffled description. The people of Illinois were being worked up in party feeling by a discussion which contributed little to the practical solution even of such a matter as slaves in Kansas.

The debate was a spectacle, a drama, an exhibition, almost a sporting event. In addition it was a serious matter, but its dramatic quality could not be ignored, and that quality would perhaps have been lost if the speakers had not used the language of controversy. In other words, the Lincoln-Douglas canvass was not an effort to work out a formula of agreement. Had such an effort been made, it would have been found that these two leaders had much in common. On the broad problem of racial relations they did not fundamentally differ. Lincoln was not proposing any marked change in the depressed status of the Negro. "I am not . . . in favor of . . . the social and political equality of the

white and black races," he declared. Again he said: ". . . I am
not in favor of negro citizenship." It is not easy to put Lincoln's
actual position in a word, for it did not fit any pat formula, certainly not that of the Abolitionist. He cited Clay as showing that
equality was abstract; you could not apply it. The idea that he
favored Negro suffrage or equality, he said, was a misrepresenta-
tion. It was "untrue," a "fabrication." As if to leave no doubt on
that point he said: ". . . I did not at any time say I was in favor
of negro suffrage; . . . I declared against it."

This was not the whole of Lincoln's position on Negro rights.
He denounced the principle that "all men" did not include the
Negro. He qualified his statements carefully. While holding that
there was a "physical difference" which would "forever forbid the
two races living together on terms of social and political equality," and while favoring the "superior position assigned to the
white race," he did not believe that "the negro should be denied
everything." He did not favor "a tendency to dehumanize the
negro, to take away from him the right of ever striving to be a
man." Matters of racial equality, intermarriage and the like, he
dismissed as "false issues." The equality he was interested in was
not a matter of color or size but of inalienable rights. He believed
the Southern people entitled to a fugitive slave law. As to slavery
in the states, not only did he recognize a lack of Federal power
to overthrow it; he also disclaimed any "inclination" to "disturb"
it. He was not insisting that Missouri should emancipate its
slaves. No such thing. Such a thought was a "perversion" of his
meaning. His concern was for new societies, not old states.

As to slavery in Kansas, Lincoln wanted Kansas free by congressional prohibition; Douglas favored a program that would
inevitably have made Kansas free both as a territory by popular
sovereignty and as a state by constitutional processes. The attitude of the two men toward the Kansas policy of Buchanan was
virtually identical, though on this point the Republicans were unwilling to give Douglas credit for agreeing with them—this in
spite of the fact that some Republicans, but not Lincoln, even
spoke of Douglas as a suitable leader for their own party.

Lincoln and Douglas were also alike in deploring sectionalism.
Douglas wanted always to subordinate any issue that would split
the people North and South. For that very reason he did not want

to agitate the slavery question. Lincoln equally deplored disruptive tendencies, but he attributed the disunity to the discarding of the old concept that slavery was to remain of limited extent.

Statements flung about in the debates did not define the issue as a choice between a position taken by Lincoln and an opposite position taken by Douglas. This became evident when, early in the canvass, each candidate sought to impale his opponent upon spikes of formal interrogation. At Freeport Lincoln answered seven questions put to him by Douglas. In the first five his position differed not at all from his rival's. His answer to the seventh was noncommittal. Only on the sixth (prohibition of slavery in all the national territories) was there a difference between the two men. Yet even on that point the difference was not vital in its practical effect upon the results. That is to say, in the territories that existed or might later be organized, Lincoln's demand of congressional prohibition for slavery would produce freedom, but so also would Douglas's principle of popular sovereignty honestly applied.

Conversely, Douglas's answers to Lincoln's questions at Freeport showed him taking either a free-state position or a non-committal attitude on those points on which Lincoln was also noncommittal. Douglas's answers were as follows: (1) He would consider Kansas entitled to admission as a free state before reaching a set figure of population which Lincoln mentioned. (2) By police regulations he considered that slavery might be kept out of a territory. This was the famous question which has caused the others (on both sides) to be unjustly dwarfed. (3) Asked whether he would favor a decree of the Supreme Court that states could not exclude slavery, Douglas showed himself "amazed" at the question and clinched the matter in the free-state sense by saying that such a declaration "would be an act of moral treason that no man on the bench could ever descend to." (4) In the possible future acquisition of any new territories he would leave the people thereof free to make it slave or nonslave as they should prefer. . . .

As to red herrings and such, there was little to choose between the contestants. Both were guilty. Douglas rang the changes on "Black Republicans," on Missouri abolishing slavery and sending a "hundred thousand emancipated slaves into Illinois, to become

citizens and voters," on turning "this beautiful State into a free
negro colony," on Lincoln's fancied collusion with Trumbull, on
his alleged lack of patriotism with reference to the Mexican War,
and on his changeable doctrines, "jet-black" in the north, "a
decent mulatto" in the center, and "almost white" in Egypt. Lincoln countered with taunts as to Douglas's alleged support of a
hypothetical future Supreme Court decision that would make
slavery national, with accusations as to a conspiracy between
Stephen, Roger, *et al.*, and with charges of "fraud, . . . absolute
forgery" traceable to Charles H. Lanphier, editor of the *Illinois
State Register,* T. L. Harris, member of Congress, and Douglas.

It cannot be said that the debates as such, in any clarification of
issues, loomed large in the solution of the "vexed question" with
which the nation was bedeviled. By 1858 it was evident that slavery in Kansas had no chance. Indeed the decisive step on this
matter was taken in the free-state sense on August 2, 1858, before
the joint debates began. After that, as Professor W. O. Lynch
has shown, "there was no remaining Federal territory where the
conditions were so favorable to slavery." The fight against the
Lecompton pro-slavery constitution was won not by reason of any
debate between Lincoln and Douglas, but by the logical workings
of natural causes and by a specific contest in which, with "the aid
of Republicans, he [Douglas] won the Lecompton fight." In 1861
Kansas was admitted as a free state, but this was just as much in
accordance with Douglas's principles as with Lincoln's. In no
sense did it occur by any overruling of Douglas. It came about
while Federal law concerning slavery in the territories remained
the same as in 1854. Douglas "won" the debate, as they say; yet
the free-state objective was not only successful in Kansas before
war broke; it was successful with Douglas's free consent and outspoken leadership. On the whole, any attempt to add luster to
Lincoln's fame by belittling Douglas or by exaggerating the
seriousness of differences between the two men, would be a perversion of history. In the sequel, when the severe national crisis came,
Douglas "defended the Inaugural address of Mr. Lincoln against
the assault of opposition senators," and stood firmly with Lincoln
in upholding the union.

On their merits, said Beveridge, the debates "deserve little
notice." The same general conclusion has been reached by George

Fort Milton, who has written as follows: "Judged as debates, they do not measure up to their reputation. On neither side did the dialectic compare with that in the debates between Webster, Hayne and Calhoun." Historically, aside from their content and merit, there were two main results of the debates, both of which were revealed in 1860: (1) Douglas's position at Freeport in answer to Lincoln's second question, gave Southern extremists a handle by which to produce a fateful schism in the Democratic party. This Southern result followed not from any difference between Douglas and Lincoln but from what might be called the free-state aspect of Douglas's declaration. Douglas suffered, not from any dodge nor from Lincoln's adroitness in pinning him down to an embarrassing position, but rather by his own forthright courage in expounding an interpretation of popular sovereignty which would favor freedom where people wished it. (2) The debates so advertised Lincoln that he became a figure of national importance; without them his becoming the Republican presidential candidate in 1860 would have been far less likely. Lincoln achieved this result while taking an attitude on specific proposals that was antislavery only in the mildest and most cautious sense. He managed somehow to obtain both radical and moderate support. Dissociating himself from Abolitionists without quite repelling them, he made a telling appeal to moderates of the North. With the help of circumstances, and by a kind of irony, he made Douglas pay dearly for a position which offended the South only as far as it favored freedom, which Lincoln also favored.

CHAPTER TWELVE

"The Taste Is in My Mouth a Little"

O*NE NIGHT TOWARD THE END of the campaign of 1858 Abraham Lincoln arrived at a flag station not far from Springfield. There he found one other prospective passenger—young Henry Villard, who was reporting the canvass for the* New York Staats-Zeitung. *Rain soon forced the two men to take shelter in an empty freight car. While they waited—the train they were expecting was late—Lincoln talked freely of his life and prospects. His wife, he said, insisted he would be elected Senator, and then President. "Just think of such a Sucker as me," he said with rueful laughter, "as President."*

Yet already there were a good many men who were thinking that there would be nothing ludicrous in electing him to the presidency. Their conviction was strengthened when he spoke with outstanding success in several midwestern states during the year 1859; their faith grew strong with his address at Cooper Union and his subsequent tour of New England early in 1860. By that time he was an avowed candidate, and the number of his supporters was becoming formidable.

Experienced politicians saw that the strength of his position lay in the weaknesses of his rivals. William H. Seward, former Governor of New York, United States Senator since 1848, forthright opponent of slavery extension, acknowledged leader of the party—shrewd, opportunistic, a generous and unembittered cynic—had an immense popular following, but because of a reputation for radicalism (not wholly deserved) he was considered to be incapable of carrying several states that had to be carried. Salmon P. Chase, of Ohio, whose political career embraced two terms as governor and one in the United States Senate, was more radical than Seward, personally unpopular, and lacked the united support of his own State's delegation. Edward Bates, of Missouri, had a nativist background which the German voters, a strong element in the party, would not stomach. John McLean, of the United States Supreme Court, admired by conservatives, was simply too old.

Lincoln, on the other hand, was not well enough known to be marked indelibly as either radical or conservative. Except for his one term in Congress he had not held national office, and therefore he had neither a record that could be used against him nor the aggregation of enemies that a man long in public life acquires. His humble birth would arouse enthusiasm among the masses; his residence in one of the "doubtful" states was an important asset.

As the Republican National Convention was about to assemble in Chicago, the elements of victory lay within reach of the small group of Illinoisans who had taken charge of Lincoln's political fortunes. Could these men, novices in national politics, see those elements, grasp them, manipulate them into a majority of delegates' votes?

1

CARL SANDBURG DRAWS "a few elusive outlines" of the national scene on the eve of the Convention.

CYNICAL FOREIGNERS were saying of American politics, "On all sides one hears of nothing but the spoils." Without promises and arrangements as to offices and favors, a candidate was beaten before he began running. "Here and there the feeble voice of a philosopher or a greenhorn mutters something about principle, but his utterance is drowned in the hoarse croak of the practical men who clamor for spoils."

The editor of *Harper's* warned the country. Unless "the intelligent people" woke up and took a hand in real politics, the country might soon pass into the hands of "Vigilance Committees or an Augustus or a Bonaparte."

And yet again, looking at business and industrial America, one felt the future of America was to swarm with forces of history. The editor of *Harper's* told his million readers the future would take care of itself. There was "a common saying." It ran, "A special Providence watches over children, drunkards, and the United States."

And the editor surveyed the past. "The United States, during the last eighty years, has endowed the world with the lightning-rod, the steamboat, the photograph, the electric telegraph, the discovery of the use of inhaled ether, the sewing machine; the best and cheapest farm implements, the best carpenter's tools, the best locks, fire-engines, nails, spikes, screws, and axes; the best fire-arms, the cheapest clocks, the fastest steamers and sailing vessels, the cheapest railroads, and the lightest wagons, and many labor-saving machines. If any nation, during the same eighty years, has done more, or as much, the fact is not generally known."

In arts of peace and war America was leading the world. "In bridges we challenge the world. In lightness, elegance, and strength, some American bridges are unsurpassed; and more than one of the finest bridges in Europe were designed by an American." Four hundred plows had been invented within fifty years. "The world has produced no printing-press equal to that of Adams of Boston," wrote the editor of *Harper's*. And, "At Sebastopol both Russian and Allied officers preferred the Colt's revolver to any other holster or belt weapon; the bodyguard of the Emperor of China is said to have made the same sensible choice. Wherever men or beasts are to be shot—Sharpe's, Perry's, Wesson's—are household words." And the editor wrote how machinery had made one man as a thousand, and a thousand as a million, and as he looked at science and industry he could hear "mysterious voices whispering forth majestic prophecies of a new future." He ended a panegyric, "The age has surely come for a new order of humanity, a new answer to the anthem, 'Peace on Earth.' If the nations still follow their insane game, it will be in the face of the solemn intervention of the heralds of God's truce."

Thus ran a few elusive outlines of the civilization of the United States in the months when Davis, Fell, Swett, Dubois, Herndon, Medill, and Ray were running their dark horse, Abraham Lincoln, in the race for a presidential nomination in 1860.

2

SANDBURG MEASURES the currents and undercurrents of politics that were running in the spring of 1860 as the brash new West prepared to test its strength against the Republican stalwarts from the machine-controlled states of the East.

LINCOLN WROTE TO an Ohio delegate, of the coming national Republican Convention in Chicago, that Seward "is the very best candidate we could have for the North of Illinois, and the very *worst* for the South of it." With Chase, of Ohio, it would be likewise in Illinois. Bates, of Missouri, would be the best candidate for the South of Illinois and the worst for the North. "I am not the fittest person to answer the questions you ask about candidates. When not a very great man begins to be mentioned for a very great position, his head is very likely to be a little turned." With Senator Trumbull he could be easier in speech. "As you request, I will be entirely frank. The taste *is* in my mouth a little." He did honestly have some hankerings for the presidency. "And this, no doubt, disqualifies me, to some extent, to form correct opinions." After which he made the same points for Trumbull that he had made for the Ohio delegate.

His own philosophy of personal conduct in politics, the scrupulous caution that gave rise to the whisper of "cunning as a fox," yet which he considered sagacity, horse sense, or some quality necessary for the growth and unity of a party organization, was seen in his writing to Trumbull: "A word now for your own special benefit. You better write no letters which can possibly be distorted into opposition or quasi-opposition to me. There are men on the constant watch for such things out of which to prejudice my peculiar friends against you." The old Whig Republicans, and the former Democrats turned Republican, were sore and growling. "While I have no more suspicion of you than I have of my best friend living, I am kept in a constant struggle against suggestions of this sort. I have hesitated some to write this paragraph, lest you should suspect I do it for my own benefit, and not for yours; but on reflection I conclude you will not suspect me." He hinted at his code as to personal secrets. "Let no eye but your

own see this—not that there is anything wrong, or even ungenerous, in it; but it would be misconstrued."

The Ohio delegate wrote to Lincoln again, asking "the lay of
the land." Lincoln replied on May 2, the national Convention that
would name or reject him being just two weeks ahead: "First I
think the Illinois delegation will be unanimous for me at the start;
and no other delegation will. A few individuals in other delegations would like to go for me at the start, but may be restrained
by their colleagues. It is represented to me by men who ought to
know, that the whole of Indiana might not be difficult to get. You
know how it is in Ohio. I am certainly not the first choice there;
and yet I have not heard that anyone makes any positive objection to me. It is just so everywhere as far as I can perceive. Everywhere, except here in Illinois and possibly in Indiana, one or another is preferred to me, but there is no positive objection." On
May 12 his friends Jesse K. Dubois and Judge David Davis
would probably be in Chicago "ready to confer with friends from
other States." To an Indiana delegate and others, he wrote they
could see Dubois and Davis.

He wrote to another Ohio delegate, expressing thanks for confidence, and pointing to his one biggest advantage as a candidate:
"If I have any chance, it consists mainly in the fact that the
whole opposition would vote for me, if nominated. (I don't mean
to include the pro-slavery opposition of the South, of course.) My
name is new in the field, and I suppose I am not the first choice of
a very great many." And in two sentences there was a shading of
color, an indication of the philosophy that often governed Lincoln
in tight places. He wrote: "Our policy, then, is to give no offense
to others—leave them in a mood to come to us if they shall be
compelled to give up their first love. This, too, is dealing justly
with all, and leaving us in a mood to support heartily whoever
shall be nominated."

The Kansas politician, Mark Delahay, asked for money, Lincoln replying: "Allow me to say I can not enter the ring on a
money basis—first, because, in the main it is wrong; and secondly,
I have not, and can not get, the money. I say, in the main, the
use of money is wrong; but for certain objects, in a political contest, the use of some is both right and indispensable." He had

known Delahay a year or two. "With me, as with yourself, this long struggle has been one of great pecuniary loss." And the nub of the letter was reached: "I now distinctly say this: If you shall be appointed a delegate to Chicago, I will furnish one hundred dollars to bear the expenses of the trip." In a second letter to Delahay, he closed, "Come along to the convention, and I will do as I said about expenses."

Opposition to Lincoln for the presidential nomination came from several of his friends. Browning, of Quincy, for instance, had tried law cases associated with Lincoln, and had often spent evenings at the Lincoln home in Springfield. Browning had not changed in his view as written in his diary in February: "At night Lincoln came to my room, and we had a free talk about the Presidency. He thinks I may be right in supposing Bates to be the strongest and best man we can run—that he (Bates) can get votes even in this county that he (Lincoln) cannot get—and that there is a large class of voters in all the free States that would go for Mr. Bates, and for no other man. Dick Yates and Phillips also think Mr. Bates stronger in this State than any other man who has been named." The same view was held by the *New York Tribune*, which was backing Bates to beat Seward.

A little heart-warming piece of news came to Lincoln one day. John Hanks had come out for him for President. It was a sign. John Hanks and he had split rails, toiled in cornfield and on flatboat together, sleeping and watching in snow and rain. Their lives were bound as with leather thongs. But until now John had been a Democrat. Even two years previous John had voted for Douglas. That honest John Hanks's heart had been reached was a sign. Were the plain people seeing something? Was there an undertow of new history in the making? . . .

Yet there were peculiar undercurrents against Lincoln. Browning, for instance, who had tried cases with Lincoln and dined often at the Lincoln home, was for Bates for President. Oglesby and other delegates had walked with Lincoln out to a quiet place on a railroad track where they sat down and talked. Oglesby was in favor of cutting off Browning from the list of delegates to the Chicago National Convention. Lincoln advised that this would make an enemy of Browning and he might then do more mischief than if he were sent to Chicago as a member of a delegation instructed to vote as a unit for Lincoln's nomination. "Lincoln sat on one of the railroad rails and his legs nearly reached clean across to the other rail," said Oglesby, telling later about the railroad-track conference that guided the Decatur convention.

Only two weeks earlier, the national Democratic Convention had met in Charleston, South Carolina, and the Douglas delegates, holding a majority control, but lacking the necessary two-thirds to nominate their man for President, had split the party, and two separate wings of it were planning conventions in June; the powerful political body that had controlled the Government practically thirty years was staggering. The answers of Douglas to Lincoln in the Freeport debate had shown him to be a straddler; the trust of the South in him, once so loyal, was gone; he was slippery, greased with expedients; with Douglas their property was not safe.

Yancey, of Alabama, tall, slender, with long black hair, spoke in a soft, musical voice for the minority, the first time in generations of men that the South was in a minority and without the votes to name the candidate for President. The Southern gentlemen had cheered, the Southern ladies filling the galleries had waved handkerchiefs. It was a moment of history. Yancey pronounced a swan song. "We came here with one great purpose, to save our Constitutional rights. We are in the minority, as we have been taunted here today. In the progress of civilization, the Northwest has grown up from an infant in swaddling clothes into the free proportions of a giant people. We therefore, as the minority, take the rights, the mission, and the position of the minority."

Yancey was dealing with the fact. The Northwest had grown up; Douglas had captured it politically, and thereby made the South a political minority, in the Democratic party; and Douglas had swung its power as a big stick, and was calling for a platform pledge to abide by the Dred Scott decision or any future decision of the Supreme Court on the rights of property in the states or territories.

"The proposition you make," said Yancey, "will bankrupt us of the South. Ours is the property invaded—ours the interests at stake. The honor of our children, the honor of our females, the lives of our men, all rest upon you. You would make a great seething caldron of passion and crime if you were able to consummate your measures."

Douglas men blamed the Convention chairman, Caleb Cushing, the Boston lawyer, and close friend of Jefferson Davis, for rulings; a Douglas rhymer wrote, "A poisonous reptile, many-scaled, and with most subtle fang, Crawled forward, Caleb Cush, while behind his rattles rang."

Ten days of speeches, ballots, wrangles, brought adjournment to Baltimore in June. Caleb Cushing uttered the dirge, "I fondly trust that we shall continue to march on forever, the hope of nations in the old world as in the new."

And little Alexander Stephens, weighing less than ninety pounds, with black eyes smoldering, "the little pale star from Georgia," blazed out, in a talk with a friend: "Men will be cutting one another's throats in a little while. In twelve months we shall be in a war, the bloodiest in history." But why civil war, even if a Republican President were elected? "Because," murmured the Little Pale Star, "there are not virtue and patriotism and sense enough left in the country to avoid it."

In the Senate at Washington, Davis and Douglas clashed. "I would sooner have an honest man on any sort of a rickety platform than to have a man I did not trust on the best platform which could be made," said Davis, drawing from Douglas the question, "Why did you not tell us in the beginning that the whole fight was against the man and not upon the platform?"

Senator Seward of New York gazed on what was happening and felt satisfied. He had started for his home in Auburn, New York, to write his letter accepting the Republican nomination for President. Would he not have more delegates to start with than any other candidate, and was not there a trend for him even in the Illinois and Indiana delegations? And his manager, Thurlow Weed, was rigging a plan which, according to a letter of William Cullen Bryant, was "to give charters for a set of city railways in New York, for which those who receive them are to furnish a fund of from four to six hundred thousand dollars, to be expended for the Republican cause in the next Presidential election"? Bankers, railroad presidents, business men who wanted government grants were putting their trust in Weed.

In Springfield, Judge Logan, the little frowsy-headed lawyer who used to sit on the circuit court bench and hold court in a gray linen shirt without a necktie, was having a new silk hat made by Adams, the hatter. Other delegates were outfitting with silk hats and broadcloth suits of clothes, to go to the Chicago convention on May 16. Lincoln wrote to Solomon Sturges, the Chicago banker, thanks for proffered hospitality during the Convention. He had decided to stay home. "I am a little too much a candidate to stay home and not quite enough a candidate to go."

3

RICHARD J. OGLESBY of Decatur, Illinois, a bluff, friendly man who was later to be commissioned a major general of volunteers and to be elected Governor and United States senator, tells how Lincoln came to be called the "Rail Splitter." The nick-name grew out of the Illinois State Republican Convention, held at Decatur the week before the National Convention met in Chicago.

I HAD KNOWN John Hanks all my life. He was a Democrat, but a great friend of Lincoln. Years before they had gone together on a flatboating expedition down the Mississippi. He had wanted to vote for Lincoln for United States Senator, but he could not do this without voting for the local Republican candidates for the Legislature. As soon as he heard that Lincoln might be nominated for President, he was bound to vote for "old Abe."

One day I was talking with John about Abe, and he said that in 1830 they made a clearing twelve miles west of Decatur. There was a patch of timber—fifteen or twenty acres—and they had cleared it; they had built a cabin, cut the trees, hauled rails, and put up a fence.

"John," said I, "did you split rails down there with old Abe?"

"Yes; every day," he replied.

"Do you suppose you could find any of them now?"

"Yes," he said. "The last time I was down there, ten years ago, there were plenty of them left. . . ."

The next day we drove out to the old clearing. We turned in by the timber, and John said:

"Dick, if I don't find any black walnut rails, nor any honey locust rails, I won't claim it's the fence Abe and I built."

Presently John said, "There's the fence!"

"But look at these great trees," said I.

"Certainly," he answered. "They have all grown up since."

John got out. I sat in the buggy. John kneeled down and commenced chipping the rails of the old fence with his knife. Soon he came back with black walnut shavings and honey locust shavings.

"There they are!" said he, triumphantly, holding out the shavings. "They are the identical rails we made."

Then I got out and made an examination of the fence. There were many black walnut and honey locust rails. . . .

We took two of the rails and tied them under the hind axletree of my new buggy, and started for town. People would occasionally pass and think something had broken. We let them think so, for we didn't wish to tell anybody just what we were doing. We kept right on until we got to my barn. There we hid the rails until the day of the Convention.

Before the Convention met I talked with several Republicans about my plan, and we fixed it up that old John Hanks should take the rails into the Convention. We made a banner, attached to a board across the top of the rails, with the inscription:

ABRAHAM LINCOLN
The Rail Candidate
For President in 1860.
Two rails from a lot of 3000 made in 1830 by
John Hanks and Abe Lincoln, whose father
was the first pioneer of Macon County.

After the Convention got under way, I arose and announced that an old Democrat desired to make a contribution to the Convention. The proceedings stopped, and all was expectancy and excitement. Then in walked old John with the rails. Lincoln was there in a corner, trying to escape observation.

"How are you, Abe?" said John, familiarly, as he passed.

"How are you, John?" Lincoln answered with equal familiarity.

Then the Convention cheered and cheered. There were loud and persistent calls for a speech from Lincoln. Abe had not known that the rails were to be brought in. He hardly knew what to say about them.

"Gentlemen," he finally said, "John and I did make some rails down there; and if these aren't the identical rails we made, they certainly look very much like them."

From that time forward the rail was ever present in the campaign. There was a great demand for Lincoln rails. John Hanks sold the two that he brought into the Convention. A man from Kentucky gave him five dollars for one. The next day he went out and got a wagonload, and put them in my barn. He sold them for a dollar apiece. Then other people went into the business, and the supply seemed inexhaustible.

4

THE OPENING SESSION of the Republican National Convention is portrayed in the words of Murat Halstead, who reported it for his paper, the *Cincinnati Commercial*. Only thirty-one, Halstead had not yet acquired the reputation that his brilliant reporting of the Conventions of 1860—a high mark in the annals of American journalism—and his war correspondence, were soon to bring him. The young city of Chicago, playing host to a national political convention for the first time, was a subject of almost as much interest as the Convention itself.

Chicago, May 15.

THE CROWD IS this evening becoming prodigious. The Tremont House is so crammed that it is with much difficulty people get about in it from one room to another. Near fifteen hundred people will sleep in it tonight. The principal lions in this house are Horace Greeley and Frank P. Blair, Sr. The way Greeley is stared at as he shuffles about, looking as innocent as ever, is itself a sight. Whenever he appears there is a crowd gaping at him, and if he stops to talk a minute with some one who wishes to consult him as the oracle, the crowd becomes dense as possible, and there is the most eager desire to hear the words of wisdom that are supposed to fall on such occasions.

The curiosity of the town—next to the Wigwam—is a bowie knife seven feet long, weighing over forty pounds. It bears on one side the inscription, *"Presented to John F. Potter by the Republicans of Missouri."* On the other side is this motto, *"Will always keep a 'Pryor' engagement."* This curiosity is gaped at almost as

much as Greeley, and it is a strange and dreadful looking concern.
It is to be formally presented to Potter at Washington by a committee from Missouri.

The city of Chicago is attending to this Convention in magnificent style. It is a great place for large hotels, and all have their
capacity for accommodation tested. The great feature is the Wigwam erected within the past month, expressly for the use of the
Convention, by the Republicans of Chicago, at a cost of seven
thousand dollars. It is a small edition of the New York Crystal
Palace, built of boards, and will hold ten thousand persons comfortably—and is admirable for its accoustic excellence. An ordinary voice can be heard through the whole structure with ease.

The political news is the utter failure of the Ohio delegation to
come to any agreement, and the loss of influence by that State.

Chicago, May 16th.

This is the morning of the first day of the Convention. The
crowd is prodigious. The hotel-keepers say there are more people
here now than during the National Fair last year, and then it
was estimated that thirty thousand strangers were in the city.
This figure was probably too high, but there are, beyond doubt,
more than twenty-five thousand persons here in attendance upon
the Convention. . . .

As in the case of all other conventions, the amount of idle talking that is done is amazing. Men gather in little groups, and with
their arms about each other, and chatter and whisper as if the fate
of the country depended upon their immediate delivery of the
mighty political secrets with which their imaginations are big.
There are a thousand rumors afloat, and things of incalculable
moment are communicated to you confidentially, at intervals of
five minutes. There are now at least a thousand men packed together in the halls of the Tremont House, crushing each other's
ribs, tramping each other's toes, and titillating each other with
the gossip of the day; and the probability is, not one is possessed
of a single political fact not known to the whole which is of the
slightest consequence to any human being.

The current of the universal twaddle this morning is that "Old
Abe" will be the nominee.

The Bates movement, the McLean movement, the Cameron

movement, the Banks movement, are all nowhere. They have gone down like lead in the mighty waters. "Old Abe" and "Old Ben" are in the field against Seward. Abe and Ben are representatives of the conservatism, the respectability, the availability, and all that sort of thing.

The out-and-out friends of Mr. Chase here are very much embittered against the Wade movement. They are mistaken about it in some particulars. While this movement has certainly been used to slaughter Mr. Chase, it was not, in my judgment, originated with any such purpose.

The roommates, the pleasure of whose society I am enjoying, were in magnificent condition last night. They were "glorious," — "o'er all the ills of life victorious," and, to use the expression which is here in everybody's mouth every minute, they were irrepressible until a late hour. And this morning I was aroused by a vehement debate among them, and rubbing my eyes, discovered that they were sitting up in bed playing cards to see who should pay for gin cocktails all around, the cocktails being an indispensable preliminary to breakfast.

The badges of different candidates are making their appearance, and a good many of the dunces of the occasion go about duly labeled. I saw an old man this morning with a woodcut of Edward Bates pasted outside his hat. The Seward men have badges of silk with his likeness and name, and some wag pinned one of them to Horace Greeley's back yesterday, and he created even an unusual sensation as he hitched about with the Seward mark upon him.

The hour for the meeting of the Convention approaches, and the agitation of the city is exceedingly great. Vast as the Wigwam is, not one-fifth of those who would be glad to get inside can be accommodated.

5

DURING THE FIRST TWO DAYS the Convention organized and adopted a platform. That document denied the right of any authority to give legal existence to slavery in the national territories, denounced popular sovereignty, called for the admission of Kansas as a state, and advocated protective tariffs, a homestead law, and the construction, with federal aid, of a railroad to the Pacific. Behind the scenes party managers argued, cajoled, and traded with desperation. By the third day the stage was set for the nomination. Halstead relates what happened.

THE SEWARD MEN generally abounded in confidence Friday morning. The air was full of rumors of the caucusing the night before, but the opposition of the doubtful states to Seward was an old story; and after the distress of Pennsylvania, Indiana & Co., on the subject of Seward's availability, had been so freely and ineffectually expressed from the start, it was not imagined their protests would suddenly become effective. The Sewardites marched as usual from their headquarters at the Richmond House after their magnificent band, which was brilliantly uniformed — epaulets shining on their shoulders, and white and scarlet feathers waving from their caps — marched under the orders of recognized leaders, in a style that would have done credit to many volunteer military companies. They were about a thousand strong, and, protracting their march a little too far, were not all able to get into the Wigwam. This was their first misfortune. They were not where they could scream with the best effect in responding to the mention of the name of William H. Seward.

When the Convention was called to order, breathless attention was given the proceedings. There was not a space a foot square in the Wigwam unoccupied. There were tens of thousands still outside, and torrents of men had rushed in at the three broad doors until not another one could squeeze in.

The first thing of interest was a fight regarding the Maryland delegation. A rule had been adopted that no delegation should cast more votes than there were duly accredited delegates. The Maryland delegation had not been full, and Mr. Montgomery Blair of that state now wanted to fill up the delegation. Three of the delegates, who were Seward men, opposed filling up the ranks with men, as one of them said, "God Almighty only knows where they come from." Here was another Seward triumph, for the Blairs were not allowed to add to the strength of their Maryland delegation. It might be said of the Blairs and the Maryland delegation as Thaddeus Stevens said of the Union and Constitutional Convention at Baltimore, "It was a family party—*it was all there.*"

Everybody was now impatient to begin the work. Mr. Evarts,

of New York, nominated Mr. Seward. Mr. Judd, of Illinois, nominated Mr. Lincoln. Mr. Dudley, of New Jersey, nominated Mr. Dayton. Mr. Reeder, of Pennsylvania, nominated Simon Cameron. Mr. Cartter, of Ohio, nominated Salmon P. Chase. Mr. Caleb Smith, of Indiana, seconded the nomination of Lincoln. Mr. Blair, of Missouri, nominated Edward Bates. Mr. Blair, of Michigan, seconded the nomination of William H. Seward. Mr. Corwin, of Ohio, nominated John McLean. Mr. Schurz, of Wisconsin, seconded the nomination of Seward. Mr. Delano, of Ohio, seconded the nomination of Lincoln. The only names that produced "tremendous applause," were those of Seward and Lincoln.

Everybody felt that the fight was between them, and yelled accordingly.

The applause, when Mr. Evarts named Seward, was enthusiastic. When Mr. Judd named Lincoln, the response was prodigious, rising and raging far beyond the Seward shriek. Presently, upon Caleb B. Smith's seconding the nomination of Lincoln, the response was absolutely terrific. It now became the Seward men to make another effort, and, when Blair of Michigan seconded his nomination,

> "At once there rose so wild a yell,
> Within that dark and narrow dell;
> As all the fiends from heaven that fell
> Had pealed the banner cry of hell."

The effect was startling. Hundreds of persons stopped their ears in pain. The shouting was absolutely frantic, shrill and wild. No Camanches, no panthers ever struck a higher note, or gave screams with more infernal intensity. Looking from the stage over the vast amphitheatre, nothing was to be seen below but thousands of hats—a black, mighty swarm of hats—flying with the velocity of hornets over a mass of human heads, most of the mouths of which were open. Above, all around the galleries, hats and handkerchiefs were flying in the tempest together. The wonder of the thing was, that the Seward outside pressure should, so far from New York, be so powerful.

Now the Lincoln men had to try it again, and as Mr. Delano, of Ohio, on behalf "of a portion of the delegation of that State," seconded the nomination of Lincoln, the uproar was beyond description. Imagine all the hogs ever slaughtered in Cincinnati giving their death squeals together, a score of big steam whistles going (steam at 160 lbs. per inch), and you conceive something of the same nature. I thought the Seward yell could not be surpassed; but the Lincoln boys were clearly ahead, and feeling their victory, as there was a lull in the storm, took deep breaths all around, and gave a concentrated shriek that was positively awful, and accompanied it with stamping that made every plank and pillar in the building quiver.

Henry S. Lane, of Indiana, leaped upon a table, and, swinging hat and cane, performed like an acrobat. The presumption is he shrieked with the rest, as his mouth was desperately wide open; but no one will ever be able to testify that he has positive knowledge of the fact that he made a particle of noise. His individual voice was lost in the aggregate hurricane.

The New York, Michigan and Wisconsin delegations sat together, and were in this tempest very quiet. Many of their faces whitened as the Lincoln *yawp* swelled into a wild hozanna of victory.

The Convention now proceeded to business. The New England States were called first, and it was manifest that Seward had not the strength that had been claimed for him there. Maine gave nearly half her vote for Lincoln. New Hampshire gave seven out of her ten votes for Lincoln. Vermont gave her vote to her Senator Collamer, which was understood to be merely complimentary. It appeared, however, that her delegation was hostile or indifferent to Seward, otherwise there would have been no complimentary vote to another. Massachusetts was divided. Rhode Island and Connecticut did not give Seward a vote. So much for the caucusing the night before. Mr. Evarts of New York rose and gave the vote of that State, calmly, but with a swelling tone of pride in his voice—"The State of *New York* casts her *seventy votes* for *William H. Seward!*" The seventy votes were a plumper, and there was slight applause and that rustle and vibration in the audience indicating a sensation. The most significant vote was that of Virginia, which had been expected solid for Seward, and which now gave him but eight and gave Lincoln fourteen. The New Yorkers looked significantly at each other as this was announced. Then Indiana gave her twenty-six votes for Lincoln. This solid vote was a startler, and the keen little eyes of Henry S. Lane glittered as it was given. He was responsible for it. It was his opinion that the man of all the land to carry the State of Indiana was Judge John McLean. He also thought Bates had eminent qualifications. But when he found that the contest was between Seward and Lincoln, he worked for the latter as if life itself depended upon success. The division of the first vote caused a fall in Seward stock. It was seen that Lincoln, Cameron and Bates had the strength to defeat Seward, and it was known that the greater part of the Chase vote would go for Lincoln.

The Secretary announced the vote:

William H. Seward, of New York, 173½.

Abraham Lincoln, of Illinois, 102.

Edward Bates, of Missouri, 48.

Simon Cameron, of Pennsylvania, 50½.

John McLean, of Ohio, 12.

Salmon P. Chase, of Ohio, 49.

Benjamin F. Wade, of Ohio, 3.

William L. Dayton, of New Jersey, 14.

John M. Reed, of Pennsylvania, 1.

Jacob Collamer, of Vermont, 10.

Charles Sumner, of Massachusetts, 1.

John C. Fremont, of California, 1.

Whole number of votes cast, 465; necessary to a choice, 233.

The Convention proceeded to a second ballot. Every man was fiercely enlisted in the struggle. The partisans of the various candidates were strung up to such a pitch of excitement as to render them incapable of patience, and the cries of "Call the roll" were fairly hissed through their teeth. The first gain for Lincoln was in New Hampshire. The Chase and the Fremont vote from that State were given him. His next gain was the whole vote of Vermont. This was a blighting blow upon the Seward interest. The New Yorkers started as if an Orsini bomb had exploded. And presently the Cameron vote of Pennsylvania was thrown for Lincoln, increasing his strength by forty-four votes. The fate of the day was now determined. New York saw "checkmate" next move, and sullenly proceeded with the game, assuming unconsciousness of her inevitable doom. On this ballot Lincoln gained 79 votes! Seward had 184½ votes; Lincoln 181.

(Great confusion while the ballot was being counted.)

The Secretary announced the result of the second ballot as follows:

For William H. Seward, of New York, 184½. [Applause.]

For Abraham Lincoln, of Illinois, 181. [Tremendous applause, checked by the Speaker.]

For Edward Bates, of Missouri, 35.

For Simon Cameron, of Pennsylvania, 2.

For John McLean, of Ohio, 8.

For Salmon P. Chase, of Ohio, 42½.

For William L. Dayton, of New Jersey, 10.

For Cassius M. Clay, of Kentucky, 2.

It now dawned upon the multitude, that the presumption entertained the night before, that the Seward men would have every thing their own way, was a mistake. Even persons unused to making the calculations and considering the combinations attendant upon such scenes, could not fail to observe that while the strength of Seward and Lincoln was almost even at the moment, the reserved votes, by which the contest must be decided, were inclined to the latter. There, for instance, was the Bates vote, 35; the McLean vote, 8; the Dayton vote, 10—all impending for Lincoln —and 42 Chase votes, the greater part going the same way. . . .

While this ballot [the third] was taken amid excitement that tested the nerves, the fatal defection from Seward in New England still further appeared—four votes going over from Seward to Lincoln in Massachusetts. The latter received four additional votes from Pennsylvania and fifteen additional votes from Ohio. It was whispered about—"Lincoln's the coming man—will be nominated this ballot." When the roll of states and territories had been called, I had ceased to give attention to any votes but those for Lincoln, and had his vote added up as it was given. The number of votes necessary to a choice were 233, and I saw under my pencil as the Lincoln column was completed, the figure 231½— one vote and a half to give him the nomination. In a moment the fact was whispered about. A hundred pencils had told the same story. The news went over the house wonderfully, and there was a pause. There are always men anxious to distinguish themselves on such occasions. There is nothing that politicians like better than a crisis. I looked up to see who would be the man to give the decisive vote. The man for the crisis in the Cincinnati Convention

—all will remember—was Colonel Preston of Kentucky. He broke
the Douglas line and precipitated the nomination of Buchanan,
and was rewarded with a foreign mission. In about ten ticks of a
watch, Cartter, of Ohio, was up. I had imagined Ohio would be
slippery enough for the crisis. And sure enough! Every eye was
on Cartter, and everybody who understood the matter at all knew
what he was about to do. He is a large man with rather striking
features, a shock of bristling, black hair, large and shining eyes,
and is terribly marked with the smallpox. He has also an impediment in his speech, which amounts to a stutter; and his selection
as chairman of the Ohio delegation was, considering its condition,
altogether appropriate. He had been quite noisy during the sessions of the Convention, but had never commanded, when mounting his chair, such attention as now. He said, "I rise (eh), Mr.
Chairman (eh), to announce the change of four votes of Ohio
from Mr. Chase to Mr. Lincoln." The deed was done. There was
a moment's silence. The nerves of the thousands, which through
the hours of suspense had been subjected to terrible tension, re-
laxed, and as deep breaths of relief were taken, there was a noise
in the Wigwam like the rush of a great wind in the van of a storm
—and in another breath, the storm was there. There were thousands cheering with the energy of insanity.

A man who had been on the roof, and was engaged in communicating the results of the ballotings to the mighty mass of out-
siders, now demanded by gestures at the skylight over the stage,
to know what had happened. One of the secretaries, with a tally
sheet in his hands, shouted—"Fire the salute! Abe Lincoln is
nominated!" As the cheering inside the Wigwam subsided, we
could hear that outside, where the news of the nomination had just
been announced. And the roar, like the breaking up of the fountains of the great deep, that was heard, gave a new impulse to the
enthusiasm inside. Then the thunder of the salute rose above the
din, and the shouting was repeated with such tremendous fury that
some discharges of the cannon were absolutely not heard by those
on the stage. Puffs of smoke, drifting by the open doors, and the
smell of gunpowder, told what was going on.

The moment that half a dozen men who were on their chairs
making motions at the President could be heard, they changed the
votes of their states to Mr. Lincoln. This was a mere formality,

and was a cheap way for men to distinguish themselves. The proper and orderly proceeding would have been to announce the vote, and then for a motion to come from New York to make the nomination unanimous. New York was prepared to make this motion, but not out of order. Missouri, Iowa, Kentucky, Minnesota, Virginia, California, Texas, District of Columbia, Kansas, Nebraska and Oregon insisted upon casting unanimous votes for Old Abe Lincoln before the vote was declared.

While these votes were being given, the applause continued, and a photograph of Abe Lincoln which had hung in one of the side rooms was brought in, and held up before the surging and screaming masses. The places of the various delegations were indicated by staffs, to which were attached the names of the states, printed in large black letters on pasteboard. As the Lincoln enthusiasm increased, delegates tore these standards of the states from their places and swung them about their heads. A rush was made to get the New York standard and swing it with the rest, but the New Yorkers would not allow it to be moved, and were wrathful at the suggestion.

When the vote was declared, Mr. Evarts, the New York spokesman, mounted the secretaries' table and handsomely and impressively expressed his grief at the failure of the Convention to nominate Seward—and, in melancholy tones, moved that the nomination be made unanimous. . . .

After a rather dull speech from Mr. Browning of Illinois, responding in behalf of Lincoln, the nomination was made unanimous, and the Convention adjourned for dinner. The town was full of the news of Lincoln's nomination, and could hardly contain itself. There were bands of music playing, and processions marching, and joyous cries heard on every hand, from the army of trumpeters for Lincoln of Illinois, and the thousands who are always enthusiastic on the winning side. But hundreds of men who had been in the Wigwam were so prostrated by the excitement they had endured, and by their exertions in shrieking for Seward or Lincoln, that they were hardly able to walk to their hotels. There were men who had not tasted liquor, who staggered about like drunkards, unable to manage themselves. The Seward men were terribly stricken down. They were mortified beyond all expression, and walked thoughtfully and silently away from the slaughterhouse, more ashamed than embittered. They acquiesced in the nomination, but did not pretend to be pleased with it; and the tone of their conversations, as to the prospect of electing the candidate, was not hopeful. It was their funeral, and they would not make merry.

A Lincoln man who could hardly believe that the "Old Abe" of his adoration was really the Republican nominee for the presidency, took a chair at the dinner table at the Tremont House, and began talking to those around him, with none of whom he was acquainted, of the greatness of the events of the day. One of his expressions was, "Talk of your money and bring on your bullies with you!—the immortal principles of the everlasting people are with Abe Lincoln, of the people, by—." "Abe Lincoln has no money and no bullies, but he has the people by—." A servant approached the eloquent patriot and asked what he would have to eat. Being thus recalled to temporal things, he glared scornfully at the servant and roared out, "Go to the devil—what do I want to eat for? Abe Lincoln is nominated, G—d—it; and I'm going to live on air—the air of Liberty by—." But in a moment he inquired for the bill of fare, and then ordered "a great deal of every thing," saying if he must eat he might as well eat "the whole bill." He swore he felt as if he could "devour and digest an Illinois prairie." And this was one of thousands. . . .

The city was wild with delight. The "Old Abe" men formed processions, and bore rails through the streets. Torrents of liquor were poured down the hoarse throats of the multitude. A hundred guns were fired from the top of the Tremont House. The *Chicago Press and Tribune* office was illuminated. That paper says:

"On each side of the counting-room door stood a *rail*—out of the three thousand split by 'honest Old Abe' thirty years ago on the Sangamon River bottoms. On the inside were two more, brilliantly hung with tapers."

I left the city on the night train on the Fort Wayne and Chicago road. The train consisted of eleven cars, with every seat full and people standing in the aisles and corners. I never before saw a company of persons so prostrated by continued excitement. The Lincoln men were not able to respond to the cheers which went up along the road for Old Abe. They had not only done their duty in that respect, but exhausted their capacity. At every station where there was a village, until after two o'clock, there were tar barrels burning, drums beating, boys carrying rails, and guns, great and small, banging away. The weary passengers were allowed no rest, but were plagued by the thundering jar of cannon, the clamor of drums, the glare of bonfires, and the whooping of the boys, who were delighted with the idea of a candidate for the presidency who thirty years ago split rails on the Sangamon River—classic stream now and forevermore—and whose neighbors named him "honest."

6

BACK IN SPRINGFIELD, life centered around the communication lines from Chicago. Ward Hill Lamon describes how Lincoln accepted the news of his nomination.

A LL THAT DAY [May 17] and all the day previous Mr. Lincoln was in Springfield, trying to behave as usual, but watching the proceedings of the Convention, as they were reported by telegraph, with nervous anxiety. Mr. Baker, the friend who had taken the *Missouri Democrat* to Chicago with Mr. Lincoln's pregnant indorsement upon it, returned on the night of the 18th. Early in the morning, he and Mr. Lincoln went to the ball alley to play at "fives"; but the alley was pre-engaged. They went to an "excellent and neat beer saloon" to play a game of billiards; but the table was occupied. In this strait they contented themselves with a glass of beer, and repaired to the *Journal* office for news.

C. C. Brown says that Lincoln played ball a great deal that day, notwithstanding the disappointment when he went with Baker; and Mr. Zane informs us that he was engaged in the same way the greater part of the day previous. It is probable that he took this physical mode of working off or keeping down the unnatural excitement that threatened to possess him.

About nine o'clock in the morning [of May 18], Mr. Lincoln came to the office of Lincoln and Herndon. Mr. Zane was then conversing with a student. "Well, boys," said Mr. Lincoln, "what do you know?" "Mr. Rosette," answered Zane, "who came from Chicago this morning, thinks your chances for the nomination are good." Mr. Lincoln wished to know what Mr. Rosette's opinion was founded upon; and, while Zane was explaining, Mr. Baker entered with a telegram, which said the names of the candidates for nomination had been announced, and that Mr. Lincoln's had been received with more applause than any other. Mr. Lincoln lay down on a sofa to rest. Soon after, Mr. Brown entered; and Mr. Lincoln said to him, "Well, Brown, do you know anything?" Brown did not know much; and so Mr. Lincoln, secretly nervous and impatient, rose and exclaimed, "Let's go to the telegraph office." After waiting some time at the office, the result of the first ballot came over the wire. It was apparent to all present that Mr. Lincoln thought it very favorable. He believed that if Mr. Seward failed to get the nomination, or to "come very near it" on the first ballot, he would fail altogether. Presently the news of the second ballot arrived, and Mr. Lincoln showed by his manner that he considered the contest no longer doubtful. "I've got him," said he. He then went over to the office of the *Journal*, where other friends were awaiting decisive intelligence. The local editor of that paper, Mr. Zane, and others, remained behind to receive the expected dispatch. In due time it came. The operator was intensely excited; at first he threw down his pencil, but, seizing it again, wrote off the news that threw Springfield into a frenzy of delight. The local editor picked it up, and rushed to the *Journal* office. Upon entering the room, he called for three cheers for the next President. They were given, and then the dispatch was read. Mr. Lincoln seemed to be calm, but a close observer could detect in his countenance the indications of deep emotion. In the meantime cheers for Lincoln swelled up from the streets, and began to be heard throughout the town. Some one remarked, "Mr. Lincoln, I suppose now we will soon have a book containing your life." "There is not much," he replied, "in my past life about which to write a book, as it seems to me." Having received the hearty congratulations of the company in the office, he descended to the street, where he was immediately surrounded by "Irish and American citizens"; and, so long as he was willing to receive it, there was great handshaking and felicitating. "Gentlemen," said the great man with a happy twinkle in his eye, "you had better come up and shake my hand while you can; honors elevate some men, you know." But he soon bethought him of a person who was of more importance to him than all this crowd. Looking toward his house, he said, "Well,

gentlemen, there is a little short woman at our house who is probably more interested in this dispatch than I am; and, if you will
excuse me, I will take it up and let her see it."

During the day a hundred guns were fired at Springfield; and
in the evening a great mass meeting "ratified" the nomination,
and, after doing so, adjourned to the house of the nominee. Mr.
Lincoln appeared, made a "model" speech, and invited into his
house everybody that could get in. To this the immense crowd
responded that they would give him a larger house the next year,
and in the mean time beset the one he had until after midnight.

7

IN CHICAGO, the Convention speedily nominated Hannibal Hamlin
for the vice-presidency and then adjourned. On the following day,
May 19, the committee which had been appointed to give Lincoln
formal notice of the nomination reached Springfield. Charles Carleton Coffin, western correspondent of the *Boston Journal,* gives an
account of the reception accorded to the delegation.

I T   W A S   P A S T   E I G H T   O ' C L O C K   Saturday evening when the
committee called upon Mr. Lincoln at his home—a plain, comfortable, two-storied house, a hallway in the center, a plain white
paling in front. The arrival of the committee had aroused no
enthusiasm on the part of the townspeople. A dozen citizens gathered in the street. One of Mr. Lincoln's sons was perched on the
gatepost. The committee entered the room at the left hand of the
hall. Mr. Lincoln was standing in front of the fireplace, wearing
a black frock coat. He bowed, but it was not gracefully done.
There was an evident constraint and embarrassment. He stood
erect, in a stiff and unnatural position, with downcast eyes. There
was a diffidence like that of an ungainly schoolboy standing alone
before a critical audience. Mr. Ashmun stated briefly the action
of the convention and the errand of the committee. Then came the
reply. . . . It was a sympathetic voice, with an indescribable
charm in the tones. There was no study of inflection or cadence for
effect, but a sincerity which won instant confidence. The lines
upon his face, the large ears, sunken cheeks, enormous nose,
shaggy hair, the deep-set eyes, which sparkled with humor, and

which seemed to be looking far away, were distinguishing facial marks. I do not know that any member of the company, other than Mr. Tuck, of New Hampshire, and some of the Western men, had ever seen him before, but there was that about him which commanded instant admiration. A stranger meeting him on a country road, ignorant of his history, would have said, "He is no ordinary man."

Mr. Lincoln's reply was equally brief. With the utterance of the last syllable his manner instantly changed. A smile, like the sun shining through the rift of a passing cloud sweeping over the landscape, illuminated his face, lighting up every homely feature, as he grasped the hand of Mr. Kelly.

"You are a tall man, Judge. What is your height?"

"Six feet three."

"I beat you. I am six feet four without my high-heeled boots."

"Pennsylvania bows to Illinois. I am glad that we have found a candidate for the presidency whom we can look up to, for we have been informed that there were only *little giants* in Illinois," was Mr. Kelly's graceful reply.

All embarrassment was gone. Mr. Lincoln was no longer the ungainly schoolboy. The unnatural dignity which he had assumed for the moment, as a barrister of the English bar assumes gown and horsehair wig in court, was laid aside. Conversation flowed as freely and laughingly as a meadow brook. There was a bubbling up of quaint humor, fragrant with Western idiom, making the hour exceedingly enjoyable.

"Mrs. Lincoln will be pleased to see you, gentlemen," said Mr. Lincoln. "You will find her in the other room. You must be thirsty after your long ride. You will find a pitcher of water in the library."

I crossed the hall and entered the library. There were miscellaneous books on the shelves, two globes, celestial and terrestrial, in the corners of the room, a plain table with writing materials upon it, a pitcher of cold water, and glasses, but no wines or liquors. There was humor in the invitation to take a glass of water, which was explained to me by a citizen, who said that when it was known that the committee was coming, several citizens called upon Mr. Lincoln and informed him that some entertainment must be provided.

"Yes, that is so. What ought to be done? Just let me know and I will attend to it," he said.

"O, we will supply the needful liquors," said his friends.

"Gentlemen," said Mr. Lincoln, "I thank you for your kind intentions, but must respectfully decline your offer. I have no liquors in my house, and have never been in the habit of entertaining my friends in that way. I cannot permit my friends to do for me what I will not myself do. I shall provide cold water—nothing else."

What Mr. Lincoln's feelings may have been over his nomination will never be known; doubtless he was gratified, but there was no visible elation. After the momentarily assumed dignity he was himself again—plain Abraham Lincoln—man of the people.

8

THE NOMINATION OF LINCOLN, Halstead commented, "was the triumph of a presumption of availability over pre-eminence in intellect and unrivalled fame—a success of the ruder qualities of manhood and the more homely attributes of popularity, over the arts of a consummate politician, and the splendor of accomplished statesmanship." From the perspective of another country and another century, Lord Charnwood confirms his appraisal.

On the whole, if we can put aside the illusion which besets us, who read the preceding history if at all in the light of Lincoln's speeches, and to whom his competitors are mere names, this was the most surprising nomination ever made in America. Other presidential candidates have been born in poverty, but none ever wore the scars of poverty so plainly; others have been intrinsically more obscure, but these have usually been chosen as bearing the hallmark of eminent prosperity or gentility. Lincoln had indeed at this time displayed brilliant ability in the debates with Douglas, and he had really shown a statesman's grasp of the situation more than any other Republican leader. The friends in Illinois who put him forward—men like David Davis, who was a man of distinction himself—did so from a true appreciation of his powers. But this does not seem to have been the case with the bulk of the delegates from other states. The explanation given us of their action is

‚curious. The choice was not the result of merit; on the other hand, it was not the work of the ordinary wicked wire-puller, for what may be called the machine was working for Seward. The choice was made by plain, representative Americans who set to themselves this question: "With what candidate can we beat Douglas?" and who found the answer in the prevalence of a popular impression concerning Lincoln and Seward, which was in fact wholly mistaken. There was, it happens, earnest opposition to Seward among some Eastern Republicans on the good ground that he was a clean man but with doubtful associates. This opposition could not by itself have defeated him. What did defeat him was his reputation at the moment as a very advanced Republican who would scare away the support of the weaker brethren. He was, for instance, the author of the alarming phrase about "irrepressible conflict," and he had spoken once, in a phrase that was misinterpreted, about a "higher law than the Constitution." Lincoln had in action taken a far stronger line than Seward; he was also the author of the phrase about the house divided against itself; but then, besides the fact that Lincoln was well regarded just where Douglas was most 'popular, Lincoln was a less noted man than Seward and his stronger words occasioned less wide alarm. So, to please those who liked compromise, the Convention rejected a man who would certainly have compromised, and chose one who would give all that moderation demanded and die before he yielded one further inch. Many Americans have been disposed to trace in the raising up of Lincoln the hand of a Providence protecting their country in its worst need. It would be affectation to set their idea altogether aside; it is, at any rate, a memorable incident in the history of a democracy, permeated with excellent intentions but often hopelessly subject to inferior influences, that at this critical moment the fit man was chosen on the very ground of his supposed unfitness.

CHAPTER THIRTEEN

Candidate and President–elect

WHILE LINCOLN QUIETLY WORE the *fame that the nomination had brought to him the Democratic party proceeded to make his election a certainty. Three weeks before the Chicago Convention the Democrats had met at Charleston to find their differences irreconcilable. When Northern delegates refused the demand of the Southerners that the platform include a plank to the effect that it was the duty of the Federal government to pass legislation protecting slave property in the territories, delegations from several slave states left the Convention. Even then discord continued to prevail, for in fifty-seven ballots Douglas was never able to muster the two-thirds majority necessary for his nomination. Finally, on May 3, the Convention adjourned, to meet at Baltimore six weeks later.*

That interval failed to soften animosities, and the Baltimore Convention, like its predecessor, fell apart. Once more the intransigents withdrew. Only then could the remaining delegates bring about what they had determined upon at the beginning—the nomination of Stephen A. Douglas.

Before the month of May was out, however, two more candidates for the presidency were in the field. One was John C. Breckinridge, nominated by the seceders from the Convention which had finally named Douglas; and John Bell, chosen by Old Whigs and others calling themselves the Constitutional Union Party. With the field thus di-

*vided, Lincoln could win the presidency simply by not
making mistakes.*

*That, however, was more difficult than it appears to a
later generation. The crisis over secession was developing,
and a foolish move could easily precipitate it. More immediate was the pressure for offices. The Republican party
had never been in power, and thousands of its members
were looking with covetous eyes on the spoils which they
expected November to put within reach. Claims of the
faithful had to be weighed with the utmost care, and decisions deferred as long as possible.*

*The election over, these twin cares pressed more and
more heavily upon the man who was now confronted, as he
himself said, with a task greater than that which rested
upon Washington. But visitors to the daily receptions
which he continued to hold in the Governor's room of the
Illinois State House and notables whom he received at his
home found him unchanged by his responsibilities: found
him still a plain and kindly man who could put old friends
at ease, find time for a long last talk with his law partner,
and take leave of his fellow townsmen with simple words of
farewell which the future would prove to be tragically
final.*

1

SIX WEEKS AFTER the Convention, Lincoln wrote a letter to
Dr. A. G. Henry, one of his few close friends, who was now living in
Oregon Territory. In it, he surveys his prospects—and reveals that
not even candidates for the presidency are immune to family cares.

Springfield, Illinois, July 4, 1860.
My dear Doctor: Your very agreeable letter of May 15th was
received three days ago. . . .

Long before this you have learned who was nominated at Chicago. We know not what a day may bring forth, but to-day it
looks as if the Chicago ticket will be elected. I think the chances
were more than equal that we could have beaten the Democracy
united. Divided as it is, its chance appears indeed very slim. But
great is Democracy in resources; and it may yet give its fortunes

a turn. It is under great temptation to do something; but what can it do which was not thought of, and found impracticable, at Charleston and Baltimore? The signs now are that Douglas and Breckinridge will each have a ticket in every State. They are driven to this to keep up their bombastic claims of nationality, and to avoid the charge of sectionalism which they have so much lavished upon us.

It is an amusing fact, after all Douglas has said about nationality and sectionalism, that I had more votes from the southern section at Chicago than he had at Baltimore! In fact, there was more of the southern section represented at Chicago than in the Douglas rump concern at Baltimore!

Our boy, in his tenth year (the baby when you left), has just had a hard and tedious spell of scarlet fever, and he is not yet beyond all danger. I have a headache and a sore throat upon me now, inducing me to suspect that I have an inferior type of the same thing.

Our eldest boy, Bob, has been away from us now nearly a year at school, and will enter Harvard University this month. He promises very well, considering we never controlled him much. Write again when you receive this. Mary joins in sending our kindest regards to Mrs. H., yourself, and all the family.

Your friend, as ever,

A. LINCOLN

2

HELEN NICOLAY, whose father became Lincoln's secretary soon after the nomination, recounts the Republican candidate's life and activities during the campaign summer of 1860.

BEING A PRESIDENTIAL CANDIDATE made astonishingly little difference in Mr. Lincoln's daily habits. More people rang the bell of the plain but comfortable house on Eighth Street. He opened the door himself if no one else was there to do it. More people stayed to dinner or supper on invitation of the host or the proud hostess, sitting down to a typically abundant Western table. When he appeared upon the street people came up to shake his hand—but they had been doing that for years.

Today it would be impossible for a man to achieve nomination without running the gauntlet of innumerable cameras. A gentleman who visited Springfield to congratulate Mr. Lincoln "and form his personal acquaintance" ventured to ask him "for a good likeness." He replied that he had no satisfactory picture—"But then," he said, "we will walk out together, and I will sit for one." Result: one ambrotype!

The headquarters of the National Committee remained as usual in New York. No "literary bureau," or other electioneering organization existed at Springfield. The local telegraph office, an inconvenient little apartment on the second floor of an office building near the Public Square, was not even enlarged. Lincoln wrote no public letters, and made no set or impromptu speeches, with the exception of speaking a word of greeting once or twice to passing street parades. Even the strictly confidential letters in which he gave advice on points in the campaign did not exceed a dozen in number.

The Legislature not being in session, the Governor's room in the State House was set aside for his use, and here he received his visitors, coming in usually between nine and ten o'clock in the morning, bringing with him the mail he had received at his own home. His office force consisted of one quiet young secretary, who assisted him with his correspondence in the intervals of greeting visitors; and wrote wonderingly to a correspondent of his own that Mr. Lincoln's mail averaged as many as fifty letters a day.

Many of them, being merely congratulatory, needed no answer. Letters from personal friends Mr. Lincoln acknowledged with his own hand; and in these he showed from the first considerable confidence of success. Governor Chase was the only one of his rivals in the Convention to write him. His letter, among the first to arrive, gave Lincoln much pleasure. "Holding myself the humblest of all those whose names were before the convention," he wrote in reply, "I feel especial need of the assistance of all; and I am glad—very glad—of the indication that you stand ready."

Cassius M. Clay, who had hoped to be nominated for Vice-President, wrote breezily:

"Well, you have cleaned us all out. The Gods favor you, and

we must with good grace submit. After your nomination for the first post, my chances were of course ruined for becoming heir to your old clothes. It became necessary to choose a Vice-president from the Northeast, and of Democratic antecedents. But after Old Kentucky had come so liberally to your rescue, I think you might have complimented us with more than two votes! Still we won't quarrel with you on that account. Nature does not aggregate her gifts; and as some of us are better-looking men than yourself, we must cheerfully award you the post of honor.

"Allow me to congratulate you, and believe me truly devoted to your success, and command my poor services if needed."

One letter of congratulation, quite apart from the rest, came from an old comrade in the Black Hawk War.

"Respected Sir: In view of the intimacy that at one time subsisted between you and me, I deem it my duty as well as privilege, now that the intensity of the excitement of recent transactions is a little passed from you and from me, after the crowd of congratulations already received from many friends, also to offer you my heartfelt gratulation on your very exalted position in the great Republican party. No doubt but that you will become tired of the flattery of cringing selfish adulators. But I think you will know that what I say I feel. For the attachment in the Black Hawk campaign while we messed together with Johnston, Faucher, and Wyatt, when we ground our coffee in the same cup with the hatchet handle—baked our bread on our ramrod around the same fire—ate our fried meat off the same piece of elm bark—slept in the same tent every night—traveled together by day and by night in search of the savage foe—and together scoured the tall grass on the battleground of the skirmish near Gratiot's Grove in search of the slain—with very many incidents too tedious to name—and consummated in our afoot and canoe journey home, must render us incapable of deception. Since the time mentioned, our pursuits have called us to operate a little apart; yours, as you formerly hinted, to a course of political and legal struggle; mine to agriculture and medicine. The success that we have both enjoyed, I am happy to know, is very encouraging. I am also glad to know, although we must act in vastly different spheres, that we are enlisted for the promotion of the same great cause—the cause which, next to revealed religion (which is humility and love) is most dear, the cause of Liberty, as set forth by true Republicanism and not rank abolitionism.

"Then let us go on in the discharge of duty, trusting for aid to the Great Universal Ruler.

"Yours truly,
GEORGE M. HARRISON."

Among the letters were many requests for his opinion on points of party doctrine. For these he prepared a polite form, explaining why he could not comply. There were also many letters of advice. William Cullen Bryant, whom we are wont to consider a poet rather than a politician, wrote with "the frankness of an old campaigner," to warn him against making speeches or promises—even to be chary of kind words. Joshua R. Giddings eloquently recommended John Quincy Adams as the model for an untried Westerner to follow. Such letters Lincoln answered with modest sincerity. "I appreciate the danger against which you would guard me," he wrote Bryant, "nor am I wanting in the purpose to avoid it. I thank you for the additional strength your words give me to maintain that purpose. . . ."

After two months had gone by, and Lincoln had received no word from his companion on the ticket, he sent him the following characteristic little note:

Hon. Hannibal Hamlin,

My Dear Sir: It appears to me that you and I ought to be acquainted, and accordingly I write this as a sort of introduction of myself to you. You first entered the Senate during the single term I was a member of the House of Representatives, but I have no recollection that we were introduced. I shall be pleased to receive a line from you.

The prospect of Republican success now appears very flattering, so far as I can perceive. Do you see anything to the contrary?

Yours truly,
A. LINCOLN.

The simplicity and friendliness of this were duplicated in the simplicity and friendliness with which he met his visitors—the neighbors who trusted him, political friends who admired him, and doubters come from afar to see what manner of Westerner a freak of popular fancy had made candidate of the vigorous young Republican party. They passed in and out of his door all day long, and each felt instinctively the kindness and honesty that shone from his deeply furrowed face. That wonderful expressive face, mirthful, shrewd, melancholy, and suffused with emotion by turns; so homely in its rugged uncompromising lines, so sad in moments of repose; on occasion so tenderly beautiful in expression. Neighbors who knew it of old loved it, though they would probably have called it ugly. Newcomers marveled at it, but soon forgot to question if it were handsome or not.

It seems odd that such a marked face could have been unknown to any one seeking him, yet there were those who met Mr. Lincoln and failed to recognize him. My father's notes tell of a stranger who asked the way to the State House. The tall man of whom he inquired said he was going there himself and offered to act as guide. Then, on reaching the Governor's room, turned upon him with a merry smile and quite inimitable gesture of apology, saying, "I am Lincoln."

Artists got permission to paint his portrait, and set up their easels in the Governor's room, doing their work as well as they could for the constant interruption of callers, and the marauding forays of Mr. Lincoln's two little boys, who appeared at intervals and got inextricably mixed with the paints, to the stifled wrath of the artist. Mr. Lincoln's mild, "Boys, boys, you mustn't meddle! Now run home and have your faces washed," seemed lamentably inadequate.

Jones, of Cincinnati, established a sculptor's studio near by, and made a bust of Mr. Lincoln, to which the candidate referred jokingly as his "mud-head." The sculptor Volk also made studies for a statue. On a certain Sunday morning he went by appointment to the house on Eighth Street to make casts of Mr. Lincoln's hands. Being asked to hold a stick, or something of the kind, he disappeared into the woodshed, the sound of sawing was heard, and he reappeared, whittling the edges of a piece of broom handle. Mr. Volk explained that it was not necessary to trim off the edges so carefully. "Oh, well," he said, "I thought I would like to have it nice."

Presents of a symbolic nature were showered upon the candidate until the room at the State House took on the aspect of a museum. Mr. Lincoln used the axes, wedges, log chains, and other implements as texts for explanations and anecdotes of pioneer craft; thus making them serve a double purpose in amusing his visitors and keeping the conversation away from politics.

For in all this exchange of friendly greeting, and under all the campaign enthusiasm, was a note of increasing anxiety. The South was making ugly threats. It behooved Lincoln to keep silence on party questions, and even more on the problems of national politics which loomed ever larger and darker as the summer advanced.

He was begged to issue some statement to allay the growing unrest in the South—to say something to reassure the men "honestly alarmed." "There are no such men," he answered stoutly. "It is the trick by which the South breaks down every Northern man. If I yielded to their entreaties I would go to Washington without the support of the men who now support me. I would be as powerless as a block of buckeye wood. The honest men—you are talking of honest men—will find in our platform everything I could say now, or which they would ask me to say."

So he went on talking pleasantries and pioneer days to his visitors, watching meanwhile the ever-growing menace behind the circle of their friendly faces.

The anxiety took on a personal note. In October his secretary wrote: "Among the many things said to Mr. Lincoln by his visitors there is nearly always an expressed hope that he will not be so unfortunate as were Harrison and Taylor, to be killed off by the cares of the Presidency—or as is sometimes hinted, by foul means. It is astonishing how the popular sympathy for Mr. Lincoln draws fearful forebodings from these two examples, which, after all, were only a natural coincidence. Not only do visitors mention the matter, but a great many letters have been written to Mr. Lincoln on the subject."

Another manifestation of the same feeling was noted by the Reverend Albert Hale, one of the pastors of Springfield, as he sat in the Governor's room, waiting to speak to Mr. Lincoln. "Several weeks ago," he wrote, "two country boys came along the dark passage that leads to his room. One of them looked in at the door, and then called to his fellow behind, saying, 'Come on, he is here.' The boys entered and he spoke to them. Immediately one of them said that it was reported in their neighborhood that he (Mr. Lincoln) had been poisoned, and their father had sent them to see if the report was true. 'And,' said the boy with all earnestness, 'Dad says you must look out and eat nothing only what your old woman cooks for you—and Mother says so too!' "

3

THROUGHOUT THE CAMPAIGN, rallies and political meetings were held almost nightly in Springfield. As a rule, Lincoln abstained from attendance, but when Carl Schurz spoke on July 24 he made an exception and attended. Schurz's version of the meeting and his visit with Lincoln reveals characteristics of the candidate that disturbed many "well bred" leaders, but appealed irresistibly to the lower ranks of party members.

W HILE ''STUMPING'' in Illinois I had an appointment to address an afternoon open-air meeting in the Capitol grounds in Springfield, Mr. Lincoln's place of residence. He asked me to take dinner with him at his house. At table we conversed about the course and the incidents of the campaign, and his genial and simple-hearted way of expressing himself would hardly permit me to remember that he was a great man and a candidate for the presidency of the United States. He was in the best of humor, and we laughed much. The inevitable brass band took position in front of the house and struck up a lively tune, admonishing us that the time for the business of the day had arrived. "I will go with you to the meeting," said Mr. Lincoln, "and hear what you have to say." The day was blazing hot. Mr. Lincoln expressed his regret that I had to exert myself in such a temperature, and suggested that I make myself comfortable. He indeed "made himself comfortable" in a way which surprised me not a little, but which was thoroughly characteristic of his rustic habits. When he presented himself for the march to the Capitol grounds I observed that he had divested himself of his waistcoat and put on, as his sole garment, a linen duster, the back of which had been marked

by repeated perspirations and looked somewhat like a rough map
of the two hemispheres. On his head he wore a well-battered
stovepipe hat which evidently had seen several years of hard
service. In this attire he marched with me behind the brass band,
after us, the local campaign committee and the Wide-Awakes.[1] Of
course, he was utterly unconscious of his grotesque appearance.
Nothing could have been farther from his mind than the thought
that the world-conspicuous distinction bestowed upon him by
his nomination for the presidency should have obliged him to
"put on dignity" among his neighbors. Those neighbors who, from
the windows and the sidewalks on that hot afternoon, watched and
cheered him as he walked by in the procession behind the brass
band, may have regarded him, the future President, with a new
feeling of reverential admiration, or awe; but he appeared before and among them entirely unconcerned, as if nothing had
happened, and so he nodded to his acquaintances, as he recognized
them in the crowd, with a: "How are you, Dan?" or "Glad to
see you, Ned!" or "How d'ye do, Bill?" and so on—just as he
had been accustomed to do. Having arrived at the place of
meeting, he declined to sit on the platform, but took a seat in the
front row of the audience. He did not join in the applause which
from time to time rewarded me, but occasionally he gave me a
nod and a broad smile. When I had finished, a few voices called
upon Mr. Lincoln for a speech, but he simply shook his head, and
the crowd instantly respected the proprieties of the situation,
some even shouting: "No, no!" at which he gratefully signified
his assent. Then the brass band, and the committee, and the Wide-
Awakes, in the same order in which we had come, escorted us back
to his house, the multitude cheering tumultuously for "Lincoln
and Hamlin," or more endearingly for "Old Abe."

4

THE PRESIDENTIAL ELECTION took place on November 6,
1860. Baringer chronicles Lincoln's day, as he cast his vote and
received the returns of the election.

---

[1] The Republican marching clubs that sprang up everywhere during the campaign of 1860. Generally, the members wore oilcloth caps and capes to protect
themselves from the drippings of their torches.

C ONTRARY TO CUSTOM, the sixth of November, 1860,
made its appearance as Election Day with the sun out and the
weather clement. Abraham Lincoln, Republican candidate for
President, intended to remain in his campaign office at the State
House, cordially greeting callers as he had done throughout the
canvass, until the balloting was over. In many earlier elections
the candidate had not scrupled to vote for himself. But this time
he did not intend to mark a ballot. He held the opinion that a
candidate for the presidency should not vote for his own electors.
On the morning of Election Day, however, Lincoln received a
suggestion from his law partner. Herndon proposed the expedient
of clipping the list of presidential electors from the ballot and
voting for the rest of the Republican ticket, arguing that his
vote might be needed to elect the state candidates. After some
argument the candidate assented. Picking up a Republican ballot
he trimmed the sheet. . . .

When the afternoon was half gone, Lincoln decided it was time
to cast his headless ballot. He left his office accompanied by
Herndon, Ward Lamon, of Bloomington, and Col. Elmer Ellsworth, of Chicago, went downstairs and across the street to
the Sangamon County Court House. At the poll he found a large
crowd (Herndon having spread the information that his partner
would vote) which gave voice to loud cheers as the candidate's
tall figure was seen approaching. Before the voter of note could
make his way out through the admiring throng of Republicans
and even Democrats who had been carried away by the infectious
enthusiasm of the occasion, he was obliged to doff his hat, smile,
shake hands and chat with numerous well-wishers. Back at the
Governor's room of the State House, Lincoln entertained callers
until the polls closed at sunset. Then he went immediately to the
telegraph office where preparations were made for giving him
returns as rapidly as possible, and for notifying him when important results began coming over the wire.

Shortly before nine o'clock a summons to the telegraph reached
Lincoln and a small group of friends in his borrowed office in the
State House, bringing a welcome end to the anxious lull which
follows the closing of the polls. Lincoln and party reached the

telegraph office as "the returns began to tap in" (in the words of the *New York Tribune's* special correspondent), the candidate establishing himself comfortably near the chattering machinery.

"The first fragments of intelligence were caught by the Superintendent as they ticked off at the table, and . . . were full of good cheer. Excepting Mr. Lincoln, whose interest was not so actively manifested, everybody present showed great excitement over each fresh bit of news. . . . Mr. Lincoln sat or reclined upon a sofa, while his companions mostly stood clustering around him. . . . As the evening advanced, other excitements were afforded by batches of private messages which came rushing in, mostly addressed to Mr. Lincoln, but in some cases to Senator Trumbull. . . . Whenever the information was of a peculiarly gratifying character, as it often was, the documents would be taken out by some thoughtful friend of the populace outside, and read aloud in the State House, or elsewhere, to large crowds which had met and were enjoying celebrations on the strength of their own convictions that the expected news would be sure to justify them. Occasionally, a line or two would come with so much force of encouragement as to set the little group beside itself with elation. A confident declaration from Gen. S. Cameron, promising abundance of good things from Pennsylvania, produced a sensation. . . . Some superb items which came just after, . . . setting aside all possibility of doubt as to New York, aroused demonstrations still more gleeful. There was just one person, however, who accepted everything with almost an immovable tranquility. Not that Mr. Lincoln undertook to conceal . . . the keen interest he felt in every new development; but, while he seemed to absorb it all with great satisfaction, the intelligence moved him to less energetic display of gratification. . . . His only departure from perfect quiet throughout the night was on hearing, just before he withdrew, of the complete success of the Republican ticket in his own precinct."

Until about midnight the returns came from the North and were generally good. Then the southern states were heard from. "Now," remarked Lincoln, "we should get a few licks back." Soon the news was entirely from the South, and "as the repetitions became a little monotonous, and as all this intelligence simply followed a foregone conclusion, Mr. Lincoln and the party went over at half-past twelve o'clock to a little gathering . . . which had been . . . prepared by the ladies of Springfield in anticipation of a long and weary night." Mrs. Lincoln was among those who had arranged the nocturnal victory feast of coffee and sandwiches, and had been on hand even for early returns. The ladies lionized Lincoln as President-elect. He was greeted with a chorus of "How do you do, Mr. President," and shook hands around while many enthusiasts expressed their emotions by rendering campaign ballads popular in the late canvass. "If Mr. Lincoln left the telegraph office for the purpose of taking a little refreshment," wrote a St. Louis correspondent, "he came as near to being killed by kindness as a man can conveniently be without serious results."

"At the State House the scene was five times as bad. Men pushed each other, threw up their hats, hurrahed, cheered for Lincoln, cheered for Trumbull, cheered for New York, cheered for everybody; and some actually laid down on the carpeted floor, and rolled over and over. It was some time before order could be restored to read the [following] dispatch . . . a second time. New York, 50,000 majority for Lincoln! And then another scene. . . . As this was the culminating point of doubt, groups commenced to leave—not to go to bed—but to let the town know the result. Some went one way and some another, yelling like demons. . . . And Springfield went off like one immense cannon report, with shouting from houses, shouting from stores, shouting from housetops, and shouting everywhere. Parties ran through the streets singing, Ain't I glad I've joined the Republicans, till they were too hoarse to speak."

During this tempest Lincoln shook hands, drank coffee, and wondered if the early news from Pennsylvania and New York would hold. At one o'clock he returned to the telegraph and stayed a half hour, until he was certain of the result. Then he went home through unquiet streets and to bed. But not to sleep. The jollification meetings did not break up until dawn. At four in the morning Republican joy was so energetic that "there was nothing to satisfy it but to bring out the big gun and make it thunder rejoicings for the crowd." Democratic headquarters had closed long before midnight.

5

SOON AFTER THE ELECTION Henry Villard, now representing the *New York Herald*, came to Springfield and began a series of daily dispatches that constitutes the best extant account of the President-elect. One of Villard's first letters, dated November 17, concerns the public receptions which Lincoln held each day.

S MALL AS THE NUMBER of attendants has been for some days—not over 160 per day—the receptions of the President-elect are nevertheless highly interesting and worthy of detailed notice. They are held daily from ten A.M. to 12 Noon and from three P.M. to half-past five P.M. in the Governor's room at the the State House, which has been for some time given up to the wants of Mr. Lincoln. . . .

The appointed hour having arrived, the crowd moves up stairs into the second story, in the southeast corner of which the reception room is located. Passing through a rather dark sort of doorway, the clear voice and often ringing laughter of the President-elect usually guide them to the right door. The boldest of the party having knocked, a ready "Come in" invites to enter. On opening the door the tall, lean form of Old Abe directly confronts the leader of the party. Seizing the latter's hand with a hearty shake, he leads him in, and bids the rest to follow suit by an encouraging "Get in, all of you." The whole party being in, he will ask for their names, and then immediately start a running conversation. . . . Although he is naturally more listened to than talked to, he does not allow a pause to become protracted. He is never at a loss as to the subjects that please the different classes of visitors, and there is a certain quaintness and originality about all he has to say, so that one cannot help feeling interested. His talk is not brilliant. His phrases are not ceremoniously set, but pervaded with a humorousness and, at times, a grotesque joviality, that will always please. I think it would be hard to find one who tells better jokes, enjoys them better and laughs oftener, than Abraham Lincoln.

The room of the Governor of the State of Illinois cannot be said to indicate the vast territorial extent of that commonwealth. It is altogether inadequate for the accommodation of Mr. Lincoln's visitors. Twenty persons will not find standing room in it, and the simultaneous presence of a dozen only will cause inconvenience.

The room is furnished with a sofa, a half dozen armchairs, a table and a desk, the latter being assigned to the private secretary, who is always present during visiting hours. These, together with countless letters and files of newspapers, and quite an assortment of odd presents, constitute the only adornments of the apartment.

No restrictions whatever being exercised as to visitors, the crowd that daily waits on the President-elect is always of a motley description. Everybody that lives in this vicinity or passes through this place goes to take a look at Old Abe. Muddy boots and hickory shirts are just as frequent as broadcloth, fine linen, etc. The ladies, however, are usually dressed up in their very best, although they cannot hope to make an impression on old married Lincoln.

Offensively democratic exhibitions of free manners occur every once in a while. Churlish fellows will obtrude themselves with their hats on, lighted cigars, and their pantaloons tucked into their boots. Dropping into chairs, they will sit puffing away and trying to gorgonize the President with their silent stares, until their boorish curiosity is fully satisfied.

Formal presentations are dispensed with in most cases. Nearly everybody finds his own way in and introduces himself. Sometimes half a dozen rustics rush in, break their way through other visitors up to the object of their search, and, after calling their names and touching the Presidential fingers, back out again without delay.

6

ON NOVEMBER 20, the Republicans of Illinois celebrated their victory in the election. Villard's letter of that day to the *Herald* pictures Lincoln beset by well meaning but troublesome admirers.

TODAY'S WORK WAS the hardest Old Abe did since his election. He had hardly appeared at the State House when he was beset by an eager crowd that had been on the lookout for him ever since daylight. They gave him no time to occupy himself the usual two hours previous to the morning receptions with his private secretary, but clung to his coattail with an obstinacy worthy of a better cause. He had to admit them at once into his apartment, and then submit for nearly ten long, weary hours to the importunities of a steady tide of callers. Limited as the space required by the lean proportions of the President-elect is, he found it a most difficult task to find sufficient standing room. By constant entreaties to make room he maintained himself in close proximity to the door, which position he had chosen with a view to facilitating the inevitable handshakings. But he found to his intense bodily inconvenience that this deference to the comfort of the callers was not the most practical plan he might have adopted. The curious defiled past him, after squeezing the presidential fingers, into the room, and settled either on the sofa or chairs or remained standing for protracted observation. Only after having stared with open mouths to their heart's content—many employed hours in that agreeable pastime—would they move out of the room and enable others to gain admittance. A tight jam prevailed, therefore, all day around the President-elect, who found himself frequently "driven to the wall."

. . . Many Sangamon County youths brought their sweethearts along and presented them to Old Abe, who was at times wholly surrounded by robust beauty. Place seekers were in despair all day. In vain, they tried to gain the presidential ear. It was monopolized from early in the morning until late in the evening by the "people."

. . . Although Old Abe had been nearly tortured to death during the daytime, the people gave him no rest after dark, even at his private residence. At half-past six he was once more crowded upon in his parlor, and had to undergo another agony of presentations. The whole lower story of the building was filled all the evening with well-dressed ladies and gentlemen, whose comfort was, however, greatly diminished by the constant influx of an ill-mannered populace. Mrs. Lincoln had to endure as many importunities as the head of the family. She often had to hear callers ask each other, "Is that the old woman?" The President-elect's offspring, however, seemed to enjoy the fuss hugely. The cheering outside was always responded to by their juvenile yells. . . .

The Republican jollification of today was, as to display of

enthusiasm and number of attendants, a comparative failure, although held at the capital of the State and the home of the President-elect. The American people are known not to be able to foster a protracted excitement on one particular subject. Having been treated *ad nauseam* to Wide-Awake processions, meetings, speeches, fireworks, etc., during the campaign, they are now sick of all such empty demonstrations, and wish to see no more of them for some time. The aggregate number of attendants from abroad did not exceed two thousand, and that of actual participants fell below five hundred.

7

ONE OF THE CELEBRITIES who attended the jollification of November 20 was Donn Piatt, of Ohio, journalist and Republican politician. He gives a not-too-sympathetic account of his meetings with Lincoln, as well as reflections on the rapidly-developing secession crisis.

GENERAL ROBERT E. SCHENCK and I had been selected to canvass Southern Illinois in behalf of Free-Soil and Abraham Lincoln. That part of Illinois was then known as Egypt, and in our missionary labors we learned there that the American eagle sometimes lays rotten eggs. Our labors on the stump were closed in the wigwam at Springfield a few nights previous to the election. Mr. Lincoln was present, and listened with intense interest to Mr. Schenck's able argument. I followed in a cheerful review of the situation that seemed to amuse the crowd, and none more so than our candidate for the presidency. We were both invited to return to Springfield for the jubilee, should success make such rejoicing proper. We did return, for this homely son of toil was elected, and we found Springfield drunk with delight. On the day of our arrival we were invited to a supper at the house of the President-elect. It was a plain, comfortable frame structure, and the supper was an old-fashioned mess of indigestion, composed mainly of cake, pies and chickens, the last evidently killed in the morning, to be eaten, as best they might, that evening.

After the supper, we sat far into the night, talking over the situation. Mr. Lincoln was the homeliest man I ever saw. His body seemed to me a huge skeleton in clothes. Tall as he was, his hands and feet looked out of proportion, so long and clumsy were they. Every movement was awkward in the extreme. He sat with one leg thrown over the other, and the pendant foot swung almost to the floor. And all the while two little boys, his sons, clambered over those legs, patted his cheeks, pulled his nose, and poked their fingers in his eyes, without causing reprimand or even notice. He had a face that defied artistic skill to soften or idealize. The multiplicity of photographs and engravings makes it familiar to the public. It was capable of few expressions, but those were extremely striking. When in repose, his face was dull, heavy, and repellent. It brightened like a lit lantern when animated. His dull eyes would fairly sparkle with fun, or express as kindly a look as I ever saw, when moved by some matter of human interest.

I soon discovered that this strange and strangely gifted man, while not at all cynical, was a skeptic. His view of human nature was low, but good-natured. I could not call it suspicious, but he believed only what he saw. This low estimate of humanity blinded him to the South. He could not understand that men would get up in their wrath and fight for an idea. He considered the movement South as a sort of political game of bluff, gotten up by politicians, and meant solely to frighten the North. He believed that when the leaders saw their efforts in that direction were unavailing, the tumult would subside. "They won't give up the offices," I remember he said, and added, "Were it believed that vacant places could be had at the North Pole, the road there would be lined with dead Virginians."

. . . Mr. Lincoln did not believe, could not be made to believe, that the South meant secession and war. When I told him, subsequently to this conversation, at a dinner table in Chicago, where the Hon. Hannibal Hamlin, General Schenck, and others, were guests, that the Southern people were in dead earnest, meant war, and I doubted whether he would be inaugurated at Washington, he laughed and said the fall of pork at Cincinnati had affected me. I became somewhat irritated, and told him that in ninety days the land would be whitened with tents. He said in reply:

"Well, we won't jump that ditch until we come to it," and then, after a pause, added, "I must run the machine as I find it."

I take no credit to myself for this power of prophecy; I only said what everyone acquainted with the Southern people knew, and the wonder is that Mr. Lincoln should have been so blind to the coming storm.

The epigrammatic force of his expressions was remarkable, as was also the singular purity of his language. What he said was so original that I reduced much of it to writing at the time. One of these sayings was this on secession:

"If our Southern friends are right in their claim the framers of the Government carefully planned the rot that now threatens their work with destruction. If one state has the right to withdraw at will, certainly a majority have the right, and we have the result given us of the states being able to force out one state. That is logical."

. . . Subsequent to the supper we had gatherings at Mr. Lincoln's old law office and at the political headquarters, at which men only formed the company; and before those good honest citizens, who fairly worshipped their distinguished neighbor, Mr. Lincoln gave way to his natural bent for fun, and told very amusing stories, always in quaint illustration of the subject under discussion, no one of which will bear printing. They were coarse, and were saved from vulgarity only by being so strangely in point, and told not for the sake of the telling as if he enjoyed the stories themselves, but that they were, as I have said, so quaintly illustrative.

8

ON DECEMBER 19, just one day before South Carolina passed the Ordinance of Secession, the problem of disunion, personalized, intruded upon Lincoln. Henry Villard reports the incident.

CONSIDERABLE SENSATION was produced today in the Capitol by the appearance of a live disunionist, wearing the emblem of secession. The gentleman, who called himself D. E. Ray, and claimed to be from Yazoo, Mississippi, stalked into Mr. Lincoln's reception room with a blue cockade displayed upon his hat. He walked in with a sullen air, introduced himself and plunged into a corner of a sofa, where he reposed for at least a quarter of an hour, without uttering a word, and with his eyes down, but all the while manipulating his tile so as to fasten the President-elect's eye upon the cockade. Mr. Lincoln at first hardly noticed him; but one of the other visitors at last addressed some questions to the scowling Southerner that induced him to open his lips. The conversation soon turned to the secession issue. In its course the Mississippian remarked gruffly that they were not afraid down South of Mr. Lincoln himself, but of those who followed him.

The President-elect hereupon joined in the talk, and soon found occasion to remark "that the main differences between Northerners and Southerners were that the former held slavery to be wrong and opposed its further extension, while the latter thought it right and endeavored to spread it; that, although the republicans were anti-extensionists, they would not interfere with slavery where it existed, and that as to his own intentions, the slave States would find that their slave property would be as secure from encroachment as it had been under Mr. Buchanan." The Southerner, having evidently softened down under the influence of these peaceful declarations, requested of Mr. Lincoln a copy of the debates with Senator Douglas, which was duly given him, with an inscription by the donor on the title page. Mr. Lincoln remarked, on handing the book to him, that he hoped its possession would not give him any trouble on his return to Mississippi.

9

INEVITABLY, the ever-mounting threat of secession was much on Lincoln's mind, although the intrigues and machinations of politicians for places in the cabinet were matters of more open concern. On both subjects Villard wrote numerous letters which he epitomized later in his *Memoirs*.

THERE WERE TWO QUESTIONS in which the public, of course, felt the deepest interest, and upon which I was expected to supply light, *viz.*, the composition of his [Lincoln's] Cabinet, and his views upon the secession movement that was daily growing in extent and strength. As to the former, he gave me to understand early, by indirection, that, as everybody expected, William H. Seward and S. P. Chase, his competitors for the presidential nomination, would be among his constitutional advisers. It was hardly possible for him not to recognize them, and he steadily turned a deaf ear to the remonstrances that were made against them as "extreme men" by leading politicians from the Border States, particularly from Kentucky and Missouri. As to the remaining members of his Cabinet, they were definitely selected much later, and after a protracted and wearisome tussle with the delegations of various States that came to Springfield to urge the claims of their favorite sons. . . .

No one who heard him talk upon the other question could fail to discover his other side, and to be impressed with his deep earnestness, his anxious contemplation of public affairs, and his thorough sense of the extraordinary responsibilities that were coming upon him. He never refused to talk with me about secession, but generally evaded answers to specific interrogatories, and confined himself to generalizations. I was present at a number of conversations which he had with leading public men upon the same subject, when he showed the same reserve. He did not hesitate to say that the Union ought to, and in his opinion would, be preserved, and to go into long arguments in support of the proposition, based upon the history of the Republic, the homogeneity of the population, the natural features of the country, such as the common coast, the rivers and mountains, that compelled political and commercial unity. But he could not be got to say what he would do in the face of Southern secession, except that as President he should be sworn to maintain the Constitution of the United States, and that he was therefore bound to fulfil that duty. He met in the same general way the frequent questions whether he should consider it his duty to resort to coercion by force of arms against the states engaged in attempts to secede. In connection therewith I understood him, however, several times to express doubts as to the practicability of holding the slave states in the Union by main force, if they were all determined to break it up. He was often embarrassed by efforts of radical antislavery men to get something out of him in encouragement of their hopes that the crisis would result in the abolition of slavery. He did not respond as they wished, and made it clear that he did not desire to be considered an Abolitionist, and that he still held the opinion that property in slaves was entitled to protection under the Constitution, and that its owners could not be deprived of it without due compensation. Consciously or unconsciously, he, like everybody else, must have been influenced in his views by current events. As political passion in the South rose higher and higher, and actual defiance of Federal authority by deeds of violence occurred almost daily after his election, culminating in the formal secession of seven states and the establishment of the Southern Confederacy under Jefferson Davis at Montgomery, Alabama, the belief, which he doubtless had originally, that by a conciliatory course as President he could pacify the rebellious states, must have become shaken. Still, I think I interpret his views up to the time of his departure for Washington correctly in saying that he had not lost faith in the preservation of peace between the North and the South. . . .

The Jacksonian doctrine that to the "victors belong the spoils," was still so universally the creed of all politicians that it was taken for granted there would be a change not only in all the principal, but also in all the minor, Federal offices. It was also expected that the other time-honored party practice of a division of executive patronage among the several states would be carried out. Accordingly, there appeared deputations from all the Northern and Border States at Springfield to put in their respective claims for recognition. Some of them came not only once, but several times. From a number of states several delegations turned up, representing rival factions in the Republican ranks, each pretending to be the rightful claimant. Almost every state presented candidates for the Cabinet and for the principal diplomatic and departmental offices. The hotel was the principal haunt of the place-hunters. The tricks, the intrigues, and the manoeuvres that were practised by them in pursuit of their aims, came nearly all within the range of my observation, as it was my duty to furnish the earliest possible news of their success or failure. As a rule, the various sets of spoilsmen were very willing to take me into their confidence, but it was not always easy to distinguish what was true in their communications from what they wished me to say to the press purely in furtherance of their interests. Among the political visitors, the most prominent I met were: Simon Cameron, S. P. Chase, Thurlow Weed, Lyman Trumbull, N. B. Judd, Richard J. Oglesby, Francis P. Blair, Sr. and Jr., and B. Gratz

Brown, William Dennison, D. C. Cartter, of Ohio, Henry J. Winter and Oliver P. Morton. Thurlow Weed was by far the most interesting figure and the most astute operator among them all.

From what I have said, it will be understood that the President-elect had a hard time of it with the office-seekers. But as he himself was a thorough believer in the doctrine of rotation in office, he felt it his duty to submit to this tribulation. The cabinet appointments, other than those already named, were especially troublesome to him. There was an intense struggle between Indiana and Illinois, most embarrassing inasmuch as there were several candidates from his own State, all intimate personal friends. Then came the bitter contest between the Border States of Kentucky, Missouri, and Maryland, and the Pennsylvania cabal pro and contra Simon Cameron. Amid all his perplexities, Lincoln displayed a good deal of patience and shrewdness in dealing with these personal problems. His never-failing stories helped many times to heal wounded feelings and mitigate disappointments. But he gradually showed the wear and tear of these continuous visitations, and finally looked so careworn as to excite one's compassion.

10

BEFORE LEAVING for Washington, Lincoln had a filial duty to perform—a visit to his stepmother, Sarah Bush Lincoln, who was still living on a small farm near Charleston, Illinois. Among those who called on him while he stayed at the home of a friend in Charleston was a young lawyer of that city, James A. Connolly. Years afterward Connolly gave his impressions of the President-elect to Jesse W. Weik.

IN THE CLOSING DAYS of January, 1861, word came to Charleston that Mr. Lincoln was coming down from Springfield to pay a farewell visit to his aged stepmother at her home in the the country. On hearing this I went down to the railroad station to witness his arrival, only to learn that he had failed to make connection with the regular passenger train at Mattoon and was therefore forced to come over from that place on the evening freight. We waited a long time and, when the train finally drew in and stopped, the locomotive was about opposite the station and the caboose, or car which carried the passengers, was some distance down the track. Presently, looking in that direction, we saw a tall man wearing a coat or shawl, descend from the steps of the car and patiently make his way through the long expanse of slush and ice beside the track as far as the station platform. I think he wore a plug hat. I remember I was surprised that a railroad company, with so distinguished a passenger aboard its train as the President-elect of the United States, did not manifest interest enough in his dignity and comfort to deliver him at the station instead of dropping him off in the mud several hundred feet down the track. In addition to myself quite a crowd of natives were gathered on the platform to see him. I confess I was not favorably impressed. His awkward, if not ungainly figure and his appearance generally, failed to attract me, but this was doubtless due to the fact that I was a great admirer of Douglas whose cause I had earnestly supported. There were no formalities. Mr Lincoln shook hands with a number of persons, whom he recognized or who greeted him, and in a few minutes left for the residence of a friend, where, it was understood, he was to spend the night. On the way uptown from the station I was joined by Colonel A. P. Dunbar, an old lawyer, who told me that he intended to call on Mr. Lincoln at the residence where the latter was expected to spend the night, and invited me to accompany him. I accepted the invitation and later we walked out to the house together. We timed our call so as to meet Mr. Lincoln after he had eaten his supper. On the way I remember Dunbar expressed a doubt as to how he should approach or address Mr. Lincoln. He told me they were old friends and associates at the bar, but now, since Mr. Lincoln had risen in life and was President-elect, Dunbar felt that he must keep within the proprieties of the occasion. There was therefore some question in his mind as to his own manner and behavior. He dared not betray any familiarity in addressing him for fear of offending good taste, and yet there had always been the greatest freedom in their intercourse with each other. Finally he announced that his conduct would depend on Lincoln's attitude. "If he is noticeably dignified and formal," said Dunbar, "I must act accordingly."

When we reached the house the family were still at the supper table, but Mr. Lincoln himself had withdrawn and was in the front room sitting before the fire. In response to our knock the door opened and who should step forward to greet us but Lincoln himself. Grasping Dunbar's outstretched palm with one hand and resting the other hand on his shoulder, he exclaimed in a burst of animation, "Lord A'mighty, Aleck, how glad I am to see you!" That broke the spell; and if any stiffness or formality was intended it disappeared like magic. I was introduced and presently we were all sitting together and facing the fire. Lincoln did most of the talking. He was cheerful and communicative. After an exchange of ideas and recollections of the past with Dunbar, he was soon telling stories. Apparently there was a flood of them, one following another and each invariably funnier than its predecessor. It was a novel experience for me. I certainly never before heard anything like it. I shall never forget the one story which he had evidently reserved for the last, for he announced that it was the strangest and most amusing incident he had ever witnessed. I knew it would be interesting and was, therefore, all attention. It was about a girl whose duty it was to find and drive home the family cow. "One day," said Mr. Lincoln, "she rode a horse bareback to the woods. On the way home the horse, frightened by a dog or something which darted from behind a bush, made a wild dash ahead, the girl still astride when suddenly—" at this point Mr. Lincoln halted a moment, for some one was knocking at the door. He stepped across the room and opened it, when lo, there stood the Presbyterian preacher, his wife, and two other ladies. Of course Mr. Lincoln had to suspend his narrative. Meanwhile other callers arrived and in a short time the house began to fill with them, whereupon Dunbar and I decided to withdraw. As we made our way downtown Dunbar, well knowing what an admirer of Douglas I was, inquired: "Now that you have seen and heard the long-legged individual whom our friend Douglas defeated for Senator, what do you think of him?" I had to confess that he was a marvel—a charming story-teller and in other respects one of the most remarkable men I ever listened to. "But he was guilty of one thing I shall never cease to regret," I said. "What was it?" he asked. "He failed to relate the closing chapter of that last story," I answered.

11

ONE OF LINCOLN'S last acts in Springfield was a final visit to his law office. William H. Herndon, his partner since 1844, recalls the leave-taking.

Early in February the last item of preparation for the journey to Washington had been made. Mr. Lincoln had disposed of his household goods and furniture to a neighbor, had rented his house; and as these constituted all the property he owned in Illinois there was no further occasion for concern on that score. In the afternoon of his last day in Springfield he came down to our office to examine some papers and confer with me about certain legal matters in which he still felt some interest. On several previous occasions he had told me he was coming over to the office "to have a long talk with me," as he expressed it. We ran over the books and arranged for the completion of all unsettled and unfinished matters. In some cases he had certain requests to make — certain lines of procedure he wished me to observe. After these things were all disposed of he crossed to the opposite side of the room and threw himself down on the old office sofa, which, after many years of service, had been moved against the wall for support. He lay for some moments, his face towards the ceiling, without either of us speaking. Presently he inquired, "Billy—" he always called me by that name—"how long have we been together?" "Over sixteen years," I answered. "We've never had a cross word during all that time, have we?" to which I returned a vehement, "No, indeed we have not." He then recalled some incidents of his early practice and took great pleasure in delineating the ludicrous features of many a lawsuit on the circuit. It was at this last interview in Springfield that he told me of the efforts that had been made by other lawyers to supplant me in the partnership with him. He insisted that such men were weak creatures, who, to use his own language, "hoped to secure a law practice by hanging to his coat-tail." I never saw him in a more cheerful mood. He gathered a bundle of books and papers he wished to take with him and started to go; but before leaving he made the strange request that the signboard which swung on its rusty hinges at the foot of the stairway should remain. "Let it hang there undisturbed," he said, with a significant lowering of his voice. "Give our clients to understand that the election of a President makes no change in the firm of Lincoln and Herndon. If I live I'm coming back some time, and then we'll go right on practising law as if nothing had ever happened." He lingered for a moment as if to take a last look at the old quarters, and then passed through the door into the narrow hallway. I accompanied him downstairs. On the way he spoke of the unpleasant features surrounding the presidential office. "I am sick of office-holding already," he complained, "and I shudder when I think of the tasks that are still ahead." He said the sorrow of parting from his old associations was deeper than most persons would imagine, but it was more marked in his case because of the feeling which had become irrepressible that he would never return alive. I argued against the thought, characterizing it as an illusory notion not in harmony or keeping with the popular ideal of a President. "But it is in keeping with my philosophy," was his quick retort. Our conversation was frequently broken in upon by the interruptions of passers-by, who, each in succession, seemed desirous of claiming his attention. At length he broke away from them all. Grasping my hand warmly and with a fervent "Good-bye," he disappeared down the street, and never came back to the office again.

12

LINCOLN'S DEPARTURE for Washington is pictured by Philip Van Doren Stern.

THE NEXT MORNING [February 11] dawned rainy and cheerless. The presidential train was to leave early, and Mrs. Lincoln and the children were to be on it. Something went amiss. According to the story told by a New York newspaper correspondent, Mary Lincoln quarreled with her husband that morning over a political appointment she wanted him to make. When the time for departure came, she was lying on the floor of her hotel room, screaming with hysterical rage that she would not leave for Washington unless her husband granted her wishes.

The President-elect entered his carriage without his family. He was driven through the muddy streets to a railroad station that was only a few blocks away from his old home. This was supposed to be his day of triumph, the auspicious beginning of a progress toward fame and success. The rain poured down as he rode through the familiar streets of Springfield; it drummed on the roof of his carriage and streaked down the window glass, obscuring the faces of people who had gathered along the sidewalks to see him pass.

Many of his old friends were at the railroad station. Some of them doubtless inquired about Mrs. Lincoln, and the man whose heart was breaking at this miserable farewell to his own past had to parry off their questions and explain elaborately that she had changed her plans. He went through the waiting room to the platform, where he was greeted with cheers. Soldiers lined his passageway; friends stopped him to shake hands for the last time.

Heavily, tiredly, he mounted the steps to the observation platform at the end of the train. He stood for a moment at the rail, looking in silence at the people he had known so well—people whose lives had been so long intertwined with his. Then he spoke to them out of the fullness of his heart:

"My friends: No one, not in my situation, can appreciate my feeling of sadness at this parting. To this place, and the kindness of these people, I owe everything. Here I have lived a quarter of a century, and have passed from a young to an old man. Here my children have been born, and one is buried. I now leave, not knowing when or whether ever I may return, with a task before me greater than that which rested upon Washington. Without the assistance of that Divine Being who ever attended him, I cannot succeed. With that assistance, I cannot fail. Trusting in Him who can go with me, and remain with you, and be everywhere for good, let us confidently hope that all will yet be well. To His care commending you, as I hope in your prayers you will commend me, I bid you an affectionate farewell."

The rain fell fast upon him, glistening on his cheeks as he spoke. The engine whistle blew. He turned and went into the car, and the train moved off toward Washington, toward civil war and death.

The people of Springfield waited, standing bareheaded in the rain, watching the train recede into the distance. They were never to see their fellow townsman alive again.

CHAPTER FOURTEEN

The New President

BEFORE LEAVING SPRINGFIELD, *Lincoln received numerous invitations to visit state capitals and other cities on his way to Washington. Doubtless he would have preferred to make the trip as quietly and quickly as possible, but with the country on edge, he felt that he might allay public excitement by a number of personal appearances. Accordingly, a zigzag itinerary through Indiana, Ohio, New York, New Jersey, and Pennsylvania was scheduled for the presidential train. The trip was to take two weeks instead of two or three days.*

It turned out to be a major ordeal. There were welcoming committees to be met, crowded receptions to be endured, speeches to be made several times daily, the mislaid manuscript of the inaugural address to be recovered, and young girls, like the one who had suggested that the President-elect grow whiskers, to be remembered and greeted. At Buffalo ex-President Fillmore entertained the man who was soon to occupy the same high office which he had held. New York City was difficult: the crowds which turned out for a glimpse of Lincoln were lukewarm, and opera, which the tall midwesterner attended for the first time, was clearly a social hazard.

But in spite of the frayed state of the public mind, there was nothing in the long, wearisome progression to arouse apprehension. Nothing, that is, until the party reached Philadelphia ten days after the departure from Springfield.

1

WARD HILL LAMON, traveling with Lincoln in the dual capacity of friend and bodyguard—he was a hulk of a man whose huge muscles had not been softened by years of law practice and free living—tells the story of a plot and the way in which it was circumvented.

W HILE MR. LINCOLN, in the midst of his suite of attend-ants, was being borne in triumph through the streets of Phila-delphia, and a countless multitude of people were shouting them-selves hoarse, and jostling and crushing each other round his carriage, Mr. Felton, the president of the Philadelphia, Wilming-ton, and Baltimore Railway, was engaged with a private detective [Allan Pinkerton] discussing the details of an alleged conspiracy to murder him at Baltimore. At various places along the route Mr. Judd, who was supposed to exercise unbounded influence over the President-elect, had received vague hints of the impending danger.

Mr. Lincoln reached Philadelphia on the afternoon of the twenty-first [of February]. The detective had arrived in the morning, and improved the interval to impress and enlist Mr. Felton. In the evening he got Mr. Judd and Mr. Felton into his room at the St. Louis Hotel, and told them all he had learned. Mr. Judd was very much startled, and was sure that it would be extremely imprudent for Mr. Lincoln to pass through Baltimore in open daylight, according to the published program. But he thought the detective ought to see the President-elect himself; and, as it was wearing toward nine o'clock, there was no time to lose. It was agreed that the part taken by the detective and Mr. Felton should be kept secret from every one but the President-elect. Mr. Sanford, president of the American Telegraph Com-pany, had also been co-operating in the business, and the same stipulation was made with regard to him.

Mr. Judd went to his own room at the Continental, and the detective followed. The crowd in the hotel was very dense, and it took some time to get a message to Mr. Lincoln. But it finally reached him, and he responded in person. Mr. Judd introduced the detective; and the latter told his story again. Mr. Judd and the detective wanted Mr. Lincoln to leave for Washington that

night. This he flatly refused to do. He had engagements with the
people, he said, to raise a flag over Independence Hall in the
morning, and to exhibit himself at Harrisburg in the afternoon—
and these engagements he would not break in any event. But he
would raise the flag, go to Harrisburg, get away quietly in the
evening, and permit himself to be carried to Washington in the
way they thought best. Even this, however, he conceded with great
reluctance. He condescended to cross-examine the detective on
some parts of his narrative; but at no time did he seem in the least
degree alarmed. He was earnestly requested not to communicate
the change of plan to any member of his party except Mr. Judd,
nor permit even a suspicion of it to cross the mind of another.

In the meantime, Mr. Seward had also discovered the conspiracy, and dispatched his son to Philadelphia to warn the President-
elect of the terrible snare into whose meshes he was about to run.
Mr. Lincoln turned him over to Judd, and Judd told him they
already knew about it. He went away with just enough information to enable his father to anticipate the exact moment of Mr.
Lincoln's surreptitious arrival in Washington.

Early in the morning of the twenty-second, Mr. Lincoln raised
the flag over Independence Hall, and departed for Harrisburg.
On the way, Mr. Judd gave him a full and precise detail of the
arrangements that had been made the previous night. After the
conference with the detective, Mr. Sanford, Colonel Scott, Mr.
Felton, and the railroad and telegraph officials had been sent for,
and came to Mr. Judd's room. They occupied nearly the whole of
the night in perfecting the plan. It was finally agreed that about
six o'clock the next evening Mr. Lincoln should slip away from
the Jones Hotel at Harrisburg, in company with a single member
of his party. A special car and engine was to be provided for him
on the track outside the depot; all other trains on the road were
to be side-tracked until this one had passed. Mr. Sanford was to
forward skilled "telegraph-climbers," and see that all the wires
leading out of Harrisburg were cut at six o'clock, and kept down
until it was known that Mr. Lincoln had reached Washington in
safety. The detective was to meet Mr. Lincoln at the West Philadelphia Station with a carriage, and conduct him by a circuitous
route to the Philadelphia, Wilmington, and Baltimore Station.
Berths for four were to be pre-engaged in the sleeping car at-

tached to the regular midnight train for Baltimore. This train Mr. Felton was to cause to be detained until the conductor should receive a package, containing important "government despatches," addressed to "E. J. Allen, Willard's Hotel, Washington." This package was to be made up of old newspapers, carefully wrapped and sealed, and delivered to the detective to be used as soon as Mr. Lincoln was lodged in the car.

Mr. Lincoln acquiesced in this plan. Then Mr. Judd, forgetting the secrecy which the spy had so impressively enjoined, told Mr. Lincoln that the step he was about to take was one of such transcendent importance that he thought "it should be communicated to the other gentlemen of the party." Therefore, when they had arrived at Harrisburg, and the public ceremonies and speechmaking were over, Mr. Lincoln retired to a private parlor in the Jones House; and Mr. Judd summoned to meet him there Judge Davis, Colonel Sumner, Major Hunter, Captain Pope, and myself. Judd began the conference by stating the alleged fact of the Baltimore conspiracy, how it was detected, and how it was proposed to thwart it by a midnight expedition to Washington by way of Philadelphia. It was a great surprise to all of us.

Colonel Sumner was the first to break the silence. "That proceeding," said he, "will be a damned piece of cowardice."

Mr. Judd considered this a "pointed hit," but replied that "that view of the case had already been presented to Mr. Lincoln." Then there was a general interchange of opinions, which Sumner interrupted by saying,

"I'll get a squad of cavalry, sir, and *cut* our way to Washington, sir!"

"Probably before that day comes," said Mr. Judd, "the Inauguration Day will have passed. It is important that Mr. Lincoln should be in Washington on that day."

Thus far Judge Davis had expressed no opinion, but had put various questions to test the truthfulness of the story. He now turned to Mr. Lincoln, and said, "You personally heard the detective's story. You have heard this discussion. What is your judgment in the matter?"

"I have thought over this matter considerably since I went over the ground with the detective last night. The appearance of Mr. Frederick Seward with warning from another source confirms my belief in the detective's statement. Unless there are some other reasons besides fear of ridicule, I am disposed to carry out Judd's plan."

There was no longer any dissent as to the plan itself; but one question still remained to be disposed of. Who should accompany the President-elect on his perilous ride? Mr. Judd again took the lead, declaring that he and Mr. Lincoln had previously determined that but one man ought to go, and that I had been selected as the proper person. To this Sumner violently demurred. "*I* have undertaken," he exclaimed, "to see Mr. Lincoln to Washington!"

Mr. Lincoln was dining when a closed carriage was brought to the side door of the hotel. He was called, hurried to his room, changed his coat and hat, and passed rapidly through the hall and out of the door. As he was stepping into the carriage, it became manifest that Sumner was determined to get in also. "Hurry with him!" whispered Judd to me; and at the same time, placing his hand on Sumner's shoulder, he said aloud, "One moment, Colonel!" Sumner turned round, and in that moment the carriage drove rapidly away. "A madder man," says Mr. Judd, "you never saw."

We got on board the car without discovery or mishap. Besides ourselves, there was no one in or about the car except Mr. Lewis, general superintendent of the Pennsylvania Central Railroad, and Mr. Franciscus, superintendent of the division over which we were about to pass. The arrangements for the special train were made ostensibly to take these two gentlemen to Philadelphia.

At ten o'clock we reached West Philadelphia, and were met by the detective and one Mr. Kenney, an underofficial of the Philadelphia, Wilmington, and Baltimore Railroad, from whose hands the "important parcel" was to be delivered to the conductor of the 10.50 P.M. train. Mr. Lincoln, the detective, and myself seated ourselves in a carriage which stood in waiting; and Mr. Kenney sat upon the box with the driver. It was nearly an hour before the Baltimore train was to start; and Mr. Kenney found it necessary to consume the time by driving northward in search of some imaginary person.

As the moment for the departure of the Baltimore train drew near, the carriage paused in the dark shadows of the depot building. It was not considered prudent to approach the entrance.

We were directed to the sleeping car. Mr. Kenney ran forward and delivered the "important package," and in three minutes the train was in motion. The tickets for the whole party had been procured by George R. Dunn, an express agent, who had selected berths in the rear of the car, and had insisted that the rear door of the car should be opened on the plea that one of the party was an invalid, who would arrive late, and did not desire to be carried through the narrow passageway of the crowded car. Mr. Lincoln got into his berth immediately, the curtains were carefully closed, and the rest of the party waited until the conductor came round, when the detective handed him the "sick man's" ticket. During the night Mr. Lincoln indulged in a joke or two, in an undertone; but with that exception the two sections occupied by us were perfectly silent. The detective said he had men stationed at various places along the road to let him know if all was right; and he rose and went to the platform occasionally to observe their signals, returning each time with a favorable report.

At half past three the train reached Baltimore. One of the spy's assistants came on board and informed him in a whisper that "all was right." Mr. Lincoln lay still in his berth; and in a few moments the car was being slowly drawn through the quiet streets of the city toward the Washington depot. There again was another pause, but no sound more alarming than the noise of shifting cars and engines. The passengers, tucked away on their narrow shelves, dozed on as peacefully as if Mr. Lincoln had never been born, until they were awakened by the loud strokes of a huge club against a night watchman's box, which stood within the depot and close to the track. It was an Irishman, trying to arouse a sleepy ticket agent comfortably ensconced within. For twenty minutes the Irishman pounded the box with ever-increasing vigor, and at each blow shouted at the top of his voice, "Captain! it's four o'clock! it's four o'clock!" The Irishman seemed to think that time had ceased to run at four o'clock, and making no allowance for the period consumed by his futile exercises, repeated to the last his original statement that it was four o'clock. The passengers were intensely amused; and their jokes and laughter at the Irishman's expense were not lost upon the occupants of the two sections in the rear.

In due time the train sped out of the suburbs of Baltimore, and the apprehensions of the President-elect and his friends diminished with each welcome revolution of the wheels. At six o'clock the dome of the Capitol came in sight, and a moment later we rolled into that long, unsightly building, the Washington depot.

2

IN WASHINGTON, only William H. Seward and Lincoln's old friend, Elihu B. Washburne, now a member of the House of Representatives, knew that the President-elect might arrive ahead of schedule. Anxious, Washburne decided to meet each train from the north. Tension and subsequent relief pervade his account of Lincoln's arrival.

ON THE AFTERNOON of the twenty-third [of February], Mr. Seward came to my seat in the House of Representatives, and told me he had no information from his son nor any one else in respect of Mr. Lincoln's movements, and that he could have none as the wires were all cut, but he thought it very probable he would arrive in the regular train from Philadelphia, and he suggested that we would meet at the depot to receive him. We were promptly on hand; the train arrived in time, and with strained eyes we watched the descent of the passengers. But there was no Mr. Lincoln among them; though his arrival was by no means certain, yet we were much disappointed. But as there was no telegraphic connection, it was impossible for us to have any information. It was no use to speculate—sad, disappointed, and under the empire of conflicting emotions we separated to go to our respective homes, but agreed to be at the depot on the arrival of the New York train the next morning before daylight, hoping either to meet the President-elect or get some information as to his movements. I was on hand in season, but to my great disappointment Governor Seward did not appear. I planted myself behind one of the great pillars in the Washington depot, where I could see and not be observed. Presently the train came rumbling in on time. . . . When it came to a stop I watched with fear and trembling to see the passengers descend. I saw every car emptied and there was no Mr. Lincoln. I was well-nigh in despair when, as I was about to leave, I saw slowly emerge from the last sleeping car three persons. I could not mistake the long, lank form of Mr. Lincoln, and my heart bounded with joy and gratitude. He had on a soft low-crowned hat, a muffler around his neck, and a short bob-tailed overcoat. Any one who knew him at that time could not have failed to recognize him at once, but, I must confess, he looked more like a well-to-do farmer from one of the back towns of Jo Daviess County coming to Washington to see the city, take out his land warrant, and get the patent for his farm, than the President-elect of the United States.

The only persons that accompanied Mr. Lincoln were Pinkerton, the well-known detective, and Ward Hill Lamon. When they were fairly on the platform and a short distance from the car, I stepped forward and accosted the President-elect: "How are you, Lincoln?"

At this unexpected and rather familiar salutation the gentlemen were apparently somewhat startled, but Mr. Lincoln, who had recognized me, relieved them at once by remarking in his peculiar voice: "This is only Washburne!"

Then we all exchanged congratulations and walked out to the front of the depot, where I had a carriage in waiting. Entering the carriage (all four of us) we drove rapidly to Willard's Hotel, entering on Fourteenth Street, before it was fairly daylight. The porter showed us into the little receiving room at the head of the stairs, and at my direction went to the office to have Mr. Lincoln assigned a room.

We had not been in the hotel more than two minutes before Governor Seward hurriedly entered, much out of breath and somewhat chagrined to think he had not been up in season to be at the depot on the arrival of the train. The meeting of those two great men under the extraordinary circumstances which surrounded them was full of emotion and thankfulness. I soon took my leave, but not before promising Governor Seward that I would take breakfast with him at eight o'clock; and as I passed out the outside door the Irish porter said to me with a smiling face:

"And by faith it is you who have brought us a Prisidint."

3

THE CITY OF WASHINGTON had not changed much in the dozen years which had passed since Lincoln had lived there as the

lone Whig Congressman from Illinois. Albert G. Riddle, a member
of the House of Representatives from Ohio's Western Reserve, pictures the Capital as Lincoln saw it on the murky morning of his
arrival.

I T WAS THEN as unattractive, straggling, sodden a town, wandering up and down the left bank of the yellow Potomac, as
the fancy can sketch. Pennsylvania Avenue, twelve rods wide,
stretched drearily over the mile between the unfinished Capitol
and the unfinished Treasury building on Fifteenth Street, West,
where it turned north for a square, and took its melancholy way
to Georgetown, across the really once very beautiful Rock Creek.
Illy paved with cobblestones, it was the only paved street of the
town. The other streets, which were long stretches of mud or
deserts of dust and sand, with here and there clumps of poorly
built residences with long gaps between them, passing little deserts of open lands, where their lines were lost, wandered from the
highlands north towards the Potomac, and from the Eastern
Branch (Anacosta) to Rock Creek. Not a sewer blessed the town,
nor off of Pennsylvania Avenue was there a paved gutter. Each
house had an open drain from its rear, out across the sidewalk. As
may be supposed, the Capital of the Republic had more malodors
than the poet Coleridge ascribed to ancient Cologne. There was
then the open canal, a branch of the Chesapeake and Ohio, from
Rock Creek to Anacosta, breeding malaria, tadpoles, and mosquitoes. The Tiber of the day, ancient "Goose Creek," stagnated
from the highlands through the Botanic Gardens, and Slash Run
overflowed the northwest wastes of the swampy city plat.

The President's house, the little dingy State Department, set
squat on the ground now occupied by the north wing of the Treasury building, the War and Navy on Seventeenth Street, the Post
Office Department, and the Interior, were the only completed public edifices of the Capital. The Washington Monument, the Capitol, and the Treasury building were melancholy specimens of arrested development.

The walls of the two wings of the Capitol had not been per-
fected, and the little old jug-like dome of the old central structure
still occupied its place, utterly lost in the expanse of the acres of
roof that it could not dominate. The building was placed at the

west margin of a tableland that sloped westward, facing the east, with the surface rising several feet in the distance of one hundred and fifty yards. This was a fenced square filled with a heavy growth of forest trees, mostly the short-lived southern maple. The west approach was up an earthern terrace, which sloped down into another timbered enclosure. North and South A Streets were then in place, and each was built up compactly on the sides facing the Capitol with low, mean structures.

Save for the enclosed east and west spaces, the western slope of Capitol Hill was open ground. Pennsylvania Avenue passed around the north wing of the Capitol on its eastern way, and all that open ground was covered with the remains of building stone, lumber, and timber, and loaded over at every place of access with the huge iron plates for the great Capitol dome, doomed in the counsels of the slavery hosts never to be set in place. Nothing more conclusively showed the predetermined destruction of the Republic than this deliberate suspension of the completion of the Capitol and Treasury building, then limited to the portion represented by the colonnade fronting Fifteenth Street. The Capitol was unfinished on the inside. All during the Thirty-seventh Congress the old hall of the House was a mere lumber room, unsightly and offensive.

So also the bridges across the Potomac were found to be in a ruinous condition, as was everything dependent upon the will of the retiring Administration. Indeed it had borrowed money for its current expenses, and this loan we had to provide for.

Politically, the city—the fixed population—was intensely Southern, as much so as Richmond or Baltimore. Very few men of culture, and none below that grade, were Republicans at the advent of "Lincoln and his Northern myrmidons," as they were called in 1860–61. . . .

The population of the District was then about 75,000, of which the city of Washington contained 61,000; 15,000 of these were colored, including a fraction over 3,000 slaves.

4

LINCOLN'S FIRST DAY in the national capital was a busy one. Margaret Leech reviews the crowded hours.

T HE FIRST DUTY of the President-elect was to pay his respects at the Executive Mansion. A special meeting of the Cabinet
was in session, when the doorkeeper handed Mr. Buchanan a
startling card. "Uncle Abe is downstairs!" the President cried,
and hurriedly descended to the Red Room. He soon returned with
the two Republicans. Mr. Lincoln was presented to the Cabinet,
and paused for a few minutes' conversation before leaving to call
on General Scott. One of the members, Attorney General Stanton,
had a sneering contempt for Mr. Lincoln. Some years earlier,
they had been associated as counsel for the defense in a famous
case, a suit brought for infringement of patent rights by Cyrus
McCormick, the inventor of the reaping machine. Stanton had
snubbed and humiliated the backwoods lawyer, and Lincoln had
not forgotten his mortification; but he had also retained a vivid
impression of Edwin M. Stanton's abilities.

Mr. Lincoln was familiarly acquainted with Washington, where
he had served a term as Congressman from Illinois, but the capital
could not return the compliment. In spite of his extraordinary figure, no one glanced a second time at the ungainly Westerner, as
he walked with Mr. Seward through the streets. Rumors that he
was in town caused unprecedented sales of the *Evening Star*,
which was out in the early afternoon with a description of his arrival at Willard's. Many people still remained skeptical. Republicans declared that the story was a dodge to keep them from the
cars; and, mounting on top of a big furniture wagon laden with
their banners, they proceeded to decorate their wigwam to impress
Mr. Lincoln on his way from the depot. Later, "squads of the
incredulous" surged through the rain to meet the special train, and
the Fourteenth Street entrance to Willard's was surrounded. The
crowds were rewarded by the sight of the weary presidential
party, oppressed by the gloom of the Maryland threats and Lincoln's sudden departure. Mrs. Lincoln had become hysterical over
the separation from her husband. Colonel Edwin Sumner was a
very angry old soldier, thwarted in the performance of his duty;
and Colonel Ellsworth had expected their train to be mobbed in
Baltimore. To counteract the depression, Bob Lincoln had led the
party in the rendition of "The Star-Spangled Banner" as the
cars crossed the Maryland line.

Leaning on the arm of Mr. Seward, Mrs. Lincoln entered the hotel, and was received in the thronged hallway by the Messrs. Willard in person. Upstairs, the President-elect sprawled in an armchair with a beaming face, while his two spoiled boys, Willie and Tad, climbed over him. He had had a busy afternoon, for the tide of visitors had already set toward Parlor Number 6. General Scott, whom he had missed in the morning, had returned his call in full uniform, sweeping his instep with the yellow plumes of his hat as he bowed. Headed by Stephen A. Douglas, the Illinois Senators and Congressmen had paid their respects. Old Francis P. Blair had come in with his hatchet-faced son, Montgomery, who was hoping to be appointed Postmaster General. The Blair family, father and two sons, were a power in the Republican party. They were a fighting clan from the border slave states, Democrats who had swung into opposition to slavery. The elder Blair, formerly a famous newspaper editor and a member of Jackson's "Kitchen Cabinet," was an acute politician who still wielded great influence behind the scenes. Frank, Jr., former Congressman, recently re-elected, was a Free-Soil leader in Missouri; while Montgomery, like his father, now lived and intrigued in Maryland. Mr. Lincoln reposed great confidence in the senior Blair, and submitted to him, as well as to his chief adviser, Mr. Seward, a copy of his inaugural address.

Soon after his family's arrival, Lincoln was informed that the delegates to the Peace Conference desired to wait on him. He appointed the hour of nine to receive them, and drove off to a seven o'clock dinner at Seward's, where the Vice-President-elect, Hannibal Hamlin, was also present. The long parlor hall at Willard's was lined with people when he returned; and, shaking hands on both sides, he was so interested, said the *New York Herald*, that he forgot to remove his shiny, new silk hat.

Ex-President Tyler and the Honorable Salmon P. Chase, of Ohio, led the Peace delegates up the stairs to Parlor Number 6. Chase was as pompous as General Scott, and very nearly as antipathetic to slavery as Senator Sumner. Re-elected to the Senate after serving as Governor of his State, he was the most prominent of the former Democrats in the Republican party. His rumored appointment to the Cabinet would satisfy the radicals, who were disgruntled with the conciliatory Seward. He was tall, imposing and handsome, with the noble brow of a statesman. As he stood beside Mr. Lincoln, presenting the delegates, it was Chase who looked the part of President of the United States, and Chase would have been the first to think so.

Curious and prejudiced, Easterners and men from the border slave states scrutinized the phenomenon from the prairies. The long, lean, sallow frontier lawyer was a shock to people who were unused to the Western type; and his homely phrases and mispronunciations grated on Eastern ears. It was impossible that Lincoln should have inspired confidence or admiration; but some saw shrewdness, honesty, and even a natural dignity in his face. Its ugliness was partially redeemed by his eyes, though their dreamy, meditative expression did not bespeak either firmness or force. He had a pleasant, kindly smile, and was thought to be not so ill-favored and hard-looking as his pictures represented him. Chatting informally with the delegates, remembering like a good politician their claims to fame and their middle initials, Lincoln made on the whole a not unfavorable impression.

5

LINCOLN'S MEETING with the members of the Peace Conference—that futile effort of delegates from twenty-one states to restore unity to a nation already divided—deserves more than passing mention. From the questions of the delegates and Lincoln's replies to them one gets a sense of the awful imminence of civil war. The report is by L. E. Chittenden, a member of the Vermont delegation.

M R. LINCOLN'S RECEPTION of the delegates was of an entirely informal character. There was no crowded approach, nor hurried disappearance; no procession of the members beyond where he stood. *There* was a point of attraction—not of repulsion. As the guests were successively and cordially received, they gathered round him in a circle, which enlarged and widened, until it comprised most of the delegates. His tall figure and animated face towered above them, the most striking in a group of noted Americans. His words arrested the attention; his wonderful vivacity surprised every spectator. He spoke apparently without premeditation, with a singular ease of manner and facility of expression.

He had some apt observation for each person ready the moment
he heard his name. "You are a smaller man than I supposed—I
mean in person: every one is acquainted with the greatness of your
intellect. It is, indeed, pleasant to meet one who has so honorably
represented his country in Congress and abroad." Such was his
greeting to William C. Rives, of Virginia, a most cultivated and
polished gentleman. "Your name is all the endorsement you require," he said to James B. Clay. "From my boyhood the name
of Henry Clay has been an inspiration to me." "You cannot be
a disunionist, unless your nature has changed since we met in
Congress!" he exclaimed as he recognized the strong face of
George W. Summers, of Western Virginia. "Does liberty still
thrive in the mountains of Tennessee?" he inquired as Mr. Zollicoffer's figure, almost as tall as his own, came into view. After so
many years, much that he said is forgotten, but it is remembered
that he had for every delegation, almost for every man, some appropriate remark, which was forcible, and apparently unstudied.

There was only one occurrence which threatened to disturb the
harmony and good humor of the reception. In reply to a complimentary remark by Mr. Lincoln, Mr. Rives had said that, although he had retired from public life, he could not decline the
request of the Governor of Virginia that he should unite in this
effort to save the Union. "But," he continued, "the clouds that
hang over it are very dark. I have no longer the courage of my
younger days. I can do little—you can do much. Everything now
depends upon you."

"I cannot agree to that," replied Mr. Lincoln. "My course is as
plain as a turnpike road. It is marked out by the Constitution.
I am in no doubt which way to go. Suppose now we all stop discussing and try the experiment of obedience to the Constitution
and the laws. Don't you think it would work?"

"Permit me to answer that suggestion," interposed Mr. Summers. "Yes, it will work. If the Constitution is your light, I will
follow it with you, and the people of the South will go with us."

"It is not of your professions we complain," sharply struck in
Mr. Seddon's sepulchral voice. "It is of your sins of omission—of
your failure to enforce the laws—to suppress your John Browns
and your Garrisons, who preach insurrection and make war upon
our property!"

"I believe John Brown was hung and Mr. Garrison imprisoned," dryly remarked Mr. Lincoln. "You cannot justly charge the North with disobedience to statutes or with failing to enforce them. You have made some which were very offensive, but they have been enforced, notwithstanding."

"You do not enforce the laws," persisted Mr. Seddon. "You refuse to execute the statute for the return of fugitive slaves. Your leading men openly declare that they will not assist the marshals to capture or return slaves."

"You are wrong in your facts again," said Mr. Lincoln. "Your slaves have been returned, yes, from the shadow of Faneuil Hall in the heart of Boston. Our people do not like the work, I know. They will do what the law commands, but they will not volunteer to act as tip-staves or bum-bailiffs. The instinct is natural to the race. Is it not true of the South? Would you join in the pursuit of a fugitive slave if you could avoid it? Is such the work of gentlemen?"

"Your press is incendiary!" said Mr. Seddon, changing his base. "It advocates servile insurrection, and advises our slaves to cut their masters' throats. You do not suppress your newspapers. You encourage their violence."

"I beg your pardon, Mr. Seddon," replied Mr. Lincoln. "I intend no offence, but I will not suffer such a statement to pass unchallenged, because it is not true. No Northern newspaper, not the most ultra, has advocated a slave insurrection or advised the slaves to cut their masters' throats. A gentleman of your intelligence should not make such assertions. We do maintain the freedom of the press—we deem it necessary to a free government. Are we peculiar in that respect? Is not the same doctrine held in the South?"

It was reserved for the delegation from New York to call out from Mr. Lincoln his first expression touching the great controversy of the hour. He exchanged remarks with ex-Governor King, Judge James, William Curtis Noyes, and Francis Granger. William E. Dodge had stood, awaiting his turn. As soon as his opportunity came, he raised his voice enough to be heard by all present, and, addressing Mr. Lincoln, declared that the whole country in great anxiety was awaiting his inaugural address, and then added: "It is for you, sir, to say whether the whole nation shall be plunged into bankruptcy; whether the grass shall grow in the streets of our commercial cities."

"Then I say it shall not," he answered, with a merry twinkle of his eye. "If it depends upon me, the grass will not grow anywhere except in the fields and the meadows."

"Then you will yield to the just demands of the South. You will leave her to control her own institutions. You will admit slave states into the Union on the same conditions as free states. You will not go to war on account of slavery!"

A sad but stern expression swept over Mr. Lincoln's face. "I do not know that I understand your meaning, Mr. Dodge," he said, without raising his voice, "nor do I know what my acts or my opinions may be in the future, beyond this. If I shall ever come to the great office of President of the United States, I shall take an oath. I shall swear that I will faithfully execute the office of President of the United States, of all the United States, and that I will, to the best of my ability, preserve, protect, and defend the Constitution of the United States. This is a great and solemn duty. With the support of the people and the assistance of the Almighty I shall undertake to perform it. I have full faith that I shall perform it. It is not the Constitution as I would like to have it, but as it *is*, that is to be defended. The Constitution will not be preserved and defended until it is enforced and obeyed in every part of every one of the United States. It must be so respected, obeyed, enforced, and defended, let the grass grow where it may."

Not a word or a whisper broke the silence while these words of weighty import were slowly falling from his lips. They were so comprehensive and unstudied, they exhibited such inherent authority, that they seemed a statement of a sovereign decree, rather than one of fact which admitted of debate. Comment or criticism upon them seemed out of order. Mr. Dodge attempted no reply. The faces of the Republicans wore an expression of surprised satisfaction. Some of the more ardent Southerners silently left the room. They were unable to comprehend the situation. The ignorant countryman they had come to ridicule threatened no crime but obedience to the Constitution. This was not the entertainment to which they were invited, and it was uninteresting. For the more

conservative Southern delegates, the statesmen, Mr. Lincoln
seemed to offer an attraction. They remained until he finally
retired.

6

SECESSION WAS ONLY ONE of the problems torturing Lincoln while he waited for the fourth of March. The composition of his
Cabinet was another. He had made his selections, but in the absence of
a public announcement the friends and enemies of prospective ap-
pointees still pressed their intrigues. The machinations of Seward
supporters, who were determined to exclude Salmon P. Chase, are
reported in the *Diary of a Public Man*—that anonymous and baffling
record which, whether synthetic or genuine, faithfully reflects events
of the time.

M ARCH 2. There can be no doubt about it any longer. This
man from Illinois is not in the hands of Mr. Seward. Heaven
grant that he may not be in other hands—not to be thought of
with patience! These New York men have done just what they
have been saying they would do, and with just the result which I
have from the first expected; though I own there are points in the
upshot which puzzle me. I can not feel even sure now that Mr.
Seward will be nominated at all on Tuesday; and certainly he
neither is nor after this can be the real head of the Administration,
even if his name is on the list of the Cabinet. Such folly on the part
of those who assume to be the especial friends of the one man in
whose ability and moderation the conservative people at the North
have most confidence; and such folly at this moment might almost
indeed make one despair of the Republic!

——has just left me. He was one of the party who called on
Mr. Lincoln today to bring matters to a head, and prevent the
nomination of Chase at all hazards. A nice mess they have made
of it! Mr. Lincoln received them civilly enough, and listened to all
they had to say. Speaking one after another, they all urged the
absolutely essential importance of the presence of Mr. Seward in
the Cabinet, to secure for it either the support of the North or
any hearing at the South; and they all set forth the downright
danger to the cause of the Union of putting into the Cabinet a

man like Mr. Chase, identified with and supported by men who did not desire to see the Union maintained on its existing and original basis at all, and who would rather take their chances with a Northern Republic, extending itself to Canada, than see the Union of our fathers kept up on the principles of our fathers. After they had all said their say in this vein, Mr. Lincoln, who had sat watching them one after another, and just dropping in a word here and there, waited a moment, and then asked what they wanted him to do, or to forbear. They all replied that they wished him to forbear from nominating Mr. Chase as a member of his Cabinet, because it would not be possible for Mr. Seward to sit in the same Administration with Mr. Chase. He wouldn't wish it, and his friends and his State would not tolerate it—couldn't tolerate it—it must not be.

Then Mr. Lincoln sat looking very much distressed for a few moments, after which he began speaking in a low voice, like a man quite oppressed and worn down, saying, it was very hard to reconcile conflicting claims and interests; that he only desired to form an Administration that would command the confidence of the country and the party; that he had the deepest respect for Mr. Seward, his services, his genius, and all that sort of thing; that Mr. Chase has great claims also, which no one could contest —perhaps not so great as Mr. Seward; but what the party and country wanted was the hearty co-operation of all good men and of all sections, and so on, and so on, for some time. They all thought he was weakening, and they were sure of it, when after a pause he opened a table drawer and took out a paper, saying: "I had written out my choice here of Secretaries in the Cabinet after a great deal of pains and trouble; and now you tell me I must break the slate and begin all over!"

He went on then to admit, which still more encouraged them, that he had sometimes feared that it would be as they said it was —that he might be forced to reconsider his matured and he thought judicious conclusions. In view of that possibility, he said he had constructed an alternative list of his Cabinet. He did not like it half as well as the one of his own deliberate preference, in which he would frankly say he had hoped to see Mr. Seward sitting as Secretary of State, and Mr. Chase sitting as Secretary of the Treasury—not half as well; but he could not expect to have things exactly as he liked them; and much more to the same effect, which set the listeners quite agog with suppressed expectations of carrying their great point.

"This being the case, gentlemen," he said, finally, after giving the company time to drink in all he had said, "—this being the case, gentlemen, how would it do for us to agree upon a change like this?" Everybody, of course, was all attention. "How would it do to ask Mr. Chase to take the Treasury, and to offer the State Department to Mr. William L. Dayton, of New Jersey?"

— —told me you could have knocked him or any man in the room down with a feather. Not one of them could speak. Mr. Lincoln went on in a moment, expatiating on his thoughtfulness about Mr. Seward. Mr. Dayton, he said, was an old Whig, like himself and like Mr. Seward. He was from New Jersey, which "is next door to New York." He had been the Vice-Presidential candidate with General Fremont, and was a most conservative, able, and sensible man. Mr. Seward could go as Minister to England, where his genius would find great scope in keeping Europe straight as to the troubles here, and so on, and so forth, for twenty minutes.

When he got through, one of the company spoke, and said he thought they had better thank him for his kindness in listening to them and retire for consultation, which they did. But I fear from the tone and the language of— —that there is more cursing than consultation going on just now. I must own that I heard him with something like consternation. Whether this prefigures an exclusion of Mr. Seward from the Cabinet, who can tell? Nor does that possibility alone make it alarming. It does not prefigure—it proves that the new Administration will be pitched on a dangerous and not on a safe key. It makes what was dark enough before midnight black. What is to come of it all?

7

WHILE LINCOLN STRUGGLED with political patronage and national policy, his secretaries and the members of his family responded to the excitement of new surroundings and the approaching inauguration. Margaret Leech carries life in the Lincoln retinue and preparations in Washington for the impending ceremonies to the morning of March 4.

I N SPITE OF THE PALL of the national crisis, the President-elect's party was not wanting in high spirits. Besides his oldest boy, Bob, a Harvard student of eighteen, it included three young men who had been law students in Mr. Lincoln's Springfield office, and he was on warmly affectionate terms with them all. John George Nicolay, capable, Teutonic, nearly thirty, was the private secretary. John Hay, the assistant secretary, was a clever, flippant, good-looking college graduate of twenty-two. The handsome little Zouave, Ellsworth, was not much older, and he had a magnetic boyish enthusiasm. He had worked out a plan for reforming the state militia system, and bringing it under Federal control; and he was hoping to be appointed to the chief clerkship of the War Department. Bob Lincoln had been educated at Phillips Exeter, and showed in speech and manner that he had enjoyed more advantages than his father. As a pendant to the campaign publicity for The Rail Splitter, Bob had been facetiously nicknamed "The Prince of Rails." Some people inevitably called him proud and affected, but he conducted himself sensibly during a prolonged ordeal of popular attention and flattery.

Nicolay thought that the bevy of ladies in the parlors made it seem like having a party every night. He was, however, occupied with the President's correspondence, while Ellsworth, though schoolgirls sighed over his black curls, was a moralist and a Spartan. John Hay and Bob Lincoln were the merry, carefree members of the party. Hay made a new friend in Henry Adams, another private secretary, who would soon be going off with his father to the Court of St. James's. In the evening, Bob sometimes tarried downstairs in the smoking room, listening to the music of the harpists and enjoying a cigar with the other men. Some disunionists, on one of these occasions, induced the musicians to play "Dixie," which Secessia had adopted as its national air; but the harpists quickly followed it with "Hail, Columbia." In Parlor Number 6, Mrs. Lincoln, attended by her sister, Mrs. Ninian Edwards, her two nieces and her cousin, Mrs. Grimsley, received a deferential throng in her stylish Springfield toilettes. The President-elect's Kentucky wife was arrogantly pleased with her position, fancied herself of great importance in politics, and referred in company to Mr. Seward as a "dirty abolition sneak."

Every night, the new squads of militia were drilling in the open spaces of the city, but the fears of revolution had largely subsided. Many patriotic men thought that it would be ill-advised to make an ostentatious display of armed force at the inauguration. The threats to his own life, however, had convinced General Scott that the ceremony was a hazardous undertaking, and he prepared to guard the incoming President with every soldier in the city. He now had, exclusive of the marines at the Navy Yard, 653 regulars at his command. He thought of Mr. Lincoln's drive from Willard's to the Capitol as a movement, and he planned to place a picked body of men, the sappers and miners from West Point, in the van. A squadron of District cavalry would ride on either side of the Presidential carriage, and infantry companies of militia would march in its rear. Squads of riflemen and a small number of United States cavalry were ordered to posts along the route. The main force of the regulars, headed by Scott in his coupé, was assigned to "flanking the movement" in F Street.

While one battery of artillery was situated near the Treasury building, two were stationed outside the north entrance to the Capitol grounds. At this latter important point, Scott himself proposed to remain during the ceremonies, and there, too, would be Major General John E. Wool, the thin, little old man who was the commander of the Department of the East.

On Saturday and Sunday, strangers, almost all men, were pouring into town in anticipation of the ceremonies on Monday. Baltimore plugs, tippling and shrieking their rallying cries, were but a noisy minority in the swelling influx of the Republicans. There were dignitaries among them—twenty-seven Governors and ex-Governors of States, and many former Senators and Congressmen—and there were also militia and civic organizations. Largest by far in number, however, were the plain men of the West—a type only recently familiar to Washington—who dodged forlornly about the city in travel-stained clothes, looking for a place to sleep. Hotel rooms were all pre-empted. The best accommodation to be had was a cot or a mattress in a parlor. The newcomers were not a spendthrift lot. Bonifaces noted that they were a cold-water army. Hack drivers and porters complained that they were given to walking and carrying their own carpetbags, reluctant to part with a quarter-dollar.

Sunday, with its roving crowds, did not seem like the Sabbath. In the morning, there was a rush to Fourteenth Street to see the President-elect depart for church. So many people congregated around the ladies' entrance to Willard's that police had difficulty in clearing a passage on the sidewalk. All tall men of only moderately good looks, said the tactful *Star*, were closely scanned, as they passed from the hotel. Uncle Abe, however, did not appear, and the sight-seers had to content themselves with the spectacle of the pugilist, John Morrissey, promenading in a stovepipe hat.

Willard's dined fifteen hundred on Sunday, and a thousand feasted at the National. In the evening, laborers were industriously scraping the entire width of the Avenue between the Capitol and the White House, a herculean assignment which they had been unable to finish on Saturday night. The wind whirled the thick dust into clouds, and, though there was now a water supply sufficient for the purpose, the city had no system for dampening the streets. At dusk, crowds of manifestly secular intention were walking toward the lighted Capitol, where the Senate flag was flying. Hundreds of homeless visitors slept on market stalls and lumber piles, or strolled about the streets all night. Orderlies and cavalry platoons rode through the dark. A rumor had reached Scott's headquarters that an attempt would be made to blow up the platform which had been erected at the east portico of the Capitol. A guard was placed under the floor of the stand, and at daybreak a battalion of District troops marched to form a semicircle around the foot of the steps.

The city was early astir with unaccommodated strangers, assembling to perform their toilets at the public fountains. People began to turn out for the parade. Boys screamed the morning newspapers, and there were lithographs of Uncle Abe's features, damp from the press. The sidewalks of the Avenue were filled from building line to curbstone. In the crush, Newton Leonard, aged four, with blue eyes and a full face, dressed in a plaid suit with tight knees, strayed from his parents, and was advertised for next day in the *National Intelligencer*.

In spite of bright sunshine, it was a raw, disagreeable day. Whipped by the gusty wind, the people stood waiting, while soldiers and District militia formed in line. It was not a festive gathering. The city seemed anxious and depressed. Few buildings had

been decorated in honor of the inauguration. Some houses along
the route had closed shutters, and many unfriendly faces frowned
from balconies and windows.

8

CARL SANDBURG sketches the preliminaries of the inauguration,
and its principal participants.

PRESIDENT BUCHANAN in a room at the Capitol that morning signed bills and disposed of matters that had kept the Senate
in session till six o'clock that morning. He had just managed to
close up his affairs when noon came, and he drove with Senator
Baker, of Oregon, and Senator Pearce, of Maryland, from the
White House to Willard's in an open carriage. (An *Evening Star*
reporter wrote with perhaps fantastic surmise that Buchanan had
offered Lincoln a closed carriage and Lincoln answered that he
would ride in the open.) Buchanan stepped out of the barouche,
disappeared into the doorway of Willard's, and soon returned
arm in arm with Lincoln as police kept a path for them. Then the
procession, headed by Marshal in Chief Major French, with aides
in blue scarfs and white rosettes, carrying blue batons with gilt
ends, their saddlecloths blue and white, moved down Pennsylvania
Avenue with representations from the judiciary; the clergy; foreign Ministers; the diplomatic corps; members of Congress; the
Peace Convention delegates; heads of bureaus; governors of
States; the army, navy, marine corps, militia; veterans of the
Revolutionary War and the War of 1812 in carriages, followed
by a variety of organizations and citizens afoot.

In the presidential carriage the crowds saw Buchanan and Lincoln side-by-side facing frontward and Senators Baker and Pearce
seated opposite. Double files of a squadron of District of Columbia
cavalry rode alongside the carriage. A company of West Point
sappers and miners marched in front of it, and infantry and riflemen of the District of Columbia followed it. There were cheers and
there were silences along the sidewalks. Washington was still a
Southern city—overrun by newly arrived Northern elements.

Four milk-white horses drew the float of the Republican Association, with thirty-four pretty girls in white frocks, one pretty girl for each State in the Union. Several newspapers reported that Lincoln took occasion later in the day to kiss each pretty girl, giving one kiss for each State, which made interesting reading but was neither true nor important.

In the Senate chamber, packed with officials and civilians, Buchanan and Lincoln witnessed the swearing-in of Hannibal Hamlin as Vice-President. A new procession was formed to escort the President-elect through a corridor to the east portico and the platform outdoors, where a crowd of at least 10,000 had waited long and finally gave its applause and scattering cheers as the actors in the solemn ceremony took places on the platform. Their eyes saw the Senate Committee of Arrangements, the outgoing President, the President-elect and his family, the Chief Justice in his black robes, the Clerk of the Court with the Bible, from the central group on the front of the platform. Gathered round and back were other Justices in robes, Senators, Representatives, officials, and eminent guests in tall silk hats and black swallowtail coats.

Senator Douglas took a seat, and as he looked over the crowd could have said that he and Lincoln had spoken to larger audiences on the prairies of Illinois. This, however, was a more genteel crowd, and one comment ran that rather than a sea of upturned faces it was a sea of silk hats and white shirt bosoms.

Lincoln in a new tall hat, new black suit of clothes and black boots, expansive white shirt bosom, carrying an ebony cane with a gold head the size of a hen's egg, had the crowd matched. Before taking a seat he looked around, hesitated and peered, then pushed the cane into a corner of the platform railing. His hat, too, needed a place. Young Henry Watterson, a press writer from Louisville, put out his hand for the hat, but Senator Douglas, just behind, outreached Watterson, received the hat from Lincoln's hand, and held it a half hour.

Two riflemen lurked hidden at each window of the Capitol wings flanking the inaugural stand, watching for any interference.

The Senator from Oregon stepped forward, Edward Dickinson Baker, of whom Lincoln had long ago told the story that Baker when a boy was found crying his eyes out one day because he had just learned that as an English-born child he could never be President of the United States.

Baker's silver-bell voice rang out: "Fellow-citizens, I introduce to you Abraham Lincoln, the President-elect of the United States." The applause was a slight ripple. Then came the inaugural address, which Lincoln drew from his inside coat pocket and read deliberately.

9

IN HIS ADDRESS LINCOLN DISAVOWED his intention of interfering with slavery in the states where it already existed, and argued temperately against the right of secession. At the same time he announced that the government would "hold, occupy, and possess" —he did not say "repossess"—its forts and property. He closed with argument and appeal of unsurpassed eloquence.

PHYSICALLY SPEAKING, we cannot separate. We cannot remove our respective sections from each other, nor build an impassable wall between them. A husband and wife may be divorced, and go out of the presence and beyond the reach of each other; but the different parts of our country cannot do this. They cannot but remain face to face, and intercourse, either amicable or hostile, must continue between them. Is it possible, then, to make that intercourse more advantageous or more satisfactory after separation than before? Can aliens make treaties easier than friends can make laws? Can treaties be more faithfully enforced between aliens than laws can among friends? Suppose you go to war, you cannot fight always; and when, after much loss on both sides, and no gain on either, you cease fighting, the identical old questions as to terms of intercourse are again upon you. . . .

The chief magistrate derives all his authority from the people, and they have conferred none upon him to fix terms for the separation of the States. The people themselves can do this also if they choose; but the executive, as such, has nothing to do with it. His duty is to administer the present government, as it came to his hands.

Why should there not be a patient confidence in the ultimate justice of the people? Is there any better or equal hope in the world? In our present differences is either party without faith of being in the right? If the Almighty Ruler of Nations, with his eternal truth and justice, be on your side of the North, or on yours of the South, that truth and that justice will surely prevail by the judgment of this great tribunal of the American people.

By the frame of the government under which we live, this same people have wisely given their public servants but little power for mischief; and have, with equal wisdom, provided for the return of that little to their own hands at very short intervals. While the people retain their virtue and vigilance, no administration, by any extreme of wickedness or folly, can very seriously injure the government in the short space of four years.

My countrymen, one and all, think calmly and well upon this whole subject. Nothing valuable can be lost by taking time. If there be an object to hurry any of you in hot haste to a step which you would never take deliberately, that object will be frustrated by taking time; but no good object can be frustrated by it. Such of you as are now dissatisfied, still have the old Constitution unimpaired, and, on the sensitive point, the laws of your own framing under it; while the new administration will have no immediate power, if it would, to change either. If it were admitted that you who are dissatisfied hold the right side in the dispute, there still is no single good reason for precipitate action. Intelligence, patriotism, Christianity, and a firm reliance on Him who has never yet forsaken this favored land, are still competent to adjust in the best way all our present difficulty.

In your hands, my dissatisfied fellow-countrymen, and not in mine, is the momentous issue of civil war. The government will not assail you. You can have no conflict without being yourselves the aggressors. You have no oath registered in heaven to destroy the government, while I shall have the most solemn one to "preserve, protect, and defend it."

I am loath to close. We are not enemies, but friends. We must not be enemies. Though passion may have strained, it must not break our bonds of affection. The mystic chords of memory, stretching from every battle-field and patriot grave to every living heart and hearthstone all over this broad land, will yet swell the chorus of the Union when again touched, as surely they will be, by the better angels of our nature.

10

"THEN," writes Carl Sandburg,

stepped forward Chief Justice Taney, worn, shrunken, odd, with "the face of a galvanized corpse," said Mrs. Clay of Alabama. His hands shook with age, emotion, both, as he held out an open Bible toward the ninth President to be sworn in by him.

Lincoln laid his left hand on the Bible, raised his right hand, and repeated after the Chief Justice the oath prescribed by the Constitution: "I do solemnly swear that I will faithfully execute the office of President of the United States, and will, to the best of my ability, preserve, protect, and defend the Constitution of the United States."

The artillery over on the slope boomed with all its guns a salute of thunder to the sixteenth President of the United States.

That was all. The inauguration was over. Men wrote their wives, former Lieutenant Governor Gustave Koerner of Illinois writing: "Dearest Sophie: Lincoln is President. In the presence of ten thousand people he took the oath and read with a firm voice his inaugural. I stood close to his chair; next to me stood Douglas. Douglas had no overcoat and I saw he was shivering. I had a thick shawl which I flung over him." Grenville M. Dodge of Council Bluffs, Iowa, dreaming as ever of a railroad to the Pacific, wrote to his wife: "Old Abe delivered the greatest speech of the age. It is backbone all over. The city bristles with bayonets." Henry Watterson wrote: "I stood just near enough to the speaker's elbow not to obstruct any gestures he might make. He delivered that inaugural as if he had been delivering inaugural addresses all his life."

CHAPTER FIFTEEN

The Momentous Issue

WHILE *ABRAHAM LINCOLN was in-
specting the White House on the afternoon of the
fourth of March, 1861, while he was shaking hands that
night at the Union Ball, his thoughts must have turned
more than once to his first Cabinet crisis—a crisis that
had developed before he had even revealed the names of
his advisers. Two days earlier Seward, apparently convinced that Chase was going to dominate the Cabinet, had
asked leave to withdraw his own acceptance, promised
months earlier. Lincoln had promptly asked him to coun-
termand the withdrawal, and had requested a reply by
nine o'clock on the morning of the fifth. "I can't afford to
let Seward take the first trick," the chief executive had remarked to one of his secretaries. But what would be the
answer?*

*Even more often his thoughts must have been upon Fort
Sumter in Charleston Harbor, where a garrison of U. S.
regulars under Major Robert Anderson continued to fly
the flag of the United States in the face of shore batteries
hastily erected by Confederate forces under General
P. G. T. Beauregard, who had resigned the superintend-
ency of the United States Military Academy less than two
weeks earlier.*

*Small wonder that young Henry Adams found the ball
a "melancholy function" and saw in the "plain, ploughed
face" of the President "the same painful sense of becoming
educated and of needing education" that was his own torment.*

1

EARLY ON THE MORNING of March 5, Lincoln learned that he
had won the first trick; Seward was retracting his letter of withdrawal. Whereupon the President performed his first official act;
he sent to the Senate, convened in extra session, the names of his
Cabinet. Margaret Leech offers quick sketches of the seven members.

A T THE HEAD of his advisers was Mr. Seward, balanced by
the radical Mr. Chase, who was to be Secretary of the Treasury.
Two selections had been virtually forced on Lincoln by bargains
which his managers had made at the Republican convention which
had nominated him. One was Caleb B. Smith, of Indiana, the Secretary of the Interior, a prosaic-looking, lisping conservative.
The other was Senator Simon Cameron, of Pennsylvania, whom
Mr. Lincoln had with much reluctance appointed Secretary of
War. Cameron was the Republican leader in his own State, but
his reputation for unscrupulous political practices shed no luster
on the new Cabinet.

As a sop to New England, Mr. Lincoln had made Gideon Welles,
of Connecticut, his Secretary of the Navy. He was tall and "ven-
erably insignificant," with a flowing beard and a huge gray wig.
Welles had been a newspaperman in Hartford, and did not know
the stem from the stern of a ship, but he was an industrious and
capable administrator. He was also very irritable, and those who
undervalued him did not know that, with a pen dipped in gall, he
kept a diary. In one respect, Welles was unique among the Cabinet members—he did not think himself a better man than the
President.

The Attorney General, Mr. Edward Bates, of Missouri, had
been one of Mr. Lincoln's earliest selections. He was a former
slaveholder, worthy, legalistic and reverential of the Constitution. The choice of the Marylander, Montgomery Blair, gave Lincoln two advisers from the border slave states. Blair was courageous, and had won Abolitionist acclaim by acting as counsel for
the slave, Dred Scott. However, while scarcely anyone could object to polite old Mr. Bates, the pinched and vindictive Montgomery had a host of enemies. He was detested by the radical
wing of the Republicans, and disliked as an uncompromising and

warmongering extremist by the moderates. He had plenty of secessionist relatives, and voiced his Union sympathies with challenge and defiance.

2

EVEN BEFORE the make-up of the Cabinet had been announced,
Lincoln learned that the crisis at Fort Sumter was far more imminent than he had realized. Nicolay and Hay explain the disturbing
revelation which marked the very beginning of the new Administration.

WHEN ON THE MORNING of the fifth of March Lincoln
went to his office in the Executive Mansion, he found a letter from
Mr. Holt, still acting as Secretary of War, giving him news of
vital importance received on the morning of the inauguration—
namely, that Fort Sumter must, in the lapse of a few weeks at
most, be strongly re-enforced or summarily abandoned. Major
Anderson had in the previous week made an examination of his
provisions. There was bread for twenty-eight days; pork for a
somewhat longer time; beans, rice, coffee, and sugar for different
periods from eight to forty days.

He had at the same time consulted his officers on the prospects
and possibilities of relief and re-enforcement. They unanimously
reported that before Sumter could be permanently or effectively
succored a combined land and naval force must attack and carry
the besieging forts and batteries, and hold the secession militia at
bay, and that such an undertaking would at once concentrate at
Charleston all the volunteers, not alone of South Carolina, but of
the adjacent states as well. "I confess," wrote Anderson, transmit-
ting the reports and estimates of his nine officers, "that I would
not be willing to risk my reputation on an attempt to throw re-
enforcements into this harbor within the time for our relief rendered necessary by the limited supply of our provisions, and with
a view of holding possession of the same, with a force of less than
twenty thousand good and well-disciplined men." Mr. Holt, quoting from previous instructions to and reports from the Major,
added that this declaration "takes the Department by surprise, as
his previous correspondence contained no such intimation."

. . . Here was a most portentous complication, not of Lincoln's own creating, but which he must nevertheless meet and overcome. He had counted on the soothing aid of time; time, on the contrary, was in this emergency working in the interest of rebellion. General Scott was at once called into council, but his sagacity and experience could afford neither suggestion nor encouragement. That same night he returned the papers to the President with a somewhat lengthy indorsement reciting the several events which led to, and his own personal efforts to avert, this contingency, but ending with the gloomy conclusion: "Evacuation seems almost inevitable, and in this view our distinguished Chief Engineer (Brigadier Totten) concurs—if indeed the worn-out garrison be not assaulted and carried in the present week."

This was a disheartening, almost a disastrous, beginning for the Administration. The Cabinet had only that day been appointed and confirmed. The presidential advisers had not yet taken their posts—all had not even signified their acceptance. There was an impatient multitude clamoring for audience, and behind these swarmed an army of office-seekers. Everything was urgency and confusion, everywhere was ignorance of method and routine. Rancor and hatred filled the breasts of political opponents departing from power; suspicion and rivalry possessed partisan adherents seeking advantage and promotion. As yet, Lincoln virtually stood alone, face to face with the appalling problems of the present and the threatening responsibilities of the future. Doubtless in this juncture he remembered and acted upon a Biblical precedent which in after days of trouble and despondency he was wont to quote for justification or consolation. When the children of Israel murmured on the shore of the Red Sea, Moses told them to "stand still and see the salvation of the Lord." Here, at the very threshold of his presidential career, Lincoln had need to practice the virtue of patience—one of the cardinal elements of his character, acquired in many a personal and political tribulation.

He referred the papers back to General Scott to make a more thorough investigation of all the questions involved. At the same time he gave him a verbal order touching his future policy, which a few days later was reduced to writing, and on the installation of the new Secretary of War transmitted by that functionary to the General in Chief through the regular official channels, as follows:

"I am directed by the President to say he desires you to exercise all possible vigilance for the maintenance of all the places within the military department of the United States, and to promptly call upon all the departments of the Government for the means necessary to that end."

3

TWO DAYS LATER, the Public Man finds Lincoln still deeply disturbed about Sumter—and at the same time facetious about the office-seekers who were swarming around him.

M A R C H 7th. Early this morning I received a message from the President, making an appointment for this afternoon. I called for——at his hotel and we drove to the White House. I could not help observing the disorderly appearance of the place, and the slovenly way in which the service was done. We were kept waiting but a few moments, however, and found Mr. Lincoln quite alone. He received us very kindly, but I was struck and pained by the haggard, worn look of his face, which scarcely left it during the whole time of our visit. I told the President, in a few words, why we had asked for this interview, and——then fully explained to him, as he had to me yesterday, the situation at Fort Sumter. It seemed to me that the information did not take the President entirely by surprise, though he asked—two or three times over—whether he was quite sure about Major Anderson's ideas as to his duty, in case of any action by Kentucky; and, when——had repeated to him exactly what he had told me as to the language used to himself by Major Anderson, Mr. Lincoln sat quite silent for a little while in a sort of brooding way, and then, looking up, suddenly said: "Well, you say Major Anderson is a good man, and I have no doubt he is; but if he is right it will be a bad job for me if Kentucky secedes. When he goes out of Fort Sumter, I shall have to go out of the White House." We could not resist a laugh at this quaint way of putting the case, but the gloomy, careworn look settled back very soon on the President's face, and he said little more except to ask——some questions about Montgomery, not I thought of a very relevant or important kind, and we soon took our leave. He walked into the corridor with us; and, as he bade us goodby, and thanked— —for what he had told him, he again brightened up for a moment and asked him in an abrupt kind of way, laying his hand as he spoke with a queer but not uncivil familiarity on his shoulder, "You haven't such a thing as a postmaster in your pocket, have you?"— —stared at him in astonishment, and I thought a little in alarm, as if he suspected a sudden attack of insanity, when Mr. Lincoln went on: "You see it seems to me kind of unnatural that you shouldn't have at least a postmaster in your pocket. Everybody I've seen for days past has had foreign ministers, and collectors, and all kinds, and I thought you couldn't have got in here without having at least a postmaster get into your pocket!" We assured him he need have no concern on that point, and left the house, both of us, I think, feeling, as I certainly felt, more anxious and disturbed than when we entered it. Not one word had Mr. Lincoln said to throw any real light either on his own views of the situation or on the effect of — —'s communication upon those views. But it was plain that he is deeply disturbed and puzzled by the problem of this wretched fort, to which circumstances are giving an importance so entirely disproportionate to its real significance, either political or military.

4

THE DIARY of Edward Bates, Lincoln's attorney general, records Cabinet discussions concerning Fort Sumter.

M AR. 9. SATURDAY NIGHT. A Cabinet Council upon the state of the country. I was astonished to be informed that Fort Sumter, in Charleston harbor *must* be evacuated, and that General Scott, Genl. Totten and Major Anderson concur in opinion, that, as the place has but 28 days' provision, it must be relieved, if at all, in that time; and that it will take a force of 20,000 men at least, and a bloody battle, to relieve it!

[NOTE ADDED LATER] For several days after this, consultations were held as to the feasibility of relieving Fort Sumter, at which were present, explaining and aiding, Gen. Scott, Gen. Totten, Commodore Stringham, and Mr. Fox [Asst. Secretary of the Navy] who seems to be *au fait* in both nautical and military matters. The *army* officers and *navy* officers differ widely about the degree of danger to rapid moving vessels passing under the fire of land batteries. The *army* officers think destruction almost inevitable, where the *navy* officers think the danger but slight. The one believes that Sumter cannot be relieved—not even provisioned —without an army of 20,000 men and a bloody battle: the other (the naval) believes that with light, rapid vessels, they can cross the bar at high tide of a dark night, run the enemy's forts (Moultrie and Cummings' Point) and reach Sumter with little risk. They say that the greatest danger will be in landing at Sumter, upon which point there may be a concentrated fire. They do not doubt that the place *can* be and *ought* to be relieved. Mr. Fox is anxious to risk his life in leading the relief, and Commodore Stringham seems equally confident of success.

The naval men have convinced me fully that the thing can be done, and yet, as the doing of it would be almost certain to *begin the war*, and as Charleston is of little importance, as compared with the chief points in the Gulf, I am willing to yield to the *military* counsel and evacuate Fort Sumter, at the same time strengthening the forts in the Gulf, so as to *look down* opposition, and guarding the coast, with all our naval power, if need be, so as to close any port at pleasure.

5

DURING MARCH AND EARLY APRIL, Lincoln's policy, molded partly by purpose, partly by circumstance, took concrete form. James G. Randall summarizes it.

THE MOST IMPORTANT ISSUES confronting the new President were the problem of conciliating the upper South so as to halt the secession movement, and the closely related problem of what to do at Fort Sumter. Major Anderson . . . had moved his force from Moultrie to Sumter, and his action was sustained by the Buchanan Administration. Supplies and re-enforcements were sent, but were not landed because of the attack upon the *Star of the West* [January 9]. To the end of his administration Buchanan refused to evacuate Sumter in compliance with the demands of South Carolina. Meanwhile perverse fate had given to "the Sumter question" an undeserved importance, and had packed it with all the dynamite of mass psychology. A striking feature of the prewar situation was the ease with which Union surrender of Southern forts and arsenals was accomplished *in general*, contrasted with the intense emotion and disturbance that raged around Sumter, whose evacuation would after all have been merely typical of what was happening all over the seceded states. One after another of the Federal strongholds and properties had fallen into Southern hands; but such incidents had been passed over by Buchanan without being treated as acts of war. This was because of Buchanan's general policy of non-aggression and of placing reliance on measures of conciliation and schemes of readjustment. On the assumption that these schemes had a fair chance of success it was expected that the places seized would come once more into Federal control. Fort Moultrie and Castle Pinckney had been taken over by South Carolina late in December, 1860; and the state authorities had proceeded to the general strengthening of various defenses at Charleston. Fort Pulaski at Savannah was seized by Georgia state troops on January 3. Fort Morgan at Mobile was taken on January 4 by Alabama troops, and a strong garrison was put in charge. At Pensacola, though Fort Pickens was kept in Union possession, the Federal Navy yard and Fort Barrancas were seized by Alabama and Florida troops, being surrendered by the Federal authorities (January 12) without a struggle. . . .

In addition, a number of post offices, custom houses, hospitals, and other public property had been occupied; the mint at New Orleans had been taken over; United States revenue cutters and other ships had been seized; and batteries in Charleston harbor had fired on a schooner (the *R. H. Shannon*) displaying the "Stars and Stripes." Of the forts in the seceded states the only ones remaining in Union hands in April, 1861, were Fort Sumter, Fort Pickens in Pensacola Bay, and two minor forts (Taylor and Jefferson) off the Florida coast. This Southern seizure of Federal forts, however, had occurred before Lincoln took office; and, while Lincoln had deliberately avoided threatening the repossession of places already taken, many in the North looked upon Sumter as a test of the President's adherence to his inaugural pronouncement that further surrenders would not take place.

In a peculiar sense the "two sides" faced each other at Sumter.

Should measures be taken there which appeared aggressive, there was real danger that the lower South would become inflamed to the point of fighting, and that, once war was started, the upper South could no longer be held in the Union. Peace thus hung upon a trigger; and to make matters worse a time limit was added to the situation by the fact that Major Anderson's supplies were low and the garrison would have to withdraw unless relieved by the middle of April. For the President to withdraw the garrison was not so easy a solution as it seemed. It was sure to be heralded as an evidence of weakness, if not a deliberate evasion of presidential duty. By such a step the Executive would have sacrificed many of his best supporters in the North.

Lincoln sought advice from various quarters. General Winfield Scott, veteran head of the army, advised that the sending of a sufficiently powerful provisioning or re-enforcing expedition was impracticable. Turning to his Cabinet, Lincoln found that only two of his ministers—Chase and Blair—favored an expedition intended to supply food to the garrison. Blair was sure that such an expedition would demonstrate the "firmness" of the administration; Chase, though approving the expedition, opposed such a move if it should inaugurate civil war. Seward blamed South Carolina for the "revolution," but declared that he "would not initiate war to regain a useless and unnecessary position. . . ." Cameron advised that an attempt to relieve the fort would be "unwise." Welles, Smith, and Bates also advised against a relief expedition.

Though Lincoln himself had announced in his inaugural the policy of holding the forts, the suggestion was made to him that he might yield at Sumter and still carry out his announced policy by remaining "firm" at Pickens where the psychology of the situation was less threatening. Furthermore, there were various developments in the early weeks of his administration which gave the distinct impression that the government at Washington was planning the evacuation of Sumter. Indirect communications occurred between Seward, widely regarded as the spokesman of the administration, and the Confederate commissioners at Washington. Though Seward did not actually "recognize" the Confederacy by receiving these commissioners officially, he did deal with them through go-betweens, especially Justices Nelson and Campbell of the United States Supreme Court. To these men, who were going back and forth between the commissioners and himself, Seward gave assurances in harmony with his own sincere wish that Sumter should be evacuated. This was regarded by the commissioners and by Southern leaders generally as a "promise" that the garrison would be withdrawn, though Lincoln himself had given no such promise.

It appears, however, that Lincoln, despite his inaugural declaration, seriously pondered the possibility of evacuating the fort. In conversation with Summers and Baldwin, unionist members of the Virginia Secession Convention who sought an interview with him, he is reported to have made a conditional suggestion to withdraw from Sumter if by this means the secession of Virginia could be prevented. "A State for a fort," he is reported to have said, "is no bad business." He had sent his Illinois friend Ward Hill Lamon to Charleston to observe and report; and Lamon, though without authority to commit the Washington government, had given both Governor Pickens of South Carolina and Major Anderson the impression that the intention was to evacuate the fort. Another factor in the complex situation was the action of a certain James E. Harvey, a Northerner who sent assurances to Charleston leaders that Anderson would be withdrawn, and that Sumter would not be re-enforced.

Having tested the possibilities that lay in the policy of evacuation, and having sounded public opinion on the subject, Lincoln, after what seemed like vacillation, decided as early as April 4 that two relief expeditions must be sent, one designed for Sumter and the other for Pickens. In making this decision, which he did independently of his Cabinet, the President had regard for the desirability of upholding the authority of the government in the South, after investigation had convinced him that evacuation would not offer a satisfactory solution of the sectional difficulty. He knew that no action was possible which would preserve the precise *status quo.* The approaching exhaustion of supplies in the fort made some change in the situation inevitable; and Lincoln's course offered the nearest approach to the preservation of the *status quo* which was possible. For it must be remembered that the purpose of the Sumter expedition was primarily to supply food to the garrison. Re-enforcements were to be landed only in case of attack.

The non-aggressive character of the expedition was emphasized by the care which Lincoln took to avoid the element of hostile surprise; for word of the expedition, with a statement of its pacific purpose, was sent to the Governor of South Carolina. That purpose was not understood in the Southern states and under these circumstances the decision to relieve Sumter was one of the most far-reaching and fateful actions in all American history. Lincoln's refusal to relax the tension on the forts at a time when such an easing of tension would have been understandable and even pleasing to many of his own followers was like a veritable declaration of war to the South.

6

ON APRIL 12 THE STORM BROKE. Stephen D. Lee, an officer in the Confederate forces stationed in Charleston harbor, narrates the event that precipitated the American Civil War.

S o s o o n . . . as it was clearly understood that the authorities at Washington had abandoned peaceful views, and would assert the power of the United States to supply Fort Sumter, General Beauregard . . . in obedience to the command of his government at Montgomery, proceeded to reduce the fort. His arrangements were about complete, and on April 11 he demanded of Major Anderson the evacuation of Fort Sumter. He offered to transport Major Anderson and his command to any port in the United States; and to allow him to move out of the fort with company arms and property, and all private property, and to salute his flag in lowering it. This demand was delivered to Major Anderson at 3:45 P.M. by two aides of General Beauregard, James Chesnut, Jr., and myself. At 4:30 P.M. he handed us his reply, refusing to accede to the demand, but adding, "Gentlemen, if you do not batter the fort to pieces about us, we shall be starved out in a few days."

The reply of Major Anderson was put in General Beauregard's hands at 5:15 P.M., and he was also told of this informal remark. Anderson's reply and remark were communicated to the Confederate authorities at Montgomery. The Secretary of War, L. P. Walker, replied to Beauregard as follows:

"Do not desire needlessly to bombard Fort Sumter. If Major Anderson will state the time at which, as indicated by him, he will evacuate, and agree that in the meantime he will not use his guns against us, unless ours should be employed against Fort Sumter, you are authorized thus to avoid the effusion of blood. If this, or its equivalent, be refused, reduce the fort as your judgment decides to be most practicable."

The same aides bore a second communication to Major Anderson, based on the above instructions, which was placed in his hands at 12:45 A.M., April 12. His reply indicated that he would evacuate the fort on the fifteenth, provided he did not in the meantime receive contradictory instructions from his government, or additional supplies, but he declined to agree not to open his guns upon the Confederate troops in the event of any hostile demonstration on their part against his flag. Major Anderson made every possible effort to retain the aides till daylight, making one excuse and then another for not replying. Finally, at 3:15 A.M., he delivered his reply. In accordance with their instructions, the aides read it and, finding it unsatisfactory, gave Major Anderson this notification:

"Fort Sumter, S. C., April 12, 1861, 3:20 A.M.—Sir: By authority of Brigadier-General Beauregard, commanding the Provisional Forces of the Confederate States, we have the honor to notify you that he will open the fire of his batteries on Fort Sumter in one hour from this time. We have the honor to be very respectfully, Your obedient servants, James Chesnut, Jr., *Aide-de-camp.* Stephen D. Lee, *Captain C. S. Army, Aide-de-camp.*"

The above note was written in one of the casemates of the fort, and in the presence of Major Anderson and several of his officers. On receiving it, he was much affected. He seemed to realize the full import of the consequences, and the great responsibility of his position. Escorting us to the boat at the wharf, he cordially pressed our hands in farewell, remarking, "If we never meet in this world again, God grant that we may meet in the next."

The boat containing the two aides and also Roger A. Pryor, of Virginia, and A. R. Chisolm, of South Carolina, who were also members of General Beauregard's staff, went immediately to Fort Johnson on James Island, and the order to fire the signal gun was given to Captain George S. James, commanding the battery at that point. It was then 4 A.M. Captain James at once aroused his command, and arranged to carry out the order. He was a great admirer of Roger A. Pryor, and said to him, "You are the only man to whom I would give up the honor of firing the first gun of the war"; and he offered to allow him to fire it. Pryor, on receiving the offer, was very much agitated. With a husky voice he said, "I could not fire the first gun of the war." His manner was almost similar to that of Major Anderson as we left him a few moments before on the wharf at Fort Sumter. Captain James would allow no one else but himself to fire the gun.

The boat with the aides of General Beauregard left Fort Johnson before arrangements were complete for the firing of the gun, and laid on its oars about one-third the distance between the fort and Sumter, there to witness the firing of "the first gun of the war" between the states. It was fired from a ten-inch mortar at 4:30 A.M., April 12, 1861. Captain James was a skillful officer, and the firing of the shell was a success. It burst immediately over the fort, apparently about one hundred feet above. The firing of the mortar woke the echoes from every nook and corner of the harbor, and in this the dead hour of night, before dawn, that shot was a sound of alarm that brought every soldier in the harbor to his feet, and every man, woman, and child in the city of Charleston from their beds. A thrill went through the whole city. It was felt that the Rubicon was passed. No one thought of going home; unused as their ears were to the appalling sounds, or the vivid flashes from the batteries, they stood for hours fascinated with horror. After the second shell the different batteries opened their fire on Fort Sumter, and by 4:45 A.M. the firing was general and regular. It was a hazy, foggy morning. About daylight, the boat with the aides reached Charleston, and they reported to General Beauregard.

Fort Sumter did not respond with her guns till 7:30 A.M. The firing from this fort, during the entire bombardment, was slow and deliberate, and marked with little accuracy. The firing continued without intermission during the twelfth, and more slowly during the night of the twelfth and thirteenth. No material change was noticed till 8 A.M. on the thirteenth, when the barracks in Fort

Sumter were set on fire by hot shot from the guns of Fort Moultrie. As soon as this was discovered, the Confederate batteries redoubled their efforts, to prevent the fire being extinguished. Fort Sumter fired at little longer intervals, to enable the garrison to fight the flames. This brave action, under such a trying ordeal, aroused great sympathy and admiration on the part of the Confederates for Major Anderson and his gallant garrison; this feeling was shown by cheers whenever a gun was fired from Sumter. It was shown also by loud reflections on the "men-of-war" outside the harbor.

About 12:30 the flag staff of Fort Sumter was shot down, but it was soon replaced. As soon as General Beauregard heard that the flag was no longer flying, he sent three of his aides, William Porcher Miles, Pryor, and myself, to offer, and also to see if Major Anderson would receive or needed, assistance, in subduing the flames inside the fort. Before we reached it, we saw the United States flag again floating over it, and began to return to the city. Before going far, however, we saw the Stars and Stripes replaced by a white flag. We turned about at once and rowed rapidly to the fort. We were directed, from an embrasure, not to go to the wharf, as it was mined, and the fire was near it. We were assisted through an embrasure and conducted to Major Anderson. Our mission being made known to him, he replied, "Present my compliments to General Beauregard, and say to him I thank him for his kindness, but need no assistance." He further remarked that he hoped the worst was over, that the fire had settled over the magazine, and, as it had not exploded, he thought the real danger was about over. Continuing, he said, "Gentlemen, do I understand you come direct from General Beauregard?" The reply was in the affirmative. He then said, "Why! Colonel Wigfall has just been here as an aide too, and by authority of General Beauregard, and proposed the same terms of evacuation offered on the eleventh instant." We informed the Major that we were not authorized to offer terms; that we were direct from General Beauregard, and that Colonel Wigfall, although an aide-de-camp to the General, had been detached, and had not seen the General for several days. Major Anderson at once stated, "There is a misunderstanding on my part, and I will at once run up my flag and open fire again." After consultation, we requested him not to do so, until the matter was explained to General Beauregard, and requested Major Anderson to reduce to writing his understanding with Colonel Wigfall, which he did. However, before we left the fort, a boat arrived from Charleston, bearing Major D. R. Jones, Assistant Adjutant-General on General Beauregard's staff, who offered substantially the same terms to Major Anderson as those offered on the eleventh, and also by Colonel Wigfall, and which were now accepted.

Thus fell Fort Sumter, April 13, 1861. At this time fire was still raging in the barracks, and settling steadily over the magazine. All egress was cut off except through the lower embrasures. Many shells from the Confederate batteries, which had fallen in the fort and had not exploded, as well as the hand grenades used for defense, were exploding as they were reached by the fire. The wind was driving the heat and smoke down into the fort and into the casemates, almost causing suffocation. Major Anderson, his officers, and men were blackened by smoke and cinders, and showed signs of fatigue and exhaustion from the trying ordeal through which they had passed.

It was soon discovered, by conversation, that it was a bloodless battle; not a man had been killed or seriously wounded on either side during the entire bombardment of nearly forty hours. Congratulations were exchanged on so happy a result. Major Anderson stated that he had instructed his officers only to fire on the batteries and forts, and not to fire on private property.

The terms of evacuation offered by General Beauregard were generous, and were appreciated by Major Anderson. The garrison was to embark on the fourteenth, after running up and saluting the United States flag, and to be carried to the United States fleet. A soldier killed during the salute was buried inside the fort, the new Confederate garrison uncovering during the impressive ceremonies. Major Anderson and his command left the harbor, bearing with them the respect and admiration of the Confederate soldiers. It was conceded that he had done his duty as a soldier holding a most delicate trust.

7

WHILE THE GUNS were giving the signal for one of the bloodiest wars in history, Lincoln—who knew the meaning of their message better than most—remained unperturbed in the White House. So, at least, Nicolay and Hay observe.

On the morning of Saturday, April 13, the newspapers of Washington, like those of every other city in the Union, North and South, were filled with the startling headlines and thrilling details of the beginning and progress of an actual bombardment.

That day there was little change in the business routine of the Executive Office. Mr. Lincoln was never liable to sudden excitement or sudden activity. Through all his life, and through all the unexpected and stirring events of the rebellion, his personal manner was one of steadiness of word and act. It was this quality which, in the earlier stages of the War, conveyed to many of his visitors the false impression of his indifference. His sagacity gave him a marked advantage over other men in enabling him to forecast probable events; and when they took place, his great caution restrained his comments and controlled his outward bearing. Oftentimes, when men came to him in the rage and transport of a first indignation over some untoward incident, they were surprised to find him quiet, even serene—perhaps with a smile on his face and a jest on his lips—engaged in routine work, and prone to talk of other and more commonplace matters. Of all things the exhibition of mock heroism was foreign to his nature. Generally it happened that when others in this mood sought him, his spirit had already been through the fiery trial of resentment—but giving no outward sign, except at times with lowered eyebrow, a slight nodding and shaking of the head, a muttering motion or hard compression of the lips, and, rarely, an emphatic downward gesture with the clenched right hand. His judgment, like his perception, far outran the average mind. While others fumed and fretted at things that were, all his inner consciousness was abroad in the wide realm of possibilities, busily searching out the dim and difficult path towards things to be. His easy and natural attention to ordinary occupations afforded no indication of the double mental process which was habitual with him.

So, while the Sumter telegrams were on every tongue and revengeful indignation was in every heart, there was little variation in the business of the Executive Mansion on that eventful Saturday. The miscellaneous gathering was larger there, as it was larger at the Departments, the newspaper and telegraph offices, and the hotels. More leading men and officials called to learn or to impart news. The Cabinet, as by a common impulse, came together and deliberated. All talk, however, was brief, sententious, informal. The issue had not yet been reached. Sumter was still under fire. Nevertheless, the main question required no discussion, not even decision, scarcely an announcement. Jefferson Davis's order and Beauregard's guns had sufficiently defined the coming action of the government. After this functionaries and people had but a single purpose, a single duty. Lincoln said but little beyond making inquiries about the current reports and criticizing the probability or accuracy of their details, and went on as usual receiving visitors, listening to suggestions, and signing routine papers throughout the day.

8

BUT LINCOLN'S DEMEANOR was deceptive. The real temper in which he received news of the bombardment became apparent, appropriately enough, on July 4, when his message to Congress, assembled in special session, was read before that body. After describing the incidents leading to the attack on the fort, he continued:

I T I S T H U S S E E N that the assault upon and reduction of Fort Sumter was in no sense a matter of self-defense on the part of the assailants. They well knew that the garrison in the fort could by no possibility commit aggression upon them. They knew—they were expressly notified—that the giving of bread to the few brave and hungry men of the garrison was all which would on that occasion be attempted, unless themselves, by resisting so much, should provoke more. They knew that this government desired to keep the garrison in the fort, not to assail them, but merely to maintain visible possession, and thus to preserve the Union from actual and immediate dissolution—trusting, as hereinbefore stated, to time, discussion, and the ballot-box for final adjustment; and they assailed and reduced the fort for precisely the reverse object—to drive out the visible authority of the Federal Union, and thus force it to immediate dissolution. That this was their object the Executive well understood; and having said to them in the in-

augural address, "You can have no conflict without being yourselves the aggressors," he took pains not only to keep this declaration good, but also to keep the case so free from the power of
ingenious sophistry that the world should not be able to misunderstand it. By the affair at Fort Sumter, with its surrounding circumstances, that point was reached. Then and thereby the assailants of the government began the conflict of arms, without a gun
in sight or in expectancy to return their fire, save only the few
in the fort sent to that harbor years before for their own protection, and still ready to give that protection in whatever was lawful.
In this act, discarding all else, they have forced upon the country
the distinct issue, "immediate dissolution or blood."

And this issue embraces more than the fate of these United
States. It presents to the whole family of man the question whether
a constitutional republic or democracy—a government of the people by the same people—can or cannot maintain its territorial
integrity against its own domestic foes. It presents the question
whether discontented individuals, too few in numbers to control
administration according to organic law in any case, can always,
upon the pretenses made in this case, or on any other pretenses,
or arbitrarily without any pretense, break up their government,
and thus practically put an end to free government upon the
earth. It forces us to ask: "Is there, in all republics, this inherent
and fatal weakness?" "Must a government, of necessity, be too
strong for the liberties of its own people, or too weak to maintain
its own existence?"

So viewing the issue, no choice was left but to call out the war
power of the government; and so to resist force employed for its
destruction, by force for its preservation.

CHAPTER SIXTEEN

The War Begins

*T*HE FIRING ON FORT SUMTER
*snapped a tension that was tighter than most of those
who had been enduring it realized. On April 15, one day
after Anderson's surrender, Lincoln issued his proclamation calling out the militia to the number of 75,000. The
North responded almost as one man. Mass meetings convened, wealthy citizens subscribed money to equip troops,
and military companies vied with one another to be the
first to fill their complements. Fife and drum sounded day
and night in hamlet as well as city, while women wore out
their eyes and fingers sewing flags and uniforms. Had the
call been for five times 75,000, the quota would still have
been met with men to spare.*

1

ONE REASON—a primary one—for the response of the North
was the stand taken by the man who had been Abraham Lincoln's
political rival for almost a quarter of a century. Though defeated
for the presidency, Stephen A. Douglas was still the leader of the
Northern wing of the Democratic party and idolized by vast numbers of its members. The way in which he subordinated personal
and political considerations to patriotism is delineated by George
Ashmun, of Massachusetts, who had presided over the Republican
National Convention which nominated Lincoln. Ashmun's analysis
was written in October, 1864, when the events it related were still
vivid in his memory.

On sunday, April 14, 1861, Washington was agitated by the spread of the information of the fall of Fort Sumter, the news of which had arrived the night before. Such an event could not but produce a profound feeling at the seat of government, and discussions of the event largely displaced all the ordinary Sunday ceremonies. The course which the new Administration would take was then quite unknown, and gave ground for much anxiety. For myself, I felt that the occasion was one which demanded prompt action and the cordial support of the whole people of the North, and that this would be greatly ensured by a public declaration from Mr. Douglas. The friendly personal relations which had long existed between us justified an effort in that direction on my part; and late in the afternoon I decided to make it. On driving to his house, I found him surrounded by quite a number of political friends, whom he, however, soon dismissed with an easy grace on a suggestion of the errand which had brought me there. Our interview lasted an hour or more, and in the course of it the whole nature of his relations to Mr. Lincoln's administration, and his duty to the country, were fully discussed. His first impulse was decidedly against my purposes. I desired him to go with me at once to the President, and make a declaration of his determination to sustain him in the needful measures which the exigency of the hour demanded, to put down the Rebellion which had thus fiercely flamed out in Charleston harbor. I well remember his first reply: "Mr. Lincoln had dealt hardly with me in removing some of my friends from office, and I don't know as he wants my advice or aid." My answer was that Mr. Lincoln had probably followed Democratic precedents in making removals; but that the question now presented rose to a higher dignity than could belong to any possible party question; and that it was now in his (Mr. Douglas's) power to render such a service to his country as would not only give him a title to its lasting gratitude, but would at the same time show that in the hour of his country's need he could trample all partisan considerations and resentments under foot. The discussion in this vein continued for some time, and resulted in his emphatic declaration that he would go with me to the President and offer a cordial and earnest support. But I shall never forget that before it was concluded his beautiful and noble wife came into the room and gave the whole weight of her affectionate influence toward the result which was reached. My carriage was waiting at the door, and it was almost dark when we started for the President's house. We fortunately found Mr. Lincoln alone, and, upon my stating the errand on which we had come, he was most cordial in his welcome, and immediately prepared the way for the conversation which followed, by taking from his drawer and reading to us the draft of the proclamation which he had decided to issue, and which was given to the country the next morning.

As soon as the reading was ended, Mr. Douglas rose from the chair and said: "Mr. President, I cordially concur in every word of that document, except that instead of a call for seventy-five thousand men I would make it two hundred thousand. You do not know the dishonest purposes of those men (the Rebels) as well as I do—" and he then asked us to look with him at the map which hung at one end of the President's room, where in much detail he pointed out the principal strategic points which should be at once strengthened for the coming contest. Among the most prominent were Fortress Monroe, Washington, Harper's Ferry and Cairo. He enlarged at length upon the firm, warlike footing which ought to be pursued, and found in Mr. Lincoln an earnest and gratified listener. It would be impossible to give in detail all the points presented by him and discussed with the President; but I venture to say that no two men in the United States parted that night with a more cordial feeling of a united, friendly and patriotic purpose than Mr. Lincoln and Mr. Douglas.

After leaving, and while on our way homeward, I said to Mr. Douglas. "You have done justice to your own reputation and to the President, and the country must know it. The proclamation will go by telegraph all over the country in the morning, and the account of this interview must go with it. I shall send it either in my own language or yours. I prefer that you should give your own version." He at once said: "Drive to your room at Willard's and I will give it shape." We did so, and he wrote the following, the original of which now lies before me, in his own handwriting. I copied it, and gave an exact copy to the agent of the Associated Press, and on the next morning it was read all over the North, in company with the President's proclamation, to the great gratification of his friends and the friends of the government. The original is still preserved, as cherished evidence of the highest character, that whoever else may have fallen by the wayside, in the hour of our country's peril from "false brethern," Mr. Douglas was not one of them:

"DISPATCH TO THE PRESS BY MR. DOUGLAS, "SUNDAY EVENING, APRIL 14, 1861.

"Mr. Douglas called on the President this evening and had an interesting conversation on the present condition of the country. The substance of the conversation was that while Mr. Douglas was unalterably opposed to the administration on all its political issues, he was prepared to sustain the President in the exercise of all his constitutional functions to preserve the Union, and maintain the government and defend the Federal capital. A firm policy and prompt action was necessary. The capital of our country was in danger and must be defended at all hazards, and at any expense of men and money. He spoke of the present and future without reference to the past."

All honor, then, to the memory of the man who thus threw party considerations to the winds and gave himself wholly and unreservedly to his country!

2

THE FIRST UNION REGIMENT to start for Washington, where a Confederate attack was feared momentarily, was the Sixth Massachusetts. While passing through Baltimore on April 19, the troops were mobbed by Confederate sympathizers. Four of their number were killed and many more were wounded, but the regiment succeeded in making its way to Washington, where it was quartered in the Capitol. The scene there, a day after the riot, found its way into the diary of John Hay.

APRIL 20, 1861. The streets were full of the talk of Baltimore. It seems to be generally thought that a mere handful of men has raised this storm that now threatens the loyalty of a state.

I went up with Nicolay, Pangborn, and Whitely to see the Massachusetts troops quartered in the Capitol. The scene was very novel. The contrast was very painful between the grey-haired dignity that filled the Senate Chamber when I saw it last and the present throng of bright-looking Yankee boys, the most of them bearing the signs of New England rusticity in voice and manner, scattered over the desks, chairs, and galleries, some loafing, many writing letters, slowly and with plough-hardened hands, or with rapid glancing clerkly fingers, while Grow stood patiently by the desk and franked for everybody. The Hall of Representatives is as yet empty. Lying on a sofa and looking upward, the magnificence of the barracks made me envy the soldiery who should be quartered there. The wide-spreading skylights overarching the vast hall like Heaven blushed and blazed with gold and the heraldic devices of the married states, while all around it the eye was rested by the massive simple splendor of the stalagmitic bronze reliefs. The spirit of our institutions seemed visibly present to inspire and nerve the acolyte, sleeping in her temple beside his unfleshed sword. . . .

The Massachusetts men drilled tonight on the Avenue. They afford a happy contrast to the unlicked patriotism that has poured ragged and unarmed out of Pennsylvania. They step together well and look as if they meant business.

3

AFTER THE BALTIMORE RIOT, troops on the way to Washington were shunted to routes which led them around that city rather than through it. But their passage was slow, and in the Capital's isolation—telegraph wires had been cut—gravest apprehension prevailed. The chronicle of Nicolay and Hay catches the excitement, the near panic, of the time.

A NOTHER NIGHT of feverish public unrest, another day of anxiety to the President—Wednesday, April 24. There was indeed no attack on the city; but, on the other hand, no arrival of troops to place its security beyond doubt. Repetition of routine duties; repetition of unsubstantial rumors; long faces in the streets; a holiday quiet over the city; closed shutters and locked doors of business houses; the occasional clatter of a squad of cavalry from point to point; sentinels about the departments; sentinels about the Executive Mansion; Willard's Hotel, which a week before was swarming with busy crowds, now deserted as if smitten by a plague, with only furtive servants to wake echoes along the vacant corridors—an oppressive contrast to the throng of fashion and beauty which had so lately made it a scene of festivity from midday to midnight.

Ever since the telegraph stopped on Sunday night, the Washington operators had been listening for the ticking of their instruments, and had occasionally caught fugitive dispatches passing between Maryland Secessionists, which were for the greater part immediately known to be untrustworthy; for General Scott kept up a series of military scouts along the Baltimore railroad as far as Annapolis Junction, twenty miles from Washington, from which point a branch railroad ran at a right angle to the former, twenty miles to Annapolis, on Chesapeake Bay. The general dared not risk a detachment permanently to hold the Junction; no considerable Secessionist force had been encountered, and the railroad was yet safe. But it was known, or at least strongly probable, that the volunteers from the North had been at Annapolis since Sunday morning. Why did they not land? Why did they not advance? The Annapolis road was known to be damaged; but could they not march twenty miles?

The previous day (April 23) had, by some lucky chance, brought a New York mail three days old. The newspapers in it contained breezy premonitions of the Northern storm—Anderson's enthusiastic reception; the departure of the Seventh New York regiment; the sailing of Governor Sprague with his Rhode Islanders; the monster meeting in Union Square, with the outpouring of half a million of people in processions and listening to speeches from half a dozen different stands; the energetic measures of the New York Common Council; the formation of the Union Defense Committee; whole columns of orders and proclamations; the flag-raisings; the enlistments; the chartering and freighting of ships; and from all quarters news of the wild, jubilant uprising of the whole immense population of the free states. All this was gratifying, pride-kindling, reassuring; and yet, read and reread with avidity in Washington that day, it would always bring after it the galling reflection that all this magnificent outburst of patriotism was paralyzed by the obstacle of a twenty miles' march between Annapolis and the junction. Had the men of the North no legs?

Lincoln, by nature and habit so calm, so equable, so undemonstrative, nevertheless passed this period of interrupted communication and isolation from the North in a state of nervous tension which put all his great powers of mental and physical endurance to their severest trial. General Scott's reports, though invariably expressing his confidence in successful defense, frankly admitted the evident danger; and the President, with his acuteness of observation and his rapidity and correctness of inference, lost no single one of the external indications of doubt and apprehension. Day after day prediction failed and hope was deferred; troops did not come, ships did not arrive, railroads remained broken, messengers failed to reach their destination. That fact itself demonstrated that he was environed by the unknown—and that whether a Union or a Secession army would first reach the capital was at best an uncertainty.

To a coarse or vulgar nature such a situation would have brought only one of two feelings—either overpowering personal fear, or overweening bravado. But Lincoln, almost a giant in physical stature and strength, combined in his intellectual nature a masculine courage and power of logic with an ideal sensitiveness of conscience and a sentimental tenderness as delicate as a woman's. This presidential trust which he had assumed was to him not a mere regalia of rank and honor. Its terrible duties and responsibilities seemed rather a coat of steel armor, heavy to bear, and cutting remorselessly in to the quick flesh. That one of the successors of Washington should find himself even to this degree in the hands of his enemies was personally humiliating; but that the majesty of a great nation should be thus insulted and its visible symbols of authority be placed in jeopardy; above all, that the hitherto glorious example of the Republic to other nations should stand in this peril of surprise and possible sudden collapse, the Constitution be scoffed, and human freedom become a byword and reproach—this must have begot in him an anxiety approaching torture.

In the eyes of his countrymen and of the world he was holding the scales of national destiny; he alone knew that for the moment the forces which made the beam vibrate with such uncertainty were beyond his control. In others' society he gave no sign of these inner emotions. But once, on the afternoon of the twenty-third, the business of the day being over, the Executive Office deserted, after walking the floor alone in silent thought for nearly half an hour, he stopped and gazed long and wistfully out of the window down the Potomac in the direction of the expected ships; and, unconscious of other presence in the room, at length broke out with irrepressible anguish in the repeated exclamation, "Why don't they come! Why don't they come!"

One additional manifestation of this bitterness of soul occurred on the day following, though in a more subdued manner. The wounded soldiers of the Sixth Massachusetts, including several officers, came to pay a visit to the President. They were a little shy when they entered the room—having the traditional New England awe of authorities and rulers. Lincoln received them with sympathetic kindness which put them at ease after the interchange of the first greetings. His words of sincere thanks for their patriotism and their suffering, his warm praise of their courage, his hearty recognition of their great service to the public, and his earnestly expressed confidence in their further devotion, quickly won their trust. He spoke to them of the position and prospect of the city, contrasting their prompt arrival with the unexplained delay which seemed to have befallen the regiments supposed to be somewhere on their way from the various states. Pursuing this theme, he finally fell into a tone of irony to which only intense feeling ever drove him. "I begin to believe," said he, "that there is no North. The Seventh regiment is a myth. Rhode Island is another. You are the only real thing." There are few parchment brevets as precious as such a compliment, at such a time, from such a man. . . .

Wednesday morning, April 24, being the fourth day at Annapolis for the Eighth Massachusetts and the third for the Seventh New York, they started on their twenty miles' march to the junction. . . . All the previous rumors had taught them that here they might expect a rebel force and fight. The anticipation proved groundless; they learned, on the contrary, that a train from Washington had come to this place for them the day before. It soon again made its appearance; and, quickly embarking on it, by noon the Seventh New York was at its destination.

Those who were in the Federal capital on that Thursday, April 25, will never, during their lives, forget the event. An indescribable gloom had hung over Washington nearly a week, paralyzing its traffic and crushing out its life. As soon as the arrival was known, an immense crowd gathered at the depot to obtain ocular evidence that relief had at length reached the city. Promptly debarking and forming, the Seventh marched up Pennsylvania Avenue to the White House. As they passed up the magnificent street, with their well-formed ranks, their exact military step, their soldierly bearing, their gayly floating flags, and the inspiring music of their splendid regimental band, they seemed to sweep all thought of danger and all taint of treason out of that great national thoroughfare and out of every human heart in the Federal city. The presence of this single regiment seemed to turn the scales of fate. Cheer upon cheer greeted them; windows were thrown up; houses opened; the population came forth upon the streets as for a holiday. It was an epoch in American history. For the first time, the combined spirit and power of liberty entered the nation's Capital.

4

THE ARRIVAL OF the Seventh New York broke the jam; thereafter troops moved into Washington in an unbroken stream. Their increasing numbers, however, failed to diminish popular interest in a 24-year-old colonel of a Zouave regiment recruited from New York firemen. Elmer Ellsworth had won national renown from the performances of a Chicago military company which he had trained; a brief period as a student in Lincoln's law office, and the President's known fondness for him, made him even more of a celebrity. John Hay portrays him and his men on their arrival in Washington.

MAY 2, 1861. Tonight Ellsworth and his stalwart troup arrived. He was dressed like his men, red cap, red shirt, grey breeches, grey jacket. In his belt, a sword, a very heavy revolver, and what was still more significant of the measures necessary with the turbulent spirits under his command, an enormously large and bloodthirsty looking bowie knife, more than a foot long in the blade and with body enough to go through a man's head from crown to chin as you would split an apple. His hair was cut short, his face thin from constant labor and excitement. His voice had assumed that tone of hoarse strength that I recognized at the end of the triumphant trip last year. He seemed contented and at ease about his regiment. He indulged in a little mild blasphemy when he found that no suitable quarters had been provided but was mollified by the offer of the Sixty-ninth's rooms and the Capitol.

I went up. It was a jolly, gay set of blackguards. They had reduced their hair to a war footing. There was not a pound of capillary integument in the house. Their noses were concave, their mouths vulgar but good-humored, their eyes, small, crafty and furtive.

They were in a pretty complete state of don't-care-a-damn, modified by an affectionate and respectful deference to the Colonel. He thought only of his men. We went, after making all possible provisions for their suppers, to hammocks. The Zouave could not enjoy his tea, as he thought it unbecoming an officer to eat before his men.

He spoke with honest exultation of the fruitless attempt made to stop him the morning of embarkation.

MAY 7, 1861. In the afternoon we went up to see Ellsworth's Zouave firemen. They are the largest, sturdiest, and, physically, the most magnificent men I ever saw collected together. They played over the sward like kittens, lithe and agile in their strength.

Ellsworth has been intensely disgusted at the wild yarns afloat about them which are, for the most part, utterly untrue. A few graceless rascals have been caught in various lapses. These are in irons. One horrible story which has been terrifying all the maiden antiques of the city for several days, has the element of horror pretty well eliminated today by the injured fair, who proves a most yielding seducee, offering to settle the matter for twenty-five dollars. Other yarns are due to the restless brains of the press gang.

The youthful Colonel formed his men in a hollow square, and made a great speech at them. There was more common sense, dramatic power, tact, energy, and that eloquence that naturally flowers into deeds, in *le petit* Colonel's fifteen-minute harangue than in all the speeches that stripped the plumes from our unfortunate ensign in the spread-eagle days of the Congress that has flitted. He spoke to them as men; made them proud in their good name; spoke bitterly and witheringly of the disgrace of the recreant; contrasted with cutting emphasis, which his men delighted in, the enlistment of the dandy regiment for thirty days with *theirs* for the war; spoke solemnly and impressively of the disgrace of expulsion; roused them to wild enthusiasm by announcing that he had heard of one officer who treated his men with less consideration than himself and that, if on inquiry the rumor proved true, he would strip him and send him home in irons. The men yelled with delight, clapped their hands, and shouted "Bully for you." He closed with wonderful tact and dramatic spirit by saying, "Now laddies, if anyone of you wants to go home, he had better sneak around the back alleys, crawl over fences, and get out of sight before we see him," which got them again. He must have run with this crowd sometime in his varied career. He knows them and handles them so perfectly.

5

LESS THAN A MONTH after Hay's light-hearted diary entry, Ellsworth was dead—the first Northern officer to fall in violence, the first Northern hero. Details of the tragedy are supplied by Lincoln's secretaries—both his friends.

IN THE BRIGHT MOONLIGHT at two o'clock of the morning of May 24, the march was begun; three regiments crossing the Aqueduct Bridge at Georgetown, and four regiments the Long Bridge at Washington. Squads of cavalry, dashing across in advance, took quick possession of the Virginia end of each of these bridges, as also of the Chain Bridge four miles above Georgetown, and forestalled any attempt by the enemy to destroy them. The movement proved a complete surprise, and found no opposing force. Once across, the outposts were pushed several miles beyond the river; by sunrise of the twenty-fourth, the engineers had traced their lines and the volunteers were busy with pick and spade throwing up fortifications. Here was begun that formidable system of earthworks, crowning every hill in an irregular line of perhaps ten miles, extending from the river bend above Georgetown to the bay into which Hunting Creek flows below Alexandria, which constituted such an immense military strength and so important a moral support to the Army of the Potomac, and indeed to the Union sentiment of the whole country during the entire war.

The capture of Alexandria and its garrison formed part of the projected work. It had been agreed that the First Michigan regiment should march directly from the Long Bridge to the rear of that city, while steamers should convey the Eleventh New York Regiment, commanded by Colonel Ellsworth, from their camp on Giesboro's Point and land them on the Alexandria wharves, under cover of the guns of the war steamer *Pawnee,* anchored in the river. The march, the embarkation, and the landing were successfully executed, but the expected capture of the rebel garrison was frustrated. The rebel commander had already been notified by his pickets of the crossing at the Chain Bridge, and suspecting a general movement, had his five hundred infantrymen under arms. He hurried his detachment out of the back streets to a waiting train of cars just as the Michigan volunteers were entering the city; and though the rebel rear guard and the Union advance guard were not more that two hundred yards apart, the detachment made its escape. A small troop of rebel cavalry, still lingering under orders to watch further movements, was easily captured. A few harmless shots had been exchanged between the landing troops and the retiring rebel sentries, and the whole movement seemed on the point of completion without bloodshed when a tragedy occurred which startled the country. This was the assassination of Colonel Ellsworth.

He had led his regiment into the place, and personally superintended posting it to secure order and prevent surprise. This task finished in the gray of the morning, his eye caught the rebel flag hoisted over the principal hotel, which had so long flaunted defiance at the national Capital. In the ardor of youthful patriotism he was seized with the wish to take it down with his own hands. Entering with only three companions, he mounted to the roof, cut the halyards, and started down the narrow winding stairs with a

soldier preceding and another following him. As Ellsworth was
about to pass a doorway, the hotelkeeper sprang from conceal-
ment and discharged the contents of a double-barreled shotgun
full in the colonel's heart. Retribution was instantaneous. As
Ellsworth fell forward, his foremost companion, Private Francis
E. Brownell, dealt out immediate death to the assassin with both
rifle shot and bayonet thrust.

To the people of the North, already strung to high nervous
tension, this drama stood out in vivid relief from the swift-moving
incidents of rebellion. Ellsworth was not only the first sacrifice of
the war; his youth, his knight-errant qualities of character, his
high ambition, and his talent for leadership had made him extremely popular. Upon President Lincoln his untimely death fell
with the force of a personal bereavement. He had brought Ellsworth to Washington among his suite of friends; had seen his
magnetic power to control the crowds that thronged every foot-
step of the President-elect; the echoes of his cheery and manly
voice seemed yet to linger in the corridors and rooms of the
Executive Mansion, from which he had so recently looked upon
this identical flag of treason now stained with his blood. When
the Colonel's comrades returned with the body, Lincoln ordered
that it should lie in state in the East Room, where Cabinet, diplo-
mats, and military and naval dignitaries attended the impressive
funeral ceremonies.

6

TO THE HARASSED MAN in the White House, driven almost
to despair by concern for the national safety, saddened by the
death of Ellsworth and by the knowledge that his was only the
first sacrifice, the spoils system added its own heavy burden. Helen
Nicolay records Lincoln's tribulations at the hands of office seekers.

IN SPITE OF THE WAR, daily life went on, as daily life
must, in a round of incidents trivial in themselves. The tragic
background was made endurable by a great hope, and against it
details of commonplace living etched a curious, inconsequent,
never-ending pattern.

Lincoln was servant of the people equally by heart's impulse and in fulfillment of his oath. Every hour was dedicated to their service. His day began early, and ended only when physical weariness drove him to his bed. Frequently at night he could not sleep, and rose to wander from room to room.

At first all his time was taken up with office seekers. "The grounds, halls, stairways, closets, are filled with applicants, who render ingress and egress difficult," Secretary Seward wrote. Mr. Lincoln began by trying to receive these importunates and attend to official business twelve full hours a day. Later his reception hours were limited, in theory, from ten o'clock to one; but it was in theory only.

"I am looking forward with a good deal of eagerness to when I shall have time to at least read and write my letters in peace without being haunted continually by some one who 'wants to see the President *for only five minutes.*' At present this request meets me from almost every man, woman and child I see, whether by day or by night, in the house, or on the street," my father wrote when they had been in Washington three weeks.

That day of leisure never came. Before the office seekers had been disposed of, war filled the house with a totally different class of visitors—men who wanted commissions, others who wished to furnish stores to the Army, inventors with improved engines of destruction, and a never-ending stream of officers in search of promotion.

Although, with the voluntary resignations of officials who went south to join the rebellion, and the countless military appointments made necessary by the new armies, no President has had such an increase in the number of places at his disposal, they were not nearly enough for the hungry hordes. "Gentlemen," he said to a group who urged the benefit of the climate as additional reason for appointing their candidate Commissioner to the Sandwich Islands, "I am sorry to say that there are eight other applicants for the place, all sicker than your man."

That was long before the days of civil service reform, but Lincoln's ideas of fairness gave a full equivalent. The patient thoroughness he lavished on his appointments has inspired many reminiscences.

"What is the matter?" a friend asked in alarm, coming upon him sad and depressed. "Have you bad news from the army?"

"No, it isn't the army," he replied with one of his weary, humorous smiles. "It is the post-office at Brownsville, Missouri."

7

WHILE REPUBLICAN POLITICIANS pulled wires for offices, the North went about the business of raising an army. By early summer, 1861, 35,000 Federal troops under Major General Irvin McDowell were under arms near Centreville, twenty miles southwest of Washington. Public clamor for an advance on Richmond became irresistible. On July 21, McDowell attacked the Confederate forces under Beauregard at Manassas Junction. In the initial fighting, the Union Army was successful, but the unexpected arrival of a part of Joseph E. Johnston's army turned the battle into a Confederate victory. One of the many noncombatants who witnessed the Battle of Bull Run was William H. Russell, correspondent of the *London Times*. In the superheated patriotism then prevailing, his dispatch aroused deep resentment in the North and led to his early departure for England.

I T WAS A STRANGE SCENE before us. From the hill, a densely wooded country, dotted at intervals with green fields and cleared lands, spread five or six miles in front, bounded by a line of blue and purple ridges, terminating abruptly in escarpments towards the left front, and swelling gradually towards the right into the lower spines of an offshoot from the Blue Ridge mountains. On our left, the view was circumscribed by a forest which clothed the side of the ridge on which we stood, and covered its shoulder far down into the plain. A gap in the nearest chain of the hills in our front was pointed out by the bystanders as the Pass of Manassas, by which the railway from the West is carried into the plain, and still nearer at hand, before us, is the junction of that rail with the line from Alexandria, and with the railway leading southwards to Richmond. The intervening space was not a dead level; undulating lines of forest marked the course of the streams which intersected it, and gave, by their variety of color and shading, an additional charm to the landscape which, enclosed in a framework of blue and purple hills, softened into violet in the extreme distance, presented one of the most agreeable displays of simple pastoral woodland scenery that could be conceived.

But the sounds which came upon the breeze, and the sights which met our eyes, were in terrible variance with the tranquil character of the landscape. The woods far and near echoed to the roar of cannon, and thin, frayed lines of blue smoke marked the spots whence came the muttering sound of rolling musketry; the white puffs of smoke burst high above the treetops, and the gunners' rings from shell and howitzer marked the fire of the artillery.

Clouds of dust shifted and moved through the forest; and, through the wavering mists of light blue smoke and the thicker masses which rose commingling from the feet of men and the mouths of cannon, I could see the gleam of arms and the twinkling of bayonets.

On the hill beside me there was a crowd of civilians on horseback, and in all sorts of vehicles, with a few of the fairer, if not gentler, sex. A few officers and some soldiers, who had straggled from the regiments in reserve, moved about among the spectators, and pretended to explain the movements of the troops below, of which they were profoundly ignorant.

The cannonade and musketry, had been exaggerated by the distance and by the rolling echoes of the hills; and sweeping the position narrowly with my glass from point to point, I failed to discover any traces of close encounter or very severe fighting. The spectators were all excited, and a lady with an opera glass who was near me was quite beside herself when an unusually heavy discharge roused the current of her blood—"That is splendid. Oh, my! Is not that first-rate? I guess we will be in Richmond this time tomorrow." These, mingled with coarser exclamations, burst from the politicians who had come out to see the triumph of the Union arms. I was particularly irritated by constant applications for the loan of my glass. One broken-down looking soldier, observing my flask, asked me for a drink, and took a startling pull, which left but little between the bottom and utter vacuity.

"Stranger, that's good stuff and no mistake. I have not had such a drink since I come South. I feel now as if I'd like to whip ten Seceshers. . . ."

Notwithstanding all the exultation and boastings of the people at Centreville, I was well convinced no advance of any importance or any great success had been achieved, because the ammunition and baggage wagons had never moved, nor had the reserves received any orders to follow in the line of the army. . . .

Loud cheers suddenly burst from the spectators as a man dressed in the uniform of an officer, whom I had seen riding violently across the plain in an open space below, galloped along the front, waving his cap and shouting at the top of his voice. He was brought up by the press of people round his horse close to where I stood. "We've whipped them on all points," he cried. "We have taken all their batteries. They are retreating as fast as they can, and we are after them." Such cheers as rent the welkin! The Congressmen shook hands with each other and cried out, "Bully for us. Bravo, didn't I tell you so." The Germans uttered their martial cheers and the Irish hurrahed wildly. At this moment my horse was brought up the hill, and I mounted and turned towards the road to the front. . . .

I had ridden between three and a half and four miles, as well as I could judge, when I was obliged to turn for the third and fourth time into the road by a considerable stream, which was spanned by a bridge, towards which I was threading my way, when my attention was attracted by loud shouts in advance, and I perceived several wagons coming from the direction of the battlefield, the drivers of which were endeavoring to force their horses past the ammunition carts going in the contrary direction near the bridge; a thick cloud of dust rose behind them, and running by the side of the wagons were a number of men in uniform whom I supposed to be the guard. My first impression was that the wagons were returning for fresh supplies of ammunition. But, every moment the crowd increased, drivers and men cried out with the most vehement gestures, "Turn back! Turn back! We are whipped." They seized the heads of the horses and swore at the opposing drivers. Emerging from the crowd a breathless man in the uniform of an officer with an empty scabbard dangling by his side, was cut off by getting between my horse and a cart for a moment. "What is the matter, sir? What is all this about?" "Why it means we are pretty badly whipped, that's the truth," he gasped, and continued.

By this time the confusion had been communicating itself through the line of wagons toward the rear, and the drivers endeavored to turn round their vehicles in the narrow road, which caused the usual amount of imprecations from the men and plunging and kicking from the horses.

The crowd from the front continually increased; the heat, the uproar, and the dust were beyond description; and these were augmented when some cavalry soldiers, flourishing their sabers and preceded by an officer, who cried out, "Make way there—make way there for the General," attempted to force a covered wagon, in which was seated a man with a bloody handkerchief round his head, through the press.

I had succeeded in getting across the bridge with great difficulty before the wagon came up, and I saw the crowd on the road was still gathering thicker and thicker. Again I asked an officer, who was on foot, with his sword under his arm, "What is all this for?" "We are whipped, sir. We are all in retreat. You are all to go back." "Can you tell me where I can find General M'Dowell?" "No! nor can any one else."

A few shells could be heard bursting not very far off, but there was nothing to account for such an extraordinary scene. A third officer, however, confirmed the report that the whole Army was in retreat, and that the Federals were beaten on all points, but there was nothing in this disorder to indicate a general rout. All these things took place in a few seconds. I got up out of the road into a cornfield, through which men were hastily walking or running, their faces streaming with perspiration, and generally without arms, and worked my way for about half a mile or so, as well as I could judge, against an increasing stream of fugitives, the ground being strewed with coats, blankets, firelocks, cooking tins, caps, belts, bayonets, asking in vain where General McDowell was.

Again I was compelled by the condition of the fields to come into the road; and having passed a piece of wood and a regiment which seemed to be moving back in column of march in tolerably good order, I turned once more into an opening close to a white house, not far from the lane, beyond which there was a belt of forest. Two fieldpieces, unlimbered near the house, with panting horses in the rear, were pointed towards the front, and along the road beside them there swept a tolerably steady column of men mingled with field ambulances and light baggage carts, back to

EMANCIPATION OF THE SLAVES

Proclamed on the 22d September 1862, by ABRAHAM LINCOLN, President of the United States of North America

Published by J. Waeshle, N° 162. North Third S! Philad!

CHICAGO HISTORICAL SOCIETY

The Proclamation of Emancipation as it appeared to the plain people of Lincoln's time.

FREEDOM TO SLAVES!

Whereas, the President of the United States did, on the first day of the present month, issue his *Proclamation* declaring "that *all persons held as Slaves in certain designated States, and parts of States, are, and hencefor-ward shall be free,*" and that the Executive Government of the United States, including the Military and Naval authorities thereof, would recognize and maintain the freedom of said persons. *And Whereas,* the county of *Frede-rick* is included in the territory designated by the Proclamation of the Presi-dent, in which the *Slaves should become free,* I therefore hereby notify the citizens of the city of Winchester, and of said County, of said Proclamation, and of my intention to maintain and enforce the same.

I expect all citizens to yield a ready compliance with the Proclamation of the Chief Executive, and I admonish all persons disposed to resist its peaceful enforcement, that upon manifesting such disposition by acts, they will be regarded as rebels in arms against the lawful authority of the Federal Government and dealt with accordingly.

All persons liberated by said Proclamation are admonished to abstain from all violence, and immediately betake themselves to useful occupations.

The officers of this command are admonished and ordered to act in accord-ance with said proclamation and to yield their ready co-operation in its enforcement.

R. H. Milroy,
Brig. Gen'l Commanding.

Jan. 5th, 1863.

Where the war was being fought, the Emancipation Proclamation became an effective weapon. This handbill shows the use that was made of it by a commander in the field.

Civil War Washington, 1863. The Capitol, its dome still unfinished, as it appeared from Indiana Avenue at 3 St. N. W. Trinity Methodist Church in the foreground.

Lincoln and McClellan in the General's tent a few days after the battle of Antietam.

Lieutenant General Ulysses Simpson Grant.

THE TRUE ISSUE OR "THATS WHATS THE MATTER".

An anti-Lincoln cartoon of the 1864 campaign. Lincoln and Jefferson Davis are shown as pulling the nation apart, with Mc-Clellan, the Democratic candidate, in the guise of peacemaker.

Fellow Countrymen: At this second appearing to take the oath of the presidential office, there is less occasion for an extended address than there was at the first. Then, a statement, somewhat in detail, of a course to be pursued, seemed fitting and proper. Now, at the expiration of four years, during which public declarations have been constantly called forth on every point and phase of the great contest which still absorbs the attention and engrosses the energies of the nation, little that is new could be presented. The progress of our arms, upon which all else chiefly depends, is as well known to the public as to myself; and it is, I trust, reasonably satisfactory and encouraging to all. With high hope for the future, no prediction in regard to it is ventured.

On the occasion corresponding to this four years ago, all thoughts were anxiously directed to an impending civil war. All dreaded it—all sought to avert it. While the inaugural address was being delivered from this place, devoted altogether to saving the Union without war, insurgent agents were in the city seeking to destroy it without war—seeking to dissolve the Union, and divide effects, by negotiation. Both parties deprecated war; but one of them would make war rather than let the nation survive; and the other would accept war rather than let it perish. And the war came.

One-eighth of the whole population were colored slaves, not distributed generally over the Union, but localized in the southern part of it. These slaves constituted a peculiar and powerful interest. All knew that this interest was, somehow, the cause of the war. To strengthen, perpetuate and extend this interest, was the object for which the insurgents would rend the Union, even by war; while the government claimed no right to do more than to restrict the territorial enlargement of it. Neither party expected for the war, the magnitude, or the duration, which it has already attained.

Neither anticipated that the cause of the conflict might cease with, or even before, the conflict itself should cease. Each looked for an easier triumph, and a result less fundamental and astounding. Both read the same Bible, and pray to the same God; and each invokes His aid against the other. It may seem strange that any men should dare to ask a just God's assistance in wringing their bread from the sweat of other men's faces; but let us judge not, that we be not judged. The prayers of both could not be answered—that of neither has been answered fully. The Almighty has His own purposes. "Woe unto the world because of offences! for it must needs be that offences come; but woe to that man by whom the offence cometh." If we shall suppose that American slavery is one of those offences which, in the providence of God, must needs come, but which, having continued through His appointed time, He now wills to remove, and that He gives to both north and south this terrible war as the woe due to those by whom the offence came, shall we discern therein any departure from those divine attributes which the believers in a living God always ascribe to Him? Fondly do we hope—fervently do we pray—that this mighty scourge of war may speedily pass away. Yet, if God wills that it continue until all the wealth piled by the bondman's two hundred and fifty years of unrequited toil shall be sunk, and until every drop of blood drawn with the lash, shall be paid by another drawn with the sword, as was said three thousand years ago, so still it must be said "the judgments of the Lord are true and righteous altogether."

With malice toward none; with charity for all; with firmness in the right, as God gives us to see the right, let us strive on to finish the work we are in; to bind up the nation's wounds; to care for him who shall have borne the battle, and for his widow, and his orphan—to do all which may achieve and cherish a just and a lasting peace, among ourselves, and with all nations.

"Abraham Lincoln, rising tall and gaunt among the groups about him, stepped forward and read his inaugural address, which was printed in two broad columns upon a single page of large paper."—Noah Brooks.

The railroad car that carried Lincoln to City Point, Virginia, when he visited Grant's army during the final days of the war.

L. C. HANDY STUDIOS, WASHINGTON

Lincoln saw Richmond with the Confederate Capitol still intact above fire-gutted buildings.

He saw as well the slaves who now were free.

L. C. HANDY STUDIOS, WASHINGTON

The last photograph.

Ford's Theatre, where John Wilkes Booth shot Lincoln on the evening of April 14, 1865.

Over the same street where Lincoln rode on March 4, 1861, a solemn procession carries his body from the White House to the Capitol.

Chicago and Alton Railroad Company.

TIME TABLE

FOR THE SPECIAL TRAIN, CONVEYING THE FUNERAL CORTEGE WITH THE REMAINS OF
THE LATE

PRESIDENT

FROM

CHICAGO TO SPRINGFIELD,

Tuesday, May 2, 1865.

Total Distance.	Dist. betw'n Stations.			
		CHICAGO	Leave	9:30 P. M.
1.7	1.7	FORT WAYNE JUNCTION	"	9:45 "
3.5	1.8	BRIDGEPORT	"	9:55 "
12.0	8.5	SUMMIT	"	10:21 "
17.6	5.0	JOY'S	"	10:34 "
25.5	8.0	LEMONT	"	10:58 "
32.5	7.0	LOCKPORT	"	11:18 "
37.7	5.2	JOLIET	"	11:33 "
46.4	8.7	ELWOOD	"	11:58 "
48.6	2.2	HAMPTON	"	12:04 A. M.
53.0	4.5	WILMINGTON	"	12:16 "
58.0	4.8	STEWART'S GROVE	"	12:30 "
61.4	3.5	BRACEVILLE	"	12:40 "
65.0	3.8	GARDNER	"	12:51 "
74.0	9.0	DWIGHT	"	1:16 "
82.0	8.0	ODELL	"	1:38 "
87.4	5.2	CAYUGA	"	1:53 "
92.4	5.0	PONTIAC	"	2:07 "
97.8	5.6	OCOYA	"	2:22 "
102.6	4.7	CHENOA	"	2:35 "
110.6	8.0	LEXINGTON	"	2:58 "
118.5	7.9	TOWANDA	"	3:20 "
124.0	5.7	ILL. CENTRAL R. R. JUNCTION	"	3:36 "
126.0	2.0	BLOOMINGTON	"	3:42 "
133.0	6.8	SHIRLEY	"	4:05 "
136.5	3.6	FUNK'S GROVE	"	4:15 "
141.4	4.8	McLEAN	"	4:28 "
146.0	4.8	ATLANTA	"	4:42 "
150.0	4.9	LAWN DALE	"	4:53 "
156.8	6.7	LINCOLN	"	5:12 "
164.0	7.1	BROADWELL	"	5:32 "
167.6	3.7	ELKHART	"	5:43 "
173.5	5.9	WILLIAMSVILLE	"	5:58 "
178.3	4.8	SHERMAN	"	6:12 "
180.0	2.1	SANGAMON	"	6:18 "
185.0	5.0	SPRINGFIELD	Arrive	6:30 "

The following instructions are to be observed for the above train:

1. All other Trains on this Road must be kept thirty minutes out of the way of the time of this Train.
2. All Telegraph Stations must be kept open during the passage of this Train.
3. A Guard with one red and one white light will be stationed at all road crossings by night; and with a white flag draped by day, or after day-light, on Wednesday morning.
4. A Pilot Engine will run upon this time, which is to be followed by the Funeral Train, ten minutes behind.
5. Pilot Engine must not pass any Telegraph Station, unless a white flag by day, or one red and one white light by night, shall be exhibited, which will signify that the Funeral Train has passed the nearest Telegraph Station. In the absence of said signals, the Pilot Engine will stop until definite information is received in regard to the Funeral Train.
6. The Funeral Train will pass all Stations slowly, at which time the bell of the Locomotive must be tolled.

By order of BREVET BRIGADIER GENERAL D. C. McCULLUM, 2d Div., in charge of Military Railroads.

ROBERT HALE,
General Superintendent.

*Behind these windows, draped with crepe, Lincoln the Lawyer
had become Lincoln the President.*

The burial of Lincoln, Oak Ridge Cemetery, May 3, 1865.

Life mask by Leonard Volk, 1860.

Centreville. I had just stretched out my hand to get a cigar light from a German gunner, when the dropping shots which had been sounding through the woods in front of us suddenly swelled into an animated fire. In a few seconds a crowd of men rushed out of the wood down towards the guns, and the artillerymen near me seized the trail of a piece and were wheeling it round to fire when an officer or sergeant called out, "Stop! stop! They are our own men"; and in two or three minutes the whole battalion came sweeping past the guns at the double, and in the utmost disorder. Some of the artillerymen dragged the horses out of the tumbrils; and for a moment the confusion was so great I could not understand what had taken place; but a soldier whom I stopped, said, "We are pursued by their cavalry; they have cut us all to pieces. . . ."

There was nothing left for it but to go with the current one could not stem. . . . On arriving at the place where a small rivulet crossed the road, the throng increased still more. The ground over which I had passed going out was now covered with arms, clothing of all kinds, accoutrements thrown off and left to be trampled in the dust under the hoofs of men and horses. The runaways ran alongside the wagons, striving to force themselves in among the occupants, who resisted tooth and nail. The drivers spurred and whipped and urged the horses to the utmost of their bent. . . . As I rode in the crowd with men clinging to the stirrup leathers or holding on by anything they could lay hands on, so that I had some apprehension of being pulled off, I spoke to the men and asked them over and over again not to be in such a hurry. "There's no enemy to pursue you. All the cavalry in the world could not get at you." But I might as well have talked to the stones.

8

THUS BULL RUN. Lincoln's reception of the bitter news is observed by Nicolay and Hay.

I T MAY WELL BE SUPPOSED that President Lincoln suffered great anxiety during that eventful Sunday; but General Scott talked confidently of success, and Lincoln bore his impatience without any visible sign, and quietly went to church at eleven o'clock. Soon after noon, copies of telegrams began to come to him at the Executive Mansion from the War Department and from Army headquarters. They brought, however, no certain information, as they came only from the nearest station to the battlefield, and simply gave what the operator saw and heard. Towards three o'clock, they became more frequent and reported considerable fluctuation in the apparent course and progress of the cannonade. The President went to the office of General Scott, where he found the General asleep and woke him to talk over the news. Scott said such reports were worth nothing as indications either way—that the changes in the currents of wind and the variation of the echoes made it impossible for a distant listener to determine the course of battle. He still expressed his confidence in a successful result, and composed himself for another nap when the President left.

Dispatches continued to come about every ten or fifteen minutes, still based on hearing and hearsay, the rumors growing more cheering and definite. They reported that the battle had extended along nearly the whole line; that there had been considerable loss; but that the Secession lines had been driven back two or three miles, some of the dispatches said, to the Junction. One of General Scott's aides also brought the telegram of an engineer, repeating that McDowell had driven the enemy before him, that he had ordered the reserves to cross Bull Run, and wanted re-enforcements without delay.

The aide further stated substantially that the General was satisfied of the truth of this report, and that McDowell would immediately attack and capture the Junction, perhaps tonight, but certainly by tomorrow noon. Deeming all doubt at an end, President Lincoln ordered his carriage and went out to take his usual evening drive.

He had not returned when, at six o'clock, Secretary Seward came to the Executive Mansion, pale and haggard. "Where is the President?" he asked hoarsely of the private secretaries. "Gone to drive," they answered. "Have you any late news?" he continued. They read him the telegrams which announced victory. "Tell no one," said he. "That is not true. The battle is lost. The telegram says that McDowell is in full retreat, and calls on General

Scott to save the capital. Find the President and tell him to come immediately to General Scott's."

Half an hour later the President returned from his drive, and his private secretaries gave him Seward's message, the first intimation he received of the trying news. He listened in silence, without the slightest change of feature or expression, and walked away to army headquarters. There he read the unwelcome report in a telegram from a captain of engineers: "General McDowell's army in full retreat through Centreville. The day is lost. Save Washington and the remnants of this army. . . . The routed troops will not re-form." This information was such an irreconcilable contradiction of the former telegram that General Scott utterly refused to believe it. That one officer should report the army beyond Bull Run, driving the enemy and ordering up reserves, and another immediately report it three miles this side of Bull Run, in hopeless retreat and demoralization, seemed an impossibility. Yet the impossible had indeed come to pass; and the apparent change of fortune had been nearly as sudden on the battlefield as in Washington.

The President and the Cabinet met at General Scott's office, and awaited further news in feverish suspense, until a telegram from McDowell confirmed the disaster. Discussion was now necessarily turned to preparation for the future. All available troops were hurried forward to McDowell's support; Baltimore was put on the alert; telegrams were sent to the recruiting stations of the nearest Northern states to lose no time in sending all their organized regiments to Washington; McClellan was ordered to "come down to the Shenandoah Valley with such troops as can be spared from Western Virginia."

A great number of civilians, newspaper correspondents, and several Senators and Representatives had followed McDowell's army to Centreville. . . . Such of these noncombatants as had been fortunate enough to keep their horses and vehicles were the first to reach Washington, arriving about midnight. President Lincoln had returned to the Executive Mansion, and, reclining on a lounge in the Cabinet room he heard from several of these eyewitnesses their excited and exaggerated narratives, in which the rush and terror and unseemly stampede of lookers-on and army teamsters were altogether disproportionate and almost exclusive features. The President did not go to his bed that night; morning found him still on his lounge in the Executive Office, hearing repetitions of these recitals and making memoranda of his own conclusions.

As the night elapsed, the news seemed to grow worse. McDowell's first dispatch stated that he would hold Centreville. His second, that "the larger part of the men are a confused mob, entirely demoralized;" but he said that he would attempt to make a stand at Fairfax Court House. His third reported from that point that "many of the volunteers did not wait for authority to proceed to the Potomac, but left on their own decision. They are now pouring through this place in a state of utter disorganization. . . . I think now, as all of my commanders thought at Centreville, there is no alternative but to fall back to the Potomac." Reports from other points generally confirmed the prevalence of confusion and disorganization. Monday morning the scattered fugitives reached the bridges over the Potomac, and began rushing across them into Washington. It was a gloomy and dismal day. A drizzling rain set in which lasted thirty-six hours. Many a panic-stricken volunteer remembered afterwards with gratitude, that when he was wandering footsore, exhausted, and hungry through the streets of the Capital, her loyal families opened their cheerful doors to give him food, rest, and encouragement. . . .

By noon of Monday the worst aspects of the late defeat were known; and especially the reassuring fact that the enemy was making no pursuit; and so far as possible immediate dangers were provided against. The War Department was soon able to reply to anxious inquiries from New York: "Our loss is much less than was at first represented, and the troops have reached the forts in much better condition than we expected." "We are making most vigorous efforts to concentrate a large and irresistible army at this point. Regiments are arriving. . . . Our works on the south bank of the Potomac are impregnable, being well manned with reenforcements. The capital is safe." On the following day Lincoln in person visited some of the forts and camps about Arlington Heights, and addressed the regiments with words of cheer and confidence.

CHAPTER SEVENTEEN

Search for a General

A FTER BULL RUN, *the country demanded that the army be entrusted to a new commander. Lincoln lost no time in making his choice, for the course of the war had already raised one officer to clear pre-eminence. That was Major General George B. McClellan who, in a few short weeks, had won a series of minor victories in western Virginia and had cleared that region of Confederate troops. To the North, hungry for a hero, he was already the counterpart of Napoleon. Lincoln at once ordered him to Washington and gave him McDowell's command.*

The new commander was thirty-five years old. He had graduated from West Point in 1846, just in time to serve with distinction in the Mexican War. He remained in the army until 1857, when he resigned to become Chief Engineer of the Illinois Central Railroad. In 1861, he was President of the Ohio and Mississippi Railroad, but, immediately after Sumter, he gave up this position to accept appointment as Major General of Ohio Volunteers. The following month he was given the same rank in the Regular Army of the United States.

Coming east, McClellan found the army completely demoralized. By tightening discipline and subjecting the new recruits who were pouring in by the thousands to rigorous training, he quickly rebuilt it as a fighting force. At the same time, he strengthened greatly the defenses of the Capital. When General Scott retired on November 1, he was promoted to General in Chief.

McClellan now had full authority, and his army was in

fine condition—well-trained, well-equipped, its morale re-stored. Yet he gave no sign that he was considering a forward movement. As time went on many of those who had seen him as the Nation's deliverer turned into critics, and even the patient President became restive. Winter was fast approaching, and the time for action growing very short.

1

JOHN HAY enters in his diary an ominous occurrence.

Novem ber 13, 1861. I wish here to record what I consider a portent of evil to come. The President, Governor Seward, and I, went over to McClellan's house tonight. The servant at the door said the General was at the wedding of Colonel Wheaton at General Buell's, and would soon return. We went in, and after we had waited about an hour, McClellan came in and, without paying any particular attention to the porter, who told him the President was waiting to see him, went upstairs, passing the door of the room where the President and Secretary of State were seated. They waited about half an hour, and sent once more a servant to tell the General they were there, and the answer coolly came that the General had gone to bed.

I merely record this unparalleled insolence of epaulettes without comment. It is the first indication I have yet seen of the threatened supremacy of the military authorities.

Coming home, I spoke to the President about the matter but he seemed not to have noticed it especially, saying it was better at this time not to be making points of etiquette and personal dignity.

2

WITH POPULAR AND OFFICIAL IMPATIENCE increasing rapidly, McClellan became seriously ill. For several weeks the army was paralyzed. Finally Lincoln became convinced that the situation had reached the limits of tolerance. What happened is related by Montgomery C. Meigs, Quartermaster General of the Union forces.

On friday, January 10, 1862, the President, in great distress, entered my office. He took a chair in front of the open fire and said, "General, what shall I do? The people are impatient; Chase has no money and he tells me he can raise no more; the General of the Army has typhoid fever. The bottom is out of the tub. What shall I do?"

I said, "If General McClellan has typhoid fever, that is an affair of six weeks at least; he will not be able sooner to command. In the meantime, if the enemy in our front is as strong as he believes, they may attack on any day, and I think you should see some of those upon whom in such case, or in case any forward movement becomes necessary, the control must fall. Send for them to meet you soon and consult with them; perhaps you may select the responsible commander for such an event."

The council was called. On Sunday, January 12, McDowell and Franklin called on me with a summons to the White House for 1:00 P.M. These officers, and Messrs. Seward, Chase, Blair, of the Cabinet, attended. The President announced that he had called this meeting in consequence of the sickness of General Mc-Clellan, but he had that morning heard from him that he was better, and would be able to be present the next day; and that, on this promise, he adjourned the discussion for twenty-four hours.

The next day, January 13, the same persons and General McClellan appeared at the rendezvous. The President opened the proceedings by making a statement of the cause of his calling the council. Mr. Chase and Mr. Blair, if memory is accurate, both spoke. All looked to McClellan, who sat still with his head hanging down, and mute. The situation grew awkward. The President spoke again a few words. One of the Generals said something; McClellan said something which evidently did not please the speaker and again was mute.

I moved my chair to the side of McClellan's and urged him, saying, "The President evidently expects you to speak; can you not promise some movement towards Manassas? You are strong." He replied, "I cannot move on them with as great a force as they have." "Why, you have near 200,000 men, how many have they?" "Not less than 175,000 according to my advices." I said, "Do you think so?" and, "the President expects something from you." He replied, "If I tell him my plans they will be in the *New York Herald* tomorrow morning. He can't keep a secret, he will tell them to Tad." I said: "That is a pity, but he is the President—

the Commander in Chief; he has a right to know; it is not respectful to sit mute when he so clearly requires you to speak. He is
superior to all."

After some further urging, McClellan moved, and seemed to
prepare to speak. He declined to give his plans in detail, but
thought it best to press the movement of Buell's troops in the
central line of operation. After a few words that brought out
nothing more, Mr. Lincoln said, "Well, on this assurance of the
General that he will press the advance in Kentucky, I will be
satisfied, and will adjourn this council."

3

McCLELLAN RECOVERED, and in the early spring of 1862
made plans for an advance on Richmond. His troops were to be trans-
ported by water to the peninsula between the York and James rivers,
whence they were to move by land against the Confederate capital.
Suddenly the Confederate frigate *Virginia*—the old Union ship
Merrimac newly clad with iron—threatened to make any campaign
which depended on water transport an impossibility. The *Merrimac's*
story, and how she was checkmated by the *Monitor*, is told by L. E.
Chittenden, whom Lincoln had appointed Register of the Treasury.

SATURDAY, MARCH 8, was a day of calamities. The news came
over the wires that the *Merrimac* had come out of Norfolk, attended by a numerous bodyguard of smaller vessels, and at one
o'clock was leisurely entering upon her brief career of destruction. Within two hours we knew that projectiles from our heaviest
guns had realized the apprehensions of Captain Fox by re-
bounding from her uninjured side like rubber balls; that she had
sent the fine sloop-of-war, the *Cumberland*, to the bottom of the
James River; that she had torn the frigate *Congress* in pieces
with her shot and shell, and left her a grounded wreck on the
shore; that two brave ships' companies had been immolated to
the demon of rebellion, and that the ironclad destroyer, satisfied
with her labors for that afternoon, had retired into the harbor of
Norfolk, leaving our third and most valuable frigate, the *Minnesota*, aground and ready for the next morning's sacrifice. There
had been no former day of such disaster. As I left the Treasury,

I involuntarily walked in the direction of the War Department, where I supposed the President would be found. At the door, I met him returning to the Executive Mansion.

He was as cheerful as he had been on the morning of the previous day. The battle was over for the day, he said, and the *Merrimac* had gone into port, probably to repair some temporary damages. Nothing had been heard from Captain Fox or the *Monitor*. He regretted deeply the loss of so many brave men; our first lesson in the value of ironclads for fighting purposes had been costly, but the Almighty ruled, and it would all come right somehow. I remember most distinctly, for it made a deep impression at the time, that he said that we should probably find that the *Merrimac* was at the end of her destructive mission, and would not sink another vessel.

Aware that it would be useless to expect sleep that night and anxious for news from Captain Fox, I returned late in the evening to the Navy Department. It was nearly midnight before his dispatch came. It was in cipher, and, being translated, informed us that he reached Newport News about nine o'clock, and went immediately on board the *Minnesota*. Everyone on the vessel was demoralized. She had been stripped; it had been decided to burn her, and in a few moments more the torch would have been applied. Captain Fox's arrival had saved the vessel. His inquiry, whether it would not be wiser to wait until it was seen whether the *Merrimac* came out of Norfolk again before setting on fire the finest ship in the Navy and destroying property to the value of a million and a half dollars, recalled the officers to their senses, and the conclusion to defer the application of the torch was speedily reached. I remained at the Department until after two o'clock, when, receiving no news from the *Monitor* nor any further dispatches from Captain Fox, all left the Naval Office for their respective homes.

The Sunday forenoon was as gloomy as any that Washington had experienced since the beginning of the war. There was no excitement, but all seemed to be overwhelmed with despondency and vague apprehension. I went to Dr. Gurley's church, where his audience was made still more uncomfortable by a very gloomy sermon. After service I called upon Secretary Chase. He had no news, and could give me no comfort. Since the President seemed to be the only officer of the government who could see any hope in the future, I went to the War Office, where he was usually to be found when any serious fighting was going on. There I found him with quite a large party, including two members of his Cabinet.

It was evident, from the general excitement, that news had been received from the James River. As I entered the room some one was saying, "Would it not be fortunate if the *Monitor* should sink her?" "It would be nothing more than I have expected," calmly observed President Lincoln. "If she does not, something else will. Many providential things are happening in this war, and this may be one of them. The loss of two good ships is an expensive lesson, but it will teach us all the value of ironclads. I have not believed at any time during the last twenty-four hours that the *Merrimac* would go right on destroying right and left without any obstruction. Since we knew that the *Monitor* had got there, I have felt that she was the vessel we wanted." I then learned that the *Monitor* had arrived at Fortress Monroe on Saturday evening; without waiting for any preparation, she had steamed up to Newport News, and laid herself alongside the grounded *Minnesota.* The *Merrimac* had made her appearance shortly after daylight; Captain Worden had promptly advanced to make her acquaintance, and had ever since been sticking to her closer than a brother. It was also reported that the two fighters had ever since been pounding each other terrifically, and that the *Monitor* as yet showed no signs of weakness. Time passes quickly in such an excitement. Very soon came a message that evoked cheers from everybody. Its substance was that the *Merrimac* had withdrawn, and was again steaming for Norfolk. Even this news, which stirred the enthusiasm of every one else, so that all burst into a long-continued volley of applause, did not seem to elate the President. "I am glad the *Monitor* has done herself credit for Worden's sake—for all our sakes," was all he said. He then walked slowly to the White House.

4

THE *Merrimac's* threat removed, the Peninsular expedition was undertaken. This narrative of the most controversial of all Civil War campaigns is Lord Charnwood's.

On APRIL 2, 1862, McClellan himself landed to begin the celebrated Peninsular campaign. . . .

Before the troops were sent to the Peninsula several things were to be done. An expedition to restore communication westward by the Baltimore and Ohio Railway involved bridging the Potomac with boats which were to be brought by canal. It collapsed because McClellan's boats were six inches too wide for the canal locks. Then Lincoln had insisted that the navigation of the lower Potomac should be made free from the menace of Confederate batteries which, if McClellan would have co-operated with the Navy Department, would have been cleared away long before. This was now done. . . . The President had been emphatic in his orders that a sufficient force should be left to make Washington safe, and supposed that he had come to a precise understanding on this point. He suddenly discovered that McClellan, who had now left for Fort Monroe, had ordered McDowell to follow him with a force so large that it would not leave the required number behind. Lincoln immediately ordered McDowell and his whole corps to remain, though he subsequently sent a part of it to McClellan. McClellan's story later gives reason for thinking that he had intended no deception; but, if so, he had expressed himself with unpardonable vagueness, and he had not in fact left Washington secure. Now and throughout this campaign, Lincoln took the line that Washington must be kept safe—safe in the judgment of all the best military authorities available.

McClellan's progress up the Peninsula was slow. He had not informed himself correctly as to the geography; he found the enemy not so unprepared as he had supposed; he wasted, it is agreed, a month in regular approaches to their thinly manned fortifications at Yorktown, when he might have carried them by assault. He was soon confronted by Joseph Johnston, and he seems both to have exaggerated Johnston's numbers and to have been unprepared for his movements. The Administration does not seem to have spared any effort to support him. In addition to the 100,000 troops he took with him, 40,000 altogether were before long dispatched to him. He was operating in a very difficult country, but he was opposed at first by not half his own number. Lincoln, in friendly letters, urged upon him that delay enabled the enemy to strengthen himself both in numbers and in fortifications. The War Department did its best for him. The whole of his incessant complaints on this score are rendered unconvincing by the language of his private letters about that "sink of iniquity, Washington," "those treacherous hounds," the civil authorities, who were at least honest and intelligent men, and the "Abolitionists and other scoundrels," who, he supposed, wished the destruction of his army. The criticism in Congress of himself and his generals was no doubt free, but so, as Lincoln reminded him, was the criticism of Lincoln himself. Justly or not, there were complaints of his relations with Corps commanders. Lincoln gave no weight to them, but wrote him a manly and a kindly warning. The points of controversy which McClellan bequeathed to writers on the Civil War are innumerable, but no one can read his correspondence at this stage without concluding that he was almost impossible to deal with, and that the whole of his evidence in his own case was vitiated by a sheer hallucination that people wished him to fail. He had been nearly two months in the Peninsula when he was attacked at a disadvantage by Johnston, but defeated him on May 31 and June 1 in a battle which gave confidence and prestige to the Northern side, but which he did not follow up. A part of his army pursued the enemy to within four miles of Richmond, and it has been contended that if he had acted with energy he could at this time have taken that city. His delay, to whatever it was due, gave the enemy time to strengthen himself greatly both in men and in fortifications. The capable Johnston was severely wounded in the battle, and was replaced by the inspired Lee. According to McClellan's own account, which English writers have followed, his movements had been greatly embarrassed by the false hope given him that McDowell was now to march overland and join him. His statement that he was influenced by this is refuted by his own letters at the time. McClellan, however, suffered a great disappointment. The front of Washington was now clear of the enemy and Lincoln had determined to send McDowell, when he was induced to keep him back by a diversion in the war which he had not expected, and which indeed McClellan had advised him not to expect.

"Stonewall" Jackson's most famous campaign happened at this juncture. . . . With a small force, surrounded by other forces, each of which, if concentrated, should have outnumbered him, he caught each in turn at a disadvantage, inflicted on them several damaging blows, and put the startled President and Secretary of War in fear for the safety of Washington. There seemed to be no one available who could immediately be charged with the supreme command of these three Northern forces, unless McDowell could have been spared from where he was; so Lincoln with Stanton's help took upon himself to ensure the co-operation of their three commanders by orders from Washington. His self-reliance had now begun to reach its full stature; his military good sense in comparison with McClellan's was proving greater than he had supposed, and he had probably not discovered its limitations. . . . Jackson, having successfully kept McDowell from McClellan, had before the end of June escaped safely southward. . . .

McClellan was slowly but steadily nearing Richmond. From June 26 to July 2, there took place a series of engagements between Lee and McClellan, or rather the commanders under him, known as the Seven Days' Battles. The fortunes of the fighting varied greatly, but the upshot is that, though the corps on McClellan's left won a strong position not far from Richmond, the sudden approach of Jackson's forces upon McClellan's right flank, which began on the twenty-sixth, placed him in what appears to have been, as he himself thought it, a situation of great danger. Lee is said to have "read McClellan like an open book," playing upon his caution, which made him, while his subordinates fought, more anxious to secure their retreat than to seize upon any advantage they gained. But Lee's reading deceived him in one respect. He had counted upon McClellan's retreating, but thought he would retreat under difficulties right down the Peninsula to his original base and be thoroughly cut up on the way. But on July 2, McClellan with great skill withdrew his whole army to Harrison's Landing far up the James estuary, having effected with the Navy a complete transference of his base. Here his army lay in a position of security; they might yet threaten Richmond, and McClellan's soldiers still believed in him. But the South was led by a great commander and had now learned to give him unbounded confidence; there was some excuse for a panic in Wall Street, and every reason for dejection in the North.

On the third of the Seven Days, McClellan, much moved by the sight of dead and wounded comrades, sent a gloomy telegram to the Secretary of War, appealing with excessive eloquence for more men. "I only wish to say to the President," he remarked in it, "that I think he is wrong in regarding me as ungenerous when I said that my force was too weak." He concluded: "If I save the army now, I tell you plainly that I owe no thanks to you nor to any other persons in Washington. You have done your best to sacrifice this army." Stanton still expressed the extraordinary hope that Richmond would fall in a day or two. He had lately committed the folly of suspending enlistment, an act which, though, of course, there is an explanation of it, must rank as the one first-rate blunder of Lincoln's administration. He was now negotiating through the astute Seward for offers from the state governors of a levy of 300,000 men to follow up McClellan's success. Lincoln, as was his way, feared the worst. He seems at one moment to have had fears for McClellan's sanity. But he telegraphed, himself, an answer to him, which affords as fair an example as can be given of his characteristic manner. "Save your army at all events. Will send reinforcements as fast as we can. Of course they cannot reach you to-day or to-morrow, or next day. I have not said you were ungenerous for saying you needed reinforcements. I thought you were ungenerous in assuming that I did not send them as fast as I could. I feel any misfortune to you and your army quite as keenly as you feel it yourself. If you have had a drawn battle or repulse, it is the price we pay for the enemy not being in Washington. We protected Washington and the enemy concentrated on you. Had we stripped Washington, he would have been upon us before the troops could have gotten to you. Less than a week ago you notified us reinforcements were leaving Richmond to come in front of us. It is the nature of the case, and neither you nor the government are to blame. Please tell me at once the present condition and aspect of things."

Demands for an impossible number of reinforcements continued. Lincoln explained to McClellan a few days later that they were impossible, and added: "If in your frequent mention of responsibility you have the impression that I blame you for not doing more than you can, please be relieved of such an impression. I only beg that, in like manner, you will not ask impossibilities of me." Much argument upon Lincoln's next important act may be saved by the simple observations that the problem in regard to the defense of Washington was real, that McClellan's propensity to ask for the impossible was also real, and that Lincoln's patient and loyal attitude to him was real, too.

Five days after his arrival at Harrison's Landing, McClellan wrote Lincoln a long letter. It was a treatise upon Lincoln's political duties. It was written as "on the brink of eternity." He was not then in fact in any danger, and possibly he had composed it seven days before as his political testament; and apprehensions, free from personal fear, excuse, without quite redeeming, its inappropriateness. The President is before all things not to abandon the cause. But the cause should be fought for upon Christian principles. Christian principles exclude warfare on private property. More especially do they exclude measures for emancipating slaves. And if the President gives way to radical views on slavery, he will get no soldiers. Then follows a mandate to the President to appoint a Commander in Chief, not necessarily the writer. Such a summary does injustice to a certain elevation of tone in the letter, but that elevation is itself slightly strained. McClellan, whatever his private opinions, had not meddled with politics before he left Washington. The question why in this military crisis he should have written what a Democratic politician might have composed as a party manifesto must later have caused Lincoln some thought, but it apparently did not enter into the decision he next took. He arrived himself at Harrison's Landing next day. McClellan handed him the letter. Lincoln read it, and said that he was obliged to him. McClellan sent a copy to his wife as "a very important record."

Lincoln had come in order to learn the views of McClellan and all his corps commanders. They differed a good deal on important points, but a majority of them were naturally anxious to stay and fight there. Lincoln was left in some anxiety as to how the health of the troops would stand the climate of the coming months if they had to wait long where they were. He was also disturbed by McClellan's vagueness about the number of his men, for he now returned as present for duty a number which far exceeded that which some of his recent telegrams had given and yet fell short of the number sent him by an amount which no reasonable estimate of killed, wounded, and sick could explain. This added to Lincoln's doubt on the main question presented to him. McClellan believed that he could take Richmond, but he demanded for this very large reinforcements. Some part of them were already being collected, but the rest could by no means be given him without leaving Washington with far fewer troops to defend it than McClellan or anybody else had hitherto thought necessary.

On July 24, the day after his arrival at Washington, Halleck [1] was sent to consult with McClellan and his generals. The record of their consultations sufficiently shows the intricacy of the problem to be decided. The question of the health of the climate in August weighed much with Halleck, but the most striking feature of their conversation was the fluctuation of McClellan's own opinion upon each important point. . . . When Halleck returned to Washington McClellan telegraphed in passionate anxiety to be left in the Peninsula and reinforced. On the other hand, some of the officers of highest rank with him wrote strongly urging withdrawal. This latter was the course on which Lincoln and Halleck decided. In the circumstances it was certainly the simplest course to concentrate all available forces in an attack upon the enemy from the direction of Washington which would keep that capital covered all the while. It was in any case no hasty and no indefensible decision, nor is there any justification for the frequent assertion that some malignant influence brought it about. It is one of the steps taken by Lincoln which have been the most often lamented. But if McClellan had had all he demanded to take Richmond and had made good his promise, what would Lee have done? Lee's own answer to a similar question later was, "We would swap queens"; that is, he would have taken Washington. If so the Confederacy would not have fallen, but in all probability the North would have collapsed, and European Powers would at the least have recognized the Confederacy.

5

WHILE McCLELLAN WAS operating on the Peninsula, Major General John Pope, who had won a reputation in the West, was

[1] Major General Henry W. Halleck, whom Lincoln appointed his military adviser on July 11, 1862.

brought east and given command of the forces protecting Washington. As McClellan's troops were brought north they were added to Pope's command to form the Army of Virginia. During the last days of August, Pope met a shattering defeat in the Second Battle of Bull Run. Once again John Hay was forced to record the way in which word of disaster came to Lincoln.

SEPTEMBER 1, 1862. Saturday morning, the thirtieth of August, I rode out into the country and turned in at the Soldiers' Home. The President's horse was standing by the door and in a moment the President appeared and we rode into town together.

We talked about the state of things by Bull Run and Pope's prospect. The President was very outspoken in regard to McClellan's present conduct. He said it really seemed to him that McClellan wanted Pope defeated. He mentioned to me a dispatch of McClellan in which he proposed, as one plan of action, to "leave Pope to get out of his own scrape, and devote ourselves to securing Washington " He spoke also of McClellan's dreadful cowardice in the matter of Chain Bridge, which he had ordered blown up the night before, but which order had been countermanded; and also of his incomprehensible interference with Franklin's corps, which he recalled once, and then when they had been sent ahead by Halleck's order, begged permission to recall them again and only desisted after Halleck's sharp injunction to push them ahead till they whipped something or got whipped themselves. The President seemed to think him a little crazy. Envy, jealousy, and spite are probably a better explanation of his present conduct. He is constantly sending despatches to the President and Halleck asking what is his real position and command. He acts as chief alarmist and grand marplot of the army.

The President, on my asking if Halleck had any prejudices, rejoined, "No! Halleck is wholly for the service. He does not care who succeeds or who fails so the service is benefited."

Later in the day we were in Halleck's room. Halleck was at dinner and Stanton came in while we were waiting for him and carried us off to dinner. A pleasant little dinner and a pretty wife as white and cold and motionless as marble, whose rare smiles seemed to pain her. Stanton was loud about the McClellan business. He was unqualifiedly severe upon McClellan. He said that after these battles there should be one court-martial, if never any more. He said that nothing but foul play could lose us this battle and that it rested with McClellan and his friends. Stanton seemed to believe very strongly in Pope. So did the President for that matter. We went back to the Headquarters and found General Halleck. He seemed quiet and somewhat confident. He said the greatest battle of the century was now being fought. He said he had sent every man that could go to the field. At the War Department we found that Mr. Stanton had sent a vast army of Volunteer Nurses out to the field, probably utterly useless, over which he gave General Wadsworth command.

Everything seemed to be going well and hilarious on Saturday and we went to bed expecting glad tidings at sunrise. But about eight o'clock the President came to my room as I was dressing and, calling me out, said, "Well, John, we are whipped again, I am afraid. The enemy reinforced on Pope and drove back his left wing and he has retired to Centreville where he says he will be able to hold his men. I don't like that expression. I don't like to hear him admit that his men need 'holding.' "

After a while, however, things began to look better and people's spirits rose as the heavens cleared. The President was in a singularly defiant tone of mind. He often repeated, "We must hurt this enemy before it gets away." And this morning, Monday, he said to me when I made a remark in regard to the bad look of things, "No, Mr. Hay, we must whip these people now. Pope must fight them. If they are too strong for him, he can gradually retire to these fortifications. If this be not so, if we are really whipped and to be whipped, we may as well stop fighting."

6

IMMEDIATELY AFTER POPE'S DEFEAT, in which an army of 90,000 had been routed by 55,000 Confederates, Lincoln restored McClellan to command; no other officer, he believed, could rebuild the demoralized army. His action was met by bitter disapproval on the part of his advisers. The diary of Gideon Welles recalls the consternation of the Cabinet, as well as the rumors and fears which stirred Washington in the anxious days following the Second Bull Run.

SEPTEMBER 2, Tuesday. At Cabinet meeting all but Seward were present. . . . Stanton said, in a suppressed voice, trembling with excitement, he was informed McClellan had been ordered to take command of the forces in Washington. General surprise was expressed. When the President came in and heard the subject matter of our conversation, he said he had done what seemed to him best and would be responsible for what he had done to the country. Halleck had agreed to it. McClellan knows this whole ground; he is a good engineer, all admit; there is no better organizer; he can be trusted to act on the defensive; but he is troubled with the "slows," and good for nothing for an onward movement. Much was said. There was a more disturbed and desponding feeling than I have ever witnessed in council; the President was greatly distressed. There was a general conversation as regarded the infirmities of McClellan, but it was claimed, by Blair and the President, he had beyond any officer the confidence of the army. Though deficient in the positive qualities which are necessary for an energetic commander, his organizing powers could be made temporarily available till the troops were rallied.

These, the President said, were General Halleck's views, as well as his own, and some who were dissatisfied with his action, and had thought Halleck was the man for General in Chief, felt that there was nothing to do but acquiesce, yet Chase earnestly and emphatically stated his conviction that it would prove a national calamity. . . .

Stanton and Halleck are apprehensive that Washington is in danger. Am sorry to see this fear, for I do not believe it among remote possibilities. . . .

September 3, Wednesday. Washington is full of exciting, vague, and absurd rumors. There is some cause for it. Our great army comes retreating to the banks of the Potomac, driven back to the intrenchments by the rebels.

The army has no head. Halleck is here in the Department, a military director, not a General, a man of some scholastic attainments, but without soldierly capacity. McClellan is an intelligent engineer and officer, but not a commander to head a great army in the field. To attack or advance with energy or power is not in him; to fight is not his forte. I sometimes fear his heart is not earnest in the cause, yet I do not entertain the thought that he is unfaithful. The study of military operations interests and amuses him. It flatters him to have on his staff French princes and men of wealth and position; he likes show, parade, and power—wishes to outgeneral the rebels, but not to kill and destroy them. In a conversation which I had with him in May last at Cumberland on the Pamunkey, he said he desired of all things to capture Charleston; he would demolish and annihilate the city. He detested, he said, both South Carolina and Massachusetts, and should rejoice to see both states extinguished. Both were and always had been ultra and mischievous, and he could not tell which he hated most. These were the remarks of the General in Chief at the head of our armies then in the field, when as large a proportion of his troops were from Massachusetts as from any state in the Union, and while as large a proportion of those opposed, who were fighting the Union, were from South Carolina as from any state. He was leading the men of Massachusetts against the men of South Carolina, yet he, the General, detests them alike. . . .

September 6, Saturday. We have information that the rebels have crossed the Potomac in considerable force, with a view to invading Maryland and pushing on into Pennsylvania. The War Department is bewildered, knows but little, does nothing, proposes nothing.

Our army is passing north. This evening some twenty or thirty thousand passed my house within three hours. There was design in having them come up from Pennsylvania Avenue to H Street, and pass by McClellan's house, which is at the corner of H and Fifteenth. They cheered the General lustily, instead of passing by the White House and honoring the President. . . .

McClellan and his partisans have ascendancy in the army, but he has lost ground in the confidence of the country, chiefly from delays, or what the President aptly terms the "slows."

September 7. . . . My convictions are with the President that McClellan and his generals are this day stronger than the Administration with a considerable portion of this Army of the Potomac. It is not so elsewhere with the soldiers, or in the country, where McClellan has lost favor. The people are disappointed in him, but his leading generals have contrived to strengthen him in the hearts of the soldiers in front of Washington. . . .

When taking a walk this Sunday evening with my son Edgar, we met on Pennsylvania Avenue, near the junction of H Street, what I thought at first sight a squad of cavalry or mounted men, some twenty or thirty in number. I remarked as they approached that they seemed better mounted than usual, but Edgar said the cavalcade was General McClellan and his staff. I raised my hand to salute him as they were dashing past, but the General, recognizing us, halted the troop and rode up to me by the sidewalk, to shake hands, he said, and bid me farewell. I asked which way. He said he was proceeding to take command of the onward movement. "Then," I added, "you go up the river." He said yes, he had just started to take charge of the army and of the operations above. "Well," said I, "onward, General, is now the word; the country will expect you to go forward." "That," he answered, "is my intention." "Success to you, then, General, with all my heart." With a mutual farewell we parted.

This was our first meeting since we parted at Cumberland on the Pamunkey in June, for we each had been so occupied during the three or four days he had been in Washington that we had made no calls. On several occasions we missed each other. In fact, I had no particular desire to fall in with any of the officers who had contributed to the disasters that had befallen us, or who had in any respect failed to do their whole duty in this great crisis. . . . I think his management has been generally unfortunate, to say the least, and culpably wrong since his return from the Peninsula.

He has now been placed in a position where he may retrieve himself, and return to Washington a victor in triumph, or he may, as he has from the beginning, wilt away in tame delays and criminal inaction. I would not have given him the command, nor have advised it, strong as he is with the army, had I been consulted; and I feel sad that he has been so intrusted. It may, however, be for the best. There are difficulties in the matter that can scarcely be appreciated by those who do not know all the circumstances. The army is, I fear, much demoralized, and its demoralization is much of it to be attributed to the officers whose highest duty it is to prevent it. To have placed any other general than McClellan, or one of his circle, in command would be to risk disaster. It is painful to entertain the idea that the country is in the hands of such men. I hope I mistake them.

7

LEE FOLLOWED UP his victory over Pope by crossing the Potomac into Maryland. On September 17 and 18, McClellan turned back the invasion in the Battle of Antietam. Soon, however, the Federal commander's unwillingness to move again became evident. This time Lincoln's patience was shorter. When, under repeated urging, McClellan found endless reasons for inaction he was superseded by Major General Ambrose E. Burnside. Burnside took command of the Army of the Potomac on November 10, 1862. On December 13, he crossed the Rappahannock at Fredericksburg to attack Lee's army. In numbers, the odds were in his favor—he had 122,000 men to 78,000—but the Confederates had a strong position and the advantage of the defensive. Two days later, after his army had suffered 10,000 casualties, Burnside withdrew. In January, 1863, Lincoln relieved him. To Joseph Hooker, "Fighting Joe"—tall, handsome, aggressive to the point of rashness—the chance was now given to succeed where McClellan, Pope, and Burnside had failed. In the spring of 1863, the prospect seemed good—at least that is the inference which one draws from Noah Brooks's version of Lincoln's visit to the army in April.

Eᴀʀʟʏ ɪɴ ᴀᴘʀɪʟ, 1863, I accompanied the President, Mrs. Lincoln, and their youngest son, Tad, on a visit to the Army of the Potomac—Hooker then being in command, with headquarters on Falmouth Heights, opposite Fredericksburg. Attorney General Bates and an old friend of Mr. Lincoln—Dr. A. G. Henry, of Washington Territory—were also in the party. . . .

At Hooker's headquarters we were provided with three large hospital tents, floored, and furnished with camp bedsteads and such rude appliances for nightly occupation as were in reach. During our stay with the army there were several grand reviews, that of the entire cavalry corps of the Army of the Potomac, on April 6, being the most impressive of the whole series. The cavalry was now for the first time massed as one corps instead of being scattered around among the various army corps, as it had been heretofore; it was commanded by General Stoneman. The entire cavalry force was rated at 17,000 men, and Hooker proudly said that it was the biggest army of men and horses ever seen in the world, bigger even than the famous body of cavalry commanded by Marshal Murat.

The cavalcade on the way from headquarters to the reviewing field was a brilliant one. The President, wearing a high hat and riding like a veteran, with General Hooker by his side, headed the flying column; next came several major-generals, a host of brigadiers, staff officers, and colonels, and lesser functionaries innumerable. The flank of this long train was decorated by the showy uniforms and accoutrements of the Philadelphia Lancers, who acted as a guard of honor to the President during that visit to the Army of the Potomac. The uneven ground was soft with melting snow, and the mud flew in every direction under the hurrying feet of the cavalcade. On the skirts of this cloud of cavalry rode the President's little son, Tad, in charge of a mounted orderly, his gray cloak flying in the gusty wind like the plume of Henry of Navarre. The President and the reviewing party rode past the long lines of cavalry standing at rest, and then the march past began. It was a grand sight to look upon, this immense body of cavalry, with banners waving, music crashing, and horses prancing, as the vast column came winding like a huge serpent over the hills past the reviewing party, and then stretching far away out of sight.

The President went through the hospital tents of the corps that lay nearest to headquarters, and insisted upon stopping and speaking to nearly every man, shaking hands with many of them, asking a question or two here and there, and leaving a kind word as he moved from cot to cot. More than once, as I followed the President through the long lines of weary sufferers, I noticed tears of gladness stealing down their pale faces; for they were made happy by looking into Lincoln's sympathetic countenance, touching his hand, and hearing his gentle voice; and when we rode away from the camp to Hooker's headquarters, tremendous cheers rent the air from the soldiers, who stood in groups, eager to see the good President.

The infantry reviews were held on several different days. On April 8, was the review of the Fifth Corps, under Meade; the Second, under Couch; the Third, under Sickles; and the Sixth, under Sedgwick. It was reckoned that these four corps numbered some 60,000 men, and it was a splendid sight to witness their grand martial array as they wound over hills and rolling ground, coming from miles around, their arms shining in the distance, and their bayonets bristling like a forest on the horizon as they marched away. The President expressed himself as delighted with the appearance of the soldiery, and he was much impressed by the parade of the great reserve artillery force, some eighty guns, commanded by Colonel De Russy. One picturesque feature of the review on that day was the appearance of the Zouave regiments, whose dress formed a sharp contrast to the regulation uniform of the other troops. General Hooker, being asked by the President if fancy uniforms were not undesirable on account of the conspicuousness which they gave as targets to the enemy's fire, said that these uniforms had the effect of inciting a spirit of pride and neatness among the men. It was noticeable that the President merely touched his hat in return salute to the officers, but uncovered to the men in the ranks. As they sat in the chilly wind, in the presence of the shot-riddled colors of the army and the gallant men who bore them, he and the group of distinguished officers around him formed a notable historic spectacle. After a few days the weather grew warm and bright; and, although the scanty driblets of news from Charleston that were filtered to us through the rebel lines did not throw much sunshine into the military situation, the President became more cheerful and even jocular. I remarked this, one evening as we sat in Hooker's headquarters, after a long and laborious day of reviewing. Lincoln replied: "It is a great relief to get away from Washington and the politicians. But nothing touches the tired spot."

On the ninth, the First Corps, commanded by General Reynolds, was reviewed by the President on a beautiful plain at the north of Potomac Creek, about eight miles from Hooker's headquarters. We rode thither in an ambulance over a rough corduroy road; and, as we passed over some of the more difficult portions of the jolting way, the ambulance driver, who sat well in front, occasionally let fly a volley of suppressed oaths at his wild team of six mules. Finally Mr. Lincoln, leaning forward, touched the man on the shoulder, and said:

"Excuse me, my friend, are you an Episcopalian?"

The man, greatly startled, looked around and replied:

"No, Mr. President; I am a Methodist."

"Well," said Lincoln, "I thought you must be an Episcopalian, because you swear just like Governor Seward, who is a church-warden." The driver swore no more.

As we plunged and dashed through the woods, Lincoln called attention to the stumps left by the men who had cut down the trees, and with great discrimination pointed out where an experienced axman made what he called "a good butt," or where a tyro had left conclusive evidence of being a poor chopper. Lincoln was delighted with the superb and inspiring spectacle of the review that day. A noticeable feature of the doings was the martial music of the corps; and on the following day the President, who loved military music, was warm in his praise of the performances of the bands of the Eleventh Corps, under General Howard, and the Twelfth, under General Slocum. In these two corps the greater portion of the music was furnished by drums, trumpets, and fifes, and with most stirring and thrilling effect. In the division commanded by General Schurz was a magnificent array of drums and trumpets, and his men impressed us as the best drilled and most soldierly of all who passed before us during our stay.

I recall with sadness the easy confidence and nonchalance which Hooker showed in all his conversations with the President and his little party while we were at his headquarters. The General seemed to regard the whole business of command as if it were a larger sort of picnic. He was then, by all odds, the handsomest soldier I ever laid my eyes upon . . . tall, shapely, well-dressed, though not natty in appearance; his fair red and white complexion glowing with health, his bright blue eyes sparkling with intelligence and animation, and his auburn hair tossed back upon his well-shaped head. His nose was aquiline, and the expression of his somewhat small mouth was one of much sweetness, though rather irresolute, it seemed to me. He was a gay cavalier, alert and confident, overflowing with animal spirits, and as cheery as a boy. One of his most frequent expressions when talking with the President was, "When I get to Richmond," or "After we have taken Richmond," etc. The President, noting this, said to me confidentially, and with a sigh: "That is the most depressing thing about Hooker. It seems to me that he is overconfident."

One night when Hooker and I were alone in his hut, which was partly canvas and partly logs, with a spacious fireplace and chimney, he stood in his favorite attitude with his back to the fire, and, looking quizzically at me, said, "The President tells me that you know all about the letter he wrote to me when he put me in command of this army." I replied that Mr. Lincoln had read it to me; whereupon, Hooker drew the letter from his pocket, and said, "Wouldn't you like to hear it again?" I told him that I should, although I had been so much impressed by its first reading that I believed I could repeat the greater part of it from memory. That letter has now become historic; then it had not been made public. As Hooker read on, he came to this sentence:

"You are ambitious, which, within reasonable bounds, does good rather than harm; but I think during Burnside's command of the army you took counsel of your ambition, and thwarted him as much as you could, in which you did a great wrong to the country and to a most meritorious and honorable brother officer."

Here Hooker stopped, and vehemently said: "The President is mistaken. I never thwarted Burnside in any way, shape, or manner. Burnside was pre-eminently a man of deportment; he fought the battle of Fredericksburg on his deportment; he was defeated on his deportment; and he took his deportment with him out of the Army of the Potomac, thank God!" Resuming the reading of Lincoln's letter, Hooker's tone immediately softened, and he finished it almost with tears in his eyes; and as he folded it, and put it back in the breast of his coat, he said, "That is just such a letter as a father might write to his son. It is a beautiful letter, and, although I think he was harder on me than I deserved, I will say that I love the man who wrote it." Then he added, "After I have got to Richmond, I shall give that letter to you to have published."

8

WITHIN A MONTH, Brooks sat with Lincoln while news of Hooker's first—and last—great battle came to the White House.

I WAS AT the White House on Wednesday, May 6, and the President, who seemed anxious and harassed beyond any power of description, said that while still without any positive information as to the result of the fighting at Chancellorsville, he was certain in his own mind that "Hooker had been licked." He was only then wondering whether Hooker would be able to recover himself and renew the fight. The President asked me to go into the room then occupied by his friend Dr. Henry, who was a guest in the house, saying possibly we might get some news later on.

In an hour or so, while the doctor and I sat talking, say about three o'clock in the afternoon, the door opened, and Lincoln came into the room. I shall never forget that picture of despair. He held a telegram in his hand, and as he closed the door and came toward us, I mechanically noticed that his face, usually sallow, was ashen in hue. The paper on the wall behind him was of the tint known as "French gray," and even in that moment of sorrow and dread expectation I vaguely took in the thought that the complexion of the anguished President's visage was almost exactly like that of the wall. He gave me the telegram, and in a voice trembling with emotion, said, "Read it—news from the army." The dispatch was from General Butterfield, Hooker's Chief of Staff, addressed to the War Department, and was to the effect that the army had been withdrawn from the south side of the Rappahannock, and was then "safely encamped" in its former position. The appearance of the President, as I read aloud these fateful words, was piteous. Never, as long as I knew him, did he seem to be so broken, so dispirited, and so ghostlike. Clasping his hands behind his back, he walked up and down the room, saying, "My God! My God! What will the country say! What will the country say!"

9

WHILE COMMANDERS in the East were losing one battle after another, Lincoln must have thought often of a man in the West who was winning them. Ulysses S. Grant, retired West Pointer who was clerking in his brothers' leather store at Galena, Illinois, when the war broke out, had gone back into the army as Colonel of a regiment of Illinois volunteers. As Brigadier General he had captured Fort Henry and Fort Donelson, on the Tennessee and Cumberland rivers, in February, 1862, and had been rewarded with a major general's commission. Then, in early April, came the bloody Battle of Shiloh, and a popular reaction that almost ended his career. How

Lincoln, with providential foresight, stood by his Western commander is developed by A. K. McClure, Pennsylvania Republican and journalist.

THE FIRST DAY'S BATTLE at Shiloh was a serious disaster to the Union Army commanded by Grant, who was driven from his position, which seems to have been selected without any special reference to resisting an attack from the enemy, and, although his army fought most gallantly in various separate encounters, the day closed with the field in possession of the enemy and Grant's army driven back to the river. Fortunately, the advance of Buell's army formed a junction with Grant late in the evening, and that night all of Buell's army arrived, consisting of three divisions. The two Generals arranged their plans for an offensive movement early the next morning, and, after another stubborn battle, the lost field was regained and the enemy compelled to retreat with the loss of their commander, General Albert Sidney Johnston, who had fallen early in the first day's action, and with a larger aggregate loss of killed, wounded, and missing than Grant suffered. The first reports from the Shiloh battlefield created profound alarm throughout the entire country, and the wildest exaggerations were spread in a flood tide of vituperation against Grant. It was freely charged that he had neglected his command because of dissipation, that his army had been surprised and defeated, and that it was saved from annihilation only by the timely arrival of Buell.

The few of today who can recall the inflamed condition of public sentiment against Grant caused by the disastrous first day's battle at Shiloh will remember that he was denounced as incompetent for his command by the public journals of all parties in the North, and with almost entire unanimity by Senators and Congressmen without regard to political faith. Not only Washington, but throughout the loyal states, public sentiment seemed to crystallize into an earnest demand for Grant's dismissal from the army. His victories of Forts Henry and Donelson, which had thrilled the country a short time before, seemed to have been forgotten, and on every side could be heard the emphatic denunciation of Grant because of his alleged reckless exposure of the army, while Buell was universally credited with having saved it. It is needless to say that owing to the excited condition of the public mind most extravagant reports gained ready credence, and it was not uncommon to hear Grant denounced on the streets and in all circles as unfitted by both habit and temperament for an important military command. The clamor for Grant's removal, and often for his summary dismissal, from the army surged against the President from every side, and he was harshly criticized for not promptly dismissing Grant, or at least relieving him from his command. I can recall but a single Republican member of Congress who boldly defended Grant at that time. Elihu B. Washburne, whose home was in Galena, where Grant had lived before he went into the army, stood nearly, or quite, alone among the members of the House in wholly justifying Grant at Shiloh, while a large majority of the Republicans of Congress were outspoken and earnest in condemning him.

I did not know Grant at that time; had neither partiality nor prejudice to influence my judgment, nor had I any favorite general who might be benefited by Grant's overthrow, but I shared the almost universal conviction of the President's friends that he could not sustain himself if he attempted to sustain Grant by continuing him in command. Looking solely to the interests of Lincoln, feeling that the tide of popular resentment was so overwhelming against Grant that Lincoln must yield to it, I had repeated conferences with some of his closest friends, including Swett and Lamon, all of whom agreed that Grant must be removed from his command, and complained of Lincoln for his manifest injustice to himself by his failure to act promptly in Grant's removal. So much was I impressed with the importance of prompt action on the part of the President after spending a day and evening in Washington that I called on Lincoln at eleven o'clock at night and sat with him alone until after one o'clock in the morning. He was, as usual, worn out with the day's exacting duties, but he did not permit me to depart until the Grant matter had been gone over and many other things relating to the war that he wished to discuss. I pressed upon him with all the earnestness I could command the immediate removal of Grant as an imperious necessity to sustain himself. As was his custom, he said but little, only enough to make me continue the discussion until it was exhausted. He sat before the open fire in the old Cabinet room, most of the time with his feet up on the high marble mantel, and exhibited unusual distress at the complicated condition of military affairs. Nearly every day brought some new and perplexing military complication. He had gone through a long winter of terrible strain with McClellan and the Army of the Potomac; and from the day that Grant started on his Southern expedition until the battle of Shiloh he had had little else than jarring and confusion among his generals in the West. He knew that I had no ends to serve in urging Grant's removal, beyond the single desire to make him be just to himself, and he listened patiently.

I appealed to Lincoln for his own sake to remove Grant at once, and, in giving my reasons for it, I simply voiced the admittedly overwhelming protest from the loyal people of the land against Grant's continuance in command. I could form no judgment during the conversation as to what effect my arguments had upon him beyond the fact that he was greatly distressed at this new complication. When I had said everything that could be said from my standpoint, we lapsed into silence. Lincoln remained silent for what seemed a very long time. He then gathered himself up in his chair and said in a tone of earnestness that I shall never forget: *"I can't spare this man; he fights."*

CHAPTER EIGHTEEN

Emancipation

AT THE VERY BEGINNING *of his first inaugural address Abraham Lincoln quoted and reaffirmed a statement he had made in the first of his joint debates with Douglas. "I have no purpose," he asserted, "directly or indirectly, to interfere with the institution of slavery in the States where it exists. I believe I have no lawful right to do so, and I have no inclination to do so." To that declaration he adhered strictly for more than a year. When Fremont, in the summer of 1861, issued a military proclamation freeing the slaves of all persons in Missouri who were supporting the Confederacy, Lincoln overruled him—and brought upon himself the bitter wrath of the country's Abolitionists. When General David Hunter, commanding the Department of the South, issued a similar order in May, 1862, it met a similar fate. As late as August, 1862, Lincoln wrote an open letter to Horace Greeley, editor of the* New York Tribune, *in which he declared:"My paramount object in this struggle is to save the Union, and is not either to save or to destroy slavery. If I could save the Union without freeing any slave, I would do it; and if I could save it by freeing all the slaves, I would do it; and if I could save it by freeing some and leaving others alone, I would also do that."*

But at least two months before this letter was written Lincoln had come to the conclusion that the freeing of some slaves would aid the cause of Union. The reasons which led to his decision must, in the main, be inferred. Undoubtedly he saw that the slave population constituted a great source of military manpower which the North could tap if a sufficient inducement were offered. It could be nothing short of freedom. And beyond question, the attitude of foreign governments was another factor. If McClellan's Peninsular campaign failed, as Lincoln feared it would, and if that reverse were followed by others, both England and France were likely to recognize the Confederacy. On the other hand, if the North made the end of slavery a concomitant of victory, neither nation would dare to accord even diplomatic aid to the South.

Whatever the reason or combination of reasons, Lincoln made his decision in the early summer of 1862.

1

THOMAS T. ECKERT, Superintendent of Military Telegraph, Department of the Potomac, emphasizes the painstaking care with which Lincoln wrote a mysterious document in Eckert's office.

THE PRESIDENT CAME to the office every day and invariably sat at my desk while there. Upon his arrival early one morning in June, 1862, shortly after McClellan's Seven Days' Battles, he asked me for some paper, as he wanted to write something special. I procured some foolscap and handed it to him. He then sat down and began to write. I do not recall whether the sheets were loose or had been made into a pad. There must have been at least a quire. He would look out of the window a while and then put his pen to paper, but he did not write much at once. He would study between times and when he had made up his mind he would put down a line or two, and then sit quiet for a few minutes. After a time, he would resume his writing, only to stop again at intervals to make some remark to me or to one of the cipher operators as a fresh dispatch from the front was handed to him.

Once his eye was arrested by the sight of a large spiderweb stretched from the lintel of the portico to the side of the outer window sill. This spiderweb was an institution of the cipher room and harbored a large colony of exceptionally big ones. We frequently watched their antics, and Assistant Secretary Watson dubbed them "Major Eckert's lieutenants." Lincoln commented on the web, and I told him that my lieutenants would soon report and pay their respects to the President. Not long after a big spider appeared at the crossroads and tapped several times on the strands, whereupon five or six others came out from different directions. Then what seemed to be a great confab took place, after which they separated, each on a different strand of the web. Lincoln was much interested in the performance and thereafter, while working at the desk, would often watch for the appearance of his visitors.

On the first day, Lincoln did not cover one sheet of his special writing paper (nor indeed on any subsequent day). When ready to leave, he asked me to take charge of what he had written and not allow any one to see it. I told him I would do this with pleasure and would not read it myself. "Well," he said, "I should be glad to know that no one will see it, although there is no objection to your looking at it; but please keep it locked up until I call for it tomorrow." I said his wishes would be strictly complied with.

When he came to the office on the following day he asked for the papers, and I unlocked my desk and handed them to him and he again sat down to write. This he did nearly every day for several weeks, always handing me what he had written when ready to leave the office each day. Sometimes he would not write more than a line or two, and once I observed that he had put question marks on the margin of what he had written. He would read over each day all the matter he had previously written and revise it, studying carefully each sentence.

On one occasion, he took the papers away with him, but he brought them back a day or two later. I became much interested in the matter and was impressed with the idea that he was engaged upon something of great importance, but did not know what it was until he had finished the document and then for the first time he told me that he had been writing an order giving freedom to the slaves in the South, for the purpose of hastening the end of the war.

2

LINCOLN FIRST REVEALED his intention to issue a proclamation of emancipation to Seward and Welles of his Cabinet. The occasion found its way into Welles' diary.

O n s u n d a y , the thirteenth of July, 1862, President Lincoln invited me to accompany him in his carriage to the funeral of an infant child of Mr. Stanton. Secretary Seward and Mrs. Frederick Seward were also in the carriage. . . . It was on this occasion and on this ride that he first mentioned to Mr. Seward and myself the subject of emancipating the slaves by proclamation in case the rebels did not cease to persist in their war on the government and the Union, of which he saw no evidence. He dwelt earnestly on the gravity, importance, and delicacy of the movement, said he had given it much thought and had about come to the conclusion that it was a military necessity absolutely essential for the salvation of the Union, that we must free the slaves or be ourselves subdued, etc., etc.

This was, he said, the first occasion upon which he had mentioned the subject to any one, and wished us to frankly state how the proposition struck us. Mr. Seward said the subject involved consequences so vast and momentous that he should wish to bestow on it mature reflection before giving a decisive answer, but his present opinion inclined to the measure as justifiable, and perhaps he might say expedient and necessary. These were also my views. Two or three times on that ride the subject, which was of course an absorbing one for each and all, was adverted to, and, before separating, the President desired us to give the question special and deliberate attention, for he was earnest in the conviction that something must be done. It was a new departure for the President, for until this time, in all our previous interviews, whenever the question of emancipation or the mitigation of slavery had been in any way alluded to, he had been prompt and emphatic in denouncing any interference by the general government with the subject. This was, I think, the sentiment of every member of the Cabinet, all of whom, including the President, considered it a local, domestic question appertaining to the states respectively, who had never parted with their authority over it. But the reverses before Richmond and the formidable power and dimensions of the insurrection, which extended through all the slave states and had combined most of them in a confederacy to destroy the Union, impelled the Administration to adopt extraordinary measures to preserve the national existence. The slaves, if not armed and disciplined, were

ın the service of those who were, not only as field laborers and pro-
ducers, but thousands of them were in attendance upon the armies
in the field, employed as waiters and teamsters; and the fortifications and intrenchments were constructed by them.

3

LINCOLN'S NEXT STEP was to present the matter of emancipation to the Cabinet. The outcome he himself reconstructed a year
or so later for Francis B. Carpenter, who had obtained permission
to make the signing of the Proclamation the subject of a painting.

I T HAD GOT TO BE midsummer, 1862. Things had gone on
from bad to worse, until I felt that we had reached the end of our
rope on the plan of operations we had been pursuing; that we had
about played our last card, and must change our tactics, or lose
the game! I now determined upon the adoption of the emancipation policy; and, without consultation with, or the knowledge of
the Cabinet, I prepared the original draft of the proclamation,
and, after much anxious thought, called a Cabinet meeting upon
the subject. This was the last of July, or the first part of the
month of August, 1862.

This Cabinet meeting took place, I think, upon a Saturday. All
were present, excepting Mr. Blair, the Postmaster-General, who
was absent at the opening of the discussion, but came in subsequently. I said to the Cabinet that I had resolved upon this step,
and had not called them together to ask their advice, but to lay
the subject-matter of a proclamation before them; suggestions as
to which would be in order, after they had heard it read. . . .
Various suggestions were offered. Secretary Chase wished the
language stronger in reference to the arming of the blacks.
Mr. Blair, after he came in, deprecated the policy, on the ground
that it would cost the Administration the fall elections. Nothing,
however, was offered that I had not already fully anticipated and
settled in my own mind, until Secretary Seward spoke. He said in
substance: "Mr. President, I approve of the proclamation, but I
question the expedience of its issue at this juncture. The depression of the public mind, consequent upon our repeated reverses, is
so great that I fear the effect of so important a step. It may be

viewed as the last measure of an exhausted government, a cry for
help; the government stretching forth its hands to Ethiopia, instead of Ethiopia stretching forth her hands to the government."
His idea was that it would be considered our last *shriek*, on the
retreat. (This was his precise expression.) "Now," continued
Mr. Seward, "while I approve the measure, I suggest, sir, that
you postpone its issue, until you can give it to the country supported by military success, instead of issuing it, as would be the
case now, upon the greatest disasters of the war!" The wisdom of
the view of the Secretary of State struck me with very great force.
It was an aspect of the case that, in all my thought upon the
subject, I had entirely overlooked. The result was that I put the
draft of the proclamation aside, as you do your sketch for a picture, waiting for a victory.

4

ALTHOUGH HE HAD DECIDED definitely on his course, Lincoln
allowed no inkling of his intention to reach the public. When, on
September 13, 1862, a delegation representing the religious denominations of Chicago called on him to ask that he proclaim emancipation, he argued the subject pro and con as if it were still an open
question. What he said on that occasion emphasizes his power of
silence, and also reveals the patient, careful reflection out of which
his decision grew.

THE SUBJECT PRESENTED in the memorial is one upon
which I have thought much for weeks past, and I may even say for
months. I am approached with the most opposite opinions and
advice, and that by religious men who are equally certain that
they represent the divine will. I am sure that either the one or the
other class is mistaken in that belief, and perhaps in some respects
both. I hope it will not be irreverent for me to say that if it is
probable that God would reveal his will to others on a point so
connected with my duty, it might be supposed he would reveal it
directly to me; for, unless I am more deceived in myself than I
often am, it is my earnest desire to know the will of Providence in
this matter, . . .

What good would a proclamation of emancipation from me do, especially as we are now situated? I do not want to issue a document that the whole world will see must necessarily be inoperative, like the Pope's bull against the comet. Would my word free the slaves, when I cannot even enforce the Constitution in the rebel States? Is there a single court, or magistrate, or individual that would be influenced by it there? And what reason is there to think it would have any greater effect upon the slaves than the late law of Congress, which I approved, and which offers protection and freedom to the slaves of rebel masters who come within our lines? Yet I cannot learn that that law has caused a single slave to come over to us. And suppose they could be induced by a proclamation of freedom from me to throw themselves upon us, what should we do with them? How can we feed and care for such a multitude? General Butler wrote me a few days since that he was issuing more rations to the slaves who have rushed to him than to all the white troops under his command. They eat, and that is all; though it is true General Butler is feeding the whites also by the thousand, for it nearly amounts to a famine there. If, now, the pressure of the war should call off our forces from New Orleans to defend some other point, what is to prevent the masters from reducing the blacks to slavery again? For I am told that whenever the rebels take any black prisoners, free or slave, they immediately auction them off. They did so with those they took from a boat that was aground in the Tennessee River a few days ago. And then I am very ungenerously attacked for it! For instance, when, after the late battles at and near Bull Run, an expedition went out from Washington under a flag of truce to bury the dead and bring in the wounded, and the rebels seized the blacks who went along to help, and sent them into slavery, Horace Greeley said in his paper that the government would probably do nothing about it. What could I do?

Now, then, tell me, if you please, what possible result of good would follow the issuing of such a proclamation as you desire? Understand, I raise no objections against it on legal or constitutional grounds; for, as commander-in-chief of the army and navy, in time of war I suppose I have a right to take any measure which may best subdue the enemy; nor do I urge objections of a moral nature, in view of possible consequences of insurrection and massacre at the South. I view this matter as a practical war measure, to be decided on according to the advantages or disadvantages it may offer to the suppression of the rebellion.

I admit that slavery is the root of the rebellion, or at least its *sine qua non*. The ambition of politicians may have instigated them to act, but they would have been impotent without slavery as their instrument. I will also concede that emancipation would help us in Europe, and convince them that we are incited by something more than ambition. I grant, further, that it would help somewhat at the North, though not so much, I fear, as you and those you represent imagine. Still, some additional strength would be added in that way to the war, and then, unquestionably, it would weaken the rebels by drawing off their laborers, which is of great importance; but I am not so sure we could do much with the blacks. If we were to arm them, I fear that in a few weeks the arms would be in the hands of the rebels; and, indeed, thus far we have not had arms enough to equip our white troops. I will mention another thing, though it meet only your scorn and contempt. There are fifty thousand bayonets in the Union armies from the border slave States. It would be a serious matter if, in consequence of a proclamation such as you desire, they should go over to the rebels. I do not think they all would—not so many to-day as yesterday. Every day increases their Union feeling. They are also getting their pride enlisted, and want to beat the rebels. Let me say one thing more: I think you should admit that we already have an important principle to rally and unite the people, in the fact that constitutional government is at stake. This is a fundamental idea going down about as deep as anything.

Do not misunderstand me because I have mentioned these objections. They indicate the difficulties that have thus far prevented my action in some such way as you desire. I have not decided against a proclamation of liberty to the slaves, but hold the matter under advisement; and I can assure you that the subject is on my mind, by day and night, more than any other. Whatever shall appear to be God's will, I will do. I trust that in the freedom with which I have canvassed your views I have not in any respect injured your feelings.

5

THE BATTLE OF ANTIETAM, though far from a clear-cut victory, gave Lincoln the military excuse for which he had been looking. Five days after it was fought he called the Cabinet together. The record of the meeting is Secretary Chase's.

Monday, Sept. 22, 1862.

To Department about nine. State Department messenger came, with notice to Heads of Departments to meet at 12. Received sundry callers. Went to White House.

All the members of the Cabinet were in attendance. There was some general talk; President mentioned that Artemus Ward had sent him his book. Proposed to read a chapter which he thought very funny. Read it, and seemed to enjoy it very much—the Heads also (except Stanton), of course. The chapter was *High-handed Outrage at Utica.*

The President then took a graver tone and said:

"Gentlemen: I have, as you are aware, thought a great deal about the relation of this war to Slavery: and you all remember that, several weeks ago, I read to you an Order I had prepared on this subject, which, on account of objections made by some of you, was not issued. Ever since then, my mind has been much occupied with this subject, and I have thought all along that the time for acting on it might very probably come. I think the time has come now. I wish it were a better time. I wish that we were in a better condition. The action of the army against the rebels has not been quite what I should have best liked. But they have been driven out of Maryland, and Pennsylvania is no longer in danger of invasion. When the rebel army was at Frederick, I determined, as soon as it should be driven out of Maryland, to issue a Proclamation of Emancipation such as I thought most likely to be useful. I said nothing to any one; but I made the promise to myself, and (hesitating a little)—to my Maker. The rebel army is now driven out, and I am going to fulfill that promise. I have got you together to hear what I have written down. I do not wish your advice about the main matter—for that I have determined for myself. This I say without intending anything but respect for any one of you. But I already know the views of each on this question. They have been heretofore expressed, and I have considered them as thoroughly and carefully as I can. What I have written is that which my reflections have determined me to say. If there is anything in the expressions I use, or in any other minor matter, which any one of you thinks had best be changed, I shall be glad to receive the suggestions. One other observation I will make. I know very well that many others might, in this matter, as in others, do better than I can; and if I were satisfied that the public confidence was more fully possessed by any one of them than by me, and knew of any Constitutional way in which he could be put in my place, he should have it. I would gladly yield it to him. But though I believe that I have not so much of the confidence of the people as I had some time since, I do not know that, all things considered, any other person has more; and, however this may be, there is no way in which I can have any other man put where I am. I am here. I must do the best I can, and bear the responsibility of taking the course which I feel I ought to take."

The President then proceeded to read his Emancipation Proclamation, making remarks on the several parts as he went on, and showing that he had fully considered the whole subject, in all the lights under which it had been presented to him.

After he had closed, Governor Seward said: "The general question having been decided, nothing can be said further about that. Would it not, however, make the Proclamation more clear and decided, to leave out all reference to the act being sustained during the incumbency of the present President; and not merely say that the Government 'recognizes,' but that it will maintain the freedom it proclaims?"

I followed, saying: "What you have said, Mr. President, fully satisfies me that you have given to every proposition which has been made a kind and candid consideration. And you have now expressed the conclusion to which you have arrived clearly and distinctly. This it was your right, and, under your oath of office, your duty to do. The Proclamation does not, indeed, mark out exactly the course I should myself prefer. But I am ready to take it just as it is written, and to stand by it with all my heart. I think, however, the suggestions of Governor Seward very judicious, and shall be glad to have them adopted."

The President then asked us severally our opinions as to the modifications proposed, saying that he did not care much about the phrases he had used. Everyone favored the modification and it was adopted. Governor Seward then proposed that in the passage relating to colonization, some language should be introduced to show that the colonization proposed was to be only with the consent of the colonists, and the consent of the States in which colonies might be attempted. This, too, was agreed to; and no other modification was proposed. Mr. Blair then said that the question having been decided, he would make no objection to issuing the Proclamation; but he would ask to have his paper, presented some days since against the policy, filed with the Proclamation. The President consented to this readily. And then Mr. Blair went on to say that he was afraid of the influence of the Proclamation on the Border States and on the army, and stated at some length the grounds of his apprehensions. He disclaimed most expressly, however, all objection to emancipation per se, saying he had always been personally in favor of it—always ready for immediate emancipation in the midst of slave states, rather than submit to the perpetuation of the system.

6

THAT VERY DAY—September 22, 1862—saw the issuance of the first, or preliminary, Proclamation of Emancipation. In it, Lincoln warned that if the States then in rebellion did not return to their allegiance by January 1, 1863, he would issue a second proclamation declaring the slaves in those States to be "forever free." The warning was ignored, as he was certain it would be. Therefore, as the year came to its end, he prepared to carry out his promise. Nicolay and Hay follow his actions.

I T IS A CUSTOM in the Executive Mansion to hold on New Year's Day an official and public reception, beginning at eleven o'clock in the morning, which keeps the President at his post in the Blue Room until two in the afternoon. The hour for this reception came before Mr. Lincoln had entirely finished revising the engrossed copy of the Proclamation, and he was compelled to hurry away from his office to friendly handshaking and festal greeting with the rapidly arriving official and diplomatic guests. The rigid laws of etiquette held him to this duty for the space of three hours. Had actual necessity required it, he could of course have left such mere social occupation at any moment; but the President saw no occasion for precipitancy. On the other hand, he probably deemed it wise that the completion of this momentous executive act should be attended by every circumstance of deliberation.

Vast as were its consequences, the act itself was only the simplest and briefest formality. It could in no wise be made sensational or dramatic. . . . No ceremony was made or attempted of this final official signing. The afternoon was well advanced when Mr. Lincoln went back from his New Year's greetings with his right hand so fatigued that it was an effort to hold the pen. There was no special convocation of the Cabinet or of prominent officials. Those who were in the house came to the Executive Office merely from the personal impulse of curiosity joined to momentary convenience. His signature was attached to one of the greatest and most beneficent military decrees of history in the presence of less than a dozen persons; after which it was carried to the Department of State to be attested by the great seal and deposited among the archives of the government.

CHAPTER NINETEEN

Life in the White House

NOT ONLY IN POLITICS and national policy did the fourth of March, 1861, mark a revolutionary break with the past; the White House became the scene of changes equally significant. During the administration of Buchanan, an elderly bachelor, it had been a sedate place; now it was a family home, with the laughter of children ringing through its rooms. In the social functions held there, the wives of government officers from North and West soon displaced the Southern women who had long dominated Washington society; before all women in the Capital, the President's wife was always on trial. Most noteworthy of all, however, was the President himself, whose homely, simple habits stood in sharp contrast to the stiff conventionality of his predecessor.

1

LINCOLN'S STRUGGLES with the clothes demanded by his new position are revealed by Ward Hill Lamon, who considered himself, by virtue of old friendship and his new office as Marshal of the District of Columbia, a capable mentor on all subjects.

SHORTLY AFTER THE ELECTION of Mr. Lincoln, I talked with him earnestly about the habits, manners, customs, and style of the people with whom he had now to associate, and the difference between his present surroundings and those of his Illinois life, and wherein his plain, practical, common-sense actions dif-

fered from the polite, graceful, and elegant bearing of the cultivated diplomat and cultured gentlemen of polite society. Thanks
to his confidence in my friendship and his affectionate forbearance
with me, he would listen to me with the most attentive interest, always evincing the strongest desire to correct anything in which
he failed to be and appear like the people with whom he acted; for
it was one of the cardinal traits of his character to be like, of, and
for the people, whether in exalted or humble life.

A New Hampshire lady having presented to him a soft felt hat
of her own manufacture, he was at a loss what to do on his arrival
in Washington, as the felt hat seemed unbecoming for a President-
elect. He therefore said to me: "Hill, this hat of mine won't do. It
is a felt one, and I have been uncomfortable in it ever since we left
Harrisburg. Give me that plug of yours, until you can go out in
the city and buy one either for yourself or for me. I think your
hat is about the style. I may have to do some trotting around
soon, and if I can't feel natural with a different hat, I may at least
look respectable in it."

I went to a store near by and purchased a hat and, by the
ironing process, soon had it shaped to my satisfaction; and I must
say that, when Mr. Lincoln put it on, he looked more presentable
and more like a President than I had ever seen him. He had very
defective taste in the choice of hats, the item of dress that does
more than any other for the improvement of one's personal appearance.

After the hat reform, I think Mr. Lincoln still suffered much
annoyance from the tyranny of fashion in the matter of gloves. His
hat for years served the double purpose of an ornamental head-
gear and a kind of office or receptacle for his private papers and
memoranda. But the necessity to wear gloves he regarded as an
affliction, a violation of the statute against "cruelty to animals."
Many amusing stories could be told of Mr. Lincoln and his gloves.
At about the time of his third reception, he had on a tight-fitting
pair of white kids, which he had with difficulty gotten on. He saw
approaching in the distance an old Illinois friend named Simpson,
whom he welcomed with a genuine Sangamon County shake, which
resulted in bursting his white kid glove with an audible sound.
Then, raising his brawny hand up before him, looking at it with
an indescribable expression, he said—while the whole procession

was checked, witnessing this scene—"Well, my old friend, this is a general bustification. You and I were never intended to wear these things. If they were stronger they might do well enough to keep out the cold, but they are a failure to shake hands with between old friends like us. Stand aside, Captain, and I'll see you shortly." The procession then advanced. Simpson stood aside, and, after the unwelcome pageantry was terminated, he rejoined his old Illinois friend in familiar intercourse.

Mr. Lincoln was always delighted to see his Western friends, and always gave them a cordial welcome; and when the proprieties justified it, he met them on the old familiar footing, entertaining them with anecdotes in unrestrained, free-and-easy conversation. He never spoke of himself as President—always referred to his office as "this place"; would often say to an old friend, "Call me Lincoln; 'Mr. President' is entirely too formal for us." Shortly after the first inauguration, an old and respected friend accompanied by his wife visited Washington, and as a matter of course paid their respects to the President and his family, having been on intimate social terms with them for many years. It was proposed that at a certain time Mr. and Mrs. Lincoln should call at the hotel where they were stopping and take them out for a ride in the presidential carriage—a gorgeous and grandly caparisoned coach, the like of which the visitors had seldom seen before that time. As close as the intimacy was, the two men had never seen each other with gloves on in their lives, except as a protection from the cold. Both gentlemen, realizing the propriety of their use in the changed condition of things, discussed the matter with their respective wives, who decided that gloves were the proper things. Mr. Lincoln reluctantly yielded to this decree, and placed his in his pocket, to be used or not according to circumstances. On arriving at the hotel he found his friend, who doubtless had yielded to his wife's persuasion, gloved in the most approved style. The friend, taking in the situation, was hardly seated in the carriage when he began to take off the clinging kids; and at the same time Mr. Lincoln began to draw his on—seeing which, they both burst into a hearty laugh, and Mr. Lincoln exclaimed, "Oh, why should the spirit of mortals be proud?" Then he added, "I suppose it is polite to wear these things, but it is positively uncomfortable for me to do so. Let us put them in our pockets; that is the best place for them, and we shall be able to act more like folks in our bare hands." After this the ride was as enjoyable as any one they had ever taken in early days in a lumber wagon over the prairies of Illinois.

2

ONE OF THOSE who accompanied the Lincolns to Washington was Elizabeth Todd Grimsley, a cousin of Mrs. Lincoln. In her memories of her visit, the first state dinners and receptions of the new Administration occupied a prominent place.

SOON THE SUBJECT of our first reception came up for settlement, as Mr. Seward indicated that he proposed to lead off. To this Mrs. Lincoln objected, urging that the first official entertainment should be given by the President. . . . The question was, however, soon settled and the reception announced for the eighth of the month, at the Executive Mansion. And what a crush and jam it was!

But the young private secretaries, Nicolay and Hay, managed the introductions to the President and the receiving party wonderfully well. The handshaking was a thing long to be remembered by the President, and, while it was gratifying, we must confess to a sigh of relief when we heard the Marine Band strike up "Yankee Doodle," the signal for retiring. The President took me on his arm and we made the circuit of the East Room, a custom as old as the house itself, I believe, and a silly one, in that the wife of the President is relegated to the escort of another gentleman.

We were amused at the many remarks we overheard, such as, "The President bears himself well, and does not seem the least embarrassed." "How much alike the President and Mrs. Grimsley are!" "Yes! brother and sister. They must belong to a very tall family."

And so ended that memorable reception, the last in which North and South would mingle for many years.

The next day there was a diplomatic reception, but the legations were not out in full force, nor did they come together in a body as was their custom. The French Minister, Mercier, was absent. Lord Lyons was coldly dignified—already the nations were looking at us askance.

The first state dinner, March 28 as I remember it, was not a very gay affair, as there were very few ladies of the Cabinet there in Washington. Secretary Seward's house was presided over by Mrs. Frederick Seward, his daughter-in-law, a lovely, charming woman. Secretary Chase had not then brought his fascinating daughter, Miss Kate, afterward wife of Governor Sprague, of Rhode Island. Mrs. Bates, the wife of the Attorney General, a dear, domestic, motherly woman, left her daughters to represent her. Besides the lady guests in the Mansion, who were soon to leave us, there were few others.

Society was already beginning to feel the upheaval—avowed Secessionists, false friends (who were worse) were in every department. A new party jubilant over success, part of an old party who had been debarred for nearly thirty years and naturally felt the unwonted exhilaration of power and place, had stepped in, and it is well known there was an element who rushed in clamoring for position, even at that early period of the Lincoln administration, who could not by any possibility lay claim to social recognition on any other ground than rapidly accumulated wealth.

The process of disintegration went on rapidly, and in a few weeks there was a thorough change socially. By degrees we ceased to meet at our informal receptions the Maryland and Virginia families, who had always held sway and dominated Washington society. Easy, suave, charming in manner, descended from a long line of aristocratic families, accustomed to wealth and all the amenities of social life and etiquette, they resented the introduction of these new elements, and withdrew to go into the Confederacy, where all their sympathies centered.

These were in time replaced by members of cultivated, refined, intellectual and wealthy people from the Northern cities, and officers of the army and navy with their wives; these, with several ladies of the legation, notably Russian and Chilian, with our many Western friends, gave a new life to home parties.

But the feeling of danger was lurking in the air; threats of assassination were made; warning letters written to the family; and, by order of General Scott, guards were placed around and in the White House, much to the President's dissatisfaction, who "had great faith in the people." One night every member of the family except the servants was taken ill; physicians were hastily summoned; and for a time whisperings of "poison" were heard, but it proved to be only an overindulgence in Potomac shad, a new and tempting dish to Western palates. Of course, there was no gaiety going on, save as formality demanded a few receptions and Cabinet dinners. However, Commodore Franklin Buchanan, then in command of the navy guard, insisted upon the honor of the President's presence at the marriage of his daughter. Though without precedent, Secretary Seward advised the acceptance of the invitation—White House etiquette demanded that the President's wife should not appear at social functions outside of the Mansion—so the President and I, attended by the Secretary of State and the private secretaries, went to the marriage feast in due formality.

It was a gay, brilliant affair, where we met the *crème de la crème* of society and were feasted and toasted as only distinguished guests could be. But it was only a seeming cordiality and respect, for, in less than three weeks, Commodore Buchanan most unceremoniously left the Navy Yard in command of Commodore J. A. Dahlgren, and went into the Confederacy. . . .

Secretary Seward called one morning in August to tell the President and Mrs. Lincoln of the expected visit of the French Prince Napoleon and suite, and to arrange for his reception at the Executive Mansion; and, after ceremonials, a dinner must be given, some receptions, drives, etc., and if the President preferred, he, Mr. Seward, would give the dinner the evening following the Prince's arrival. Mrs. Lincoln did not fail to make a prompt objection to this suggestion, which seemed an echo of an earlier one which I have mentioned, and she at once caused one of the private secretaries to be summoned and charged with arranging for a formal dinner on the day of the Prince's presentation to the President. It was at the same time settled that Mr. Seward should give an evening reception in honor of the Prince on a subsequent day.

Saturday at noon, Prince "Plon Plon," as he was widely known, attended by his suite, was presented to the President by Count Mercier, the French Minister.

At seven o'clock they returned and were ushered into the Blue Room just as the Marine Band struck up "Yankee Doodle", with which the usual Saturday afternoon crowd was dismissed. The whole party was invited out to the balcony, much to the gratification of the people, who feasted their eyes on His Imperial Highness, while he, in turn, had a view of the "American Sovereigns." The grouping was effective. The Prince, in full dress, his breast a flame of decoration, over which was crossed the broad crimson sash of a Marshal of the Empire, stood in the center of his suite, in the attitude always assumed by his uncle, the first Consul, so easily recognized. . . .

After their return to the drawing room, the home party, composed of the President, Mrs. Lincoln, Robert, myself, and the private secretaries, Nicolay and Hay, entered the room. Presentations and conversation were in order before the other dinner guests should appear. Soon came the Cabinet officers, and the last to enter was General Scott, magnificent old man, leaning on the arm of McClellan. Six-foot-four expressed it, "History waiting on prophecy, memory upon Hope." Then came the entrance to the dining room, the President leading, I upon his arm, Mrs. Lincoln with the Prince, the other guests following in the usual order of precedence. A beautiful dinner, beautifully served, and gay conversation in which the French tongue predominated, led Prince Napoleon to remark gallantly that, after enjoying the elegant hospitality of Washington and especially of those presiding in the Executive Mansion, he should be forced to confess that "Paris is not all the world," while General Scott said to the President, "I have dined with every President since Jefferson, and that, in my mind, the last should be first."

Secretary Seward's Tuesday evening reception was a brilliant entertainment, worthily in honor of his princely guests, and it gave "Plon Plon" some new ideas perhaps, of the elegance, beauty, and refinement to be found in American society.

In close proximity to such gaiety came harrowing scenes of wretchedness, full of pathos; and, indeed, we all felt as if it were no time for "eating, drinking, and making merry," but policy demanded a show and pretence of cheer and hopefulness we were far from feeling.

3

ONE WASHINGTON RESIDENT who quickly made the acquaintance of the new family in the White House was Julia Taft, a girl in
her teens. In her story, qualities of Mrs. Lincoln which were to cause
much unfriendly gossip—her fondness for clothes, her insistence,
often pettish, upon her prerogatives as first lady of the land—become
apparent.

I HAVE A VERY TENDER MEMORY of Mrs. Lincoln, who
was always so good to me. More than once she said, "I wish I had
a little girl like you, Julia." She always called me Julia, although
the boys, like their father, usually changed my name to Julie. I
think both she and the President would have been glad to have a
daughter. She told me about her little son, Edward, who was between Robert and Willie, and who had died in infancy, and we
wept together as she told me about his death. Once, a long time
after this, I spoke of a boy friend who had joined the Confederate
army and she said, "Yes, dear, it is sad when our friends are in
the rebel army." I had heard that two brothers of Mrs. Lincoln
were in that army and she may have been thinking of them when
she comforted me, but I never heard her actually speak of them.
She said rebel army, not Southern or Confederate army but
"rebel." Mrs. Lincoln was wickedly maligned by people's saying
that she was in sympathy with the South, but I am sure she was
unreservedly for the Union and at one with her husband. I showed
her an impassioned appeal from this boy friend to, "fly with me
to the Southern clime before Washington is destroyed." I would
not have dared to annoy my lady-mother with such trivial things,
but the first lady was not too exalted to sympathize with my story
and give kind advice.

She would ask me to play my pieces of music to her. When I
was asked to play, I had to play, no doubt of that. My parents
had drilled into me the idea that it was an unforgivable breach of
etiquette to refuse. I never practiced if I could help it, and I
would leave out a part of my piece if I could get by with it. If I
heard talking behind me, I went on fairly well, but if they actually
listened, I nearly fell off the piano stool. When I played for
Mrs. Lincoln, she would stand beside me to the last note, turning

the leaves of my music. Somehow I never minded playing for her. . . .

Mrs. Lincoln was very particular in the matter of clothes. She dressed well, as befitted her position, and, when she happened to see a fabric, or a ribbon, or a certain style that pleased her fancy, she would make life miserable for her dressmaker or milliner until it was added to her wardrobe. . . . This amiable feminine weakness—if it was a weakness—was responsible for a little incident in which the bonnets of my mother and Mrs. Lincoln played an amusing part. . . .

My mother's bonnet—we call them hats now, but, in the spring of 1861, they were bonnets—was, her friends all agreed, one of Willian's most ideal creations. Willian was the fashionable milliner on Pennsylvania Avenue, where everybody who was anybody went for bonnets, also dresses. They had not begun to be gowns, though they were always "robes" to Willian. This bonnet, a delicate straw, was lavishly trimmed with purple ribbon embroidered with small, black figures. It had long strings which tied with a bow under the chin. On the next Wednesday after the bonnet was sent home, I accompanied my mother to the promenade concert on the White House grounds. . . .

My mother, of course, wore the bonnet, together with a purple and white silk over a moderate crinoline, and lavender kid gloves. . . . The band had been playing for some time, and, after we had walked about for a while, exchanging greetings with friends, the first notes of the national anthem brought those sitting to their feet; gentlemen removed their hats; and all stood at attention. Many people have the idea that this custom originated somewhat later, but it certainly was the custom in 1861, as I well remember. At the close of the concert my mother and I went up to the south front, where the presidential party was sitting, to pay our respects. I noticed Mrs. Lincoln looking intently at my mother's bonnet. After a few words of greeting, she took my mother aside and talked with her for a moment. While I could not hear their conversation, I knew someway that they were talking about my mother's bonnet, and I was a bit puzzled at the look of amazement on my mother's face. I did not see why my mother should look so surprised at a passing compliment from Mrs. Lincoln.

It was nearly dinnertime when we arrived home. My father was reading his *Star* in the back parlor. There were back parlors then, you know. Mother went up to him and said, "Horatio, Mrs. Lincoln made a most peculiar request of me today."

"What was it?" said my father.

She leaned forward and said something I could not hear, but as she stepped back and untied her bonnet strings I heard her say, "Willian trimmed her bonnet with this same ribbon but is unable to get enough for the strings."

"Well," said my father, "what will you do about it?"

"Why," answered my mother, "I suppose I'll have to let her have it, and it's provoking, for I really did like this bonnet." Then she noticed I was listening and said, "Take your flat upstairs, Julia, and put it in the box." I went. We went when we were told in those days.

Next day, we went to Willian's for the fitting of my first long dress. . . . I heard Willian say to my mother, "You is veree kind, Mrs. Taft. The Madame she want only that ribbon, not any other. If you give up ze strings, I retrim ze bonnet with lavender ribbon so it will be complete." So Willian sent for my mother's bonnet and in a few days it came back, more beautiful than at first, but now trimmed with lavender white-embroidered ribbon, instead of purple. . . .

Not long after this exchange of bonnet strings I reported to my mother, "Mrs. Lincoln wore a purple dress and those strings which were on your bonnet at first." My mother reproved me sharply.

"Never let me hear you make any remark about Mrs. Lincoln's clothes, Julia. The wife of the President should be above petty gossip."

4

THE QUALITIES of Mrs. Lincoln which young Julia Taft revealed, perhaps unwittingly, stand out in sharper relief in Elizabeth Keckley's explanation of her first employment at the White House. Elizabeth Keckley was a mulatto dressmaker who became Mrs. Lincoln's close confidante.

Tuesday morning, at eight o'clock, I crossed the threshold of the White House for the first time. I was shown into a waiting room, and informed that Mrs. Lincoln was at breakfast. In the waiting room I found no less than three mantuamakers waiting for an interview with the wife of the new President. It seems that Mrs. Lincoln had told several of her lady friends that she had urgent need for a dressmaker, and that each of these friends had sent her mantuamaker to the White House. Hope fell at once. With so many rivals for the position sought after, I regarded my chances for success as extremely doubtful. I was the last one summoned to Mrs. Lincoln's presence. All the others had a hearing, and were dismissed. I went upstairs timidly, and entering the room with nervous steps, discovered the wife of the President standing by a window, looking out, and engaged in lively conversation with a lady, Mrs. Grimsley, as I afterwards learned. Mrs. Lincoln came forward, and greeted me warmly.

"You have come at last. Mrs. Keckley, who have you worked for in the city?"

"Among others, Mrs. Senator Davis has been one of my best patrons," was my reply.

"Mrs. Davis! So you have worked for her, have you? Of course you gave satisfaction; so far, good. Can you do my work?"

"Yes, Mrs. Lincoln. Will you have much work for me to do?"

"That, Mrs. Keckley, will depend altogether upon your prices. I trust that your terms are reasonable. I cannot afford to be extravagant. We are just from the West, and are poor. If you do not charge too much, I shall be able to give you all my work."

"I do not think there will be any difficulty about charges, Mrs. Lincoln; my terms are reasonable."

"Well, if you will work cheap, you shall have plenty to do. I can't afford to pay big prices, so I frankly tell you so in the beginning."

The terms were satisfactorily arranged, and I measured Mrs. Lincoln, took the dress with me, a bright, rose-colored moire-antique, and returned the next day to fit it on her. A number of ladies were in the room, all making preparations for the levee to come off on Friday night. These ladies, I learned, were relatives of Mrs. Lincoln's—Mrs. Edwards and Mrs. Kellogg, her own sisters, and Elizabeth Edwards and Julia Baker, her nieces. Mrs. Lincoln this morning was dressed in a cashmere wrapper, quilted down the front; and she wore a simple headdress. The other ladies wore morning robes.

I was hard at work on the dress, when I was informed that the levee had been postponed from Friday night till Tuesday night. This, of course, gave me more time to complete my task. Mrs. Lincoln sent for me, and suggested some alteration in style, which was made. She also requested that I make a waist of blue-watered silk for Mrs. Grimsley, as work on the dress would not require all my time.

Tuesday evening came, and I had taken the last stitches on the dress. I folded it and carried it to the White House, with the waist for Mrs. Grimsley. When I went upstairs I found the ladies in a terrible state of excitement. Mrs. Lincoln was protesting that she could not go down, for the reason that she had nothing to wear.

"Mrs. Keckley, you have disappointed me—deceived me. Why do you bring my dress at this late hour?"

"Because I have just finished it, and I thought I should be in time."

"But you are not in time, Mrs. Keckley; you have bitterly disappointed me. I have no time now to dress, and, what is more, I will not dress, and go downstairs."

"I am sorry if I have disappointed you, Mrs. Lincoln, for I intended to be in time. Will you let me dress you? I can have you ready in a few minutes."

"No, I won't be dressed. I will stay in my room. Mr. Lincoln can go down with the other ladies."

"But there is plenty of time for you to dress, Mary," joined in Mrs. Grimsley and Mrs. Edwards. "Let Mrs. Keckley assist you, and she will soon have you ready."

Thus urged, she consented. I dressed her hair, and arranged the dress on her. It fitted nicely, and she was pleased. Mr. Lincoln came in, threw himself on the sofa, laughed with Willie and little Tad, and then commenced pulling on his gloves, quoting poetry all the while.

"You seem to be in a poetical mood tonight," said his wife.

"Yes, mother, these are poetical times," was his pleasant reply. "I declare, you look charming in that dress. Mrs. Keckley has met with great success." And then he proceeded to compliment the other ladies.

Mrs. Lincoln looked elegant in her rose-colored moire-antique. She wore a pearl necklace, pearl earrings, pearl bracelets, and red roses in her hair. Mrs. Baker was dressed in lemon-colored silk; Mrs. Kellogg in a drab silk, ashes of rose; Mrs. Edwards in a brown and black silk; Miss Edwards in crimson, and Mrs. Grimsley in blue-watered silk. Just before they started downstairs, Mrs. Lincoln's lace handkerchief was the object of search. It had been misplaced by Tad, who was mischievous and hard to restrain. The handkerchief found, all became serene. Mrs. Lincoln took the President's arm, and with smiling face led the train below. I was surprised at her grace and composure. I had heard so much, in current and malicious report, of her low life, of her ignorance and vulgarity, that I expected to see her embarrassed on this occasion. Report, I soon saw, was wrong. No queen, accustomed to the usages of royalty all her life, could have comported herself with more calmness and dignity than did the wife of the President.

5

BUT MRS. LINCOLN, for all her haughtiness, was a devoted mother. The loss of one child—Edward Baker—had, if anything, intensified her love for the three who remained. In February, 1862, William Wallace, a bright and promising youngster of eleven years, was taken ill. Mrs. Keckley recalls the Lincolns' vigil.

THE FIRST PUBLIC APPEARANCE of Mrs. Lincoln that winter was at the reception on New Year's Day. This reception was shortly followed by a brilliant levee. The day after the levee, I went to the White House, and, while fitting a dress to Mrs. Lincoln, she said:

"Lizabeth"—she had learned to drop the "E"—"Lizabeth, I have an idea. These are war times, and we must be as economical as possible. You know the President is expected to give a series of state dinners every winter, and these dinners are very costly. Now I want to avoid this expense; and my idea is that, if I give three large receptions, the state dinners can be scratched from the program. What do you think, Lizabeth?"

"I think that you are right, Mrs. Lincoln."

"I am glad to hear you say so. If I can make Mr. Lincoln take the same view of the case, I shall not fail to put the idea into practice."

Before I left her room that day, Mr. Lincoln came in. She at once stated the case to him. . . . The question was decided, and arrangements were made for the first reception. It now was January, and cards were issued for February.

The children, Tad and Willie, were constantly receiving presents. Willie was so delighted with a little pony, that he insisted on riding it every day. The weather was changeable, and exposure resulted in a severe cold, which deepened into fever. He was very sick, and I was summoned to his bedside. It was sad to see the poor boy suffer. Always of a delicate constitution, he could not resist the strong inroads of disease. The days dragged wearily by, and he grew weaker and more shadow-like. . . .

Finding that Willie continued to grow worse, Mrs. Lincoln determined to withdraw her cards of invitation and postpone the reception. Mr. Lincoln thought that the cards had better not be withdrawn. At least, he advised that the doctor be consulted before any steps were taken. Accordingly, Dr. Stone was called in. He pronounced Willie better, and said that there was every reason for an early recovery. He thought, since the invitations had been issued, it would be best to go on with the reception. Willie, he insisted, was in no immediate danger. Mrs. Lincoln was guided by these counsels, and no postponement was announced. On the evening of the reception, Willie was suddenly taken worse. His mother sat by his bedside a long while, holding his feverish hand in her own, and watching his labored breathing. The doctor claimed there was no cause for alarm. I arranged Mrs. Lincoln's hair, then assisted her to dress. Her dress was white satin, trimmed with black lace. The trail was very long, and as she swept through the room, Mr. Lincoln was standing with his back to the fire, his hands behind him and his eyes on the carpet. His face wore a thoughtful, solemn look. The rustling of the satin dress attracted his attention.

He looked at it a few moments, then, in his quaint, quiet way remarked,

"Whew! our cat has a long tail tonight."

Mrs. Lincoln did not reply. The President added:

"Mother, it is my opinion, if some of that tail was nearer the head, it would be in better style"; and he glanced at her bare arms and neck. She had a beautiful neck and arms, and low dresses were becoming to her. She turned away with a look of offended dignity, and presently took the President's arm, and both went downstairs to their guests, leaving me alone with the sick boy.

The reception was a large and brilliant one, and the rich notes of the Marine Band in the apartments below came to the sickroom in soft, subdued murmurs, like the wild, faint sobbing of far-off spirits. Some of the young people had suggested dancing, but Mr. Lincoln met the suggestion with an emphatic veto. The brilliance of the scene could not dispel the sadness that rested upon the face of Mrs. Lincoln. During the evening she came upstairs several times, and stood by the bedside of the suffering boy. She loved him with a mother's heart, and her anxiety was great. The night passed slowly; morning came; and Willie was worse. He lingered a few days, and died. God called the beautiful spirit home, and the house of joy was turned into the house of mourning. I was worn out with watching, and was not in the room when Willie died, but was immediately sent for. I assisted in washing him and dressing him, and then laid him on the bed when Mr. Lincoln came in. I never saw a man so bowed down with grief. He came to the bed, lifted the cover from the face of his child, gazed at it long and earnestly, murmuring, "My poor boy, he was too good for this earth. God has called him home. I know that he is much better off in heaven, but then we loved him so. It is hard, hard to have him die!"

Great sobs choked his utterance. He buried his head in his hands, and his tall frame was convulsed with emotion. I stood at the foot of the bed, my eyes full of tears, looking at the man in silent, awe-stricken wonder. His grief unnerved him, and made him a weak, passive child. I did not dream that his rugged nature could be so moved. I shall never forget those solemn moments— genius and greatness weeping over love's idol lost. . . .

Mrs. Lincoln's grief was inconsolable. The pale face of her dead boy threw her into convulsions. Around him, love's tendrils had been twined, and now that he was dressed for the tomb, it was like tearing the tendrils out of the heart by their roots. Willie, she often said, if spared by Providence, would be the hope and stay of her old age. But Providence had not spared him. The light faded from his eyes, and the death dew had gathered on his brow.

In one of her paroxysms of grief, the President kindly bent over his wife, took her by the arm, and gently led her to the window. With a stately, solemn gesture, he pointed to the lunatic asylum.

"Mother, do you see that large white building on the hill yonder? Try and control your grief, or it will drive you mad, and we may have to send you there."

6

AFTER THE DEATH of Willie Lincoln, the affections of the grief-stricken parents were lavished on the one boy who remained at home—Thomas, or, as he was invariably called, Tad. Noah Brooks characterizes this sprite-like youngster, who won the hearts of all who knew him.

TAD WAS EIGHT YEARS OLD when he was taken to Washington with the rest of the family. He had a curious impediment in his speech which rather heightened the effect of his droll sayings; and the difficulty which he had in pronouncing his own name gave him the odd nickname by which he was always known. . . .

Perhaps it was heaviness of grief at the loss of Willie that made it well-nigh impossible for Lincoln to treat Tad's innumerable escapades with severity. While the family lived in Washington, the lad was allowed his own way almost without check. His father was to the last degree indulgent, although when he chose to exercise his paternal authority, the boy was readily amenable to discipline or reproof. Much of the time it was impossible that he should not be left to run at large. He was caressed and petted by people who wanted favors of his father, and who took this way of making a friend in the family, as they thought; and he was living in the midst of a most exciting epoch in the country's history, when a boy in the White House was in a strange and somewhat unnatural atmosphere. But I am bound to say that Tad, although

he doubtless had his wits sharpened by being in such strange surroundings, was never anything else, while I knew him, but a
boisterous, rollicking, and absolutely real boy. He was not "old for
his years," as we sometimes say of precocious children, nor was he
burdened with care before his time. He was a big-hearted and
fresh-faced youngster. . . .

Very soon after he began life in the White House, Tad learned
what an office-seeker was. All day long, unless the President was
absent from the building, the office-seekers lined the upper corridors and passages; and sometimes the lines extended all the way
down the stairs and nearly to the main entrance. When other di-
versions failed him, Tad liked to go around among these waiting
place-hunters and institute inquiries on his own account. He would
ask what they wanted, how long they had been there, and how
much longer they proposed to wait. Some of these men came day
after day, and for many successive days; with these Tad became
acquainted, and to them he would give much sympathetic advice
in his own whimsical but sincere way. Once he mounted guard at
the foot of the public staircase, and exacted toll of all who passed
up. "Five cents for the benefit of the Sanitary Fund," he explained to the visitors, who were not unwilling to have a friend
at court for so small a price.

He organized for himself, after the custom of the day, a Sanitary Fair. Beginning with a little table, which he set in the grand
corridor of the White House and stocked with small purchases of
fruit and odds and ends begged from the pantry of the house, he
extended his operations in a second venture. He secured from a
carpenter a pair of trestles and a wide board, on which he spread
the entire stock of an old woman who sold apples, gingerbread, and
candy, near the Treasury building, bought out with the lad's
carefully saved pocket-money. The Fair was set up just within the
portico of the White House, where the place-seekers, whose
patronage the shrewd boy catered for, would be sure to pass on
their way to the fountain of power. Tad's enterprise was highly
successful, but the proceeds of his sales were speedily dispersed by
his open-handed generosity. Before night, capital and profits had
been spent, and the little speculator went penniless to bed.

Everything that Tad did was done with a certain rush and
rude strength which was peculiar to him. I was once sitting with

the President in the library, when Tad tore into the room in search of something, and, having found it, he threw himself on his father like a small thunderbolt, gave him one wild, fierce hug, and, without a word, fled from the room before his father could put out his hand to detain him. With all his boyish roughness, Tad had a warm heart and a tender conscience. He abhorred falsehood as he did books and study. Tutors came and went, like changes of the moon. None stayed long enough to learn much about the boy; but he knew them before they had been one day in the house. "Let him run," his father would say; "there's time enough yet for him to learn his letters and get poky. Bob was just such a little rascal, and now he is a very decent boy."

It was curious, however, to see how Tad comprehended many practical realities that are far beyond the grasp of most boys. Even when he could scarcely read, he knew much about the cost of things, the details of trade, the principles of mechanics, and the habits of animals, all of which showed the activity of his mind and the odd turn of his thoughts. His father took great interest in everything that concerned Tad, and when the long day's work was done, and the little chap had related to the President all that had moved him or had taken up his attention during the daylight hours, and had finally fallen asleep under a drowsy cross-examination, the weary father would turn once more to his desk, and work on into the night, for his cares never ended. Then, shouldering the sleeping child, the man for whom millions of good men and women nightly prayed took his way through the silent corridors and passages to his boy's bedchamber.

7

OF THE PRESIDENT HIMSELF—his daily routine, his living habits, his simple and infrequent amusements—no one was better fitted to write than John Hay. His portrayal follows:

T HE DAILY LIFE of the White House during the momentous years of Lincoln's presidency had a character of its own, different from that of any previous or subsequent time. In the first days after the inauguration there was the unprecedented rush of office-seekers, inspired by a strange mixture of enthusiasm and greed, pushed by motives which were perhaps at bottom selfish, but which had nevertheless a curious touch of that deep emotion which had stirred the heart of the nation in the late election. They were not all ignoble; among that dense crowd that swarmed in the staircases and the corridors, there were many well-to-do men who were seeking office to their own evident damage, simply because they wished to be a part, however humble, of a government which they had aided to put in power and to which they were sincerely devoted. Many of the visitors who presented so piteous a figure in those early days of 1861 afterwards marched, with the independent dignity of a private soldier, in the ranks of the Union Army, or rode at the head of their regiments like men born to command. There were few who had not a story worth listening to, if there were time and opportunity. But the numbers were so great, the competition was so keen, that they ceased for the moment to be regarded as individuals, drowned as they were in the general sea of solicitation.

Few of them received office; when, after weeks of waiting, one of them got access to the President, he was received with kindness by a tall, melancholy-looking man sitting at a desk with his back to a window which opened upon a fair view of the Potomac, who heard his story with a gentle patience, took his papers and referred them to one of the Departments, and that was all; the fatal pigeonholes devoured them. As time wore on and the offices were filled, the throng of eager aspirants diminished and faded away. When the war burst out an immediate transformation took place. The house was again invaded and overrun by a different class of visitors—youths who wanted commissions in the regulars; men who wished to raise irregular regiments or battalions without regard to their state authorities; men who wanted to furnish stores to the army; inventors full of great ideas and in despair at the apathy of the world; later, an endless stream of officers in search of promotion or desirable assignments. And, from first to last, there were the politicians and statesmen in Congress and out, each of whom felt that he had the right by virtue of his representative capacity to as much of the President's time as he chose, and who never considered that he and his kind were many, and that the President was but one.

It would be hard to imagine a state of things less conducive to serious and effective work, yet in one way or another the work was done. In the midst of a crowd of visitors who began to arrive early in the morning and who were put out, grumbling, by the servants who closed the doors at midnight, the President pursued those labors which'will carry his name to distant ages. There was little order or system about it; those around him strove from beginning to end to erect barriers to defend him against constant inter- ruption, but the President himself was always the first to break them down. He disliked anything that kept people from him who wanted to see him, and although the continual contact with im- portunity which he could not satisfy, and with distress which he could not always relieve, wore terribly upon him and made him an old man before his time, he would never take the necessary measures to defend himself. He continued to the end receiving these swarms of visitors, every one of whom, even the most wel- come, took something from him in the way of wasted nervous force. Henry Wilson once remonstrated with him about it: "You will wear yourself out." He replied, with one of those smiles in which there was so much of sadness, "They don't want much; they get but little, and I must see them." In most cases he could do them no good, and it afflicted him to see he could not make them understand the impossibility of granting their requests. One hot afternoon a private soldier, who had somehow got access to him, persisted, after repeated explanations that his case was one to be settled by his immediate superiors, in begging that the President would give it his personal attention. Lincoln at last burst out: "Now, my man, go away! I cannot attend to all these details. I could as easily bail out the Potomac with a spoon."

Of course it was not all pure waste; Mr. Lincoln gained much of information, something of cheer and encouragement, from these visits. He particularly enjoyed conversing with officers of the army and navy, newly arrived from the field or from sea. He listened with the eagerness of a child over a fairy tale to Garfield's graphic account of the Battle of Chickamauga; he was always delighted with the wise and witty sailor-talk of John A. Dahlgren, Gustavus V. Fox, and Commander Henry A. Wise. Sometimes a word fitly spoken had its results. When R. B. Ayres called on him in company with Senator Harris, and was introduced as a captain of artillery who had taken part in a recent unsuccessful engage- ment, he asked, "How many guns did you take in?" "Six," Ayres answered. "How many did you bring out?" the President asked, maliciously. "Eight." This unexpected reply did much to gain Ayres his merited promotion.

The President rose early, as his sleep was light and capricious. In the summer, when he lived at the Soldiers' Home, he would take his frugal breakfast and ride into town in time to be at his desk at eight o'clock. He began to receive visits nominally at ten o'clock, but long before that hour struck the doors were besieged by anxious crowds, through whom the people of importance, Senators and members of Congress, elbowed their way after the fashion which still survives. On days when the Cabinet met, Tuesdays and Fridays, the hour of noon closed the interviews of the morning. On other days it was the President's custom, at about that hour, to order the doors to be opened and all who were waiting to be admitted. The crowd would rush in, thronging the narrow room, and one by one would make their wants known. Some came merely to shake hands, to wish him Godspeed; their errand was soon done. Others came asking help or mercy; they usually pressed forward, careless, in their pain, as to what ears should overhear their prayer. But there were many who lingered in the rear and leaned against the wall, hoping each to be the last, that they might in *tête-à-tête* unfold their schemes for their own advantage or their neighbors' hurt. These were often disconcerted by the President's loud and hearty, "Well, friend, what can I do for you?" which compelled them to speak, or retire and wait for a more convenient season.

The inventors were more a source of amusement than annoyance. They were usually men of some originality of character, not infrequently carried to eccentricity. Lincoln had a quick comprehension of mechanical principles, and often detected a flaw in an invention which the contriver had overlooked. He would sometimes go out into the waste fields that then lay south of the Executive Mansion to test an experimental gun or torpedo. He used to quote with much merriment the solemn dictum of one rural inventor that "a gun ought not to rekyle; if it rekyled at all, it ought to rekyle a little forrid." He was particularly interested in the first rude attempts at the afterwards famous mitrailleuses; on one occasion he worked one with his own hands at the Arsenal, and sent forth peals of Homeric laughter as the balls, which had not power to penetrate the target set up at a little distance, came bounding back among the shins of the bystanders. He accompanied Colonel Hiram Berdan one day to the camp of his sharpshooters and there practised in the trenches his long-disused skill with the rifle. A few fortunate shots from his own gun, and pleasure at the still better marksmanship of Berdan, led to the arming of that admirable regiment with breechloaders.

At luncheon time, he had literally to run the gantlet through the crowds who filled the corridors between his office and the rooms at the west end of the house occupied by the family. The afternoon wore away in much the same manner as the morning; late in the day he usually drove out for an hour's airing; at six o'clock he dined. He was one of the most abstemious of men; the pleasures of the table had few attractions for him. His breakfast was an egg and a cup of coffee; at luncheon he rarely took more than a biscuit and a glass of milk, a plate of fruit in its season; at dinner he ate sparingly of one or two courses. He drank little or no wine; not that he remained always on principle a total abstainer, as he was during a part of his early life in the fervor of the Washingtonian reform; but he never cared for wine. . . .

Mr. Lincoln's life was almost devoid of recreation. He sometimes went to the theater, and was particularly fond of a play of Shakespeare well acted. He was so delighted with Hackett in "Falstaff" that he wrote him a letter of warm congratulation which pleased the veteran actor so much that he gave it to the *New York Herald*, which printed it with abusive comments. Hackett was greatly mortified and made suitable apologies; upon which the President wrote to him again in the kindliest manner, saying:

"Give yourself no uneasiness on the subject. . . . I certainly did not expect to see my note in print; yet I have not been much shocked by the comments upon it. They are a fair specimen of what has occurred to me through life. I have endured a great deal of ridicule, without much malice; and have received a great deal of kindness, not quite free from ridicule. I am used to it."

This incident had the usual sequel; the veteran comedian asked for an office, which the President was not able to give him, and the pleasant acquaintance ceased. A hundred times this experience was repeated; a man whose disposition and talk were agreeable would be introduced to the President; he took pleasure in his conversation for two or three interviews; and then this congenial person would ask some favor impossible to grant, and go away in bitterness of spirit. It is a cross that every President must bear.

Mr. Lincoln spent most of his evenings in his office, though occasionally he remained in the drawing room after dinner, conversing with visitors or listening to music, for which he had an especial liking, though he was not versed in the science, and preferred simple ballads to more elaborate compositions. In his office he was not often suffered to be alone; he frequently passed the evening there with a few friends in frank and free conversation. If the company was all of one sort he was at his best; his wit and rich humor had free play; he was once more the Lincoln of the Eighth Circuit, the cheeriest of talkers, the riskiest of story tellers; but if a stranger came in, he put on in an instant his whole armor of dignity and reserve. He had a singular discernment of men; he would talk of the most important political and military concerns with a freedom which often amazed his intimates; but we do not recall an instance in which this confidence was misplaced.

Where only one or two were present he was fond of reading aloud. He passed many of the summer evenings in this way when occupying his cottage at the Soldiers' Home. . . . He read Shakespeare more than all other writers together. He made no attempt to keep pace with the ordinary literature of the day. Sometimes, he read a scientific work with keen appreciation, but he pursued no systematic course. He owed less to reading than most men. He delighted in Burns; he said one day after reading those exquisite lines to Glencairn, beginning, "The bridegroom may forget the bride," that "Burns never touched a sentiment without carrying it to its ultimate expression and leaving nothing further to be said." Of Thomas Hood he was also excessively fond. He often read aloud "The Haunted House." He would go to bed with a volume of Hood in his hand, and would sometimes rise at midnight and, traversing the long halls of the Executive Mansion in his night clothes, would come to his secretary's room and read a. ud something that especially pleased him. He wanted to share his enjoyment of the writers; it was dull pleasure to him to laugh alone. He read Bryant and Whittier with appreciation; there were many poems of Holmes's that he read with intense relish. *The*

Last Leaf was one of his favorites; he knew it by heart, and used often to repeat with deep feeling:

> The mossy marbles rest
> On the lips that he has pressed
>   In their bloom,
> And the names he loved to hear
> Have been carved for many a year
>   On the tomb;

giving the marked Southwestern pronunciation of the words "hear" and "year." A poem by William Knox, "Oh, why should the Spirit of Mortal be Proud?" he learned by heart in his youth, and used to repeat all his life. . . .

As time wore on and the war held its terrible course, upon no one of all those who lived through it was its effect more apparent than upon the President. He 'bore the sorrows of the Nation in his own heart; he suffered deeply not only from disappointments, from treachery, from hope deferred, from the open assaults of enemies, and from the sincere anger of discontented friends, but also from the world-wide distress and affliction which flowed from the great conflict in which he was engaged and which he could not evade. One of the most tender and compassionate of men, he was forced to give orders which cost thousands of lives; by nature a man of order and thrift, he saw the daily spectacle of unutterable waste and destruction which he could not prevent. The cry of the widow and the orphan was always in his ears; the awful responsibility resting upon him as the protector of an imperiled republic kept him true to his duty, but could not make him unmindful of the intimate details of that vast sum of human misery involved in a civil war.

Under this frightful ordeal his demeanor and disposition changed — so gradually that it would be impossible to say when the change began; but he was in mind, body, and nerves a very different man at the second inauguration from the one who had taken the oath in 1861. He continued always the same kindly, genial, and cordial spirit he had been at first; but the boisterous laughter became less frequent year by year; the eye grew veiled by constant meditation on momentous subjects; the air of reserve and detachment from his surroundings increased. He aged with great rapidity.

CHAPTER TWENTY

Gettysburg

S *OON AFTER the Battle of Chancellorsville, Lee
took the exultant Army of Northern Virginia across
the Potomac and started north. Perhaps his ultimate objective was Washington, perhaps it was the rich cities of
Pennsylvania, where dwindling supplies might be replen-
ished. No one knew. Hooker, whose army had not been demoralized by defeat, started north at the same time, skillfully disposing his troops so that they would stand as a
shield between the Confederates and the national Capital.*

*Early in the morning of June 28, 1863, George Gordon
Meade, commanding Hooker's Fifth Corps, was awakened
by a messenger from the President placing him in command of the Army of the Potomac. Four days later his forward elements stumbled into Lee's advance guard, and the
Battle of Gettysburg began. For three days Lee sent troops
hitherto invincible against blue lines that at first yielded
and then stood firm. When it was over, his army, bled by
20,000 casualties, had lost one of the decisive battles of
history.*

1

CARL SANDBURG recounts the first great victory of the Army
of the Potomac.

F ROM DAY TO DAY neither Meade nor Lee had been certain
where the other was. Lee would rather have taken Harrisburg, its
stores and supplies, and then battled Meade on the way to Phila-

delphia. In that case Lee would have had ammunition enough to keep his artillery firing with no letup, no orders during an infantry charge that ammunition was running low and must be saved.

Lee rode his horse along roads winding through bright summer landscapes to find himself suddenly looking at the smoke of a battle he had not ordered nor planned. Some of his own marching divisions had become entangled with enemy columns, traded shots, and a battle had begun that Lee could draw away from or carry on. He decided to carry on. He said Yes. His troops in their last two battles and on general form looked unbeatable. Against him was an untried commander with a jealous staff that had never worked as smoothly as his own. If he could repeat his performances with his men at Fredericksburg and Chancellorsville, he could then march to Harrisburg, use the State Capitol for barracks, replenish his needs, march on to Philadelphia, Baltimore, and Washington, lay hold of money, supplies, munitions, win European recognition, and end the war.

The stakes were immense, the chances fair. The new enemy commander had never planned a battle nor handled a big army in the wild upsets of frontal combat on a wide line. Also fifty-eight regiments of Northern veterans who had fought at Antietam, Fredericksburg, Chancellorsville, had gone home, their time up, their places filled by militia and raw recruits.

One factor was against Lee: he would have to tell his cannoneers to go slow and count their shells, while Meade's artillery could fire on and on from an endless supply. Another factor, too, was against Lee: he was away from his Virginia, where he knew the ground and the people, while Meade's men were fighting for their homes, women, barns, cattle, and fields against invaders and strangers, as Meade saw and felt it.

To Lee's words, "If the enemy is there, we must attack him," Longstreet who now replaced Stonewall Jackson, spoke sharply, "If he is there, it will be because he is anxious that we should attack him—a good reason, in my judgment, for not doing so." This vague and involved feeling Longstreet nursed in his breast; attack was unwise, and his advice rejected. It resulted in hours of delay and wasted time that might have counted.

Lee hammered at the Union left wing the first day, the right wing the second day, Meade on that day sending word to Lincoln that the enemy was "repulsed at all points." On the third day, July 3, 1863, Lee smashed at Meade's center. Under Longstreet's command, General George Edward Pickett, a tall arrow of a man, with mustache and goatee, with long ringlets of auburn hair flying as he galloped his horse, headed 15,000 men, who had nearly a mile to go up a slow slope of land to reach the Union center. Pickett might have had thoughts in his blanket under the stars some night that week of how long ago it was, twenty-one years, since he, a Virginia boy schooled in Richmond, had been studying law in his uncle's office in Quincy, Illinois, seeing men daily who tried cases with the young attorney Abraham Lincoln. And the Pickett boy had gone on to West Point, graduated at the bottom of his class, the last of all, though later he had been first to go over the parapets at Chapultepec in 1847, and still later, in 1859, had taken possession of San Juan Island at Puget Sound on the delicate mission of accommodating officials of the Buchanan administration in bringing on a war with Great Britain, with the hope of saving his country from a threatened civil war by welding its divided sections. British diplomacy achieved joint occupation of the island by troops of two nations and thus averted war. On the Peninsula, Pickett's men had earned the nickname of "The Game Cock Brigade," and he considered love of woman second only to the passion for war.

Before starting his men on their charge to the Union center, Pickett handed Longstreet a letter to a girl in Richmond he was to marry if he lived. Longstreet had ordered Pickett to go forward and Pickett had penciled on the back of the envelope, "If Old Peter's (Longstreet's) nod means death, good-by, and God bless you, little one!" An officer held out a flask of whiskey to Pickett: "Take a drink with me; in an hour you'll be in hell or glory." And Pickett said No; he had promised "the little girl" he wouldn't.

Across the long rise of open ground, with the blue flag of Virginia floating ahead, over field and meadow Pickett's 15,000 marched steadily and smoothly, almost as if on a drill ground. Solid shot, grape and canister, from the Union artillery plowed through them, and later a wild rain of rifle bullets. Seven-eighths of a mile they marched in the open sunlight, every man a target for the Union marksmen behind stone fences and breastworks. They obeyed orders; Uncle Robert had said they would go anywhere and do anything.

As men fell their places were filled, the ranks closed up. As officers tumbled off horses it was taken as expected in battle.

Perhaps half who started reached the Union lines surmounting Cemetery Ridge.

Then came cold steel, the bayonet, the clubbed musket. The strongest and last line of the enemy was reached. "The Confederate battle flag waved over his defences," said a Confederate major, "and the fighting over the wall became hand to hand, but more than half having already fallen, our line was too weak to rout the enemy."

Meade rode up white-faced to hear it was a repulse and cried, "Thank God!" Lee commented: "They deserved success as far as it can be deserved by human valor and fortitude. More may have been required of them than they were able to perform." To one of his colonels, Lee said, "This has been a sad day for us, a sad day, but we cannot expect always to gain victories."

As a heavy rainfall came on the night of July 4, Lee ordered a retreat toward the Potomac.

2

CEMETERIES MARK BATTLEFIELDS. How that at Gettysburg came to be created, and how Lincoln was invited to dedicate it, are related by Clark E. Carr, the Illinois member of the cemetery commission.

SCARCELY HAD THE REVERBERATIONS of the guns of the battle died away when the Honorable David Wills, a citizen of Gettysburg, wrote to the Honorable Andrew G. Curtin, the great war Governor of Pennsylvania, suggesting that a plot of ground in the midst of the battlefield be at once purchased and set apart as a soldiers' national cemetery, and that the remains of the dead be exhumed and placed in this cemetery. He suggested that the ground to be selected should be on what was known as Cemetery

Hill, so called because adjoining it is the local cemetery of Gettysburg. . . .

Governor Curtin at once approved of the recommendation of Mr. Wills, and correspondence was opened with the governors of the loyal States whose troops had engaged in the battle, asking them to co-operate in the movement. The grounds proposed by Mr. Wills . . . were at once purchased. . . .

It was proposed, as the work proceeded, that memorial dedicatory exercises be held to consecrate this sacred ground, which was finally determined upon. The day first fixed upon for these exercises was the twenty-third of October, 1863.

The Honorable Edward Everett, of Massachusetts, was then regarded as the greatest living American orator, and it was decided to invite him to deliver the oration; and this was done. But he replied that it was wholly out of his power to make the necessary preparation by the twenty-third of October. So desirous were we all to have Mr. Everett that the dedication was postponed to Thursday, the nineteenth of November, 1863—nearly a month— to suit Mr. Everett's convenience. The dedication took place on that day.

A formal invitation to be present was sent to the President of the United States and his Cabinet, to Major General George G. Meade . . . and to the officers and soldiers who had participated in, and gained, the memorable victory. Invitations were also sent to the venerable Lieutenant General Winfield Scott and to Admiral Charles Stewart, the distinguished and time-honored representatives of the army and navy, to the diplomatic corps, representing foreign governments, to the members of both Houses of Congress, and to other distinguished personages.

All these invitations and all arrangements for the dedicatory exercises—as was the case with everything relating to the cemetery—were considered and decided upon by our Board of Commissioners, and were, insofar as he was able, under the direction of the Board, carried into effect by Mr. Wills, our president. As we were all representing and speaking for the governors of our respective States, by whom we were appointed, we made all the invitations in their names.

The proposition to ask Mr. Lincoln to speak at the Gettysburg ceremonies was an afterthought. The President of the United States had, like the other distinguished personages, been invited to be present, but Mr. Lincoln was not, at that time, invited to speak. In fact, it did not seem to occur to any one that he could speak upon such an occasion.

Scarcely any member of the Board, excepting the member representing Illinois, had ever heard him speak at all, and no other member had ever heard, or read from him, anything except political discussions. When the suggestion was made that he be invited to speak, while all expressed high appreciation of his great abilities as a political speaker, as shown in his debates with Senator Douglas, and in his Cooper Institute address, the question was raised as to his ability to speak upon such a grave and solemn occasion as that of the memorial services. Besides, it was said that, with his important duties and responsibilities, he could not possibly have the leisure to prepare an address for such an occasion. In answer to this it was urged that he himself, better than any one else, could determine as to these questions, and that, if he were invited to speak, he was sure to do what, under the circumstances, would be right and proper. . . .

It was finally decided to ask President Lincoln "after the oration" (that is to say, after Mr. Everett's oration), as Chief Executive of the nation, "to set apart formally these grounds to their sacred use by a few appropriate remarks." This was done in the name of the governors of the States, as was the case with others, by Mr. Wills; but the invitation was not settled upon and sent to Mr. Lincoln until the second of November, more than six weeks after Mr. Everett had been invited to speak, and but a little more than two weeks before the exercises were held.

3

TARDY AS IT WAS, the invitation to speak was promptly accepted by the President. On November 18, 1863, he and his party proceeded from Washington to Gettysburg by special train. Of that trip and the preliminaries of the dedicatory exercises, John Hay preserved much in his diary, at the same time demonstrating that a man with a finely developed literary instinct does not always recognize a masterpiece when he hears it.

O N   O U R   T R A I N were the President, Seward, Usher and Blair; Nicolay and myself; Mercier and Admiral Reynaud; Bertinatti and Capt. Isola and Lt. Martinez and Cora; Mrs. Wise; Wayne MacVeagh; McDougal of Canada, and one or two others. We had a pleasant sort of a trip. . . .

At Gettysburg the President went to Mr. Wills who expected him, and our party broke like a drop of quicksilver spilled. Mac-Veagh, young Stanton, and I foraged around for awhile—walked out to the college, got a chafing dish of oysters then some supper, and finally loafing around to the Court House where Lamon was holding a meeting of marshals, we found Forney and went around to his place, Mr. Fahnestock's, and drank a little whisky with him. He had been drinking a good deal during the day and was getting to feel a little ugly and dangerous. He was particularly bitter on Montgomery Blair. MacVeagh was telling him that he pitched into the Tycoon coming up, and told him some truths. He said the President got a good deal of that from time to time and needed it. . . .

We went out after a while following the music to hear the serenades. The President appeared at the door and said half a dozen words meaning nothing and went in. Seward, who was staying around the corner at Harper's, was called out, and spoke so indistinctly that I did not hear a word of what he was saying. Forney and MacVeagh were still growling about Blair.

We went back to Forney's room, having picked up Nicolay, and drank more whisky. Nicolay sang his little song of the "Three Thieves," and we then sang "John Brown." At last we proposed that Forney should make a speech and two or three started out, ·Shannon and Behan and Nicolay, to get a band to serenade him. I stayed with him. So did Stanton and MacVeagh. He still growled quietly and I thought he was going to do something imprudent. He said, "If I speak, I will speak my mind." The music sounded in the street, and the fuglers came rushing up imploring him to come down. He smiled quietly, told them to keep cool, and asked, "Are the recorders there?" "I suppose so of course," shouted the fugler. "Ascertain," said the imperturbable Forney. "Hay, we'll take a drink." They shouted and begged him to come down. The thing would be a failure—it would be his fault, etc. "Are the recorders congenial?" he calmly insisted on knowing. Somebody commended prudence. He said sternly, "I am always prudent." I walked downstairs with him.

The crowd was large and clamorous. The fuglers stood by the door in an agony. The reporters squatted at a little stand in the entry. Forney stood on the threshold, John Young and I by him. The crowd shouted as the door opened. Forney said, "My friends, these are the first hearty cheers I have heard tonight. You gave no such cheers to your President down the street. Do you know what you owe to that great man? You owe your country—you owe your name as American citizens."

He went on blackguarding the crowd for their apathy and then diverged to his own record, saying he had been for Lincoln in his heart in 1860—that open advocacy was not as effectual as the course he took—dividing the most corrupt organization that ever existed—the proslavery Democratic party. He dwelled at length on this question and then went back to the eulogy of the President, that great, wonderful, mysterious, inexplicable man who holds in his single hands the reins of the Republic; who keeps his own counsels; who does his own purpose in his own way, no matter what temporizing minister in his Cabinet sets himself up in opposition to the progress of the age.

And very much of this.

After him Wayne MacVeagh made a most touching and beautiful speech of five minutes and Judge Shannon of Pittsburgh spoke effectively and acceptably to the people.

"That speech must not be written out yet," says Young. "He will see further about it when he gets sober," as we went upstairs. We sang more of "John Brown" and went home.

In the morning I got a beast and rode out with the President's suite to the Cemetery in the procession. The procession formed itself in an orphanly sort of way and moved out with very little help from anybody, and after a little delay, Mr. Everett took his place on the stand—and Mr. Stockton made a prayer which thought it was an oration; and Mr. Everett spoke as he always does, perfectly—and the President, in a fine, free way, with more grace than is his wont, said his half dozen words of consecration, and the music wailed and we went home through crowded and cheering streets. And all the particulars are in the daily papers.

4

HERE ARE the "half dozen words of consecration."

FOURSCORE AND SEVEN YEARS AGO our fathers brought forth on this continent a new nation, conceived in liberty, and dedicated to the proposition that all men are created equal.

Now we are engaged in a great civil war, testing whether that nation, or any nation so conceived and so dedicated, can long endure. We are met on a great battlefield of that war. We have come to dedicate a portion of that field as a final resting-place for those who here gave their lives that that nation might live. It is altogether fitting and proper that we should do this.

But in a larger sense, we cannot dedicate—we cannot consecrate—we cannot hallow—this ground. The brave men, living and dead, who struggled here, have consecrated it far above our poor power to add or detract. The world will little note nor long remember what we say here, but it can never forget what they did here. It is for us, the living, rather, to be dedicated here to the unfinished work which they who fought here have thus far so nobly advanced. It is rather for us to be here dedicated to the great task remaining before us—that from these honored dead we take increased devotion to that cause for which they gave the last full measure of devotion; that we here highly resolve that these dead shall not have died in vain; that this nation, under God, shall have a new birth of freedom; and that government of the people, by the people, for the people, shall not perish from the earth.

5

IN PROSE only less memorable than Lincoln's own, Carl Sandburg has written the epilogue to Gettysburg.

AFTER THE CEREMONIES at Gettysburg, Lincoln lunched with Governor Curtin, Mr. Everett, and others at the Wills home, held a reception that had not been planned, handshaking nearly an hour, looking gloomy and listless but brightening sometimes as a small boy or girl came in line, and stopping one tall man for remarks as to just how high up he reached. At five o'clock he attended a patriotic meeting in the Presbyterian church, walking arm-in-arm with old John Burns, and listening to an address by Lieutenant Governor-elect Anderson of Ohio. At six-thirty he was on the departing Washington train. In the dining car his secretary, John Hay, ate with Simon Cameron and Wayne MacVeagh. Hay had thought Cameron and MacVeagh hated each other, but he noted: "I was more than usually struck by the intimate jovial relations that existed between men that hate and detest each other as cordially as do the Pennsylvania politicians."

The ride to Washington took until midnight. Lincoln was weary, talked little, stretched out on one of the side seats in the drawing room and had a wet towel laid across his eyes and fore-head.

He had stood that day, the world's foremost spokesman of popular government, saying that democracy was yet worth fight-ing for. He had spoken as one in mist who might head on deeper yet into mist. He incarnated the assurances and pretenses of popular government, implied that it could and might perish from the earth. What he meant by "a new birth of freedom" for the nation could have a thousand interpretations. The taller riddles of democracy stood up out of the address. It had the dream touch of vast and furious events epitomized for any foreteller to read what was to come. He did not assume that the drafted soldiers, substitutes, and bounty-paid privates had died willingly under Lee's shot and shell, in deliberate consecration of themselves to the Union cause. His cadences sang the ancient song that where there is freedom men have fought and sacrificed for it, and that freedom is worth men's dying for. For the first time since he became Presi-dent he had on a dramatic occasion declaimed, howsoever it might be read, Jefferson's proposition which had been a slogan of the Revolutionary War—"All men are created equal"—leaving no other inference than that he regarded the Negro slave as a man. His outwardly smooth sentences were inside of them gnarled and tough with the enigmas of the American experiment.

Back at Gettysburg the blue haze of the Cumberland Moun-tains had dimmed till it was a blur in a nocturne. The moon was up and fell with a bland golden benevolence on the new-made graves of soldiers, on the sepulchers of old settlers, on the horse carcasses of which the onrush of war had not yet permitted removal. The *New York Herald* man walked amid them and ended the story he sent his paper: "The air, the trees, the graves are silent. Even the relic hunters are gone now. And the soldiers here never wake to the sound of reveille."

In many a country cottage over the land, a tall old clock in a quiet corner told time in a tick-tock deliberation. Whether the orchard branches hung with pink-spray blossoms or icicles of sleet, whether the outside news was seedtime or harvest, rain or drouth, births or deaths, the swing of the pendulum was right and left and right and left in a tick-tock deliberation.

The face and dial of the clock had known the eyes of a boy who listened to its tick-tock and learned to read its minute and hour hands. And the boy had seen years measured off by the swinging pendulum, and grown to man size, had gone away. And the people in the cottage knew that the clock would stand there and the boy never again come into the room and look at the clock with the query, "What is the time?"

In a row of graves of the Unidentified the boy would sleep long in the dedicated final resting place at Gettysburg. Why he had gone away and why he would never come back had roots in some mystery of flags and drums, of national fate in which individuals sink as in a deep sea, of men swallowed and vanished in a man-made storm of smoke and steel.

The mystery deepened and moved with ancient music and inviolable consolation because a solemn Man of Authority had stood at the graves of the Unidentified and spoken the words "We cannot consecrate—we cannot hallow—this ground. The brave men, living and dead, who struggled here, have consecrated it far above our poor power to add or detract. . . . From these honored dead we take increased devotion to that cause for which they gave the last full measure of devotion."

To the backward and forward pendulum swing of a tall old clock in a quiet corner they might read those cadenced words while outside the windows the first flurry of snow blew across the orchard and down over the meadow, the beginnings of winter in a gun-metal gloaming to be later arched with a star-flung sky.

CHAPTER TWENTY-ONE

Years of Victory

W HEN PICKETT'S CHARGE BROKE
against the steady Federal lines on Cemetery Ridge,
the final fate of the Confederacy was settled. But Gettysburg was only one of two simultaneous turning points.
The other, a thousand miles distant, came one day later.

For two years the Eastern theater of war, with Washington and Richmond the shining prizes of victory, had
almost monopolized the attention of the millions who were
watching the American struggle. But all the while, events
of far-reaching importance had been taking place in the
West. By moving into Missouri immediately after the out-
break of the war, the North had protected itself from attack. At the same time, Lincoln's masterly diplomacy kept
Kentucky from secession. Grant's capture of Fort Henry
and Fort Donelson early in 1862 pushed back the area occupied by the Confederacy, and Shiloh, bloody as it was,
parried a major threat. In ensuing months the Union
Navy cleared the Mississippi as far south as Vicksburg,
and Federal forces occupied New Orleans. By the spring
of 1863, only a short stretch of the Mississippi was in
Confederate hands. That, however, was of critical importance.

1

LORD CHARNWOOD TRACES the campaign which gave the
North another great victory to pair with Gettysburg.

V ICKSBURG . . . lies one hundred and seventy-five to one hundred and eighty miles south of Memphis. . . . At Vicksburg itself, and for some distance south of it, a line of bluffs or steep-sided hills lying east of the Mississippi comes right up to the edge of the river. The river as it approaches these bluffs makes a sudden bend to the northeast and then again to the southwest, so that two successive reaches of the stream, each from three to four miles long, were commanded by the Vicksburg guns, two hundred feet above the valley; the eastward or landward side of the fortress was also well situated for defense. To the north of Vicksburg the country on the east side of the Mississippi is cut up by innumerable streams and "bayous" or marshy creeks, winding and intersecting amid a dense growth of cedars. The North, with a flotilla under Admiral Porter, commanded the Mississippi itself, and the Northern forces could freely move along its western shore to the impregnable river face of Vicksburg beyond. But the question of how to get safely to the assailable side of Vicksburg presented formidable difficulty to Grant and to the government.

Grant's operations began in November, 1862. Advancing directly southward along the railway from Memphis with the bulk of his forces, he after a while detached Sherman with a force which proceeded down the Mississippi to the mouth of the Yazoo, a little northwest of Vicksburg. Here Sherman was to land, and, it was hoped, surprise the enemy at Vicksburg itself while the bulk of the enemy's forces were fully occupied by Grant's advance from the north. But Grant's lengthening communications were cut up by a cavalry raid, and he had to retreat, while Sherman came upon an enemy fully prepared and sustained a defeat a fortnight after Burnside's defeat at Fredericksburg. This was the first of a long series of failures. . . .

In the first three months of 1863, while the Army of the Potomac, shattered at Fredericksburg, was being prepared for the fresh attack upon Lee which ended at Chancellorsville, and while Bragg and Rosecrans lay confronting each other in middle Tennessee, each content that the other was afraid to weaken himself by sending troops to the Mississippi, Grant was occupied in a series of enterprises apparently more cautious than that in which he eventually succeeded, but each in its turn futile. An attempt was made to render Vicksburg useless by a canal cutting across the bend of the Mississippi to the west of that fortress. Then Grant endeavored, with the able co-operation of Admiral Porter and his flotilla, to secure a safe landing on the Yazoo, which enters the Mississippi a little above Vicksburg, so that he could move his army to the rear of Vicksburg by this route. Next, Grant and Porter tried to establish a sure line of water communication from a point far up the Mississippi through an old canal, then somehow obstructed, into the upper waters of the Yazoo and so to a point on that river thirty or forty miles to the northeast of Vicksburg, by which they would have turned the right of the main Confederate force; but this was frustrated by the Confederates, who succeeded in establishing a strong fort further up the Yazoo. Yet a further effort was made to establish a waterway by a canal quitting the Mississippi about forty miles north of Vicksburg and communicating, through lakes, bayous and smaller rivers, with its great tributary, the Red River, far to the south. This, like the first canal attempted, would have rendered Vicksburg useless.

Each of these projects failed in turn. The tedious engineering work which two of them involved was rendered more depressing by adverse conditions of weather and by ill-health among Grant's men. Natural grumbling among the troops was repeated and exaggerated in the North . . . It is melancholy to add that a good many newspapers at this time began to print statements that Grant had again taken to drink. It is certain that he was at this time a total abstainer. It is said that he had offended the authors of this villainy by the restrictions which he had long before found necessary to put upon information to the press. Some of the men freely confessed afterwards that they had been convinced of his sobriety, and added the marvelous apology that their business was to give the public "the news." Able and more honest journalists urged that Grant had proved his incompetence. Secretary Chase took up their complaints and pressed that Grant should be removed. Lincoln, before the outcry against Grant had risen to its height, had felt the need of closer information than he possessed about the situation on the Mississippi; and had hit upon the happy expedient of sending an able official of the War Department, who deserved and obtained the confidence of Grant and his officers, to accompany the Western army and report to him.

Apart, however, from the reports he thus received, he had always treated the attacks on Grant with contempt. . . . In reply to complaints that Grant drank, he inquired (adapting, as he knew, George II's famous saying about Wolfe) what whisky he drank, explaining that he wished to send barrels of it to some of his other generals. His attitude is remarkable, because in his own mind he had not thought well of any of Grant's plans after his first failure in December; he had himself wished from an early day that Grant would take the very course by which he ultimately succeeded. He let him go his own way, as he afterwards told him, from "a general hope that you know better than I."

At the end of March Grant took a memorable determination to transfer his whole force to the south of Vicksburg and approach it from that direction. He was urged by Sherman to give up any further attempt to use the river, and, instead, to bring his whole army back to Memphis and begin a necessarily slow approach on Vicksburg by the railway. He declared himself that on ordinary grounds of military prudence this would have been the proper course, but he decided for himself that the depressing effect of the retreat to Memphis would be politically disastrous. At Grand Gulf, thirty miles south of Vicksburg, the South possessed another fortified post on the river; to reach this Grant required the help of the navy, not only in crossing from the western bank of the river, but in transporting the supplies for which the roads west of the river were inadequate. Admiral Porter, with his gunboats and laden barges, successfully ran the gantlet of the Vicksburg batteries by night without serious damage. Grand Gulf was taken on May 3, and Grant's army established at this new base. . . . He had with him 35,000 men. General Pemberton, to whom he had so far been opposed, lay covering Vicksburg with 20,000 and a further force in the city; Joseph Johnston, whom he afterwards described as the Southern general who in all the war gave him most trouble, had been sent by Jefferson Davis to take supreme command in the West, and had collected 11,000 men at Jackson, the capital of Mississippi, forty-five miles east of Vicksburg. Grant was able to take his enemy in detail. Having broken up Johnston's force he defeated Pemberton in a series of battles. His victory at Champion's Hill on May 16, not a fortnight after Chancellorsville, conveyed to his mind the assurance that the North would win the war. An assault on Vicksburg failed with heavy loss. Pemberton was at last closely invested in Vicksburg, and Grant could establish safe communications with the North by way of the lower Yazoo and up the Mississippi above its mouth. There had been dissension between Pemberton and Johnston, who, seeing that gunboats proved able to pass Vicksburg in any case, thought that Pemberton, whom he could not at the moment hope to relieve, should abandon Vicksburg and try to save his army. Long before Johnston could be sufficiently reinforced to attack Grant, Grant's force had been raised to 71,000. On July 4, 1863 . . . Vicksburg was surrendered. Its garrison, which had suffered severely, was well victualled by Grant and allowed to go free on parole. Pemberton in his vexation treated Grant with peculiar insolence, which provoked a singular exhibition of the conqueror's good temper to him; and in his dispatches to the President, Grant mentioned nothing with greater pride than the absence of a word or a sign on the part of his men which could hurt the feelings of the fallen. Johnston was forced to abandon the town of Jackson, with its large stores, to Sherman, but could not be pursued in his retreat. On July 9, five days later, the defender of Port Hudson, invested shortly before by Banks, who had not force enough for an assault, heard the news of Vicksburg and surrendered. Lincoln could now boast to the North that "the Father of Waters again goes unvexed to the sea."

2

LINCOLN, elated by two major Union victories, believed that the war could be ended if Meade would strike Lee's army before its commander could get it across the Potomac. When Meade failed to follow up his advantage as Lincoln saw it, the President was as deeply perturbed as he ever was in four years that held many bitter disappointments. Gideon Welles pictures his dejection.

J U L Y 14, Tuesday. . . . The Cabinet meeting was not full today. Two or three of us were there when Stanton came in with some haste and asked to see the President alone. The two were absent about three minutes in the library. When they returned, the President's countenance indicated trouble and distress; Stanton was disturbed, disconcerted. Usher asked Stanton if he had bad news. He said, "No." Something was said of the report that Lee had crossed the river. Stanton said abruptly and curtly he knew nothing of Lee's crossing. "I do," said the President emphatically, with a look of painful rebuke to Stanton. "If he has not got all of his men across, he soon will."

The President said he did not believe we could take up anything in Cabinet today. Probably none of us were in a right frame of mind for deliberation; he was not. He wanted to see General Halleck at once. Stanton left abruptly. I retired slowly. The President hurried and overtook me. We walked together across the lawn to the Departments and stopped and conversed a few moments at the gate. He said, with a voice and countenance which I shall never forget, that he had dreaded yet expected this; that there has seemed to him for a full week a determination that Lee, though we had him in our hands, should escape with his force and plunder. "And that, my God, is the last of this Army of the Potomac! There is bad faith somewhere. Meade has been pressed and urged, but only one of his generals was for an immediate attack, was ready to pounce on Lee; the rest held back. What does it mean, Mr. Welles? Great God! what does it mean?" I asked what orders had gone from him while our troops had been quiet with a defeated and broken army in front, almost destitute of ammunition, and an impassable river to prevent their escape. He could not say that anything positive had been done, but both Stanton and Halleck professed to agree with him, and he thought Stanton did. Halleck was all the time wanting to hear from Meade. "Why," said I, "he is within four hours of Meade. Is it not strange that he has not been up there to advise and encourage him?" I stated I had observed the inertness, if not incapacity, of the General in Chief, and had hoped that he, who had better and more correct views, would issue peremptory orders. The President immediately softened his tone, and said: "Halleck knows better than I what to do. He is a military man, has had a military education. I brought him here to give me military advice. His views and mine are widely different. It is better that I, who am not a military man, should defer to him, rather than he to me." I told the President I did not profess to be a military man, but there were some things on which I could form perhaps as correct an opinion as

General Halleck, and I believed that he, the President, could more correctly, certainly more energetically, direct military movements than Halleck, who, it appeared to me, could originate nothing, and was, as now, all the time waiting to hear from Meade, or whoever was in command.

I can see that the shadows which have crossed my mind have clouded the President's also. On only one or two occasions have I ever seen the President so troubled, so dejected and discouraged.

3

IN THE FALL of 1863, while the armies in the East lay quiescent, Rosecrans, commanding the Union Army of the Cumberland, lost the Battle of Chickamauga to Bragg, retreated to Chattanooga, and had to be extricated by Grant, whose reputation was growing steadily. At the same time, as Lord Charnwood points out, Lincoln's confidence in his own military judgment was reaching fullness.

THE AUTUMN MONTHS of 1863 witnessed in the Middle West a varying conflict ending in a Northern victory hardly less memorable than those of Gettysburg and Vicksburg. At last, after the fall of Vicksburg, Rosecrans in middle Tennessee found himself ready to advance. By skillful maneuvers, in the difficult country where the Tennessee River cuts the Cumberland mountains and the parallel ranges which run from northeast to southwest behind, he turned the flank of Bragg's position at Chattanooga and compelled him to evacuate that town in the beginning of September. Bragg, as he retreated, succeeded in getting false reports as to his movements and the condition of his army conveyed to Rosecrans, who accordingly followed him up in an incautious manner. By this time the bulk of the forces that had been used against Vicksburg should have been brought to support Rosecrans. . . . For the Confederate authorities, eager to retrieve their losses, sent every available reinforcement to Bragg, and he was shortly able to turn back towards Chattanooga with over 71,000 men against the 57,000 with which Rosecrans, scattering his troops in false security, was pursuing him. The two armies came upon one another, without clear expectation, upon the Chickamauga Creek beyond the ridge which lies southeast of Chatta-

nooga. The battle, fought among the woods and hills by Chickamauga on September 19 and 20, surpassed any other in the war
in the heaviness of the loss on each side. On the second day Bragg's
maneuvers broke Rosecrans' line, and only an extraordinarily gallant stand by Thomas with a part of the line, in successive positions of retreat, prevented Bragg from turning the hasty retirement of the remainder into a disastrous rout. As it was, Rosecrans
made good his retreat to Chattanooga, but there he was in danger
of being completely cut off. A corps was promptly detached from
Meade in Virginia, placed under Hooker, and sent to relieve him.
Rosecrans, who in a situation of real difficulty seems to have had
no resourcefulness, was replaced in his command by Thomas.
Grant was appointed to supreme command of all the forces in the
West and ordered to Chattanooga. There, after many intricate
operations on either side, a great battle was eventually fought on
November 24 and 25, 1863. Grant had about 60,000 men; Bragg,
who had detached Longstreet for his vain attack on Burnside, had
only 33,000, but he had one steep and entrenched ridge behind
another on which to stand. The fight was marked by notable incidents—Hooker's "battle above the clouds"; and the impulse by
which, apparently with no word of command, Thomas's corps,
tired of waiting while Sherman advanced upon the one flank and
Hooker upon the other, arose and carried a ridge which the enemy
and Grant himself had regarded as impregnable. It ended in a
rout of the Confederates, which was energetically followed up.
Bragg's army was broken and driven right back into Georgia. To
sum up the events of the year, the one serious invasion of the
North by the South had failed, and the dominion on which the
Confederacy had any real hold was now restricted to the Atlantic
states, Alabama, and a part of the State of Mississippi.

At this point, at which the issue of the war, if it were only pursued, could not be doubted, and at which, as it happens, the need
of Lincoln's personal intervention in military matters became
greatly diminished, we may try to obtain a general impression of
his wisdom, or want of it, in such affairs. The closeness and keen
intelligence with which he followed the war is undoubted, but
could only be demonstrated by a lengthy accumulation of evidence. The larger strategy of the North, sound in the main, was
of course the product of more than one co-operating mind, but, as

his was undoubtedly the dominant will of his administration, so, too, it seems likely that, with his early and sustained grasp of the general problem, he contributed not a little to the clearness and consistency of the strategical plans. The amount of the forces raised was for long, as we shall see later, beyond his control, and, in the distribution of what he had to the best effect, his own want of knowledge and the poor judgment of his earlier advisers seem to have caused some errors. He started with the evident desire to put himself almost unreservedly in the hands of the competent military counsellors, and he was able in the end to do so; but for a long intermediate period, as we have seen, he was compelled as a responsible statesman to forego this wish. It was all that time his function, first, to pick out, with very little to go by, the best officers he could find, replacing them with better when he could; and, secondly, to give them just so much direction, and no more, as his wisdom at a distance and their more expert skill upon the spot made proper. In each of these respects his occasional mistakes are plain enough, but the evidence, upon which he has often been thought capable of setting aside sound military considerations causelessly or in obedience to interested pressure, breaks down when the facts of any imputed instance are known. It is manifest that he gained rapidly both in knowledge of the men he dealt with and in the firm kindness with which he treated them. It is remarkable that, with his ever-burning desire to see vigor and ability displayed, he could watch so constantly as he did for the precise opportunity or the urgent necessity before he made changes in command. It is equally remarkable that, with his decided and often right views as to what should be done, his advice was always offered with equal deference and plainness. "Quite possibly I was wrong both then and now," he once wrote to Hooker, "but in the great responsibility resting upon me, I cannot be entirely silent. Now, all I ask is that you will be in such mood that we can get into action the best cordial judgment of yourself and General Halleck, with my poor mite added, if indeed he and you shall think it entitled to any consideration at all." The man whose habitual attitude was this, and who yet could upon the instant take his own decision, may be presumed to have been wise in many cases where we do not know his reasons. Few statesmen, perhaps, have so often stood waiting and refrained themselves from a firm will

and not from the want of it, and for the sake of the rare moment
of action.

4

GRANT'S REWARD for victory at Chattanooga was promotion
and command of all the Union armies. Nicolay and Hay, after recall-
ing how the honor was deliberated before it was conferred, describe
the simple ceremonies which marked Grant's acceptance.

I MMEDIATELY AFTER THE VICTORIES at Chattanooga
Mr. Washburne, of Illinois, the devoted friend and firm supporter
of General Grant through good and evil report, introduced a bill
in Congress to revive the grade of Lieutenant General in the
army. The measure occasioned a good deal of discussion. This
high rank had never been conferred on any citizen of the Republic
except Washington, who held it for a short time before his death.
It was discontinued for more than half a century and then conferred by brevet only upon General Scott. There were those who
feared, or affected to fear, that so high military rank was threatening to the liberties of the Republic. The great majority of Congress, however, considered the liberties of the Republic more robust than this fear would indicate, and the bill was finally passed
on the twenty-sixth of February, and received the approval of
the President on the twenty-ninth of February. It provided for the
revival of the grade of Lieutenant General, and authorized the
President "to appoint, by and with the advice and consent of the
Senate, a lieutenant-general, to be selected from among those officers in the military service of the United States not below the
grade of major-general, most distinguished for courage, skill, and
ability, who, being commissioned as lieutenant-general, may be
authorized, under the direction and during the pleasure of the
President, to command the armies of the United States." Immediately upon signing the bill the President nominated Grant to the
Senate for the office created by it.

Although the bill, of course, mentioned the name of no general,
there was no pretense from the beginning that any one else was
thought of in connection with the place. The Administration exercised no influence in the matter, neither helping nor hindering the

progress of the bill through the Houses of Congress. It had already become clearly manifest that General Halleck, although an officer of great learning and ability, was not fitted by character or temperament for the assumption of such weighty responsibilities as the military situation required. The President himself said about this time: "When it appeared that McClellan was incompetent to the work of handling the army and we sent for Halleck to take command, he stipulated that it should be with the full powers and responsibilities of general-in-chief. He kept that attitude until Pope's defeat, but ever since that event he has shrunk from responsibility whenever it was possible." So that in the mind of the President, as well as in the intention of Congress and the acquiescence of the public, there was no thought of nominating any one but Grant to the chief command of all the armies. Whether he was or was not the ablest of all our generals is a question which can never be decided; perhaps there were legionaries in the Army of Gaul as able as Caesar if occasion had been given them to show it. The success and fame of generals is the joint result of merit and of opportunity; and Grant was, beyond all comparison, the most fortunate of American soldiers. Whatever criticism might be made on his character, his learning, or his methods, the fact was not to be denied that he had reaped the most substantial successes of the war; he had captured two armies and utterly defeated a third; he was justly entitled, by virtue of the *spolia opima* with which he had presented the Republic, to his triumph, to be celebrated with all the pomp and circumstance possible.

The Senate immediately confirmed his nomination, and on the third of March the Secretary of War directed him to report in person to the War Department as early as practicable, considering the condition of his command. . . .

Grant proceeded on his way to the Capital as quietly as possible, but the rumors of his coming went everywhere before him, and his train moved through a continual storm of cheering and enthusiasm from Nashville to Washington. He reached there on the evening of the eighth of March. There was to be a reception at the Executive Mansion and, as Grant's arrival was expected, the throng was very great. At about half past nine Grant entered, and he and the President met for the first time. A certain movement and rumor in the crowd heralded the approach of the most famous guest of the evening, and, when General Grant stood before Mr. Lincoln, they recognized each other without formal presentation and cordially shook hands. The thronging crowd, with instinctive deference, stood back for a moment, while the President and the General exchanged a few words of conversation. Lincoln then introduced Seward to Grant, and the Secretary of State took him away to present him to Mrs. Lincoln. He then went on to the East Room, where his presence excited a feeling which burst the bonds of etiquette, and cheer after cheer rose from the assembled crowd. Hot and blushing with embarrassment, he was forced to mount a sofa from which he could shake hands with the eager admirers who rushed upon him from all sides of the great room.

It was an hour before he could return to the small drawing room, where, after the departure of the crowd, the President awaited him. The President here made an appointment with him for the formal presentation next day of his commission as lieutenant general. "I shall make a very short speech to you," said Lincoln, "to which I desire you to reply, for an object; and that you may be properly prepared to do so I have written what I shall say, only four sentences in all, which I will read from my manuscript as an example which you may fellow and also read your reply—as you are perhaps not so much accustomed to public speaking as I am; and I therefore give you what I shall say so that you may consider it. There are two points that I would like to have you make in your answer: First, to say something which shall prevent or obviate any jealousy of you from any of the other generals in the service; and second, something which shall put you on as good terms as possible with the Army of the Potomac. If you see any objection to doing this, be under no restraint whatever in expressing that objection to the Secretary of War."

General Grant and Mr. Stanton left the room together. The next day, at one o'clock, in presence of the Cabinet, General Halleck, two members of Grant's staff, and the President's private secretary, the commission of lieutenant general was formally delivered by the President. Mr. Lincoln said: "General Grant, the nation's appreciation of what you have done, and its reliance upon you for what remains to do in the existing great struggle, are now presented, with this commission constituting you Lieutenant-General in the Army of the United States. With this high honor devolves upon you, also, a corresponding responsibility. As the country herein trusts you, so, under God, it will sustain you. I scarcely need to add that with what I here speak for the nation, goes my own hearty personal concurrence." The General had hurriedly and almost illegibly written his speech on half of a sheet of note paper in lead pencil. His embarrassment was evident and extreme; he found his own writing very difficult to read; but what he said could hardly have been improved: "Mr. President, I accept this commission with gratitude for the high honor conferred. With the aid of the noble armies that have fought on so many fields for our common country, it will be my earnest endeavor not to disappoint your expectations. I feel the full weight of the responsibilities now devolving on me; and I know that if they are met, it will be due to those armies, and above all to the favor of that Providence which leads both nations and men."

5

GIVEN FULL POWER, Grant moved at once to carry out the strategical conceptions which he had matured in three years of command. His plan was simple: the Union armies would attack on all fronts, and never let up the pressure until the opposing forces were destroyed. The plan is evident in John G. Nicolay's summary of the fighting in the East that followed.

THE UNION ARMY, under Grant, 122,000 strong, on April 30 was encamped north of the Rapidan River. The Confederate Army under Lee, numbering 62,000, lay south of that stream. Nearly three years before, these opposing armies had fought their first battle of Bull Run, only a comparatively short distance north of where they now confronted each other. Campaign and battle between them had surged far to the north and to the south, but neither could as yet claim over the other any considerable gain of ground or of final advantage in the conflict. Broadly speaking, relative advance and retreat, as well as relative loss and gain of battlefields substantially balanced each other. Severe as had been their struggles in the past, a more arduous trial of strength was before them. Grant had two to one in numbers; Lee, the advantage of a defensive campaign. He could retire toward cumulative reserves, and into prepared fortifications; knew almost by heart every road, hill, and forest of Virginia; had for his friendly scout every white inhabitant. Perhaps his greatest element of strength lay in the conscious pride of the Confederate Army that, through all fluctuations of success and failure, it had for three years effectually barred the way of the Army of the Potomac to Richmond. But to offset this there now menaced it what was before absent in every encounter, the grim, unflinching will of the new Union commander.

General Grant devised no plan of complicated strategy for the problem before him, but proposed to solve it by plain, hard, persistent fighting. He would endeavor to crush the army of Lee before it could reach Richmond or unite with the army of Johnston; or, failing in that, he would shut it up in that stronghold and reduce it by a siege. With this in view, he instructed Meade at the very outset: "Lee's army will be your objective point. Where Lee goes, there you will go, also." Everything being ready, on the night of May 4 Meade threw five bridges across the Rapidan, and before the following night the whole Union army, with its trains, was across the stream moving southward by the left flank, past the right flank of the Confederates.

Sudden as was the advance, it did not escape the vigilant observation of Lee, who instantly threw his force against the flanks of the Union columns, and for two days there raged in that difficult, broken, and tangled region known as the Wilderness, a furious battle of detachments along a line five miles in length. Thickets, swamps, and ravines, rendered intelligent direction and concerted maneuvering impossible, and furious and bloody as was the conflict, its results were indecisive. No enemy appearing on the seventh, Grant boldly started to Spottsylvania Court House, only, however, to find the Confederates ahead of him; and on the eighth and ninth these turned their position, already strong by nature, into an impregnable intrenched camp. Grant assaulted their works on the tenth, fiercely, but unsuccessfully. There followed one day of inactivity, during which Grant wrote his report, only claiming that after six days of hard fighting and heavy losses "the result up to this time is much in our favor"; but expressing, in the phrase which immediately became celebrated, his firm resolution to "fight it out on this line if it takes all summer."

On May 12, 1864, Grant ordered a yet more determined attack in which, with fearful carnage on both sides, the Union forces finally stormed the earthworks which have become known as the "bloody angle." But finding that other and more formidable intrenchments still resisted his entrance to the Confederate camp, Grant once more moved by the left flank past his enemy toward Richmond. Lee followed with equal swiftness along the interior lines. Days passed in an intermitting, and about equally matched, contest of strategy and fighting. The difference was that Grant was always advancing and Lee always retiring. On May 26, Grant reported to Washington:

"Lee's army is really whipped. The prisoners we now take show it, and the action of his army shows it unmistakably. A battle with them outside of intrenchments cannot be had. Our men feel that they have gained the *morale* over the enemy, and attack him with confidence. I may be mistaken, but I feel that our success over Lee's army is already assured."

That same night, Grant's advance crossed the Pamunkey River at Hanover Town, and, during another week, with a succession of marching, flanking, and fighting, Grant pushed the Union army forward to Cold Harbor. Here Lee's intrenched army was again between him and Richmond, and, on June 3, Grant ordered another determined attack in front, to break through that constantly resisting barrier. But a disastrous repulse was the consequence. Its effect upon the campaign is best given in Grant's own letter, written to Washington on June 5:

"My idea from the start has been to beat Lee's army, if possible, north of Richmond; then, after destroying his lines of communication on the north side of the James River, to transfer the army to the south side and besiege Lee in Richmond, or follow him south if he should retreat. I now find, after over thirty days of trial, the enemy deems it of the first importance to run no risks with the armies they now have. They act purely on the defensive behind breastworks, or feebly on the offensive immediately in front of them, and where, in case of repulse, they can instantly retire behind them. Without a greater sacrifice of human life than I am willing to make, all cannot be accomplished that I had designed outside of the city."

During the week succeeding the severe repulse at Cold Harbor, which closed what may be summed up as Grant's campaign against Richmond, he made his preparations to enter upon the second element of his general plan, which may be most distinctively denominated the siege of Petersburg, though, in fuller phraseology, it might be called the siege of Petersburg and Richmond combined. But the amplification is not essential; for though the operation and the siegeworks embraced both cities, Petersburg was the vital and vulnerable point. When Petersburg fell, Richmond fell of necessity. The reason was that Lee's army, inclosed within the combined fortifications, could only be fed by the use of three railroads centering at Petersburg; one from the southeast, one from the south, and one with general access from the southwest. Between these, two plank roads added a partial means of supply. Thus far, Grant's active campaign, though failing to destroy Lee's army, had nevertheless driven it into Richmond, and obviously his next step was either to dislodge it, or compel it to surrender.

Cold Harbor was about ten miles from Richmond, and that city was inclosed on the Washington side by two circles of fortifications devised with the best engineering skill. On June 13, Grant threw forward an army corps across the Chickahominy, deceiving Lee into the belief that he was making a real direct advance upon the city; and so skillfully concealed his intention that by midnight of the sixteenth he had moved the whole Union Army with its artillery and trains about twenty miles directly south and across the James River, on a pontoon bridge over two thousand feet long, to City Point. General Butler, with an expedition from Fortress Monroe, moving early in May, had been ordered to capture Petersburg; and, though he failed in this, he had nevertheless seized and held City Point, and Grant thus effected an immediate junction with Butler's force of 32,000. Butler's second attempt to seize Petersburg while Grant was marching to join him also failed, and Grant, unwilling to make any needless sacrifice, now limited his operations to the processes of a regular siege.

This involved a complete change of method. The campaign

against Richmond, from the crossing of the Rapidan and battle of the Wilderness, to Cold Harbor, and the change of base to City Point, occupied a period of about six weeks of almost constant swift marching and hard fighting. The siege of Petersburg was destined to involve more than nine months of mingled engineering and fighting. The Confederate Army forming the combined garrisons of Richmond and Petersburg numbered about 70,000. The army under Grant, though in its six weeks' campaign it had lost over 60,000 in killed, wounded, and missing, was again raised by the reinforcements sent to it, and by its junction with Butler, to a total of about 150,000. With this superiority of numbers, Grant pursued the policy of alternately threatening the defenses of Lee, sometimes south, sometimes north of the James River, and at every favorable opportunity pushing his siegeworks westward in order to gradually gain and command the three railroads and two plank roads that brought the bulk of absolutely necessary food and supplies to the Confederate armies and the inhabitants of Petersburg and Richmond. It is estimated that this gradual westward extension of Grant's lines, redoubts, and trenches, when added to those threatening Richmond and Petersburg on the east, finally reached a total development of about forty miles. The catastrophe came when Lee's army grew insufficient to man his defensive line along this entire length, and Grant, finding the weakened places, eventually broke through it, compelling the Confederate General and Army to evacuate and abandon both cities and seek safety in flight.

6

IN THE SUMMER of 1864, in an effort to shake off Grant's grip, Lee sent Jubal A. Early north to raid Washington. For the first and only time during the war, Lincoln was under fire. The narrative is Carl Sandburg's.

ONCE MORE GENERAL ROBERT E. LEE played a bold defensive game and struck fear into the heart of the Union cause. He gave Jubal A. Early and John C. Breckinridge an army of 20,000 men. Sheltered by the Blue Ridge Mountains, they marched up the Shenandoah Valley, slipped through a pass, headed for

Washington, and, only by a nod of fate as whimsical as a throw of dice, John C. Breckinridge failed to pay that visit he had in the spring of 1861 promised his kinswoman in the White House.

Early's men had legs and grit, could march thirty miles a day, and in their stride toward Washington their commander collected $20,000 cash at Hagerstown, and from Frederick City, Maryland, which he threatened to lay in ashes, came $200,000 more. The foot soldiers tore up twenty-four miles of Baltimore and Ohio Railroad tracks, wrecked and burned mills, workshops, factories, while Early's horsemen got as far as the environs of Baltimore and burned the home of Governor Bradford of Maryland. Turning their horses toward Washington, they reached Silver Spring, and in sight of the Capitol dome seized private papers, valuables, whisky, in the homes of Postmaster General Blair and Old Man Blair, and then set the houses afire.

"Baltimore is in great peril," telegraphed a mayor's committee to President Lincoln, asking for troops. From Philadelphia arrived a telegram that some "assuring announcement" must come from Washington to quiet the public mind. A Confederate army of 75,000 to 100,000 under Lee himself was again foot-loose and aiming for a strangle hold on Washington, ran another telegram that tumbled into Washington. Gustavus Vasa Fox, without the President's knowing it, had a steamer docked and ready for him in case the city was taken. In the Gold Room in New York, the wild-eyed gamblers saw gold on June 11 go to its peak price of 285. "The panic here is heavy and increasing," telegraphed Lew Wallace, department commander at Baltimore. "Do not think there is just cause for it." To the Baltimore mayor's committee Lincoln wired: "I have not a single soldier but whom is being disposed by the military for the best protection of all. By latest accounts the enemy is moving on Washington. They cannot fly to either place. Let us be vigilant, but keep cool. I hope neither Baltimore nor Washington will be sacked."

Wallace had marched troops out to Monocacy, fought a battle, and, heavily outnumbered, was routed. His defeat delayed Early's army one day. That one day, it was generally admitted, saved Washington from the disgrace of capture. At Point Lookout near by were 17,000 Confederate prisoners whom Lee hoped Early would free and arm. But Early didn't find time. Every hour counted. His objective, as he later told of it, was practically the same as reported by a Union prisoner, Artificer N. A. Fitts, who escaped from Early's men and informed the War Department, "They claimed the object of their raid was to get horses and provisions, that they did not expect to take Washington and hold it, but thought they could raid through the city and capture the President, if there, and draw Grant's forces from Petersburg."

Raw troops and soldiers just out of hospital made up the 20,-000 men scraped together for manning the forts around Washington against Early, who had cut all wires north and July 11 marched his men on the Seventh Street Road that would lead him straight to the offices, the arsenals, the gold and silver, of the United States Government. Early halted his men just a little over two miles from the Soldiers' Home, where Lincoln the night before had gone to bed when a squad from the War Department arrived with word from Stanton that he must get back into the city in a hurry. The President put on his clothes and rode tб the Executive Mansion.

The next day would decide whether a Confederate flag was for once to be run up over the Capitol dome. The next day the President looked from the south windows of the White House and saw through a glass transport steamers at Alexandria coming to unload two magnificent divisions of veteran troops fresh from Grant at City Point. The President met them at the wharf, touched his hat to them, and they cheered and he waved his hand and smiled and they sent up more and more cheers.

Out on the Seventh Street Road the same day Jubal Early sat his horse and looked at Fort Stevens (later Stephens), which blocked his path. The fort was "feebly manned," as he saw it. And he was correct. But, while he was still gazing, and while the attack he had ordered was getting under way, his eye caught a column of men in blue filing into the works. The fort guns began speaking. A line of skirmishers strung out in front. On one of the parapets Lincoln was a watcher and saw the first shots traded. He was too tall a target, said officers, who insisted till he put himself below the danger line.

Early stopped his attack, sent his cavalry to hunt another door into the city. That night, while Early held a council of war just north of Washington, more newly arrived troops at the south stepped off transports and tramped through the streets with a certainty that the Capitol dome the next day would be saved from a Confederate flag over it. The sun was throwing long slants of gold over that dome the next morning as Jubal Early looked at it and wondered what this day of July 12 would bring.

No mail, no telegrams, arrived from the outer world that day of July 12 in Washington. At a noon Cabinet meeting the President was signing a batch of commissions. "The President," wrote Welles, "said he and Seward had visited several of the fortifications. I asked where the Rebels were in force. He said he did not know with certainty, but he thought the main body at Silver Spring. I expressed a doubt whether there was any large force at any one point, but that they were in squads of from 500 to perhaps 1,500 scattered along . . . the Potomac. . . . The President did not respond farther than to again remark he thought there must be a pretty large force in the neighborhood of Silver Spring."

From where Lincoln stood on a Fort Stevens rampart that afternoon, he could see the swaying skirmish lines and later the marching brigade of General Daniel Davidson Bidwell, a police justice from Buffalo, New York, who had enlisted in 1861 as a private, was a colonel through the Seven Days' Battles and Malvern Hill, and with his men had heard the bullets sing from Antietam through Gettysburg and the Wilderness. Out across parched fields, dust, and a haze of summer heat, marched Bidwell's men in perfect order to drive the enemy from a house and orchard near the Silver Spring Road. Up a rise of ground in the face of a withering fire, they moved and took their point and pushed the enemy pickets back for a mile. The cost was 280 men killed and wounded.

For the first time in his life Abraham Lincoln saw men in battle action go to their knees and sprawl on the earth with cold lead in their vitals, with holes plowed by metal through their heads. Before this day he had seen them marching away, cheering and laughing, and he had seen them return in ambulances, and had met them on crutches and in slings and casts; and in hospitals he had held their hands and talked with them. Now for the first time he saw them as the rain of enemy rifle shots picked them off.

While he stood watching this bloody drama, a bullet whizzed

five feet from him, was deflected, and struck Surgeon Crawford of the one hundred and second Pennsylvania in the ankle. While he yet stood there, within three feet of the President, an officer fell with a death wound. Those who were there that afternoon said he was cool and thoughtful, seemed unconscious of danger, and looked like a Commander in Chief.

In officially reporting the afternoon's losses at 300, Halleck wrote that "a few men in the trenches were picked off by rebel sharpshooters." The fire of those who came near picking off Lincoln was at long range, it would seem from the report of a chief of staff, who suggested to Major General Augur, in command, the driving away of "a thin line of the enemy (not more than 500), who occupy a crest and house near our line and 1,100 yards only from Fort Stevens," the special object being "to put them out of a large house occupied by sharpshooters." So it was probable the men 1,100 yards away were shooting that day at a man, any man on a rampart or in a trench who made a good target, though they would concede that a man six feet four in height was a shade the easier to draw a bead on. Twice they nearly got the tall man. "Amid the whizzing bullets," wrote Nicolay and Hay, the President held to his place "with . . . grave and passive countenance," till finally "General Wright peremptorily represented to him the needless risk he was running."

7

WHILE GRANT, with the Army of the Potomac, smashed relentlessly at Lee, Sherman began in the West the forward movement that finally brought the South to its last extremity. John G. Nicolay's chronicle covers the main events of one of the most remarkable campaigns in all history.

WHILE GRANT was making his marches, fighting his battles, and carrying on his siege operations in Virginia, Sherman in the West was performing the task assigned to him by his chief, to pursue, destroy, or capture the principal western Confederate army, now commanded by General Johnston. The forces which, under Bragg, had been defeated in the previous autumn at Lookout

Mountain and Missionary Ridge, had halted as soon as pursuit ceased, and remained in winter quarters at and about Dalton, only twenty-eight or thirty miles on the railroad southeast of Chattanooga, where their new commander, Johnston, had, in the spring of 1864, about 68,000 men with which to oppose the Union advance. . . .

Sherman prepared himself by uniting at Chattanooga the best material of the three Union armies, that of the Cumberland, that of the Tennessee, and that of the Ohio, forming a force of nearly 100,000 men with 254 guns. They were seasoned veterans, whom three years of campaigning had taught how to endure every privation and avail themselves of every resource. They were provided with every essential supply, but carried with them not a pound of useless baggage or impedimenta that could retard the rapidity of their movements.

Sherman had received no specific instructions from Grant, except to fight the enemy and damage the war resources of the South; but the situation before him clearly indicated the city of Atlanta, Georgia, as his first objective, and as his necessary route, the railroad leading there from Chattanooga. It was obviously a difficult line of approach, for it traversed a belt of the Alleghanies forty miles in width, and, in addition to the natural obstacles they presented, the Confederate commander, anticipating his movement, had prepared elaborate defensive works at the several most available points.

As agreed upon with Grant, Sherman began his march on May 5, 1864, the day following that on which Grant entered upon his Wilderness campaign in Virginia. These pages do not afford space to describe his progress. It is enough to say that with his double numbers he pursued the policy of making strong demonstrations in front, with effective flank movements to threaten the railroad in the Confederate rear, by which means he forced back the enemy successively from point to point, until by the middle of July he was in the vicinity of Atlanta, having during his advance made only one serious front attack, in which he met a costly repulse. His progress was by no means one of mere strategical maneuver. Sherman says that during the month of May, across nearly one hundred miles of as difficult country as was ever fought over by civilized armies, the fighting was continuous, almost daily, among trees and bushes, on ground where one could rarely see one hundred yards ahead.

However skillful and meritorious may have been the retreat into which Johnston had been forced, it was so unwelcome to the Richmond authorities and damaging to the Confederate cause that, about the middle of July, Jefferson Davis relieved him, and appointed one of his corps commanders, General J. B. Hood, in his place; his personal qualities and free criticism of his superior led them to expect a change from a defensive to an aggressive campaign. Responding to this expectation, Hood almost immediately took the offensive, and made vigorous attacks on the Union positions, but met disastrous repulse, and found himself fully occupied in guarding the defenses of Atlanta. For some weeks each army tried ineffectual methods to seize the other's railroad communications. But, toward the end of August, Sherman's flank movements gained such a hold of the Macon railroad at Jonesboro, twenty-five miles south of Atlanta, as to endanger Hood's security; and when, in addition, a detachment sent to dislodge Sherman was defeated, Hood had no alternative but to order an evacuation. On September 3, Sherman telegraphed to Washington:

"Atlanta is ours, and fairly won. . . . Since May 5 we have been in one constant battle or skirmish, and need rest." . . .

Up to his occupation of Atlanta, Sherman's further plans had neither been arranged by Grant nor determined by himself, and for a while remained somewhat undecided. For the time being, he was perfectly secure in the new stronghold he had captured and completed. But his supplies depended upon a line of about 120 miles of railroad from Atlanta to Chattanooga, and very near 150 miles more from Chattanooga to Nashville. Hood, held at bay at Lovejoy's Station, was not strong enough to venture a direct attack or undertake a siege, but chose the more feasible policy of operating systematically against Sherman's long line of communications. In the course of some weeks both sides grew weary of the mere waste of time and military strength consumed in attacking and defending railroad stations, and interrupting and re-establishing the regularities of provision trains. Toward the end of

September, Jefferson Davis visited Hood, and, in rearranging some army assignments, united Hood's and an adjoining Confederate department under the command of Beauregard, partly with a view to adding the counsels of the latter to the always energetic and bold, but sometimes rash, military judgment of Hood.

Between these two, Hood's eccentric and futile operations against Sherman's communications were gradually shaded off into a plan for a Confederate invasion of Tennessee. Sherman, on his part, finally matured his judgment that instead of losing 1,000 men a month merely defending the railroad, without other advantage, he would divide his army, send back a portion of it under the command of General Thomas to defend the State of Tennessee against the impending invasion, and, abandoning the whole line of railroad from Chattanooga to Atlanta and cutting entirely loose from his base of supplies, march with the remainder to the sea, living upon the country, and "making the interior of Georgia feel the weight of war." Grant did not immediately fall in with Sherman's suggestion; and Sherman prudently waited until the Confederate plan of invading Tennessee became further developed. It turned out as he hoped and expected. Having gradually ceased his raids upon the railroad, Hood, by the end of October, moved westward to Tuscumbia on the Tennessee River, where he gathered an army of about 35,000, to which a cavalry force under Forrest of 10,000 more was soon added.

Under Beauregard's orders to assume the offensive, he began a rapid march northward, and, for a time, with a promise of cutting off some advanced Union detachments. We need not follow the fortunes of this campaign further than to state that the Confederate invasion of Tennessee ended in a disastrous failure. It was severely checked at the battle of Franklin on November 30; and when, in spite of this reverse, Hood pushed forward and set his army down before Nashville, as if for attack or siege, the Union army, concentrated and reinforced to about 55,000, was ready. A severe storm of rain and sleet held the confronting armies in forced immobility for a week; but, on the morning of December 15, 1864, General Thomas moved forward to an attack in which, on that and the following day, he inflicted so terrible a defeat upon his adversary that the Confederate Army not only retreated in rout and panic, but soon literally went to pieces in disorganization and disappeared as a military entity from the western conflict.

Long before this, Sherman had started on his famous march to the sea. His explanations to Grant were so convincing that the General in Chief on November 2 telegraphed him: "Go on as you propose." In anticipation of this permission, he had been preparing himself ever since Hood left him a clear path by starting westward on his campaign of invasion. From Atlanta, he sent back his sick and wounded and surplus stores to Chattanooga, withdrew the garrisons, burned the bridges, broke up the railroad, and destroyed the mills, foundries, shops and public buildings in Atlanta. With 60,000 of his best soldiers, and 65 guns, he started on November 15 on his march of 300 miles to the Atlantic. They carried with them 20 days' supplies of provisions, 5 days' supply of forage, and 200 rounds of ammunition, of which each man carried 40 rounds.

With perfect confidence in their leader, with perfect trust in each others' valor, endurance and good comradeship, in the fine weather of the Southern autumn, and singing the inspiring melody of "John Brown's Body," Sherman's army began its "marching through Georgia" as gaily as if it were starting on a holiday. And, indeed, it may almost be said such was their experience, in comparison with the hardships of war which many of these veterans had seen in their varied campaigning. They marched as nearly as might be in four parallel columns abreast, making an average of about fifteen miles a day. Kilpatrick's admirable cavalry kept their front and flanks free from the improvised militia and irregular troopers of the enemy. Carefully organized foraging parties brought in their daily supply of miscellaneous provisions—corn, meat, poultry, and sweet potatoes, of which the season had yielded an abundant harvest along their route.

The Confederate authorities issued excited proclamations and orders, calling on the people to "fly to arms," and to "assail the invader in front, flank, and rear, by night and by day." But no rising occurred that in any way checked the constant progress of the march. The Southern whites were, of course, silent and sullen, but the Negroes received the Yankees with demonstrations of welcome and good will, and in spite of Sherman's efforts, followed in such numbers as to embarrass his progress. As he proceeded, he destroyed the railroads by filling up cuts, burning ties, heating the rails red-hot, and twisting them around trees and into irreparable spirals. Threatening the principal cities to the right and left, he marched skillfully between and past them.

He reached the outer defenses of Savannah on December 10, easily driving before him about 10,000 of the enemy. On December 13, he stormed Fort McAllister, and communicated with the Union fleet through Ossabaw Sound, reporting to Washington that his march had been most agreeable, that he had not lost a wagon on the trip, that he had utterly destroyed over 200 miles of rails, and consumed stores and provisions that were essential to Lee's and Hood's armies. With pardonable exultation General Sherman telegraphed to President Lincoln on December 22:

"I beg to present to you as a Christmas gift the city of Savannah, with one hundred and fifty heavy guns and plenty of ammunition. Also about twenty-five thousand bales of cotton."

He had reason to be gratified with the warm acknowledgment which President Lincoln wrote him in the following letter:

"My Dear General Sherman: Many, many thanks for your Christmas gift, the capture of Savannah. When you were about leaving Atlanta for the Atlantic coast I was anxious, if not fearful; but feeling that you were the better judge, and remembering that 'nothing risked, nothing gained,' I did not interfere. Now, the undertaking being a success, the honor is all yours, for I believe none of us went farther than to acquiesce. And taking the work of General Thomas into the count, as it should be taken, it is, indeed, a great success. Not only does it afford the obvious and immediate military advantages, but in showing to the world that your army could be divided, putting the stronger part to an important new service, and yet leaving enough to vanquish the old opposing force of the whole—Hood's army—it brings those who sat in darkness to see a great light. But what next? I suppose it will be safe if I leave General Grant and yourself to decide. Please make my grateful acknowledgments to your whole army, officers and men."

CHAPTER TWENTY-TWO

The Second Election

WHILE GRANT AND MEADE *in the East drove forward slowly but relentlessly, while Sherman, with tactical brilliance rarely equalled, moved steadily towards Atlanta, Lincoln's first term neared its end. Politics, therefore, claimed a large share of public interest in the spring and summer of 1864.*

Politically, the course of the Administration had been anything but smooth. The military reverses of 1862, coupled with widespread disapproval of the Proclamation of Emancipation, had caused heavy Republican losses in the Congressional and state elections of that year. Typical of the trend was the result in Lincoln's own Congressional district, where John T. Stuart, his first law partner, now a political opponent, decisively defeated Leonard Swett, who ran as an Administration candidate.

By 1862, moreover, the factional cleavage in the party, exemplified at the beginning of the Administration by the rivalry between Seward and Chase, had become deep and sharp. As time went on, the radicals gained both in the cohesion and in the boldness of their opposition to Lincoln. Military failures — Fredericksburg, Chancellorsville, Lee's escape after Gettysburg — fanned popular discontent. The heavy casualties of Grant's drive towards Richmond threw an even darker cloud over Republican prospects.

But the opposition to Lincoln, extensive as it was, remained inept and unorganized. For a time it appeared that Chase might rally the discontented — even though a Cabinet member, he had carefully furthered his own Presi-

dential aspirations—but his candidacy, launched by his
friends early in 1864, speedily collapsed. The Administra-
tion, on the other hand, controlled the party machinery.
So smoothly was this manipulated that by the time the
convention was ready to meet—at Baltimore, on June 7
—Lincoln's nomination was a certainty.

1

NOAH BROOKS PORTRAYS Lincoln's second nomination.

THE MOST TERRIFIC CONTESTS were made when sundry
well-meaning persons were almost ready to fly at one another's
throats in their anxiety to have the honor of nominating Abraham
Lincoln for the presidency. As one sat on the platform, looking
over the tempest-tossed assemblage, watching with amusement the
frantic efforts of a score of men to climb over one another's heads,
as it were, and snatch for themselves this inestimable privilege, one
could not help thinking of the frequently repeated assertion of
certain small politicians that Lincoln could not possibly be nominated by that convention. The most conspicuous claimants for the
honor of naming Lincoln were Simon Cameron, of Pennsylvania,
Governor Stone, of Iowa, B. C. Cook, of Illinois, and Thompson
Campbell, of California. The last-named gentleman, who had
known Lincoln intimately during his young manhood in Springfield, Illinois, was especially desirous that he might be permitted
to speak for Illinois, California, and his own native state, Kentucky. This had been virtually agreed upon, but, before he could
secure the floor, Simon Cameron got in ahead of him and sent up
to the clerk's desk a written resolution which he demanded should
be read. When the clerk opened the paper and read its contents, it
was found that the resolution demanded the renomination of Abraham Lincoln, of Illinois, and Hannibal Hamlin, of Maine. No
sooner had the clerk finished reading the resolution than a frightful clamor shook the hall. Almost every delegate was on his feet
objecting or hurrahing or in other ways making his emotions and
his wishes known in stentorian tones. For a few minutes pandemonium reigned, and in the midst of it Cameron stood with his
arms folded, grimly smiling, regarding with composure the storm

that he had raised. After the turmoil had spent itself, Henry J. Raymond, of New York, in an incisive, clear-cut speech, advocated making nominations by a call of states. He urged that, as entire unanimity in the choice of the Presidential candidate was expected, the moral effect would be better if no noisy acclamation were made, which would give slanderers an opportunity to say that the nomination was rushed through by the overwhelming of all opposition, however small. Before the applause which followed the adoption of Raymond's resolution had entirely subsided, B. C. Cook, of Illinois, mounted a settee and cried: "Illinois once more presents to the nation the name of Abraham Lincoln—God bless him!" Another roar of applause swept through the theater, and Stone, of Iowa, succeeded in gaining his point by seconding Cook's nomination; but Thompson Campbell, of California, who had been unfairly deprived of his coveted privilege of making the nomination, leaped upon a settee and addressed the chair. He was constantly interrupted with catcalls and cries of "No speeches," "Get down," "Dry up," and "Call the roll," etc. In the midst of the confusion, however, Campbell, who was a tall, spare man with a saturnine visage and tremendous lung power, kept on speaking in dumb show, wildly gesticulating, not a word of his speech being audible. Campbell was evidently beside himself with rage and disappointment; but those nearest him finally succeeded in coaxing him off his perch, and he sat down, sullen with anger.

That was a business convention, and, when the roll call began, Maine simply announced its sixteen votes for Abraham Lincoln. New Hampshire, coming next, attempted to ring in a little speech with its vote, but was summarily choked off with cries of "No speeches," and the call proceeded in an orderly manner, no delegation venturing to make any other announcement than that of its vote. The convention struck a snag when Missouri was reached and the chairman of the united delegations made a brief speech in which he said that the radical delegation was under positive instructions to cast its twenty-two votes for U. S. Grant; that he and his associates would support any nominee of the convention, but they must obey orders from home. This caused a sensation, and growls of disapproval arose from all parts of the convention; for it was evident that this unfortunate complication might prevent a unanimous vote for Lincoln. The Missouri radical delegates, it should be understood, had been chosen many weeks before the nomination of Lincoln became inevitable. There never was any recall of the instructions given at a time when it was apparently among the possibilities that another than Lincoln might be the nominee of the National Convention. When the clerk of the convention announced the result of the roll call, it was found that Abraham Lincoln had 507 votes and U. S. Grant 22 votes. Thereupon Mr. Hume, chairman of the Missouri delegation, immediately moved that the nomination be declared unanimous. This was done. Straightway, the long pent-up enthusiasm burst forth in a scene of the wildest confusion. Men hurrahed, embraced one another, threw up their hats, danced in the aisles or on the platform, jumped on the benches, waved flags, yelled, and committed every possible extravagance to demonstrate the exuberance of their joy. One of the most comical sights which I beheld was that of Horace Maynard and Henry J. Raymond alternately hugging each other and shaking hands, apparently unable to utter a word, so full of emotion were they. And when the big brass band burst out with "Hail Columbia" the racket was so intolerable that I involuntarily looked up to see if the roof of the theater were not lifted by the volume of sound. When quiet was restored and other business was about to. be resumed, the band struck up "Yankee Doodle" in its liveliest manner and another torrent of enthusiasm broke forth; and it was a long time before the excited and jubilant assemblage could be quieted down and order restored.

2

THE CONVENTION which renominated Lincoln was not, strictly speaking, a Republican convention. In an effort to attract War Democrats, the party had taken the name of Union party. John G. Nicolay, in Baltimore as Lincoln's personal representative, reveals how the party lived up to its new name, and strengthened the President's candidacy, by nominating a War Democrat for Vice-President.

FOR SEVERAL DAYS before the convention met, Mr. Lincoln had been besieged by inquiries as to his personal wishes in regard to his associate on the ticket. He had persistently refused to give the slightest intimation of such wish. His private secretary, Mr. Nicolay, who was at Baltimore in attendance at the convention, was well acquainted with this attitude; but at last, overborne by the solicitations of the chairman of the Illinois delegation, who had been perplexed at the advocacy of Joseph Holt by Leonard Swett, one of the President's most intimate friends, Mr. Nicolay wrote to Mr. Hay, who had been left in charge of the Executive Office in his absence:

"Cook wants to know, confidentially, whether Swett is all right; whether in urging Holt for Vice-President he reflects the President's wishes; whether the President has any preference, either personal or on the score of policy; or whether he wishes not even to interfere by a confidential intimation. . . . Please get this information for me, if possible."

The letter was shown to the President, who indorsed upon it:

"Swett is unquestionably all right. Mr. Holt is a good man, but I had not heard or thought of him for V. P. Wish not to interfere about V. P. Cannot interfere about platform. Convention must judge for itself."

This positive and final instruction was sent at once to Mr. Nicolay, and by him communicated to the President's most intimate friends in the convention. It was therefore with minds absolutely untrammeled by even any knowledge of the President's wishes that the convention went about its work of selecting his associate on the ticket. It is altogether probable that the ticket of 1860 would have been nominated without a contest had it not been for the general impression, in and out of the convention, that it would be advisable to select as a candidate for the vice-presidency a War Democrat. Mr. Dickinson, while not putting himself forward as a candidate, had sanctioned the use of his name on the special ground that his candidacy might attract to the support of the Union party many Democrats who would have been unwilling to support a ticket avowedly Republican; but these considerations weighed with still greater force in favor of Mr. Johnson, who was not only a Democrat, but also a citizen of a slave State. The first ballot showed that Mr. Johnson had received 200 votes, Mr. Hamlin, 150, and Mr. Dickinson, 108; and before the result was announced almost the whole convention turned their votes to Johnson; whereupon his nomination was declared unanimous. The work was so quickly done that Mr. Lincoln received notice of the action of the convention only a few minutes after the telegram announcing his own renomination had reached him.

3

TO WIN A NOMINATION without opposition was one thing; to carry the election was another. A week before the Baltimore convention, Radical die-hards met at Cleveland and nominated John C. Fremont as their presidential canidate. The Democrats waited until the end of August, and then chose George B. McClellan, with George H. Pendleton, of Ohio, as his running mate, to oppose Lincoln and Johnson. By that time the defeat of the Administration looked like a certainty. Grant's losses, in the spring and summer, had been terrific; now, in the trenches before Petersburg, he was at a standstill. In the West, Sherman had cut his way through Tennessee and northwestern Georgia, but his objective—Atlanta—still held out. So pessimistic were the Republicans that a number of party leaders actually made plans to force Lincoln to withdraw in favor of another candidate.

Then, almost overnight, the situation changed. Atlanta fell on September 1, and over the North despondency gave way to hope. Maine and Vermont, voting in September, turned in good Republican majorities. On September 22, Fremont withdrew as a candidate. All signs pointed to victory. But it was not until October 11, when Pennsylvania, Ohio, and Indiana held their state elections, that the result in November was forecast with certainty. John Hay describes how Lincoln received the election returns from the three "October states."

O CTOBER 11. At eight o'clock the President went over to the War Department to watch for dispatches. I went with him. We found the building in a state of preparation for siege. Stanton had locked the doors and taken the keys upstairs so that it was impossible even to send a card to him. A shivering messenger was pacing to and fro in the moonlight over the withered leaves; catching sight of the President, he took us around by the Navy Department and conducted us into the War Office by a side door.

The first dispatch we received contained the welcome intelligence of the election of Eggleston and Hays in the Cincinnati districts. This was from Stager, at Cleveland, who also promised considerable gains in Indiana, made good a few minutes after by a statement of 400 gain in Noble County. Then came in a dispatch from Sandford, stating we had 2,500 in the city of Philadelphia and that leading Democrats had given up the State. Then Shallabarger was seen to be crowding Sam Cox very hard in the Columbus district, in some places increasing Brough's colossal vote of last year.

The President, in a lull of dispatches, took from his pocket the *Nasby Papers* and read several chapters of the experiences of the saint and martyr, Petroleum V. They were immensely amusing. Stanton and Dana enjoyed them scarcely less than the President, who read on, *con amore,* until nine o'clock. At this time I went to Seward's to keep my engagement. I found there Banks and his wife, Colonels Clark and Wilson, Asta Burnaga and Madame, the New Orleans people, and a young Briton, who was nephew to the Earl of Dorset, somebody said, and would like to enter our army before we finish this thing up. Dennison was also there. We broke up very early. Dennison and I went back to the Department.

We found the good Indiana news had become better and the Pennsylvania had begun to be streaked with lean. Before long the dispatches announced with some certainty of tone that Morton was elected by a safe working majority. The scattering reports from Pennsylvania showed about equal gains and losses. But the estimates and flyers all claimed gains on the Congressmen. A dispatch from Puleston says, "We have gained 4 or five or even 6 Cong^m. I am going to New York to sleep a few days." Not a word came from any authorized source. Cameron and the State Committee silent as the grave. It was suggested that Cameron had gone home to Harrisburg to vote. It looked a little ominous, his silence. The President telegraphed to him but got no answer.

Reports began to come in from the hospitals and camps in the vicinity, the Ohio troops about ten to one for Union and the Pennsylvanians less than three to one. Carver Hospital, by which Stanton and Lincoln pass every day on their way to the country, gave the heaviest opposition vote—about one out of three. Lincoln says, "That's hard on us, Stanton—they know us better than the others." Co. K, 150 P.V., the President's personal escort, voted 63 to 11 Union.

An enthusiastic dispatch announcing 30,000 for Morton came in, signed McKim. "Who is that?" "A quartermaster of mine," he added, "a very healthy sentiment is growing up among the quartermasters. Allen is attending all the Republican meetings, so is Myers. A nephew of Brough's that I placed at Louisville and made a Colonel, I reduced to a Captain and ordered him South the other day. He was caught betting against Morton." A murmur of adhesion filled the apartment.

I suggested to the Secretary what Dorsheimer had told me about Dandy's regiment being all for McClellan. I added that Dandy wanted promotion. "He will get it," said the Secretary, puffing a long blue spiral wreath of smoke from his stern lips. Colonel Dandy's dream of stars passed away in that smoke. . . .

I am deeply thankful for the result in Indiana. I believe it saves Illinois in November. I believe it rescues Indiana from sedition and civil war. A Copperhead governor would have afforded a grand central rallying point for that lurking treason whose existence Carrington has already so clearly demonstrated, which, growing bolder by the popular seal and sanction, would have dared to lift its head from the dust and measure strength with the government. The defection of the executive governments of those two great States, Illinois and Indiana, from the general Administration would have been disastrous and paralyzing. I should have been willing to sacrifice something in Pennsylvania to avert that calamity. I said as much to the President. He said he was anxious about Pennsylvania because of her enormous weight and influence which, cast definitely into the scale, would close the campaign and leave the people free to look again with their whole hearts to the cause of the country.

4

A MONTH LATER Lincoln sat at the telegraph and heard the promise of October fulfilled. Again the picture is John Hay's.

N o v e m b e r 8. The house has been still and almost deserted today. Everybody in Washington, not at home voting, seems ashamed of it and stays away from the President.

I was talking with him today. He said, "It is a little singular that I, who am not a vindictive man, should have always been before the people for election in canvasses marked for their bitterness; always but once: when I came to Congress it was a quiet time. But always besides that the contests in which I have been prominent have been marked with great rancor. . . ."

During the afternoon few dispatches were received.

At night, at seven o'clock we started over to the War Department to spend the evening. Just as we started we received the first gun from Indianapolis, showing a majority of 8,000 there, a gain of 1,500 over Morton's vote. The vote itself seemed an enormous one for a town of that size and can only be accounted for by considering the great influx since the war of voting men from the country into the state centers where a great deal of army business is done. There was less significance in this vote on account of the October victory which had disheartened the enemy and destroyed their incentive to work.

The night was rainy, steamy, and dark. We splashed through the grounds to the side door of the War Department where a soaked and smoking sentinel was standing in his own vapor with his huddled-up frame covered with a rubber cloak. Inside a half dozen idle orderlies, upstairs the clerks of the telegraph. As the President entered they handed him a dispatch from Forney claiming a 10,000 Union majority in Philadelphia. "Forney is a little excitable." Another comes from Felton, Baltimore, giving us "15,000 in the city, 5,000 in the state. All Hail, Free Maryland." That is superb. A message from Rice to Fox, followed instantly by one from Sumner to Lincoln, claiming Boston by 5,000, and Rice's and Hooper's elections by majorities of 4,000 apiece. A magnificent advance on the chilly dozens of 1862.

Eckert came in, shaking the rain from his cloak, with trousers very disreputably muddy. We sternly demanded an explanation. He had slipped, he said, and tumbled prone, crossing the street. He had done it watching a fellow being ahead and chuckling at his uncertain footing. Which reminded the Tycoon, of course. The President said, "For such an awkward fellow, I am pretty surefooted. It used to take a pretty dextrous man to throw me. I remember, the evening of the day in 1858 that decided the contest for the Senate between Mr. Douglas and myself was something like this, dark, rainy, and gloomy. I had been reading the returns, and had ascertained that we had lost the Legislature and started to go home. The path had been worn hog-back and was slippery. My foot slipped from under me, knocking the other one out of the way, but I recovered myself and lit square, and I said to myself, 'It's a slip and not a fall.' "

The President sent over the first fruits to Mrs. Lincoln. He said, "She is more anxious than I."

We went into the Secretary's room. Mr. Welles and Fox soon came in. They were especially happy over the election of Rice, regarding it as a great triumph for the Navy Department. Says Fox, "There are two fellows that have been especially malignant to us, and retribution has come upon them both, Hale and Winter Davis." "You have more of that feeling of personal resentment than I," said Lincoln. "Perhaps I may have too little of it, but I never thought it paid. A man has not time to spend half his life in quarrels. If any man ceases to attack me, I never remember the past against him. It has seemed to me recently that Winter Davis was growing more sensible to his own true interests and has ceased wasting his time by attacking me. I hope for his own good he has. He has been very malicious against me but has only injured himself by it. His conduct has been very strange to me. I came here, his friend, wishing to continue so. I had heard nothing but good of him; he was the cousin of my intimate friend Judge Davis. But he had scarcely been elected when I began to learn of his attacking me on all possible occasions. It is very much the same with Hickman. I was much disappointed that he failed to be my friend. But my greatest disappointment of all has been with Grimes. Before I came here, I certainly expected to rely upon Grimes more than any other one man in the Senate. I like him very much. He is a great strong fellow. He is a valuable friend, a dangerous enemy. He carries too many guns not to be respected in any point of view. But he got wrong against me, I do not clearly know how, and has always been cool and almost hostile to me. I am glad he has always been the friend of the Navy and generally of the administration."

Dispatches kept coming in all the evening showing a splendid triumph in Indiana, showing steady, small gains all over Pennsylvania, enough to give a fair majority this time on the home vote. Guesses from New York and Albany which boiled down to about the estimated majority against us in the city, 35,000, and left the result in the State still doubtful.

A dispatch from Butler was picked up and sent by Sanford, saying that the city had gone 35,000 McClellan and the State 40,000. This looked impossible. The State had been carefully canvassed and such a result was impossible except in view of some monstrous and undreamed-of frauds. After a while another came from Sanford correcting the former one and giving us the 40,000 in the State.

Sanford's dispatches all the evening continued most jubilant, especially when he announced that most startling majority of 80,000 in Massachusetts.

General Eaton came in and waited for news with us. I had not before known he was with us. His denunciations of Seymour were especially hearty and vigorous.

Toward midnight we had supper, provided by Eckert. The President went awkwardly and hospitably to work shovelling out the fried oysters. He was most agreeable and genial all the evening in fact. Fox was abusing the coffee for being so hot—saying quaintly, it kept hot all the way down to the bottom of the cup as a piece of ice stayed cold till you finished eating it.

We got later in the evening a scattering dispatch from the West, giving us Michigan; one from Fox promising Missouri certainly; but a loss in the first district from that miserable split of Knox and Johnson; one promising Delaware; and one, too good for ready credence, saying Raymond and Dodge and Darling had been elected in New York City.

Captain Thomas came up with a band about half past two, and made some music and a small hifalute.

The President answered from the window with rather unusual dignity and effect, and we came home. . . .

W. H. L. [Ward Hill Lamon] came to my room to talk over the chief justiceship; he goes in for Stanton, and thinks, as I am inclined to think, that the President cannot afford to place an enemy in a position so momentous for good or evil.

He took a glass of whisky and then, refusing my offer of a bed, went out and, rolling himself up in his cloak, lay down at the President's door, passing the night in that attitude of touching and dumb fidelity, with a small arsenal of pistols and bowie knives around him. In the morning he went away leaving my blankets at my door, before I or the President were awake.

5

IN HIS DIARY three days after the election, John Hay makes note of a strange occurrence.

A T THE MEETING of the Cabinet today, the President took out a paper from his desk and said, "Gentlemen, do you remember last summer I asked you all to sign your names to the back of a paper of which I did not show you the inside? This is it. Now, Mr. Hay, see if you can get this open without tearing it?" He had pasted it up in so singular a style that it required some cutting to get it open. He then read as follows:

Executive Mansion
Washington, Aug. 23, 1864

This morning, as for some days past, it seems exceedingly probable that this Administration will not be re-elected. Then it will be my duty to so cooperate with the President-elect, as to save the Union between the election and the inauguration; as he will have secured his election on such ground that he cannot possibly save it afterwards.

A. LINCOLN

This was indorsed:

> William H. Seward
> W. P. Fessenden
> Edwin M. Stanton
> Gideon Welles
> Edw Bates
> M. Blair
> J. P. Usher

August 23, 1864

The President said, "You will remember that this was written at a time (6 days before the Chicago nominating Convention) when as yet we had no adversary, and seemed to have no friends. I then solemnly resolved on the course of action indicated above.

I resolved, in case of the election of General McClellan, being certain that he would be the candidate, that I would see him and talk matters over with him. I would say, "General, the election has demostrated that you are stronger, have more influence with the American people than I. Now let us together, you with your influence and I with all the executive power of the government, try to save the country. You raise as many troops as you possibly can for this final trial, and I will devote all my energies to assisting and finishing the war."

Seward said, "And the General would answer you 'Yes, Yes;' and the next day when you saw him again and pressed these views upon him, he would say, 'Yes, Yes'; and so on forever, and would have done nothing at all."

"At least," added Lincoln, "I should have done my duty and have stood clear before my own conscience."

6

FOUR MONTHS PASSED, and Lincoln again stood before the people to take the oath of office. Noah Brooks reviews the ceremonies.

THE DAY of Lincoln's second inauguration, March 4, 1865, was as somber and drizzly as the November day of his second election. When the hour of noon arrived, great crowds of men and women streamed around the Capitol building in most wretched plight. The mud in the city of Washington on that day certainly excelled all the other varieties I have ever seen before or since, and the greatest test of feminine heroism—the spoiling of their clothes—redounded amply to the credit of the women who were so bedraggled and drenched on that memorable day. The only entrance to the Senate wing, where the preliminary ceremonies were held, was by the main or eastern portico, the other entrances being used only by privileged persons. From the reporters' gallery one could see that the Senators were all massed on one side of their chamber, the other side being left for the members of the House and the few notables who should come in later. When the doors of the gallery were opened, and the crowd of women had finally been admitted, the sight was a beautiful one. Senator Foote, of Vermont, was in the chair, and was greatly discomfited to find that the fair ladies in the gallery had not the slightest idea that they were invading a session of the Senate. They chattered and clattered like zephyrs among the reeds of a waterside. The presiding officer in vain tapped with his ivory mallet. The gay people in the galleries talked on just as though there was no Senate in session in the United States; but when the attention of the fair mob was diverted by the arrival of eminent personages, something like a calm prevailed, and there was a silent gazing. There was Hooker, handsome, rosy, and gorgeous in full uniform; "the dear old Admiral," as the women used to call Farragut; Mrs. Lincoln in the diplomatic gallery, attended by gallant Senator Anthony; a gorgeous array of foreign ministers in full court costume; and a considerable group of military and naval officers, brilliant in gold lace and epaulets. There was a buzz when the Justices of the Supreme Court came in, attired in their robes of office, Chief Justice Chase looking very young and also very queer, carrying a stovepipe hat and wearing his long black silk gown. The foreign ministers occupied seats at the right of the chair behind the Supreme Court Justices; and behind these were the members of the House. The members of the Cabinet had front seats at the left of the chair, Seward at the head, followed by Stanton, Welles, Speed, and Dennison. Usher was detained by illness, and Fessenden occupied his old seat in the Senate. Lincoln sat in the middle of the front row.

All eyes were turned to the main entrance, where, precisely on the stroke of twelve, appeared Andrew Johnson, Vice-President-elect, arm in arm with Hannibal Hamlin, whose term of office was now expiring. They took seats together on the dais of the presiding officer, and Hamlin made a brief and sensible speech, and Andrew Johnson, whose face was extraordinarily red, was presented to take the oath. It is needless to say here that the unfortunate gentleman, who had been very ill, was not altogether sober at this most important moment of his life. In order to strengthen himself for the physical and mental ordeal through which he was about to pass, he had taken a stiff drink of whisky in the room of the Vice-President, and the warmth of the Senate chamber, with possibly other physical conditions, had sent the fiery liquor to his brain. He was evidently intoxicated. As he went on with his speech, he turned upon the Cabinet officers and

addressed them as "Mr. Stanton," "Mr. Seward," etc., without
the official handles to their names. Forgetting Mr. Welles's name,
he said, "and you, too, Mr.— —," then, leaning over to Colonel
Forney, he said, "What is the name of the Secretary of the Navy?"
and then continued as though nothing had happened. Once in a
while, from the reporters' gallery, I could observe Hamlin nudging
Johnson from behind, reminding him that the hour for the inauguration ceremony had passed. The speaker kept on, although
President Lincoln sat before him, patiently waiting for his extraordinary harangue to be over.

The study of the faces below was interesting. Seward was as
bland and serene as a summer day; Stanton appeared to be petri-
fied; Welles' face was usually void of any expression; Speed sat
with his eyes closed; Dennison was red and white by turns. Among
the Union Senators, Henry Wilson's face was flushed; Sumner
wore a saturnine and sarcastic smile; and most of the others
turned and twisted in their senatorial chairs as if in long-drawn
agony. Of the Supreme Bench, Judge Nelson only was apparently
moved, his lower jaw being dropped clean down in blank horror.
Chase was marble, adamant, granite in immobility until Johnson
turned his back upon the Senate to take the oath, when he exchanged glances with Nelson, who then closed up his mouth.
When Johnson had repeated inaudibly the oath of office, his hand
upon the Book, he turned and took the Bible in his hand, and,
facing the audience, said, with a loud, theatrical voice and gesture,
"I kiss this Book in the face of my nation of the United States."

This painful incident being over, Colonel Forney, the Secretary
of the Senate, read the proclamation of the President convoking
an extra session, and called the names of the members-elect. Thereupon the newly chosen Senators were sworn in, and the procession
for the inauguration platform, which had been built on the east
front of the Capitol, was formed. There was a sea of heads in the
great plaza in front of the Capitol, as far as the eye could reach,
and breaking in waves along its outer edges among the budding
foliage of the grounds beyond. When the President and the procession of notables appeared, a tremendous shout, prolonged
and loud, arose from the surging ocean of humanity around the
Capitol building. Then the Sergeant-at-Arms of the Senate, the
historic Brown, arose and bowed, with his shining black hat in

hand, in dumb show before the crowd, which thereupon became still, and Abraham Lincoln, rising tall and gaunt among the groups about him, stepped forward and read his inaugural address, which was printed in two broad columns upon a single page of large paper. As he advanced from his seat, a roar of applause shook the air, and, again and again repeated, finally died far away on the outer fringe of the throng, like a sweeping wave upon the shore. Just at that moment the sun, which had been obscured all day, burst forth in its unclouded meridian splendor, and flooded the spectacle with glory and with light. Every heart beat quicker at the unexpected omen, and doubtless not a few mentally prayed that so might the darkness which had obscured the past four years be now dissipated by the sun of prosperity,

> Till danger's troubled night depart,
> And the star of peace return.

7

THEN, his voice clear and audible to the limits of the huge hushed crowd, Abraham Lincoln said:

Fellow-countrymen : At this second appearing to take the oath of the presidential office, there is less occasion for an extended address than there was at the first. Then a statement, somewhat in detail, of a course to be pursued, seemed fitting and proper. Now, at the expiration of four years, during which public declarations have been constantly called forth on every point and phase of the great contest which still absorbs the attention and engrosses the energies of the nation, little that is new could be presented. The progress of our arms, upon which all else chiefly depends, is as well known to the public as to myself; and it is, I trust, reasonably satisfactory and encouraging to all. With high hope for the future, no prediction in regard to it is ventured.

On the occasion corresponding to this four years ago, all thoughts were anxiously directed to an impending civil war. All dreaded it—all sought to avert it. While the inaugural address was being delivered from this place, devoted altogether to saving the Union without war, insurgent agents were in the city seeking to destroy it without war—seeking to dissolve the Union, and divide effects, by negotiation. Both parties deprecated war; but one of them would make war rather than let the nation survive; and the other would accept war rather than let it perish. And the war came.

One-eighth of the whole population were colored slaves, not distributed generally over the Union, but localized in the Southern part of it. These slaves constituted a peculiar and powerful interest. All knew that this interest was, somehow, the cause of the war. To strengthen, perpetuate, and extend this interest was the object for which the insurgents would rend the Union, even by war; while the government claimed no right to do more than to restrict the territorial enlargement of it.

Neither party expected for the war the magnitude or the duration which it has already attained. Neither anticipated that the cause of the conflict might cease with, or even before, the conflict itself should cease. Each looked for an easier triumph, and a result less fundamental and astounding. Both read the same Bible, and pray to the same God; and each invokes his aid against the other. It may seem strange that any men should dare to ask a just God's assistance in wringing their bread from the sweat of other men's faces; but let us judge not, that we be not judged. The prayers of both could not be answered—that of neither has been answered fully.

The Almighty has his own purposes. "Woe unto the world because of offenses! for it must needs be that offenses come; but woe to that man by whom the offense cometh." If we shall suppose that American slavery is one of those offenses which, in the providence of God, must needs come, but which, having continued through his appointed time, he now wills to remove, and that he gives to both North and South this terrible war, as the woe due to those by whom the offense came, shall we discern therein any departure from those divine attributes which the believers in a living God always ascribe to him? Fondly do we hope—fervently do we pray—that this mighty scourge of war may speedily pass away. Yet, if God wills that it continue until all the wealth piled by the bondman's two hundred and fifty years of unrequited toil shall be sunk, and until every drop of blood drawn with the lash shall be paid by another drawn with the sword, as was said three thousand years ago, so still it must be said, "The judgments of the Lord are true and righteous altogether."

With malice toward none; with charity for all; with firmness in the right, as God gives us to see the right, let us strive on to finish the work we are in; to bind up the nation's wounds; to care for him who shall have borne the battle, and for his widow, and his orphan—to do all which may achieve and cherish a just and lasting peace among ourselves, and with all nations.

8

TO LORD CHARNWOOD, Lincoln's Second Inaugural Address was a profession of faith as well as a great state paper.

PROBABLY NO OTHER SPEECH of a modern statesman uses so unreservedly the language of intense religious feeling. The occasion made it natural; neither the thought nor the words are in any way conventional; no sensible reader now could entertain a suspicion that the orator spoke to the heart of the people but did not speak from his own heart. But an old Illinois attorney, who thought he knew the real Lincoln behind the President, might have wondered whether the real Lincoln spoke here. For Lincoln's religion, like everything else in his character, became, when he was famous, a stock subject of discussion among his old associates. Many said "he was a Christian but did not know it." Some hinted, with an air of great sagacity, that "so far from his being a Christian or a religious man, the less said about it the better." In early manhood he broke away forever from the scheme of Christian theology which was probably more or less common to the very various churches which surrounded him. He had avowed this sweeping denial with a freedom which pained some friends, perhaps rather by its rashness than by its impiety, and he was apt to regard the procedure of theologians as a blasphemous twisting of the words of Christ. He rejected that belief in miracles and in the literally inspired accuracy of the Bible narrative which was no doubt held as fundamental by all these churches. He rejected no less any attempt to substitute for this foundation the belief in any priestly authority or in the authority of any formal and earthly society called the Church. With this total independence of the expressed creeds of his neighbors, he still went and took his boys to Presbyterian public worship—their mother was an Episcopalian and his own parents had been Baptists. He loved the Bible and knew it intimately—he is said also by the way to have stored in his memory a large number of hymns. In the year before his death he wrote to Speed: "I am profitably engaged in reading the Bible. Take all of this book upon reason that you can and the balance upon faith and you will live and die a better man." It was not so much the Old Testament as the New Testament and what he called "the true spirit of Christ" that he loved especially, and took with all possible seriousness as the rule of life. His theology, in the narrower sense, may be said to have been limited to an intense belief in a vast and overruling Providence—the lighter forms of superstitious feelings which he is known to have had in common with most frontiersmen were apparently of no importance in his life. And this Providence, darkly spoken of, was certainly conceived by him as intimately and kindly related to his own life. In his presidential candidature, when he owned to someone that the opposition of clergymen hurt him deeply, he is said to have confessed to being no Christian and to have continued, "I know that there is a God and that He hates injustice and slavery. I see the storm coming and I know that His hand is in it. If He has a place and work for me, and I think He has, I believe I am ready. I am nothing, but truth is everything; I know I am right because I know that liberty is right, for Christ teaches it, and Christ is God. I have told them that a house divided against itself cannot stand, and Christ and reason say the same, and they will find it so." When old acquaintances said that he had no religion they based their opinion on such remarks as that the God, of whom he had just been speaking solemnly, was "not a person." It would be unprofitable to inquire what he, and many others, meant by this expression, but, later at any rate, this "impersonal" power was one with which he could hold commune. His robust intellect, impatient of unproved assertion, was unlikely to rest in the common assumption that things dimly seen may be treated as not being there. So humorous a man was also unlikely to be too conceited to say his prayers. At any rate he said them; said them intently; valued the fact that others prayed for him and for the nation; and, as in official proclamations (concerning days of national religious observance) he could wield, like no other modern writer, the language of the Prayer Book, so he would speak of prayer without the smallest embarrassment in talk with a general or a statesman. It is possible that this was a development of later years. Lincoln did not, like most of us, arrest his growth. To Mrs. Lincoln it seemed that with the death of their child, Willie, a change came over his whole religious outlook. It well might; and since that grief, which came while his troubles were beginning, much else had come to Lincoln; and now through four years of unsurpassed trial his capacity had steadily grown, and his delicate fairness, his pitifulness, his patience, his modesty had grown therewith. Here is one of the few speeches ever delivered by a great man at the crisis of his fate on the sort of occasion which a tragedian telling his story would have devised for him. This man had stood alone in the dark. He had done justice; he had loved mercy; he had walked humbly with his God. The reader to whom religious utterance makes little appeal will not suppose that his imaginative words stand for no real experience. The reader whose piety knows no questions will not be pained to think that this man had professed no faith.

CHAPTER TWENTY-THREE

Peace

I N THE SUMMER OF 1864, with the North
sick of war and the South foreseeing defeat ever more
clearly, men's thoughts turned increasingly often to the
possibility of peace. With Lincoln's blessing, Horace Greeley traveled to Canada for the purpose of meeting Confederate emissaries, only to learn that the reputed diplo-
mats had no authority even to begin a negotiation. Soon
afterward two other Northerners, James F. Jaquess and
J. R. Gilmore, armed with Lincoln's unofficial assurance
that peace could be made on the basis of the restoration of
the Union and the abandonment of slavery, conferred with
Jefferson Davis at Richmond, where they learned at first
hand that the Confederate President was still insistent
upon full Southern independence. There would have to be
more blood-letting before the war could end.

More blood-letting there was—at Franklin and Nashville, Tennessee, where the Union commanders Schofield
and Thomas literally shattered Hood's fine army; in the
trenches before Petersburg, where Grant was slowly stran-
gling the once-proud Army of Northern Virginia; in
Georgia, where Sherman's columns left a wide belt of destruction in their march from Atlanta to Savannah. As the
new year opened, peace, by force of arms if not by man's
good will, was measurably closer.

1

EARLY IN JANUARY, 1865, old Francis P. Blair, still a power in
politics, visited Richmond and conferred with Davis. His effort called

forth a letter in which the Confederate President expressed his willingness to negotiate with a view to bringing peace to "the two countries." Lincoln, having seen the letter, wrote that he would be glad to see peace come to "our one common country." Thus the deadlock continued. Nevertheless, Lincoln thought enough of the overture to invite Confederate representatives to a conference within the Union lines. On February 2, the President himself, with his Secretary of State, met Alexander H. Stephens, R. M. T. Hunter, and J. A. Campbell on the Union transport *River Queen* in Hampton Roads. Carl Sandburg tells the story of the conference.

F IVE ASTUTE MEN of politics and law talked four hours in a steamboat saloon. At the outset Lincoln's instructions to Seward marked off three areas where there could be no discussion. The three Confederate commissioners made many approaches trying to get a foot or a toe into some one of these areas. The Federal President and Secretary of State always ruled they were out of bounds, said discussion was impossible. What went on in the minds of the five men, the tangled cross-purposes underlying the words of their mouths, no onlooker could have caught and reported.

As between drinking men Seward on his arrival had sent the commissioners three bottles of whisky, though aware that Stephens never took more than a teaspoon of it at a time. Hunter, who had spent most of his life in Washington, genially asked Seward: "Governor, how is the Capitol? Is it finished?" Whereupon Seward described the new dome and the great brass door.

Stephens's account ran that greetings were cordial between those who had met before, that Lincoln and he spoke as old friends and at once asked about acquaintances of the Mexican War days when Lincoln and Stephens were in Congress together. There was good feeling and harmony between the States and sections then, Stephens suggested, with a query, "Mr. President, is there no way of putting an end to the present trouble?" Lincoln replied to the Confederate Vice-President that he knew of only one way and that was for those who were resisting the laws of the Union to cease that resistance.

There might be a "continental question" on which they could adjust the strife, Stephens once led off, Lincoln rejoining that

Mr. Blair in Richmond on matters in Mexico had spoken with no authority from him. Often the talk ranged around States' Rights and slavery, courteously, respectfully, even-tempered— with deep chasms of disagreement. At one point, according to Stephens, Lincoln said it was not his intention in the beginning to interfere with slavery; necessity had compelled it; he had interfered only when driven to it; he had favored no extension of slavery into the Territories but did not think that the Federal government had power over slavery in the States except as a war measure; he had always been in favor of emancipation, but not immediate emancipation, even by the States.

The people of the North were as responsible for slavery as the people of the South (as Stephens heard Lincoln say it) and "He knew some [in the North] who were in favor of an appropriation as high as four hundred millions of dollars for this purpose [of paying owners for the loss of their slaves]. 'I could mention persons,' said he, 'whose names would astonish you, who are willing to do this if the war shall now cease.' "

On Hunter's saying it seemed that Lincoln's terms forced the Confederate people to choose nothing else than unconditional surrender and submission, Seward with quiet dignity insisted that "no words like unconditional submission had been used" nor any harsh phrases meaning degradation or humiliation. With peace, said Seward, the Southern people would again be under the Constitution "with all their rights secured thereby."

Campbell had a feeling that Stephens along with Davis was "duped" by Blair into hopes of somehow using Mexico. "I was incredulous," wrote Campbell. "Mr. Hunter did not have faith. Mr. Stephens supposed Blair to be 'the mentor of the administration and the Republican party.' " Of course Campbell, as a man of no vivid streaks and whimsical blends such as ran through Stephens, failed to credit Stephens with using the only prop and lever allowed them by Davis's instructions. The opening query of the conference had come from Stephens to Lincoln: "Well, Mr. President, is there no way of putting an end to the present trouble . . . existing between the different States and sections of *the country?*" In this Stephens did not go so far as Lincoln's term "our one common country," but he did with intention and meaning as his first stroke at the conference abandon the Davis phrase "two countries." Could Davis have listened in, he would have suspected the Stephens motive.

Stripping the discussions of the language of diplomacy and briefing it, Stephens in effect asked why not stop fighting among ourselves and take on a war in Mexico together? Lincoln answered in effect that we would take on another war only after the question of Union was settled. Campbell raised questions of how the Confederates might return armies to peace, of what would be done about the new freedom of the slaves, of Senators and Congressmen elected to go to Washington from seceded States returning to the Union, of Virginia now divided into two States, of claims for Southern property taken or wrecked in the war. Lincoln and Seward answered that some of these points were covered in the President's December message to Congress, other points would have to go to the courts, and Congress might be liberal in handling property claims after the war fever had cooled down. West Virginia would stay as a separate State. The new freedom of the Negroes would be passed on by courts; the Emancipation Proclamation would stand with no change from Lincoln. And it was news to the Confederate commissioners that the United States Congress on January 31 had passed the Thirteenth Amendment to the Constitution and when this should also pass threefourths of the state legislatures, it would outlaw and abolish slavery.

Lincoln often had to make it clear that as the Executive he might personally wish to do some things, but under the Constitution those things would have to go to Congress or the courts of the States. Once he stressed the point that even if the Confederate States should consider coming back into the Union, he could not make any bargains with armed forces making war on his government; until the war was over some things could not begin to commence.

At this Hunter reached back into history for a parallel. Hunter pointed to King Charles I of England and how that monarch bargained with people in arms against his government. Hunter's argument was long and elaborate, insisting that peace could come through Lincoln's recognizing the right of Davis to make a treaty.

"Mr. Lincoln's face," ran a later newspaper account by

Stephens, "then wore that indescribable expression which generally preceded his hardest hits, and he remarked: 'Upon questions of history I must refer you to Mr. Seward, for he is posted in such things, and I don't pretend to be bright. My only distinct recollection of the matter is that Charles lost his head.' That settled Mr. Hunter for a while."

. . . Hunter was to go away and report to a Richmond mass meeting, "Mr. Lincoln told us, told me, that while we could send representatives to the Yankee Congress, yet it rested with that Congress to say whether they would receive them or not." This was correct. "Thus," proceeded Hunter, "we would cast every thing away, and go to them as a subdued, subjugated and degraded people, to be held in subjection by their soldiery." That this was the spirit of Congress, and not the animus of Lincoln and Seward during the conference, failed to get into Hunter's report. None of the three commissioners reported to their people that Lincoln had said he could mention "persons whose names would astonish you" who favored a $400,000,000 appropriation for compensation to the South for its lost slave property. Stephens, according to the *Augusta Chronicle*, "thought he was doing a favor to Mr. Lincoln" in not publishing this matter of compensation, "for it would be used to the injury of Mr. Lincoln."

No good would have come to the commissioners from publishing part of the informal proceedings which came to Lamon's ear, it seemed, from Lincoln himself. A hush fell over the conference at one point where Lincoln found himself required to contradict gravely and directly remarks made by the Confederate commissioners. His words were measured and sounded like doom, for he was saying that the conduct of certain rebel leaders had been such that they had plainly forfeited all right to immunity from punishment for the highest crime known to law. He had come to the brink of saying they should be strung up for treason, hang high and lonesome as traitors.

There was a hush and a pause. Hunter gave Lincoln a steady, searching look, and then very deliberately: "Mr. President, if we understand you correctly, you think that we of the Confederacy have committed treason; that we are traitors to your government; that we have forfeited our rights, and are proper subjects for the hangman. Is not that about what your words imply?"

"Yes," rejoined Lincoln. "You have stated the proposition better than I did. That is about the size of it!"

Another hush and a somewhat painful pause, then Hunter with a pleasant smile: "Well, Mr. Lincoln, we have about concluded that we shall not be hanged as long as you are President—if we behave ourselves."

. . . Hunter was the one Confederate conferee who stirred smoldering fire in Lincoln. An *Augusta* (Georgia) *Chronicle* interview with Stephens later related: "Hunter declared that he had never entertained any fears for his person or life from so mild a government as that of the United States. To which Mr. Lincoln retorted that he, also, had felt easy as to the Rebels, but not always so easy about the lamp-posts around Washington City—a hint that he had already done more favors for the Rebels than was exactly popular with the radical men of his own party. Mr. Lincoln's manner had now grown more positive. He suggested that it would be better for the Rebel States to return at once than to risk the chances of continuing the war, and the increasing bitterness of feeling in Congress. The time might come, he said, when they would not be considered as an erring people invited back to citizenship, but would be looked upon as enemies to be exterminated or ruined. During the conference, the amendment to the Federal Constitution, which has just been adopted by Congress, was read, providing that neither slavery nor involuntary servitude, except for crime, should exist within the United States, or any place within its jurisdiction, and Congress should have power to enforce the amendment by appropriate legislation."

A fellowship resting on thin fire, in a far cavern of gloom, seemed to have renewal between Lincoln and Stephens. Stephens came aboard the steamer wearing a coarse gray woolen overcoat of newly improvised Southern manufacture. The thick cloth of this garment came down nearly to his feet and he looked almost like an average-sized man, though his weight was only ninety pounds. Lincoln, a foot taller than Stephens and nearly twice his weight, had come into the steamer saloon and stood watching the dwarfish Georgian shake loose and step out of his huge overcoat, unwinding a long wool muffler and several shawls. Lincoln moved toward Little Aleck, whom he had. not seen in sixteen years, and with a smiling handshake: "Never have I seen so small a nubbin come out of so much husk. . . ."

Once during the conference someone spoke of an Illinois Congressman who had gone to the Mexican War. This drew from Stephens a story touching on how, in a House session, the Illinois members themselves could not agree on how to pronounce the name of their State. Some insisted it was "Illi-*noy*" others that it was "Illi-*nois*." One of them appealed to the venerable John Quincy Adams, who with a malicious smile thrust out: "If one were to judge from the character of the representatives in this Congress from that State, I should decide unhesitatingly that the proper pronunciation was 'All noise!' " Thus Stephens's anecdote was relayed by Lincoln to Carpenter as a piece of brightness worth passing on.

Lincoln tried free straightaway peace talk on Stephens only— as though they might be alone on the wide, heaving Atlantic and no listener but a gray sea as melancholy as their own two worn hearts. Lincoln spoke his personal judgments about immediate emancipation. "Many evils attending this appeared to him," wrote Stephens. A gradual emancipation across perhaps a five-year period would better enable the two races to work out their codes and designs for living together than emancipation at one sweep. Stephens wrote of this mood and what followed, that after pausing for some time, his head rather bent down, as if in deep reflection, while all were silent, Lincoln rose and used these words, almost, if not quite, exactly:

"Stephens, if I were in Georgia, and entertained the sentiments I do—though, I suppose, I should not be permitted to stay there long with them; but if I resided in Georgia, with my present sentiments, I'll tell you what I would do, if I were in your place: I would go home and get the Governor of the State to call the Legislature together, and get them to recall all the State troops from the war; elect Senators and Members to Congress, and ratify this Constitutional Amendment [outlawing and abolishing slavery] *prospectively*, so as to take effect—say in five years. Such a ratification would be valid in my opinion. I have looked into the subject, and think such a prospective ratification would be valid. Whatever may have been the views of your people before the war, they must be convinced now, that slavery is doomed. It cannòt last long in any event, and the best course, it seems to me, for your public men to pursue, would be to adopt such a policy as will avoid, as far as possible, the evils of immediate emancipation. This would be my course, if I were in your place."

Lincoln spoke this as though Stephens had a genius for suffering that might gather and use an appeal to suffer more yet. The two men had a like melancholy, Stephens once recording: "Sometimes I have thought that of all men I was most miserable; that I was especially doomed to misfortune, to melancholy, to grief. . . . The misery, the deep agony of spirit I have suffered, no mortal knows, nor ever will. . . . The torture of body is severe; I have had my share of that. . . . But all these are slight when compared with the pangs of an offended or wounded spirit. The heart alone knoweth its own sorrow. I have borne it these many years. I have borne it all my life." Lincoln knew deeply the same mood. They were the two most somber figures at this five-man conference. And by paradox they laughed more through the discussions than any two of the five.

Now came the friendly handshakings of saying good-by, of ending the Hampton Roads conference, a world of nations and people watching, a horde of journalists and politicians puzzling. Stephens again asked Lincoln to reconsider Blair's stalking horse, the plan of an armistice on the basis of a Mexican expedition commanded by Jeff Davis. Lincoln: "Well, Stephens, I will reconsider it; but I do not think my mind will change."

Nothing more seemed worth saying. The President of the United States said to the Vice-President of the Confederacy: "Well, Stephens, there has been nothing we could do for our country. Is there anything I can do for you personally?"

"Nothing." Then Little Aleck's pale face brightened. "Unless you can send me my nephew who has been for twenty months a prisoner on Johnson's Island."

Lincoln's face too brightened. "I shall be glad to do it. Let me have his name." And he wrote it down in a notebook.

After handshakings all round, the Confederate commissioners were put in a rowboat and taken to their steamer for return to their own army lines. They were getting ready to steam away when they saw a rowboat with a Negro at the oars heading for their steamer. He reached their deck with a basket of champagne and a note with the compliments of Mr. Seward. The commissioners read the note, waved their handkerchiefs in acknowledgment. Then they saw Mr. Seward, speaking through a boatswain's trumpet. The words of the Secretary of State came clear. He was saying, "*Keep the champagne, but return the negro!*" Thus ran the final informal words of the Hampton Roads conference, which was quite informal but not at all final.

"To-day they returned to Richmond," wrote General Meade to his wife, "but what was the result of their visit no one knows. At the present moment, 8 P.M., the artillery on our lines is in full blast, clearly proving that at this moment there is no peace."

2

A FEW WEEKS MORE, and the doom of the Confederacy was clear to all except the willfully blind. Lincoln, knowing the end to be at hand, proceeded to Grant's headquarters at City Point. There Sherman, who had left his army, now in Carolina, for a few days, found him. Once more the *River Queen* was the scene of historic conferences, this time depicted by Sherman himself.

My ARMY WAS HARD UP for food and clothing, which could only reach us from the coast, and my chief attention was given to the reconstruction of the two railroads which meet at Goldsboro, from Newbern and Wilmington, so as to reclothe the men, and get provisions enough with which to continue our march to Burksville, Virginia, where we would come into communication with General Grant's army, then investing Richmond and Petersburg. I had written to General Grant several times, and had received leters from him, but it seemed to me all important that I should have a personal interview. Accordingly, on the twenty-fifth of March, leaving General Schofield in command, I took the first locomotive which had come over the repaired railroad, back to Newbern and Morehead City, where I got the small steamer *Russia* to convey me to City Point. We arrived during the after-

noon of March 27, and I found General Grant and staff occupying
a neat set of log huts, on a bluff overlooking the James River. The
General's family was with him. We had quite a long and friendly
talk, when he remarked that the President, Mr. Lincoln, was
near by in a steamer lying at the dock, and he proposed that we
should call at once. We did so, and found Mr. Lincoln on board
the *River Queen*. We had met in the early part of the war, and
he recognized me, and received me with a warmth of manner and
expression that was most grateful. We then sat some time in the
after-cabin, and Mr. Lincoln made many inquiries about the
events which attended the march from Savannah to Goldsboro, and
seemed to enjoy the humorous stories about "our bummers," of
which he had heard much. When in lively conversation, his face
brightened wonderfully; but if the conversation flagged, his
face assumed a sad and sorrowful expression.

General Grant and I explained to him that my next move
from Goldsboro would bring my army, increased to 80,000 men
by Schofield's and Terry's reinforcements, in close communication
with General Grant's army, then investing Lee in Richmond, and
that unless Lee could effect his escape, and make junction with
Johnston in North Carolina, he would soon be shut up in Richmond with no possibility of supplies, and would have to surrender. Mr. Lincoln was extremely interested in this view of the
case, and when we explained that Lee's only chance was to escape,
join Johnston, and, being then between me in North Carolina and
Grant in Virginia, could choose which to fight. Mr. Lincoln
seemed unusually impressed with this, but General Grant explained that, at the very moment of our conversation, General
Sheridan was passing his cavalry across James River from the
north to the south, that he would, with this cavalry, so extend
his left below Petersburg as to meet the South Shore Road, and
that if Lee should "let go" his fortified lines, he (Grant) would
follow him so close that he could not possibly fall on me alone in
North Carolina. I, in like manner, expressed the fullest confidence
that my army in North Carolina was willing to cope with Lee
and Johnston combined, till Grant could come up. But we both
agreed that one more bloody battle was likely to occur before the
close of the war.

Mr. Lincoln repeatedly inquired as to General Schofield's ability, in my absence, and seemed anxious that I should return to North Carolina, and more than once exclaimed: "Must more blood be shed? Cannot this last bloody battle be avoided?" We explained that we had to presume that General Lee was a real general; that he must see that Johnston alone was no barrier to my progress; and that, if my army of 80,000 veterans should reach Burksville, he was lost in Richmond, and that we were forced to believe he would not await that inevitable conclusion, but make one more desperate effort.

I think we were with Mr. Lincoln an hour or more, and then returned to General Grant's quarters, where Mrs. Grant had prepared us some coffee, or tea. During this meal, Mrs. Grant inquired if we had seen Mrs. Lincoln. I answered: "No, I did not know she was on board." "Now," said Mrs. Grant, "you are a pretty pair," and went on to explain that we had been guilty of a piece of unpardonable rudeness; but the General said, "Never mind. We will repeat the visit to-morrow, and can then see Mrs. Lincoln."

The next morning a good many officers called to see me, among them Generals Meade and Ord, also Admiral Porter. The latter inquired as to the *Russia*, in which I had come up from Morehead City, and explained that she was a slow tub, and he would send me back in the steamer *Bat*, Captain Barnes, U. S. Navy, because she was very fleet, and could make seventeen knots an hour. Of course I did not object, and fixed that afternoon to start back.

Meantime we had to repeat our call on Mr. Lincoln on board the *River Queen*, then anchored out in the stream at some distance from the wharf. Admiral Porter went along, and we took a tug at the wharf, which conveyed us off to the *River Queen*. Mr. Lincoln met us all in the same hearty manner as on the previous occasion, and this time we did not forget Mrs. Lincoln. General Grant inquired for her, and the President explained that she was not well, but he stepped to her stateroom and returned to us asking us to excuse her. We all took seats in the after-cabin, and the conversation became general. I explained to Mr. Lincoln that Admiral Porter had given me the *Bat*, a very fleet vessel, to carry me back to Newbern, and that I was ready to start back then. It seemed to relieve him, as he was afraid that something might go wrong at Goldsboro in my absence. I had no such fears, and the most perfect confidence in General Schofield, and doubt not I said as much.

I ought not, and must not, attempt to recall the words of that conversation. Of course none of us then foresaw the tragic end of the principal figure of that group so near at hand; and none of us saw the exact manner in which the war was to close; but I knew that I felt, and I believe the others did, that the end of the war was near.

The imminent danger was that Lee, seeing the meshes closing surely around him, would not remain passive, but would make one more desperate effort; and General Grant was providing for it, by getting General Sheridan's cavalry well to his left flank, so as to watch the first symptoms, and to bring the rebel army to bay till the infantry could come up. Meantime I only asked two weeks' delay, the *status quo*, when we would have our wagons loaded, and would start from Goldsboro for Burksville, via Raleigh. Though I cannot attempt to recall the words spoken by any one of the persons present on that occasion, I know we talked generally about what was to be done when Lee's and Johnston's armies were beaten and dispersed. On this point Mr. Lincoln was very full. He said that he had long thought of it, that he hoped this end could be reached without more bloodshed, but in any event he wanted us to get the deluded men of the rebel armies disarmed and back to their homes; that he contemplated no revenge; no harsh measures, but quite the contrary, and that their suffering and hardships during the war would make them the more submissive to law. I cannot say that Mr. Lincoln, or anybody else, used this language; but I know I left his presence with the conviction that he had in his mind, or that his Cabinet had, some plan of settlement ready for application the moment Lee and Johnston were defeated.

3

ON APRIL 2, five days after Lincoln's last meeting with Grant and Sherman, Lee ordered the evacuation of Petersburg. Richmond fell simultaneously. Lincoln, escorted by Admiral D. D. Porter and a small party, proceeded without delay to the Confederate Capital. Porter recounts what must have been the high point of Lincoln's life.

GENERAL WEITZEL, who commanded the army on the left of the James, was marching into Richmond, and the whole tragedy was over.

"Thank God," said the President, fervently, "that I have lived to see this! It seems to me that I have been dreaming a horrid dream for four years, and now the nightmare is gone. I want to see Richmond."

"If there is any of it left," I added. "There is black smoke over the city, but before we can go up we must remove all the torpedoes [mines]; the river is full of them above Hewlit's Battery."

. . . When the channel was reported clear of torpedoes (a large number of which were taken up), I proceeded up to Richmond in the *Malvern*, with President Lincoln on board the *River Queen*. . . . Every vessel that got through the obstructions wished to be the first one up, and pushed ahead with all steam; but they grounded, one after another, the *Malvern* passing them all, until she also took the ground. Not to be delayed, I took the President in my barge, and, with a tug ahead with a file of marines on board, we continued on up to the city. . . .

There was a small house on this landing, and behind it were some twelve Negroes digging with spades. The leader of them was an old man sixty years of age. He raised himself to an upright position as we landed, and put his hands up to his eyes. Then he dropped his spade and sprang forward. "Bress de Lord," he said, "dere is de great Messiah! I knowed him as soon as I seed him. He's bin in my heart fo' long yeahs, an' he' cum at las' to free his chillun from deir bondage! Glory, Hallelujah!" And he fell upon his knees before the President and kissed his feet. The others followed his example, and in a minute Mr. Lincoln was surrounded by these people, who had treasured up the recollection of him caught from a photograph, and had looked up to him for four years as the one who was to lead them out of captivity. . . .

Mr. Lincoln looked down at the poor creatures at his feet; he was much embarrassed at his position. "Don't kneel to me," he said. "That is not right. You must kneel to God only, and thank him for the liberty you will hereafter enjoy. I am but God's humble instrument; but you may rest assured that as long as I live no one shall put a shackle to your limbs, and you shall have all the rights which God has given to every other free citizen of this Republic."

His face was lit up with a divine look as he uttered these words. Though not a handsome man, and ungainly in his person, yet in his enthusiasm he seemed the personification of manly beauty, and that sad face of his looked down in kindness upon these ignorant blacks with a grace that could not be excelled. He really seemed of another world. . . .

It was a minute or two before I could get the Negroes to rise and leave the President. The scene was so touching that I hated to disturb it, yet we could not stay there all day; we had to move on; so I requested the patriarch to withdraw from about the President with his companions and let us pass on.

"Yess, Massa," said the old man, "but after bein' so many years in de desert widout water, it's mighty pleasant to be lookin' at las' on our spring of life. 'Scuse us, sir; we means no disrespec' to Mass' Lincoln; we means all love and gratitude." And then, joining hands together in a ring, the Negroes sang the following hymn with melodious and touching voices only possessed by the Negroes of the South:

"Oh, all ye people clap your hands,
    And with triumphant voices sing;
No force the mighty power withstands
    Of God, the universal King."

The President and all of us listened respectfully while the hymn was being sung. Four minutes at most had passed away since we first landed at a point where, as far as the eye could reach, the streets were entirely deserted, but now what a different scene appeared as that hymn went forth from the Negroes' lips! The streets seemed to be suddenly alive with the colored race. They seemed to spring from the earth. They came, tumbling and shouting, from over the hills and from the waterside, where no one was seen as we had passed. . . .

While some were rushing forward to try and touch the man they had talked of and dreamed of for four long years, others stood off a little way and looked on in awe and wonder. Others turned somersaults, and many yelled for joy. Half of them acted as though demented, and could find no way of testifying their delight. . . . The Negroes, in their ecstasy, could not be made to understand that they were detaining the President; they looked upon him as belonging to them, and that he had come to put the crowning act to the great work he had commenced. They would not feel that they were free in reality until they heard it from his own lips.

At length he spoke. He could not move for the mass of people— he had to do something.

"My poor friends," he said, "you are free—free as air. You can cast off the name of slave and trample upon it; it will come to you no more. Liberty is your birthright. God gave it to you as he gave it to others, and it is a sin that you have been deprived of it for so many years. But you must try to deserve this priceless boon. Let the world see that you merit it, and are able to maintain it by your good works. Don't let your joy carry you into excesses. Learn the laws and obey them; obey God's commandments and thank him for giving you liberty, for to him you owe all things. There, now, let me pass on; I have but little time to spare. I want to see the capital, and must return at once to Washington to secure to you that liberty which you seem to prize so highly. . . ."

At length we were able to move on. . . . Our progress was very slow; we did not move a mile an hour, and the crowd was still increasing. Many poor whites joined the throng, and sent up their shouts with the rest. We were nearly half an hour getting from abreast of Libby Prison to the edge of the city. The President stopped a moment to look on the horrid bastile where so many Union soldiers had dragged out a dreadful existence, and were subjected to all the cruelty the minds of brutal jailers could devise.

"We will pull it down," cried the crowd, seeing where his look fell.

"No," he said, "leave it as a monument. . . ."

It was a warm day, and the streets were dusty, owing to the immense gathering which covered every part of them, kicking up the dirt. The atmosphere was suffocating, but Mr. Lincoln could be seen plainly by every man, woman, and child, towering head and shoulders above the crowd; he overtopped every man there. He carried his hat in his hand, fanning his face, from which the perspiration was pouring. He looked as if he would have given his presidency for a glass of water—I would have given my commission for half that.

Now came another phase in the procession. As we entered the city every window flew up, from ground to roof, and every one was filled with eager, peering faces, which turned one to another and seemed to ask, "Is this large man, with soft eyes and kind, benevolent face, the one who has been held up to us as the incarnation of wickedness, the destroyer of the South?" I think that illusion vanished, if it was ever harbored by any one there. . . . There was nothing like taunt or defiance in the faces of those who were gazing from the windows or craning their necks from the sidewalks to catch a view of the President. The look of every one was that of eager curiosity—nothing more.

While we were stopped for a moment by the crowd, a white man in his shirt sleeves rushed from the sidewalk toward the President. His looks were so eager that I questioned his friendship, and prepared to receive him on the point of my sword; but when he got within ten feet of us he suddenly stopped short, took off his hat, and cried out, "Abraham Lincoln, God bless you! You are the poor man's friend!" Then he tried to force his way to the President to shake hands with him. He would not take No for an answer until I had to treat him rather roughly, when he stood off, with his arms folded, and looked intently after us. The last I saw of him he was throwing his hat into the air.

Just after this a beautiful girl came from the sidewalk, with a large bouquet of roses in her hand, and advanced, struggling through the crowd toward the President. The mass of people endeavored to open to let her pass, but she had a hard time in reaching him. Her clothes were very much disarranged in making the journey across the street. . . . Although nearly stifled with the dust, she gracefuly presented her bouquet to the President and made a neat little speech, while he held her hand. The beauty and youth of the girl—for she was only about seventeen—made the presentation very touching. . . .

At length I got hold of a cavalryman. He was sitting his horse near the sidewalk, blocked in by the people, and looking on with the same expression of interest as the others. He was the only soldier I had seen since we landed. . . . There was only guard enough posted about the streets to protect property and to prevent irregularities.

"Go to the General," I said to the trooper, "and tell him to send a military escort here to guard the President and get him through this crowd!"

"Is that old Abe?" asked the soldier, his eyes as large as saucers. The sight of the President was as strange to him as to the inhabitants; but off he went as fast as the crowd would allow him, and, some twenty minutes later, I heard the clatter of horses' hoofs over the stones as a troop of cavalry came galloping and clearing the street, which they did, however, as mildly as if for a parade.

For the first time since starting from the landing we were able to walk along uninterruptedly. In a short time we reached the mansion of Mr. Davis, President of the Confederacy. . . . It was quite a small affair compared with the White House, and modest in all its appointments, showing that while President Davis was engaged heart and soul in endeavoring to effect the division of the States, he was not, at least, surrounding himself with regal style, but was living in a modest, comfortable way, like any other citizen. . . .

General Shepley made us a speech and gave us a lunch, after which we entered a carriage and visited the State House—the late seat of the Confederate Congress. It was in dreadful disorder, betokening a sudden and unexpected flight; members' tables were upset, bales of Confederate scrip were lying about the floor, and many official documents of some value were scattered about. It was strange to me that they had not set fire to the building before they departed, to bury in oblivion every record that might remain relating to the events of the past four years.

After this inspection I urged the President to go on board the *Malvern*. . . . He was glad to go; he was tired out, and wanted the quiet of the flagship. We took leave of our hosts and departed.

4

SIX DAYS LATER, Lee's army was definitely, inescapably trapped. To have fired one more round would have been a senseless waste of life. Lee surrendered. Lloyd Lewis draws a picture of the memorable scene.

I T W A S S T R A N G E L Y Q U I E T even for Sunday, this ninth day of April, 1865, as Ulysses S. Grant jogged along the Virginia road that led to Appomattox Court House, his head drooping on his stubby little body.

The big guns were still. Through the woods on either side of the white road, two armies sat motionless, waiting.

One of them was his, the bruised but powerful Army of the Potomac, the other was that of his enemies, the Army of Northern Virginia, bled white and exhausted.

Four years of war were done. Eleven States of the South that had been fighting so frenziedly to tear their way out of the United States of America had fallen gasping across their guns. They hadn't the strength to make their get-away. Secession was a gone dream, a lost cause.

Grant, always solemn, more solemn now than ever, was riding to receive Robert E. Lee's surrender, and it made him sad. At Lee and at Lee's desperate Army of Northern Virginia, last hope of the South, he had been pounding all spring, all the winter before, and the summer before that. Now the end had come. He was glad it was over, but compassion for the brave old foe drowned all the elation of his own triumph. . . .

Into a two-story brick house on the edge of a tiny village he went as to his own surrender, dust and ashes over his mussy uniform, a private's stained overcoat upon his back, looking, as he entered, like a Missouri farmer who had by mistake crawled into a blouse that carried, unnoticed, three little silver stars on its shoulders.

Awaiting him was Lee, who of all men knew that those stars were no mistake, Lee in his own resplendent uniform, handsome, aristocratic, perfect model of the old army manners and professional culture to which both Grant and he had been trained at West Point—ideals which he had remembered and which Grant, luckily for the Union, had so soon forgotten.

The aristocrat wore a sword, the democrat none, and, noticing this, the democrat, with a grave courtesy that somehow shamed the lofty hauteur of the cavalier, explained that he had not had time to bring out his official blade and get fixed up for the ceremony.

As simply and naturally as though at an ordinary meeting of officers, Grant presented his staff, and the Union men, admiring the great Confederate, made gracious attempts to ease the situation with small, pleasant talk. But to them Lee, who had been an officer all his life, could be only stiff and cold, and when his eye fell on Grant's military secretary, Colonel Ely S. Parker, full-blooded Indian chief of the Six Nations, he stared in amazement, evidently thinking that the Yankees had brought in a Negro officer to humiliate him.

But under the gentle voice of his plain, slouching conqueror, Lee's proud reserve began to thaw. Grant talked of the Mexican War, in which both had served, and would have gone on in such informal fashion if Lee had not brought up the business of the day —surrender.

Grant silently wrote out the terms. They were simple: the enlisted men were to surrender their arms, the officers to retain theirs, all were to give their paroles and go home, not to be disturbed by United States authority so long as they kept their promise not to fight the government again. He handed them to his adversary and waited. Lee wiped his glasses, adjusted them to his nose, and began reading.

The sweeping generosity of the terms, considering what the Southern politicians had told their soldiers about the bloodthirst of the North, must have been plain in their full significance to Lee.

His face lit up when he came to the clause which allowed the officers to keep their property, and when he had finished he said with a little ring in his voice, "This will have a very happy effect upon my army."

Grant wanted the whole thing to be happy and asked if Lee had anything more to suggest. The Confederate wondered if his cavalrymen and artillerymen, who owned their horses, would be permitted to keep them. "No, the terms as written don't permit it," said Grant. He hadn't known the Southern army was thus organized. But he would allow it anyway and do better than that, he said; he would tell his officers to let every man claim a horse or mule and take it home. The Confederate privates were mostly small farmers, that he knew, and with their land overrun by two armies they would find times hard, indeed, without work horses.

At this Lee melted entirely.

"This will have the best possible effect upon the men," he said, warming to so unmartial a conquistador. "It will be very gratifying and will do much toward conciliating our people."

Then as staff officers copied the letters of surrender and the terms, Lee bent toward Grant, as in embarrassment, and whispered in his rival's ear that his men hadn't had anything but parched corn to eat in several days. It was like one brother confiding in another. Grant turned to his staff officers: "You go to the Twenty-fourth, you to the Fiftieth," and so on, naming his various corps, "and ask every man who has three rations to turn over two of them. Go to the commissaries, go to the quartermasters. General Lee's army is on the point of starvation."

Away rode the officers and Lee's men received the food, which they wanted, almost as soon as the news of the surrender which, exhausted though they were, they did not want.

Through the Union lines went the word like a spring wind. Guns began to boom salutes of victory. Grant, hearing them, ordered all celebration to stop. "The rebels are our countrymen again; the best sign of rejoicing after the victory will be to abstain from all demonstrations on the field," he said.

Grant rode one way, Lee the other, such a sight as the world never saw before, the victor as depressed as the vanquished. Around Lee pressed his ragged starvelings, weeping, holding his hand, calling upon God to bless him. He wept, too, saying, "I have done the best I could for you."

The surrender itself was quietly done—no ceremonies, no humiliations of ceremonious capitulation. Confederate officers signed paroles for the Army of Northern Virginia, 26,765 men—all that were left from the 49,000 who had begun the Appomattox campaign. Death and desertion had both been busy. A few of the Union fighters felt a little cheated at not being able to behold a formal ceremony such as had been celebrated at Yorktown in 1781, with the defeated enemy marching without guns between long lines of their conquerors, but no such nonsense lived in the mass of Northern troops, who were content to feed the Confederates, slap them on the back, and call Good-by as they crawled on their horses and scattered southward.

Grant, in whose iron face a faint trace of easiness was now apparent, sat down in his camp. He was silent for a time and his staff was silent, too, watching him. At length Grant spoke up, addressing his quartermaster: "Ingalls, do you remember that old white mule that So-and-So used to ride when we were in the City of Mexico?"

Of course Ingalls remembered it. His business was to remember things that his idol wanted. That was what a quartermaster was for.

And as the Spring twilight came down, Grant talked on and on —his officers no doubt squirming with their desire to rehash and gossip about the great surrender—his mind rambling on back across twenty years to center and cling to the antics of an old white mule on the road to Popocatapetl.

5

ON THAT SAME APRIL 9, a weary President returned to Washington and went at once to the home of Secretary Seward, who had been seriously injured when thrown from his carriage a few days earlier. Margaret Leech portrays Lincoln's reception—and the Capital's—of the news that the war was over.

SEWARD LAY ON THE SIDE of the bed away from the door, precariously stretched along the edge, so that his painful broken arm projected, free from any pressure. His face, swathed in bandages, was so swollen and discolored as to be nearly unrecognizable. He managed to whisper, "You are back from Richmond?" "Yes," the President told him, "and I think we are near the end, at last." Lincoln sprawled across the bed, resting on his elbow with his face close to Seward's, and related the story of the last two weeks. At last, the Secretary of State fell into a feverish sleep, and Lincoln slipped softly from the room.

Before he went to rest, the President learned from Stanton that Lee's army had surrendered that morning at Appomattox. Few were abroad in the dark and damp to join the jollification of the newspaper reporters. Most people in the Capital were informed of the surrender when, at daybreak next morning, their beds were shaken by the repercussions of the guns. The battery was stationed on Massachusetts Avenue, behind Lafayette Square, and cracking windowpanes in that aristocratic neighborhood provoked some of the residents to wish an end to the Union's rejoicing. A large crowd of patriots was soon hurrahing in the bleak dawn. Many loyal persons, however, remained abed, satisfied to know that the tongues of the guns proclaimed victory for General Grant.

The morning newspapers brought full details to Washington breakfast tables. . . . The rainy April morning was lighted by the promise of peace. The capitulation of the Southern chieftain foretold the end of the rebellion, for it must quickly be followed by the surrender of Joe Johnston's army to Sherman and the collapse of the other scattered remnants of the Confederate forces. For a second time, Monday was given over to celebration. At an early hour, flags were waving in the rain. The government offices and many business firms granted their employees another holiday, and again the Capital was in an uproar of salutes, bells, music, cheers and speeches.

There was not the wild hysteria that had greeted the fall of Richmond. Popular emotion had been too freely spent to repeat that outburst in a single week. Yet there was one new factor which made for the strongest excitement on April 10. The President was back in Washington, and to the White House, from breakfast time on, people went running like joyful children eager to see their father. Several times, Lincoln, hard at work in his office, sent out word to disperse the crowds, but twice he appeared briefly at the window. In the forenoon, a procession followed in the wake of the Navy Yard workmen, who had been rampaging through the streets with bands and noisy boat howitzers. While the little show-off, Tad, waved a captured rebel flag, there were shouts for a speech. The President's appearance was the signal for pandemonium. Throwing their hats in the air again and again, men gave vent to throat-splitting yells of exultation. Lincoln briefly excused himself. He supposed that there would be some general demonstration, and he would say something then. He called on the musicians to play the good old tune of "Dixie," which he declared had now become the lawful property of the Union.

Late in the afternoon, he again responded to rousing calls by saying that he would defer his remarks; preferably until the following evening, as he would then be better prepared.

The President's features had lost their look of illness and fatigue. His thin face was shining. The burden of "this great trouble" was about to be lifted from his shoulders; but there was no elation in his happiness. Absorbed in thoughts of rebuilding the Union, his joy was sobered by the heavy responsibilities of victory.

It was announced that the Government buildings would again be illuminated on Tuesday evening, and Washington prepared to give the President a grand ovation on the occasion of his promised speech. Its general tenor should not have been hard to anticipate. The President had become widely beloved as a man of mercy. Charity for all had been the keynote of his recent inaugural address. His conferences with Grant had been followed by generous terms to the defeated enemy. On Tuesday evening, across the Potomac, General Lee's mansion blazed with lights, and a host of freedmen trampled the lawn, chanting "The Year of Jubilee."

. . . While the illuminations turned a shrouding mist to gold, an immense throng gathered before the White House, filling the grounds and obstructing the sidewalks on Pennsylvania Avenue. As Lincoln stepped to the window, cheers surged and broke, and surged again. An observer felt that "there was something terrible in the enthusiasm. . . ." The crowd was vibrating with emotion, which a word from the President could have turned to frenzy.

Lincoln, however, scarcely dwelt on the victory which was the reason for the demonstration. At this jubilant moment of his country's history, his mind was fixed on the resumption of the relations between the Union and the rebellious States. As though he were addressing a persuasive message to the Congress which had already rejected his policies, he read from a carefully prepared manuscript an elucidation of his views on reconstruction, and their practical application in the case of Louisiana. His address was a defense and a plea; reasonable, expository, lacking in eloquence. It was a noble speech, and one quite unsuited to the humor of his auditors. Some reporters heard cheers, and cheers there must have been—for a personality and an occasion. Others said that the serenaders stood silent, surprised at finding their elation punctured by the arguments of statesmanship. On the subject of Negro suffrage, the President's opinions were far too moderate to suit the radicals of his party; yet his statement that he favored giving the vote to certain colored men, the very intelligent and the soldiers, must have fallen with chilling effect on a part of his audience. . . .

Senator James Harlan, of Iowa, designate for the post of Secretary of the Interior, followed the President at the window, and evoked an outburst by asking what should "be done with these brethren of ours." "Hang 'em!" cried the crowd. There were shouts of "Never! never!" when he suggested that Mr. Lincoln might exercise the pardoning power. The crowd, however, sustained Harlan in supposing the mass of the rebels innocent. It was only the punishment of the leaders that they cheered; and there was great and prolonged applause for Harlan's concluding statement, that he was willing to trust the future to the President.

Calls for other speakers were interrupted when a band struck up "The Battle Cry." The misty drizzle thickened into raindrops, and the multitude began to disperse.

CHAPTER TWENTY-FOUR

Death—and a People's Grief

E *NOUGH LIVES have been sacrificed; we must extinguish our resentments if we expect harmony and union." Thus spoke Lincoln to his Cabinet on the 14th of April, 1865.*

1

WARD HILL LAMON tells the strange story of a dream.

THE MOST STARTLING INCIDENT in the life of Mr. Lincoln was a dream he had only a few days before his assassination. To him it was a thing of deadly import, and certainly no vision was ever fashioned more exactly like a dread reality. . . . After worrying over it for some days, Mr. Lincoln seemed no longer able to keep the secret. I give it as nearly in his own words as I can, from notes which I made immediately after its recital. There were only two or three persons present. The President was in a melancholy, meditative mood, and had been silent for some time. Mrs. Lincoln, who was present, rallied him on his solemn visage and want of spirit. This seemed to arouse him, and without seeming to notice her sally he said, in slow and measured tones:

"It seems strange how much there is in the Bible about dreams. There are, I think, some sixteen chapters in the Old Testament and four or five in the New in which dreams are mentioned; and there are many other passages scattered throughout the book which refer to visions. If we believe the Bible, we must accept the fact that in the old days God and His angels came to men in their sleep and made themselves known in dreams. Nowadays dreams are regarded as very foolish, and are seldom told, except by old women and by young men and maidens in love."

Mrs. Lincoln here remarked: "Why, you look dreadfully solemn; do *you* believe in dreams?"

"I can't say that I do," returned Mr. Lincoln; "but I had one the other night which has haunted me ever since. After it occurred, the first time I opened the Bible, strange as it may appear, it was at the twenty-eighth chapter of Genesis, which relates the wonderful dream Jacob had. I turned to other passages, and seemed to encounter a dream or a vision wherever I looked. I kept on turning the leaves of the old book, and everywhere my eye fell upon passages recording matters strangely· in keeping with my own thoughts—supernatural visitations, dreams, visions, etc."

He now looked so serious and disturbed that Mrs. Lincoln exclaimed: "You frighten me! What is the matter?"

"I am afraid," said Mr. Lincoln, observing the effect his words had upon his wife, "that I have done wrong to mention the subject at all; but somehow the thing has got possession of me, and, like Banquo's ghost, it will not down."

This only inflamed Mrs. Lincoln's curiosity the more, and while bravely disclaiming any belief in dreams, she strongly urged him to tell the dream which seemed to have such a hold upon him, being seconded in this by another listener. Mr. Lincoln hesitated, but at length commenced very deliberately, his brow overcast with a shade of melancholy.

"About ten days ago," said he, "I retired very late. I had been up waiting for important dispatches from the front. I could not have been long in bed when I fell into a slumber, for I was weary. I soon began to dream. There seemed to be a death-like stillness about me. Then I heard subdued sobs, as if a number of people were weeping. I thought I left my bed and wandered downstairs. There the silence was broken by the same pitiful sobbing, but the mourners were invisible. I went from room to room; no living person was in sight, but the same mournful sounds of distress met me as I passed along. It was light in all the rooms; every object was familiar to me; but where were all the people who were grieving as if their hearts would break? I was puzzled and alarmed. What could be the meaning of this? Determined to find the cause of a state of things so mysterious and so shocking, I kept on until I arrived at the East Room, which I entered. There I met with a sickening surprise. Before me was a catafalque, on which rested a corpse wrapped in funeral vestments. Around it were stationed soldiers who were acting as guards; and there was a throng of people, some gazing mournfully upon the corpse, whose face was covered, others weeping pitifully. 'Who is dead in the White House?' I demanded of one of the soldiers. 'The President,' was his answer; 'he was killed by an assassin!' Then came a loud burst of grief from the crowd, which awoke me from my dream. I slept no more that night; and although it was only a dream, I have been strangely annoyed by it ever since."

"That is horrid!" said Mrs. Lincoln. "I wish you had not told it. I am glad I don't believe in dreams, or I should be in terror from this time forth."

"Well," responded Mr. Lincoln, thoughtfully, "it is only a dream, Mary. Let us say no more about it, and try to forget it."

This dream was so horrible, so real, and so in keeping with other dreams and threatening presentiments of his, that Mr. Lincoln was profoundly disturbed by it. During its recital he was grave, gloomy, and at times visibly pale, but perfectly calm. He spoke slowly, with measured accents and deep feeling. In conversations with me he referred to it afterward, closing one with this quotation from *Hamlet*: "To sleep; perchance to dream! ay, *there's the rub!*" with a strong accent on the last three words.

Once the President alluded to this terrible dream with some show of playful humor. "Hill," said he, "your apprehension of harm to me from some hidden enemy is downright foolishness. For a long time you have been trying to keep somebody—the Lord knows who—from killing me. Don't you see how it will turn out? In this dream it was not me, but some other fellow, that was killed. It seems that this ghostly assassin tried his hand on some one else. And this reminds me of an old farmer in Illinois whose family were made sick by eating greens. Some poisonous herb had got into the mess, and members of the family were in danger of dying. There was a half-witted boy in the family called Jake; and always afterward when they had greens the old man would say, 'Now, afore we risk these greens, *let's try 'em on Jake. If he stands 'em*, we're all right.' Just so with me. As long as this imaginary assassin continues to exercise himself on others *I* can stand it." He then became serious and said: "Well, let it go. I think the Lord in His own good time and way will work this out all right. God knows what is best."

These words he spoke with a sigh, and rather in a tone of soliloquy, as if hardly noting my presence.

2

ON THE MORNING of April 14, Lincoln asked Frederick W. Seward, acting as Secretary of State during his father's incapacity, to call the Cabinet together at eleven o'clock. Again there was talk of a dream. Seward recalls the occasion.

I sent out the notices, and at the appointed hour came Secretaries McCulloch and Welles; Postmaster General Dennison and Attorney General Speed soon arrived, and I appeared as representative of the State Department. Mr. Lincoln, with an expression of visible relief and content upon his face, sat in his study chair, by the south window, chatting with us over "the great news." Some curiosity was expressed as to what had become of the heads of the rebel government—whether they would escape from the country, or would remain to be captured and tried; and if tried, what penalty would be visited upon them?

All those present thought that, for the sake of general amity and good will, it was desirable to have as few judicial proceedings as possible. Yet would it be wise to let the leaders in treason go entirely unpunished? Mr. Speed remarked that it would be a difficult problem if it should occur.

"I suppose, Mr. President," said Governor Dennison, "you would not be sorry to have them escape out of the country?"

"Well," said Mr. Lincoln slowly, "I should not be sorry to have them out of the country; but I should be for following them up pretty close, to make sure of their going."

The conversation turning upon the subject of sleep, Mr. Lincoln remarked that a peculiar dream of the previous night was one that had occurred several times in his life—a vague sense of floating—floating away on some vast and indistinct expanse, toward an unknown shore. The dream itself was not so strange as the coincidence that each of its previous recurrences had been followed by some important event or disaster, which he mentioned.

The usual comments were made by his auditors. One thought it was merely a matter of coincidences.

Another laughingly remarked, "At any rate it cannot presage a victory nor a defeat this time, for the war is over."

I suggested, "Perhaps at each of these periods there were possibilities of great change or disaster, and the vague feeling of uncertainty may have led to the dim vision in sleep."

"Perhaps," said Mr. Lincoln, thoughtfully, "perhaps that is the explanation."

Mr. Stanton was the last to arrive. He brought with him a large roll of paper, upon which he had been at work.

General Grant entered, in accordance with the President's invitation, and was received with cordial welcomes and congratulations. He briefly and modestly narrated the incidents of the surrender. Mr. Lincoln's face glowed with approval when, in reply to his inquiry, "What terms did you make for the common soldiers?" General Grant said, "I told them to go back to their homes and families, and they would not be molested, if they did nothing more."

Kindly feeling toward the vanquished, and hearty desire to restore peace and safety at the South, with as little harm as possible to the feelings or the property of the inhabitants, pervaded the whole discussion.

At such a meeting, in such a time, there could be but one question—the restoration or re-establishment of the Federal Union.

The conference was long and earnest, with little diversity of opinion, except as to details. One of the difficulties of the problem was, who should be recognized as State authorities? There was a loyal governor in Virginia. There were military governors in some of the other States. But the Southern legislatures were for the most part avowedly treasonable. Whether they should be allowed to continue until they committed some new overt act of hostility; whether the governors should be requested to order new elections; whether such elections should be ordered by the general government—all these were questions raised.

Among many similar expressions of the President, was the remark: "We can't undertake to run State governments in all these Southern States. Their people must do that—though I reckon that at first some of them may do it badly."

The Secretary of War then unrolled his sheets of paper, on which he had drafted the outlines of reconstruction, embodying the President's views, and, as it was understood, those of the other members of the Cabinet. In substance it was that the Treasury Department should take possession of the custom houses, and proceed to collect the revenues; that the War Department should garrison or destroy the forts; that the Navy Department should, in like manner, occupy the harbors, take possession of navy yards, ships, and ordnance; that the Interior Department should send out its surveyors, land, pension, and Indian agents and set them at work; that the Postmaster General should reopen his post-offices and re-establish his mail routes; that the Attorney General should look after the re-establishment of the Federal courts, with their judges, marshals, and attorneys: in short, that the machinery of the United States government should be set in motion; that its laws should be faithfully observed and enforced; that anything like domestic violence or insurrection should be repressed; but that public authorities and private citizens should remain unmolested, if not found in actual hostility to the government of the Union.

It must have been about two o'clock when the Cabinet meeting ended. At its close, the President remarked that he had been urged to visit the theatre that evening, and asked General Grant if he would join the party. The General excused himself, as he had a previous engagement. He took his leave, and some of the others followed him.

Then I said, "Mr. President, we have a new British Minister, Sir Frederick Bruce. He has arrived in Washington, and is awaiting presentation. At what time will it be convenient for you to receive him?"

He paused a moment in thought, and replied:

"Tomorrow at two o'clock."

"In the Blue Room, I suppose?"

"Yes, in the Blue Room," and then added with a smile,

"Don't forget to send up the speeches beforehand. I would like to look them over."

I promised to do so, and then took my leave—I never saw him afterwards.

3

AFTER THE CABINET MEETING, Lincoln went for a drive with Mrs. Lincoln, asking that no one should accompany them. During the afternoon he spoke of the future. "Mary," said he, "we have had a hard time of it since we came to Washington, but the war is over, and with God's blessing we may hope for four years of peace and happiness, and then we will go back to Illinois and pass the rest of our lives in quiet."

That evening, as they had planned, Mr. and Mrs. Lincoln went to the theater. John G. Nicolay describes the tragic sequel.

IT WAS ONLY ABOUT NOON of the fourteenth that Booth learned that the President was to go to Ford's Theater that night to see the play *Our American Cousin*. It has always been a matter of surprise in Europe that he should have been at a place of amusement on Good Friday; but the day was not kept sacred in America, except by the members of certain churches. The President was fond of the theater. It was one of his few means of recreation. Besides, the town was thronged with soldiers and officers, all eager to see him; by appearing in public he would gratify many people whom he could not otherwise meet. Mrs. Lincoln had asked General and Mrs. Grant to accompany her; they had accepted, and the announcement that they would be present had been made in the evening papers; but they changed their plans, and went north by an afternoon train. Mrs. Lincoln then invited in their stead Miss Harris and Major Rathbone, the daughter and the stepson of Senator Ira Harris. Being detained by visitors, the play had made some progress when the President appeared. The band struck up "Hail to the Chief," the actors ceased playing, the audience rose, cheering tumultuously, the President bowed in acknowledgment, and the play went on.

From the moment he learned of the President's intention, Booth's every action was alert and energetic. He and his confederates were seen on horseback in every part of the city. He had a hurried conference with Mrs. Surratt before she started for Lloyd's tavern. He intrusted to an actor named Matthews a carefully prepared statement of his reasons for committing the murder, which he charged him to give to the publisher of the *National Intelligencer*, but which Matthews, in the terror and dismay of the night, burned without showing to any one. Booth was perfectly at home in Ford's Theater. Either by himself, or with the aid of friends, he arranged his whole plan of attack and escape during the afternoon. He counted upon address and audacity to gain access to the small passage behind the President's box. Once there, he guarded against interference by an arrangement of a wooden bar to be fastened by a simple mortise in the angle of the wall and the door by which he had entered, so that the door could not be opened from without. He even provided for the contingency of not gaining entrance to the box by boring a hole in its door, through which he might either observe the occupants, or take aim and shoot. He hired at a livery stable a small, fleet horse.

A few minutes before ten o'clock, leaving his horse at the rear of the theater in charge of a callboy, he went into a neighboring saloon, took a drink of brandy, and, entering the theater, passed rapidly to the little hallway leading to the President's box. Showing a card to the servant in attendance, he was allowed to enter, closed the door noiselessly, and secured it with the wooden bar he had previously made ready, without disturbing any of the occupants of the box, between whom and himself yet remained the partition and the door through which he had made the hole.

No one, not even the comedian who uttered them, could ever remember the last words of the piece that were spoken that night —the last Abraham Lincoln heard upon earth. The tragedy in the box turned play and players to the most unsubstantial of phantoms. . . . The murderer seemed to himself to be taking part in a play. Hate and brandy had for weeks kept his brain in a morbid state. Holding a pistol in one hand and a knife in the other, he opened the box door, put the pistol to the President's head, and fired. Major Rathbone sprang to grapple with him, and received a savage knife wound in the arm. Then, rushing forward, Booth placed his hand on the railing of the box and vaulted to the stage. It was a high leap, but nothing to such an athlete. He would have got safely away but for his spur catching in the flag that draped the front of the box. He fell, the torn flag trailing on his spur; but, though the fall had broken his leg, he rose instantly, and brandishing his knife and shouting, "Sic Semper Tyrannis!" fled rapidly across the stage and out of sight. Major Rathbone called, "Stop him!" The cry rang out, "He has shot the President!" and from the audience, stupid at first with surprise, and wild afterward with excitement and horror, two or three men jumped upon the stage in pursuit of the assassin. But he ran through the familiar passages, leaped upon his horse, rewarding with a kick and a curse the boy who held him, and escaped into the night.

The President scarcely moved; his head drooped forward slightly, his eyes closed. Major Rathbone, not regarding his own grievous hurt, rushed to the door of the box to summon aid. He found it barred, and someone on the outside beating and clamoring for admittance. It was at once seen that the President's wound was mortal. A large derringer bullet had entered the back of the head, on the left side, and, passing through the brain, lodged just behind the left eye. He was carried to a house across the street, and laid upon a bed in a small room at the rear of the hall on the ground floor. Mrs. Lincoln followed, tenderly cared for by Miss Harris. Rathbone, exhausted by loss of blood, fainted, and was taken home. Messengers were sent for the Cabinet, for the Surgeon General, for Dr. Stone, Mr. Lincoln's family physician, and for others whose official or private relations to the President gave them the right to be there. A crowd of people rushed instinctively to the White House, and, bursting through the doors, shouted the dreadful news to Robert Lincoln and Major Hay, who sat together in an upper room. They ran downstairs, and as they were entering a carriage to drive to Tenth Street, a friend came up and told them that Mr. Seward and most of the Cabinet had been murdered. The news seemed so improbable that they hoped it was all untrue; but, on reaching Tenth Street, the excitement and the gathering crowds prepared them for the worst. In a few moments those who had been sent for and many others were assembled in the little chamber where the chief of the state lay in his agony. His son was met at the door by Dr. Stone, who with grave tenderness informed him that there was no hope.

4

NO FIRSTHAND ACCOUNT conveys the tensions, the fears, and the pathos of the long hours that followed Booth's pistol shot as does that which Gideon Welles entrusted to his diary.

I HAD RETIRED TO BED about half past ten on the evening of the fourteenth of April, and was just getting asleep when Mrs. Welles, my wife, said someone was at our door. Sitting up in bed, I heard a voice twice call to John, my son, whose sleeping room was on the second floor directly over the front entrance. I arose at once and raised a window, when my messenger, James Smith, called to me that Mr. Lincoln, the President, had been shot, and said Secretary Seward and his son, Assistant Secretary Frederick Seward, were assassinated. James was very much alarmed and excited. I told him his story was very incoherent and improbable, and that he was associating men who were not together and liable to attack at the same time. "Where," I inquired, "was the President when shot?" James said he was at Ford's Theatre on Tenth Street. "Well," said I, "Secretary Seward is an invalid in bed in his house yonder on Fifteenth Street." James said he had been there, stopped in at the house to make inquiry before alarming me.

I immediately dressed myself, and, against the earnest remonstrance and appeals of my wife, went directly to Mr. Seward, whose residence was on the east side of the square, mine being on the north. James accompanied me. . . . Entering the house, I found the lower hall and office full of persons, and among them most of the foreign legations, all anxiously inquiring what truth there was in the horrible rumors afloat. I replied that my object was to ascertain the facts. Proceeding through the hall to the stairs, I found one, and I think two, of the servants there holding the crowd in check. The servants were frightened and appeared relieved to see me. I hastily asked what truth there was in the story that an assassin or assassins had entered the house and assaulted the Secretary. They said it was true, and that Mr. Frederick was also badly injured. They wished me to go up, but no others. At the head of the first stairs I met the elder Mrs. Seward, who was scarcely able to speak but desired me to proceed up to Mr. Seward's room. I met Mrs. Frederick Seward on the third story, who, although in extreme distress, was, under the circumstances, exceedingly composed. I asked for the Secretary's room, which she pointed out—the southwest room. As I entered, I met Miss Fanny Seward, with whom I exchanged a single word, and proceeded to the foot of the bed. Dr. Verdi and, I think, two others were there. The bed was saturated with blood. The Secretary was lying on his back, the upper part of his head covered by a cloth, which extended down over his eyes. His mouth was open, the lower jaw dropping down. I exchanged a few whispered words with Dr. V. Secretary Stanton, who came after but almost simultaneously with me, made inquiries in a louder tone till admonished by a word from one of the physicians. We almost immediately withdrew and went into the adjoining front room, where lay Frederick Seward. His eyes were open but he did not move them, nor a limb, nor did he speak. Doctor White, who was in attendance, told me he was unconscious and more dangerously injured than his father.

As we descended the stairs, I asked Stanton what he had heard in regard to the President that was reliable. He said the President was shot at Ford's Theatre, that he had seen a man who was present and witnessed the occurrence. I said I would go immediately to the White House. Stanton told me the President was not there but was at the theatre. "Then," said I, "let us go immediately there." He said that was his intention, and asked me, if I had not a carriage, to go with him. In the lower hall we met General Meigs, whom he requested to take charge of the house, and to clear out all who did not belong there. General Meigs begged Stanton not to go down to Tenth Street; others also remonstrated against our going. Stanton, I thought, hesitated. Hurrying forward, I remarked that I should go immediately, and I thought it his duty also. He said he should certainly go, but the remonstrants increased and gathered round him. I said we were wasting time, and, pressing through the crowd, entered the carriage and urged Stanton, who was detained by others after he had placed his foot on the step. I was impatient. Stanton, as soon as he had seated himself, turned round, rose partly, and said the carriage was not his. I said that was no objection. He invited Meigs to go with us, and Judge Cartter of the Supreme Court [of the District of Columbia] mounted with the driver. At this moment Major Eckert rode up on horseback beside the carriage and protested vehemently against Stanton's going to Tenth Street; said he had just come from there, that there were thousands of people of all sorts there, and he considered it very unsafe for the Secretary of War to expose himself. I replied that I knew not where he would be more safe, and that the duty of both of us was to attend the President immediately. Stanton concurred. Meigs called to some soldiers to go with us, and there was one on each side of the carriage. The streets were full of people. Not only the sidewalk but the carriage-way was to some extent occupied, all or nearly all hurrying towards Tenth Street. When we entered that street we found it pretty closely packed.

The President had been carried across the street from the theatre, to the house of a Mr. Peterson. We entered by ascending a flight of steps above the basement and passing through a long hall to the rear, where the President lay extended on a bed, breathing heavily. Several surgeons were present, at least six, I should think more. Among them I was glad to observe Dr. Hall, who, however, soon left. I inquired of Dr. Hall, as I entered, the true condition of the President. He replied the President was dead to all intents, although he might live three hours or perhaps longer.

The giant sufferer lay extended diagonally across the bed, which was not long enough for him. He had been stripped of his clothes. His large arms, which were occasionally exposed, were of a size which one would scarce have expected from his spare appearance. His slow, full respiration lifted the clothes with each breath that he took. His features were calm and striking. I had never seen them appear to better advantage than for the first hour, perhaps, that I was there. After that, his right eye began to swell and that part of his face became discolored.

Senator Sumner was there, I think, when I entered. If not he came in soon after, as did Speaker Colfax, Secretary McCulloch, and the other members of the Cabinet, with the exception of Mr. Seward. A double guard was stationed at the door and on the sidewalk to repress the crowd, which was of course highly excited and anxious. The room was small and overcrowded. The surgeons and members of the Cabinet were as many as should have been in the room, but there were many more, and the hall and other rooms in the front or main house were full. One of these rooms was occupied by Mrs. Lincoln and her attendants, with Miss Harris. Mrs. Dixon and Mrs. Kinney came to her about twelve o'clock. About once an hour Mrs. Lincoln would repair to the bedside of her dying husband and with lamentation and tears remain until overcome by emotion.

(APRIL 15.) A door which opened upon a porch or gallery, and also the windows, were kept open for fresh air. The night was dark, cloudy, and damp, and about six it began to rain. I remained in the room until then without sitting or leaving it, when, there being a vacant chair which someone left at the foot of the bed, I occupied it for nearly two hours, listening to the heavy groans, and witnessing the wasting life of the good and great man who was expiring before me.

About 6 A.M. I experienced a feeling of faintness and for the first time after entering the room, a little past eleven, I left it and the house, and took a short walk in the open air. It was a dark and gloomy morning, and rain set in before I returned to the house, some fifteen minutes (later). Large groups of people were gathered every few rods, all anxious and solicitous. Some one or more from each group stepped forward as I passed, to inquire into the condition of the President, and to ask if there was no hope. Intense grief was on every countenance when I replied that the President could survive but a short time. The colored people especially —and there were at this time more of them, perhaps, than of whites—were overwhelmed with grief.

Returning to the house, I seated myself in the back parlor, where the Attorney General and others had been engaged in taking evidence concerning the assassination. Stanton, and Speed, and Usher were there, the latter asleep on the bed. There were three or four others also in the room. While I did not feel inclined to sleep, as many did, I was somewhat indisposed. I had been so for several days. The excitement and bad atmosphere from the crowded rooms oppressed me physically.

A little before seven, I went into the room where the dying President was rapidly drawing near the closing moments. His wife soon after made her last visit to him. The death-struggle had begun. Robert, his son, stood with several others at the head of the bed. He bore himself well, but on two occasions gave way to overpowering grief and sobbed aloud, turning his head and leaning on the shoulder of Senator Sumner. The respiration of the President became suspended at intervals, and at last entirely ceased at twenty-two minutes past seven.

5

IN BEAUTIFULLY CADENCED PROSE Carl Sandburg describes the funeral ceremonies held in Washington.

I N   T H E   E A S T   R O O M of the White House lay the body of a man, embalmed and prepared for a journey. Sweet roses, early magnolias, and the balmiest of lilies were strewn for an effect as though the flowers had begun to bloom even from his coffin. On a platform under a canopy of folds and loops of black silk and crape rested the coffin. Six feet six was the coffin in length, one foot and a half across the shoulders. The wood was mahogany, lined with lead, covered with black broadcloth, at the sides four massive silver handles. Tassels, shamrock leaves, silver stars and silver cords could be seen on facings and edges. A shield with a silver plate had the inscription:

ABRAHAM LINCOLN
SIXTEENTH PRESIDENT OF THE UNITED STATES
BORN FEB. 12, 1809
DIED APRIL 15, 1865

On a pillow of white silk lay the head, on plaited satin rested the body, dressed in the black suit in which the first inaugural was delivered, with its references to "fellow citizens," to "my dissatisfied countrymen," to "better angels," as though even among angels there are the worse and the better. The chandeliers at each end of the East Room drooped with black alpaca. The eight grand mirrors of the room spoke sorrow with nightshade silk gauze. The doors, the windows too, drooped with black alpaca.

It was Tuesday, April 18, and outside surged the largest mass of people that ever thronged the White House lawn. In two columns they filed through the East Room, moving along the two sides of the coffin, many pale and limping soldiers out of the convalescent wards of the hospitals, many women and children sobbing and weeping aloud as they passed pausing only the slightest

moment for a look. Those counting estimated twenty-five thousand. If it had been a hundred thousand or ten thousand the impression of any beholder would have been much the same.

On Wednesday, April 19, arrived sixty clergymen, the Cabinet
members, the Supreme Court Justices, important officials from
coast to coast, foreign ministers spangled in color and costume,
General Grant with white sash across his breast, Admiral Farragut
as a model of composure and quiet valor, the new President Andrew Johnson—six hundred dignitaries in all—crowded and
squeezed amid the chandeliers and eight grand mirrors of the
East Room. Mrs. Lincoln was still too distracted to be present.
Robert Lincoln had come—and Tad with a drawn, tear-swollen
face—it was not easy for them to be there.

To responsive, imaginative little Tad it was perhaps dreamlike,
a living nightmare softened by festoons of black silk, by an illusion
of black moonlight falling into a room where the tongue of no one
could possibly compete with the loud, persistent, pervasive silence
of one tongue stilled behind the shut lips amid the plaited white
satin.

"Hear my prayer, O Lord . . . I am a stranger with Thee, and
a sojourner, as all my fathers were," intoned the Reverend Dr.
C. H. Hall, rector of the Church of the Epiphany. "For a thousand years in Thy sight are but as yesterday. . . . As soon as Thou
scatterest them they are even as a sleep; and fade away suddenly
like the grass. In the morning it is green, and groweth up; but in
the evening it is cut down, dried up, and withered."

The great poem of Anglo-Saxon speech comprised in the fifteenth chapter of the first Epistle of St. Paul to the Corinthians
made the Lesson for the day. Man is cut down as a flower. He
fleeth as a shadow. Yet death may be swallowed up in victory. . . .
"Thou knowest, Lord, the secrets of our hearts; shut not thy
merciful ears to our prayers."

Bishop Matthew Simpson of the Methodist Episcopal Church
offered prayer that smitten hearts might endure, might not be
called upon for further sacrifices, that the widow and children be
comforted. "We bless Thee that no tumult has arisen, and in peace
and harmony our government moves onward; and that Thou hast
shown that our Republican government is the strongest upon the
face of the earth. . . . Hear us while we unite in praying with

Thy Church in all lands and ages. . . . Around the remains of our beloved President may we convenant together by every possible means to give ourselves to our country's service until every vestige of this rebellion shall have been wiped out, and until slavery, its cause, shall be forever eradicated." Then the Lord's Prayer . . . Thy will be done on earth, as it is in Heaven. Give us this day our daily bread. And forgive us our debts, as we forgive our debtors . . . deliver us from evil . . . Amen.

A bitter cup from the hand of a chastening Divine Father had been given the mourning nation, said the Reverend Dr. Phineas D. Gurley, of the New York Avenue Presbyterian Church, in the funeral address. "His way is in the sea, and His path in the great waters; and His footsteps are not known. . . .We bow, we weep, we worship." The cruel assassin had brought mysterious affliction. "We will wait for His interpretation . . . He may purify us more in the furnace of trial, but He will not consume us." The people had in the late President a loving confidence. No man since Washington was so deeply enshrined in the hearts of the people. He deserved it, merited it, by his acts, by the whole tone of his life. He leaned on God, remembering that "God is in history."

Dr. Gurley recalled his leaving Springfield, saying to old and tried friends, "I leave you with this request: *pray for me*," and added, "They did pray for him; and millions of others prayed for him; nor did they pray in vain." Dr. Gurley sketched the familiar outlines of the life, said it would enter "the register of the ages . . . triumph over the injuries of time," surviving busts and statues, which are frail and perishable.

The closing invocation was spoken by a Baptist clergyman, Chaplain of the United States Senate, the Reverend Dr. E. H. Gray. He beheld a nation prostrate and in sackcloth over the remains of an illustrious and beloved chief, asked compassion for hearts wrung with agony, asked blessings for those of the government who must now sustain the government. And the final ceremonial words spoken in the White House over the mute form of the author of the second inaugural and the Louisiana reconstruction speech of April 11 were as follows: "O God, let treason, that has deluged our land with blood, and devastated our country, and bereaved our homes, and filled them with widows and orphans, and has at length culminated in the assassination of the nation's chosen ruler—God of justice, and avenger of the nation's wrong, let the work of treason cease, and let the guilty author of this horrible crime be arrested and brought to justice. O hear the cry, and the prayer, and the tears now rising from a nation's crushed and smitten heart, and deliver us from the power of all our enemies, and send speedy peace unto all our borders, through Jesus Christ our Lord. Amen."

The services were over. The pallbearers took the silver handles. The bong of big bells on cathedrals struck and the little bells of lesser steeples chimed in, as across the spring sunshine came the tolling of all the church bells of Washington and Georgetown, and Alexandria across the river. Counting the minutes with their salutes came the hoarse boom of fort guns encircling the national Capital and several batteries sent into the city.

Out of the great front door of the Executive Mansion for the last time went the mortal shape of Abraham Lincoln, sixteenth President of the United States.

6

THUS BEGAN THE LONG JOURNEY to the quiet prairies of Illinois, with pauses in Philadelphia, New York, Cleveland, Indianapolis, and other cities so that a grieving people might perform the last office of devotion. Then endless peace.

On the first of may the cortege reached Chicago, where the body was to lie for twenty-four hours. On the third it would be in Springfield.

The day [May 3] broke bright and clear. Dawn found the streets crowded—for hours special trains had been pouring thousands into the prairie Capital. By eight o'clock the Alton station was an island in a human sea, and other thousands lined the tracks beyond the limits of the town. The One Forty-sixth Illinois, with detachments from other regiments, was drawn up in line on Jefferson Street. Minute guns, fired by a Missouri battery, sounded strangely sharp against the hushed voices of the crowd.

Shortly before nine o'clock the pilot engine arrived. A strained silence was the crowd's only manifestation. A few minutes later the funeral train, nine black-draped cars, drew slowly into the station.

In absolute quiet the body was placed in the magnificent hearse which the city of St. Louis had tendered for the occasion, and the long procession started for the State House. There, in the Hall of the House of Representatives, the coffin was placed on a velvet-covered catafalque. The guard of honor took their places, the casket was opened, and the people started to file past. All day and all night the slow procession continued, until it was said that 75,000 had looked upon the face of Lincoln.

At ten o'clock on the morning of May 4 the coffin was closed. While minute guns sounded, and a choir of 250 voices sang hymns on the State House steps, the casket was placed in the hearse. With General Hooker at its head, the long procession started towards Oak Ridge. The cemetery reached, the choir sang again while the body was placed in the tomb. A minister offered a prayer, another read scripture, a third read the second inaugural. The choir sang a dirge, and Bishop Simpson pronounced the funeral oration. There was a closing prayer, the Doxology, a benediction. Slowly, silently, the vast crowd dispersed.

Epilogue

"Many great deeds had been done in the war. The greatest was the keeping of the North together in an enterprise so arduous, and an enterprise for objects so confusedly related as the Union and freedom. Abraham Lincoln did this; nobody else could have done it; to do it he bore on his sole shoulders such a weight of care and pain as few other men have borne. When it was over it seemed to the people that he had all along been thinking their real thoughts for them; but they knew that this was because he had fearlessly thought for himself. He had been able to save the nation, partly because he saw that unity was not to be sought by the way of base concession. He had been able to free the slaves, partly because he would not hasten to this object at the sacrifice of what he thought a larger purpose. This most unrelenting enemy to the project of the Confederacy was the one man who had quite purged his heart and mind from hatred or even anger towards his fellow-countrymen of the South. That fact came to be seen in the South too, and generations in America are likely to remember it when all other features of his statecraft have grown indistinct. A thousand reminiscences ludicrous or pathetic, passing into myth but enshrining hard fact, will prove to them that this great feature of his policy was a matter of more than policy. They will remember it as adding a peculiar lustre to the renovation of their national existence; as no small part of the glory, surpassing that of former wars, which has become the common heritage of North and South. For perhaps not many conquerors, and certainly few successful statesmen, have escaped the tendency of power to harden or at least to narrow their human sympathies; but in this man a natural wealth of tender compassion became richer and more tender while in the stress of deadly conflict he developed an astounding strength.

"Beyond his own country some of us recall his name as the greatest among those associated with the cause of popular government. He would have liked this tribute, and the element of truth in it is plain enough, yet it demands one final consideration. He accepted the institutions to which he was born, and he enjoyed them. His own intense experience of the weakness of democracy did not sour him, nor would any similar experience of later times have been likely to do so. Yet if he reflected much on forms of government it was with a dominant interest in something beyond them. For he was a citizen of that far country where there is neither aristocrat nor democrat. No political theory stands out from his words or actions; but they show a most unusual sense of the possible dignity of common men and common things. His humour rioted in comparisons between potent personages and Jim Jett's brother or old Judge Brown's drunken coachman, for the reason for which the rarely jesting Wordsworth found a hero in the 'Leech-Gatherer' or in Nelson and a villain in Napoleon or in Peter Bell. He could use and respect and pardon and overrule his far more accomplished ministers because he stood up to them with no more fear or cringing, with no more dislike or envy or disrespect than he had felt when he stood up long before to Jack Armstrong. He faced the difficulties and terrors of his high office with that same mind with which he had paid his way as a poor man or navigated a boat in rapids or in floods. If he had a theory of democracy it was contained in this condensed note which he wrote, perhaps as an autograph, a year or two before his Presidency: 'As I would not be a slave, so I would not be a master. This expresses my idea of democracy. Whatever differs from this, to the extent of the difference, is no democracy.—A. LINCOLN.'"

LORD CHARNWOOD

References

CHAPTER I

1: Nicolay & Hay, *Abraham Lincoln, Complete Works,* I, 638–639
2: Sandburg, *Prairie Years,* I, 14–16
3: Tarbell, *Footsteps of the Lincolns,* 96–98
4: Beveridge, *Abraham Lincoln,* I, 26–29
5: Barton, *Life,* I, 87–95

CHAPTER II

1: Nicolay & Hay, *Abraham Lincoln, A History,* I, 28–30
2: Sandburg, *Prairie Years,* I, 39–40
3: Lamon, *Life,* 29–32
4: Barton, *Life,* I, 119–123
5: Lamon, *Life,* 39–45
6: Beveridge, *Abraham Lincoln,* I, 86–89
7: Sandburg, *Prairie Years,* I, 102–104

CHAPTER III

1: Nicolay & Hay, *Abraham Lincoln, Complete works,* I, 640–641
2: *Herndon's Lincoln,* I, 76–84
3: Thomas, *Lincoln's New Salem,* 53–58
4: Nicolay & Hay, *Abraham Lincoln, A History,* I, 101–109
5: Reep, *Lincoln at New Salem,* 44–47, 65
6: Thomas, *Lincoln's New Salem,* 63–69
7: Barton, *Life,* I, 192–198
8: Thomas, *Lincoln's New Salem,* 89–90

CHAPTER IV

1: Nicolay & Hay, *Abraham Lincoln, A History,* I, 119–122
2: Pratt, *Lincoln: 1809–1839,* xxxii–xxxiii
3: *Herndon's Lincoln,* I, 162–164
4: Nicolay & Hay, *Abraham Lincoln, A History,* II, 125–128
5: Lamon, *Life,* 186–191
6: Beveridge, *Abraham Lincoln,* I, 125–128
7: *Herndon's Lincoln,* I, 173–180
8: Ford, *History of Illinois,* 186–187

CHAPTER V

1: Woldman, *Lawyer Lincoln,* 16–23
2: Angle, *100 Years of Law,* 19–25
3: Nicolay & Hay, *Abraham Lincoln, A History,* I, 157–162
4: Beveridge, *Abraham Lincoln,* I, 270–275
5: Woldman, *Lawyer Lincoln,* 36–39
6: *Ibid.,* 45–48

CHAPTER VI

1: Sandburg, *Prairie Years*, I, 185–186, 189–190
2: Nicolay & Hay, *Abraham Lincoln, Complete Works*, I, 15–17
3: *Ibid.*, I, 17–18
4: Sandburg & Angle, *Mary Lincoln*, 38–60

CHAPTER VII

1: Thomas, *Lincoln: 1847–1853*, xvi–xviii
2: *Ibid.*, xx–xxv
3: *Ibid.*, xxv–xxviii
4: Busey, *Reminiscences*, 24–27
5: Townsend, *Lincoln and His Wife's Home Town*, 164–172
6: Thomas, *Lincoln: 1847–1853*, xxxi–xxxvi
7: Nicolay & Hay, *Abraham Lincoln, A History*, I, 292–297
8: Hertz, *Hidden Lincoln*, 127–128
9: *Herndon's Lincoln*, II, 303–306

CHAPTER VIII

1: Thomas, *Lincoln: 1847–1853*, xliv–xlix
2: Whitney, *Life on the Circuit*, 43–49
3: Weik, *Real Lincoln*, 156–163
4: Woldman, *Lawyer Lincoln*, 112–116
5: Pratt, *Personal Finances*, 50–54
6: *Herndon's Lincoln*, II, 315–319
7: Browne, *Everyday Life*, 142–144

CHAPTER IX

1: Lamon, *Life*, 471–472
2: Hertz, *Hidden Lincoln*, 128–129
3: Weik, *Real Lincoln*, 53–55
4: Lamon, *Life*, 470–471
5: Sandburg & Angle, *Mary Lincoln*, 66–73
6: Barton, *Life*, I, 321–324

CHAPTER X

1: Miner, *Abraham Lincoln*, 1–4
2: Phillips, *Abraham Lincoln*, 52–57
3: Newton, *Lincoln and Herndon*, 57–62
4: Nicolay & Hay, *Abraham Lincoln*, I, 213–215
5: *Ibid.*, 216–219
6: *Herndon's Lincoln*, II, 382–385
7: Whitney, *Life on the Circuit*, 78–81
8: Brooks in *Scribner's Monthly*, Feb., 1878, 561–562
9: Sandburg, *Prairie Years*, II, 92–96

CHAPTER XI

1: *Herndon's Lincoln*, II, 396–401
2: Arnold, *Life*, 140–142
3: *Herndon's Lincoln* (1892 ed.), II, 95–96, 101–105, 108
4: Sparks, *Lincoln-Douglas Debates*, 188–190
5: *Ibid.*, 190–192
6: *Ibid.*, 203–205
7: *Schurz Reminiscences*, II, 88–94
8: *Koerner Memoirs*, II, 66–68
9: Angle, *Here I Have Lived*, 233–235
10: Randall, *Lincoln the President*, I, 121–128

CHAPTER XII

1: Sandburg, *Prairie Years*, II, 326–327
2: *Ibid.*, II, 328–335
3: *Century Magazine*, June, 1900
4: Halstead, *Caucuses of 1860*, 121–123
5: *Ibid.*, 143–154
6: Lamon, *Life*, 450–453
7: Rice, *Reminiscences*, 172–175
8: Charnwood, *Abraham Lincoln*, 167–168

CHAPTER XIII

1: Nicolay & Hay, *Abraham Lincoln, Complete Works*, I, 644-645
2: Nicolay, *Personal Traits*, 134-148
3: Schurz, *Reminiscences*, II, 196-197
4: Baringer, *House Dividing*, 3-6
5: *N. Y. Herald*, Nov. 22, 1860
6: *N. Y. Herald*, Dec. 4, 1860
7: Piatt, *Memories*, 28-30, 33-35
8: *N. Y. Herald*, Dec. 24, 1860
9: Villard, *Memoirs*, I, 144-147
10: Weik, *Real Lincoln*, 294-297
11: *Herndon's Lincoln*, III, 482-485
12: Stern, *Life and Writings*, 99-100

CHAPTER XIV

1: Lamon, *Recollections*, 38-45
2: Rice, *Reminiscences*, 112-115
3: Riddle, *Recollections*, 7-10
4: Leech, *Reveille in Washington*, 37-39
5: Chittenden, *Recollections*, 71-76
6: *Diary Public Man*, 60-63
7: Leech, *Reveille in Washington*, 40-43
8: Sandburg, *War Years*, I, 121-122
9: Nicolay & Hay, *Abraham Lincoln, Complete Works*, II, 1-7
10: Sandburg, *War Years*, I, 122-123

CHAPTER XV

1: Leech, *Reveille in Washington*, 39-40
2: Nicolay & Hay, *Abraham Lincoln, A History*, III, 376-379
3: *Diary Public Man*, 84-85
4: *Bates Diary*, 177-178
5: Randall, *Civil War*, 232-238
6: *Battles* and *Leaders*, I, 75-81
7: Nicolay & Hay, *Abraham Lincoln, A History*, IV, 70-71
8: Nicolay & Hay, *Abraham Lincoln, Complete Works*, II, 57-58

CHAPTER XVI

1: *N. Y. Tribune*, Oct. 31, 1864
2: Hay, *Diaries and Letters*, 4-5
3: Nicolay & Hay, *Abraham Lincoln, A History*, IV, 149-153, 155-157
4: Hay, *Diaries and Letters*, 17, 20-21
5: Nicolay & Hay, *Abraham Lincoln, A History*, IV, 312-314
6: Nicolay, *Personal Traits*, 181-184
7: Russell, *My Diary*, 222 ff.
8: Nicolay & Hay, *Abraham Lincoln, A History*, IV, 352-357

CHAPTER XVII

1: Hay, *Diaries and Letters*, 34-35
2: *American Historical Review*, Vol. 26, 292-293
3: Chittenden, *Recollections*, 222-225
4: Charnwood, *Abraham Lincoln*, 292-302
5: Hay, *Diaries and Letters*, 44-46
6: *Welles Diary*, I, 104-107, 111-115
7: Brooks, *Washington in Lincoln's Time*, 45-53
8: *Ibid.*, 56-58
9: McClure, *Lincoln and Men of War Times*, 193-196

CHAPTER XVIII

1: Bates, *Lincoln in Telegraph Office*, 138-141
2: *Welles Diary*, I, 70-71
3: Carpenter, *Six Months at the White House*, 20-22
4: Nicolay & Hay, *Abraham Lincoln, Complete Works*, II, 234-236
5: *Chase Diary*, 87-89
6: Nicolay & Hay, *Abraham Lincoln, A History*, VI, 421-430

CHAPTER XIX

1: Lamon, *Recollections*, 96-99
2: *Journal Illinois State Historical Society*, Vol. 19, 49-52, 69-71
3: Bayne, *Tad Lincoln's Father*, 35-37, 41-50
4: Keckley, *Behind the Scenes*, 83-89
5: *Ibid.*, 95-97, 100-105
6: Brooks, *Washington in War Time*, 278-282
7: *Century Magazine*, Nov., 1890

CHAPTER XX

1: Sandburg, *War Years*, II, 339–341
2: Carr, *Lincoln at Gettysburg*, 8–10, 18–25
3: Hay, *Diaries and Letters*, 119–121
4: Nicolay & Hay, *Abraham Lincoln, Complete Works*, II, 439
5: Sandburg, *War Years*, II, 475–477

CHAPTER XXI

1: Charnwood, *Abraham Lincoln*, 349–355
2: *Welles Diary*, II, 369–371
3: Charnwood, *Abraham Lincoln*, 359–362
4: Nicolay & Hay, *Abraham Lincoln, A History*, VIII, 334–336, 339–342
5: Nicolay, *Short Life*, 396–402
6: Sandburg, *War Years*, III, 138–142
7: Nicolay, *Short Life*, 405–413

CHAPTER XXII

1: Brooks, *Washington in Lincoln's Time*, 154–158
2: Nicolay, *Short Life*, 448–449
3: Hay, *Diaries and Letters*, 227–230
4: *Ibid.*, 232–236
5: *Ibid.*, 237–238
6: Brooks, *Washington in Lincoln's Time*, 235–239
7: Nicolay & Hay, *Abraham Lincoln, Complete Works*, II, 656–657
8: Charnwood, *Abraham Lincoln*, 439–441

CHAPTER XXIII

1: Sandburg, *War Years*, IV, 39–45
2: Arnold, *Life*, 420–423
3: Porter, *Incidents and Anecdotes*, 293 ff.
4: Lewis, *Myths After Lincoln*, 3–7
5: Leech, *Reveille in Washington*, 381–383

CHAPTER XXIV

1: Lamon, *Recollections*, 114–118
2: Seward, *Reminiscences*, 254–257
3: Nicolay, *Short Life*, 536–540
4: *Welles Diary*, II, 283–288
5: Sandburg, *War Years*, IV, 388–391
6: Angle, *Here I Have Lived*, 291–292

EPILOGUE

Charnwood, *Abraham Lincoln*, 454–456

BIBLIOGRAPHY

American Historical Review, January, 1921, XXVI, No. 2. Washington: The American Historical Association.

ANGLE, PAUL M. *"Here I Have Lived"*: *A History of Lincoln's Springfield, 1821–1865.* Springfield, Illinois: Abraham Lincoln Association, 1933.

ANGLE, PAUL M. *One Hundred Years of Law.* Springfield, Illinois: Brown, Hay and Stephens, 1928.

ARNOLD, ISAAC N. *The Life of Abraham Lincoln.* Chicago: Jansen, McClurg & Co., 1885.

BARINGER, WILLIAM E. *A House Dividing*: *Lincoln as President Elect.* Springfield, Illinois: Abraham Lincoln Association, 1945.

BARTON, WILLIAM E. *The Life of Abraham Lincoln.* Two vols. Indianapolis: Bobbs-Merrill, 1925.

BATES, DAVID HOMER. *Lincoln in the Telegraph Office.* New York: Century Co., 1907.

BATES DIARY. *Annual Report, American Historical Association, 1930.* Vol. IV. Washington: Government Printing Office, 1933.

Battles and Leaders of the Civil War. Four vols. New York: Century Co., 1887–1888.

BAYNE, JULIA TAFT. *Tad Lincoln's Father.* Boston: Little, Brown, 1931.

BEVERIDGE, ALBERT J. *Abraham Lincoln, 1809–1858.* Two vols. Boston: Houghton Mifflin, 1928.

BROOKS, NOAH. *Washington in Lincoln's Time.* New York: Century Co., 1895.

BROWNE, FRANCIS FISHER. *The Every-day Life of Abraham Lincoln.* Chicago: Browne & Howell Co., 1913.

BUSEY, SAMUEL C. *Personal Reminiscences and Recollections.* Washington: 1895.

CARPENTER, FRANCIS B. *Six Months at the White House with Abraham Lincoln.* New York: Hurd and Houghton, 1866.

CARR, CLARK E. *Lincoln at Gettysburg: An Address.* Chicago: A. C. McClurg & Co., 1906.

Century Magazine, November, 1890, XLI, No. 1; June, 1900. LX, No. 2.

CHARNWOOD, LORD GODFREY RATHBONE BENSON. *Abraham Lincoln.* New York: Holt, 1917.

CHASE DIARY. *Annual Report, American Historical Association, 1902,* Vol. II. Washington: Government Printing Office, 1903.

CHITTENDEN, LUCIUS E. *Recollections of President Lincoln and His Administration.* New York: Harper, 1891.

Diary of a Public Man. Chicago: Abraham Lincoln Book Shop, 1945.

FORD, THOMAS. *A History of Illinois from its Commencement as a State in 1818 to 1847.* Chicago: S. C. Griggs & Co., 1854.

HALSTEAD, MURAT. *Caucuses of 1860: A History of the National Conventions of the Current Presidential Campaigns.* Columbus: Follett, Foster & Co., 1860.

HAY, JOHN. *Lincoln and the Civil War in the Diaries and Letters of John Hay.* New York: Dodd, Mead & Co., 1939.

HERNDON, WILLIAM H., and WEIK, JESSE W. *Herndon's Lincoln: The True Story of a Great Life.* Three vols. Chicago: Belford, Clarke & Co., 1889. Also in two vols. with an Introduction by Horace White. New York: D. Appleton & Co., 1892.

HERTZ, EMANUEL. *The Hidden Lincoln, From the Letters and Papers of William H. Herndon.* New York: Viking Press, 1938.

Journal of the Illinois State Historical Society. Springfield, Illinois: Illinois State Historical Society.

KECKLEY, ELIZABETH. *Behind the Scenes.* New York: Carleton & Co., 1868.

KOERNER, GUSTAVE. *Memoirs of Gustave Koerner, 1809–1896.* Two vols. Cedar Rapids: Torch Press, 1909.

LAMON, WARD HILL. *The Life of Abraham Lincoln; From His Birth to His Inauguration as President.* Boston: Osgood & Co., 1872.

LAMON, WARD HILL. *Recollections of Abraham Lincoln, 1847–1865.* Chicago: A. C. McClurg & Co., 1895.

LEECH, MARGARET. *Reveille in Washington, 1860–1865.* New York: Harpers, 1941.

LEWIS, LLOYD. *Myths After Lincoln.* New York: Harcourt, Brace, 1929.

McClure, Alexander K. *Abraham Lincoln and Men of War-times*: *Some Personal Recollections of War and Politics during the Lincoln Administration.* Philadelphia: Times Publishing Co., 1892.

Miner, James. *Abraham Lincoln: Personal Reminiscences.* [1912] *New York Herald,* November 22, December 4, December 24, 1860. *New York Tribune,* October 31, 1864.

Newton, Joseph Fort. *Lincoln and Herndon.* Cedar Rapids: Torch Press, 1910.

Nicolay, Helen. *Personal Traits of Abraham Lincoln.* New York: Century Co., 1912.

Nicolay, John G. *A Short Life of Abraham Lincoln, Condensed from Nicolay & Hay's Abraham Lincoln: A History.* New York: Century Co., 1902.

Nicolay, John G., and Hay, John. *Abraham Lincoln: A History.* Ten vols. New York: Century Co., 1890.

Nicolay, John G., and Hay, John. *Abraham Lincoln, Complete Works: Comprising His Speeches, Letters, State Papers, and Miscellaneous Writings.* Two vols. New York: Century Co., 1894.

Phillips, Isaac N. *Abraham Lincoln By Some Men Who Knew Him.* Bloomington, Ill.: Pantagraph Printing & Stationery Co., 1910.

Piatt, Donn. *Memories of the Men Who Saved the Union.* New York: Belford, Clarke & Co., 1887.

Porter, David D. *Incidents and Anecdotes of the Civil War.* New York: Appleton, 1885.

Pratt, Harry E. *Lincoln, 1809–1839; Being the Day-by-Day Activities of Abraham Lincoln from February 12, 1809 to December 31, 1839.* Springfield, Illinois: Abraham Lincoln Association, 1941.

Pratt, Harry E. *The Personal Finances of Abraham Lincoln.* Springfield, Illinois: Abraham Lincoln Association, 1943.

Randall, J. G. *The Civil War and Reconstruction.* Boston: D. C. Heath & Co., 1937.

Randall, J. G. *Lincoln the President, Springfield to Gettysburg.* Two vols. New York: Dodd, Mead & Co., 1945.

Reep, Thomas P. *Lincoln at New Salem.* Petersburg, Illinois: Old Salem Lincoln League, 1927.

Rice, Charles Allen Thorndike. *Reminiscences of Abraham Lincoln by Distinguished Men of His Time.* New York: Harper & Brothers, 1909.

RIDDLE, ALBERT G. *Recollections of War Times: Reminiscences of Men and Events in Washington, 1860–1865.* New York: Putnam, 1895.

RUSSELL, WILLIAM HOWARD. *My Diary North and South.* Boston: T. O. H. P. Burnham, 1863.

SANDBURG, CARL. *Abraham Lincoln: The Prairie Years.* Two vols. New York: Harcourt, Brace, 1926.

SANDBURG, CARL. *Abraham Lincoln: The War Years.* Four vols. New York: Harcourt, Brace, 1939.

SANDBURG, CARL, and ANGLE, PAUL M. *Mary Lincoln, Wife and Widow.* New York: Harcourt, Brace, 1932.

SCHURZ, CARL. *The Reminiscences of Carl Schurz.* Three vols. New York: McClure Co., 1907–1908.

Scribner's Monthly, February, 1878, XV, No. 5.

SEWARD, FREDERICK W. *Reminiscences of a War-Time Statesman and Diplomat, 1830–1915.* New York: Putnam, 1916.

SPARKS, EDWIN ERLE. *The Lincoln-Douglas Debates of 1858.* Springfield, Illinois: Illinois State Historical Library, 1908.

STERN, PHILIP VAN DOREN. *The Life and Writings of Abraham Lincoln.* New York: Modern Library, 1942.

TARBELL, IDA M. *In the Footsteps of the Lincolns.* New York: Harper & Bros., 1924.

THOMAS, BENJAMIN P. *Lincoln, 1847–1853; Being the Day-by-Day Activities of Abraham Lincoln from January 1, 1847 to December 31, 1853.* Springfield, Ill.: Abraham Lincoln Association, 1936.

THOMAS, BENJAMIN P. *Lincoln's New Salem.* Springfield, Illinois: Abraham Lincoln Association, 1934.

TOWNSEND, WILLIAM H. *Lincoln and His Wife's Home Town.* Indianapolis: 1929.

VILLARD, HENRY. *Memoirs of Henry Villard, Journalist and Financier, 1835–1900.* Two vols. Boston: Houghton Mifflin, 1904.

WEIK, JESSE W. *The Real Lincoln: A Portrait.* Boston: Houghton Mifflin, 1922.

WELLES, GIDEON. *Diary of Gideon Welles, Secretary of the Navy under Lincoln and Johnson.* 3 vols. Boston: Houghton Mifflin, 1911.

WHITNEY, HENRY C. *Life on the Circuit with Lincoln.* Boston: Estes and Lauriat, 1892.

WOLDMAN, ALBERT A. *Lawyer Lincoln.* Boston: Houghton Mifflin, 1936.

INDEX

Able, Mrs. Bennett, 117

Abolitionism, Lincoln's position on, 84–86; McClellan opposes, 387; adherents condemn Lincoln, 403

Adams, John Quincy, 502

Adams, Henry, 329, 337

Aesop's Fables, 24

Alexandria, Va., 366

Allen, Charles, 175–76

Allen, Dr. John, 61–62, 116

Allen, ——, 209–210, 483

Allen & Stone, 95

Alley, Nelson, 56

Alton, Ill., debate, 230, 246–47; seeks state capital, 84, 87–88

Anderson, Charles, 448

Anderson, Robert, musters Lincoln into service, 45; commands at Fort Sumter, 337; asks relief for Fort Sumter, 339; loyalty questioned, 341; on Fort Sumter crisis, 342; refuses to surrender, 347–48; surrenders, 350–51

Angle, Paul M., on Stuart partnership, 94–98; on conclusion Lincoln-Douglas debates, 247–48; describes Lincoln funeral, 536–37

Angle & Sandburg, on Lincoln's marriage, 122–31

Annapolis Junction, Md., 36–63

Anthony, Senator, 489

Antietam, Md., Battle of, 394, 411

Anti-Nebraska Party, 209

Appomattox Court House, 513–15

Armstrong, Hannah, 42, 178–79

Armstrong, Hugh, 43

Armstrong, Jack, wrestling match, 42; in Lincoln's company, Black Hawk War, 43; father of "Duff," 175; Lincoln defends son, 178–79

Armstrong, Pleasant, 43

Armstrong, Robert, 61

Armstrong, William ("Duff"), 175–79

Arnold, Benedict, 138

Arnold, Isaac N., describes Lincoln in 1849, 162–63; characterizes Lincoln and Douglas, 230–31

Armies, Cumberland, 456; Northern Virginia, 439, 513–16; Potomac, 394–98, 439, 513–16; Virginia, 389–90

Ashmun, George, heads notification committee, 278; describes Douglas interview with Lincoln, 355–58

Atchison, David R., 201

Atlanta, Ga., 471, 472, 481

Augur, Christopher C., 470

Augusta, Ga., *Chronicle,* 500, 501

Ayers, R. B., 434–35

Bagley *vs.* Vanmeter, 173

Baker, Edward D., nominated for state senate, 106; elected to Congress, 132; and land office, 156–57; campaigns with Lincoln, 231; at first inauguration, 332–34; mentioned, 107

Baker, Edward L., 276

Baker, Henry L., 209–10

Baker, Julia, 426–27

Baldwin, John B., 346

Bale, Abraham, 61

Bale, Jacob, 61

Baltimore, Md., Democratic Convention, 262, 282, 284; conspiracy against Lincoln, 311–14; riots, 358–59; Early invades, 467; Union Party Convention, 477–81

Banks, Nathaniel P., vote for, in vice-presidential nomination, 219; contender for presidency, 267; takes Port Hudson, 454

Baringer, William E., describes Lincoln's election, 291–94

Barrancas, Fort, 344

Barrett, James W., 248

Barton, William E., describes life on Knob Creek, 11–15; describes Lincoln's schooling, 23–25; on Lincoln and New Salem, 60–62; on social life in Springfield, 198–200

Bat (ship), 506

Bates, Edward, contender for presidency, 256, 258, 260, 266–67; nominated, 269, 271, 272; appointed attorney general, 338; on Fort Sumter crisis, 342, 345; visits Hooker's headquarters, 394; endorses Lincoln's promise to cooperate with successor, 487

Battery (newspaper), 155

Beardstown, Ill., Lincoln at, 44; postal receipts, 59; Armstrong case, 175–79;

Lincoln speaks at, 232; Douglas speaks at, 232

Beauregard, P. G. T., commands South Carolina forces, 337; in Fort Sumter action, 347–51; at Bull Run, 369; in Tennessee campaign, 473

Beecher, Edward, 110

Bell, John, 149, 282

Benton, Thomas H., 201

Berdan, Hiram, 436

Bergen, Abram, describes Armstrong trial, 175–76, 177

Berry, Squire, 92

Berry, William F., 43, 51–55

Beveridge, Albert J., describes Knob Creek farm, 9–11; account of flatboat trip, 30–33; describes Illinois legislature, 78–82; on Harrison campaign, 102–06; quoted, 253; mentioned, xi

Bidwell, Daniel D., 469

Birney, James G., 102

Bissell, William H., 181, 216

Black Hawk War, Lincoln in, 42–46, 286–87

Black River, Wis., 45

Blackstone's Commentaries, 90

Blair, Austin, 269

Blair, Francis P., Jr., nominates Bates, 269; visits Lincoln, 303

Blair, Francis P., Sr., at Republican Convention, 265; calls on Lincoln, 303, 321; home burned, 467; peace mission, 496–97

Blair, Montgomery, at Chicago Convention, 268; calls on Lincoln, 321; appointed postmaster general, 338; on Fort Sumter crisis, 345; at military council, 379; and Emancipation Proclamation, 407, 413; at Gettysburg, 445; home burned, 467; endorses Lincoln's promise to cooperate with successor, 487

Blanchard, John, 144

Bledsoe, Albert T., 107

Bloomington, Ill., Lincoln and Douglas at, 204–05

Bogota, Colombia, consulate, 126

Booth, John Wilkes, 526–28

Bradford, A. W., 467

Bragg, Braxton, 451, 456–57

Brayman, Mason, 180

Breckinridge, John C., candidate for presidency, 282, 284; threatens Washington, 466–70

Breese, Sidney, 47

Brewster House, Freeport, Ill., 236, 238, 239

Brooks, Noah, describes campaign of 1856, 220–22; on Lincoln's visit to Hooker's headquarters, 394–98; on Hooker's defeat, 398–99; charac-

terizes Tad Lincoln, 430–32; describes Lincoln's second nomination, 477–79; describes Lincoln's second inauguration, 488–91

Brown, Christopher C., 276, 277

Brown, B. Gratz, 303–04

Browne, Thomas C., 78

Brownell, Francis E., 367

Brownfield, George, 5

Browning, Orville H., in Whig Party, 47; characterized, 81; favors Clay for President, 153; diary quoted, 198–99; Lincoln with, at Quincy, 244; favors Bates for President, 260; responds for Lincoln, 274

Browning, Mrs. Orville H., characterized, 81; letter to, from Lincoln, 119–22; calls on Lincolns, 199

Brown's Hotel, Washington, 133

Bruce, Sir Frederick, 525

Brumfield, William, 5

Bryant, William Cullen, describes Illinois Volunteers, 43; characterizes Thurlow Weed, 262; advises Lincoln, 287; poetry, Lincoln's fondness for, 437

Buchanan, James, presidential possibility, 152; elected President, 222; opposes Douglas, 227; Lincoln calls on, 320; at Lincoln inauguration, 332; Fort Sumter policy, 343–44; in White House, 415

Buchanan, Franklin, 420

Buell, Don Carlos, 400

Buena Vista, Battle of, 137, 138

"Buena Vista," 145

Bull Run, Battle of, 369–75. *See also* Second Battle of Bull Run.

Bullock, Mrs. Maria, 147

Burner, Daniel Green, 91

Burner, Isaac Green, 91

Burns, John, 448

Burns, Robert, poetry, 60, 437

Burnside, Ambrose E., 394, 398

Busey, Samuel C., describes Lincoln as member of Congress, 143–45

Butler, Benjamin F., 409, 465, 486

Butler, William, 47, 50

Butterfield, Daniel, 399

Butterfield, Justin, 78, 157

Byron's Poems, 60

Cabinet, Lincoln considers appointments, 301–03; intrigues over, 326–28, 337–38; confirmed, 340; and Fort Sumter, 342, 345; and re-appointment of McClellan, 390; and Emancipation Proclamation, 407–08, 411–13; discusses Lee's escape, 454–56; endorses Lincoln's promise to cooperate with successor, 487–88; last meeting, 523–26; attends funeral ceremonies, 534

Calhoun, John, 59, 71, 231

California, territorial government, 140, 141

Cameron, Simon, contender for Presidency, 266–67; nominated, 269, 271, 272; announces election returns, 293; seeks Cabinet place, 303, 304; appointed Secretary of War, 338; and Sumter crisis, 345; at Gettysburg, 448; and nomination of Lincoln, 1864, 477–78

Cameron Mill, 40

Campbell, Harriet, 124

Campbell, John A., 345–46, 497–504

Campbell, Thompson, 477–78

Capitol, U. S., in 1848, 134; described, 318–19; troops quartered in, 358–59, 364–65

Carlin, Thomas, 100

Carpenter, Francis B., account Emancipation Proclamation, 407–08

Carpenter, William, 58, 67, 68

Carr, Clark E., account preliminaries of Gettysburg ceremonies, 442–44

Cartter, David K., nominates Chase, 269; changes Ohio vote, 273; visits Lincoln, 304; and assassination, 530–31

Cartwright, Peter, debates with, 47; elected to legislature, 51; Lincoln defeats, 132; mentioned, 61

Carver Hospital, Washington, 482

Casparis, James, 144–45

Cass, Lewis, Lincoln satirizes, 46; presidential possibility, 152; candidate, 155

Castle Pinckney, S. C., 344

Centreville, Va., 369–73

Cerro Gordo, Battle of, 138

Champion's Hill, Battle of, 453

Chancellorsville, Battle of, 398–99

Chapman, Augustus H., 191

Chapman, Harriet. *See* Hanks, Harriet.

Charles I, Lincoln's anecdote, 499–500

Charleston, Ill., debate, 230, 242, 304–06

Charleston, S. C., Democratic Convention, 261–62, 282, 284; excitement over Sumter attack, 349

Charnwood, Lord, analyzes Lincoln's nomination, 280–81; account Peninsular campaign, 382–88; account Vicksburg campaign, 451–54; account Tennessee campaign, 456–57; on Lincoln's religion, 493–95; epilogue by, 538–39; mentioned, xi

Chase, Kate, 419

Chase, Salmon P., in Congress, 231; contender for presidential nomination, 256, 258, 267; nominated, 269,

271, 272; congratulates Lincoln, 285; appointed to Cabinet, 301–02, 338; calls on Lincoln, 303, 321–22; intrigue against, 326–28; on Sumter crisis, 345; attends military council, 379; apprehensive about *Merrimac,* 381; condemns re-appointment of McClellan, 391; and Proclamation of Emancipation, 407, 411–13; presses for Grant's removal, 452; bids for Presidency, 476–77; attends Johnson inauguration, 489, 490

Chattanooga, Tenn., relieved, 456–57

Chestnut, James, 347

Cnicago, Ill., postal receipts, 59; Lincoln speaks at, 156, 230; Douglas speaks at, 229; Republican Convention, 265–76, 284; celebrates Lincoln's nomination, 275; delegation advocates emancipation, 408

Chicago, Ill., *Times,* reports Freeport debate, 236–37

Chicago, Ill., *Tribune,* reports debates, 232, 237–39; on Lincoln's nomination, 275

Chickamauga, Battle of, 434, 456–57

Chisholm, A. R., 348

Chittenden, L. E., account Lincoln and Peace Conference, 322–26; on *Monitor* and *Merrimac,* 380–82

Chrisman Brothers, 52

City Point, Va., Butler's Army at, 465–66; Lincoln visits, 504–07; Sherman visits, 504–07

Civil War, begins, 347–51; first Northern advance, 365–67; Peninsular campaign, 382–88; end, 513–16

Clarke, C. J. F., 55–56

Clary, Bill, 41, 43

Clary, Royal, 43

Clary's Grove boys, 41–42, 43–44, 52

Clay, Cassius M., sues enemies, 150; vote for, Chicago Convention, 272; congratulates Lincoln, 285–86; describes Lincoln's inauguration, 336

Clay, Henry, dropped by Whigs, 102, 151–53; in Kentucky politics, 150; vote for, Philadelphia Convention, 153

Clay, James B., 323

Clinton, Ill., 204

Coffin, Charles Carleton, describes notification ceremony, 278–80

Cold Harbor, Va., 464–65

Coles County, Ill., Lincolns in, 37–38

Colfax, Schuyler, 531

Collamer, Jacob, 219, 270, 271

Congress, U. S., Lincoln in, 132–58; effect of, on Lincoln, 162–63

Congress (ship), 380

Conkling, James C., describes circuit

practice, 97; describes Lincoln, 125–26, 127

Connolly, James A., account of Lincoln's visit to Charleston, Ill., 304–06

Constitution, U. S., and slavery, 211–12; Lincoln to defend, 325–26

Constitutional Union Party, 282

Cook, B. C., in senatorial contest, 209–10; and second nomination of Lincoln, 477–78, 480

Cooper Institute Speech, 231

Corwin, Thomas, 138, 269

Couch, Darius N., 395

Cox, Samuel S., 482

Crawford, Andrew, 23

Crawford, Betsey, 34

Crawford, Mrs. Elizabeth, 27–28

Crawford, Josiah, 25, 33

Crittenden, John J., 150, 231

Crume, Ralph, 5

Cumberland (ship), 380

Curtin, Andrew G., 443, 447

Cushing, Caleb, 262

Dahlgren, John A., 434

Dana, Charles A., 482

"Danites," 227

David, William, 31

Davidson, William H., 81

Davis, David, characterizes Logan, 107; on Eighth Circuit, 163–64, 166–70; comment on senatorial election, 210; attends Bloomington Convention, 216; holds court at Urbana, 217–19; at Chicago Convention, 259; and assassination plot, 313; mentioned, 208, 257

Davis, Henry Winter, 485

Davis, Jefferson, clashes with Douglas, 262; Confederate President, 303; relieves Johnston, 472; puts Beauregard in command, 473; conference with Blair, 496–97; instructions for Hampton Roads conference, 498–99; home of, Lincoln visits, 512

Davis, Mrs. Jefferson, 425

Dawson, John, 67, 68, 73

Dayton, William L., proposed for Vice Presidency, 219; proposed for Presidency, 269, 271, 272; proposed for Cabinet, 328

Decatur, Ill., Lincoln cabin near, 37; seeks state capital, 84; State Republican Convention, 263–65

Declaration of Independence, 223–25

"Deep Snow," 31

Delahay, Mark W., 259–60

Delano, Columbus, 269

Democratic Party, attitude on Mexican War, 135–40; state convention, 227; conventions, 1860, 261, 282; nominates McClellan, 481

Dennison, William, visits Lincoln, 304; receives election returns, 482; at Johnson inauguration, 489, 490; at last Cabinet meeting, 523–25

Diary of a Public Man, quoted, 326–28; 341–42

Dickinson, Daniel S., 480

Dillworth's Speller, 24

District of Columbia, slavery in, 142–43

Dixon's Ferry, Ill., 44

Dodge, Grenville M., 336

Dodge, William E., 324, 325

Donelson, Fort, 399, 400, 450

Dorsey, Azel W., 23

Douglas, Stephen A., Lincoln meets, 70; introduces caucus, 72; characterized, 81–82; on Illinois debt, 83; supports internal improvement system, 84; defeated by Stuart, 94–95; in Harrison campaign, 104, 106; and Nebraska Bill, 201, 202, 213–14; in campaign of 1854, 204–07; defends Dred Scott decision, 222; in 1858 campaign, 226–54; speaks at Chicago, 229; Freeport doctrine, 241–42; described by Koerner, 246–47; re-elected to Senate, 248, 484–85; splits Democratic Convention, 261–62; candidate, 1860, 282, 284; calls on Lincoln, 321; at Lincoln's inauguration, 333, 336; offers support to administration, 355–58

Douglas, Mrs. Stephen A., 234, 356–57

Douglass, John M., 182

Dred Scott Case, 222–25

Dresser, Rev. Charles, 131, 188

Drummond, Thomas, estimate of Lincoln as lawyer, 185–87

Dubois, Jesse K., in Whig Party, 47; characterized, 79; Lincoln's relations with, 181; seeks to retain Lincoln as counsel, 182; and House Divided Speech, 228; at Chicago Convention, 259

Duchesne Plantation, 32

Dudley, Thomas H., 269

Dunaway, John, 217–18

Dunbar, A. P., 305–06

Dungey vs. Spencer, 174–75

Dunn, George R., 315

Earle, Thomas, 102

Early, Jacob M., 45, 75

Early, Jubal A., 466–70

Eckert, Thomas T., describes writing of Emancipation Proclamation, 404–05; receives election returns, 484–86; and Lincoln assassination, 531

Edgar County, Ill., in Eighth Circuit, 166

Edmonds, Alexander, 172–73

Editor (steamer), 232
Edwards, Benjamin S., 155
Edwards, Cyrus, 79, 100, 156–57
Edwards, Matilda, 125, 127
Edwards, Ninian W., elected to legislature, 73; in 1836 campaign, 74, 75, 76–77; characterized, 79; home, Lincoln married in, 131; mentioned, 107, 125
Edwards, Mrs. Ninian W., sister Mary Todd, 122; at Willard's Hotel, 329; in White House, 426–27
Egan, Dr. McIllroy, 220
Eighth Circuit, extent, 96–97; Lincoln's practice in, 163–70
Eighth Massachusetts Infantry, 362–63
Election, 1846, 132; 1848, Lincoln in, 151–56; of 1860, 291–94; of 1864, 476–88
Ellsworth, Elmer, in Lincoln's law office, 185; accompanies Lincoln to polls, 292; in Lincoln party, 320, 329; and Fire Zouaves, 363–65; death, 365–67; funeral, 367
Emancipation, Lincoln decides upon, 403–414; Lincoln discusses, 408–10; compensated, 500
Emancipation Proclamation, Lincoln writes, 404–05; preliminary, issued, 413–14; reaction against, 476; no modification of, 499
Ericsson, John, 380
Evarts, William M., 268–69, 270, 274
Everett, Edward, invited to speak at Gettysburg, 443; Gettysburg speech, 446; with Lincoln at Gettysburg, 447
Ewing, James S., 204–05
Ewing, William L. D., 71

Falmouth Heights, 394
Farragut, David G., 489, 534
"Fatal first of January," 114, 125, 130
Fell, Jesse W., 204–05, 257
Felton, S. H., 311–12, 484
Fessenden, William Pitt, 231, 487, 489
Ficklin, Orlando B., 80
Fillmore, Millard, 222, 310
First Michigan regiment, 366
Fitts, N. A., 468
Fletcher, Job, 73
Flint, Margaret, xii
Florney, T. S., 152
Foote, Henry S., 488–89
Ford, Thomas, on location of Illinois capital, 86–88; on internal improvement system, 99–100
Ford's Theatre, 526–28
Forney, John W., 445–46, 484, 490
Forquer, George, 75–76
Forrest, Nathan B., 473

Fox, Gustavus Vasa, on Sumter crisis, 342; reports *Monitor* battle, 381; Lincoln's liking for, 434; prepares to send Lincoln from Washington, 467; receives election returns, 485
Francis, Mrs. Simeon, 130
Franciscus, G. C., 314
Franklin, W. B., 379
Franklin, Battle of, 473, 496
Franklin's Autobiography, 25
Frederick City, Va., 467
Fredericksburg, Battle of, 394
Free Soil Party, 155, 156
Freeport, Ill., debate, 230, 236–41; doctrine, 241–42, 252, 254
Fremont, John C., nominated for Presidency, 218; defeated, 222; vote for in Chicago Convention, 271; emancipation proclamation overruled, 403; Radical candidate, 481
French, Benjamin B., 332
French, Edmund, 144

Galena, Ill., 45
Galesburg, Ill., 230, 239, 242
Garfield, James A., 434
General Land Office, Lincoln seeks commissionership, 156–58
Gentry, Allen, 31–33
Gentry, James, 30–33
Gentryville, Ind., founded, 31; Lincoln cabin near, 18; life in, 27–28, 62
George II, 453
Georgetown, D. C., 133
Georgia, Sherman's campaign in 471–75, 505
Gettysburg, Battle of, 439–42, 450
Gettysburg, Pa., cemetery established, 442–43; cemetery dedicated, 444–46
Giddings, Joshua R., 138, 142, 287 ·
Gillespie, Joseph, 102
Gillmore, J. R., 496
Gollihur, Isaac, 43
Gourley, James, describes Lincoln's speech, 74–75; on Lincoln's domestic life, 195–96
Graham, Mentor, 39, 59, 62
Grand Gulf, Miss., 453
Granger, Francis, 324
Grant, Ulysses S., career, 399; criticized, 400–02; supported by Lincoln, 402; successes in West, 450; Vicksburg campaign, 451–54; Tennessee campaign, 456–57; made commanding general, 459–62; Richmond campaign, 462; authorizes march through Georgia, 471, 473–74; vote for, Baltimore Convention, 478–79; Lincoln visits, 504–07; receives Lee's surrender, 513–16; at last Cabinet meeting, 524–

25; declines theater invitation, 526; attends funeral ceremonies, 534

Grant, Mrs. Ulysses S., 506, 526

Gray, Rev. E. H., 535–36

Greeley, Horace, at Chicago Convention, 265, 267; Lincoln's letter to, 403; criticizes Lincoln, 409; peace mission, 496

Green, Bowling, surety on tavern license, 54; influence on Lincoln, 61; lends books, 91; justice's court, 92; helps Lincoln, 116

Green, Mrs. Bowling, 116

Green, Duff, 144

Greene, William G., clerks for Offut, 41; describes Lincoln, 42; in Black Hawk War, 43; buys and sells store, 52–54; cares for Lincoln, 116

Grigsby, Nancy, 34

Grimes, James W., 485

Grimsley, Mrs. Elizabeth Todd, at Willard's Hotel, 329; account of visit to White House, 418–21; in White House, 426–27

Grubb *vs.* Frink & Walker, 171

Gunnell, Dr. Francis M., 143

Gurley, Rev. Phineas D., 535

Hackett, James H., 436

Hagerstown, Md., 467

Hale, Rev. Albert, 289

Hale, John P., 138, 231, 485

Hall, Rev. C. H., 534

Hall, Levi, 33

Hall, Thomas, 12

Hall, Dr., 531

Halleck, Henry W., appointed military adviser, 388; relations with McClellan, 389; expected success at Bull Run, 390; deficiencies, 391, 455–56, 460; witnesses Grant ceremonies, 461; report of Early's raid, 470

Halstead, Murat, describes Chicago Convention, 265–76; on Lincoln's nomination, 280

Hamlin, Hannibal, nominated for vice-presidency, 278; letter to, 287; guest of Seward, 321; takes oath of office, 333; re-nomination proposed, 477; attends Johnson inauguration, 489

Hammond, Abram, 160–61

Hampton Roads Conference, 497–504. *See also River Queen* Conference.

Hannegan, Edward, 161

Hanks, Dennis, at Lincoln's birth, 6–7; describes Knob Creek farm, 10–11; makes coffin, 19; on Thomas Lincoln's second marriage, 20–22; describes Lincoln, 31; removal to Illinois, 33

Hanks, Harriet, account of Lincoln home life, 190–92

Hanks, John, helps build cabin, 36; on flatboat trip, 37; describes Lincoln as speaker, 47; supports Lincoln in 1860, 260; and Rail-Splitter legend, 263–65

Hanks, Lucy, 4

Hanks, Nancy, parentage, 3–4; marriage, 5. *See also* Lincoln, Nancy Hanks.

Hardin, John J., in Whig Party, 47; rival of Douglas, 70, 72; characterized, 80–81; elected to Congress, 132; campaigns with Lincoln, 231

Hardin, Martin D., characterized, 80–81

Harlow, James, 519

Harper's Weekly, 256–57

Harriott, James, 175, 178 .

Harris, Clara W., 526, 528, 532

Harris, Ira, 434

Harris, Jasper, *vs.* Great Western Railway Co., 171

Harris, Thomas L., 154–55, 253

Harrisburg, Pa., 312–14

Harrison, George M., 45, 286–87

Harrison, Peyton L., 95

Harrison, William Henry, 102–06, 151

Harrison's Landing, Va., 385, 387

Hart, Jonathan, 174

Harvey, James E., 346

Hatch, Ozias M., 181

Havana, Ill., Lincoln at, 45; postal receipts, 59; Lincoln speaks at, 232–34; Douglas speaks at, 233–34

Hawthorne *vs.* Wooldridge, 107

Hay, John, in Lincoln party, 329; describes Sixth Massachusetts, 358–59; on Ellsworth and Zouaves, 363–65; account of McClellan's rudeness, 378; gets news of Second Bull Run, 389–90; describes daily life in White House, 432–38; account of Gettysburg ceremonies, 445–46; on receiving election returns, 481, 483–86; on Cabinet meeting, Aug. 23, 1864, 487–88; at Lincoln's deathbed, 528; mentioned, xi

Hay, Milton, 95–96, 184

Haycraft, Samuel, 10, 20, 34

Hayes, Rutherford B., 481

Hazel, Caleb (teacher), 10, 11

Hazel, Caleb (tavern keeper), 14

Helm, John B., 21

Helm, Katherine, 123

Henning, Fanny, 129

Henry, Dr. Anson G., attends Lincoln, 125–26; letter to, from Lincoln, 283–84; visits Hooker's headquarters, 394

Henry, Fort, 399, 400, 450

Herndon, Archer G., 73, 110

Herndon, James, 51
Herndon, Rowan, 39–40, 51, 110
Herndon, William H., biographical
materials, 26; on Lincoln's arrival
at New Salem, 38–42; on Lincoln in
Black Hawk War, 46; Lincoln as
postmaster, 58; Lincoln in legislature, 69–70, 82–86; partnership with
Lincoln, 109–12; letters to, on Mexican War, 139–40; letters to, on Taylor candidacy, 153–54; story of Lincoln and the Kentuckian, 158–59;
story of Lincoln and the comet,
159–60; retains firm's clients, 162;
shares circuit practice, 165–66;
"Horological Cradle" case, 172; Illinois Central fee suit, 180–181; de-
fines "antithesis," 184; Lincoln divides fee with, 185; account of
Lincoln's domestic life, 190; drawn
on, by Lamon, 192–93; describes
Lincoln's dejection, 196; arranges
escape from Republicans, 208; de-
scribes "Lost Speech," 215; on Lin-
coln's nomination for Senate, 227–29;
accompanies Lincoln to polls, 292;
last interview with Lincoln, 307–08;
mentioned, xi, 257
Hildreth vs. Turner, 171–72
Hill, Samuel, 56, 59
Hingham, Mass., 3
Hodgen's Mill, 10
Hodgenville, Ky., 6
Hoffman's Row, 94
Hogan, Rev. John, 79
Holmes, Oliver Wendell, 437
Holt, Joseph, 339, 480
Hood, John B., 472–74, 496
Hood, Thomas, 437
Hood, P. H., & Co., 150
Hooker, Joseph, commands Army of
Potomac, 394; described, 397; letters
to, from Lincoln, 398, 458; Chancel-
lorsville, 398–99; relieved of com-
mand, 439; at Battle of Chattanooga,
457; attends Johnson inauguration,
489; at funeral, 537
"Horological Cradle" case, 172–73
Howard, O. O., 397
Hubbard, Gurdon S., 78
Hubbard, T. S., 220
Hume, John F., 479
Hunter, David, 313, 403
Hunter, R. M. T., 497–504
Huntington, Judge, 161
Hurst, Charles R., 110

Iles, Elijah, 45
Illinois, Taylor campaign in, 153–54,
156; Lincoln's chances in, 1860, 258–
59

Illinois Central Railroad, fee suit,
179–83
Illinois College, 110
Illinois Constitutional Convention, 152
Illinois State Fair, 205–08
Illinois State House, Lincoln's office,
283, 285, 289, 295–98
Illinois State Journal, 139, 215, 277.
See also Sangamo Journal.
Illinois State Register, 106, 138–39,
154–56
Illinois State Republican Convention,
263–65
Illinois Supreme Court, 98
Illiopolis, Ill., 84
Inauguration, Lincoln's first, 332–36;
Lincoln's second, 490–93
Independence Hall, 312
Indiana, Lincolns in, 16; schools, 23–
25; Lincoln's chances in, 1860, 259;
delegation opposes Seward, 268;
election returns, 481–83
Indiana Revised Statutes, 90
Ingalls, Rufus, 516
Internal Improvement System, 82–84,
87–88, 99–102
Island Grove, Ill., 47

Jackson, Andrew, 47–48
Jackson, Thomas Jonathan, 384–85
Jackson, Miss., 454
Jacksonville, Ill., 59, 84, 156
James, George S., 349
James, Judge, 324
Jaquess, James F., 496
Jayne, Julia, 130
Jefferson, Fort, 344
Jefferson, Thomas, philosophy, 137
Johnson, Andrew, nominated for vice-
president, 480–81; inauguration, 489–
90; at Lincoln funeral ceremonies,
534
Johnson, Richard M., 102
Johnston, Albert Sidney, 400
Johnston, John D., in Coles County,
37–38; signs receipt, 174; mentioned,
22, 26
Johnston, Joseph E., at Bull Run,
369; in Peninsular campaign, 383;
wounded, 384; commands in West,
453–54; opposes Sherman, 470–72;
Lee attempts junction with, 505–06;
prospective surrender, 517
Johnston, Matilda, 22, 26
Johnston, Sarah Bush, 20–22. See also
Lincoln, Sarah Bush.
Johnston, Sally, 22
Jones, D. R., 351
Jones, T. D., 288
Jones, William, 31
Jonesboro, Ill., 230, 242

Joseph, Jonathan, 12

Joy, James F., 180

Judd, Norman B., in senatorial contest, 209–10; attends Bloomington Convention, 216; objects to Freeport question, 240; nominates Lincoln, 248, 269; visits Lincoln, 303; learns of assassination plot, 311–14

Kane, Elias Kent, 71

Kansas, bill to organize as territory, 201; slavery agitation in, 212–14, 250–53; Lecompton constitution, 226

Kansas-Nebraska Bill. See Nebraska Bill.

Keckley, Elizabeth, characterizes Mrs. Lincoln, 424–27; describes death of William Lincoln, 427–30

Kellogg, Mrs., 426–27

Kellogg's Grove, Ill., 45

Kelly, W. D., 279

Kelso, Jack, 60, 92

Kenney, ——, and assassination plot, 314, 315

Kentucky, Lincolns in, 16; stays in Union, 450

Kilpatrick, Judson, 474

King, Austin A., 324

King, Preston, 219

Kinney, William, 47–48

Kinzie, Robert, 96

Kirkpatrick, William, 51

Knapp, N. M., 202

Knob Creek farm, 9–15

Know Nothing Party, 214

Knox, Joseph, 220

Knox, William, poem, 438

Knoxville, postal receipts, 59

Koerner, Gustave, describes Alton debate, 246–47; describes Lincoln's inauguration, 336

Krume, Ralph, 21

Krutz, Teresa, xii

Lamborn, Josiah, 78, 107, 231

Lamon, Ward Hill, describes Thomas Lincoln's second marriage, 20–22; on Lincoln's youth in Indiana, 26–30; on Lincoln in campaign of 1836, 73–77; partner of Lincoln, 164; on Eighth Circuit, 168–69; account of Lincoln's home life, 189, 192–93; how Lincoln received news of nomination, 276–78; accompanies Lincoln to polls, 292; account of assassination plot, 311–16; escorts Lincoln to Washington, 317; visits Charleston, S. C., 346; favors Grant's removal, 401; on Lincoln's troubles with clothes, 415–18; guards Lincoln,

486–87; account of Lincoln's dream, 520–23

Lane, Ebenezer, 181–82

Lane, H. S., 270–71

Lanphier, Charles H., 248, 253

"Last Leaf, The," 437

Lecompton Constitution, 226, 253

Lee, Robert E., in Peninsular campaign, 384–85; defeats Burnside and Hooker, 394; Gettysburg campaign, 439–42; escapes from Meade, 454–55; opposes Grant, Richmond campaign, 462–66; final plans anticipated, 505; evacuates Petersburg, 507; surrender, 512–16

Lee, Stephen D., describes attack on Sumter, 347–51

Leech, Margaret, on Lincoln's first day in Washington, 319–22; describes Lincoln party on eve of inauguration, 328–32; sketches Lincoln's Cabinet, 338; account of end of war, 516–19

Legislature, Illinois, Lincoln's first campaign for, 42, 46–51; Lincoln elected to, 66–67; Lincoln in, 67–77, 82–86, 99–102; members characterized, 78–82

Leonard, Newton, 331

Levering, Mercy, letters to, from Mary Todd, 124–25, 127–29; letter to, from James C. Conkling, 125–26; describes Lincoln, 127; letter to Mary Todd, 128

Lewis, Lloyd, describes Lee's surrender, 513–16

Lewistown, Ill., 59, 234

Lexington, Ky., 133

Libby Prison, 510

Lincoln, Abraham (grandfather of the President), 3–5

Lincoln, Abraham, birth and childhood, 3–15; youth, 16–35; school attendance, 23–25; flatboat trips, 30–33, 37; first year in Illinois, 36–38; at New Salem, 36–64; in Black Hawk War, 42–46; first political campaign, 46–51, 65–66; storekeeper, 51–55; postmaster and surveyor, 55–59; at Vandalia, 67–70; in legislature, 69–73, 82–86; in campaign of 1836, 73–77; studies law, 89–93; Stuart partnership, 94–98; collapse of internal improvement system, 99–102; in Harrison campaign, 102–06; Logan partnership, 107–09; Herndon partnership, 109–12; and Ann Rutledge, 114–17; and Mary Owens, 117–22; marriage, 122–31; member of Congress, 132–58; in campaign of 1848, 151–56; Land Office appointment,

156–58; leads Illinois bar, 162–87; law office described, 183–85; fee book, 185; home life in Springfield, 188–200

Re-enters politics, 201–08; defeated for Senate, 1855, 208–11; becomes Republican, 215; speech at Bloomington, 216–17; considered for vice-presidency, 217–20; at Ogle County rally, 220–22; Dred Scott speech, 222–25; in 1858 campaign, 226–54; nominated for Senate, 227–29; House Divided speech, 227–29; Chicago speech, 229–30; challenges Douglas, 230; described by Schurz, 243–45; Alton debate, 246–47; last speech in 1858, 247–48; defeated by Douglas, 254

Nominated for Presidency, 255–81; candidate and President-Elect, 282–309; leaves Springfield, 308–09; trip to Washington, 310–17; first inauguration, 332–36; Fort Sumter policy, 343–47; gets news of attack on Sumter, 351–53; first message to Congress, 353–54; receives Douglas's pledge of support, 357–58; orders Peninsular campaign abandoned, 388; relieves McClellan, 394; visits Hooker, 394–98; letter to Hooker, 398; sustains Grant, 400–02, 452–53

Proclaims Emancipation, 403–14; difficulties with clothes, 415–18; grief at son's death, 429–30; indulges Tad, 430–32; personal habits in White House, 432–38; Gettysburg Address, 443–49; dismayed by aftermath of Gettysburg, 454–56; military capacity, 457–59; capture of, planned, 468; under fire, 469–70; congratulates Sherman, 475; nomination, 1864, 476–79; re-elected, 483–86; second inauguration, 488–91; second inaugural address, 491–93; religion, 493–95; confers with Stephens, Campbell, and Hunter, 497–504; confers with Grant and Sherman, 504–07; last speech, 518–19; ominous dreams, 520–24; last Cabinet meeting, 523–26; funeral, 533–37; meaning of life, 538–39

Lincoln, Mrs. Abraham, marriage, 122–31; accompanies Lincoln to Washington, 133; visits Lexington, 145–51; letters to, from Lincoln, 146–47, 149–51; letter to Lincoln, 147–49; home life, 188–200; characterized by Herndon, 190; characterized by Harriet Hanks, 191–92; to visit Louisville, 214; at Alton debate, 246; gets news of nomination, 278; receives election returns, 294; importuned by visitors, 297; refuses to leave Springfield, 308

In presidential party, 320; at Willard's Hotel, 321, 329; visits Hooker's headquarters, 394–98; first social functions in White House, 418–21; kindness to Julia Taft, 422–23; fondness for clothes, 423–27; grieves over son's death, 427–30; meets Grant, 461; anxiety over election, 485; attends Johnson inauguration, 489; on Lincoln's religion, 495; at Grant's headquarters, 506; concern over Lincoln's dreams, 520–22; last drive with Lincoln, 526; at Ford's Theater, 526–27; at Lincoln's deathbed, 528. See also Todd, Mary.

Lincoln, Edward Baker, birth, 194; at Lexington, 145; death, 422, 427; mentioned, 147, 148, 151

Lincoln, Isaac, 4

Lincoln, Jacob, 4

Lincoln, John, 4

Lincoln, Josiah, 5

Lincoln, Martha, 7

Lincoln, Mary (aunt of the President), 5

Lincoln, Mordecai, 4–5

Lincoln, Nancy (aunt of the President), 5

Lincoln, Nancy Hanks, marriage, 5; birth of son, 5–7; life of, 7–9; on Knob Creek farm, 12–14; death, 19–20; grave, 35. See also Hanks, Nancy.

Lincoln, Robert Todd, birth, 194; at Lexington, 145; Lincoln's attitude towards, 190, 191; at Harvard, 284; in presidential party, 320, 329; attends reception, 421; at father's deathbed, 528, 532; attends funeral ceremonies, 534; mentioned, 147, 148, 151

Lincoln, Samuel, 3, 7

Lincoln, Sarah, life of, 5; school attendance, 10, 23; household chores, 13; greets stepmother, 21–22

Lincoln, Mrs. Sarah Bush, marriage, 20–22; describes young Lincoln, 26–27; removal to Illinois, 34; Lincoln visits, 304–06

Lincoln, Thomas (1761–1819), 4

Lincoln, Thomas (father of the President), life of, 4–5; at son's birth, 5–7; on Knob Creek farm, 9–15; settles in Indiana, 16–18; makes coffin, 19; marries Sarah Bush Johnston, 20–22; son works for, 27; removal to Illinois, 33–35; settles in Coles

County, 37–38; gets Lincoln's fee, 174

Lincoln, Thomas (Tad), birth, 194; Lincoln's attitude towards, 190; pranks of, 288, 299; at Willard's Hotel, 321; at Hooker's headquarters, 394–98; celebrates Lee's surrender, 517; attends funeral ceremonies, 534

Lincoln, William Wallace, birth, 194; Lincoln's attitude towards, 190; illness, 284; pranks of, 288, 299; at Willard's Hotel, 321; death, 427–430; effect of death on Lincoln, 495

Linder, Usher F., 80, 140, 173

Little Pigeon Creek, 18

Littlefield, John H., describes Lincoln's law office, 183–85

Lockwood, Samuel D., 78

Logan, Stephen T., in Whig Party, 47; describes Lincoln, 50; partnership with Lincoln, 98, 107–09, 111, 126; defeated for Congress, 154–55; in Illinois Central case, 180; in Lincoln's law office, 184; campaigns with Lincoln, 231; plans to attend convention, 262–63

"Long Nine," 74, 84, 86, 87

Longstreet, James, 440–41

Lookout Mountain, Battle of, 470–71

Louisiana, reconstruction in, 518

Louisville, Ky., Lincoln visits, 129

Lovejoy, Elijah P., 110

Lovejoy, Owen, 208, 216

Lynch, Jesse, 152

Lynch, W. O., 253

Lyons, Lord, 419

McAllister, Fort, 475

McClellan, George B., general in chief, 377; snubs Lincoln, 378; dilatoriness, 378–79; in Peninsular campaign, 380, 382–88; criticizes Lincoln, 384–88; and Pope's defeat, 389; restored to command, 390–93; relieved of command, 394; attends reception, 421; deficiencies, 460; Democratic candidate, 481; Lincoln plans to co-operate with, 487–88

McClernand, John A., 79, 84, 148

McClure, Alexander K., records Lincoln's opinion of Grant, 400–02

McCormick, Andrew, 73

McCormick House, Danville, Ill., 169–70

McCulloch, Hugh, 523–25, 531

McDougall, James A., 107

McDowell, Irvin, at Bull Run, 369, 374–76; relieved of command, 377; attends military council, 379; ordered to defend Washington, 383, 384

McIlvaine, Abraham R., 144

McKibben, Thomas, 174

McLean, John, mentioned for presidency, 218; defeated for nomination, 219; pre-convention candidate, 1860, 256, 266–67; in Chicago Convention, 269, 271, 272; mentioned, 161

McLean County, Ill., 179–80

McNamar, John (John McNeil), 114–15

McNeil, John (John McNamar), 114–15

McWilliams, Amzi, 204

Macomb, Ill., 239

Macon County, Ill., Lincolns in, 33–37; in Eighth Circuit, 166

MacVeagh, Wayne, 445, 448

Malvern (ship), 508, 512

Manassas Junction. *See* Bull Run.

Marsh, Mathew S., 57

Mason, Lucinda, 95

Massachusetts, McClellan's opinion of, 392

Matheny, James H., 76

Mather, Lamb & Co., 95

Matteson, Joel A., 209–11

Maynard, Horace, 479

Meade, George G., commands Fifth Corps, 395; in Gettysburg campaign, 439–42; invited to Gettysburg ceremonies, 443; criticized by Lincoln, 454–56; commands Army of the Potomac, 463; reports on *River Queen* conference, 504; at Grant's headquarters, 506

Mechanicsburg, Ill., 74

Medill, Joseph, 239, 257

Meigs, Montgomery C., describes military council, 378–80; and Lincoln's assassination, 530–31

Merrimac, duel with *Monitor,* 380–82

Metzker, James P., 175–76

Mexico, war with, 135–58; Blair's proposed expedition, 498, 499, 503

Miner, James, on Lincoln in campaign of 1854, 202–03

Miles, William P., 350–51

Milton, George Fort, 254

Minnesota (ship), 380, 381

Missionary Ridge, Battle of, 471

Mississippi River, battle for, 450, 454

Missouri, remains in Union, 450

Missouri Compromise, extension proposed, 141; repeal, 201, 207, 240; repeal attacked by Lincoln, 202–03, 212–14. *See also* Nebraska Bill.

Mitchell, Col., 237

Monaghan, Jay, xii

Monitor, duel with *Merrimac,* 380–82

Monocacy, Battle of, 467

Moore, C. H., 175

Morgan, Fort, 344
Morris, Achilles, 51, 74
Morrison, Don, 209-10
Morrison, J. L. D., 157
Morrissey, John, 331
Morton, Oliver P., 304, 482, 483
Moultrie County, Ill., 166
Moultrie, Fort, 344
Muldraugh's Hill, Ky., 9, 15
Murray's English Reader, 24
Musick, Samuel, 115

Napoleon, Prince, 420-21
Nasby Papers, 482
Nashville, Battle of, 473-74, 482
National Era, 134, 141-42
National Intelligencer, 134
Neal, John, 74-75
Neale, Thomas M., 71
Nebraska Bill, introduced, 201; Lincoln attacks, 202-03, 205-08, 212-14; Douglas defends, 204, 205-07. See also Missouri Compromise.
Nelson, Samuel, 345-46, 490
Nelson, Thomas H., story of Lincoln and the comet, 160-61
Nelson, Dr., 40
New England, Lincoln in, 155
New Mexico, 140, 141
New Orleans, trips to, 32-33, 37; occupied by North, 450
New Salem, Ill., Lincoln at, 36-64
Newton, Joseph Fort, account of Lincoln's first great speech, 205-08
New Year's Day, reception, 413-14
New York City, 360
New York Fire Zouaves, 363-65
New York Herald, Villard correspondence, 295-98; quoted, 449
New York Times, 225
New York Tribune, 260, 293
Newton, ——, Lincoln meets, 150
Nicolay, Helen, describes Lincoln as candidate, 284-90; on office seekers, 367-69
Nicolay, John G., appointed secretary, 284; answers Lincoln's mail, 285-87; on threats against Lincoln, 289; in presidential party, 329; visits Sixth Massachusetts, 358; account of Richmond campaign, 462-66; account of Georgia campaign, 470-75; describes Johnson's nomination, 479-81; describes assassination, 526-28; mentioned, xi
Nicolay & Hay, describe removal to Indiana, 17-18; on Lincoln's first political campaign, 46-51; on Lincoln in legislature, 65-67, 71-73; collapse of internal improvement system, 99-102; Lincoln and Land Office appointment, 156-58; Fort Sumter crisis, 339-41; Lincoln's reception of Sumter news, 352-53; describe Lincoln's apprehension, 359-63; account of Ellsworth's death, 365-67; Lincoln's reception of Bull Run news, 373-76; describe signing of Emancipation Proclamation, 413-14; on Grant's acceptance of high command, 459-62; describe Lincoln under fire, 470
Nolin Creek, Ky., 6, 7-9, 15
Norris, James H., 175
Norton, Jesse O., 182
Noyes, William Curtis, 324

Oak Ridge Cemetery, 537
Offut, Denton, 37, 39, 40-42
Oglesby, Richard J., supports Lincoln, 260-61; originates "Rail Splitter" slogan, 263-65; visits Lincoln, 303
"Oh, why should the spirit of mortal be proud?", 438
Ohio, Lincoln's chances in, 259; election returns, 481-83
Old Soldier (newspaper), 105
Oliver Oldschool (pseud.), 144
Onstott, Henry, 91
Ord, E. O. C., 506
Ordinance of Secession, 300
Ordinance of 1787, 141
Oregon, territorial government, 140; governorship offered Lincoln, 157
Osborn, W. H., 181
Ottawa, Ill., Lincoln in, 44, 45; debate at, 230, 234-35
Ottawa Free Trader (newspaper), 138
"Our American Cousin" (play), 526
Owens, Mary, in Lincoln's life, 113; courtship of, 117-22

Paine, Thomas, Age of Reason, 61
Palfrey, John G., 142
Palmer, John M., 209-10, 219
Pantier, David, 43
Parker, Dr. Charles E., 176-77
Parker, Ely S., 514
Parker, James, 148
Parker, John, 146, 150
Parker, Mrs., 149-50
Peace Conference, members and Lincoln, 321-26
Pearce, James A., 332
Peck, Ebenezer, 72
Peck, John Mason, 140
Pekin, Ill., 59
Pemberton, John C., 453-54
Pendleton, George H., 481
Peninsular campaign, 382-88
Pennington, William, 219

Pennsylvania, opposes Seward, 268; election returns, 481–83
Pennsylvania Avenue, Washington, 133
Pensacola Navy Yard, 344
Peoria, Ill., Lincoln at, 45; postal receipts, 59; seeks state capital, 84; Lincoln speaks at, 231, 234
Perry County, Ind., Lincolns settle in, 17–18
Petersburg, Ill., 51, 56
Petersburg, Va., siege of, 465–66; Lee evacuates, 507
Peterson house, Washington, 531
Philadelphia, Convention, Lincoln attends, 150, 153; Lincoln speaks at, 311–12
Phillips, David L., 260
Phillips, Wendell, 142
Piatt, Donn, characterizes Lincoln, 298–300
Piatt County, Ill., 166
Pickens, Francis W., 346
Pickens, Fort, 344, 346–47
Pickett, George E., 441–42, 450
Pierce, Franklin, 201
Pigeon Creek, Ind., 33–35
Pilgrim's Progress, 24
Pinkerton, Allan, 311–13, 317
Polk, James K., in White House, 134; Lincoln criticizes, 135–39; veto message, 141; presidential possibility, 152
Pollack, James, 144
Pope, John, and assassination plot, 313; given Eastern command, 388; defeat, 389–90
Popular Sovereignty. *See* Missouri Compromise, Nebraska Bill.
Port Hudson, La., 454
Porter, David D., in Vicksburg campaign, 451–53; at *River Queen* conference, 506; account of Lincoln's visit to Richmond, 508–12
Posey, Francis, 17, 18
Potter, John F., 265
Potter, Nancy, 61
Pratt, Harry E., on Lincoln in legislature, 67–70; account of Illinois Central fee suit, 179–83
"Prince of Rails" (Robert T. Lincoln), 329
Pryor, Roger A., at Fort Sumter, 348–49, 350–51
Public Man, Diary, quoted, 326–28, 341–42
Pulaski, Fort, 344

Quincy, Ill., debate, 230, 242

Radford, Reuben, 52
"Rail Splitter" slogan, origin, 263–65

Randall, James G., analyzes Lincoln-Douglas debates, 248–54; analyzes Sumter crisis, 343–47; mentioned, xi
Rathbone, Henry R., 526, 527–28
Ray, Charles H., 257
Ray, D. E., 300
Raymond, Henry J., 478, 479, 486
Reed, John M., 271
Reeder, Andrew H., 269
Reep, Thomas P., describes Lincoln as storekeeper, 51–55
Religion, Lincoln's convictions, 493–95
Republican Party, organized in Illinois, 208, 216; Lincoln joins, 215; Bloomington Convention, 215; Philadelphia Convention, 217; faction favors Douglas, 226–27; Decatur Convention, 227–29; Chicago Convention, 265–76; 1860 platform, 267; radicals oppose Lincoln, 476; radicals nominate Fremont, 481; faction favors Lincoln's withdrawal, 481
Reynolds, John (governor), 43, 47–48, 78–79
Reynolds, John F. (general), 396
Richardson, William A., 135–36, 139, 151
Richland, Ill., 43
Richmond, Va., McClellan threatens, 385; Grant's campaign against, 507–08; falls, 508; Lincoln visits, 508–12
Richmond House, Chicago, 268
Riddle, Albert G., describes Washington, 318–19
Riney, Zachariah, 10
River Queen (ship), 508
River Queen Conference, 504–507. *See also* Hampton Roads Conference.
Rives, William C., 323
Robinson Crusoe, 24
Rock Island, Ill., 44
Romaine, Gideon W., 31
Rosecrans, W. S., 451, 456–57
Rosen, June, xii
Rosette, John E., 276–77
Ross, E. C., 95
Ross, Harvey L., 56, 58
Ross, Ossian, 56
Russell, William H., account of Bull Run, 369–73
Russia (ship), 504, 506
Rutgers University Press, xi
Rutledge, Ann, romance with Lincoln, 113–17; death, 117
Rutledge, David, 43
Rutledge, James, 52, 54, 61
Rutledge, John M., 43
Rutledge mill, 40

Saint-Gaudens, Augustus, 207
Sam Gaty (ship), 232

Sandburg, Carl, describes Lincoln's birth, 5–7; on death of Nancy Hanks, 18–20; describes migration to Illinois, 33–35; Ann Rutledge romance, 114–17; on Lincoln's Dred Scott speech, 222–25; outlines political situation in 1860, 256–63; account Lincoln's first inauguration, 332–33, 336; Gettysburg campaign, 439–42; epilogue to Gettysburg, 447–49; describes Lincoln under fire, 466–70; on Hampton Roads conference, 497–504; account funeral ceremonies, 533–36; mentioned, xi

Sandburg and Angle, on Lincoln's marriage, 122–31; domestic life of the Lincolns, 193–200

Sanford, Henry, 311, 312

Sangamo Journal (Springfield newspaper), Lincoln agent for, 59; campaign announcement in, 73–74; law cards in, 94, 98; Lincoln writes for, 130–31. *See also Illinois State Journal.*

Santa Anna, Antonio Lopez de, 136

Sargent, Nathan, 144

Sauk and Foxes, 42–43

Savannah, Ga., 475

Schenck, Robert E., 298

Schofield, J. M., 496, 504–06

Schouler, William, 155

Schurz, Carl, describes Quincy debate, 242–45; seconds nomination, 269; on Lincoln as candidate, 290–91; commands division, 397

Scott, Winfield, Mexican War victories, 137; vote for, in Philadelphia Convention, 153; Lincoln calls on, 320; calls on Lincoln, 321; safeguards for inauguration, 330; on Sumter crisis, 340, 342, 345; disposes troops, 360–61; confident of success at Bull Run, 373–74; retirement, 377; stations guards at White House, 419–20; attends reception, 421; invited to Gettysburg ceremonies, 443; brevet Lieutenant General, 459

Scott, Col., 312

Scripps, John Locke, 4–5

Scriven, Margaret, xii

Secession, threatened, 289; Lincoln takes lightly, 299–300; Lincoln becomes concerned over, 300–03; justification by Southerners, 323–24; Lincoln argues against, 334–36; Lincoln's policy, 343–47

Second Battle of Bull Run, 389–90. *See also Bull Run, Battle of.*

Second Inaugural Address, 491–93; Charnwood's interpretation, 493–95

Seddon, James A., 323–24

Sedgwick, John, 395

Semple, James, 71, 79–80

Seven Days' Battles, 385–86, 404

Seventh New York regiment, 360, 362–63

Seward, Fanny, 530

Seward, Frederick W., warns Lincoln of plot, 312, 313; murder reported, 529; murder attempted, 530; account of last Cabinet meeting, 523–26

Seward, Mrs. Frederick W., 419, 530

Seward, William H., Lincoln meets, 155; in Congress, 231; contender for presidential nomination, 255, 258, 267; prepares letter of acceptance, 262; loses nomination, 268–74, 281; offered Cabinet appointment, 301–02; discovers assassination plot, 312; informed of Lincoln's secret journey, 316; greets Lincoln in Washington, 317; entertains Lincoln, 321; supports intrigue against Chase, 326–28; attempts to withdraw from Cabinet, 337–38; heads Cabinet, 338; and Sumter negotiations, 345–46; on office seekers, 368; announces Bull Run defeat, 374–75; snubbed by McClellan, 378; attends military council, 379; profanity, 397; and Emancipation Proclamation, 405–08, 412–13; gives reception, 420–21; attends Gettysburg ceremonies, 445; meets Grant, 461; endorses Lincoln's promise to cooperate with successor, 487; attends Johnson inauguration, 489, 490; at Hampton Roads conference, 497–504; injured, 516; murder attempted, 528, 529

Seward, Mrs. William H., 529

Shakespeare's Works, 60, 436, 437

R. H. Shannon (ship), 344

Shaw, J. Henry, 178

Shelby County, Ill., 166

Shepley, G. F., 512

Sheridan, Philip H., 505, 507

Sherman, William T., Vicksburg campaign, 451–54; at Battle of Chattanooga, 457; Georgia campaign, 470–75; account of *River Queen* conference, 504–07

Sherwood, Mrs. John, 135

Shields, James, characterized, 80; supports internal improvement system, 84; challenges Lincoln, 130–31; Lincoln opposes, 206, 208–09

Shiloh, Battle of, 399–401, 450

Shirreff, Patrick, 55

Short, Joshua, 91

Sickles, Daniel E., 395

Silver Spring, Md., 469

Simpson, Bishop Matthew, 534–35, 537
Sixth Massachusetts regiment, 358–59, 362
Slavery, Lincoln's position on, 84–86; in District of Columbia, 134; Lincoln's attitude towards, as Congressman, 140–43; and Popular Sovereignty, 203; extension of, Lincoln's argument against, 206–08; Lincoln's attitude towards, 211–14, 223–24, 403–04; in Lincoln-Douglas debates, 249–52; abolition of, opposed by McClellan, 387; root of the rebellion, 410; discussed at Hampton Roads conference, 498
Slocum, Henry W., 397
Smith, Caleb B., 269, 338, 345
Smith, James, 529
Smith, John, 12
Smithsonian Institution, 134
Smoot, Coleman, 67
Soldiers' Home, Washington, D. C., 389, 435, 468
South Carolina, passes Ordinance of Secession, 300; seizes Federal forts, 343–44; McClellan's opinion of, 392
Sparrow, Betsy, 6–7, 18, 19
Sparrow, Tom, 6–7, 18, 19
Spears, George, 57
Speed, James, 489, 523–25, 532
Speed, Joshua F., describes Lincoln in 1836 campaign, 75–76; on Lincoln's campaign expenses, 99; Herndon clerks for, 110; counsels Lincoln on marriage, 125; letter to Mary Todd, 128; letters to, from Lincoln, 129–31, 132–33, 140, 211–14
Speed, Mrs. Joshua F., 214
Spencer County, Ind., 26–30
"Spot" Resolutions, 136–37
Sprague, William, 360
Sprigg, Mrs., 143–45
Springfield, Ill., Lincoln's first visit to, 37; postal receipts, 59; made state capital, 84, 87–88, 98, 99; Lincoln settles in, 89; Harrison rally, 103; life in, 117; Lincoln's law office, 183–85; society of, 198–200; Lincoln's first great speech, 205–08; last speech in 1858 campaign, 247–48; celebrates Lincoln's nomination, 278; 1860 campaign meeting, 290–91; Republican jollification, 296–98; Lincoln's departure from, 308–09; funeral ceremonies, 536–37
"Squatter Sovereignty." *See* Missouri Compromise, Nebraska Bill.
Stanton, Edwin M., contempt for Lincoln, 320; suspends enlistments, 386; condemns McClellan, 389–91; at Gettysburg, 445; dismayed by Lee's es-

cape, 455; meets Grant, 461; recalls Lincoln to Washington, 468; receives election returns, 481–83; advocated for chief justiceship, 486; endorses Lincoln's promise to cooperate with successor, 487; attends Johnson inauguration, 489, 490; announces Lee's surrender, 516; attends last Cabinet meeting, 524–25; at Lincoln's deathbed, 530–33
Stephens, Alexander, 262, 497–504
Stern, Philip Van Doren, describes Lincoln's departure from Springfield, 308–09
Stevens, Thaddeus, 144, 155, 268
Stevens, Fort, 468–70
Stewart, Charles, 443
Stockton, George, 171
Stockton, Thomas H., 446
Stone, Dan, 73, 85–86
Stone, Dr. Robert K., 428, 528
Stoneman, George, 394
Stringham, Silas H., 342
Strong, William, 147
Strunk, ——, 209–10
Stuart, John T., in Black Hawk War, 45; in Whig Party, 47; impressed by Lincoln, 50; elected to legislature, 51, 67; with Lincoln at Vandalia, 68; characterized, 79; urges Lincoln to study law, 89; lends law books, 91; partnership with, 94–98; letters to, from Lincoln, 105–06, 126; argues Illinois Central case, 180; protests Lincoln's affiliation with Republicans, 215; defeats Swett, 476; mentioned, 107, 155
Sturges, Solomon, 263
Summers, George W., 323, 346
Sumner, Charles, vote for vice-presidential nomination, 219; vote for, Chicago Convention, 271; sends election returns, 484; attends Johnson inauguration, 490; at Lincoln's deathbed, 531, 533
Sumner, Edwin V., 313, 314, 320
Sumter, Fort, threatened by South, 337; crisis develops, 339–42; Cabinet discusses, 342; relief expedition, 346–47; attack on, 347–51; Lincoln's account of, 353–54; effect of attack on, 355–58
Supreme Court, U. S., Dred Scott decision, 222–25; charged with conspiracy, 253
Surratt, Mrs. Anna M., 527
Sweeney, William, 23
Swett, Leonard, on Eighth Circuit, 168–69; attends Bloomington Convention, 216; criticizes House Divided speech, 229; favors Grant's removal,

401; defeated for Congress, 476; in Baltimore Convention, 480; mentioned, 257

Taft, Horatio, 424
Taft, Mrs. Horatio, 423–24
Taft, Julia, recollections of Mrs. Lincoln, 422–24
Talisman (steamer), 48, 86
Taney, Roger, 336
Tarbell, Ida M., describes life of Nancy Hanks, 7–9; mentioned, xi
Tavern license, 54
Taylor, Edmund Dick, 51, 76–77
Taylor, Zachary, resolution of thanks, 137; candidacy of, 144; defeats Clay, 150; elected President, 151–56; offers Lincoln Oregon position, 157
Taylor, Fort, 344
Temperance, Lincoln's attitude on, 204, 279–80
Texas, war with Mexico, 136–37
Theater, Lincoln's fondness for, 436
Thirteenth Amendment, U. S. Const., 499, 501–03
Thirtieth Congress, 132–58
Thomas, Benjamin P., on Lincoln in Black Hawk War, 42–46; Lincoln as postmaster and surveyor, 55–59; effect of New Salem on Lincoln, 62–64; description of Washington, 133–35; Lincoln and Mexican War, 135–40; Lincoln's attitude towards slavery, 140–43; Lincoln in 1848 campaign, 151–56; Lincoln as circuit lawyer, 163–66; mentioned, xi
Thomas, George H., 457, 473–74, 496
Thomas, Jesse B., 203
Thompkins, Patrick W., 144
Thompson, Lorenzo D., 45
Thompson, Richard W., 161
Todd, Levi, 148
Todd, Mary, in Lincoln's life, 113; Lincoln's courtship of, 122–31. *See also* Lincoln, Mrs. Abraham.
Todd, Mrs. Robert S., 148
Tolby, James, 171
Totten, Joseph G., 340, 342
Townsend, William H., account of Lincoln in Washington, 145–51
Trapp, ——, 209–10
Tremont House, Chicago, 229, 265, 266, 275
Tremont Temple, Boston, 155
Trent, Alexander, 43, 56
Trent Brothers, 54–55
Truett, H. B., 74
Trumbull, Lyman, elected to Senate, 209–11; attends Bloomington Convention, 216; in Congress with Douglas, 231; castigated by Douglas, 232; letter to, from Lincoln, 258–59; receives election returns, 293; visits Lincoln, 303
Tuck, Amos, 279
Tunstall, Warrick, 146
Turner, Thomas J., 237, 238
Tyler, John, 102, 321

Union, Lincoln determined to preserve, 302–03; assailed by attack on Sumter, 353–54; preservation of, Lincoln's supreme purpose, 403; restoration of, condition of peace, 499; Lincoln's plans for restoration, 518–19; restoration discussed, 524–25
Union Ball, 337
Union Party Convention, 477–81. *See also* Republican Party.
United States courts, 98
Usher, John P., meets Lincoln, 161; at Gettysburg, 445; at Cabinet meeting, 455; endorses Lincoln's promise to cooperate with successor, 487; at Lincoln's deathbed, 532

Van Buren, Martin, elected President, 73; candidate for Presidency, 102; ridiculed, 103–04; in 1848 campaign, 155
Vandalia, Ill., postal receipts, 59; Lincoln in, 67–70; loses capital, 84
Verdi, Dr., 530
Vicksburg campaign, 451–54
Villard, Henry, with Lincoln in 1858, 255; describes Lincoln as President-Elect, 295–98; on Lincoln's secessionist visitor, 300–01; on secession and appointments, 301–03
Virginia (ship). *See Merrimac.*
Volk, Leonard, 288
Volney's *Ruins*, 61

Wade, Benjamin F., 267, 271
Walker, L. P., 347–48
Wallace, Mrs. W. S., 147, 149, 189
Wallace, Lew, 466–67
Walters, Peggy, 6
War Democrats, 479–81
Warburton, George, 43
Ward, Artemus, 411
Washburne, Elihu B., describes Logan, 108; letters to, from Lincoln, 152, 209–11, 227; objects to Freeport question, 240; describes Lincoln's arrival in Washington, 316–17; defends Grant, 401; secures Grant's promotion, 459
Washington, George, 168, 459

Washington, D. C., in 1848, 133–35; Lincoln in, as Congressman, 145–51; in 1861, 318–19; apprehension in, 356, 359–63, 375–76, 381, 391; necessity of protecting, 386–87; capture threatened, 466–70; celebrates end of war, 517–19; Lincoln funeral ceremonies, 533–36

Watkins, ——, in Armstrong trial, 177, 178

Watson, P. H., 404

Watterson, Henry, 333, 336

Webb, Edwin B., 79, 128, 149

Webber, T. R., 179–80

Webster, Daniel, 231

Webster's Speller, 24

Weed, Thurlow, 262, 303–04

Weems' *Life of Washington*, 24, 25

Weems' *Life of Marion*, 25

Weik, Jesse W., letters to, from Herndon, 158–59, 190; on Lincoln's law practice, 170–75; letter to, from Harriet Hanks, 191–92

Weitzel, Godfrey, 508

Weldon, Lawrence, 174–75, 204

Welles, Gideon, Secretary of Navy, 338; and Sumter question, 345; distrust of McClellan, 390–93; on first mention of Emancipation Proclamation, 405–06; describes Lincoln's distress after Gettysburg, 454–56; describes Lincoln during Early's raid, 469; receives election returns, 485; endorses Lincoln's promise to cooperate with successor, 487; attends Johnson inauguration, 489, 490; attends last Cabinet meeting, 523–25; account of Lincoln's death, 529–33

Welles, Mrs. Gideon, 529

Welles, John, 529

"Whig Junto," 104

Whig Party, Lincoln joins, 46–48; carries Sangamon County, 77; defends banks, 101–02; attitude on Mexican War, 135–40; wins 1848 election, 151–56; Lincoln attends national convention, 153; Lincoln still member of, 214

White, Albert S., 161

White, Alexander, 45

White, Horace, describes Lincoln's first great speech, 207–08; describes 1858 campaign, 232–35

White, Hugh L., 74, 77, 102

White, Dr., 530

White House, in 1848, 134; Lincoln family in, 415–38; funeral ceremonies, 533–36

Whiteside, Samuel, 44

Whitney, Henry C., pictures life on Eighth Circuit, 166–70; excerpt from, 217–20

Whittier's Poems, 437

Wide-Awakes, 291

Wigfall, Louis T., 35–51

Wigwam, Chicago, 266

Wilderness, Battle of, 463–64

Wiley and Wood, case of, 95

Willard's Hotel, Washington, 317, 321

Williams, Archibald, 80, 152, 153

Willian, Washington milliner, 423–24

Wills, David, 442–43, 445, 447

Wilmot Proviso, 140, 144, 214

Wilson, Henry, 219, 434, 490

Wilson, Robert L., 73, 75, 84

Wilson, William, 78

Winchester, Ill., 202–03

Winter, Henry J., 304

Wise, Henry A., 434

Wise, Mrs., 445

Woldman, Albert A., on Lincoln's study of law, 89–93; on partnership with Logan, 107–09; on Herndon partnership, 109–12; on Armstrong case, 175–79

Wood, William, 31

Wool, John E., 330

Worden, John L., 382

Wright, Horatio G., 470

Yancey, William L., 261–62

Yates, Richard, at Winchester meeting, 202; attends Bloomington Convention, 216; speaks at Springfield, 248; favors Bates for President, 260

Yazoo River, canal, 452

Yorktown, Va., 383

Young, John, 446

Young Men's Lyceum, 111

Zane, Charles S., 276–77

Zollicoffer, Felix K., 323